The Book of
Common Prayer
and Administration of the
Sacraments,
and other
Rites and Ceremonies
of the
Church
Proposed for the Use in
the Antiochian Western Rite Vicariate

Together with the Psalter

or

Psalms of David

Apologia Anglicana
Boston, Massachusetts
A. D. MMXXV

Table of Contents

Copyright	i
Dedication	iii
Foreword	iv
Editor's Preface	vii
Rubrics	viii
Rankings of Days	xvi
Kalendar of the Church Year	xx
Daily Office Lectionary	xxxiii
Proper of Season	xxxiv
Feasts of the Year	lxvi
Common of Saints	lxxiii
Alternative Psalter Arrangement	lxxiv
Daily Office	1
Fore-Office	2
The Order for Daily Morning Prayer	8
Old Testament Canticles	21
Hour of Prime	30
Pretiosa	35
Commemoration of the Faithful Departed	36
Athanasian Creed	37
Hour of Terce	40
Hour of Sext	45
Hour of None	49
The Order for Daily Evening Prayer	53
Hour of Compline	60
Marian Anthems	65
Prayers & Thanksgivings	69
Prayers	70
Thanksgivings	82

Litanies & Offices — 85
- Great Litany 86
- A Penitential Office 91
- Blessing of Baptismal Waters 94
- Litany of Saints 98

Office of the Dead — 105
- Vespers of the Dead 106
- Matins of the Dead 111
- Lauds of the Dead 126

Eucharistic Devotions — 133
- Benediction of the Blessed Sacrament 134
- Preparation for Holy Communion 137
- Thanksgiving for Holy Communion 150
- Aspersion of the People 152
- Prayers at the Foot of the Altar 154

Holy Mass — 157
- Liturgy of St. Tikhon 158
- Pre-Communion Hymn 184
- Prefaces for the Mass 185

Propers of the Church Year — 189
- Proper of the Season 190
- Proper of Saints 412
- Table of Prayers 541

Votive Masses — 565
- Our Lady on Saturday 566
- Mass of the Angels 575
- Holy Matrimony 578
- Masses for the Dead 582

Pastoral Rites — 587
- Sacrament of Baptism for Infants 588
- Sacrament of Baptism for Adults 596
- Sacrament of Penance 622
- Reception of Converts 623
- Sacrament of Confirmation 629
- Sacrament of Matrimony 633

Purification of Women after Childbirth 640
Sacrament of Holy Unction 642
Communion of the Sick 651
The Order for the Burial of the Dead 654
At the Burial of a Child 668

Forms of Prayer to be used in Families   673
Morning Prayer 674
Evening Prayer 676
A Shorter Form of Morning Prayer 678
A Shorter Form of Evening Prayer 679
Additional Prayers 680

Psalter of David   685

Copyright

The 2025 Proposed Book of Common Prayer (© 2025 Apologia Anglicana, LLC) is licenced under CC BY-SA 4.0. To view a copy of this license, visit `https://creativecommons.org/licenses/by-sa/4.0/`

ISBN: 978-1-969461-04-0 (Personal Size Hardcover)
ISBN: 978-1-969461-05-7 (Altar Size Hardcover)
ISBN: 978-1-969461-06-4 (eBook)

Library of Congress Control Number: 2025920564

Edited by J. P. 'Augustine' Watson (Augustine@ApologiaAnglicana.org).
Front cover designed by Matthew Taylor (@semperadiuvans).

PLEASE NOTE THAT THIS IS NOT CURRENTLY AN OFFICIAL TEXT OF THE ANTIOCHIAN WESTERN RITE VICARIATE.

We are thankful to have such great giants upon whose shoulders we stand. These works are used in this Book according to fair use, where their content is not already in the public domain. What was used from the book, or in what way it was consulted, is described under each citation.

A Manual for Priests. 5th edition. Athens: Anglican Parishes Association, 2004.
The Burial rites.

Davis, C. Lance, ed. *The Anglican Office Book*. 2nd edition. Chester: Whithorn Press, 2023.
Lessons and Psalms in the Daily Office Lectionary, which are not provided in the 1928 Book of Common Prayer. The Invitatory antiphon for Septuagesimatide. Some of the text and Rubrics for the Minor Hours. Other Daily Office propers.

The American Missal: Revised & Expanded. Glendale: Lancelot Andrewes Press, 2010.
The propers for Our Lady of Walsingham.

The Armed Forces Division of the Protestant Episcopal Church. *The Armed Forces Prayer Book*. New York: The Church Pension Fund, 1951.
The Prayer for the Armed Forces.

Copyright

The English Missal for the Laity. London: W. Knott & Sons Limited, 1933.
Mass Rubrics. The Litany of Saints. The Thanksgiving for Holy Communion. Parts of the Mass not found in the Prayer Book Tradition. Propers not found in the Prayer Book Tradition nor used from other books.

The General Synod of the Anglican Church of Canada. *The Book of Common Prayer.* Toronto: Anglican Book Centre, 1962.
The Invitatory Antiphon for Lent.

The Monastic Diurnal. Oxford University Press, 1932.
Office Rubrics. Ranking of Feast Days. Marian Anthems. Office of the Dead. Sacrament of Penance. Preparation for Holy Communion.

Orthodox Ritual. St. Luke's Priory Press, 2016.
Translations for some of the prayers in the Sacraments of Baptism and Confirmation, as well as in other Pastoral Rites.

Dedication

This *Book of Common Prayer* is dedicated to Patriarch JOHN X, 171st Successor of St. Peter, Head of the Church, and Patriarch of Antioch.

And we are beyond thankful for our Christ-loving, God-fearing, and faithful-caring Chief Bishop and Metropolitan SABA. For his support of the Western Rite continues our endeavours, lightens our hearts, and shows his divine charity for his flock.

And for our faithful, compassionate, and righteous Bishop JOHN, we must send up everlasting praise and thanksgiving unto the Most Holy Trinity. For through him has the daily care, discipline, and concern for the Vicariate been carried. Through him have so many of us flocked for refuge under the See of St. Peter within the Holy Orthodox Catholic Church. And through him have we been intimately cared and nourished.

Finally, we must thank our Lord and God and Saviour Jesus Christ for our beloved Priests, Deacons, and all Clergy in the Vicariate for their tireless care, concern, and work for our salvation. Chiefly among them must surely be our pious and religious Abbot Theodore of Ladyminster, as well as our blessed archpriests, The Very Reverend Fathers Edward Hughes, John Fenton, Lester Bundy, Patrick Cardine, and Christopher Nerreau.

We also wish to express our deep love for our brethren in the British Isles, keeping the life of the Western Rite, Fathers Augustine and James.

Let us for ever bless the Father and the Son and the Holy Ghost, together with all the Saints, chiefly of blessed Mary ever-Virgin, blessed John Baptist, and the holy Apostles Peter and Paul, for our fathers in the faith. May God, through the merits and prayers of the Saints, bless and preserve us now and for ever. Amen.

AND I SAY ALSO UNTO THEE, THAT THOU ART PETER, AND UPON THIS ROCK I WILL BUILD MY CHURCH; AND THE GATES OF HELL SHALL NOT PREVAIL AGAINST IT. AND I WILL GIVE UNTO THEE THE KEYS OF THE KINGDOM OF HEAVEN: AND WHATSOEVER THOU SHALT BIND ON EARTH SHALL BE BOUND IN HEAVEN: AND WHATSOEVER THOU SHALT LOOSE ON EARTH SHALL BE LOOSED IN HEAVEN.

Foreword

THE publication of this edition of the Book of Common Prayer, carefully edited and directed toward those in the Antiochian Western Rite Vicariate, marks a contemplative moment of continued growth of the Orthodox Catholic faith in North America and in the territories of British Christendom. Much has already been written about the nearly universal acceptance of the Western Rite among our Holy Fathers in modern times, and so this foreword is not concerned with such a topic. The message I hope to leave with the faithful is the importance of beauty, and the importance of Orthodox Christianity being the Great Healer of nations.

The Orthodox Church has always emphasized the importance of beauty in the salvation of mankind, for as it says in the Epistle of James,

> Every good gift and every perfect gift is from above, and cometh down from the Father of lights, with whom is no variableness, neither shadow of turning. —James 1:17

In our homeland of North America, many of us have been led to Orthodoxy by the beauty of the English tradition of prayer which was given to our forefathers (according to the flesh) by way of our English and Scottish heritage. As the peoples of the British Isles arrived in the colonial New World, so too did their prayer tradition which was rooted in a deep connection to the blessed Dowry of Mary, that is, the Albion of Saint Alfred and the Three Holy Patrons: St. Edmund, St. Edward, and St. Gregory the Great. Even the Congregationalists, Puritans, and "Low Churchmen" could not avoid retaining an echo of the ancient Liturgy within their houses of prayer.

This deep connection to the England once known as Mary's Dowry is what allowed for beauty to thrive in a deeply desolate new world. Amidst the darkness of isolation and uncertainty, New Englanders and Southern Americans built lasting houses of prayer adorned with the beauty of Christ's Name and images of His saints. Within those halls, the men and women of an uncertain new world prayed the collects, hymns, and prayers of an ancient inheritance, albeit commingled with new and unfamiliar doctrines and liturgics that set a broad path against what was once dedicated to the very Narrow Way of Christ. In modern times, the Christians of the English tradition have found themselves near shipwreck and in danger of losing the beauty of their rich past. Though the valuable buildings, real-estate, and stained glass have passed on to "the Religion of the Future," as our holy father St. Seraphim of Platina called it, the prayers and liturgical life of English Christians can be still be made firm in the life giving

Foreword

Water of Christ. This life giving water runs out from the side of the Living Christ, from His Church, which boldly proclaims the Catholic faith without shame.

The thirst for the living water of the ancient Orthodoxy of the Christian life was never fully stomped out by the errors of the dialectical tension of Roman Catholicism and Anglicanism. Much has been said before about the elegant writing of William Laud, Richard Hooker, Lancelot Andrewes, and George Herbert. And so I wish to offer a sometimes forgotten example from the Right Reverend William Seabury of Connecticut. Rt. Rev. Seabury was the first Anglican bishop consecrated in the United States and, writing in favor of aligning the American Anglican ethos with that of the Scottish prayerbook, he wrote:

> The grand fault in that [1662] office [of Holy Communion] is the deficiency of a more formal oblation of the elements, and of the invocation of the Holy Ghost to sanctify and bless them. The Consecration is made to consist merely in the Priest's laying his hands on the elements and pronouncing "This is my body," etc., which words are not consecration at all, nor were they addressed by Christ to the Father, but were declarative to the Apostles . . . The efficacy of Baptism, of Confirmation, of Orders, is ascribed to the Holy Ghost, and His energy is implored for that purpose; and why he should not be invoked in the consecration of the Eucharist, especially as all the old Liturgies are full to the point, I cannot conceive. —*The Life and Correspondence of Samuel Seabury*, p. 354

We see in this early American bishop a desire to return to the ancient liturgies, to live within the uncreated energies experienced and preached by St. Paul, and to find what had been lost after the Great Schism and the deeply regrettable brother wars of the Reformation which led to the destruction, desolation, and murder of European Christianity.

Herein we find the purpose of the 2025 Proposed Book of Common Prayer: to bring forth the Good, to let go of all that which is contrary to the Truth, and to heal what is infirm. Following carefully the recommendations of the fathers of the Antiochian and Russian Orthodox Churches, the 2025 Proposed Book of Common Prayer has only sought to remain loyal to what the Orthodox Church has already observed and ruled. Recalling the conclusion to the Russian Observations on the American Prayerbook, it is worth restating their findings:

Foreword

The committee, after reviewing these "Observations," allowed in general the possibility that if Orthodox parishes, composed of former Anglicans, were organized in America, they might be allowed, at their desire, to perform their worship according to the "Book of Common Prayer," but only on condition that the following corrections were made in the spirit of the Orthodox Church. —*Russian Observations upon the American Prayer Book* 2:VI

The 2025 Proposed Book of Common Prayer is not a restoration project, nor is it a historical recreation. Rather it is a spiritual surgery for those of the Anglican patrimony who seek communion with the One, Holy, Catholic, and Apostolic Church and to retain that which the ancient Church provided, influenced, and now attempts to sustain.

Continued prayers are also asked for all those of the Western Rite, so that a spirit of pretest, pride, or confusion may never yoke itself to the Latin and English presence within the Orthodox world. All things are submitted to the Holy Church so that Christ may judge, through His living Mystical Body.

The Blessings of Our Lord Jesus Christ,

The Reverend Father Justin Slaughter Doty
Priest, St. Euphemia Orthodox Christian Church
Overseeing St. Botolph Orthodox Chapel

Editor's Preface

WE rejoice on the occasion of the publication of this edition of the Book of Common Prayer. As Orthodox Catholics, we have been blessed to have received the Gospel and full membership within the Mystical Body of Christ. And by the undeserved gift bestowed upon us, we offer unto the Almighty Father 'our worship and praise and thanksgiving'. In light of so great a gift, it is only fitting that we have a Book for so great a worship.

The Proposed 2025 Book of Common Prayer is a revision of the 1928 Book of Common Prayer for use within the Orthodox Church, specifically the Antiochian Western Rite Vicariate. Where the 1928 BCP was deficient, it was changed or supplemented, either from the Prayer Book Tradition itself or other books, such as the Roman Missal and the Monastic Office.

For those familiar with the Anglican tradition, this Book will be very familiar. We took great care to not remove or change anything unless necessary or truly expedient. And where we changed or removed, we took even greater care to not follow our personal eccentricities or idiosyncrasies. Therefore, this Book stands as a true successor within the Prayer Book Tradition: both an integral expression of the English Rite as well as truly and wholly Orthodox.

We are thankful for all the support we have received. This Book simply would not be possible without the many laymen who spent their money, time, and energy to buy draft copies, use them in their prayer life, and offer corrections and suggestions. This is to say nothing of the priests and other clergy who offered their valuable time (of which they do not have much) to review the Book of Common Prayer and give indispensable feedback. We are especially thankful for the priests who took the time to study and use the Book of Common Prayer. And above all, thanksgiving must be given to the Right Reverend JOHN of Worcester who oversees the Antiochian Western Rite Vicariate with the greatest charity and prudence, and who has pastorally cared for those involved with this project.

Please pray for this project, that this Book may, in the end, receive official approbation and full reception within the Vicariate. And please pray for our salvation as we pray for yours.

On the Feast of the Motherhood of the Blessed Virgin Mary

Pax Christi,

Mr. Augustine Watson, MSt
Chief Editor, Apologia Anglicana

Rubrics

PREFACE

In the Christian life, the Holy Sacrifice of the Mass and the Daily Office serve as the highest modes of prayer. Due to their solemnity, it is important to attend carefully to their proper celebration.

Through the Mass, the highest sacrifice is offered unto the Most Holy Trinity, and Christ is made substantially present upon the Altar. In the Office, the Christian obediently, faithfully, and joyfully observes the Sacred Scriptures' exhortation to offer the morning and evening sacrifice.

The Christian who prays this Book, both layman and cleric, must keep the rubrics and their purpose within these prayers in mind. At the same time, however, the rubrics are to help the Christian offer his Sacrifice with loving care and faithfulness, not to bog him down with obligations. The Rites and Rubrics in this Book are laid out in a manner that should be accessible, especially after a few uses, lest 'there be more business to find out what should be read, than to read it when it be found out.'

GENERAL RUBRICS

Amen When the word *Amen* is in italics, it should be said by the Congregation in response to the Minister's prayer.

Antecommunion It may occur that a community lacks a Priest on Sunday or another day where the Service of Holy Communion is desired. In such a case, Mattins and the Great Litany should first be said. Then, the Holy Mass may be said from the *Collect for Purity* until the Sermon, inclusive, concluding with the Additional Collects (p. 79).

NOTE, Mattins, the Great Litany, and Antecommunion should all be led by the Minister in the same place as the Office, not at the Altar.

Collects When several proper Collects (or Secrets, or Postcommunions) are said, only the first and the last receive the full ending.

NOTE, In the Mass, the *Lord be with you* is only said to introduce the first and second collects.

Commemorations When multiple Feast Days overlap on the same day, the Office will be of the Feast Day of highest rank. The other Feast Day(s) will then be commemorated (or, in some cases, suppressed or transferred). Commemoration consists of praying the highest-ranking Feast Day's collect first followed by the lower ranking Feast Day(s)' collect. In the Mass, this also applies to the Secret and Postcommunion.

Rubrics

Conclusion of Collects When the Collect is addressed to God the Father, the ending is 'Through Jesus Christ thy Son our Lord, who liveth and reigneth with thee, in the unity of the Holy Ghost, God, throughout all ages, world without end. Amen.'

If in the beginning of the Collect the Son be mentioned: 'Through the same Jesus Christ thy Son our Lord; who liveth and reigneth with thee in the unity of the Holy Ghost, God, throughout all ages, world without end. Amen.'

If at the end of the Collect the Son be mentioned: 'Who liveth and reigneth with thee in the unity of the Holy Ghost, God, throughout all ages, world without end. Amen.'

If the Collect be addressed to the Son: 'Who livest and reignest with the Father, in the unity of the Holy Ghost, God, throughout all ages, world without end. Amen.'

If the Collect be addressed to the Holy Spirit: 'Who livest and reignest with the Father and the Son, God, throughout all ages, world without end. Amen.'

When the Holy Spirit is mentioned in the Collect: 'In the unity of the same Holy Ghost, etc.'

Dominus Vobiscum The Minister may only proclaim the *Dominus vobiscum* (The Lord be with you) if he be in Major Orders. Otherwise, he must instead lead with the *Domine, exaudi orationem nostram* (O Lord, hear our prayer) wherever the *Dominus vobiscum* appears, or omit it entirely if it would be said twice consecutively.

Ferial Commemorations In Advent & Lent, the propers for the First Sunday of Advent and Ash Wednesday may be said when commemoration of their season's respective Feria is indicated.

Gloria Patri During Passiontide, the *Gloria Patri* is omitted in the Invitatory of Mattins, Responsory of the Minor Hours, Aspersion of the People, Introit, and Lavabo. During the Sacred Triduum, the *Gloria Patri* is wholly omitted.

Latin In much of this Book, Latin is provided alongside the English. The Latin may always be used instead of the English, unless otherwise determined by the Ordinary. When Latin is not provided, but great devotion exists for the Latin language, the Latin which serves as the base text (such as the Liber Precum Publicarum, Breviarium Monasticum, Missale, & Rituale)

Rubrics

may be used, with great concern for the catechesis and participation of the People.

Liturgical Seasons For the purpose of the rubrics, these festive seasons are referenced:

- Christmastide: From I Evensong of Christmas Day until I Evensong of Epiphany Day, exclusive.
- Epiphanytide: From I Evensong of Epiphany Day until I Evensong of Septuagesima Sunday, exclusive.
- Septuagesimatide (Pre-Lent): From I Evensong of Septuagesima Sunday until Mattins of Ash Wednesday, exclusive.
- Lent: From Mattins of Ash Wednesday until I Evensong of Passion Sunday, exclusive.
- Passiontide: From I Evensong of Passion Sunday until Mattins of Maundy Thursday, exclusive.
- Sacred Triduum: From Mattins of Maundy Thursday until I Evensong of Easter Sunday, exclusive.
- Eastertide (Paschaltide): From I Evensong of Easter Sunday until I Evensong of Trinity Sunday, exclusive.
- Trinitytide: From I Evensong of Trinity Sunday until I Evensong of the First Sunday of Advent, exclusive.

Minor Feast Days Since only I and II Doubles are provided here in this Book (with some exceptions), the rubrics will be geared towards those. When the Office or Mass is celebrated with the rest of the Feast Days, the rubrics of the *Prayer Book Hymnal* should be consulted.

Mode of Recitation Wherever it is indicated something be read, it may also be chanted, except for the Fore-Office and the Prayers after the Third Collect.

Office Rubrics

Collects The Collect to be said during the Office is provided in the relevant Proper. The Seasonal Prayers are to be said during Mass as indicated. The Seasonal Prayers (only its Collects) may be said as additional Prayers during the Office.

Rubrics

Ferial Days The Ferial Office, that is, the Simple Office of the occurrent Season, is always said on weekdays in Lent, on Ember Days, and on Rogation Monday, unless a I or II Double occur, in which case the Office is of the Feast with Commemoration of the Feria.

On weekdays in Advent and between Septuagesima and Ash Wednesday, and on Common Vigils, the Ferial Office is always said unless a Double Feast or Octave occur, and then Commemoration is made of such Ferias.

If a Simple Octave Day occur on one of these Ferias, it is only commemorated.

In like manner throughout the year the Office is of the Feria on those weekdays on which there does not occur a Double Feast, an Octave, or the Office of St. Mary on Saturday.

Gloria Patri After every Psalm and the indicated Canticles, except in the Office of the Dead or where otherwise indicated, the *Gloria Patri* should be said.

It is customary to reverence the Trinity by bowing one's head during the *Gloria Patri*, instead of crossing oneself.

Lectionary The Lessons and Psalms for the days of the Church Year are provided in the lectionary, according to the Rankings of Feast Days (p. xvi).

NOTE, The proper psalms for Second Class and lower Sundays are optional.

Octaves The Office of an Octave is said (or Commemoration thereof made, when it is hindered by a Feast or a Sunday) through eight continuous days in Octaves of Feasts of the I Class. Octaves of Feasts of the II Class, which are Simple Octaves, are kept only on the Octave Day itself, with the rite of a Simple, unless hindered by a more worthy Office; but no notice is taken of the days within the Octave. If any Octave is not ended before Ash Wednesday, the Vigil of Pentecost, or 17 December, no notice is taken of it thenceforth.

A Simple Octave Day occurring within an Octave is only commemorated.

Octave Days On the Octave Day, except for the proper Psalms and Lessons, the Office is said as on the day of the Feast, unless otherwise noted. On a Simple Octave Day the Office is Simple.

On Sundays within Privileged Octaves, the Office is said as directed in the Proper of Season. On Sundays within Common Octaves, the Office is of the Sunday with Commemoration of the Octave.

Rubrics

Office of the Dead The Office of the Dead may be prayed in addition to the Daily Office. It may also be prayed instead of the Daily Office on an ordinary Feria, a Memorial, or a Feast of Simple rank.

The Office of the Dead may also replace the Daily Office of rank Double or lower on the day of death and the day of burial.

Office of the Dead Antiphons The Antiphons are not doubled except on 2 November; on the day of a burial; on the day after receiving tidings of a death; on the third, seventh, and thirtieth days; on the anniversary (even when transferred); and whenever the Office is celebrated solemnly.

Office of the Dead Lessons The lessons are always read without introduction or conclusion.

Office of Our Lady on Saturday On all Saturdays—except in Advent, Septuagesimatide, Lent, and on Ember Days—unless the Office be of a Double Feast (even transferred), or of an occurrent Octave or Vigil, or of a Sunday anticipated according to the rubrics, the Office is of St. Mary.

Scripture Verse Numbers When a lesson or psalm is listed with only one verse (such as John 1:45 or Psalm 102:15), the Minister reads the that verse and the verses following for the rest of the chapter.

Suffrages The Suffrages in the Minor Hours are not said on Feast Days Double or higher.

Sunday Collects If the Office be of a Feria without a proper Collect, then the Sunday Collect is read. Otherwise, the Collect for the Feast Day is read instead.

Third Lesson In accordance with pious custom, after the Second Canticle in the Major Hours, but before the Creed, it is fitting for a patristic lesson to be read from the Feast Day's Second or Third Nocturn in Monastic or Sarum Matins.

Vigils The Office of a Vigil is only said at Mattins.

If a Vigil fall on a Sunday (except for the Vigils of Nativity & Epiphany), it is said or commemorated on the preceding Saturday.

Rubrics

Mass Rubrics

Chant The Priest should be aware which parts of the liturgy, according to the solemnity of the Mass and the rank of the Feast Day, should be chanted.

Conventual Masses Since this Book is oriented towards use in a parish church, it assumes the Mass being said is a 'non-conventual Mass'.

Gloria in excelsis The *Gloria in excelsis* is said in the Mass on Feast Days of Double rank and higher. It is also said on all Sundays, except in Advent, Septuagesimatide, and Lent.

NOTE, For special rubrics regarding Votive Masses and Ferias, the *Ordo* or Missal Rubrics should be consulted.

Introduction of the Epistle The Epistle is introduced according to manner specified in the rubric, preferably using the title of the book as given in the 1611 King James Bible.

Introit The Introit for each Mass is provided. The Introit is said as written, followed by the *Gloria Patri* (except in Passiontide) and the Introit repeated up to the '*Ps*' or '*Cant.*'

Nicene Creed The Nicene Creed is said after the Gospel on all Sundays throughout the year, even if the Mass is of a Feast on which it would not otherwise be said. On all Feast Days of the Apostles, St. Joseph, Our Lady, the Holy Cross, and our Lord, and through their Octaves. From Christmas until the Octave of St. John, inclusive. On the Feast of the Epiphany and its Octave. Maundy Thursday. On Feasts of Angels, St. Mary Magdalene, St. Gregory, St. Ambrose, St. Augustine of Hippo, St. Jerome, St. Hilary, St. Isidore, Pope St. Leo I, St. Bede the Venerable, St. Peter Chrysologus, St. Athanasius, St. Basil, St. Cyril of Alexandria, St. Cyril of Jerusalem, St. Ephram Syrus, St. Gregory Nazianzen, St. John Chrysostom, St. John Damascene, St. Lawrence, St. John Baptist and his Octave Day. On All Hallows' Day and through its Octave, on the Dedication of St. Saviour, and of the Holy Apostles Peter and Paul. As well as on the anniversary of the dedication of a Church, and through its Octave; on the day of consecration of a Church, or of an Altar; on the Feasts of the Patron Saint of a Church, and on the day of a Saint where his Body or a considerable Relic is preserved; on the day of the creation and coronation of the Chief Bishop, and on the anniversary of such day; on the day, and the anniversary, of the election and consecration of a bishop.

Rubrics

Also, the Creed is said in Votive Masses, which are celebrated solemnly for a grave matter or for a public Church cause, even if they are said in violet vestments on a Sunday.

Prefaces The Prefaces with Solemn Chant are to be used in all Masses of at least Semidouble rank, and in Votive Masses for a grave and public cause.

NOTE, When the Mass is of a Feast Day and has a proper Preface, its Preface is said in preference to the Season's.

NOTE, When a Mass does not have a proper Preface, and a Feast Day with a proper Preface is commemorated, the Commemoration's Preface may be said, the Feasts of Our Lord always receiving priority.

NOTE, When no proper Preface is said, the Priest proceeds immediately from *Almighty, Everlasting God.* to *Therefore, with Angels and Archangels.*

Reciting the Propers When a clerk of appropriate rank is not available, a clerk of higher rank shall fulfil his role, such as the Priest chanting the Gospel or a Deacon chanting the Epistle.

Requiem Mass On the first day of each month (outside Advent, Lent, and Eastertide) not hindered by a Semidouble or higher Feast Day, the Mass is said generally for departed Priests, Benefactors, and others. But if no day occur in the week on which it can be said, a general commemoration of the departed shall be said, except during Lent and Eastertide.

NOTE, The *Dies irae* is said on All Souls' Day and on the day of the burial in all sung Masses. However, in other Masses, it may either be recited or omitted at the pleasure of the celebrant.

Seasonal Prayers Throughout the year, as indicated in the rubrics, additional Collects, Secrets, and Postcommunions are to be said, assigned for the different seasons even within Octaves or on Vigils. On Marian Feast Days (or Feast Days which include her commemoration), when the second seasonal collect would be of St. Mary, it is instead of the Holy Ghost.

NOTE, The propers chosen for the Collect should match for the Secret and Postcommunion.

Signs of the Cross In the Mass, when ✠ appears, unless otherwise indicated or manifestly evident, it indicates the manual act of making the sign of the Cross.

Rubrics

In the Canon, if there be a cross (✠) in reference to Bread or Body, it indicates a sign of the cross made over the Host. Likewise, if there be a cross (✠) in reference to Wine or Cup, it indicates a sign of the cross made over the Cup. Otherwise, it indicates a sign of the cross made over the Gifts generally, unless otherwise stated.

When the rubrics tell the Priest to make the sign of the Cross on himself, unless otherwise indicated or manifestly evident, it indicates making the sign of the Cross from forehead to breast.

Votive Mass of Our Lady on Saturday On Saturdays not hindered by a Double or Semidouble Feast, Octave, Vigil, Lenten Feria, or Ember Day, or by the Office of a Sunday anticipated, Mass is said of our Lady according to the season, as given in the Missal.

Ranking of Days

FEAST Days are ranked in order of priority. This is important, since it determines both what is prayed in the changeable parts of the Office (the Propers) and how to determine which Feast outranks the other(s) when Feast Days overlap on the same day.

The rankings for all of the Feast Days throughout the year are provided in the Kalendar (p. xx). However, there are some rankings which are not provided there or may need to be explained. For most people, it is expedient to order a yearly Ordo from the Antiochian Western Rite Vicariate which lays out the correct ordering for each day. However, to determine it without an Ordo, important rankings are described here.

- Feast Days

    First Class Double (I Double)

    Second Class Double (II Double)

    Greater Double

    Double Feasts of Double and higher have I and II Evensong, beginning with I Evensong and ending with Compline of the following day.

    Semidouble Sundays and days within Common Octaves are Semidouble. The Semidouble Office begins with I Evensong and ends with Compline of the following day.

    Memorial No Office is to be said for a Memorial, but on the day on which they are noted in the Kalendar, Commemoration only is made of them at I Evensong and Mattins; except on II Doubles, on which Commemoration of the Memorial is omitted at Evensong; and on I Doubles, on which no Commemoration is made of Memorials.

    Simple The Office is Simple on weekdays when the Office is of the Feria, and on the Octave Day of a Simple Octave.

    The Simple Office begins with I Evensong, and ends with None of the following day.

- Ferial Days

    First Class Feria No Feast Day may be celebrated. Begins at Mattins.
    - Ash Wednesday
    - Holy Monday
    - Holy Tuesday

Ranking of Days

- Holy Wednesday

Second Class Feria Only I and II Doubles may be celebrated, lesser Feast Days being commemorated. Begins at Mattins.

- Ember Days
- Rogation Monday
- Weekdays in Lent & Passion Week

Greater Feria Begins at Mattins.

- Weekdays in Advent

Feria Begins when the Office of the preceding day ceases. The Ferial Office ends at None if a Double or Simple follow.

- Octaves
  - Privileged Octaves

    First Order Privileged Octaves The Feast Day, and second & third days of the Octave, are I Double. The rest of the Octave until the Octave Day is Semidouble. The Octave Day is I Double. Feast Days cannot outrank the Days within the Octave, nor the Octave Day.
    A I or II Double is transferred to the first unhindered day after the Octave; other Feasts are commemorated, except on the Feast Day and the two following days.
    * Easter Octave
    * Whitsun Octave

    Second Order Privileged Octaves The Feast Day is I Double. The Days within the Octave are Semidouble, being only outranked by I Double, with the Octave commemorated. The Octave Day is Greater Double, and gives place only to a I Double of universal observance.
    * Epiphany Octave
    * Corpus Christi Octave

    Third Order Privileged Octaves Days within the Octave are trumped by any feast over Simple. Any Double Feast within this Octave has its Office with Commemoration of the Octave, but on the Octave Day of the Ascension only a I or II Double is kept, with Commemoration of the Octave.
    * Christmas Octave

Ranking of Days

  - * Ascension Octave
- – Common Octaves

  The Days within the Octave are Semidouble. A Double Feast occurring within a Common Octave has its Office with Commemoration of the Octave, unless otherwise noted.

  NOTE, Common Octaves are not commemorated during Lent.

    - * Conception of the BVM Octave
    - * Assumption Octave
    - * Nativity of St. John Baptist Octave
    - * Solemnity of St. Joseph Octave
    - * Sts. Peter & Paul Octave
    - * All Hallows Octave
    - * The Octave of the principal patron saint of a church, cathedral, order, town, diocese, province, or nation.

- – Simple Octaves

  The Feast Day is II Double. The Octave Day is Simple. The Days within the Octave are not commemorated.

    - * St. Stephen Octave
    - * St. John the Evangelist Octave
    - * Holy Innocents Octave
    - * St. Lawrence Octave
    - * Nativity of the B.V.M. Octave
    - * Divine Compassion Octave
    - * An Octave of Secondary Patrons

- Sundays

  First Class Sundays of the First Class give place to no Feast. A I or II Double Feast Day falling on a Sunday of the First Class is transferred to the first unhindered day.

  NOTE, When I or II Double Feast Day falls on (or is transferred to) Monday, I Evensong is of the Feast Day with a commemoration of the Sunday. Otherwise, it is of the Sunday with a commemoration of the Feast Day.

    - – First Sunday of Advent
    - – Sundays in Lent & Passiontide

Ranking of Days

- Easter Sunday
- Low Sunday
- Whitsunday

Second Class Sundays of the Second Class give place only to I Doubles, and the Sunday is commemorated.

- Second Sunday of Advent
- Third Sunday of Advent
- Fourth Sunday of Advent
- Septuagesima Sunday
- Sexagesima Sunday
- Quinquagesima Sunday

All Other Sundays On lesser Sundays, the Office is of the Sunday unless a Double I or II Class occur thereon, when the Office is of the Feast with Commemoration of the Sunday.

- Privileged Vigils

  First Class Vigils of the First Class are preferred over any other Feast Day.

  - Vigil of the Nativity of Our Lord
  - Vigil of Whitsunday

  Second Class Vigils of the Second Class are preferred over any Feast Day, except I & II Doubles and Feasts of Our Lord.

  - Vigil of Epiphany

- Common Vigils

  Non-privileged Vigils are preferred over any Feast Day, except Doubles & above or an Octave.

Kalendar of the Church Year

January
1. Circumcision of Our Lord, *2nd Double*
   (Octave Day of the Nativity)
2. Most Holy Name of Jesus, *2nd Double*
   Octave Day of St. Stephen, Protomartyr, *Simple*
3. Octave Day of St. John, Apostle & Evangelist, *Simple*
4. Octave Day of the Holy Innocents, *Simple*
   St. Titus, Bishop & Confessor, *Memorial*
5. The Vigil of the Epiphany, *2nd Vigil*
   Pope St. Telesphorus of Rome, Bishop & Martyr, *Memorial*
6. The Epiphany of Our Lord, *1st Double*, *2nd Octave*
7. Day II within the Octave of the Epiphany, *Semidouble*
8. Day III within the Octave of the Epiphany, *Semidouble*
9. Day IV within the Octave of the Epiphany, *Semidouble*
10. Day V within the Octave of the Epiphany, *Semidouble*
    St. Paul the First Hermit, *Memorial*
11. Day VI within the Octave of the Epiphany, *Semidouble*
    Pope St. Hyginus of Rome, Bishop & Martyr, *Memorial*
12. Day VII within the Octave of the Epiphany, *Semidouble*
    St. Benedict Biscop, Abbot, *Memorial*
13. Baptism of Our Lord, *Greater Double*
    (Octave Day of the Epiphany)
14. St. Hilary, Bishop, Confessor & Doctor, *Double*
    St. Felix of Nola, Priest & Martyr, *Memorial*
15. St. Maurus, Abbot, *Greater Double*
16. Pope St. Marcellus I of Rome, Bishop & Martyr, *Memorial*
17. St. Anthony, Abbot, *Double*
18. Chair of St. Peter in Rome, *Greater Double*
    Commemoration of St. Paul, *Commemoration*
    St. Prisca of Rome, Virgin Martyress, *Memorial*
19. Sts. Marius, Martha, Audifax, & Abachum, Martyrs, *Memorial*
    St. Mark of Ephesus, Bishop & Confessor, *Memorial*
20. Sts. Fabian (Bishop) & Sebastian, Martyrs, *Double*
21. St. Agnes of Rome, Virgin Martyress, *Greater Double*
22. Sts. Vincent (Deacon) & Anastasius, Martyrs, *Memorial*
23. St. Emerentiana, Virgin Martyress, *Memorial*
24. St. Timothy, Bishop & Martyr, *Double*
25. The Conversion of St. Paul the Apostle, *Greater Double*
    Commemoration of St. Peter, *Commemoration*

Kalendar of the Church Year

26 | St. Polycarp of Smyrna, Bishop & Martyr, *Memorial*
27 | St. John Chrysostom, Bishop, Confessor, & Doctor, *Double*
28 | St. Cyril of Alexandria, Bishop, Confessor, & Doctor, *Double*
    | The Second Feast of St. Agnes, Virgin Martyress, *Memorial*
29 |
30 | St. Martina, Virgin Martyress, *Memorial*
31 | (Earliest Date of Septuagesima)

FEBRUARY

1 | St. Ignatius of Antioch, Bishop & Martyr, *Double*
  | St. Bridget of Ireland, Virgin, *Memorial*
2 | Purification of the Blessed Virgin Mary, 2nd *Double*
3 | St. Blaise, Bishop & Martyr, *Memorial*
4 | The New Martyrs of Russia, *Memorial*
  | St. Joseph of Aleppo, Martyr, *Memorial*
5 | St. Agatha, Virgin Martyress, *Greater Double*
6 | St. Dorothea, Virgin Martyress, *Memorial*
  | St. Photius, Bishop & Confessor, *Memorial*
7 | St. Romuald, Abbot, *Double*
8 |
9 | St. Apollonia of Alexandria, Virgin Martyress, *Memorial*
10 | St. Scholastica, Virgin, 2nd *Double*
11 | Pope St. Gregory II, Bishop & Confessor, *Memorial*
12 |
13 |
14 | St. Valentine, Priest & Martyr, *Memorial*
15 | Sts. Faustinus & Jovita, Martyrs, *Memorial*
16 |
17 | (Earliest Date of Lent)
18 | St. Simeon of Jerusalem, Bishop & Martyr, *Memorial*
19 |
20 |
21 |
22 | Chair of St. Peter at Antioch, 2nd *Double*
    | Commemoration of St. Paul, *Commemoration*
23 | Vigil of St. Matthias, *Vigil*
24 | St. Matthias, Apostle, 2nd *Double*
25 | St. Walburga of Heidenheim, Virgin, *Memorial*
26 | Pope St. Alexander of Alexandria, Bishop & Confessor, *Memorial*
27 | St. Raphael of Brooklyn, Bishop & Confessor, *Greater Double*

Kalendar of the Church Year

28 |

MARCH

1 | St. David of Wales, Bishop & Confessor, *Memorial*
2 | St. Chad, Bishop & Confessor, *Memorial*
3 |
4 | Pope St. Lucius I, Bishop & Martyr, *Memorial*
5 |
6 | St. Perpetua & Felicitas, Martyrs, *Double*
  | (Latest Date of Septuagesima)
7 |
8 |
9 | St. Gregory of Nyssa, Bishop, Confessor, & Doctor, *Memorial*
10 | The Forty Holy Martyrs, *Memorial*
11 |
12 | Pope St. Gregory, Bishop, Confessor, & Martyr, 2nd *Double*
13 |
14 |
15 |
16 |
17 | St. Patrick, Bishop & Confessor, *Double*
   | St. Joseph of Arimathea, Confessor, *Memorial*
18 | St. Cyril of Jerusalem, Bishop, Confessor, & Doctor, *Double*
   | St. Edward, King & Martyr, *Memorial*
19 | St. Joseph, Spouse of the Blessed Virgin Mary, Confessor, 1st *Double*
20 | St. Cuthbert, Bishop & Confessor, *Double*
21 | St. Benedict, Abbot, 2nd *Double*
22 |
23 | (Latest Date of Lent)
24 | St. Gabriel the Archangel, *Greater Double*
25 | The Annunciation of the Blessed Virgin Mary, 1st *Double*
26 |
27 | St. John Damascene, Confessor & Doctor, *Double*
28 |
29 |
30 | St. John Climacus, Abbot, *Memorial*
31 | St. Innocent of Alaska, Bishop & Confessor, *Memorial*

APRIL

1 |
2 |

Kalendar of the Church Year

3	
4	St. Isidore of Seville, Bishop, Confessor, & Doctor, *Double* (Earliest Date of Easter)
5	
6	
7	St. Tikhon of Moscow, Bishop & Confessor, *1st Double*, Common Octave
8	
9	
10	
11	Pope St. Leo the Great, Bishop, Confessor, & Doctor, *Double*
12	
13	St. Hermengild, Martyr, *Memorial*
14	St. Justin, Martyr, *Memorial*
	St. Tiburtius, Valerian, & Maximus, Martyrs, *Memorial*
15	
16	
17	Pope St. Anicetus, Bishop & Martyr, *Memorial*
18	
19	
20	
21	
22	Pope Sts. Soter & Caius, Bishops & Martyrs, *Memorial*
23	St. George, Martyr, *1st Double*, Common Octave
24	Day II within the Octave of St. George, *Semidouble*
25	St. Mark, Evangelist, *2nd Double*
	Day III within the Octave of St. George, *Semidouble*
26	Day IV within the Octave of St. George, *Semidouble*
	Sts. Cletus & Marcellinus, Martyrs, *Memorial*
27	Day V within the Octave of St. George, *Semidouble*
28	Day VI within the Octave of St. George, *Semidouble*
	St. Vitalis, Martyr, *Memorial*
29	Day VII within the Octave of St. George, *Semidouble*
30	Octave Day of St. George, *Greater Double*

May

1	Sts. Philip & James, Apostles, *2nd Double*
2	St. Athanasius, Bishop, Confessor, & Doctor, *Double*
3	Invention of the Holy Cross, *2nd Double*
	Sts. Pope Alexander (Bishop), Eventius, Theodulus (Martyrs), & Juvenalis (Bishop & Confessor), *Memorial*

Kalendar of the Church Year

4	St. Monica, Widow, *Memorial*
5	
6	St. John before the Latin Gate, *Greater Double*
7	St. Alexis Toth, Priest & Confessor, *Memorial*
8	The Apparition of St. Michael the Archangel, *Greater Double*
	Pope St. Boniface IV, Bishop & Confessor, *Memorial*
	(Latest Date of Easter)
9	St. Gregory Nazianzen, Bishop, Confessor, & Doctor, *Double*
10	Sts. Gordian & Epimachus, Martyrs, *Memorial*
11	
12	Sts. Nereus, Achilles, Domitilla, & Pancras, Martyrs, *Memorial*
13	
14	St. Boniface of Tarsus, Martyr, *Memorial*
15	
16	
17	
18	St. Venantius, Martyr, *Double*
19	St. Pudentiana, Virgin, *Memorial*
20	
21	
22	St. Romanus, Abbot, *Memorial*
23	
24	St. Vincent of Lerins, Confessor, *Memorial*
25	Pope St. Urban, Bishop & Martyr, *Memorial*
26	St. Augustine of Canterbury, Bishop & Confessor, *Double*
	Pope St. Eleutherius, Bishop & Martyr, *Memorial*
27	St. Bede the Venerable, Confessor & Doctor, *Double*
	Pope St. John I, Bishop & Martyr, *Memorial*
28	
29	
30	Pope St. Felix I, Bishop & Martyr, *Memorial*
31	St. Petronilla, Virgin, *Memorial*

JUNE

1	
2	St. Marcellinus, Peter, & Erasmus, Martyrs, *Memorial*
3	
4	
5	St. Boniface, Bishop & Martyr, *Double*
6	
7	

Kalendar of the Church Year

8	
9	St. Columba of Iona, Abbot, *Double*
	Sts. Primus & Felician, Martyrs, *Memorial*
10	St. Margaret of Scotland, Queen & Widow, *Memorial*
11	St. Barnabas, Apostle, *Greater Double*
12	Sts. Basilides, Cyrinus, Nabor, & Nazarius, Martyrs, *Memorial*
13	
14	St. Basil the Great, Bishop, Confessor, & Doctor, *Greater Double*
15	Sts. Vitus, Modestus, & Crescentia, Martyrs, *Memorial*
16	
17	
18	St. Ephrem the Syrian, Deacon, Confessor, & Doctor, *Double*
	Sts. Marcus & Marcellianus, Martyrs, *Memorial*
19	Sts. Gervase & Protase, Martyrs, *Memorial*
20	Pope St. Silverius, Bishop & Martyr, *Memorial*
21	
22	St. Alban, Protomartyr of England, *Double*
	St. Paulinus, Bishop & Confessor, *Memorial*
23	Vigil of St. John Baptist, *Vigil*
	St. Etheldreda, Queen & Virgin, *Memorial*
24	Nativity of St. John Baptist, 1st *Double*, Common Octave
25	Day II within the Octave of St. John Baptist, *Semidouble*
26	Sts. John & Paul, Martyrs, *Double*
	Day III within the Octave of St. John Baptist, *Semidouble*
27	Day IV within the Octave of St. John Baptist, *Semidouble*
28	Day V within the Octave of St. John Baptist, *Semidouble*
	Vigil of Sts. Peter & Paul, *Vigil*
	Pope St. Leo II, Bishop & Confessor, *Memorial*
29	Sts. Peter & Paul, Apostles, 1st *Double*, Common Octave
	Day VI within the Octave of St. John Baptist, *Semidouble*
30	Commemoration of St. Paul, Apostle, *Greater Double*
	Commemoration of St. Peter, Apostle, *Commemoration*
	Day VII within the Octave of St. John Baptist, *Semidouble*

JULY

1	Most Precious Blood of Our Lord Jesus Christ, 2nd *Double*
	Octave Day of St. John Baptist, *Greater Double*
	Day III within the Octave of Sts. Peter & Paul, *Semidouble*
2	Visitation of the Blessed Virgin Mary, 2nd *Double*
	St. John of San Francisco, Bishop & Confessor, *Memorial*

Kalendar of the Church Year

	Sts. Processus & Martinian, Martyrs, *Memorial*
	Day IV within the Octave of Sts. Peter & Paul, *Semidouble*
3	St. Irenæus of Lyon, Bishop & Martyr, *Double*
	Day V within the Octave of Sts. Peter & Paul, *Semidouble*
4	Day VI within the Octave of Sts. Peter & Paul, *Semidouble*
5	Day VII within the Octave of Sts. Peter & Paul, *Semidouble*
6	The Octave Day of Sts. Peter & Paul, *Greater Double*
7	Sts. Cyril & Methodius, Bishops & Confessors, *Double*
8	
9	
10	Seven Holy Brothers, with Sts. Rufina & Secunda, Martyrs, *Memorial*
	Sts. Joseph of Damascus (Priest) & Companions, Martyrs, *Memorial*
11	Pope St. Pius I, Bishop & Martyr, *Memorial*
	[Solemnity of St. Benedict (Monastics & Oblates only)], *Greater Double*
12	Sts. Nabor & Felix, Martyrs, *Memorial*
13	Pope St. Anacletus, Bishop & Martyr, *Memorial*
14	
15	St. Vladimir of Kiev, King & Confessor, *Double*
16	Sts. Nicholas & Habib Khasha, Martyrs, *Memorial*
17	St. Alexius, Confessor, *Memorial*
18	Translation of St. Raphael of Brooklyn, *Double*
	St. Sergius of Radonezh, Abbot, *Memorial*
	Sts. Symphorosa & Her Seven Sons, Martyrs, *Memorial*
19	St. Seraphim of Sarov, Priest & Confessor, *Memorial*
20	St. Elias the Prophet, Confessor, *Double*
	St. Margaret of Antioch, Virgin Martyress, *Memorial*
21	St. Praxedes, Virgin, *Memorial*
22	St. Mary Magdalene, Penitent, *Greater Double*
23	St. John Cassian, Abbot, *Memorial*
	St. Apollinaris of Ravenna, Bishop & Martyr, *Memorial*
	St. Liborius, Bishop & Confessor, *Memorial*
24	Vigil of St. James, *Vigil*
	St. Christina, Virgin Martyress, *Memorial*
25	St. James, Apostle, *2nd Double*
	St. Christopher, Martyr, *Memorial*
26	St. Anne, Mother of the Blessed Virgin Mary, *2nd Double*
27	St. Pantaleon, Martyr, *Memorial*
28	Sts. Nazarius, Celsus, Martyrs; Pope St. Victor, Bishop & Martyr; & Pope St. Innocent, Bishop & Confessor, *Memorial*

Kalendar of the Church Year

29 | St. Martha of Bethany, Virgin, *Double*
   | Sts. Pope Felix II (Bishop), Simplicius, Faustinus, & Beatrice, Martyrs, *Memorial*
30 | Sts. Abdon & Sennen, Martyrs, *Memorial*
31 |

August

1 | Chains of St. Peter, Apostle, *Greater Double*
  | Commemoration of St. Paul, Apostle, *Commemoration*
  | Holy Maccabees, Martyrs, *Memorial*
2 | Pope St. Stephen, Bishop & Martyr, *Memorial*
3 | The Invention of St. Stephen, Protomartyr, *Double*
4 |
5 | Dedication of Our Lady of the Snows, *Greater Double*
  | St. Oswald, King & Martyr, *Memorial*
6 | Transfiguration of Our Lord Jesus Christ, *2nd Double*
  | Sts. Pope Sixtus II (Bishop & Martyr), Felicissimus, & Agapitus (Deacons), Martyrs, *Memorial*
7 | Most Holy Name of Jesus, *2nd Double*
  | St. Donatus, Bishop & Martyr, *Memorial*
8 | Sts. Cyriacus, Largus, & Smaragdus, Martyrs, *Memorial*
9 | Vigil of St. Lawrence, *Vigil*
  | St. Romanus, Martyr, *Memorial*
10 | St. Lawrence, Deacon & Martyr, *2nd Double*, Simple Octave
11 | Sts. Tiburtius & Susanna, Martyrs, *Memorial*
12 |
13 | St. Maximus of Constantinople, Confessor, *Double*
   | Sts. Hippolytus & Cassian, Martyrs, *Memorial*
14 | Vigil of the Assumption, *Vigil*
   | St. Eusebius, Priest & Confessor, *Memorial*
15 | Assumption of the Blessed Virgin Mary, *1st Double*, Common Octave
16 | St. Joachim, Father of the Blessed Virgin Mary, *2nd Double*
17 | Day III within the Octave of the Assumption, *Semidouble*
   | Octave Day of St. Lawrence, *Simple*
18 | Day IV within the Octave of the Assumption, *Semidouble*
   | St. Helen, Empress, *Memorial*
   | St. Agapitus, Martyr, *Memorial*
19 | Day V within the Octave of the Assumption, *Semidouble*
20 | Day VI within the Octave of the Assumption, *Semidouble*
21 | Day VII within the Octave of the Assumption, *Semidouble*

Kalendar of the Church Year

22	Octave Day of the Assumption, *Greater Double*
	St. Timothy (Bishop), Hippolytus, & Symphorian, Martyrs, *Memorial*
23	Vigil of St. Bartholomew, *Vigil*
24	St. Bartholomew, Apostle, *2nd Double*
25	
26	Pope St. Zephyrinus, Bishop & Martyr, *Memorial*
27	
28	St. Augustine of Hippo, Bishop, Confessor, & Doctor, *Greater Double*
	St. Hermes, Martyr, *Memorial*
29	Decollation of St. John Baptist, *Greater Double*
	St. Sabina, Martyr, *Memorial*
30	Sts. Felix & Adauctus, Martyrs, *Memorial*
31	St. Aidan of Lindisfarne, Bishop & Confessor, *Memorial*

SEPTEMBER

1	St. Giles, Abbot, *Memorial*
	Twelve Holy Brothers, Martyrs, *Memorial*
2	St. Stephen of Hungary, King & Confessor, *Memorial*
3	
4	St. Gorazde of Prague, Bishop & Martyr, *Double*
5	
6	
7	
8	Nativity of the Blessed Virgin Mary, *2nd Double*, Simple Octave
	St. Hadrian, Martyr, *Memorial*
9	St. Gorgonius, Martyr, *Memorial*
10	
11	Sts. Protus & Hyacinth, Martyrs, *Memorial*
12	Most Holy Name of Mary, *Greater Double*
13	
14	Exaltation of the Holy Cross, *Greater Double*
15	Seven Sorrows of the Blessed Virgin Mary, *2nd Double*
	St. Nicomedes, Martyr, *Memorial*
16	Sts. Pope Cornelius & Cyprian, Bishops and Martyrs, *Double*
	Sts. Euphemia, Lucy, & Geminian, Martyrs, *Memorial*
17	
18	
19	Sts. Januarius & Companions, Martyrs, *Double*
	St. Theodore of Canterbury, Bishop & Confessor, *Memorial*
20	Sts. Eustace & Companions, Martyrs, *Double*

Kalendar of the Church Year

	Vigil of St. Matthew, *Vigil*
21	St. Matthew, Apostle & Evangelist, *2nd Double*
22	Sts. Maurice & Companions, Martyrs, *Memorial*
23	Pope St. Linus, Bishop & Martyr, *Memorial*
	St. Thecla, Virgin Martyress, *Memorial*
24	
25	
26	Sts. Cyprian & Justina, Martyrs, *Memorial*
27	Sts. Cosmas & Damian, Martyrs, *Memorial*
28	St. Wenceslaus, Martyr, *Memorial*
29	Dedication of St. Michael the Archangel, *1st Double*
30	St. Jerome, Priest, Confessor, & Doctor, *Greater Double*
	St. Gregory of Armenia, Bishop & Confessor, *Memorial*

October

1	St. Remigius, Bishop & Confessor, *Memorial*
2	Holy Guardian Angels, *Greater Double*
3	
4	
5	Sts. Placidus & Companions, Martyrs, *Double*
6	
7	The Holy Rosary of the Blessed Virgin Mary, *Greater Double*
	Pope St. Mark of Rome, Bishop & Confessor, *Memorial*
	Sts. Sergius, Bacchus, Marcellus, & Apuleius, Martyrs, *Memorial*
8	
9	Sts. Denys, Rusticus, & Eleutherius, Martyrs, *Memorial*
10	
11	Motherhood of the Blessed Virgin Mary, *2nd Double*
12	St. Wilfrid, Bishop & Confessor, *Memorial*
13	St. Edward, King & Confessor, *Memorial*
14	Pope St. Callistus, Bishop & Martyr, *Double*
15	Our Lady of Walsingham, *Double*
16	
17	
18	St. Luke, Evangelist, *2nd Double*
19	St. Frideswide, Virgin, *Memorial*
20	
21	St. Hilarion, Abbot, *Memorial*
	Sts. Ursula & Companions, Martyrs, *Memorial*
22	

Kalendar of the Church Year

23	
24	St. Raphael the Archangel, *Greater Double*
25	Sts. Chrysanthus & Daria, Martyrs, *Memorial*
26	Pope St. Evaristus, Bishop & Martyr, *Memorial*
27	Vigil of Sts. Simon & Jude, *Vigil*
28	Sts. Simon & Jude, Apostles, 2nd *Double*
29	
30	
31	Vigil of All Hallows, *Vigil*

November

1	All Hallows, 1st *Double*, Common Octave
2	All Souls, *Double*
	Day II within the Octave of All Hallows, *Semidouble*
3	Day III within the Octave of All Hallows, *Semidouble*
	St. Winifred, Virgin Martyress, *Memorial*
4	Day IV within the Octave of All Hallows, *Semidouble*
	Sts. Vitalis & Agricola, Martyrs, *Memorial*
5	Day V within the Octave of All Hallows, *Semidouble*
	St. Elizabeth, Mother of St. John Baptist, *Memorial*
6	Day VI within the Octave of All Hallows, *Semidouble*
7	Day VII within the Octave of All Hallows, *Semidouble*
	St. Willibrord, Bishop & Confessor, *Memorial*
8	Octave Day of All Hallows, *Greater Double*
	Four Crowned Martyrs, *Memorial*
9	Dedication of the Basilica of St. Saviour, *Greater Double*
	St. Theodore Tyro, Martyr, *Memorial*
10	Sts. Tryphon, Respicius, & Nympha, Martyrs, *Memorial*
11	St. Martin of Tours, Bishop & Confessor, *Greater Double*
	St. Mennas, Martyr, *Memorial*
12	Pope St. Martin I, Bishop & Martyr, *Memorial*
13	St. Britius of Tours, Bishop & Confessor, *Memorial*
14	St. Gregory Palamas, Bishop & Confessor, *Memorial*
15	
16	
17	St. Gregory the Wonder-worker, Bishop & Confessor, *Memorial*
	St. Hilda of Whitby, Virgin, *Memorial*
18	Dedication of the Basilica of the Holy Apostles Peter & Paul, *Greater Double*
19	Pope St. Pontianus, Bishop & Martyr, *Memorial*

Kalendar of the Church Year

20	St. Edmund, King & Martyr, *Double*
21	Presentation of the Blessed Virgin Mary, *Greater Double*
	St. Gelasius, Bishop & Confessor, *Memorial*
	St. Columbanus, Abbot, *Memorial*
22	St. Cecilia, Virgin Martyress, *Greater Double*
23	Pope St. Clement, Bishop & Martyr, *Double*
	St. Felicitas, Martyr, *Memorial*
24	St. Chrysogonus, Martyr *Memorial*
25	St. Catherine of Alexandria, Virgin Martyress, *Double*
26	St. Peter of Alexandria, Bishop & Martyr, *Memorial*
27	
28	
29	Vigil of St. Andrew, *Vigil*
	St. Saturninus, Bishop & Martyr, *Memorial*
30	St. Andrew, Apostle, 2nd *Double*

December

1	
2	St. Peter Chrysologus, Bishop, Confessor, & Doctor, *Double*
	St. Bibiana, Virgin Martyress, *Memorial*
3	
4	St. Barbara, Virgin Martyress, *Memorial*
5	St. Sabbas of Judæa, Abbot , *Memorial*
6	St. Nicholas, Bishop & Confessor, *Double*
7	St. Ambrose of Milan, Bishop, Confessor, & Doctor, *Greater Double*
8	Conception of the Blessed Virgin Mary, 2nd *Double*, Common Octave
9	Day II within the Octave of the Conception, *Semidouble*
10	Day III within the Octave of the Conception, *Semidouble*
	Pope St. Melchiades, Bishop & Martyr, *Memorial*
11	Day IV within the Octave of the Conception, *Semidouble*
	Pope St. Damasus, Bishop & Confessor, *Memorial*
12	Day V within the Octave of the Conception, *Semidouble*
13	St. Lucy, Virgin Martyress, *Greater Double*
	Day VI within the Octave of the Conception, *Semidouble*
	St. Herman of Alaska, Priest & Confessor, *Memorial*
14	Day VII within the Octave of the Conception, *Semidouble*
15	Octave Day of the Conception of the Blessed Virgin Mary, *Greater Double*
16	St. Eusebius of Vercelli, Bishop & Martyr, *Memorial*
17	

Kalendar of the Church Year

18	Expectation of the Blessed Virgin Mary, *Double*
19	
20	Vigil of St. Thomas, *Vigil*
21	St. Thomas, Apostle, 2nd *Double*
22	
23	
24	Vigil of the Nativity of Our Lord, 1st *Vigil*
25	Nativity of Our Lord, 1st *Double*, 3rd Octave
	St. Anastasia, Virgin Martyress, *Commemoration*
26	St. Stephen, Protomartyr, 2nd *Double*, Simple Octave
	Day II within the Nativity Octave, *Semidouble*
27	St. John, Apostle & Evangelist, 2nd *Double*, Simple Octave
	Day III within the Nativity Octave, *Semidouble*
28	Holy Innocents, Martyrs, 2nd *Double*, Simple Octave
	Day IV within the Nativity Octave, *Semidouble*
29	Day V within the Nativity Octave, *Semidouble*
30	Day VI within the Nativity Octave, *Semidouble*
31	St. Sylvester, Bishop & Confessor, *Double*
	Day VII within the Nativity Octave, *Semidouble*

Daily Office Lectionary

Lectionary

Proper of Season

Day	Psalms	Lesson 1	Lesson 2
ADVENT I			
Mattins	8,50	Is 55	Lk 1:57
Evensong	96,97	Is 60:1-11,18-end	Jn 1:15-28
Monday			
Mattins	-	Gn 1:1-2:3	Mk 1:1-20
Evensong	-	1 Kgs 11:1-25	Rev 4
Tuesday			
Mattins	-	Gn 2:4-14	Mk 1:21
Evensong	-	1 Kgs 11:26	Rev 5
Wednesday			
Mattins	-	Gn 2:15	Mk 2
Evensong	-	1 Kgs 12	Rev 6
Thursday			
Mattins	-	Gn 3	Mk 3
Evensong	-	1 Kgs 13	Rev 7
Friday			
Mattins	-	Gn 4:1-15	Mk 4:1-34
Evensong	-	1 Kgs 14:1-20	Rev 8
Saturday			
Mattins	-	Gn 4:16	Mk 4:35-5:20
ADVENT II			
Evensong	36,57	1 Kgs 15:25-16:7	Rev 9
Mattins	80,82	Is 35	Lk 4:14-32
Evensong	25,26	Jdgs 16:21	Lk 6:27-42
Monday			
Mattins	-	Gn 6	Mk 5:21
Evensong	-	1 Kgs 16:8	Rev 10
Tuesday			
Mattins	-	Gn 7:1-12	Mk 6:1-29
Evensong	-	1 Kgs 17	Rev 11:1-18
Wednesday			
Mattins	-	Gn 7:13	Mk 6:30
Evensong	-	1 Kgs 18	Rev 11:19-12:end
Thursday			
Mattins	-	Gn 8:1-19	Mk 7

Lectionary *Proper of Season*

Day	Psalms	Lesson 1	Lesson 2
Evensong	-	1 Kgs 19	Rev 13
Friday			
Mattins	-	Gn 8:20-9:19	Mk
Evensong	-	1 Kgs 20:1-25	Rev 14
Saturday			
Mattins	-	Gn 9:20 & 11:1-9	Mk 8:1-21
ADVENT III			
Evensong	96,97,98	1 Kgs 20:26	Rev 15-16
Mattins	52,53	Is 40:1-11	Lk 3:1-18
Evensong	93,94	Is 61	Mt 9:35-10:7
Monday			
Mattins	-	2 Esd 6:38-55	Mk 8:22-9:1
Evensong	-	1 Kgs 21	Rev 17
Tuesday			
Mattins	-	Ecclus 42:15-43:10	Mk 9:2-37
Evensong	-	1 Kgs 22:1-28	Rev 18
Ember Wednesday			
Mattins	15,24,26	Mal 1:6-2:7	Jn 1:29
Evensong	84,132,134	Dt 18:13	2 Tim 1:1-2:7
Thursday			
Mattins	-	Ecclus 16:24-17:15	Mk 9:38-10:16
Evensong	-	1 Kgs 22:29	Rev 19
Ember Friday			
Mattins	15,24,26	Mal 3:1-12	Mt 9:1-17
Evensong	84,132,134	1 Sam 3	2 Tim 2:8
Ember Saturday			
Mattins	15,24,26	Mal 3:13-4:end	Lk 6:12-23
Evensong	84,132,134	Jer 1	2 Tim 3:14-4:8
ADVENT IV			
Mattins	98,99	Is 52:1-10	Mt 25:1-13
Evensong	101,103	1 Kgs 17:1-16	Mt 3:1-12
Monday			
Mattins	-	Is 1:1-20	Mk 10:17
Evensong	-	Dt 18:9	Rev 20-21:8
Tuesday			
Mattins	-	Is 2:1-21	Mk 11:
Evensong	-	Mic 3:5-4:7	Rev 21:9-22:end
Wednesday			
Mattins	-	Is 2:22-3:15	Mk 12:1-27

Proper of Season # Lectionary

Day	Psalms	Lesson 1	Lesson 2
Evensong	-	Joel 3:9	Lk 1:1-25
Thursday			
Mattins	-	Is 5:1-17	Mk 12:28
Evensong	-	Ezek 12:21	Lk 1:26-38
Friday			
Mattins	-	Is 5:18	Mk 13
Evensong	-	Zech 2:10	Lk 1:39-56
Saturday			
Mattins	-	Is 9:8-10:4	Mt 1:18
CHRISTMAS			
Evensong	2,8,144	Mic 5:2-7	Lk 1:57
Mattins	19,45,85	Is 9:2-7	Lk 2:1-20
Evensong	89:1-30,110,132	Is 7:10-16	Titus 2:11-3:7
ST. STEPHEN			
Mattins	118	2 Chron 24:15-25	Acts 6
Evensong	30,31:1-6	Wis 4:7-15	Acts 7:59-8:8
ST. JOHN EVANGELIST			
Mattins	23,24	Ex 33:7	Jn 13:20-35
Evensong	97	Is 6:1-8	Rev 4
HOLY INNOCENTS			
Mattins	8,26	Jer 31:1-17	Mt 18:1-14
Evensong	19,126	2 Chron 22:8	Mk 10:13-27
CHRISTMAS I			
Mattins	2,8	1 Sam 1:20	Lk 2:22-40
Evensong	89:1-30	Is 9:2-7	Lk 2:1-19
29 December			
Mattins	-	Is 10:33-11:9	1 Jn 1:1-2:6
Evensong	-	Ezek 34:1-16	Lk 2:21-40
30 December			
Mattins	-	Is 11:10-12:end	1 Jn 2:7-17
Evensong	-	Ezek 34:17	Mt 2:1-12
31 December			
Mattins	-	Is 25:1-9	1 Jn 2:18
CIRCUMCISION			
Evensong	105	Dt 10:12-11:1	Mt 2:13
Mattins	40:1-16,90	Ex 6:2-8	Mt 1:18
Evensong	65,103	Gn 32:22-30	Rev 19:11-16
CHRISTMAS II			
Mattins	85,87	Ex 2:1-10	Mt 2:13

Lectionary *Proper of Season*

Day	Psalms	Lesson 1	Lesson 2
Evensong	90,91	Prv 31:10-29	Lk 2:15-32
Most Holy Name of Jesus			
Evensong	146,147	Is 7:10-14	Phil 2:5-11
Mattins	9,19,24	Is 28:9-22	1 Jn 3
Evensong	110,111,112	Jer 23:1-6	Lk 2:41
3 January			
Mattins	-	Is 29:9-19	1 Jn 3:18-4:6
Evensong	-	Jer 30:1-11	Jn 1:1-28
4 January			
Mattins	-	Is 32:1-8,16-18	1 Jn 4:7
Evensong	-	Jer 30:15-22	Jn 1:29
5 January			
Mattins	-	Is 35	1 Jn 5
Epiphany			
Evensong	19,67	Num 24:15-24	Mt 28:16
Mattins	46,47,48	Is 60	Mt 3:13
Evensong	72,117,135	Is 49:1-13	Jn 2:1-11
Monday			
Mattins	-	Is 42:5-12	Gal 1
Evensong	-	Jer 31:1-9	Jn 2:12
Tuesday			
Mattins	-	Is 45:11-23	Gal 2
Evensong	-	Jer 31:27-37	Jn 3:1-21
Wednesday			
Mattins	-	Is 55	Gal 3
Evensong	-	Jer 33:14	Jn 3:22
Thursday			
Mattins	-	Is 56:1-8	Gal 4:1-5:1
Evensong	-	Ezek 36:1-15	Jn 4:1-26
Friday			
Mattins	-	Is 61	Gal 5:2
Evensong	-	Zeph 3:7	Jn 4:27
Saturday			
Mattins	-	Is 66:1-2,10-14,18-23	Gal 6
Evensong	-	Zech 14:1-9	Jn 5:1-24
Epiphany I			
Mattins	47,48	Gn 28:10	Mt 2:1-11
Evensong	66,67	1 Sam 2:1-11,26	Mt 18:1-5,10-14

Proper of Season

Lectionary

Day	Psalms	Lesson 1	Lesson 2
Monday			
Mattins	-	Gn 11:27-12:9	Rom 1:1-15
Evensong	-	2 Kgs 1	Jn 5:25
Tuesday			
Mattins	-	Gn 12:10	Rom 1:16
Evensong	-	2 Kgs 2	Jn 6:1-21
Wednesday			
Mattins	-	Gn 13	Rom 2:1-16
Evensong	-	2 Kgs 3	Jn 6:22-40
Thursday			
Mattins	-	Gn 14	Rom 2:17
Evensong	-	2 Kgs 4:1-25a	Jn 6:41
Friday			
Mattins	-	Gn 15	Rom 3:1-18
Evensong	-	2 Kgs 4:25b	Jn 7:1-30
Saturday			
Mattins	-	Gn 16	Rom 3:19
Evensong	-	2 Kgs 5	Jn 7:31
EPIPHANY II			
Mattins	96,97	Ex 3:1-15	Mk 9:2-13
Evensong	45,46	Neh 2:1-11	Acts 5:17-32
Monday			
Mattins	-	Gn 17	Rom 4:1-13
Evensong	-	2 Kgs 6	Jn 8:1-30
Tuesday			
Mattins	-	Gn 18	Rom 4:14
Evensong	-	2 Kgs 7	Jn 8:31
Wednesday			
Mattins	-	Gn 19:1-29	Rom 5:1-11
Evensong	-	2 Kgs 8	Jn 9:1-23
Thursday			
Mattins	-	Gn 19:30-20:end	Rom 5:12
Evensong	-	2 Kgs 9	Jn 9:24
Friday			
Mattins	-	Gn 21:1-21	Rom 6:1-14
Evensong	-	2 Kgs 10	Jn 10:1-21
Saturday			
Mattins	-	Gn 21:22	Rom 6:15
Evensong	-	2 Kgs 11	Jn 10:22

Lectionary *Proper of Season*

Day	Psalms	Lesson 1	Lesson 2
EPIPHANY III			
Mattins	20,21	1 Sam 3:1-18	Mk 10:13-16,35-45
Evensong	27,29	Jonah 3-4	Acts 10:1-35,44-end
Monday			
Mattins	-	Gn 22	Rom 7:1-12
Evensong	-	2 Kgs 12	Jn 11:1-27
Tuesday			
Mattins	-	Gn 23	Rom 7:13
Evensong	-	Jonah 1-2	Jn 11:28-44
Wednesday			
Mattins	-	Gn 24:1-28	Rom 8:1-11
Evensong	-	Jonah 3-4	Jn 11:45
Thursday			
Mattins	-	Gn 24:29-52	Rom 8:11-25
Evensong	-	2 Kgs 13	Jn 12:1-19
Friday			
Mattins	-	Gn 24:53	Rom 8:26
Evensong	-	Amos 1:1-2:3	Jn 12:20-36
Saturday			
Mattins	-	Gn 25:7-11,19-end	Rom 9:1-18
Evensong	-	Amos 2:4	Jn 12:37
EPIPHANY IV			
Mattins	75,76	1 Kgs 18:1,17-39	Mk 1:32
Evensong	107	Num 22:1-35	Matt 23:16-26
Monday			
Mattins	-	Gn 26	Rom 9:19
Evensong	-	Amos 3-4	Jn 13:1-19
Tuesday			
Mattins	-	Gn 27:1-25	Rom 10:1-10
Evensong	-	Amos 5	Jn 13:20
Wednesday			
Mattins	-	Gn 27:26	Rom 10:11
Evensong	-	Amos 6	Jn 14
Thursday			
Mattins	-	Gn 28	Rom 11:1-11
Evensong	-	Amos 7	Jn 15
Friday			
Mattins	-	Gn 29:1-20	Rom 11:12-24
Evensong	-	Amos 8	Jn 16

Proper of Season # Lectionary

Day	Psalms	Lesson 1	Lesson 2
Saturday			
Mattins	-	Gn 29:21	Rom 11:25
Evensong	-	Amos 9	Jn 17
EPIPHANY V			
Mattins	63, 65	1 Kgs 18:41-19:end	Mk 8:22-9:1
Evensong	78	Num 23:1-26	Acts 5:1-11
Monday			
Mattins	-	Gn 30:1-24	Rom 12
Evensong	-	Hos 4	Jn 18:1-27
Tuesday			
Mattins	-	Gn 30:25-31:3	Rom 13
Evensong	-	Hos 5-6	Jn 18:28-19:16
Wednesday			
Mattins	-	Gn 31:4-24	Rom 14:1-18
Evensong	-	Hos 10	Jn 19:17
Thursday			
Mattins	-	Gn 31:25	Rom 14:19-15:12
Evensong	-	Hos 11	Jn 20:1-18
Friday			
Mattins	-	Gn 32	Rom 15:13
Evensong	-	Hos 13-14	Jn 20:19
Saturday			
Mattins	-	Gn 33	Rom 16
Evensong	-	2 Kgs 14	Jn 21
EPIPHANY VI			
Mattins	146, 147	Dan 3:8	Mk 10:46
Evensong	148, 149, 150	Num 24:2	Lk 10:1-16
Monday			
Mattins	-	Wis 1:1-14, 2:23-end	2 Pet 1
Evensong	-	2 Kgs 15	Heb 1
Tuesday			
Mattins	-	Wis 4:7-15	2 Pet 2
Evensong	-	2 Kgs 17:1-23	Heb 2
Wednesday			
Mattins	-	Wis 6:1-21	2 Pet 3
Evensong	-	2 Kgs 17:24	Heb 3
Thursday			
Mattins	-	Wis 6:22-7:14	Jude
Evensong	-	Nah 1	Heb 3

Lectionary *Proper of Season*

Day	Psalms	Lesson 1	Lesson 2
Friday			
Mattins	-	Wis 8:1-18	2 Jn
Evensong	-	Nah 2	Heb 4
Saturday			
Mattins	-	Wis 9:1-16	3 Jn
Evensong	-	Nah 3	Heb 5
EPIPHANY VII			
Mattins	75, 76	2 Esd 16:53-67	Jas 4
Evensong	107	Bar 3:1-14	Mt 21:33
Monday			
Mattins	-	Prv 22:17	Mk 9:2-29
Evensong	-	Ecclus 28	Heb 6
Tuesday			
Mattins	-	Prv 23:19	Mk 9:30
Evensong	-	Ecclus 29	Heb 7:1-17
Wednesday			
Mattins	-	Prv 24:1-22	Mk 10:1-31
Evensong	-	Ecclus 35	Heb 7:18
Thursday			
Mattins	-	Prv 24:23	Mk 10:32
Evensong	-	Eccles 1	Heb 8
Friday			
Mattins	-	Prv 25	Acts 8:14
Evensong	-	Eccles 2	Heb 9:1-10
Saturday			
Mattins	-	Prv 26	Acts 9:1-22
Evensong	-	Eccles 3	Heb 9:11
EPIPHANY VIII			
Mattins	63, 65	Prayer of Manasses	Jas 5
Evensong	78	Bar 4:36-5:end	Mt 23:1-22
Monday			
Mattins	-	Prv 27	Acts 13:33
Evensong	-	Eccles 5	Heb 10:1-18
Tuesday			
Mattins	-	Prv 28	Acts 14
Evensong	-	Eccles 6:1-7:8	Heb 10:19
Wednesday			
Mattins	-	Prv 29	Rev 17
Evensong	-	Eccles 8:1-15	Heb 11:1-16

Proper of Season # Lectionary

Day	Psalms	Lesson 1	Lesson 2
Thursday			
Mattins	-	Prv 30:1-16	Rev 18
Evensong	-	Eccles 8:16-9:end	Heb 11:17
Friday			
Mattins	-	Prv 30:17	Rev 19
Evensong	-	Eccles 10	Heb 12
Saturday			
Mattins	-	Prv 31	Rev 20
Evensong	-	Eccles 11-12	Heb 13
SEPTUAGESIMA			
Mattins	8,148	Josh 6:1-21	Lk 7:1-10
Evensong	104	Lam 1:1-12	Mt 23:29-24:2
Monday			
Mattins	-	Gn 34	Phil 1:1-11
Evensong	-	1 Kgs 14:21	Mt 5:1-20
Tuesday			
Mattins	-	Gn 35-36:8	Phil 1:12
Evensong	-	1 Kgs 15:1-24	Mt 5:21
Wednesday			
Mattins	-	Gn 37	Phil 2:1-13
Evensong	-	2 Chron 19:4-end,20:30-end	Mt 6:1-18
Thursday			
Mattins	-	Gn 38	Phil 2:14
Evensong	-	2 Chron 21	Mt 6:19
Friday			
Mattins	-	Gn 39	Phil 3
Evensong	-	2 Chron 22	Mt 7:1-27
Saturday			
Mattins	-	Gn 40	Phil 4
Evensong	-	2 Chron 23	Mt 13:24-52
SEXAGESIMA			
Mattins	33,93	1 Sam 17:17	Mt 10:32-39
Evensong	139	2 Sam 22:1-12,33-36	Acts 12:1-17
Monday			
Mattins	-	Gn 41:1-36	Jas 1:1-15
Evensong	-	2 Chron 24	Mt 15:1-20
Tuesday			
Mattins	-	Gn 41:37	Jas 1:16
Evensong	-	2 Chron 25	Mt 18:1-14

Lectionary *Proper of Season*

Day	Psalms	Lesson 1	Lesson 2
Wednesday			
Mattins	-	Gn 42:1-17	Jas 2:1-12
Evensong	-	2 Chron 26:1-5-27:end	Mt 18:15
Thursday			
Mattins	-	Gn 42:18	Jas 2:12
Evensong	-	2 Kgs 16	Mt 20:1-16
Friday			
Mattins	-	Gn 43:1-14	Jas 3:1-13
Evensong	-	2 Chron 30:1-15,25-end	Mt 22:1-14
Saturday			
Mattins	-	Gn 43:15	Jas 3:13-4:6
Evensong	-	2 Chron 32:1-23	Mt 25:1-13
QUINQUAGESIMA			
Mattins	15,16	Ruth 1:1-17	Jn 15:1-17
Evensong	111,112	Is 63:7-9,14-16	1 Jn 4
Monday			
Mattins	-	Gn 44	Jas 4:7
Evensong	-	2 Kgs 20	Mt 25:14-30
Tuesday			
Mattins	-	Gn 45:1-15	Jas 5
Evensong	-	Mic 6	Mt 25:31
ASH WEDNESDAY			
Mattins	6,32,38	Is 58	Lk 15
Evensong	102,130,143	Is 1:2-20	Lk 3:1-22
Thursday			
Mattins	-	Gn 45:16	1 Cor 1
Evensong	-	2 Chron 33	Lk 4:1-29
Friday			
Mattins	-	Gn 46:1-7,26-end	1 Cor 2-3
Evensong	-	2 Kgs 22:1-23:3	Lk 4:30-5:16
Saturday			
Mattins	-	Gn 47	1 Cor 4
Evensong	-	2 Kgs 23:21-35	Lk 5:17
LENT I			
Mattins	51,54	2 Sam 11:1-12:13	Lk 18:10-14
Evensong	119:1-32	1 Sam 26:5	Mk 1:9-28
Monday			
Mattins	-	Gn 48	1 Cor 5-6:11
Evensong	-	Hab 1:1-2:4	Lk 6:1-26

Proper of Season

Lectionary

Day	Psalms	Lesson 1	Lesson 2
Tuesday			
Mattins	-	Gn 49	1 Cor 6:12-7:16
Evensong	-	Jer 13	Lk 6:27
Ember Wednesday			
Mattins	15,24,26	1 Sam 2:27-35	Lk 10:1-24
Evensong	84,132,134	Jer 26	2 Cor 3
Thursday			
Mattins	-	Gn 50	1 Cor 7:17
Evensong	-	Jer 36	Lk 7:1-23
Ember Friday			
Mattins	15,24,26	Ezek 33:1-20	Mt 10:1-23
Evensong	84,132,134	Amos 7:1-15	2 Cor 4:1-5:4
Ember Saturday			
Mattins	15,24,26	Ezek 44:4-16,23-24	Mt 10:24
Evensong	84,132,134	Neh 8:1-12	2 Cor 5:5-6:10
LENT II			
Mattins	6,38	1 Kgs 21:1-20	Mk 10:17-31
Evensong	119:33-72	1 Sam 19:1-18	Mt 21:33
Monday			
Mattins	-	Wis 9:17-10:14	1 Cor 8-9:23
Evensong	-	2 Kgs 23:36-24:17	Lk 7:24
Tuesday			
Mattins	-	Ex 1	1 Cor 9:24-10:22
Evensong	-	Jer 24	Lk 8:1-25
Wednesday			
Mattins	-	Ex 2	1 Cor 10:23-11:16
Evensong	-	Jer 29:1-14	Lk 8:26
Thursday			
Mattins	-	Ex 3	1 Cor 11:17
Evensong	-	Jer 21	Lk 9:1-17
Friday			
Mattins	-	Ex 4:1-26	1 Cor 12:1-26
Evensong	-	Jer 18	Lk 9:18-36
Saturday			
Mattins	-	Ex 4:27-5:21	1 Cor 12:27-13:end
Evensong	-	Jer 19:1-20:6	Lk 9:37
LENT III			
Mattins	56,86	Gn 50:7-21	Mt 18:21
Evensong	119:73-104	Gn 27:1-38	Mt 20:1-28

Lectionary *Proper of Season*

Day	Psalms	Lesson 1	Lesson 2
Monday			
Mattins	-	Ex 5:22-6:13	1 Cor 14:1-19
Evensong	-	Jer 27	Lk 10:1-24
Tuesday			
Mattins	-	Ex 6:28-7:25	1 Cor 14:20
Evensong	-	Jer 28	Lk 10:25
Wednesday			
Mattins	-	Ex 8:1-19	1 Cor 15:1-22
Evensong	-	Jer 34	Lk 11:1-28
Thursday			
Mattins	-	Ex 8:20	1 Cor 15:20-34
Evensong	-	Jer 35	Lk 11:29
Friday			
Mattins	-	Ex 9:1-12	1 Cor 15:35
Evensong	-	Jer 37	Lk 12:1-12
Saturday			
Mattins	-	Ex 9:13	1 Cor 16
Evensong	-	Jer 38	Lk 12:13-34
LENT IV			
Mattins	142,143	2 Sam 18:5	Lk 15:11
Evensong	119:105-144	Gn 13	Mt 7:13
Monday			
Mattins	-	Ex 10:1-20	2 Cor 1:1-22
Evensong	-	2 Kgs 24:18-25:11,20-22	Lk 12:35
Tuesday			
Mattins	-	Ex 10:21-11:10	2 Cor 1:23-2:end
Evensong	-	Jer 39:11-40:end	Lk 13:1-17
Wednesday			
Mattins	-	Ex 12:1-28	2 Cor 3:1-4:6
Evensong	-	Jer 41	Lk 13:18
Thursday			
Mattins	-	Ex 12:29	2 Cor 4:7-5:10
Evensong	-	Jer 42	Lk 14:1-24
Friday			
Mattins	-	Ex 13	2 Cor 5:11-6:10
Evensong	-	Jer 43	Lk 14:25
Saturday			
Mattins	-	Ex 14	2 Cor 6:11-7:end
Evensong	-	Jer 44	Lk 15

Proper of Season   # Lectionary

Day	Psalms	Lesson 1	Lesson 2
PASSION SUNDAY			
Mattins	42,43	Gn 22:1-13	Jn 10:1-16
Evensong	119:145-176	1 Kgs 8:22-53	Jn 17
Passion Monday			
Mattins	-	Wis 10:15-11:4	2 Cor 8:1-22
Evensong	-	Dan 1	Lk 16:1-18
Passion Tuesday			
Mattins	-	Ex 15:1-21	2 Cor 8:23-9:end
Evensong	-	Dan 3	Lk 16:19-17:10
Passion Wednesday			
Mattins	-	Ex 15:22-16:10	2 Cor 10
Evensong	-	Dan 4	Lk 17:11
Passion Thursday			
Mattins	-	Ex 16:11	2 Cor 11
Evensong	-	Dan 5	Lk 18:1-17
Passion Friday			
Mattins	-	Ex 17	2 Cor 12
Evensong	-	Dan 6	Lk 18:18
Passion Saturday			
Mattins	-	Ex 18	2 Cor 13
Evensong	-	Dan 9	Lk 19:1-28
PALM SUNDAY			
Mattins	97,110	Zech 9:9-16	Mk 11:1-11
Evensong	22,23	Is 52:13-53:end	Lk 19:28b-44
Holy Monday			
Mattins	6,32,38	Num 20:1-13	1 Cor 10:1-13
Evensong	42,43	Is 5:1-7	Lk 19:45-20:40
Holy Tuesday			
Mattins	51,55	Num 21:1-9	Jn 3:1-21
Evensong	102,130	Is 2:2-5	Lk 21
Holy Wednesday			
Mattins	138,139	Is 42:1-12	Jn 10:11-18
Evensong	140,141	Gn 37:3-28	Lk 22:1-6
Maundy Thursday			
Mattins	81,116	Jer 31:31-34	Jn 13:1-17,33-35
Evensong	142,143	Ex 16:4-15	Lk 22:7-22,39-54
Good Friday			
Mattins	22:1-19,40:1-16,54	Gn 22:1-18	Jn 18

Lectionary *Proper of Season*

Day	Psalms	Lesson 1	Lesson 2
Evensong	64,69:1-22,88	Is 52:13-53:end	Lk 23:13-47
Easter Even			
Mattins	4,16,17	Job 14:1-15	Rom 6:3-11
EASTER DAY			
Evensong	27,30,31	Ex 12:1-14	Lk 23:50
Mattins	2,57,111	Is 51:9-16	Lk 24:1-12
Evensong	113,114,118	Ex 15:1-21	Mt 28:1-10,16-end
Easter Monday			
Mattins	-	Ex 19:1-15	Mk 16:1-8
Evensong	-	Is 40	Lk 24:13-35
Easter Tuesday			
Mattins	-	Ex 19:16-20:26	Jn 20:1-18
Evensong	-	Is 41	Lk 24:36-49
Easter Wednesday			
Mattins	-	Ex 21:1-32	Mk 8:27-9:1
Evensong	-	Is 42	Jn 20:19
Easter Thursday			
Mattins	-	Ex 21:33-22:31	Mk 9:2-13,30-32
Evensong	-	Is 43	Jn 21:1-14
Easter Friday			
Mattins	-	Ex 23	Mk 10:32-45
Evensong	-	Is 44	Jn 21:15
Easter Saturday			
Mattins	-	Ex 24	Mk 14:17,22-28
Evensong	-	Is 45	Mk 16:9
EASTER I			
Mattins	110,111	2 Kgs 4:18-37	Lk 24:13-35
Evensong	2,57	Job 19:1,13-27a	Jn 14:1-14
Monday			
Mattins	-	Ex 25:1-22	1 Pet 1:1-21
Evensong	-	Is 46	Mk 5:22
Tuesday			
Mattins	-	Ex 25:23	1 Pet 1:22-2:10
Evensong	-	Is 47	Lk 7:11-16
Wednesday			
Mattins	-	Ex 31	1 Pet 2:11
Evensong	-	Is 48	Jn 11:1-44

Proper of Season # Lectionary

Day	Psalms	Lesson 1	Lesson 2
Thursday			
Mattins	-	Ex 32:1-24	1 Pet 3
Evensong	-	Is 49	Jn 5:19-30
Friday			
Mattins	-	Ex 32:25-33:23	1 Pet 4
Evensong	-	Is 50	Jn 6:25-58
Saturday			
Mattins	-	Ex 34:1-14,27-35	1 Pet 5
Evensong	-	Is 51	Mk 13:18-27
EASTER II			
Mattins	21,23	2 Sam 1:19	Jn 20:24
Evensong	116,117	Ezek 34:11-16,30-31	Jn 10:1-11
Monday			
Mattins	-	Ex 35:20-36:1	Col 1
Evensong	-	Is 52	Acts 3:12
Tuesday			
Mattins	-	Ex 40:17	Col 2
PATRONAGE OF ST. JOSEPH			
Evensong	110,117,146	Gn 39:1-5	Mt 1:18
Mattins	1,2,3	Gn 41:38-43	Mt 2:13
Evensong	112,116,126	Gn 49:22-26	Lk 2:41
Thursday			
Mattins	-	Num 9	Col 3
Evensong	-	Is 53	Acts 17:22-31
Friday			
Mattins	-	Num 10:1-13,29-end	Col 4
Evensong	-	Is 54	Acts 26:1-23
Saturday			
Mattins	-	Num 11:1-30	Philemon
Evensong	-	Is 55	Acts 9:32
EASTER III			
Mattins	120,121,122	2 Sam 12:15b-23	Jn 21:1-19
Evensong	123,124,125	Ex 14:5	Rom 6:1-18
Monday			
Mattins	-	Num 11:31-12:16	Eph 1:1-2:3
Evensong	-	Is 56	1 Cor 15:1-11
Tuesday			
Mattins	-	Num 13:1-3,17-25	Eph 2:4
Evensong	-	Is 57	1 Cor 15:12-22

Lectionary   *Proper of Season*

Day	Psalms	Lesson 1	Lesson 2
Wednesday			
Mattins	-	Num 13:26-14:10	Eph 3
Evensong	-	Is 58	2 Cor 5:5
Thursday			
Mattins	-	Num 14:11-25	Eph 4:1-16
Evensong	-	Is 59	Rom 1:1-12
Friday			
Mattins	-	Num 14:26	Eph 4:17
Evensong	-	Is 60	Rom 6:1-13
Saturday			
Mattins	-	Num 16:1-40	Eph 5:1-21
Evensong	-	Is 61	Rom 14:1-9
EASTER IV			
Mattins	126,127,128	2 Esd 2:42-47	Jn 11:17-39a,41-44
Evensong	129,130,131	Gn 8:6-12,15-16,9:8-16	Mk 12:18-27a
Monday			
Mattins	-	Num 16:41-17:11	Eph 5:22-6:9
Evensong	-	Is 62	Phil 3:7
Tuesday			
Mattins	-	Num 17:12-18:24	Eph 6:10
Evensong	-	Is 63	2 Cor 1:1-10
Wednesday			
Mattins	-	Num 20:1-21	Heb 1:1-12
Evensong	-	Is 64	2 Cor 4:6-5:1
Thursday			
Mattins	-	Num 20:22-21:9	Heb 1:13-2:13
Evensong	-	Is 65:1-12	Rom 8:1-17
Friday			
Mattins	-	Num 21:10-35	Heb 2:14-3:end
Evensong	-	Is 65:13	1 Cor 15:35
Saturday			
Mattins	-	Num 22:1-14	Heb 4:1-13
Evensong	-	Is 66	Rev 21:1-7
EASTER V			
Mattins	146,147	Ezek 37:1-14	Lk 24:36-49
Evensong	132,133,134	Job 14:1-15	Mt 19:16-29
Rogation Monday			
Mattins	-	Dt 28:1-14	Mt 6:24
Evensong	-	Dt 8	Jas 1:1-17

Proper of Season # Lectionary

Day	Psalms	Lesson 1	Lesson 2
Rogation Tuesday			
Mattins	-	Is 64	Lk 11:1-13
Evensong	-	1 Kgs 8:22-40	Jas 4
Vigil of the Ascension			
Mattins	-	Jer 14	Jn 6:27-63
Ascension Thursday			
Evensong	93,99	Gn 5:18-24	Eph 4:1-13
Mattins	8,15,21	2 Kgs 2:1-15	Heb 4:14-5:10
Evensong	24,47,108:1-6	Dan 7:9-14	Lk 24:44
Friday			
Mattins	-	Num 22:15-35	Heb 5:11-6:end
Evensong	-	Obadiah	1 Pet 3:8
Saturday			
Mattins	-	Num 22:36-23:26	Heb 7
Evensong	-	Hab 1	Phil 2:1-11
Sunday within Ascension Octave			
Mattins	108,110	2 Kgs 2:1-22	Acts 1:1-14
Evensong	46,47	Dt 34	Jn 14:15-27
Monday			
Mattins	-	Num 23:27-24:25	Heb 8:1-9:12
Evensong	-	Hab 2	Jn 14:1-14
Tuesday			
Mattins	-	Num 25	Heb 9:11
Evensong	-	Hab 3	Jn 14:15
Wednesday			
Mattins	-	Num 26:1-4,52-56,63-end; 27:12	Heb 10:1-34
Evensong	-	Zeph 1	Jn 15:1-16
Thursday			
Mattins	-	Num 32:1-33	Heb 10:35-11:22
Evensong	-	Zeph 2	Jn 15:17-16:11
Friday			
Mattins	-	Dt 31:1-13,24-26	Heb 11:23-12:2
Evensong	-	Zeph 3	Jn 16:12
Saturday			
Mattins	-	Dt 32:48-end;34	Heb 12:1-13
Whitsunday			
Evensong	46,133	2 Esd 13	Jn 17
Mattins	48,68	Joel 2:28	Jn 3:1-16
Evensong	104,145	Gn 2:7-10,15-24	Acts 2:14-24,36-39

Lectionary *Proper of Season*

Day	Psalms	Lesson 1	Lesson 2
Whit-Monday			
Mattins	-	Gn 11:1-9	Heb 12:14
Evensong	-	Ezek 11:14	Acts 2:38
Whit-Tuesday			
Mattins	-	Is 10:33-11:10	Heb 13
Evensong	-	Ezek 47:1-12	Acts 3:1-4:4
EMBER WEDNESDAY			
Mattins	15,24,26	Ezek 2:1-3:14	Eph 4:1-16
Evensong	84,132,134	Is 52:1-10	Acts 4:5-31
Whit-Thursday			
Mattins	-	Ezek 3:15	Gal 5:16-6:8
Evensong	-	Jer 31:27-37	Acts 4:32-5:11
EMBER FRIDAY			
Mattins	15,24,26	Jer 33:14	Jn 20:19-29
Evensong	84,132,134	Jer 42:1-12	Acts 5:12
EMBER SATURDAY			
Mattins	15,24,26	Is 61	Mt 28:16
Evensong	84,132,134	Zech 7:1-10	Acts 6
TRINITY SUNDAY			
Mattins	29,33	Gn 1:1-2:3	Jn 1:1-18
Evensong	93,97,150	Job 38:1-7,42:1-5	Rev 19:5-16
Monday			
Mattins	-	Josh 1	Mt 3
Evensong	-	Ezra 1	Acts 7:1-53
Tuesday			
Mattins	-	Josh 2	Mt 4
Evensong	-	Ezra 3-4:6,24	Acts 7:54-8:13
Wednesday			
Mattins	-	Josh 3-4	Mt 5:1-16
CORPUS CHRISTI			
Evensong	113,117,146	Gn 14:18-20	Mk 14:22-25
Mattins	20,23,24	Prv 9:1-6	1 Cor 10:15-17
Evensong	147,148	Ex 16:14-18	Jn 6:47-58
Friday			
Mattins	-	Josh 5	Mt 5:17-32
Evensong	-	Haggai 1-2:9	Acts 8:14
Saturday			
Mattins	-	Josh 6	Mt 5:33
Evensong	-	Haggai 2:10	Acts 9

Proper of Season # Lectionary

Day	Psalms	Lesson 1	Lesson 2
Trinity I			
Mattins	1,5	Is 6:1-8	Acts 9:1-22
Evensong	2,3,4	Is 40:12	Acts 17:16
Monday			
Mattins	-	Josh 7	Mt 6:1-18
Evensong	-	Zech 1	Acts 10
Tuesday			
Mattins	-	Josh 8	Mt 6:19
Evensong	-	Zech 2-3	Acts 11
Wednesday			
Mattins	-	Josh 9	Mt 7:1-20
Evensong	-	Zech 4	Acts 12-13:3
Thursday			
Mattins	-	Josh 10:1-28	Mt 7:21-8:13
Compassion of Our Lord			
Evensong	22,28,30	Lam 3:22-33	Eph 1:3
Mattins	34,45,72	Is 12:1-6	Jn 15:9-16
Evensong	84,85,86	Is 63:7-9	Eph 3:14-19

or

Friday			
Evensong	-	Haggai	Lk 4:16
Mattins	-	Num 34	Mk 1:40-2:12
Evensong	-	Dan 3:16	2 Tim 3

Saturday			
Mattins	-	Josh 10:29	Mt 8:14-27
Evensong	-	Zech 5-6	Acts 13:4
Trinity II			
Mattins	12,13	Gn 3	Rev 3:7
Evensong	10,11	Ex 20:1-17	Mk 12:28-34a
Monday			
Mattins	-	Josh 11	Mt 8:28-9:1
Evensong	-	Ezra 5	Acts 14
Tuesday			
Mattins	-	Josh 14	Mt 9:2-17
Evensong	-	Ezra 6:1-12	Acts 15

Lectionary *Proper of Season*

Day	Psalms	Lesson 1	Lesson 2
Wednesday			
Mattins	-	Josh 18:1-10,20:1-21:3	Mt 9:18-34
Evensong	-	Ezra 6:13	Acts 16
Thursday			
Mattins	-	Josh 21:43-22:20	Mt 9:35-10:15
Evensong	-	Zech 7	Acts 17
Friday			
Mattins	-	Josh 22:21-23:13	Mt 10:16-11:1
Evensong	-	Zech 8	Acts 18
Saturday			
Mattins	-	Josh 23:14-24:end	Mt 11:2-19
Evensong	-	Ezra 4:7-23	Acts 19
TRINITY III			
Mattins	16,17	Gn 4:2b-10	1 Cor 13
Evensong	18	Gn 18:1-10,16-19	Acts 26:1-2,8-19
Monday			
Mattins	-	Jdgs 1:1-28	Mt 11:20
Evensong	-	Neh 1	Acts 20
Tuesday			
Mattins	-	Jdgs 2	Mt 12:1-21
Evensong	-	Neh 2	Acts 21:1-16
Wednesday			
Mattins	-	Jdgs 3	Mt 12:22-37
Evensong	-	Neh 4:1-11	Acts 21:17-36
Thursday			
Mattins	-	Jdgs 4	Mt 12:38
Evensong	-	Neh 4:12	Acts 21:37-22:29
Friday			
Mattins	-	Jdgs 5	Mt 13:1-23
Evensong	-	Neh 5	Acts 22:30-23:end
Saturday			
Mattins	-	Jdgs 6:1-24	Mt 13:24-43
Evensong	-	Neh 6:1-16	Acts 24
TRINITY IV			
Mattins	19,20	Gn 37:2-35	Mt 5:1-16
Evensong	24,25	Dt 10:12-11:1	Jn 8:21-36
Monday			
Mattins	-	Jdgs 6:25	Mt 13:44
Evensong	-	Ezra 7:1,6-end	Acts 25

Proper of Season # Lectionary

Day	Psalms	Lesson 1	Lesson 2
Tuesday			
Mattins	-	Jdgs 7	Mt 14:1-21
Evensong	-	Ezra 8:15,21-32,36	Acts 26
Wednesday			
Mattins	-	Jdgs 8	Mt 14:22
Evensong	-	Ezra 9	Acts 27:1-26
Thursday			
Mattins	-	Jdgs 9:1-21	Mt 15:1-20
Evensong	-	Ezra 10:1-17	Acts 27:27
Friday			
Mattins	-	Jdgs 9:22	Mt 15:21
Evensong	-	Neh 8:1-12	Acts 28:1-15
Saturday			
Mattins	-	Jdgs 10	Mt 16:1-12
Evensong	-	Neh 8:13	Acts 28:16
TRINITY V			
Mattins	21,23	Gn 41:1-49,54-end	Mt 25:14-30
Evensong	26,27	Ex 6:1-13	Mk 9:14-29
Monday			
Mattins	-	Jdgs 11:1-17	Mt 16:13
Evensong	-	Neh 9:1-21	1 Thess 1
Tuesday			
Mattins	-	Jdgs 11:18	Mt 17:1-13
Evensong	-	Neh 9:22	1 Thess 2
Wednesday			
Mattins	-	Jdgs 12	Mt 17:14
Evensong	-	Neh 10:28-11:2	1 Thess 3
Thursday			
Mattins	-	Jdgs 13	Mt 18:1-20
Evensong	-	Neh 12:27-31,37-40,43-end	1 Thess 4:1-12
Friday			
Mattins	-	Jdgs 14	Mt 18:21
Evensong	-	Neh 13:1-14	1 Thess 4:13-5:13
Saturday			
Mattins	-	Jdgs 15	Mt 19:1-15
Evensong	-	Neh 13:15-22	1 Thess 5:14
TRINITY VI			
Mattins	28,29	Gn 42	Mt 5:38-6:15
Evensong	30,31	Ecclus 2	Mt 14:22-33

Lectionary *Proper of Season*

Day	Psalms	Lesson 1	Lesson 2
Monday			
Mattins	-	Jdgs 16	Mt 19:16
Evensong	-	Est 1	2 Thess 1
Tuesday			
Mattins	-	Jdgs 17-18:13	Mt 20:1-16
Evensong	-	Est 2	2 Thess 2
Wednesday			
Mattins	-	Jdgs 18:14	Mt 20:17
Evensong	-	Est 3	2 Thess 3
Thursday			
Mattins	-	Jdgs 19	Mt 21:1-17
Evensong	-	Est 4	Gal 1
Friday			
Mattins	-	Jdgs 20:1-36a	Mt 21:18-32
Evensong	-	Est 13:8	Gal 2
Saturday			
Mattins	-	Jdgs 20:36b-21:end	Mt 21:33
Evensong	-	Est 14	Gal 3:1-15
TRINITY VII			
Mattins	32,36	Gn 43	Mt 25:31
Evensong	33,34	Tob 4:5-11,16	Mt 6:1-4,19-21
Monday			
Mattins	-	Ruth 1	Mt 22:1-14
Evensong	-	Est 5	Gal 3:16
Tuesday			
Mattins	-	Ruth 2	Mt 22:15-33
Evensong	-	Est 6:1-12	Gal 4:1-18
Wednesday			
Mattins	-	Ruth 3	Mt 22:34
Evensong	-	Est 6:13-7:end	Gal 4:19-5:1
Thursday			
Mattins	-	Ruth 4:1-17	Mt 23:1-12
Evensong	-	Est 8	Gal 5:2-15
Friday			
Mattins	-	1 Sam 1:1-20	Mt 23:13-26
Evensong	-	Est 16	Gal 5:16
Saturday			
Mattins	-	1 Sam 1:21-2:21	Mt 23:27
Evensong	-	Est 9:20-10:end	Gal 6

Proper of Season

Lectionary

Day	Psalms	Lesson 1	Lesson 2
TRINITY VIII			
Mattins	39,41	Gn 44:18-45:15	Mt 7:1-12
Evensong	37	Gn 18:20	Lk 11:5-13
Monday			
Mattins	-	1 Sam 2:21	Mt 24:1-28
Evensong	-	Zech 9:9-16	1 Cor 1
Tuesday			
Mattins	-	1 Sam 3	Mt 24:29
Evensong	-	Zech 10	1 Cor 2
Wednesday			
Mattins	-	1 Sam 4	Mt 25:1-30
Evensong	-	Zech 11 & 13:7-end	1 Cor 3
Thursday			
Mattins	-	1 Sam 5	Mt 25:31
Evensong	-	Zech 12:1-8	1 Cor 4
Friday			
Mattins	-	1 Sam 6:1-7:2	Mt 26:1-16
Evensong	-	Zech 12:9-13:6	1 Cor 5-6:end
Saturday			
Mattins	-	1 Sam 7:3	Mt 26:17-35
Evensong	-	Zech 14	1 Cor 7:1-24
TRINITY IX			
Mattins	46,47	Ex 32:1-24	Jn 4:1-30
Evensong	44,45	Jonah 1:1-2:1,10	Acts 27:14
Monday			
Mattins	-	1 Sam 8	Mt 26:36-56
Evensong	-	Mal 1	1 Cor 7:25
Tuesday			
Mattins	-	1 Sam 9:1-10:1	Mt 26:57
Evensong	-	Mal 2:1-9	1 Cor 8
Wednesday			
Mattins	-	1 Sam 10:17-11:13	Mt 27:1-26
Evensong	-	Mal 2:10-16	1 Cor 9
Thursday			
Mattins	-	1 Sam 11:14-12:end	Mt 27:27-56
Evensong	-	Mal 2:17-3:6	1 Cor 10
Friday			
Mattins	-	1 Sam 13	Mt 27:57
Evensong	-	Mal 3:7-12	1 Cor 11

Lectionary *Proper of Season*

Day	Psalms	Lesson 1	Lesson 2
Saturday			
Mattins	-	1 Sam 14:1-23	Mt 28
Evensong	-	Mal 3:13-4:end	1 Cor 12:1-26
TRINITY X			
Mattins	61,62	Jdgs 5	Rom 12:9
Evensong	48,49	Joshua 24:14-28	Lk 9:46
Monday			
Mattins	-	1 Sam 14:24	Lk 3:1-22
Evensong	-	Dan 2:1-24	1 Cor 12:27-13:end
Tuesday			
Mattins	-	1 Sam 15	Lk 3:23-4:13
Evensong	-	Dan 2:25	1 Cor 14:1-20
Wednesday			
Mattins	-	1 Sam 16	Lk 4:14-32
Evensong	-	Dan 7	1 Cor 14:20
Thursday			
Mattins	-	1 Sam 17:1-30	Lk 4:33
Evensong	-	Dan 8	1 Cor 15:1-34
Friday			
Mattins	-	1 Sam 17:31-53	Lk 5:1-16
Evensong	-	Dan 10	1 Cor 15:35
Saturday			
Mattins	-	1 Sam 17:54-18:9	Lk 5:17
Evensong	-	Dan 11:1-4,12:1-end	1 Cor 16
TRINITY XI			
Mattins	63,64	1 Sam 16	Mk 4:35-5:20
Evensong	54,55	Gn 24:1-38,50-54,61-end	Mt 19:1-9
Monday			
Mattins	-	1 Sam 18:10	Lk 6:1-19
Evensong	-	1 Macc 1:1-28	2 Cor 1:1-22
Tuesday			
Mattins	-	1 Sam 19	Lk 6:20
Evensong	-	1 Macc 1:29-58	2 Cor 1:23-2:end
Wednesday			
Mattins	-	1 Sam 20:1-23	Lk 7:1-16
Evensong	-	1 Macc 2:1-30	2 Cor 3:1-4:6
Thursday			
Mattins	-	1 Sam 20:24	Lk 7:16-35
Evensong	-	1 Macc 2:31-48	2 Cor 4:7-5:10

Proper of Season # Lectionary

Day	Psalms	Lesson 1	Lesson 2
Friday			
Mattins	-	1 Sam 21:1-22:2	Lk 7:36
Evensong	-	1 Macc 2:49	2 Cor 5:11-6:10
Saturday			
Mattins	-	1 Sam 22:3	Lk 8:1-21
Evensong	-	1 Macc 3:1-26	2 Cor 6:11-7:end
TRINITY XII			
Mattins	76,77	1 Sam 20:11	Lk 10:25-37
Evensong	71,72	1 Sam 8	Lk 14:7-24
Monday			
Mattins	-	1 Sam 23	Lk 8:22-39
Evensong	-	1 Macc 3:42	2 Cor 8:1-22
Tuesday			
Mattins	-	1 Sam 24	Lk 8:40
Evensong	-	1 Macc 4:1-25	2 Cor 8:23-9:end
Wednesday			
Mattins	-	1 Sam 25:1-22	Lk 9:1-17
Evensong	-	1 Macc 4:36	2 Cor 10
Thursday			
Mattins	-	1 Sam 25:23	Lk 9:18-36
Evensong	-	1 Macc 6:1-16	2 Cor 11
Friday			
Mattins	-	1 Sam 26	Lk 9:37-50
Evensong	-	1 Macc 8:1-29	2 Cor 12
Saturday			
Mattins	-	1 Sam 27:1-28:2	Lk 9:51
Evensong	-	1 Macc 14:4-19,38-47	2 Cor 13
TRINITY XIII			
Mattins	81,82	1 Sam 24	Mt 5:17-26
Evensong	73	Ex 17:8-13	Acts 20:17
Monday			
Mattins	-	1 Sam 28:3	Lk 10:1-24
Evensong	-	Dt 4:1-24	Rom 1
Tuesday			
Mattins	-	1 Sam 29	Lk 10:25
Evensong	-	Dt 4:25-40	Rom 2
Wednesday			
Mattins	-	1 Sam 30	Lk 11:1-13
Evensong	-	Dt 5:1-22	Rom 3

Lectionary *Proper of Season*

Day	Psalms	Lesson 1	Lesson 2
Thursday			
Mattins	-	1 Sam 31	Lk 11:14-28
Evensong	-	Dt 5:23	Rom 4
Friday			
Mattins	-	2 Sam 1	Lk 11:29
Evensong	-	Dt 6	Rom 5
Saturday			
Mattins	-	2 Sam 2:1-11	Lk 12:1-12
Evensong	-	Dt 7:1-11	Rom 6
TRINITY XIV			
Mattins	84,85	2 Sam 23:8-17	Mt 26:1-13
Evensong	74	1 Kgs 22:10-18,29-37	Mt 11:2-19
Monday			
Mattins	-	2 Sam 2:12	Lk 12:13-34
Evensong	-	Dt 7:12	Rom 7
Tuesday			
Mattins	-	2 Sam 3:1,17-end	Lk 12:35-48
Evensong	-	Dt 8	Rom 8:1-17
Wednesday			
Mattins	-	2 Sam 4	Lk 12:49
Evensong	-	Dt 10:12-11:1	Rom 8:18
Thursday			
Mattins	-	2 Sam 5	Lk 13:1-17
Evensong	-	Dt 11:2-12	Rom 9:1-18
Friday			
Mattins	-	2 Sam 6	Lk 13:18
Evensong	-	Dt 11:13	Rom 9:19
Saturday			
Mattins	-	2 Sam 7	Lk 14:1-14
Evensong	-	Dt 12:1-14	Rom 10
TRINITY XV			
Mattins	96,97	1 Kgs 3:5	Mt 10:2-16
Evensong	79,80	1 Kgs 20:28	Mk 9:33
Monday			
Mattins	-	2 Sam 8	Lk 14:15-24
Evensong	-	Dt 12:17	Rom 11
Tuesday			
Mattins	-	2 Sam 9	Lk 14:25
Evensong	-	Dt 14:22	Rom 12

Proper of Season # Lectionary

Day	Psalms	Lesson 1	Lesson 2
Wednesday			
Mattins	-	2 Sam 10	Lk 15:1-10
Evensong	-	Dt 15:1-15	Rom 13
Thursday			
Mattins	-	2 Sam 11	Lk 15:11
Evensong	-	Dt 16:1-12	Rom 14
Friday			
Mattins	-	2 Sam 12	Lk 16:1-18
Evensong	-	Dt 16:13-20	Rom 15
Saturday			
Mattins	-	2 Sam 13	Lk 16:19
Evensong	-	Dt 17:8	Rom 16
TRINITY XVI			
Mattins	98,99	Dan 5:1-9,13-30	Lk 12:13-21
Evensong	89	Gn 32:24-30	Eph 6:10-20
Monday			
Mattins	-	2 Sam 14:1-20	Lk 17:1-10
Evensong	-	Dt 18:9	Eph 1
Tuesday			
Mattins	-	2 Sam 14:21	Lk 17:11-19
Evensong	-	Dt 19:1-15	Eph 2
Wednesday			
Mattins	-	2 Sam 15:1-12	Lk 17:20
Evensong	-	Dt 24:14	Eph 3
Thursday			
Mattins	-	2 Sam 15:13-29	Lk 18:1-14
Evensong	-	Dt 26	Eph 4:1-24
Friday			
Mattins	-	2 Sam 15:30	Lk 18:15-30
Evensong	-	Dt 27:1-10	Eph 4:25-5:14
Saturday			
Mattins	-	2 Sam 16	Lk 18:31
Evensong	-	Dt 28:1-14	Eph 5:15-6:9
TRINITY XVII			
Mattins	91,92	Dan 6:1-23	Rom 8:14-18,31-end
Evensong	105	Ruth 2	Jn 8:1-11
Monday			
Mattins	-	2 Sam 17:1-14	Lk 19:1-10
Evensong	-	Dt 29	Eph 6:10

Lectionary *Proper of Season*

Day	Psalms	Lesson 1	Lesson 2
Tuesday			
Mattins	-	2 Sam 17:15	Lk 19:11-28
Evensong	-	Dt 30	Col 1
Wednesday			
Mattins	-	2 Sam 18:1-18	Lk 19:29
Evensong	-	Dt 31:30-32:43	Col 2
Thursday			
Mattins	-	2 Sam 18:19	Lk 20:1-19
Evensong	-	Dt 33	Col 3:1-4:1
Friday			
Mattins	-	2 Sam 19:1-15	Lk 20:20-38
Evensong	-	Lev 19:1-18,32-end	Col 4:2
Saturday			
Mattins	-	2 Sam 19:16-30	Lk 20:39-21:4
Evensong	-	Lev 26:1-12	Philemon
TRINITY XVIII			
Mattins	111,112	Eccles 12	Lk 2:41
Evensong	106	Ex 34:27	1 Jn 2:24-3:2
Monday			
Mattins	-	2 Sam 19:31-20:2	Lk 21:5-24
Evensong	-	Job 1	Phil 1:1-11
Tuesday			
Mattins	-	2 Sam 20:3	Lk 21:25
Evensong	-	Job 2	Phil 1:12
Wednesday			
Mattins	-	2 Sam 21	Lk 22:1-13
Evensong	-	Job 3	Phil 2:1-13
Thursday			
Mattins	-	2 Sam 23:1-23	Lk 22:14-38
Evensong	-	Job 4	Phil 2:14
Friday			
Mattins	-	2 Sam 24	Lk 22:39-53
Evensong	-	Job 5	Phil 3
Saturday			
Mattins	-	1 Chron 21:1-17	Lk 22:54
Evensong	-	Job 6	Phil 4
TRINITY XIX			
Mattins	114,115	2 Kgs 5	Jn 13:1-15
Evensong	107	Ecclus 38:1-15	Mt 8:1-13

Proper of Season

Lectionary

Day	Psalms	Lesson 1	Lesson 2
Monday			
Mattins	-	1 Chron 21:18-22:4	Lk 23:1-26
Evensong	-	Job 8	1 Tim 1
Tuesday			
Mattins	-	1 Chron 22:5	Lk 23:27-46
Evensong	-	Job 9	1 Tim 2
Wednesday			
Mattins	-	1 Kgs 1:5-21	Lk 23:47
Evensong	-	Job 11	1 Tim 3
Thursday			
Mattins	-	1 Kgs 1:22-37	Lk 24:1-12
Evensong	-	Job 12:1-24	1 Tim 4
Friday			
Mattins	-	1 Kgs 1:38	Lk 24:13-35
Evensong	-	Job 15	1 Tim 5
Saturday			
Mattins	-	1 Chron 23:1-6,24-end	Lk 24:36
Evensong	-	Job 16	1 Tim 6
TRINITY XX			
Mattins	116,117	2 Kgs 6:8-17	Jn 9:1-38
Evensong	118	Mic 4:1-7	Jas 3
Monday			
Mattins	-	1 Chron 28	Jn 1:1-18
Evensong	-	Job 18	Titus 1:1-2:10
Tuesday			
Mattins	-	1 Chron 29:1-19	Jn 1:19-34
Evensong	-	Job 19:1-27a	Titus 2:11-3:end
Wednesday			
Mattins	-	1 Chron 29:20	Jn 1:35
Evensong	-	Job 20	2 Tim 1
Thursday			
Mattins	-	1 Kgs 2:1-27	Jn 2:1-11
Evensong	-	Job 21	2 Tim 2
Friday			
Mattins	-	1 Kgs 2:28-35	Jn 2:12
Evensong	-	Job 22	2 Tim 3
Saturday			
Mattins	-	1 Kgs 2:36	Jn 3:1-21
Evensong	-	Job 23:1-24:1	2 Tim 4

Lectionary *Proper of Season*

Day	Psalms	Lesson 1	Lesson 2
Trinity XXI			
Mattins	120,121,122	Wis 3:1-9	Rev 21:1-7,10-11a,22-end
Evensong	133,134,135	1 Kgs 19:1-18	Mt 11:16
Monday			
Mattins	-	1 Kgs 3:1-15	Jn 3:22
Evensong	-	Job 25-26	Jas 1:1-15
Tuesday			
Mattins	-	1 Kgs 3:16	Jn 4:1-26
Evensong	-	Job 28	Jas 1:16
Wednesday			
Mattins	-	1 Kgs 4:21	Jn 4:27
Evensong	-	Job 29:1-30:1	Jas 2
Thursday			
Mattins	-	1 Kgs 5:1-12	Jn 5:1-24
Evensong	-	Job 31	Jas 3
Friday			
Mattins	-	1 Kgs 5:13-6:1,11-14	Jn 5:25
Evensong	-	Job 32	Jas 4
Saturday			
Mattins	-	1 Kgs 6:37-7:14	Jn 6:1-21
Evensong	-	Job 33	Jas 5
Trinity XXII			
Mattins	123,124,125	Ecclus 44:1-14	Heb 11:1-3,17-12:2
Evensong	136,138	Is 1:10-20	Lk 5:36-6:10
Monday			
Mattins	-	1 Kgs 8:1-21	Jn 6:22-40
Evensong	-	Job 34	1 Pet 1:1-21
Tuesday			
Mattins	-	1 Kgs 8:22-53	Jn 6:41
Evensong	-	Job 36:5-25	1 Pet 1:22-2:10
Wednesday			
Mattins	-	1 Kgs 8:54	Jn 7:1-30
Evensong	-	Job 36:27-37:end	1 Pet 2:11-3:7
Thursday			
Mattins	-	1 Kgs 9:1-9	Jn 7:31
Evensong	-	Job 38:1-36	1 Pet 3:8
Friday			
Mattins	-	1 Kgs 9:10	Jn 8:1-30
Evensong	-	Job 40	1 Pet 4

Proper of Season   # Lectionary

Day	Psalms	Lesson 1	Lesson 2
Saturday			
Mattins	-	1 Kgs 10:1-15,21-24	Jn 8:31
Evensong	-	Job 42	1 Pet 5
TRINITY XXIII			
Mattins	126,127,128	Job 1:1-21	2 Cor 11:18-30
Evensong	140,141	Ex 33:7-19	Heb 1:1-12
Monday			
Mattins	-	Prv 1:1-19	Jn 9:1-23
Evensong	-	Ecclus 1:1-20	Heb 1:13-2:13
Tuesday			
Mattins	-	Prv 1:20	Jn 9:24
Evensong	-	Ecclus 1:21-2:end	Heb 2:14-3:11
Wednesday			
Mattins	-	Prv 2	Jn 10:1-21
Evensong	-	Ecclus 3:1-15	Heb 3:12-4:13
Thursday			
Mattins	-	Prv 3:1-18	Jn 10:22
Evensong	-	Ecclus 4:1-19	Heb 4:14-5:end
Friday			
Mattins	-	Prv 3:19	Jn 11:1-27
Evensong	-	Ecclus 6:4-17	Heb 6
Saturday			
Mattins	-	Prv 4:1-13	Jn 11:28-44
Evensong	-	Ecclus 6:18	Heb 7:1-17
TRINITY XXIV			
Mattins	129,130,131	Is 5:1-7	Lk 8:4-15
Evensong	144,145	1 Sam 28:7-20	Lk 16:19
Monday			
Mattins	-	Prv 4:14	Jn 11:45
Evensong	-	Ecclus 7:1-18	Heb 7:18
Tuesday			
Mattins	-	Prv 5	Jn 12:1-19
Evensong	-	Ecclus 9:15-10:8	Heb 8:1-12
Wednesday			
Mattins	-	Prv 6	Jn 12:20-36
Evensong	-	Ecclus 10:12-24	Heb 8:13-9:12
Thursday			
Mattins	-	Prv 7	Jn 12:37
Evensong	-	Ecclus 14:20-15:end	Heb 9:11

Lectionary *Proper of Season*

Day	Psalms	Lesson 1	Lesson 2
Friday			
Mattins	-	Prv 8	Jn 13:1-19
Evensong	-	Ecclus 24:1-22	Heb 10:1-18
Saturday			
Mattins	-	Prv 9	Jn 13:20
Evensong	-	Ecclus 26:1-6,13-21	Heb 10:19
SUNDAY NEXT BEFORE ADVENT			
Mattins	146,147	2 Kgs 19:14-36	Mt 6:19
Evensong	148,149,150	Mic 6:1-8	Jas 1:12
Monday			
Mattins	-	Ecclus 44:1-15	Rev 1:1-8
Evensong	-	2 Esd 3:4-27	2 Jn
Tuesday			
Mattins	-	Ecclus 44:16-45:5	Rev 1:9
Evensong	-	Ecclus 48:1-16	3 Jn
Wednesday			
Mattins	-	Ecclus 46	Rev 2:1-11
Evensong	-	Ecclus 48:17-49:end	Jude
Thursday			
Mattins	-	Ecclus 47:1-11	Rev 2:12
Evensong	-	2 Esd 2:33	2 Pet 1
Friday			
Mattins	-	Ecclus 47:12	Rev 3:1-13
Evensong	-	2 Esd 7:19-35	2 Pet 2
Saturday			
Mattins	-	2 Esd 16:54-67	Rev 3:14
Evensong	-	Tob 13	2 Pet 3

Lessons for the Autumnal Ember Days

Day	Psalms	Lesson 1	Lesson 2
Wednesday			
Mattins	15,24,26	Gn 14:13-20	Heb 4:14-5:10
Evensong	84,132,134	1 Kgs 19	1 Tim 3
Friday			
Mattins	15,24,26	Num 17:1-18:7	Lk 12:35-48
Evensong	84,132,134	2 Kgs 2:1-22	1 Tim 4
Saturday			
Mattins	15,24,26	Dt 14:22	1 Cor 9:7
Evensong	84,132,134	Ezek 34:1-16	Titus 1:1-2:8

Proper of Saints

Lectionary

Feasts of the Year

Feast	Proper Psalms	Lesson 1	Lesson 2
ST. ANDREW			
30 November			
I Evensong	102:15,117	Is 49:1-13	1 Cor 4:1-16
Mattins	34	Num 10:29	Jn 1:29-42
II Evensong	96,100	Is 55	Jn 12:20-36
CONCEPTION OF THE B.V.M.			
8 December			
I Evensong	113,122,127	Gen 3:1-15	Gal 4:1-7
Mattins	8,19,24	Mic 5:2-5	Mt 1:20-23
II Evensong	146,147	1 Sam 2:1-11	Heb 2:9
ST. THOMAS			
21 December			
I Evensong	23,121	2 Kgs 6:8-23	Jn 11:1-16
Mattins	27	2 Kgs 7	Jn 14:1-14
II Evensong	112,113	Heb 1:1-2:4	Mk 16
CONVERSION OF ST. PAUL			
25 January			
I Evensong	1,19	Wis 5:1-16	Gal 1
Mattins	66	Ecclus 39:1-10	2 Tim 3:10-4:8
II Evensong	67,138	Jer 1:1-10	Acts 26:1-23
PURIFICATION			
2 February			
I Evensong	48,138	Ex 13:11-16	Heb 10:1-10
Mattins	20,86,87	1 Sam 1:20	Gal 3:15-4:7
II Evensong	84,113,134	Lev 12	1 Jn 3:1-8
CHAIR OF ST. PETER AT ANTIOCH			
22 February			
I Evensong	146,147	Ezek 3:4-11	Acts 4:8-20
Mattins	47,61,74	Ezek 2:1-7	Acts 11:1-18
II Evensong	113,126,139	Ezek 34:11-16	Jn 21:15-22
ST. MATTHIAS			
24/25 February			
I Evensong	33	1 Kgs 2:26-31	Lk 10:1-20
Mattins	15,24	1 Sam 2:27	Lk 12:16-40
II Evensong	145	Is 22:15-24	1 Jn 2:15

Lectionary *Proper of Saints*

Feast	Proper Psalms	Lesson 1	Lesson 2
Pope St. Gregory the Great			
12 March			
I Evensong	1,2,4	Ecclus 39:1-10	Jn 21:15-17
Mattins	15,21,24	Is 61	Mt 5:13-19
II Evensong	96,97,98	Is 52:1-10	Jn 20:19-23
St. Joseph, Spouse of the B.V.M.			
19 March			
I Evensong	110,117,146	Gn 39:1-5	Mt 1:18
Mattins	1,2,3	Gn 41:38-43	Mt 2:13
II Evensong	112,116,126	Gn 49:22-26	Lk 2:41
St. Benedict			
21 March			
I Evensong	1,2,4	Ecclus 44:1-15	Jn 21:15-17
Mattins	15,21,24	Is 61	Mt 19:27-29
II Evensong	96,97,98	Is 52:1-10	Jn 20:19-23
Annunciation of the B.V.M.			
25 March			
I Evensong	113	Gn 3:1-15	Rev 12
Mattins	89:1-30	Gn 18:1-14	Jn 1:1-18
II Evensong	131,132,138	1 Sam 1:21-2:10	Lk 1:39-56
St. Tikhon			
7 April			
I Evensong	23,100	Ecclus 50:5,11-21	Jn 21:15-17
Mattins	132	Is 61	Mt 10:1-20
II Evensong	111,112	Is 52:1-10	Jn 20:19-23
St. George			
23 April			
I Evensong	1,2,4	Wis 5:1-7,15-20	Lk 21:10-19
Mattins	15,21,24	Jer 17:7-8	Jn 15:1-7
II Evensong	64,65,92	Ecclus 31:8-11	Rev 7:9
St. Mark			
25 April			
I Evensong	67,96	Ecclus 2	Acts 12:24-13:13
Mattins	102:15	Is 62	1 Pet 5
II Evensong	19,112	Ezek 1:2-14	2 Tim 4:1-18
Sts. Philip & James			
1 May			
I Evensong	119:33-48	Ecclus 14:20-15:10	Jn 6:1-14
Mattins	139	Is 43:1-12	Jn 1:45

Proper of Saints   # Lectionary

Feast	Proper Psalms	Lesson 1	Lesson 2
II Evensong	27	Is 61	Acts 15:1-31
INVENTION OF THE HOLY CROSS			
3 May			
I Evensong	8,21,24	Is 42:1-9	Phil 2:5-11
Mattins	30,47,66	Is 53:4	Col 2:9-15
II Evensong	76,96,97	Dt 21:18-23	Gal 3:10-14
ST. JOHN BEFORE THE LATIN GATE			
6 May			
I Evensong	19,34,45	Ecclus 15:1-6	Rev 1:9
Mattins	47,61,64	Ex 33:9-19	Jn 13:21-35
II Evensong	75,97,99	Is 6:1-8	1 Jn 5:1-12
ST. BARNABAS			
11 June			
I Evensong	112,146	Ecclus 31:3-11	Acts 4:23
Mattins	1,15	2 Esd 2:33	Acts 9:23-31
II Evensong	97,100	Dt 33:8-11,26-end	Acts 14
ST. JOHN BAPTIST			
24 June			
I Evensong	103	Jdgs 13	Lk 1:5-25
Mattins	82,98	Mal 3:1-12	Mt 3
II Evensong	24,96	1 Kgs 21:17	Mk 6:14-29
STS. PETER & PAUL			
29 June			
I Evensong	118	Ezek 3:4-14	Mt 4:12
Mattins	22:23,67	Ezek 34:1-16	Jn 21:1-22
II Evensong	23,146	Zech 3	1 Pet 4:12-5:11
COMMEMORATION OF ST. PAUL			
30 June			
Mattins	47,61,64	Is 45:18	2 Cor 11:18-31
II Evensong	75,97,99	Is 49:1-13	Phil 1:12-30
PRECIOUS BLOOD			
1 July			
I Evensong	1,2,3,4	Ex 12:1-14	Heb 9:11
Mattins	16,64,94	Is 63:1-9	Mt 27:1-25
II Evensong	23,30,88	Lev 3	Mt 26:20-30
VISITATION OF THE B.V.M.			
2 July			
I Evensong	113,122,127	Songs 2:1-6	Lk 1:5-25
Mattins	45,46,87	Is 7:10-14	Lk 1:26-38

Lectionary *Proper of Saints*

Feast	Proper Psalms	Lesson 1	Lesson 2
II Evensong	146,147	Songs 2:7-14	Lk 1:39-45
St. Mary Magdalene			
22 July			
I Evensong	113,117,146	Is 52:7-10	Mk 15:40-16:10
Mattins	63,93,100	Song 3:1-4,8:1-17	Lk 8:1-3
II Evensong	110,116,126	Zeph 3:14	Jn 20:1-10
St. James			
25 July			
I Evensong	112,113	1 Sam 22:6-19	Mk 1:14-22
Mattins	34	Jer 26:1-11	Mt 10:16
II Evensong	33	2 Kgs 1:1-15	Lk 9:46
St. Anne			
26 July			
I Evensong	113,122,127	Prov 31:10	2 Tim 1:1-10
Mattins	45,46,87	1 Sam 1:1-20	Rom 12:1-17
II Evensong	96,97,98	1 Sam 1:21-2:11	2 Jn
St. Peter in Chains			
1 August			
I Evensong	113,117,146	Jer 1:11-19	Acts 12:5-11
Mattins	75,97,99	Dan 3:19-28	2 Cor 1:3-11
II Evensong	116,126,139	Gn 22:1-19	1 Pet 1:13-21
Transfiguration			
6 August			
I Evensong	29,97	Ex 24	Mk 9:2-13
Mattins	27,61,93	Mal 3:16-4:end	Rev 1
II Evensong	84,99,133	Ex 34:29	2 Cor 3
Most Holy Name of Jesus			
7 August			
Evensong	146,147	Is 7:10-14	Phil 2:5-11
Mattins	9,19,24	Mic 6:3-8	Col 3:12-7
Evensong	110,111,112	Ex 34:1-8	Acts 3:1-12
St. Lawrence			
10 August			
I Evensong	1,2,4	Ecclus 51:1-12	Lk 21:10-19
Mattins	15,17,21	Ecclus 14:20-15:6	Jn 12:24-26
II Evensong	24,64,92	Job 5:8-21	Rev 7:9
Assumption of the B.V.M.			
15 August			
I Evensong	146,147	Songs 2:10	Jn 19:25-27

Proper of Saints # Lectionary

Feast	Proper Psalms	Lesson 1	Lesson 2
Mattins	45,46,87	Songs 2:1-4	Rev 11:19-12:6
II Evensong	148,149,150	Ecclus 24:7-12	Rev 7:9-17

St. Joachim
16 August

I Evensong	1,2,3	Ecclus 31:8-11	Lk 12:42-44
Mattins	4,5,8	Ecclus 32:14-16	Mt 25:31-36
II Evensong	15,21,24	Ecclus 34:13-17	Jn 13:12-17

St. Bartholomew
24 August

I Evensong	1,15	Is 66:1-2,18-23	Lk 6:12-23
Mattins	91	Gn 28:10	Jn 1:43
II Evensong	46,102:15	Mic 4:1-7	1 Pet 1:22-2:10

Decollation of St. John Baptist
29 August

I Evensong	113,117,146	Is 1:4-9	Jn 3:22-30
Mattins	63,93,100	Ezek 3:4-11	Mt 11:2-19
II Evensong	110,116,126	Wis 5:15-20	Lk 12:1-12

The Nativity of the B.V.M.
8 September

I Evensong	113,122,126	Songs 1:1-8	Lk 1:26-38
Mattins	45,46,87	Songs 1:9	Rom 1:1-4
II Evensong	146,147	Prv 9:1-6	Lk 11:27-28

Exaltation of the Holy Cross
14 September

I Evensong	8,21,24	Num 21:4-9	Jn 3:1-17
Mattins	30,47,66	Is 26:12-15	Gal 6:12-17
II Evensong	76,96,97	Is 6:1-8	Phil 2:5-11

Seven Sorrows of the B.V.M.
15 September

I Evensong	3,11,31	Lam 1:2,20-21	Lk 2:33-35
Mattins	22,56,42	Lam 2:13-18	Lk 2:41-51
II Evensong	64,6,46	Judith 13:17	Rev 11:19-12:5

St. Matthew
21 September

I Evensong	65,117	Wis 7:21-8:1	Lk 5:27-32
Mattins	119:1-16	1 Kgs 19	Mt 19:16
II Evensong	19,112	Is 52:1-10	Rom 10:1-15

Lectionary — *Proper of Saints*

Feast	Proper Psalms	Lesson 1	Lesson 2
St. Michael			
29 September			
I Evensong	8,150	Job 38	Heb 1:13-2:10
Mattins	91,103	Gn 32:24-30	Acts 12:1-17
II Evensong	34,148	Dan 12	Rev 14:1-13
Guardian Angels			
2 October			
I Evensong	8,11,15	Gn 31:45-32:2	Rev 14:6-12
Mattins	19,24,34	Ex 23:20-23	Acts 27:13-25
II Evensong	96,97,103	Is 6:1-8	Mt 4:1-11
Holy Rosary of the B.V.M.			
7 October			
I Evensong	8,19,24	Ecclus 24:7-12	Mt 1:18-25
Mattins	45,46,87	Ecclus 24:13-17	Lk 2:25-35
II Evensong	96,97,98	Ecclus 24:18-24	Gal 4:4-7
Motherhood of the B.V.M.			
11 October			
I Evensong	48,138	Ex 13:11-16	Heb 10:1-10
Mattins	20,86,87	1 Sam 1:20	Gal 3:15-4:7
II Evensong	84,113,134	Lev 12	1 Jn 3:1-8
Our Lady of Walsingham			
15 October			
I Evensong	84,87	Ex 40:17-35	Jn 2:1-22
Mattins	116,122	1 Kgs 8:1-21	Jn 19:23-27
II Evensong	132,138	Ezra 5:9-15	1 Cor 3:11-23
St. Luke			
18 October			
I Evensong	103	Ecclus 38:1-14	Acts 15:36-16:15
Mattins	67,96	Ezek 1:1-14	Lk 1:1-4
II Evensong	147	Ezek 47:1-12	Col 4:2
St. Raphael			
24 October			
I Evensong	9,11,15	Tob 4:19-5:8	Jn 5:1-4
Mattins	30,34,47	Tob 12:1-15	Rev 8:1-5
II Evensong	97,99,103	Ex 23:20-23	Rev 10:1-7
Sts. Simon & Jude			
28 October			
I Evensong	66	Is 44:1-8,21-26	Mark 6:1-13
Mattins	118	Is 28:9-16	Eph 2

Proper of Saints # Lectionary

Feast	Proper Psalms	Lesson 1	Lesson 2
II Evensong	62,121	Jer 3:12-18	Jn 14:15
CHRIST THE KING			
Last Sunday in October			
I Evensong	146,147	Jer 23:5-8	Lk 1:26-33
Mattins	72, 89:1-36	Jer 10:1-10	Rev 19:1-16
II Evensong	110,111,113	Dan 4:34-37	1 Tim 6:1-16
ALL HALLOWS			
1 November			
I Evensong	97,148	Ecclus 44:1-15	Heb 11:32-12:11
Mattins	1,15,146	Wis 3:1-9	Rev 19:1-16
II Evensong	112,121,149	Dt 33:1-5,26-end	Rev 21:1-22:5

Lectionary

Common of Saints

Common of Saints

¶ When, for some reason, a Feast Day (not mentioned in this lectionary) is elevated to II Double or higher, these Commons are used.

Feast	Proper Psalms	Lesson 1	Lesson 2
Bishop			
I Evensong	23,100	Ecclus 50:5,11-21	Jn 21:15-17
Mattins	132	Is 61	Mt 10:1-20
II Evensong	111,112	Is 52:1-10	Jn 20:19-23
Confessor			
I Evensong	121,124	Ecclus 2:1-11	Lk 12:1-12
Mattins	3,8	Jer 15:15	Eph 4:1-13
II Evensong	118	Is 49:1-12	Acts 4:5-13
Martyr			
I Evensong	138,146	Ecclus 51:7-12	Lk 21:10-19
Mattins	30	Job 19:23-27	Lk 6:20-36
II Evensong	116	Job 5:8-21	Rev 7:9
Virgin			
I Evensong	45	Jer 31:1-14	Mt 25:1-13
Mattins	96,97	Is 54:1-5,11-14	Lk 10:38
II Evensong	113,122	Joel 2:28	Mt 13:44-52
Matron			
I Evensong	148	Esth 4:1,5-17	Lk 23:50-24:10
Mattins	85	Prov 31:10	Rom 12
II Evensong	34	Is 49:14-21	2 Jn
Dedication of a Church			
I Evensong	84	Hg 2:1-9	1 Cor 3:9-17
Mattins	132	1 Kgs 8:22-30	Jn 10:22-30
II Evensong	48,122	Gn 28:10-12,16-17	Heb 10:19-25

¶ Note, For the Blessed Virgin Mary, the proper psalms and lessons from her Nativity are used.

Alternative Psalter

Daily Office

Alternative Psalter Arrangement

¶ For those who also pray the Minor Hours, it may be desired to have a more robust cursus of the Psalms during Mattins and Evensong, which do not overlap with the Psalms of the Minor Hours. The following arrangement is provided for such a situation.

¶ NOTE, The proper Psalms for Feast Days and obligatory Sundays take priority.

¶ NOTE, The First Sunday of Advent & Palm Sunday always begin 'Week 1'.

Week I

Sunday
Mattins. Psalms 63, 66, 67, 93, 96, 97.
Evensong. Psalms 84, 85, 104.

Monday
Mattins. Psalms 1, 2, 3, 5, 6, 7, 8.
Evensong. Psalms 69, 70, 71, 72.

Tuesday
Mattins. Psalms 9, 10, 11, 12, 13, 14.
Evensong. Psalms 73, 74, 75, 76, 77.

Wednesday
Mattins. Psalms 15, 16, 17, 18.
Evensong. Psalms 78, 79, 80, 81.

Thursday
Mattins. Psalms 19, 20, 21, 22, 23.
Evensong. Psalms 82, 83, 86, 87, 88.

Friday
Mattins. Psalms 24, 25, 26, 27, 28, 29.
Evensong. Psalms 89, 90, 92, 94.

Saturday
Mattins. Psalms 30, 31, 32, 33, 34.
Evensong. Psalms 101, 102, 103, 105.

Week II

Sunday
Mattins. Psalms 98, 99, 100, 148, 149, 150.
Evensong. Psalms 110, 111, 112, 113, 114, 115.

Monday
Mattins. Psalms 35, 36, 37, 38.
Evensong. Psalms 106, 107, 108, 109.

Tuesday
Mattins. Psalms 39, 40, 41, 42, 43.
Evensong. Psalms 116, 117, 118, 120, 121, 122, 123, 124.

Wednesday
Mattins. Psalms 44, 45, 46, 47, 48, 49.
Evensong. Psalms 125, 126, 127, 128, 129, 130, 131.

Thursday
Mattins. Psalms 50, 51, 52, 53, 55.
Evensong. Psalms 132, 133, 135, 136, 137, 138.

Friday
Mattins. Psalms 56, 57, 58, 59, 60, 61.
Evensong. Psalms 139, 140, 141, 142, 143.

Saturday
Mattins. Psalms 62, 64, 65, 68.
Evensong. Psalms 144, 145, 146, 147.

Daily Office

Daily Office

Fore-Office

¶ The Minister shall begin Morning and Evening Prayer by reading one or more of the following Sentences of Scripture.

¶ On any day, save a Day of Fasting or Abstinence, or on any day when the Litany or Holy Communion is immediately to follow, the Minister may, at his discretion, pass at once from the Sentences to the Lord's Prayer and Angelic Salutation, which may never be omitted.

General

When the wicked man turneth away from his wickedness that he hath committed, and doeth that which is lawful and right, he shall save his soul alive.

I acknowledge my transgressions, and my sin is ever before me.

Hide thy face from my sins, and blot out all mine iniquities.

The sacrifices of God are a broken spirit: a broken and a contrite heart, O God, thou wilt not despise.

Rend your heart, and not your garments, and turn unto the Lord your God: for he is gracious and merciful, slow to anger, and of great kindness, and repenteth him of the evil.

To the Lord our God belong mercies and forgivenesses, though we have rebelled against him; neither have we obeyed the voice of the Lord our God, to walk in his laws which he set before us.

O Lord, correct me, but with judgment; not in thine anger, lest thou bring me to nothing.

Repent ye; for the Kingdom of Heaven is at hand.

I will arise and go to my father, and will say unto him, Father, I have sinned against heaven, and before thee, and am no more worthy to be called thy son.

Enter not into judgment with thy servant, O Lord; for in thy sight shall no man living be justified.

If we say that we have no sin, we deceive ourselves, and the truth is not in us; but if we confess our sins, God is faithful and just to forgive us our sins, and to cleanse us from all unrighteousness.

Morning

The LORD is in his holy temple: let all the earth keep silence before him.

I was glad when they said unto me, We will go into the house of the LORD.

Let the words of my mouth, and the meditation of my heart, be alway acceptable in thy sight, O LORD, my strength and my redeemer.

O send out thy light and thy truth, that they may lead me, and bring me unto thy holy hill, and to thy dwelling.

Thus saith the high and lofty One that inhabiteth eternity, whose name is Holy; I dwell in the high and holy place, with him also that is of a contrite and humble spirit, to revive the spirit

Daily Office *Fore-Office*

of the humble, and to revive the heart of the contrite ones.

The hour cometh, and now is, when the true worshippers shall worship the Father in spirit and in truth: for the Father seeketh such to worship him.

Grace be unto you, and peace, from God our Father, and from the Lord Jesus Christ.

Evening

The Lord is in his holy temple: let all the earth keep silence before him.

Lord, I have loved the habitation of thy house, and the place where thine honour dwelleth.

Let my prayer be set forth in thy sight as the incense; and let the lifting up of my hands be an evening sacrifice.

O worship the Lord in the beauty of holiness; let the whole earth stand in awe of him.

Let the words of my mouth, and the meditation of my heart, be alway acceptable in thy sight, O Lord, my strength and my redeemer.

Seek ye the Lord while he may be found, call ye upon him while he is near: let the wicked forsake his way and the unrighteous man his thoughts: and let him return unto the Lord, and he will have mercy upon him: and to our God, for he will abundantly pardon.

Advent

Repent ye, for the Kingdom of heaven is at hand.

Watch ye, for ye know not when the master of the house cometh, at even, or at midnight, or at the cock-crowing, or in the morning: lest coming suddenly he find you sleeping.

Prepare ye the way of the Lord, make straight in the desert a highway for our God.

Christmastide

Behold, I bring you good tidings of great joy, which shall be to all people. For unto you is born this day in the city of David a Saviour, which is Christ the Lord.

Behold, the tabernacle of God is with men, and he will dwell with them, and they shall be his people, and God himself shall be with them, and be their God.

Herein was the love of God manifested in us, that God hath sent his only begotten Son into the world, that we might live through him.

Epiphanytide

From the rising of the sun even unto the going down of the same my Name shall be great among the Gentiles; and in every place incense shall be offered unto my Name, and a pure offering: for my Name shall be great among the heathen, saith the Lord of hosts.

And the Gentiles shall come to thy light, and kings to the brightness of thy rising.

The earth shall be filled with the knowledge of the glory of the Lord, as the waters cover the sea.

Septuagesimatide

The Lord is high above all heathen : and his glory above the heavens.

Fore-Office   # Daily Office

Lent

He shall deliver thee from the snare of the hunter. And from the noisome pestilence.

Passiontide

God commendeth his love toward us, in that, while we were yet sinners, Christ died for us.

    Is it nothing to you, all ye that pass by? behold, and see if there be any sorrow like unto my sorrow which is done unto me, wherewith the Lord hath afflicted me.

    Draw nigh unto my soul and save it. O deliver me because of mine enemies.

Eastertide

He is risen. The Lord is risen indeed.

    Thanks be to God, which giveth us the victory through our Lord Jesus Christ.

    If ye then be risen with Christ, seek those things which are above, where Christ sitteth on the right hand of God.

Ascensiontide

Seeing that we have a great High Priest, that is passed into the heavens, Jesus the Son of God, let us come boldly unto the throne of grace, that we may obtain mercy, and find grace to help in time of need.

    Christ is not entered into the holy places made with hands, which are the figures of the true; but into heaven itself, now to appear in the presence of God for us.

    I ascend to my Father, and your Father. And to my God, and your God. Alleluia.

Whitsuntide

Ye shall receive power, after that the Holy Ghost is come upon you: and ye shall be witnesses unto me both in Jerusalem, and in all Judæa, and in Samaria, and unto the uttermost part of the earth.

    There is a river, the streams whereof shall make glad the city of God, the holy place of the tabernacles of the Most High.

    The love of God hath been shed abroad in our hearts through the Holy Spirit which was given unto us.

Trinity Sunday

Holy, holy, holy, Lord God Almighty, which was, and is, and is to come.

    Holy, holy, holy, is the Lord of hosts: the whole earth is full of his glory.

    God is love; and he that abideth in love abideth in God and God in him.

Apostle

Thou hast given an heritage unto those that fear thy Name, O Lord.

Martyr

Thou hast crowned him, O Lord, with glory and worship.

Bishop, Confessor, or Doctor

The righteous shall flourish like a palm-tree: and shall spread abroad like a cedar in Libanus.

Daily Office *Fore-Office*

Abbot or Monk
O ye holy and humble men of heart, bless ye the Lord: praise and exalt him above all for ever.

Virgin
In thy grace and in thy beauty, go forth, ride prosperously and reign.

Matron
God is in the midst of her, therefore shall she not be removed : God shall help her, and that right early.

Blessed Virgin Mary
Thou art the holy Mother of God, O Mary, ever Virgin.

Blessed Sacrament
I have eaten my honeycomb with my honey. I have drunk my wine with my milk. (Alleluia.)

Dedication of a Church
My house shall be called the house of prayer.

EXHORTATION TO PENITENCE

DEARLY beloved brethren, the Scripture moveth us, in sundry places, to acknowledge and confess our manifold sins and wickedness; and that we should not dissemble nor cloak them before the face of Almighty God our heavenly Father; but confess them with an humble, lowly, penitent, and obedient heart; to the end that we may obtain forgiveness of the same, by his infinite goodness and mercy. And although we ought, at all times, humbly to acknowledge our sins before God; yet ought we chiefly so to do, when we assemble and meet together to render thanks for the great benefits that we have received at his hands, to set forth his most worthy praise, to hear his most holy Word, and to ask those things which are requisite and necessary, as well for the body as the soul. Wherefore I pray and beseech you, as many as are here present, to accompany me with a pure heart, and humble voice, unto the throne of the heavenly grace, saying—

or,

BELOVED, we are come together in the presence of Almighty God and of the whole company of heaven to offer unto him through our Lord Jesus Christ our worship and praise and thanksgiving; to make confession of our sins; to pray, as well for others as for ourselves, that we may know more truly the greatness of God's love and shew forth in our lives the fruits of his grace; and to ask on behalf of all men such things as their well-being doth require. Wherefore let us kneel in silence, and remember God's presence with us now.

¶If the exhortation be omitted, to be said in its place: Let us humbly confess our sins unto Almighty God.

Fore-Office # Daily Office

GENERAL CONFESSION

¶ To be said by the whole Congregation, after the Minister, all kneeling.

LMIGHTY and most merciful Father; We have erred, and strayed from thy ways like lost sheep. We have followed too much the devices and desires of our own hearts. We have offended against thy holy laws. We have left undone those things which we ought to have done; And we have done those things which we ought not to have done; And there is no health in us. But thou, O Lord, have mercy upon us, miserable offenders. Spare thou those, O God, who confess their faults. Restore thou those who are penitent; According to thy promises declared unto mankind in Christ Jesus our Lord. And grant, O most merciful Father, for his sake; That we may hereafter live a godly, righteous, and sober life, To the glory of thy holy Name. Amen.

DECLARATION OF ABSOLUTION

¶ To be made by the Priest alone, standing; the People still kneeling.

¶ But NOTE, That the Priest, at his discretion, may use, instead of what follows, the Absolution from the Order for the Holy Communion.

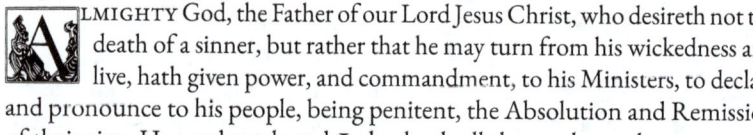LMIGHTY God, the Father of our Lord Jesus Christ, who desireth not the death of a sinner, but rather that he may turn from his wickedness and live, hath given power, and commandment, to his Ministers, to declare and pronounce to his people, being penitent, the Absolution and Remission of their sins. He pardoneth and ✠ absolveth all those who truly repent, and unfeignedly believe his holy Gospel.

Wherefore let us beseech him to grant us true repentance, and his Holy Spirit, that those things may please him which we do at this present; and that the rest of our life hereafter may be pure and holy; so that at the last we may come to his eternal joy; through Jesus Christ our Lord. *Amen.*

or,

HE Almighty and merciful Lord grant you Absolution ✠ and Remission of all your sins, true repentance, amendment of life, and the grace and consolation of the Holy Spirit. Amen.

Daily Office

Fore-Office

¶ *If no Priest be present, the Minister saying the Service shall read the following, that Minister and the People still kneeling.*

GRANT, we beseech thee, merciful Lord, to thy faithful people pardon and peace, that they may be cleansed from all their sins, and serve thee with a quiet mind. Through Jesus Christ thy Son our Lord, who liveth and reigneth with thee, in the unity of the Holy Ghost, God, throughout all ages, world without end. *Amen.*

LORD'S PRAYER & ANGELIC SALUTATION

¶ *Then the Minister shall kneel, and say the Lord's Prayer & Angelic Salutation; the People still kneeling, and repeating them with him, both here, and wheresoever else they are used in Divine Service.*

OUR Father, who art in heaven, Hallowed be thy Name. Thy kingdom come. Thy will be done on earth, As it is in heaven. Give us this day our daily bread. And forgive us our trespasses, As we forgive those who trespass against us. And lead us not into temptation; But deliver us from evil: For thine is the kingdom, and the power, and the glory, for ever and ever. Amen.

HAIL Mary, full of grace; The Lord is with thee; Blessed art thou amongst women, And blessed is the fruit of thy womb, Jesus. Holy Mary, Mother of God, Pray for us sinners, now and at the hour of our death. Amen.

Mattins

Daily Office

The Order for Daily Morning Prayer

℣. O Lord, † open thou our lips.
℟. And our mouth shall show forth thy praise.
℣. O God, ✠ make speed to save us.
℟. O Lord, make haste to help us.

℣. Dómine, † lábia nostra apéries.
℟. Et os nostrum annuntiábit laudem tuam.
℣. Deus, ✠ in adjutórium nostrum inténde.
℟. Dómine, ad adjuvándum nos festína.

¶ Here, all standing up, the Minister shall say,

℣. Glory be to the Father, and to the Son, and to the Holy Ghost.
℟. As it was in the beginning, is now, and ever shall be, world without end. Amen.
℣. Praise ye the Lord.
℟. The Lord's Name be praised.

℣. Glória Patri, et Fílio, * et Spirítui Sancto:
℟. Sicut erat in princípio, et nunc, et semper, * et in sǽcula sæculórum. Amen.
℣. Laudáte Dominum.
℟. Sit Nomen Dómini Benedíctum.

¶ Then shall be said or sung the following Psalm; except on those days for which an Anthem is appointed; and except also, when Psalm 95 may occur in the course of the Psalms.

¶ But NOTE, That on Ash Wednesday and Good Friday the **Venite** may be omitted.

¶ On the days hereafter named, immediately before and after the **Venite** may be sung or said,

Advent. Our King and Saviour draweth nigh; * O come, let us adore him.
Christmastide. Alleluia. Unto us a child is born; * O come, let us adore him. Alleluia.
Epiphanytide & Transfiguration. The Lord hath manifested forth his glory; * O come, let us adore him.
Septuagesimatide. Let us come before the presence of the Lord with thanksgiving; * O come, let us adore him.
Lent. The goodness of God leadeth to repentance; * O come, let us adore him.
Passiontide. Christ our Lord became obedient unto death; * O come, let us adore him.
Eastertide. Alleluia. The Lord is risen indeed; * O come let us adore him. Alleluia.
Ascensiontide. Alleluia. Christ the Lord ascended into heaven; * O come, let us adore him. Alleluia.
Whitsuntide. Alleluia. The Spirit of the Lord filleth the world; * O come, let us adore him. Alleluia.

Daily Office *Mattins*

Trinitytide. Father, Son, and Holy Ghost, One God; * O come, let us adore him.
Feasts of Our Lord & Our Lady. The Word was made flesh; * O come, let us adore him.
Other Feast Days of Semidouble or higher. The Lord is glorious in his saints; * O come, let us adore him.

Venite, exultemus Domino.

COME, let us sing unto the Lord : let us heartily rejoice in the strength of our salvation.

2 Let us come before his presence with thanksgiving : and shew ourselves glad in him with psalms.

3 For the Lord is a great God : and a great King above all gods.

4 In his hand are all the corners of the earth : and the strength of the hills is his also.

5 The sea is his, and he made it : and his hands prepared the dry land.

6 O come, let us worship and fall down : and kneel before the Lord our Maker.

7 For he is the Lord our God : and we are the people of his pasture, and the sheep of his hand.

8 To-day if ye will hear his voice, harden not your hearts : as in the provocation, and as in the day of temptation in the wilderness.

9 When your fathers tempted me : proved me, and saw my works.

10 Forty years long was I grieved with this generation, and said : It is a people that do err in their hearts, for they have not known my ways;

11 Unto whom I sware in my wrath : that they should not enter into my rest.

ENÍTE, exsultémus Dómino, jubilémus Deo, salutári nostro:

Præoccupémus fáciem ejus in confessióne, et in psalmis jubilémus ei.

Quóniam Deus magnus Dóminus, et Rex magnus super omnes deos, quóniam non repéllet Dóminus plebem suam:

Quia in manu ejus sunt omnes fines terræ, et altitúdines móntium ipse cónspicit.

Quóniam ipsíus est mare, et ipse fecit illud, et áridam fundavérunt manus ejus.

Veníte, adorémus, et procidámus ante Deum: plorémus coram Dómino, qui fecit nos,

Quia ipse est Dóminus, Deus noster; nos autem pópulus ejus, et oves páscuæ ejus.

Hódie, si vocem ejus audiéritis, nolíte obduráre corda vestra, sicut in exacerbatióne secúndum diem tentatiónis in desérto: ubi tentavérunt me patres vestri, probavérunt et vidérunt ópera mea.

Quadragínta annis próximus fui generatióni huic, et dixi; Semper hi errant corde, ipsi vero non cognovérunt vias meas: quibus jurávi in ira mea; Si introíbunt in réquiem meam.

Mattins # Daily Office

¶ Then shall follow a Portion of the Psalms, according to the Use of this Church. And at the end of every Psalm, and likewise at the end of the Venite, daily Old Testament Canticle, Athanasian Creed, and Benedictus, shall be sung or said the Gloria Patri.

℣. Glory be to the Father, and to the Son, * and to the Holy Ghost.
℞. As it was in the beginning, is now, and ever shall be, * world without end. Amen.

℣. Glória Patri, et Fílio, * et Spirítui Sancto:
℞. Sicut erat in princípio, et nunc, et semper, * et in sǽcula sæculórum. Amen.

¶ Verses 8-11 of the Venite may be replaced with the following.

O worship the Lord in the beauty of holiness : let the whole earth stand in awe of him.
For he cometh, for he cometh to judge the earth : and with righteousness to judge the world, and the people with his truth.

Tóllite hóstias, et introíte in átria ejus: * adoráte Dóminum in átrio sancto ejus.
Judicábit orbem terræ in æquitáte, * et pópulos in veritáte sua.

¶ After the Venite, a Hymn may be sung.

¶ Then shall be read the First Lesson, according to the Table or Calendar. And NOTE, That before every Lesson, the Minister shall say, Here beginneth *such a Chapter* (or *Verse of such a Chapter*) of *such a Book*; and after every Lesson, Here endeth the First (or Second) Lesson.

TE DEUM LAUDAMUS

¶ The Te Deum is prayed on all Sundays (outside Advent & Lent) and Feast Days (Semidouble or higher).
NOTE, The Old Testament Canticle (p. 21) may be said instead of the Te Deum.

E praise thee, O God; we acknowledge thee to be the Lord.
All the earth doth worship thee, the Father everlasting.
To thee all Angels cry aloud; the Heavens, and all the Powers therein;
To thee Cherubim and Seraphim continually do cry,
Holy, Holy, Holy, Lord God of

E Deum laudámus: * te Dóminum confitémur.
Te ætérnum Patrem * omnis terra venerátur.
Tibi omnes Ángeli, * tibi Cæli, et univérsæ Potestátes
Tibi Chérubim et Séraphim * incessábili voce proclámant:
Sanctus, Sanctus, Sanctus * Dóminus Deus Sábaoth.

Daily Office *Mattins*

Sabaoth;
  Heaven and earth are full of the Majesty of thy glory.
  The glorious company of the Apostles praise thee.
  The goodly fellowship of the Prophets praise thee.
  The noble army of Martyrs praise thee.
  The holy Church throughout all the world doth acknowledge thee;
  The Father of an infinite Majesty;
  Thine honourable, true and only Son;
  Also the Holy Ghost the Comforter.
  THOU art the King of Glory, O Christ.
  Thou art the everlasting Son of the Father.
  When thou tookest upon thee to deliver man, thou didst not abhor the Virgin's womb.
  When thou hadst overcome the sharpness of death, thou didst open the Kingdom of Heaven to all believers.
  Thou sittest at the right hand of God, in the glory of the Father.
  We believe that thou shalt come to be our Judge.
  We therefore pray thee, help thy servants, whom thou hast redeemed with thy precious blood.
  Make them to be numbered with thy Saints, in glory everlasting.
  O LORD, save thy people, and bless thine heritage.
  Govern them and lift them up for ever.

Pleni sunt cæli et terra * majestátis glóriæ tuæ.
  Te gloriósus * Apostolórum chorus,
  Te Prophetárum * laudábilis númerus,
  Te Mártyrum candidátus * laudat exércitus.
  Te per orbem terrárum * sancta confitétur Ecclésia,
  Patrem * imménsæ majestátis;
  Venerándum tuum verum * et únicum Fílium;
  Sanctum quoque * Paráclitum Spíritum.
  TU Rex glóriæ, * Christe.
  Tu Patris * sempitérnus es Fílius.
  Tu, ad liberándum susceptúrus hóminem: * non horruísti Vírginis úterum.
  Tu, devícto mortis acúleo, * aperuísti credéntibus regna cælórum.
  Tu ad déxteram Dei sedes, * in glória Patris.
  Judex créderis * esse ventúrus.
  Te ergo quǽsumus, tuis fámulis súbveni, * quos pretióso sánguine redemísti.
  Ætérna fac cum Sanctis tuis * in glória numerári.
  SALVUM fac pópulum tuum, Dómine, * et bénedic hereditáti tuæ.
  Et rege eos, * et extólle illos usque in ætérnum.
  Per síngulos dies * benedícimus te.
  Et laudámus nomen tuum in sǽculum, * et in sǽculum sǽculi.
  Dignáre, Dómine, die isto * sine peccáto nos custodíre.

Mattins   # Daily Office

Day by day we magnify thee;
And we worship thy Name ever, world without end.
Vouchsafe, O Lord, to keep us this day without sin.
O Lord, have mercy upon us, have mercy upon us.
O Lord, let thy mercy lighten upon us, as our trust is in thee.
O Lord, in thee have I trusted; let me never be confounded.

Miserére nostri, Dómine, * miserére nostri.
Fiat misericórdia tua, Dómine, super nos, * quemádmodum sperávimus in te.
In te, Dómine, sperávi: * non confúndar in ætérnum.

Benedicite, omnia opera Domini.

¶ The Benedicite is prayed on all Sundays in Advent & Lent, and on Days below Semi-double.
Note, The Old Testament Canticle (p. 21) may be said instead of the Benedicite.

ALL ye Works of the Lord, bless ye the Lord: * praise him, and magnify him for ever.
O ye Angels of the Lord, bless ye the Lord: * praise him, and magnify him for ever.
YE Heavens, bless ye the Lord: * praise him, and magnify him for ever.
O ye Waters that be above the firmament, bless ye the Lord: * praise him, and magnify him for ever.
O all ye Powers of the Lord, bless ye the Lord: * praise him, and magnify him for ever.
O ye Sun and Moon, bless ye the Lord: * praise him, and magnify him for ever.
O ye Stars of heaven, bless ye the Lord: * praise him, and magnify him for ever.
O ye Showers and Dew, bless ye the

ENEDÍCITE, ómnia ópera Dómini, Dómino: * laudáte et superexaltáte eum in sǽcula.
Benedícite, Ángeli Dómini, Dómino: * laudáte et superexaltáte eum in sǽcula.
ENEDÍCITE, cæli, Dómino: * laudáte et superexaltáte eum in sǽcula.
Benedícite, aquæ omnes, quæ super cælos sunt, Dómino: * laudáte et superexaltáte eum in sǽcula.
Benedícite, omnes virtútes Dómini, Dómino: * laudáte et superexaltáte eum in sǽcula.
Benedícite, sol et luna, Dómino: * laudáte et superexaltáte eum in sǽcula.
Benedícite, stellæ cæli, Dómino: * laudáte et superexaltáte eum in sǽcula.
Benedícite, omnis imber et ros, Dómino: * laudáte et superexaltáte eum in sǽcula.
Benedícite, omnes spíritus Dei, Dó-

Lord: * praise him, and magnify him for ever.

O ye winds of God, bless ye the Lord: * praise him, and magnify him for ever.

O ye Fire and Heat, bless ye the Lord * praise him, and magnify him for ever.

O ye Winter and Summer, bless ye the Lord: * praise him, and magnify him for ever.

O ye Dews and Frosts, bless ye the Lord: * praise him, and magnify him for ever.

O ye Frost and Cold, bless ye the Lord: * praise him, and magnify him for ever.

O ye Ice and Snow, bless ye the Lord * praise him, and magnify him for ever.

O ye Nights and Days, bless ye the Lord: * praise him, and magnify him for ever.

O ye Light and Darkness, bless ye the Lord: * praise him, and magnify him for ever.

O ye Lightnings and Clouds, bless ye the Lord * praise him, and magnify him for ever.

LET the Earth bless the Lord: * yea, let it praise him, and magnify him for ever.

O ye Mountains and Hills, bless ye the Lord: * praise him, and magnify him for ever.

O all ye Green Things upon the earth, bless ye the Lord: * praise him, and magnify him for ever.

O ye Wells, bless ye the Lord: * praise him, and magnify him for ever.

mino: * laudáte et superexaltáte eum in sǽcula.

Benedícite, ignis et æstus, Dómino: * laudáte et superexaltáte eum in sǽcula.

Benedícite, frigus et æstus, Dómino: * laudáte et superexaltáte eum in sǽcula.

Benedícite, rores et pruína, Dómino: * laudáte et superexaltáte eum in sǽcula.

Benedícite, gelu et frigus, Dómino: * laudáte et superexaltáte eum in sǽcula.

Benedícite, glácies et nives, Dómino: * laudáte et superexaltáte eum in sǽcula.

Benedícite, noctes et dies, Dómino: * laudáte et superexaltáte eum in sǽcula.

Benedícite, lux et ténebræ, Dómino: * laudáte et superexaltáte eum in sǽcula.

Benedícite, fúlgura et nubes, Dómino: * laudáte et superexaltáte eum in sǽcula.

ENEDÍCAT terra Dóminum: * laudet et superexáltet eum in sǽcula.

Benedícite, montes et colles, Dómino: * laudáte et superexaltáte eum in sǽcula.

Benedícite, univérsa germinántia in terra, Dómino: * laudáte et superexaltáte eum in sǽcula.

Benedícite, fontes, Dómino: * laudáte et superexaltáte eum in sǽcula.

Benedícite, mária et flúmina, Dómino: * laudáte et superexaltáte eum in sǽcula.

Mattins   # Daily Office

O ye Seas and Floods, bless ye the Lord: * praise him, and magnify him for ever.

O ye Whales, and all that move in the waters, bless ye the Lord: * praise him, and magnify him for ever.

O all ye Fowls of the air, bless ye the Lord: * praise him, and magnify him for ever.

O all ye Beasts and Cattle, bless ye the Lord: * praise him, and magnify him for ever.

O ye Children of Men, bless ye the Lord: * praise him, and magnify him for ever.

LET Israel bless the Lord: * praise him, and magnify him for ever.

O ye Priests of the Lord, bless ye the Lord: * praise him, and magnify him for ever.

O ye Servants of the Lord, bless ye the Lord: * praise him, and magnify him for ever.

O ye Spirits and Souls of the Righteous, bless ye the Lord: * praise him, and magnify him for ever.

O ye holy and humble Men of heart, bless ye the Lord: * praise him, and magnify him for ever.

ET us bless the Father, and the Son, and the Holy Ghost: * praise him, and magnify him for ever.

Benedícite, cete, et ómnia, quæ movéntur in aquis, Dómino: * laudáte et superexaltáte eum in sǽcula.

Benedícite, omnes vólucres cæli, Dómino: * laudáte et superexaltáte eum in sǽcula.

Benedícite, omnes béstiæ et pécora, Dómino: * laudáte et superexaltáte eum in sǽcula.

Benedícite, fílii hóminum, Dómino: * laudáte et superexaltáte eum in sǽcula.

ENEDÍCAT Israël Dóminum: * laudet et superexáltet eum in sǽcula.

Benedícite, sacerdótes Dómini, Dómino: * laudáte et superexaltáte eum in sǽcula.

Benedícite, servi Dómini, Dómino: * laudáte et superexaltáte eum in sǽcula.

Benedícite, spíritus, et ánimæ justórum, Dómino: * laudáte et superexaltáte eum in sǽcula.

Benedícite, sancti, et húmiles corde, Dómino: * laudáte et superexaltáte eum in sǽcula.

ENEDICÁMUS Patrem et Fílium cum Sancto Spíritu: * laudémus et superexaltémus eum in sǽcula.

¶ Then shall be read, in like manner, the Second Lesson, taken out of the New Testament, according to the Table or Calendar.

¶ After which may be sung or said a Hymn.

Daily Office   *Mattins*

BENEDICTUS

⁋ Then shall be sung or said the Hymn following.

LESSED ✠ be the Lord God of Israel; * for he hath visited and redeemed his people;

And hath raised up a mighty salvation for us, * in the house of his servant David;

As he spake by the mouth of his holy Prophets, * which have been since the world began;

That we should be saved from our enemies, * and from the hand of all that hate us.

To perform the mercy promised to our forefathers, * and to remember his holy covenant;

To perform the oath which he sware to our forefather Abraham, * that he would give us;

That we being delivered out of the hand of our enemies * might serve him without fear;

In holiness and righteousness before him, * all the days of our life.

And thou, child, shalt be called the prophet of the Highest: * for thou shalt go before the face of the Lord to prepare his ways;

To give knowledge of salvation unto his people * for the remission of their sins,

Through the tender mercy of our God; * whereby the day-spring from on high hath visited us;

To give light to them that sit in darkness, and in the shadow of death, * and to guide our feet into the way of peace.

ENEDÍCTUS ✠ Dóminus, Deus Israël: * quia visitávit, et fecit redemptiónem plebi suæ:

Et eréxit cornu salútis nobis: * in domo David, púeri sui.

Sicut locútus est per os sanctórum, * qui a sǽculo sunt, prophetárum ejus:

Salútem ex inimícis nostris, * et de manu ómnium, qui odérunt nos.

Ad faciéndam misericórdiam cum pátribus nostris: * et memorári testaménti sui sancti.

Jusjurándum, quod jurávit ad Ábraham patrem nostrum, * datúrum se nobis:

Ut sine timóre, de manu inimicórum nostrórum liberáti, * serviámus illi.

In sanctitáte, et justítia coram ipso, * ómnibus diébus nostris.

Et tu, puer, Prophéta Altíssimi vocáberis: * præíbis enim ante fáciem Dómini, paráre vias ejus:

Ad dandam sciéntiam salútis plebi ejus: * in remissiónem peccatórum eórum:

Per víscera misericórdiæ Dei nostri: * in quibus visitávit nos, óriens ex alto:

Illumináre his, qui in ténebris, et in umbra mortis sedent: * ad dirigéndos pedes nostros in viam pacis.

Mattins # Daily Office

Apostles' Creed

❡ Then shall be said the Apostles' Creed, by the Minister and the People, standing. Note, the Nicene Creed may be said instead of the Apostles' (p. 162).

❡ Upon these Feasts; Christmas Day, the Epiphany, Saint Matthias, Easter Day, Ascension Day, Whitsunday, Saint John Baptist, Saint James, Saint Bartholomew, Saint Matthew, Saint Simon and Saint Jude, Saint Andrew, and upon Trinity Sunday, shall be sung or said, instead of the Apostle's Creed, the Athanasian Creed (p. 37).

I BELIEVE in God the Father Almighty, Maker of heaven and earth: And in Jesus Christ his only Son our Lord: Who was conceived by the Holy Ghost, Born of the Virgin Mary: Suffered under Pontius Pilate, Was crucified, dead, and buried: He descended into hell; The third day he rose again from the dead: He ascended into heaven, And sitteth on the right hand of God the Father Almighty: From thence he shall come to judge the quick and the dead.

I believe in the Holy Ghost: The holy Catholic Church; The Communion of Saints: The Forgiveness of sins: The Resurrection of the body: ✠ And the Life everlasting. Amen.

REDO in Deum, Patrem omnipoténtem, Creatórem cæli et terræ. Et in Jesum Christum, Fílium ejus únicum, Dóminum nostrum: qui concéptus est de Spíritu Sancto, natus ex María Vírgine, passus sub Póntio Piláto, crucifíxus, mórtuus, et sepúltus: descéndit ad ínferos; tértia die resurréxit a mórtuis; ascéndit ad cælos; sedet ad déxteram Dei Patris omnipoténtis: inde ventúrus est judicáre vivos et mórtuos.

Credo in Spíritum Sanctum, sanctam Ecclésiam cathólicam, Sanctórum communiónem, remissiónem peccatórum, carnis ✠ resurrectiónem, vitam ætérnam. Amen.

❡ And after that, these Prayers following, the People devoutly kneeling; the Minister first pronouncing,

℣. The Lord be with you.
or, O Lord, hear our prayer.

℟. And with thy spirit.
or, And let our cry come unto thee.
℣. Let us pray.
℣. Lord, have mercy upon us.
℟. Christ, have mercy upon us.
℣. Lord, have mercy upon us.

℣. Dóminus vobíscum.
vel, Dómine, exáudi oratiónem nostram.
℟. Et cum spíritu tuo.
vel, Et clamor noster ad te véniat.
℣. Orémus.
℣. Kýrie, eléison.
℟. Christe, eléison.
℣. Kýrie, eléison.

Daily Office *Mattins*

Lord's Prayer

¶ Then the Minister, Clerks, and People—all kneeling—shall say the Lord's Prayer with a loud voice.

UR Father, who art in heaven, Hallowed be thy Name. Thy kingdom come. Thy will be done on earth, As it is in heaven. Give us this day our daily bread. And forgive us our trespasses, As we forgive those who trespass against us. And lead us not into temptation; But deliver us from evil. Amen.

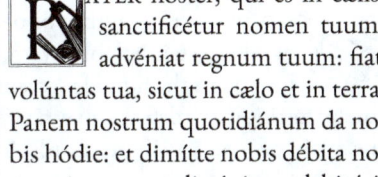ATER noster, qui es in cælis, sanctificétur nomen tuum: advéniat regnum tuum: fiat volúntas tua, sicut in cælo et in terra. Panem nostrum quotidiánum da nobis hódie: et dimítte nobis débita nostra, sicut et nos dimíttimus debitóribus nostris: et ne nos indúcas in tentatiónem: sed líbera nos a malo. Amen.

Preces

¶ Then the Minister standing up shall say,

℣. O Lord, show thy mercy upon us.
℟. And grant us thy salvation.
℣. O Lord, save the *State*.
℟. And mercifully hear us when we call upon thee.
℣. Endue thy Ministers with righteousness.
℟. And make thy chosen people joyful.
℣. O Lord, save thy people.
℟. And bless thine inheritance.
℣. Give peace in our time, O Lord.
℟. For it is thou, Lord, only, that makest us dwell in safety.
℣. O God, make clean our hearts within us.
℟. And take not thy Holy Spirit from us.

℣. Osténde nobis, Dómine, misericórdiam tuam.
℟. Et salutáre tuum da nobis.
℣. Dómine salvam fac *Civitatem*.
℟. Et exáudi nos cum invocámus te.
℣. Sacerdótes tui induántur Justítia.
℟. Et sancti tui exúltent.
℣. Salvum fac Pópulum tuum, Dómine.
℟. Et bénedic Hæreditáti tuæ.
℣. Da pacem Dómine in diébus nostris.
℟. Quóniam tu, Dómine, singuláriter in spe constituísti me.
℣. Cor mundum crea in nobis, O Deus.
℟. Et Spíritum Sanctum tuum ne áuferas a nobis.

Mattins — # Daily Office

❧ Then shall follow the Collect(s) for the Day, except when the Communion Service is read; and then the Collect(s) for the Day shall be omitted here.

A Collect for Peace

O GOD, who art the author of peace and lover of concord, in knowledge of whom standeth our eternal life, whose service is perfect freedom; Defend us thy humble servants in all assaults of our enemies; that we, surely trusting in thy defence, may not fear the power of any adversaries, through the might of Jesus Christ our Lord. *Amen.*

A Collect for Grace

O LORD, our heavenly Father, Almighty and everlasting God, who hast safely brought us to the beginning of this day; Defend us in the same with thy mighty power; and grant that this day we fall into no sin, neither run into any kind of danger; but that all our doings, being ordered by thy governance, may be righteous in thy sight; through Jesus Christ our Lord. *Amen.*

Conclusion

℣. The Lord be with you.	℣. Dóminus vobíscum.
or, O Lord, hear our prayer.	*vel,* Dómine, exáudi oratiónem nostram.
℟. And with thy spirit.	℟. Et cum spíritu tuo.
or, And let our cry come unto thee.	*vel,* Et clamor noster ad te véniat.
℣. Let us bless the Lord (alleluia, alleluia.)	℣. Benedicámus Dómino (allelúja, allelúja.)
℟. Thanks be to God (alleluia, alleluia.)	℟. Deo grátias (allelúja, allelúja.)
℣. May the souls ✠ of the faithful departed, through the mercy of God, rest in peace.	℣. Fidélium ánimæ ✠ per misericórdiam Dei requiéscant in pace.
℟. Amen.	℟. Amen.

❧ The following Prayers shall be omitted here when the Great Litany is said, and may be omitted when the Holy Communion is to follow.

❧ And NOTE, That the Minister may here end the Morning Prayer with such intercessions taken out of this Book, as he shall think fit, or with the Grace.

Daily Office   *Mattins*

After the Third Collect

¶ The Prayer for the Head of State (p. 70) is here said.

A Prayer for the Clergy and People

ALMIGHTY and everlasting God, from whom cometh every good and perfect gift; Send down upon our Bishops, and other Clergy, and upon the Congregations committed to their charge, the healthful Spirit of thy grace; and, that they may truly please thee, pour upon them the continual dew of thy blessing. Grant this, O Lord, for the honour of our Advocate and Mediator, Jesus Christ. *Amen.*

¶ Additional Prayers (p. 70) may here be said.

A Prayer for all Sorts & Conditions of Men

O GOD, the Creator and Preserver of all mankind, we humbly beseech thee for all sorts and conditions of men; that thou wouldest be pleased to make thy ways known unto them, thy saving health unto all nations. More especially we pray for thy holy Church universal; that it may be so guided and governed by thy good Spirit, that all who profess and call themselves Christians may be led into the way of truth, and hold the faith in unity of spirit, in the bond of peace, and in righteousness of life. Finally, we commend to thy fatherly goodness all those who are any ways afflicted, or distressed, in mind, body, or estate; (*especially those for whom our prayers are desired;) that it may please thee to comfort and relieve them, according to their several necessities; giving them patience under their sufferings, and a happy issue out of all their afflictions. And this we beg for Jesus Christ's sake. *Amen.*

*This may be said when any desire the prayers of the Congregation.

A General Thanksgiving

¶ The General Thanksgiving may be said by the Congregation with the Minister.

ALMIGHTY God, Father of all mercies, we, thine unworthy servants, do give thee most humble and hearty thanks for all thy goodness and loving-kindness to us and to all men; (*to those who desire now to offer up their praises and thanksgivings for thy late mercies vouchsafed unto them.) We bless thee for our creation, preservation, and all the blessings of this life; but above all, for thine inestimable love in the redemption of the world by our Lord Jesus Christ; for the means of grace, and for the hope of glory. And, we beseech thee, give us that due sense of all thy mercies, that our hearts may be unfeignedly thankful; and that we show forth thy praise, not only with our lips,

*This may be said when any desire to return thanks for mercies vouchsafed to them.

but in our lives, by giving up our selves to thy service, and by walking before thee in holiness and righteousness all our days; through Jesus Christ our Lord, to whom, with thee and the Holy Ghost, be all honour and glory, world without end. *Amen.*

¶ The Thanksgivings (p. 82) may here be offered.

A Prayer of St. Chrysostom

ALMIGHTY God, who hast given us grace at this time with one accord to make our common supplications unto thee; and dost promise that when two or three are gathered together in thy Name thou wilt grant their requests; Fulfil now, O Lord, the desires and petitions of thy servants, as may be most expedient for them; granting us in this world knowledge of thy truth, and in the world to come life everlasting. *Amen.*

The Grace

THE grace of our Lord Jesus Christ, ✠ and the love of God, and the fellowship of the Holy Ghost, be with us all evermore. *Amen.*

HERE ENDETH THE ORDER OF MORNING PRAYER.

Tuesday Ferial **Daily Office** *Old Testament Canticles*

Old Testament Canticles

❧ The Festal Canticle is prayed on Feast Days Semidouble & higher and the Saturday Office of St. Mary.

Monday Ferial Canticle

Confitebor tibi

LORD, I will praise thee, though thou wast angry with me; * thine anger is turned away, and thou comfortedst me.

Behold, God is my salvation; * I will trust, and not be afraid:

For the Lord Jehovah is my strength and my song; * he also is become my salvation.

Therefore with joy shall ye draw water out of the wells of salvation: * and in that day shall ye say, Praise the Lord, call upon his Name,

Declare his doings among the people, * make mention that his Name is exalted.

Sing unto the Lord; for he hath done excellent things: * this is known in all the earth.

Cry out and shout, thou inhabitant of Sion: * for great is the Holy One of Israel in the midst of thee.

Monday Festal Canticle

Benedictus es, Domine

LESSED be thou, Lord God of Israel * our father, for ever and ever.

Thine, O Lord is the greatness, and the power, and the glory, † and the victory, and the majesty: * for all that is in the heaven and in the earth is thine;

Thine is the kingdom, O Lord, * and thou art exalted as head above all.

Both riches and honour come of thee, * and thou reignest over all;

And in thine hand is power and might; * and in thine hand it is to make great, and to give strength unto all.

Now therefore, our God, we thank thee, and praise thy glorious name.

Tuesday Ferial Canticle

Ego dixi

SAID in the cutting off of my days, † I shall go to the gates of the grave: * I am deprived of the residue of my years.

I said, I shall not see the Lord, † even the Lord, in the land of the living: * I shall behold man no more with the inhabitants of the world.

Mine age is departed, * and is removed from me as a shepherd's tent;

I have cut off like a weaver my life: † he will cut me off with pining sickness: * from day even to night wilt thou make an end of me.

I reckoned till morning, † that, as a lion, so will he break all my bones: * from day even to night wilt thou make an end of me.

Like a crane or a swallow, so did I chatter: * I did mourn as a dove.

Mine eyes fail with looking upward: * O Lord, I am oppressed; undertake for me.

What shall I say? † he hath both spoken unto me, and himself hath done it: * I shall go softly all my years in the bitterness of my soul.

O Lord, by these things men live, † and in all these things is the life of my spirit: * so wilt thou recover me, and make me to live.

Behold, for peace I had great bitterness: † but thou hast in love to my soul delivered it from the pit of corruption: * for thou hast cast all my sins behind thy back.

For the grave cannot praise thee, † death can not celebrate thee: * they that go down into the pit cannot hope for thy truth.

The living, the living, he shall praise thee, as I do this day: * the father to the children shall make known thy truth.

The Lord was ready to save me: * therefore we will sing my songs to the stringed instruments all the days of our life in the house of the Lord.

scattered us among them.

There declare his greatness, and extol him before all the living: * for he is our Lord, and he is the God our Father for ever.

And he will scourge us for our iniquities, * and will have mercy again, and will gather us out of all nations, among whom he hath scattered us.

If ye turn to him with your whole heart, and with your whole mind, † and deal uprightly before him, * then will he turn unto you, and will not hide his face from you.

Therefore see what he will do with you, and confess him with your whole mouth, and praise the Lord of might, * and extol the everlasting King.

In the land of my captivity do I praise him, * and declare his might and majesty to a sinful nation.

O ye sinners, turn and do justice before him: * who can tell if he will accept you, and have mercy on you?

I will extol my God, * and my soul shall praise the King of heaven, and shall rejoice in his greatness.

Tuesday Festal Canticle

Magnus es, Domine

LESSED be God that liveth for ever, * and blessed be his kingdom.

For he doth scourge, and hath mercy: † he leadeth down to hell, and bringeth up again: * neither is there any that can avoid his hand.

Confess him before the Gentiles, ye children of Israel: * for he hath

Wednesday Ferial Canticle

Exsultavit cor meum

Y heart rejoiceth in the Lord, * mine horn is exalted in the Lord:

My mouth is enlarged over mine enemies; * because I rejoice in thy salvation.

There is none holy as the Lord: † for there is none beside thee: * neither is there any rock like our God.

Talk no more so exceeding proudly; * let not arrogancy come out of your mouth:

For the Lord is a God of knowledge, * and by him actions are weighed.

The bows of the mighty men are broken, * and they that stumbled are girded with strength.

They that were full have hired out themselves for bread; * and they that were hungry ceased:

So that the barren hath born seven; * and she that hath many children is waxed feeble.

The Lord killeth, and maketh alive: * he bringeth down to the grave, and bringeth up.

The Lord maketh poor, and maketh rich: * he bringeth low, and lifteth up.

He raiseth up the poor out of the dust, * and lifteth up the beggar from the dunghill,

To set them among princes, * and to make them inherit the throne of glory:

For the pillars of the earth are the Lord's, * and he hath set the world upon them.

He will keep the feet of his saints, † and the wicked shall be silent in darkness; * for by strength shall no man prevail.

The adversaries of the Lord shall be broken to pieces; * out of heaven shall he thunder upon them:

The Lord shall judge the ends of the earth; † and he shall give strength unto his King, * and exalt the horn of his Anointed.

Wednesday Festal Canticle

Hymnum cantemus

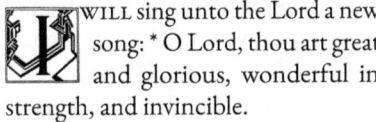WILL sing unto the Lord a new song: * O Lord, thou art great and glorious, wonderful in strength, and invincible.

Let all creatures serve thee: * for thou spakest, and they were made,

Thou didst send forth thy spirit, and it created them, * and there is none that can resist thy voice.

For the mountains shall be moved from their foundations with the waters, † the rocks shall melt as wax at thy presence: * yet thou art merciful to them that fear thee.

For all sacrifice is too little for a sweet savour unto thee: * but he that feareth the Lord is great at all times.

Woe to the nations that rise up against my kindred! * the Lord Almighty will take vengeance of them in the day of judgment.

Thursday Ferial Canticle

Cantemus Domino

I WILL sing unto the Lord, for he hath triumphed gloriously: * the horse and his rider hath he thrown into the sea.

The Lord is my strength and song, * and he is become my salvation:

He is my God, and I will prepare him an habitation; * my father's God, and I will exalt him.

The Lord is a man of war: * the Lord is his Name.

Pharaoh's chariots and his host hath he cast into the sea: * his chosen captains also are drowned in the Red Sea.

The depths have covered them: * they sank into the bottom as a stone.

Thy right hand, O Lord, is become glorious in power: * thy right hand, O Lord, hath dashed in pieces the enemy.

And in the greatness of thine excellency † thou hast overthrown them that rose up against thee: * thou sentest forth thy wrath, which consumed them as stubble.

And with the blast of thy nostrils the waters were gathered together, * the floods stood upright as an heap, and the depths were congealed in the heart of the sea.

The enemy said, † I will pursue, I will overtake, I will divide the spoil; * my lust shall be satisfied upon them;

I will draw my sword, * my hand shall destroy them.

Thou didst blow with thy wind, the sea covered them: * they sank as lead in the mighty waters.

Who is like unto thee, O Lord, among the gods? * who is like thee, glorious in holiness, fearful in praises, doing wonders?

Thou stretchedst out thy right hand, * the earth swallowed them.

Thou in thy mercy hast led forth the people which thou hast redeemed: * thou hast guided them in thy strength unto thy holy habitation.

The people shall hear, and be afraid: * sorrow shall take hold on the inhabitants of Palestina.

Then the dukes of Edom shall be amazed; * the mighty men of Moab, trembling shall take hold upon them; all the inhabitants of Canaan shall melt away.

Fear and dread shall fall upon them; † by the greatness of thine arm they shall be as still as a stone; * till thy people pass over, O Lord, till the people pass over, which thou hast purchased.

Thou shalt bring them in, and plant them in the mountain of thine inheritance, * in the place, O Lord, which thou hast made for thee to dwell in, in the Sanctuary, O Lord, which thy hands have established.

The Lord shall reign * for ever and ever.

For the horse of Pharaoh went in with his chariots and with his horsemen into the sea, * and the Lord brought again the waters of the sea upon them.

But the children of Israel went on dry land * in the midst of the sea.

Thursday Festal Canticle

Audite verbum

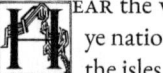EAR the word of the Lord, O ye nations, * and declare it in the isles afar off,

And say, He that scattered Israel will gather him, * and keep him, as a shepherd doth his flock.

For the Lord hath redeemed Jacob, * and ransomed him from the hand of him that was stronger than he.

Therefore they shall come and sing in the height of Sion, * and shall flow together to the goodness of the Lord,

For wheat, and for wine, and for oil, * and for the young of the flock and of the herd:

And their soul shall be as a watered garden; * and they shall not sorrow any more at all.

Then shall the virgin rejoice in the dance, * both young men and old together:

For I will turn their mourning into joy, * and will comfort them, and make them rejoice from their sorrow.

And I will satiate the soul of the priests with fatness, * and my people shall be satisfied with my goodness, saith the Lord.

Friday Ferial Canticle

Domine audivi

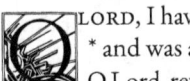O Lord, I have heard thy speech, * and was afraid:

O Lord, revive thy work in the midst of the years, † in the midst of the years make known; * in wrath remember mercy.

God came from Teman, * and the Holy One from mount Paran.

His glory covered the heavens, * and the earth was full of his praise.

And his brightness was as the light; † he had horns coming out of his hand: * and there was the hiding of his power.

Before him went the pestilence, * and burning coals went forth at his feet.

He stood, and measured the earth: * he beheld, and drove asunder the nations;

And the everlasting mountains were scattered, † the perpetual hills did bow: * his ways are everlasting.

I saw the tents of Cushan in affliction: * and the curtains of the land of Midian did tremble.

Was the Lord displeased against the rivers? * was thine anger against the rivers?

Was thy wrath against the sea, * that thou didst ride upon thine horses and thy chariots of salvation?

Thy bow was made quite naked, * according to the oaths of the tribes, even thy word.

Thou didst cleave the earth with rivers: * the mountains saw thee, and they trembled:

The overflowing of the water passed by: * the deep uttered his voice, and lifted up his hands on high.

The sun and moon stood still in their habitation: * at the light of thine arrows they went, and at the shining of thy glittering spear.

Thou didst march through the land in indignation, * thou didst thresh the heathen in anger.

Thou wentest forth for the salvation of thy people, * even for salvation with thine Anointed;

Thou woundedst the head out of the house of the wicked, * by discovering the foundation unto the neck.

Thou didst strike through with his staves the head of his villages: * they came out as a whirlwind to scatter me:

their rejoicing was as to devour the poor secretly.

Thou didst walk through the sea with thine horses, * through the heap of great waters.

When I heard, my belly trembled; * my lips quivered at the voice:

Rottenness entered into my bones, * and I trembled in myself, that I might rest in the day of trouble:

When he cometh up unto the people, * he will invade them with his troops.

Although the fig tree shall not blossom, * neither shall fruit be in the vines;

The labour of the olive shall fail, * and the fields shall yield no meat;

The flock shall be cut off from the fold, * and there shall be no herd in the stalls:

Yet I will rejoice in the Lord, * I will joy in the God of my salvation.

The Lord God is my strength, and he will make my feet like hinds' feet, * and he will make me to walk upon mine high places.

Friday Festal Canticle

Vere tu es Deus absconditus

ERILY thou art a God that hidest thyself, * O God of Israel, the Saviour.

They shall be ashamed, and also confounded, all of them: * they shall go to confusion together that are makers of idols.

But Israel shall be saved in the Lord with an everlasting salvation: * ye shall not be ashamed nor confounded world without end.

For thus saith the Lord that created the heavens; * God himself that formed the earth and made it;

He hath established it, he created it not in vain, * he formed it to be inhabited:

I am the Lord; * and there is none else.

I have not spoken in secret, * in a dark place of the earth:

I said not unto the seed of Jacob, Seek ye me in vain: * I the Lord speak righteousness, I declare things that are right.

Assemble yourselves and come; * draw near together, ye that are escaped of the nations:

They have no knowledge that set up the wood of their graven image, * and pray unto a god that cannot save.

Tell ye, and bring them near; † yea, let them take counsel together: * who hath declared this from ancient time? who hath told it from that time?

Have not I the Lord? and there is no God else beside me; * a just God and a Saviour; there is none beside me.

Look unto me, and be ye saved, all the ends of the earth: * for I am God, and there is none else.

I have sworn by myself, * the word is gone out of my mouth in righteousness, and shall not return,

That unto me every knee shall bow, * every tongue shall swear.

Surely, shall one say, in the Lord have I righteousness and strength: * even to him shall men come; and all that are incensed against him shall be ashamed.

In the Lord shall all the seed of Israel be justified, * and shall glory.

Saturday Ferial Canticle

Audite cæli

IVE ear, O ye heavens, and I will speak; * and hear, O earth, the words of my mouth.

My doctrine shall drop as the rain, † my speech shall distil as the dew, * as the small rain upon the tender herb, and as the showers upon the grass:

Because I will publish the Name of the Lord: * ascribe ye greatness unto our God.

He is the Rock, his work is perfect: * for all his ways are judgment:

A God of truth and without iniquity, * just and right is he.

They have corrupted themselves, † their spot is not the spot of his children: * they are a perverse and crooked generation.

Do ye thus requite the Lord, O foolish people and unwise? * is not he thy father that hath bought thee? hath he not made thee, and established thee?

Remember the days of old, * consider the years of many generations:

Ask thy father, and he will shew thee; * thy elders, and they will tell thee.

When the Most High divided to the nations their inheritance, * when he separated the sons of Adam,

He set the bounds of the people * according to the number of the children of Israel.

For the Lord's portion is his people; * Jacob is the lot of his inheritance.

He found him in a desert land, * and in the waste howling wilderness;

He led him about, he instructed him, * he kept him as the apple of his eye.

As an eagle stirreth up her nest, fluttereth over her young, * spreadeth abroad her wings, taketh them, beareth them on her wings:

So the Lord alone did lead him, * and there was no strange god with him.

He made him ride on the high places of the earth, * that he might eat the increase of the fields;

And he made him to suck honey out of the rock, * and oil out of the flinty rock;

Butter of kine, and milk of sheep, * with fat of lambs, and rams of the breed of Bashan,

And goats, with the fat of kidneys of wheat; * and thou didst drink the pure blood of the grape.

But Jeshurun waxed fat, and kicked: * thou art waxen fat, thou art grown thick, thou art covered with fatness;

Then he forsook God which made him, * and lightly esteemed the Rock of his salvation.

They provoked him to jealousy with strange gods, * with abominations provoked they him to anger.

They sacrificed unto devils, not to God; * to gods whom they knew not, to new gods that came newly up, whom your fathers feared not.

Of the Rock that begat thee thou art unmindful, * and hast forgotten God that formed thee.

And when the Lord saw it, he abhorred them, * because of the provoking of his sons, and of his daughters.

And he said, I will hide my face from them, † I will see what their end shall be: * for they are a very froward generation, children in whom is no faith.

They have moved me to jealousy with that which is not God; * they have provoked me to anger with their vanities:

And I will move them to jealousy with those which are not a people; * I will provoke them to anger with a foolish nation.

Ignis succensus est

FOR a fire is kindled in mine anger, † and shall burn unto the lowest hell, * and shall consume the earth with her increase, and set on fire the foundations of the mountains.

I will heap mischiefs upon them; * I will spend mine arrows upon them.

They shall be burnt with hunger, * and devoured with burning heat, and with bitter destruction:

I will also send the teeth of beasts upon them, * with the poison of serpents of the dust.

The sword without, and terror within, † shall destroy both the young man and the virgin, * the suckling also with the man of gray hairs.

I said, I would scatter them into corners, * I would make the remembrance of them to cease from among men:

Were it not that I feared the wrath of the enemy, * lest their adversaries should behave themselves strangely,

And lest they should say, Our hand is high, * and the Lord hath not done all this.

For they are a nation void of counsel, * neither is there any understanding in them.

O that they were wise, that they understood this, * that they would consider their latter end!

How should one chase a thousand, † and two put ten thousand to flight, * except their Rock had sold them, and the Lord had shut them up?

For their rock is not as our Rock, * even our enemies themselves being judges.

For their vine is of the vine of Sodom, * and of the fields of Gomorrah:

Their grapes are grapes of gall, * their clusters are bitter:

Their wine is the poison of dragons, * and the cruel venom of asps.

Is not this laid up in store with me, † and sealed up among my treasures? * to me belongeth vengeance, and recompence;

Their foot shall slide in due time: * for the day of their calamity is at hand, and the things that shall come upon them make haste.

For the Lord shall judge his people, * and repent himself for his servants,

When he seeth that their power is gone, * and there is none shut up, or left.

And he shall say, Where are their

gods, * their rock in whom they trusted,

Which did eat the fat of their sacrifices, * and drank the wine of their drink offerings?

Let them rise up and help you, *and be your protection.

See now that I, even I, am he, * and there is no god with me:

I kill, and I make alive; † I wound, and I heal: * neither is there any that can deliver out of my hand.

For I lift up my hand to heaven, and say, * I live for ever.

If I whet my glittering sword, and mine hand take hold on judgment; * I will render vengeance to mine enemies, and will reward them that hate me.

I will make mine arrows drunk with blood, † and my sword shall devour flesh; * and that with the blood of the slain and of the captives, from the beginning of revenges upon the enemy.

Rejoice, O ye nations, with his people: * for he will avenge the blood of his servants,

And will render vengeance to his adversaries, * and will be merciful unto his land, and to his people.

Saturday Festal Canticle

Miserere nostri, Deus

¶ This Canticle is also used when Sunday Mattins is anticipated on Saturday evening.

AVE mercy upon us, O Lord God of all, and behold us: * and send thy fear upon all the nations that seek not after thee.

Lift up thy hand against the strange nations, * and let them see thy power.

As thou wast sanctified in us before them: * so be thou magnified among them before us.

And let them know thee, as we have known thee, * that there is no God but only thou, O God.

Shew new signs, and repeat thy wonders: * glorify thy hand and thy right arm, that they may set forth thy wondrous works.

Raise up indignation, and pour out wrath: * take away the adversary, and destroy the enemy.

Make the time short, remember the covenant, * and let them declare thy wonderful works.

Let him that escapeth be consumed by the rage of the fire; * and let them perish that oppress the people.

Smite in sunder the heads of the rulers of the heathen, * that say, There is none other but we.

Gather all the tribes of Jacob together, * and inherit thou them, as from the beginning.

Prime

Daily Office

Hour of Prime

¶ This service may be said at any convenient time before or after the saying of Morning Prayer, but not in substitution therefor.

℣. O God, ✠ make speed to save us.
℟. O Lord, make haste to help us.
℣. Glory be to the Father, and to the Son, and to the Holy Ghost.
℟. As it was in the beginning, is now, and ever shall be, world without end. Amen.
℣. Praise ye the Lord.
℟. The Lord's Name be praised.

Jam Lucis Ordo Sidere

ow that the daylight fills the sky,
We lift our hearts to God on high,
That he, in all we do or say,
Would keep us free from harm to-day:

Would guard our hearts and tongues from strife;
From anger's din would hide our life;
From all ill sights would turn our eyes,
Would close our ears from vanities:

Would keep our inmost conscience pure;
Our souls from folly would secure;
Would bid us check the pride of sense
With due and holy abstinence.

So we, when this new day is gone,
And night in turn is drawing on,
With conscience by the world un-stained

Shall praise his name for victory gained.

All laud to God the Father be;
All praise, eternal Son, to thee;
All glory, as is ever meet,
To God the holy Paraclete. Amen.

Psalm 54. *Deus, in nomine*

ave me, O God, for thy Name's sake : and avenge me in thy strength.

2 Hear my prayer, O God : and hearken unto the words of my mouth.

3 For strangers are risen up against me : and tyrants, which have not God before their eyes, seek after my soul.

4 Behold, God is my helper : the Lord is with them that uphold my soul.

5 He shall reward evil unto mine enemies : destroy thou them in thy truth.

6 An offering of a free heart will I give thee, and praise thy Name, O Lord : because it is so comfortable.

7 For he hath delivered me out of all my trouble : and mine eye hath seen his desire upon mine enemies.

℣. Glory be to the Father, and to the Son, and to the Holy Ghost.
℟. As it was in the beginning, is now, and ever shall be, world without end. Amen.

Daily Office

Prime

Psalm 119. *Beati immaculati*

LESSED are those that are undefiled in the way : and walk in the law of the Lord.

2 Blessed are they that keep his testimonies : and seek him with their whole heart.

3 For they who do no wickedness : walk in his ways.

4 Thou hast charged : that we shall diligently keep thy commandments.

5 O that my ways were made so direct : that I might keep thy statutes!

6 So shall I not be confounded : while I have respect unto all thy commandments.

7 I will thank thee with an unfeigned heart : when I shall have learned the judgements of thy righteousness.

8 I will keep thy ceremonies : O forsake me not utterly.

℣. Glory be to the Father, and to the Son, and to the Holy Ghost.

℟. As it was in the beginning, is now, and ever shall be, world without end. Amen.

In quo corriget?

HEREWITHAL shall a young man cleanse his way : even by ruling himself after thy word.

10 With my whole heart have I sought thee : O let me not go wrong out of thy commandments.

11 Thy words have I hid within my heart : that I should not sin against thee.

12 Blessed art thou, O Lord : O teach me thy statutes.

13 With my lips have I been telling : of all the judgements of thy mouth.

14 I have had as great delight in the way of thy testimonies : as in all manner of riches.

15 I will talk of thy commandments : and have respect unto thy ways.

16 My delight shall be in thy statutes : and I will not forget thy word.

℣. Glory be to the Father, and to the Son, and to the Holy Ghost.

℟. As it was in the beginning, is now, and ever shall be, world without end. Amen.

Retribue servo tuo

DO well unto thy servant : that I may live, and keep thy word.

18 Open thou mine eyes : that I may see the wondrous things of thy law.

19 I am a stranger upon earth : O hide not thy commandments from me.

20 My soul breaketh out for the very fervent desire : that it hath alway unto thy judgements.

21 Thou hast rebuked the proud : and cursed are they that do err from thy commandments.

22 O turn from me shame and rebuke : for I have kept thy testimonies.

23 Princes also did sit and speak against me : but thy servant is occupied in thy statutes.

24 For thy testimonies are my delight : and my counsellors.

Prime

Daily Office

℣. Glory be to the Father, and to the Son, and to the Holy Ghost.

℟. As it was in the beginning, is now, and ever shall be, world without end. Amen.

Adhaesit pavimento

y soul cleaveth to the dust : O quicken thou me, according to thy word.

26 I have acknowledged my ways, and thou heardest me : O teach me thy statutes.

27 Make me to understand the way of thy commandments : and so shall I talk of thy wondrous works.

28 My soul melteth away for very heaviness : comfort thou me according unto thy word.

29 Take from me the way of lying : and cause thou me to make much of thy law.

30 I have chosen the way of truth : and thy judgements have I laid before me.

31 I have stuck unto thy testimonies : O Lord, confound me not.

32 I will run the way of thy commandments : when thou hast set my heart at liberty.

℣. Glory be to the Father, and to the Son, and to the Holy Ghost.

℟. As it was in the beginning, is now, and ever shall be, world without end. Amen.

¶ As in the ancient use of Prime, the Athanasian Creed (p. 37) may here be said, concluding with the **Gloria Patri**.

Chapter

Ferias Throughout the Year

Love the truth and peace, saith the Lord of hosts.

Sundays & Feast Days

Now unto the King eternal, immortal, invisible, the only wise God, be honour and glory for ever and ever.

Eastertide

O Lord, be gracious unto us; we have waited for thee: be thou our arm every morning, our salvation also in the time of trouble.

¶ After the Chapter is said,

℟. Thanks be to God.

Short Respond

℣. Jesu Christ, Son of the living God, have mercy upon us;

℟. Jesu Christ, Son of the living God, have mercy upon us.

℣. Thou that sittest at the right hand of the Father;

℟. Have mercy upon us.

℣. Glory be to the Father, and to the Son, and to the Holy Ghost.

℟. Jesu Christ, Son of the living God, have mercy upon us.

℣. O Lord, arise, help us;

℟. And deliver us for thy name's sake.

Daily Office — Prime

Suffrages

℣ The Suffrages are said, kneeling, on all Ferias outside of Eastertide.

℣. Lord, have mercy upon us.
℟. Christ, have mercy upon us.
℣. Lord, have mercy upon us.

Lord's Prayer

UR Father, who art in heaven, Hallowed be thy Name. Thy kingdom come. Thy will be done on earth, As it is in heaven. Give us this day our daily bread. And forgive us our trespasses, As we forgive those who trespass against us. And lead us not into temptation; But deliver us from evil. Amen.

℣ Then shall follow these Versicles and Responses.

℣. O let my mouth be filled with thy praise;
℟. That I may sing of thy glory and honour all the day long.
℣. Turn thy face from my sins, O Lord;
℟. And put out all my misdeeds.
℣. Make me a clean heart, O God;
℟. And renew a right spirit within me.
℣. Cast me not away from thy presence;
℟. And take not thy Holy Spirit from me.
℣. O give me the comfort of thy help again;
℟. And stablish me with thy free spirit.

Confession

℣ Then shall the Minister and People say together the Confession following,

CONFESS to God, to blessed Mary, to all the saints, and to you: that I have sinned exceedingly in thought, word, and deed, by my own fault. I beg holy Mary, all the Saints of God, and you, to pray for me.

℣ The Minister then stands and says,

LMIGHTY God, have mercy upon us, forgive us all our sins and deliver us from all evil, confirm and strengthen us in all goodness, and bring us to life everlasting. *Amen.*

℣ If a Priest be present, he shall stand and pronounce the following Absolution,

AY the Almighty and Merciful Lord grant unto you pardon ✠ and remission of all your sins, time for amendment of life, and the grace and comfort of the Holy Spirit. *Amen.*

℣. Wilt thou not turn again and quicken us, O God?
℟. That thy people may rejoice in thee.
℣. O Lord, show thy mercy upon us.
℟. And grant us thy salvation.
℣. Vouchsafe, O Lord, to keep us this day without sin;
℟. O Lord, have mercy upon us, have mercy upon us.

Prime   # Daily Office

Collect

℣. O Lord, hear our prayer.
℟. And let our cry come unto thee.
Let us pray.

IN this hour of this day, fill us, O Lord, with thy mercy; that going forth in thy strength, we may make our boast of thee all the day long. Through.

℣. The Lord be with you.
or, O Lord, hear our prayer.
℟. And with thy spirit.
or, And let our cry come unto thee.
℣. Let us bless the Lord.
℟. Thanks be to God.

THE Lord bless us, and preserve us from all evil, and bring us to everlasting life; and may the souls ✠ of the faithful departed, through the mercy of God, rest in peace. *Amen.*

¶ The Office of Prime may end here, or the following devotions may be added.

Daily Office

Pretiosa

¶ The Pretiosa *is a laudable custom and may be added to* Prime. *The Martyrology reading for the Day may here be read. The following is then said.*

℣. Right dear in the sight of the Lord.
℟. Is the death of his Saints.

May holy Mary and all the Saints intercede for us to the Lord: that we may be worthy to obtain from him help and salvation, who liveth and reigneth for ever and ever. *Amen.*

℣. O God, ✠ make speed to save me.
℟. O Lord, make haste to help me.
℣. O God, ✠ make speed to save me.
℟. O Lord, make haste to help me.
℣. O God, ✠ make speed to save me.
℟. O Lord, make haste to help me.

℣. Glory be to the Father, and to the Son, and to the Holy Ghost.
℟. As it was in the beginning, is now, and ever shall be, world without end. Amen.
℣. Lord, have mercy upon us.
℟. Christ, have mercy upon us.
℣. Lord, have mercy upon us.

Our Father, who art in heaven, Hallowed be thy Name. Thy kingdom come. Thy will be done on earth, As it is in heaven. Give us this day our daily bread. And forgive us our trespasses, As we forgive those who trespass against us. And lead us not into temptation; But deliver us from evil. Amen.

℣. Let thy loving mercy come also unto us, O Lord.
℟. Even thy salvation, according unto thy word.
℣. And show thy servants thy work.
℟. And their children thy glory.
℣. And the glorious Majesty of the Lord our God be upon us.
℟. And prosper thou the work of our hands upon us: O prosper thou our handy-work.

Let us pray.

Almighty Lord and Everlasting God, vouchsafe, we beseech thee, to direct, sanctify, and govern, both our hearts and bodies in the ways of thy laws and in the works of thy commandments: that through thy most mighty protection, both here and ever, we may be preserved in body and soul; through our Lord and Saviour Jesus Christ. *Amen.*

℣. May the Divine Assistance remain always with us.
℟. Amen.

Commemoration of the Faithful Departed

¶ This Commemoration is a laudable custom, which may be said after any Hour.

℣. Let us commemorate our departed kinsfolk, neighbours, friends, and benefactors.
℟. May they rest in peace.

Psalm 130. *De profundis*

UT of the deep have I called unto thee, O Lord : Lord, hear my voice.

2 O let thine ears consider well : the voice of my complaint.

3 If thou, Lord, wilt be extreme to mark what is done amiss : O Lord, who may abide it?

4 For there is mercy with thee : therefore shalt thou be feared.

5 I look for the Lord; my soul doth wait for him : in his word is my trust.

6 My soul fleeth unto the Lord : before the morning watch, I say, before the morning watch.

7 O Israel, trust in the Lord, for with the Lord there is mercy : and with him is plenteous redemption.

8 And he shall redeem Israel : from all his sins.

℣. Rest eternal * grant unto them, O Lord.
℟. And let light perpetual * shine upon them.

℣. From the gate of hell.
℟. Deliver their souls, O Lord.
℣. May they rest in peace.
℟. Amen.
℣. O Lord hear my prayer.
℟. And let my cry come unto thee.
℣. The Lord be with you.
℟. And with thy spirit.

Let us pray.

GOD, the Giver of pardon and the Author of man's salvation: we humbly beseech thy mercy to grant that our kinsfolk, neighbours, friends, and benefactors who have departed out of this world, blessed Mary ever Virgin and all thy Saints praying for them, may attain to the fellowship of everlasting blessedness. Through.

℣. Rest eternal grant unto them, O Lord.
℟. And let light perpetual shine upon them.
℣. May they rest in peace.
℟. Amen.

Athanasian Creed

HOSOEVER would be saved : needeth before all things to hold fast the Catholick Faith.

2 Which Faith except a man keep whole and undefiled : without doubt he will perish eternally.

3 Now the Catholick Faith is this : that we worship one God in Trinity, and the Trinity in Unity;

4 Neither confusing the Persons : nor dividing the substance.

5 For there is one Person of the Father, another of the Son : another of the Holy Ghost;

6 But the Godhead of the Father, and of the Son, and of the Holy Ghost is all one : the glory equal, the majesty co-eternal.

7 Such as the Father is, such is the Son : and such is the Holy Ghost.

8 The Father uncreated, the Son uncreated : the Holy Ghost uncreated;

9 The Father infinite, the Son infinite : the Holy Ghost infinite;

10 The Father eternal, the Son eternal : the Holy Ghost eternal.

11 And yet there are not three eternals : but one eternal.

12 As also there are not three uncreated, nor three infinites : but one infinite, and one uncreated.

13 So likewise the Father is almighty, the Son almighty : the Holy Ghost almighty;

14 And yet there are not three almighties : but one almighty.

15 So the Father is God, the Son God

UICÚMQUE vult salvus esse, * ante ómnia opus est, ut téneat cathólicam fidem:

Quam nisi quisque íntegram inviolatámque serváverit, * absque dúbio in ætérnum períbit.

Fides autem cathólica hæc est: * ut unum Deum in Trinitáte, et Trinitátem in unitáte venerémur.

Neque confundéntes persónas, * neque substántiam separántes.

Alia est enim persóna Patris, ália Fílii, * ália Spíritus Sancti:

Sed Patris, et Fílii, et Spíritus Sancti una est divínitas, * æquális glória, coætérna majéstas.

Qualis Pater, talis Fílius, * talis Spíritus Sanctus.

Increátus Pater, increátus Fílius, * increátus Spíritus Sanctus.

Imménsus Pater, imménsus Fílius, * imménsus Spíritus Sanctus.

Ætérnus Pater, ætérnus Fílius, * ætérnus Spíritus Sanctus.

Et tamen non tres ætérni, * sed unus ætérnus.

Sicut non tres increáti, nec tres imménsi, * sed unus increátus, et unus imménsus.

Simíliter omnípotens Pater, omnípotens Fílius, * omnípotens Spíritus Sanctus.

Et tamen non tres omnipoténtes, * sed unus omnípotens.

Ita Deus Pater, Deus Fílius, * Deus Spíritus Sanctus.

Ut tamen non tres Dii, * sed unus

: the Holy Ghost God;

16 And yet there are not three Gods : but one God.

17 So the Father is Lord, the Son Lord : the Holy Ghost Lord;

18 And yet there are not three Lords : but one Lord.

19 For like as we are compelled by the Christian verity : to confess each Person by himself to be both God and Lord;

20 So are we forbidden by the Catholick religion : to speak of three Gods or three Lords.

21 The Father is made of none : nor created, nor begotten.

22 The Son is of the Father : not made, nor created, but begotten.

23 The Holy Ghost is of the Father : not made, nor created, nor begotten, but proceeding.

24 There is therefore one Father, not three Fathers; one Son, not three Sons : one Holy Ghost, not three Holy Ghosts.

25 And in this Trinity there is no before or after : no greater or less;

26 But all three Persons are co-eternal together : and co-equal.

27 So that in all ways, as is aforesaid : both the Trinity is to be worshipped in Unity, and the Unity in Trinity.

28 He therefore that would be saved : let him thus think of the Trinity.

URTHERMORE it is necessary to eternal salvation : that he also believe faithfully the Incarnation of our Lord Jesus Christ.

30 Now the right faith is that we believe and confess : that our Lord Jesus

est Deus.

Ita Dóminus Pater, Dóminus Fílius, * Dóminus Spíritus Sanctus.

Et tamen non tres Dómini, * sed unus est Dóminus.

Quia, sicut singillátim unamquámque persónam Deum ac Dóminum confitéri christiána veritáte compéllimur: * ita tres Deos aut Dóminos dícere cathólica religióne prohibémur.

Pater a nullo est factus: * nec creátus, nec génitus.

Fílius a Patre est: * non factus, nec creátus, sed génitus.

Spíritus Sanctus a Patre: * non factus, nec creátus, nec génitus, sed procédens.

Unus ergo Pater, non tres Patres: unus Fílius, non tres Fílii: * unus Spíritus Sanctus, non tres Spíritus Sancti.

Et in hac Trinitáte nihil prius aut postérius, nihil majus aut minus: * sed totæ tres persónæ coætérnæ sibi sunt et coæquáles.

Ita ut per ómnia, sicut jam supra dictum est, * et únitas in Trinitáte, et Trínitas in unitáte veneránda sit.

Qui vult ergo salvus esse, * ita de Trinitáte séntiat.

ED necessárium est ad ætérnam salútem, * ut Incarnatiónem quoque Dómini nostri Jesu Christi fidéliter credat.

Est ergo fides recta ut credámus et confiteámur, * quia Dóminus noster Jesus Christus, Dei Fílius, Deus et homo est.

Deus est ex substántia Patris ante sǽcula génitus: * et homo est ex substántia matris in sǽculo natus.

Christ, the Son of God, is both God and man.

31 He is God, of the substance of the Father, begotten before the worlds : and he is man, of the substance of his Mother, born in the world;

32 Perfect God : perfect man, of reasoning soul and human flesh subsisting;

33 Equal to the Father as touching his Godhead : less than the Father as touching his manhood.

34 Who although he be God and man : yet he is not two, but is one Christ ;

35 One however, not by conversion of Godhead into flesh : but by taking manhood into God;

36 One altogether : not by confusion of substance, but by unity of person.

37 For as reasoning soul and flesh is one man : so God and man is one Christ;

38 Who suffered for our salvation : descended into hell, rose again from the dead;

39 Ascended into heaven, sat down at the right hand of the Father : from whence he shall come to judge the quick and the dead.

40 At whose coming all men must rise again with their bodies : and shall give account for their own deeds.

41 And they that have done good will go into life eternal : they that have done evil into eternal fire.

THIS is the Catholick Faith : which except a man do faithfully and steadfastly believe, he cannot be saved.

Perféctus Deus, perféctus homo: * ex ánima rationáli et humána carne subsístens.

Æquális Patri secúndum divinitátem: * minor Patre secúndum humanitátem.

Qui licet Deus sit et homo, * non duo tamen, sed unus est Christus.

Unus autem non conversióne divinitátis in carnem, * sed assumptióne humanitátis in Deum.

Unus omníno, non confusióne substántiæ, * sed unitáte persónæ.

Nam sicut ánima rationális et caro unus est homo: * ita Deus et homo unus est Christus.

Qui passus est pro salúte nostra: descéndit ad ínferos: * tértia die resurréxit a mórtuis.

Ascéndit ad cælos, sedet ad déxteram Dei Patris omnipoténtis: * inde ventúrus est judicáre vivos et mórtuos.

Ad cujus advéntum omnes hómines resúrgere habent cum corpóribus suis; * et redditúri sunt de factis própriis ratiónem.

Et qui bona egérunt, ibunt in vitam ætérnam: * qui vero mala, in ignem ætérnum.

HÆC est fides cathólica, * quam nisi quisque fidéliter firmitérque credíderit, salvus esse non póterit.

Terce

Daily Office

Hour of Terce

℣. O God, ✠ make speed to save us.
℟. O Lord, make haste to help us.
℣. Glory be to the Father, and to the Son, and to the Holy Ghost.
℟. As it was in the beginning, is now, and ever shall be, world without end. Amen.
℣. Praise ye the Lord.
℟. The Lord's Name be praised.

Nunc Sancte

OME Holy Ghost, with God the Son,
And God the Father, ever one:
Shed forth thy grace within our breast,
And dwell with us, a ready Guest.

By every power, by heart and tongue,
By act and deed, thy praise be sung;
Inflame with perfect love each sense,
That others' souls may kindle thence.

O Father, that we ask be done,
Through Jesus Christ, thine only Son;
Who, with the Holy Ghost and thee,
Shall live and reign eternally. Amen.

Legem pone

EACH me, O Lord, the way of thy statutes : and I shall keep it unto the end.
34 Give me understanding, and I shall keep thy law : yea, I shall keep it with my whole heart.
35 Make me to go in the path of thy commandments : for therein is my desire.
36 Incline my heart unto thy testimonies : and not to covetousness.
37 O turn away mine eyes, lest they behold vanity : and quicken thou me in thy way.
38 O stablish thy word in thy servant : that I may fear thee.
39 Take away the rebuke that I am afraid of : for thy judgements are good.
40 Behold, my delight is in thy commandments : O quicken me in thy righteousness.
℣. Glory be to the Father, and to the Son, and to the Holy Ghost.
℟. As it was in the beginning, is now, and ever shall be, world without end. Amen.

Et veniat super me

ET thy loving mercy come also unto me, O Lord : even thy salvation, according unto thy word.
42 So shall I make answer unto my blasphemers : for my trust is in thy word.
43 O take not the word of thy truth utterly out of my mouth : for my hope is in thy judgements.
44 So shall I alway keep thy law : yea, for ever and ever.
45 And I will walk at liberty : for I seek thy commandments.
46 I will speak of thy testimonies also, even before kings : and will not be ashamed.
47 And my delight shall be in thy commandments : which I have loved.

Daily Office — *Terce*

48 My hands also will I lift up unto thy commandments, which I have loved : and my study shall be in thy statutes.

℣. Glory be to the Father, and to the Son, and to the Holy Ghost.

℟. As it was in the beginning, is now, and ever shall be, world without end. Amen.

Memor esto servi tui

THINK upon thy servant, as concerning thy word : wherein thou hast caused me to put my trust.

50 The same is my comfort in my trouble : for thy word hath quickened me.

51 The proud have had me exceedingly in derision : yet have I not shrinked from thy law.

52 For I remembered thine everlasting judgements, O Lord : and received comfort.

53 I am horribly afraid : for the ungodly that forsake thy law.

54 Thy statutes have been my songs : in the house of my pilgrimage.

55 I have thought upon thy Name, O Lord, in the night-season : and have kept thy law.

56 This I had : because I kept thy commandments.

℣. Glory be to the Father, and to the Son, and to the Holy Ghost.

℟. As it was in the beginning, is now, and ever shall be, world without end. Amen.

Portio mea, Domine

THOU art my portion, O Lord : I have promised to keep thy law.

58 I made my humble petition in thy presence with my whole heart : O be merciful unto me, according to thy word.

59 I called mine own ways to remembrance : and turned my feet unto thy testimonies.

60 I made haste, and prolonged not the time : to keep thy commandments.

61 The congregations of the ungodly have robbed me : but I have not forgotten thy law.

62 At midnight I will rise to give thanks unto thee : because of thy righteous judgements.

63 I am a companion of all them that fear thee : and keep thy commandments.

64 The earth, O Lord, is full of thy mercy : O teach me thy statutes.

℣. Glory be to the Father, and to the Son, and to the Holy Ghost.

℟. As it was in the beginning, is now, and ever shall be, world without end. Amen.

Bonitatem fecisti

LORD, thou hast dealt graciously with thy servant : according unto thy word.

66 O learn me true understanding and knowledge : for I have believed thy commandments.

67 Before I was troubled, I went wrong : but now have I kept thy word.

Terce

Daily Office

68 Thou art good and gracious : O teach me thy statutes.

69 The proud have imagined a lie against me : but I will keep thy commandments with my whole heart.

70 Their heart is as fat as brawn : but my delight hath been in thy law.

71 It is good for me that I have been in trouble : that I may learn thy statutes.

72 The law of thy mouth is dearer unto me : than thousands of gold and silver.

℣. Glory be to the Father, and to the Son, and to the Holy Ghost.

℞. As it was in the beginning, is now, and ever shall be, world without end. Amen.

Manus tuae fecerunt me

THY hands have made me and fashioned me : O give me understanding, that I may learn thy commandments.

74 They that fear thee will be glad when they see me : because I have put my trust in thy word.

75 I know, O Lord, that thy judgements are right : and that thou of very faithfulness hast caused me to be troubled.

76 O let thy merciful kindness be my comfort : according to thy word unto thy servant.

77 O let thy loving mercies come unto me, that I may live : for thy law is my delight.

78 Let the proud be confounded, for they go wickedly about to destroy me : but I will be occupied in thy commandments.

79 Let such as fear thee, and have known thy testimonies : be turned unto me.

80 O let my heart be sound in thy statutes : that I be not ashamed.

℣. Glory be to the Father, and to the Son, and to the Holy Ghost.

℞. As it was in the beginning, is now, and ever shall be, world without end. Amen.

Chapter

Feria Days Throughout the Year

Heal me, O Lord, and I shall be healed; save me, and I shall be saved: for thou art my praise.

Sundays & Feast Days

O the depth of the riches both of the wisdom and knowledge of God! How unsearchable are his judgements, and his ways past finding out!

Eastertide

For whatsoever is born of God overcometh the world: and this is the victory that overcometh the world, even our faith.

℞. Thanks be to God.

Short Respond

Ferias Throughout the Year

℣. Heal my soul, for I have sinned against thee.

℞. Heal my soul, for I have sinned against thee.

℣. I said, Lord, be merciful unto me.

℞. For I have sinned against thee.

Daily Office

Terce

℣. Glory be to the Father, and to the Son, and to the Holy Ghost.
℞. Heal my soul, for I have sinned against thee.

℣. Thou hast been my succour.
℞. Leave me not, neither forsake me, O God of my salvation.

<small>Sundays, Feasts, & in Eastertide</small>

℣. Incline my heart, O God, unto thy testimonies (alleluia, alleluia).
℞. Incline my heart, O God, unto thy testimonies (alleluia, alleluia).

℣. Turn away mine eyes, lest they behold vanity.
℞. Unto thy testimonies (alleluia, alleluia).

℣. Glory be to the Father, and to the Son, and to the Holy Ghost.
℞. Incline my heart, O God, unto thy testimonies (alleluia, alleluia).

℣. I said, Lord, be merciful unto me (alleluia).
℞. For I have sinned against thee (alleluia).

Suffrages

¶ The Suffrages are said, kneeling, on all Ferias outside of Eastertide.

℣. Lord, have mercy upon us.
℞. Christ, have mercy upon us.
℣. Lord, have mercy upon us.

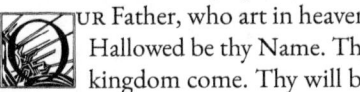OUR Father, who art in heaven, Hallowed be thy Name. Thy kingdom come. Thy will be done on earth, As it is in heaven. Give us this day our daily bread. And forgive us our trespasses, As we forgive those who trespass against us. And lead us not into temptation; But deliver us from evil. Amen.

℣. Send out thy light and thy truth, that they may lead me.
℞. And bring me unto thy holy hill, and to thy dwelling.

℣. O let us live.
℞. And we shall call upon thy Name.

℣. Turn us again, O Lord God of hosts.
℞. Show the light of thy countenance, and we shall be whole.

Collects

℣. The Lord be with you.
or, O Lord, hear our prayer.
℞. And with thy spirit.
or, And let our cry come unto thee.
℣. Let us pray.

¶ The Collect(s) of the Day is here said, followed by this memorial Collect.

HELP us this day, O God, to serve thee devoutly and the world busily. May we do our work wisely, give succour secretly, go to our meat appetitely, sit thereat discreetly, arise temperately, please our friends duly, go to our bed merrily, and sleep surely; for the joy of our Lord Jesus Christ. *Amen.*

℣. The Lord be with you.
or, O Lord, hear our prayer.
℞. And with thy spirit.
or, And let our cry come unto thee.
℣. Let us bless the Lord.
℞. Thanks be to God.

Terce

Daily Office

℣. May the souls ✠ of the faithful departed, through the mercy of God, rest in peace.

NTO him that loved us, and washed us from our sins in his own blood, and hath made us kings and priests unto God and his Father, to him be glory and dominion for ever and ever. *Amen.*

Daily Office

Sext

Hour of Sext

℣. O God, ✠ make speed to save us.
℟. O Lord, make haste to help us.
℣. Glory be to the Father, and to the Son, and to the Holy Ghost.
℟. As it was in the beginning, is now, and ever shall be, world without end. Amen.
℣. Praise ye the Lord.
℟. The Lord's Name be praised.

Rector Potens

GOD of truth, O Lord of might,
Who ord'rest time and change aright,
And send'st the early morning ray,
And light'st the glow of perfect day.

Extinguish thou each sinful fire,
And banish every ill desire:
And while thou keep'st the body whole,
Shed forth thy peace upon the soul.

O Father, that we ask be done,
Through Jesus Christ, thine only Son;
Who, with the Holy Ghost and thee,
Doth live and reign eternally. Amen.

Defecit anima mea

Y soul hath longed for thy salvation : and I have a good hope because of thy word.

82 Mine eyes long sore for thy word : saying, O when wilt thou comfort me?

83 For I am become like a bottle in the smoke : yet do I not forget thy statutes.

84 How many are the days of thy servant : when wilt thou be avenged of them that persecute me?

85 The proud have digged pits for me : which are not after thy law.

86 All thy commandments are true : they persecute me falsely; O be thou my help.

87 They had almost made an end of me upon earth : but I forsook not thy commandments.

88 O quicken me after thy lovingkindness : and so shall I keep the testimonies of thy mouth.

℣. Glory be to the Father, and to the Son, and to the Holy Ghost.
℟. As it was in the beginning, is now, and ever shall be, world without end. Amen.

In aeternum. Domine

LORD, thy word : endureth for ever in heaven.

90 Thy truth also remaineth from one generation to another : thou hast laid the foundation of the earth, and it abideth.

91 They continue this day according to thine ordinance : for all things serve thee.

92 If my delight had not been in thy law : I should have perished in my trouble.

93 I will never forget thy commandments : for with them thou hast quickened me.

94 I am thine, O save me : for I have sought thy commandments.

95 The ungodly laid wait for me to destroy me : but I will consider thy testimonies.

96 I see that all things come to an end : but thy commandment is exceeding broad.

℣. Glory be to the Father, and to the Son, and to the Holy Ghost.

℟. As it was in the beginning, is now, and ever shall be, world without end. Amen.

Quomodo dilexi!

ORD, what love have I unto thy law : all the day long is my study in it.

98 Thou through thy commandments hast made me wiser than mine enemies : for they are ever with me.

99 I have more understanding than my teachers : for thy testimonies are my study.

100 I am wiser than the aged : because I keep thy commandments.

101 I have refrained my feet from every evil way : that I may keep thy word.

102 I have not shrunk from thy judgements : for thou teachest me.

103 O how sweet are thy words unto my throat : yea, sweeter than honey unto my mouth.

104 Through thy commandments I get understanding : therefore I hate all evil ways.

℣. Glory be to the Father, and to the Son, and to the Holy Ghost.

℟. As it was in the beginning, is now, and ever shall be, world without end. Amen.

Lucerna pedibus meis

HY word is a lantern unto my feet : and a light unto my paths.

106 I have sworn, and am stedfastly purposed : to keep thy righteous judgements.

107 I am troubled above measure : quicken me, O Lord, according to thy word.

108 Let the free-will offerings of my mouth please thee, O Lord : and teach me thy judgements.

109 My soul is alway in my hand : yet do I not forget thy law.

110 The ungodly have laid a snare for me : but yet I swerved not from thy commandments.

111 Thy testimonies have I claimed as mine heritage for ever : and why? they are the very joy of my heart.

112 I have applied my heart to fulfil thy statutes alway : even unto the end.

℣. Glory be to the Father, and to the Son, and to the Holy Ghost.

℟. As it was in the beginning, is now, and ever shall be, world without end. Amen.

Iniquos odio habui

I HATE them that imagine evil things : but thy law do I love.

114 Thou art my defence and shield : and my trust is in thy word.

115 Away from me, ye wicked : I will keep the commandments of my God.

116 O stablish me according to thy word, that I may live : and let me not be disappointed of my hope.

Daily Office *Sext*

117 Hold thou me up, and I shall be safe : yea, my delight shall be ever in thy statutes.

118 Thou hast trodden down all them that depart from thy statutes : for they imagine but deceit.

119 Thou puttest away all the ungodly of the earth like dross : therefore I love thy testimonies.

120 My flesh trembleth for fear of thee : and I am afraid of thy judgements.

℣. Glory be to the Father, and to the Son, and to the Holy Ghost.

℟. As it was in the beginning, is now, and ever shall be, world without end. Amen.

Feci judicium

I DEAL with the thing that is lawful and right : O give me not over unto mine oppressors.

122 Make thou thy servant to delight in that which is good : that the proud do me no wrong.

123 Mine eyes are wasted away with looking for thy health : and for the word of thy righteousness.

124 O deal with thy servant according unto thy loving mercy : and teach me thy statutes.

125 I am thy servant, O grant me understanding : that I may know thy testimonies.

126 It is time for thee, Lord, to lay to thine hand : for they have destroyed thy law.

127 For I love thy commandments : above gold and precious stone.

128 Therefore hold I straight all thy commandments : and all false ways I utterly abhor.

℣. Glory be to the Father, and to the Son, and to the Holy Ghost.

℟. As it was in the beginning, is now, and ever shall be, world without end. Amen.

Chapter

Ferias Throughout the Year

Prove all things, hold fast to that which is good: abstain from all appearance of evil.

Sundays & Feast Days

There are three that bear record in heaven: The Father, the Word, and the Holy Ghost: and these three are one.

Eastertide

Who is he that overcometh the world, but he that believeth that Jesus is the Son of God? This is he that came by water and blood, even Jesus Christ.

℟. Thanks be to God.

Short Respond

Ferias Throughout the Year

℣. I will bless the Lord at all times.

℟. I will bless the Lord at all times.

℣. His praise shall ever be in my mouth.

℟. At all times.

℣. Glory be to the Father, and to the Son, and to the Holy Ghost.

℟. I will bless the Lord at all times.

℣. Behold, God is my helper.

℟. The Lord is with them that uphold my soul.

Sext

Daily Office

Sundays, Feasts, & in Eastertide

℣. O Lord, thy Word endureth for ever in heaven (alleluia, alleluia).

℞. O Lord, thy Word endureth for ever in heaven (alleluia, alleluia).

℣. Thy truth also remaineth from one generation to another.

℞. For ever in heaven (alleluia, alleluia).

℣. Glory be to the Father, and to the Son, and to the Holy Ghost.

℞. O Lord, thy Word endureth for ever in heaven (alleluia, alleluia).

℣. The Lord is my shepherd, therefore can I lack nothing (alleluia).

℞. He shall feed me in a green pasture (alleluia).

Suffrages

❡ *The Suffrages are said, kneeling, on all Ferias outside of Eastertide.*

℣. Lord, have mercy upon us.

℞. Christ, have mercy upon us.

℣. Lord, have mercy upon us.

UR Father, who art in heaven, Hallowed be thy Name. Thy kingdom come. Thy will be done on earth, As it is in heaven. Give us this day our daily bread. And forgive us our trespasses, As we forgive those who trespass against us. And lead us not into temptation; But deliver us from evil. Amen.

℣. Hide not thy face from thy servant, for I am in trouble.

℞. O haste thee and hear me.

℣. Draw nigh unto my soul and save it.

℞. O deliver me, because of mine enemies.

℣. Arise, O Christ, and help us.

℞. And deliver us for thy Name's sake.

Collects

℣. The Lord be with you.

or, O Lord, hear our prayer.

℞. And with thy spirit.

or, And let our cry come unto thee.

℣. Let us pray.

❡ *The Collect(s) of the Day is here said, followed by this memorial Collect.*

ORD Jesus, who didst stretch out thine arms of love on the hard wood of the Cross, that all men might come within the reach of thy saving embrace; clothe us in thy Spirit, that we, stretching forth our hands in loving labour for others, may bring those who know thee not to the knowledge and love of thee, who with the Father and the Holy Ghost livest and reignest ever one God, world without end. *Amen.*

℣. The Lord be with you.

or, O Lord, hear our prayer.

℞. And with thy spirit.

or, And let our cry come unto thee.

℣. Let us bless the Lord.

℞. Thanks be to God.

℣. May the souls ✠ of the faithful departed, through the mercy of God, rest in peace.

OW unto the King eternal, immortal, invisible, the only wise God, be honour and glory, for ever and ever. *Amen.*

Daily Office — *None*

Hour of None

℣. O God, ✠ make speed to save us.
℟. O Lord, make haste to help us.
℣. Glory be to the Father, and to the Son, and to the Holy Ghost.
℟. As it was in the beginning, is now, and ever shall be, world without end. Amen.
℣. Praise ye the Lord.
℟. The Lord's Name be praised.

Rerum Deus

O GOD, creation's secret force,
Thyself unmoved, all motion's source,
Who from the morn till evening ray,
Through all its changes guid'st the day:

Grant us, when this short life is past,
The glorious evening that shall last;
That, by a holy death attained,
Eternal glory may be gained.

O Father, that we ask be done,
Through Jesus Christ, thine only Son;
Who, with the Holy Ghost and thee,
Doth live and reign eternally. Amen.

Mirabilia

THY testimonies are wonderful : therefore doth my soul keep them.
130 When thy word goeth forth : it giveth light and understanding unto the simple.
131 I opened my mouth, and drew in my breath : for my delight was in thy commandments.
132 O look thou upon me, and be merciful unto me : as thou usest to do unto those that love thy Name.
133 Order my steps in thy word : and so shall no wickedness have dominion over me.
134 O deliver me from the wrongful dealings of men : and so shall I keep thy commandments.
135 Shew the light of thy countenance upon thy servant : and teach me thy statutes.
136 Mine eyes gush out with water : because men keep not thy law.

℣. Glory be to the Father, and to the Son, and to the Holy Ghost.
℟. As it was in the beginning, is now, and ever shall be, world without end. Amen.

Justus es, Domine

RIGHTEOUS art thou, O Lord : and true is thy judgement.
138 The testimonies that thou hast commanded : are exceeding righteous and true.
139 My zeal hath even consumed me : because mine enemies have forgotten thy words.
140 Thy word is tried to the uttermost : and thy servant loveth it.
141 I am small, and of no reputation : yet do I not forget thy commandments.
142 Thy righteousness is an everlasting righteousness : and thy law is the truth.

143 Trouble and heaviness have taken hold upon me : yet is my delight in thy commandments.

144 The righteousness of thy testimonies is everlasting : O grant me understanding, and I shall live.

℣. Glory be to the Father, and to the Son, and to the Holy Ghost.

℟. As it was in the beginning, is now, and ever shall be, world without end. Amen.

Clamavi in toto corde meo

CALL with my whole heart : hear me, O Lord, I will keep thy statutes.

146 Yea, even unto thee do I call : help me, and I shall keep thy testimonies.

147 Early in the morning do I cry unto thee : for in thy word is my trust.

148 Mine eyes prevent the night-watches : that I might be occupied in thy words.

149 Hear my voice, O Lord, according unto thy loving-kindness : quicken me, according as thou art wont.

150 They draw nigh that of malice persecute me : and are far from thy law.

151 Be thou nigh at hand, O Lord : for all thy commandments are true.

152 As concerning thy testimonies, I have known long since : that thou hast grounded them for ever.

℣. Glory be to the Father, and to the Son, and to the Holy Ghost.

℟. As it was in the beginning, is now, and ever shall be, world without end. Amen.

Vide humilitatem

CONSIDER mine adversity, and deliver me : for I do not forget thy law.

154 Avenge thou my cause, and deliver me : quicken me, according to thy word.

155 Health is far from the ungodly : for they regard not thy statutes.

156 Great is thy mercy, O Lord : quicken me, as thou art wont.

157 Many there are that trouble me, and persecute me : yet do I not swerve from thy testimonies.

158 It grieveth me when I see the transgressors : because they keep not thy law.

159 Consider, O Lord, how I love thy commandments : O quicken me, according to thy loving-kindness.

160 Thy word is true from everlasting : all the judgements of thy righteousness endure for evermore.

℣. Glory be to the Father, and to the Son, and to the Holy Ghost.

℟. As it was in the beginning, is now, and ever shall be, world without end. Amen.

Principes persecuti sunt

RINCES have persecuted me without a cause : but my heart standeth in awe of thy word.

162 I am as glad of thy word : as one that findeth great spoils.

163 As for lies, I hate and abhor them : but thy law do I love.

164 Seven times a day do I praise thee : because of thy righteous judgements.

165 Great is the peace that they have who love thy law : and they are not offended at it.

166 Lord, I have looked for thy saving health : and done after thy commandments.

167 My soul hath kept thy testimonies : and loved them exceedingly.

168 I have kept thy commandments and testimonies : for all my ways are before thee.

℣. Glory be to the Father, and to the Son, and to the Holy Ghost.

℟. As it was in the beginning, is now, and ever shall be, world without end. Amen.

Appropinquet deprecatio

ET my complaint come before thee, O Lord : give me understanding, according to thy word.

170 Let my supplication come before thee : deliver me, according to thy word.

171 My lips shall speak of thy praise : when thou hast taught me thy statutes.

172 Yea, my tongue shall sing of thy word : for all thy commandments are righteous.

173 Let thine hand help me : for I have chosen thy commandments.

174 I have longed for thy saving health, O Lord : and in thy law is my delight.

175 O let my soul live, and it shall praise thee : and thy judgements shall help me.

176 I have gone astray like a sheep that is lost : O seek thy servant, for I do not forget thy commandments.

℣. Glory be to the Father, and to the Son, and to the Holy Ghost.

℟. As it was in the beginning, is now, and ever shall be, world without end. Amen.

Chapter

Ferias Throughout the Year

Bear ye one another's burdens, and so fulfil the law of Christ.

Sundays & Feast Days

One Lord, one Faith, one Baptism, one God and Father of all, who is above all, and through all, and in you all.

Eastertide

There are three that bear witness in earth: the Spirit, and the Water, and the Blood: and these three agree in one.

℟. Thanks be to God.

Short Respond

Ferias Throughout the Year

℣. Deliver me, O Lord, and be merciful unto me.

℟. Deliver me, O Lord, and be merciful unto me.

℣. My foot standeth right; I will praise the Lord in the congregations.

℟. And be merciful unto me.

℣. Glory be to the Father, and to the Son, and to the Holy Ghost.

℟. Deliver me, O Lord, and be merciful unto me.

℣. I will praise thy Name, O Lord.

℟. For thou hast delivered me out of all my trouble.

None

Daily Office

Sundays, Feasts, & in Eastertide

℣. I call with my whole heart; hear me, O Lord (alleluia, alleluia).

℟. I call with my whole heart; hear me, O Lord (alleluia, alleluia).

℣. I will keep thy statutes.

℟. Hear me, O Lord (alleluia, alleluia).

℣. Glory be to the Father, and to the Son, and to the Holy Ghost.

℟. I will call with my whole heart; hear me, O Lord (alleluia, alleluia).

℣. Cleanse me, O Lord, from my secret faults (alleluia).

℟. Keep thy servant also from presumptuous sins (alleluia).

Suffrages

¶ The Suffrages are said, kneeling, on all Ferias outside of Eastertide.

℣. Lord, have mercy upon us.

℟. Christ, have mercy upon us.

℣. Lord, have mercy upon us.

ur Father, who art in heaven, Hallowed be thy Name. Thy kingdom come. Thy will be done on earth, As it is in heaven. Give us this day our daily bread. And forgive us our trespasses, As we forgive those who trespass against us. And lead us not into temptation; But deliver us from evil. Amen.

℣. Cast me not away in the time of age.

℟. Forsake me not when my strength faileth me.

℣. Hide not thy face from me.

℟. Lest I be like unto them that go down into the pit.

℣. Quicken me, O Lord, for thy Name's sake.

℟. And for thy righteousness' sake bring my soul out of trouble.

Collects

℣. The Lord be with you.

or, O Lord, hear our prayer.

℟. And with thy spirit.

or, And let our cry come unto thee.

℣. Let us pray.

¶ The Collect(s) of the Day is here said, followed by this memorial Collect.

ord Jesus Christ, who for our sakes didst tread the paths of death; make known to us the way of life; that as thou wast reckoned with the transgressors in thy death, and with the rich in thy burial, so we, who are dead in trespasses and sins, may be raised up by thee to the land of true riches. Who livest and reignest with the Father and the Holy Ghost, ever one God, world without end. *Amen.*

℣. The Lord be with you.

or, O Lord, hear our prayer.

℟. And with thy spirit.

or, And let our cry come unto thee.

℣. Let us bless the Lord.

℟. Thanks be to God.

℣. May the souls ✠ of the faithful departed, through the mercy of God, rest in peace.

ow unto him that is able to keep us from falling and to present us faultless before the presence of his glory with exceeding joy; to the only wise God our Saviour be glory and majesty, dominion, and power, both now and ever. *Amen.*

Daily Office *Evensong*

The Order for Daily Evening Prayer

℣. O Lord, ✝ open thou our lips.
℟. And our mouth shall show forth thy praise.
℣. O God, ✠ make speed to save us.
℟. O Lord, make haste to help us.

℣. Dómine, ✝ lábia nostra apéries.
℟. Et os nostrum annuntiábit laudem tuam.
℣. Deus, ✠ in adjutórium nostrum inténde.
℟. Dómine, ad adjuvándum nos festína.

¶ *Here, all standing up, the Minister shall say,*

℣. Glory be to the Father, and to the Son, and to the Holy Ghost.
℟. As it was in the beginning, is now, and ever shall be, world without end. Amen.
℣. Praise ye the Lord.
℟. The Lord's Name be praised.

℣. Glória Patri, et Fílio, * et Spirítui Sancto:
℟. Sicut erat in princípio, et nunc, et semper, * et in sǽcula sæculórum. Amen.
℣. Laudáte Dominum.
℟. Sit Nomen Dómini Benedíctum.

¶ *Then shall follow a Portion of the Psalms, according to the Use of this Church. And at the end of every Psalm, and likewise at the end of the* Magnificat, Nunc dimittis, *shall be sung or said the* Gloria Patri, *or else the* Gloria in excelsis, *as followeth, except during Advent, Septuagesimatide, & Lent.*

Gloria in excelsis

LORY be to God on high, and on earth peace, good will towards men. We praise thee, we bless thee, we worship thee, we glorify thee, we give thanks to thee for thy great glory, O Lord God, heavenly King, God the Father Almighty.

O Lord, the only-begotten Son, Jesus Christ; O Lord God, Lamb of God, Son of the Father, that takest away the sins of the world, have mercy upon us. Thou that takest away the sins of the world, receive our prayer. Thou that sittest at the right hand of God the Father, have mercy upon us. For thou

LÓRIA in excélsis Deo. Et in terra pax homínibus bonæ voluntátis. Laudámus te. Benedícimus te. Adorámus te. Glorificámus te. Grátias ágimus tibi propter magnam glóriam tuam. Dómine Deus, Rex cæléstis, Deus Pater omnípotens.

Dómine Fili unigénite, Jesu Christe. Dómine Deus, Agnus Dei, Fílius Patris. Qui tollis peccáta mundi, miserére nobis. Qui tollis peccáta mundi, súscipe deprecatiónem nostram. Qui sedes ad déxteram Patris, miserére nobis. Quóniam tu solus Sanctus. Tu solus Dóminus. Tu solus Altíssimus, Je-

Evensong # Daily Office

only art holy; thou only art the Lord; thou only, O Christ, with the Holy Ghost, art ✠ most high in the glory of God the Father. Amen.

su Christe. Cum Sancto Spíritu ✠ in glória Dei Patris. Amen.

¶ Then shall be read the First Lesson, according to the Table or Calendar.

¶ After which may be sung or said a Hymn.

Magnificat

¶ Then shall be sung or said the Hymn following.

y soul ✠ doth magnify the Lord, * and my spirit hath rejoiced in God my Saviour.

For he hath regarded * the lowliness of his handmaiden.

For behold, from henceforth * all generations shall call me blessed.

For he that is mighty hath magnified me; * and holy is his Name.

And his mercy is on them that fear him * throughout all generations.

He hath showed strength with his arm; * he hath scattered the proud in the imagination of their hearts.

He hath put down the mighty from their seat, * and hath exalted the humble and meek.

He hath filled the hungry with good things; * and the rich he hath sent empty away.

He remembering his mercy hath holpen his servant Israel; * as he promised to our forefathers, Abraham and his seed, for ever.

Magníficat ✠ ánima mea Dóminum.

Et exsultávit spíritus meus: * in Deo, salutári meo.

Quia respéxit humilitátem ancíllæ suæ: * ecce enim ex hoc beátam me dicent omnes generatiónes.

Quia fecit mihi magna qui potens est: * et sanctum nomen ejus.

Et misericórdia ejus, a progénie in progénies: * timéntibus eum.

Fecit poténtiam in brácchio suo: * dispérsit supérbos mente cordis sui.

Depósuit poténtes de sede: * et exaltávit húmiles.

Esuriéntes implévit bonis: * et dívites dimísit inánes.

Suscépit Israël púerum suum: * recordátus misericórdiæ suæ.

Sicut locútus est ad patres nostros: * Ábraham, et sémini ejus in sæcula.

¶ Then a Lesson of the New Testament, as it is appointed.

Daily Office — *Evensong*

Nunc dimittis

❡ And after that shall be sung or said the Hymn called Nunc dimittis, as followeth.

ORD, ✠ now lettest thou thy servant depart in peace, * according to thy word.
    For mine eyes have seen * thy salvation,
    Which thou hast prepared * before the face of all people;
    To be a light to lighten the Gentiles, * and to be the glory of thy people Israel.

UNC dimíttis ✠ servum tuum, Dómine, * secúndum verbum tuum in pace:
    Quia vidérunt óculi mei * salutáre tuum,
    Quod parásti * ante fáciem ómnium populórum,
    Lumen ad revelatiónem géntium, * et glóriam plebis tuæ Israël.

Apostles' Creed

❡ Then shall be said the Apostles' Creed, by the Minister and the People, standing.
Note, the Nicene Creed may be said instead of the Apostles' (p. 162).

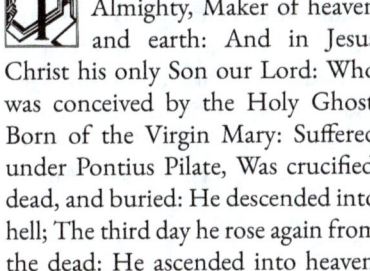 BELIEVE in God the Father Almighty, Maker of heaven and earth: And in Jesus Christ his only Son our Lord: Who was conceived by the Holy Ghost, Born of the Virgin Mary: Suffered under Pontius Pilate, Was crucified, dead, and buried: He descended into hell; The third day he rose again from the dead: He ascended into heaven, And sitteth on the right hand of God the Father Almighty: From thence he shall come to judge the quick and the dead.
    I believe in the Holy Ghost: The holy Catholic Church; The Communion of Saints: The Forgiveness of sins: The Resurrection of the body: ✠ And the Life everlasting. Amen.

REDO in Deum, Patrem omnipoténtem, Creatórem cæli et terræ. Et in Jesum Christum, Fílium ejus únicum, Dóminum nostrum: qui concéptus est de Spíritu Sancto, natus ex María Vírgine, passus sub Póntio Piláto, crucifíxus, mórtuus, et sepúltus: descéndit ad ínferos; tértia die resurréxit a mórtuis; ascéndit ad cælos; sedet ad déxteram Dei Patris omnipoténtis: inde ventúrus est judicáre vivos et mórtuos.
    Credo in Spíritum Sanctum, sanctam Ecclésiam cathólicam, Sanctórum communiónem, remissiónem peccatórum, carnis ✠ resurrectiónem, vitam ætérnam. Amen.

Evensong

Daily Office

❧ And after that, these Prayers following, the People devoutly kneeling; the Minister first pronouncing,

℣. The Lord be with you.
or, O Lord, hear our prayer.

℟. And with thy spirit.
or, And let our cry come unto thee.
℣. Let us pray.
℣. Lord, have mercy upon us.
℟. Christ, have mercy upon us.
℣. Lord, have mercy upon us.

℣. Dóminus vobíscum.
vel, Dómine, exáudi oratiónem nostram.
℟. Et cum spíritu tuo.
vel, Et clamor noster ad te véniat.
℣. Orémus.
℣. Kýrie, eléison.
℟. Christe, eléison.
℣. Kýrie, eléison.

Lord's Prayer

❧ Then the Minister, Clerks, and People—all kneeling—shall say the Lord's Prayer with a loud voice.

UR Father, who art in heaven, Hallowed be thy Name. Thy kingdom come. Thy will be done on earth, As it is in heaven. Give us this day our daily bread. And forgive us our trespasses, As we forgive those who trespass against us. And lead us not into temptation; But deliver us from evil. Amen.

PATER noster, qui es in cælis, sanctificétur nomen tuum: advéniat regnum tuum: fiat volúntas tua, sicut in cælo et in terra. Panem nostrum quotidiánum da nobis hódie: et dimítte nobis débita nostra, sicut et nos dimíttimus debitóribus nostris: et ne nos indúcas in tentatiónem: sed líbera nos a malo. Amen.

Preces

❧ Then the Minister standing up shall say

℣. O Lord, show thy mercy upon us.
℟. And grant us thy salvation.
℣. O Lord, save the *State*.
℟. And mercifully hear us when we call upon thee.
℣. Endue thy Ministers with righteousness.
℟. And make thy chosen people joyful.

℣. Osténde nobis, Dómine, misericórdiam tuam.
℟. Et salutáre tuum da nobis.
℣. Dómine salvam fac *Civitatem*.
℟. Et exáudi nos cum invocámus te.
℣. Sacerdótes tui induántur Justítia.
℟. Et sancti tui exúltent.
℣. Salvum fac Pópulum tuum, Dómine.
℟. Et bénedic Hæreditáti tuæ.

Daily Office — *Evensong*

℣. O Lord, save thy people.
℟. And bless thine inheritance.
℣. Give peace in our time, O Lord.
℟. For it is thou, Lord, only, that makest us dwell in safety.
℣. O God, make clean our hearts within us.
℟. And take not thy Holy Spirit from us.

℣. Da pacem Dómine in diébus nostris.
℟. Quóniam tu, Dómine, singuláriter in spe constituísti me.
℣. Cor mundum crea in nobis, O Deus.
℟. Et Spíritum Sanctum tuum ne áuferas a nobis.

¶ Then shall be said the Collect(s) of the Day, and after that the Collects and Prayers following.

A Collect for Peace

GOD, from whom all holy desires, all good counsels, and all just works do proceed; Give unto thy servants that peace which the world cannot give; that our hearts may be set to obey thy commandments, and also that by thee, we, being defended from the fear of our enemies, may pass our time in rest and quietness; through the merits of Jesus Christ our Saviour. *Amen.*

A Collect for Aid against Perils

LIGHTEN our darkness, we beseech thee, O Lord; and by thy great mercy defend us from all perils and dangers of this night; for the love of thy only Son, our Saviour, Jesus Christ. *Amen.*

Conclusion

℣. The Lord be with you.
or, O Lord, hear our prayer.
℟. And with thy spirit.
or, And let our cry come unto thee.
℣. Let us bless the Lord (alleluia, alleluia.)
℟. Thanks be to God (alleluia, alleluia.)
℣. May the souls ✠ of the faithful departed, through the mercy of God, rest in peace.
℟. Amen.

℣. Dóminus vobíscum.
vel, Dómine, exáudi oratiónem nostram.
℟. Et cum spíritu tuo.
vel, Et clamor noster ad te véniat.
℣. Benedicámus Dómino (allelúja, allelúja.)
℟. Deo grátias (allelúja, allelúja.)
℣. Fidélium ánimæ ✠ per misericórdiam Dei requiéscant in pace.
℟. Amen.

Evensong # Daily Office

¶ In places where it may be convenient, here followeth the Marian Anthem (p. 65).

¶ The Minister may here end the Evening Prayer with such Prayer, or Prayers, taken out of this Book, as he shall think fit.

After the Third Collect

¶ The Prayer for the Head of State (p. 70) is here said.

A Prayer for the Clergy and People

ALMIGHTY and everlasting God, from whom cometh every good and perfect gift; Send down upon our Bishops, and other Clergy, and upon the Congregations committed to their charge, the healthful Spirit of thy grace; and, that they may truly please thee, pour upon them the continual dew of thy blessing. Grant this, O Lord, for the honour of our Advocate and Mediator, Jesus Christ. *Amen.*

¶ Additional Prayers (p. 70) may here be said.

A Prayer for all Sorts & Conditions of Men

O GOD, the Creator and Preserver of all mankind, we humbly beseech thee for all sorts and conditions of men; that thou wouldest be pleased to make thy ways known unto them, thy saving health unto all nations. More especially we pray for thy holy Church universal; that it may be so guided and governed by thy good Spirit, that all who profess and call themselves Christians may be led into the way of truth, and hold the faith in unity of spirit, in the bond of peace, and in righteousness of life. Finally, we commend to thy fatherly goodness all those who are any ways afflicted, or distressed, in mind, body, or estate; (*especially those for whom our prayers are desired;) that it may please thee to comfort and relieve them, according to their several necessities; giving them patience under their sufferings, and a happy issue out of all their afflictions. And this we beg for Jesus Christ's sake. *Amen.*

*This may be said when any desire the prayers of the Congregation.

A General Thanksgiving

¶ The General Thanksgiving may be said by the Congregation with the Minister.

ALMIGHTY God, Father of all mercies, we, thine unworthy servants, do give thee most humble and hearty thanks for all thy goodness and loving-kindness to us and to all men; (*to those who desire now to offer up their praises and thanksgivings for thy late mercies vouchsafed unto

*This may be said when any desire to return thanks for mercies vouchsafed to them.

them.) We bless thee for our creation, preservation, and all the blessings of this life; but above all, for thine inestimable love in the redemption of the world by our Lord Jesus Christ; for the means of grace, and for the hope of glory. And, we beseech thee, give us that due sense of all thy mercies, that our hearts may be unfeignedly thankful; and that we show forth thy praise, not only with our lips, but in our lives, by giving up our selves to thy service, and by walking before thee in holiness and righteousness all our days; through Jesus Christ our Lord, to whom, with thee and the Holy Ghost, be all honour and glory, world without end. *Amen.*

¶ The Thanksgivings (p. 82) may here be offered.

A Prayer of St. Chrysostom

ALMIGHTY God, who hast given us grace at this time with one accord to make our common supplications unto thee; and dost promise that when two or three are gathered together in thy Name thou wilt grant their requests; Fulfil now, O Lord, the desires and petitions of thy servants, as may be most expedient for them; granting us in this world knowledge of thy truth, and in the world to come life everlasting. *Amen.*

The Grace

THE grace of our Lord Jesus Christ, ✠ and the love of God, and the fellowship of the Holy Ghost, be with us all evermore. *Amen.*

HERE ENDETH THE ORDER OF EVENING PRAYER.

Compline

Daily Office

Hour of Compline

¶ This Service may be used when Evensong has been previously said.
¶ All standing up, the Minister shall say,

HE Lord Almighty grant us a quiet night and a perfect end. ℟. Amen.

RETHREN, be sober, be vigilant; because your adversary the devil, as a roaring lion, walketh about, seeking whom he may devour : Whom resist, stedfast in the faith. (1 Peter 5:8-9.)

℣. But thou, O Lord, have mercy upon us;

℟. Thanks be to God.

INTRODUCTION

℣. O God, ✠ make speed to save us.
℟. O Lord, make haste to help us.
℣. Glory be to the Father, and to the Son, and to the Holy Ghost.
℟. As it was in the beginning, is now, and ever shall be, world without end. Amen.
℣. Praise ye the Lord.
℟. The Lord's Name be praised.

PSALM 4. *CUM INVOCAREM*

EAR me when I call, O God of my righteousness : thou hast set me at liberty when I was in trouble; have mercy upon me, and hearken unto my prayer.

2 O ye sons of men, how long will ye blaspheme mine honour : and have such pleasure in vanity, and seek after leasing?

3 Know this also, that the Lord hath chosen to himself the man that is godly : when I call upon the Lord, he will hear me.

4 Stand in awe, and sin not : commune with your own heart, and in your chamber, and be still.

5 Offer the sacrifice of righteousness : and put your trust in the Lord.

6 There be many that say : Who will shew us any good?

7 Lord, lift thou up : the light of thy countenance upon us.

8 Thou hast put gladness in my heart : since the time that their corn and wine and oil increased.

9 I will lay me down in peace, and take my rest : for it is thou, Lord, only, that makest me dwell in safety.

℣. Glory be to the Father, and to the Son, and to the Holy Ghost.

℟. As it was in the beginning, is now, and ever shall be, world without end. Amen.

PSALM 31. *IN TE, DOMINE, SPERAVI*

N thee, O Lord, have I put my trust : let me never be put to confusion, deliver me in thy righteousness.

Daily Office — *Compline*

2 Bow down thine ear to me : make haste to deliver me.

3 And be thou my strong rock, and house of defence : that thou mayest save me.

4 For thou art my strong rock, and my castle : be thou also my guide, and lead me for thy Name's sake.

5 Draw me out of the net that they have laid privily for me : for thou art my strength.

6 Into thy hands I commend my spirit : for thou hast redeemed me, O Lord, thou God of truth.

℣. Glory be to the Father, and to the Son, and to the Holy Ghost.

℟. As it was in the beginning, is now, and ever shall be, world without end. Amen.

Psalm 91. *Qui habitat*

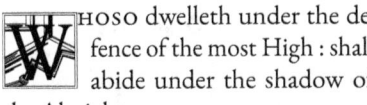HOSO dwelleth under the defence of the most High : shall abide under the shadow of the Almighty.

2 I will say unto the Lord, Thou art my hope, and my strong hold : my God, in him will I trust.

3 For he shall deliver thee from the snare of the hunter : and from the noisome pestilence.

4 He shall defend thee under his wings, and thou shalt be safe under his feathers : his faithfulness and truth shall be thy shield and buckler.

5 Thou shalt not be afraid for any terror by night : nor for the arrow that flieth by day;

6 For the pestilence that walketh in darkness : nor for the sickness that destroyeth in the noon-day.

7 A thousand shall fall beside thee, and ten thousand at thy right hand : but it shall not come nigh thee.

8 Yea, with thine eyes shalt thou behold : and see the reward of the ungodly.

9 For thou, Lord, art my hope : thou hast set thine house of defence very high.

10 There shall no evil happen unto thee : neither shall any plague come nigh thy dwelling.

11 For he shall give his angels charge over thee : to keep thee in all thy ways.

12 They shall bear thee in their hands : that thou hurt not thy foot against a stone.

13 Thou shalt go upon the lion and adder : the young lion and the dragon shalt thou tread under thy feet.

14 Because he hath set his love upon me, therefore will I deliver him : I will set him up, because he hath known my Name.

15 He shall call upon me, and I will hear him : yea, I am with him in trouble; I will deliver him, and bring him to honour.

16 With long life will I satisfy him : and shew him my salvation.

℣. Glory be to the Father, and to the Son, and to the Holy Ghost.

℟. As it was in the beginning, is now, and ever shall be, world without end. Amen.

Psalm 134. *Ecce nunc*

EHOLD now, praise the Lord : all ye servants of the Lord;
2 Ye that by night stand in the house of the Lord : even in the courts of the house of our God.
3 Lift up your hands in the sanctuary : and praise the Lord.
4 The Lord that made heaven and earth : give thee blessing out of Sion.
℣. Glory be to the Father, and to the Son, and to the Holy Ghost.
℟. As it was in the beginning, is now, and ever shall be, world without end. Amen.

Chapter

HOU, O Lord, art in the midst of us, and we are called by thy name. Leave us not, O Lord our God. ℟. Thanks be to God.

Short Respond

℣. Into thy hands, O Lord, I commend my spirit;
℟. Into thy hands, O Lord, I commend my spirit;
℣. For thou hast redeemed me, O Lord, thou God of truth.
℟. I commend my spirit.
℣. Glory be to the Father, and to the Son, and to the Holy Ghost;
℟. Into thy hands, O Lord, I commend my spirit.

Te lucis ante terminum.

EFORE the ending of the day, Creator of the world we pray, That with thy wonted favour thou
Wouldst be our guard and keeper now.

From all ill dreams defend our eyes,
From nightly fears and fantasies
Tread under foot our ghostly foe,
That no pollution we may know.

O Father, that we ask be done,
Through Jesus Christ, thine only Son;
Who, with the Holy Ghost and thee,
Doth live and reign eternally. Amen.

℣. Keep me as the apple of an eye;
℟. Hide me under the shadow of thy wings.

Nunc Dimittis

Ant. Preserve us, O Lord, waking, and guard us sleeping, that we may watch with Christ, and rest in peace.

ORD, ✠ now lettest thou thy servant depart in peace, * according to thy word.
For mine eyes have seen * thy salvation,
Which thou hast prepared * before the face of all people;
To be a light to lighten the Gentiles, * and to be the glory of thy people Israel.
℣. Glory be to the Father, and to the Son, and to the Holy Ghost.

Daily Office *Compline*

R̸. As it was in the beginning, is now, and ever shall be, world without end. Amen.

Ant. Preserve us, O Lord, waking, and guard us sleeping, that we may watch with Christ, and rest in peace.

Suffrages

¶ The Suffrages are said, kneeling, on all Ferias outside of Eastertide.

V̸. Lord, have mercy upon us.
R̸. Christ, have mercy upon us.
V̸. Lord, have mercy upon us.

Lord's Prayer

UR Father, who art in heaven, Hallowed be thy Name. Thy kingdom come. Thy will be done on earth, As it is in heaven. Give us this day our daily bread. And forgive us our trespasses, As we forgive those who trespass against us. And lead us not into temptation; But deliver us from evil. Amen.

Apostles' Creed

I BELIEVE in God the Father Almighty, Maker of heaven and earth: And in Jesus Christ his only Son our Lord: Who was conceived by the Holy Ghost, Born of the Virgin Mary: Suffered under Pontius Pilate, Was crucified, dead, and buried: He descended into hell; The third day he rose again from the dead: He ascended into heaven, And sitteth on the right hand of God the Father Almighty: From thence he shall come to judge the quick and the dead.

I believe in the Holy Ghost: The holy Catholic Church; The Communion of Saints: The Forgiveness of sins: The Resurrection of the body: ✠ And the Life everlasting. Amen.

¶ Then shall follow these Versicles and Responses.

V̸. Blessed art thou, Lord God of our fathers;
R̸. To be praised and glorified above all for ever.
V̸. Let us bless the Father, the Son, and the Holy Ghost;
R̸. Let us praise him and magnify him for ever.
V̸. Blessed art thou, O Lord, in the firmament of heaven;
R̸. To be praised and glorified above all for ever.
V̸. The Almighty and most merciful Lord guard us and give us his blessing.
R̸. Amen.

Confession

¶ Then shall the Minister and People say together the Confession following,

CONFESS to God, to blessed Mary, to all the saints, and to you: that I have sinned exceedingly in thought, word, and deed, by my own fault. I beg holy Mary, all the Saints of God, and you, to pray for me.

¶ The Minister then stands and says,

LMIGHTY God, have mercy upon us, forgive us all our sins and deliver us from all evil, confirm and strengthen us in all goodness, and bring us to life everlasting. *Amen.*

Compline — Daily Office

¶ If a Priest be present, he shall stand and pronounce the following Absolution,

MAY the almighty and merciful Lord grant unto you pardon ✠ and remission of all your sins, time for amendment of life, and the grace and comfort of the Holy Spirit. *Amen.*

℣. Wilt thou not turn again and quicken us, O God?
℟. That thy people may rejoice in thee.
℣. O Lord, show thy mercy upon us.
℟. And grant us thy salvation.
℣. Vouchsafe, O Lord, to keep us this day without sin;
℟. O Lord, have mercy upon us, have mercy upon us.

Collect

℣. O Lord, hear our prayer.
℟. And let our cry come unto thee.
Let us pray.

VISIT, we beseech thee, O Lord, this place, and drive from it all the snares of the enemy; let thy holy angels dwell herein to preserve us in peace; and may thy blessing be upon us evermore; through Jesus Christ our Lord. *Amen.*

or,

LORD Jesus Christ, Son of the living God, who at this evening hour didst rest in the sepulchre, and didst thereby sanctify the grave to be a bed of hope to thy people; Make us so to abound in sorrow for our sins, which were the cause of thy passion, that when our bodies lie in the dust, our souls may live with thee; who livest and reignest with the Father and the Holy Ghost, one God world without end. Amen.

Conclusion

℣. We will lay us down in peace and take our rest.
℟. For it is thou, Lord, only that makest us dwell in safety.
℣. The Lord be with you.
or, O Lord, hear our prayer.
℟. And with thy spirit.
or, And let our cry come unto thee.
℣. Let us bless the Lord.
℟. Thanks be to God.

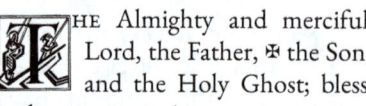

THE Almighty and merciful Lord, the Father, ✠ the Son, and the Holy Ghost; bless and preserve us. *Amen.*

¶ The appropriate Marian Anthem (p. 65) shall be said or sung here.

Marian Anthems

Alma Redemptoris Mater

From I Evensong of Advent I until II Evensong of the Purification, inclusive.

RACIOUS Mother of our Redeemer, for ever abiding Heaven's gateway, and star of ocean,
O succour the people, who, though falling, strive to rise again.
Thou Maiden who barest thy holy Creator, to the wonder of all nature;
Ever Virgin, after, as before thou receivedst that Ave
From the mouth of Gabriel; have compassion on us sinners.

In Advent

℣. The Angel of the Lord announced unto Mary.

℟. And she conceived by the Holy Ghost.

Let us pray.

E beseech thee, O Lord, pour thy grace into our hearts: that, as we have known the incarnation of thy Son Jesus Christ by the message of an angel, so by his Cross and Passion we may be brought unto the glory of his Resurrection. Through the same Christ our Lord. *Amen.*

In Christmastide

℣. After Childbearing, O Virgin, thou didst remain inviolate.

℟. Intercede for us, O Mother of God.

LMA Redemptóris Mater, quæ pérvia cæli porta manes,
Et stella maris, succúrre cadénti,
Súrgere qui curat, pópulo: tu quæ genuísti,
Natúra miránte, tuum sanctum Genitórem,
Virgo prius ac postérius, Gabriélis ab ore
Sumens illud Ave, peccatórum miserére.

In Adventu

℣. Ángelus Dómini nuntiávit Maríæ.

℟. Et concépit de Spíritu Sancto.

Orémus.

RÁTIAM tuam, quǽsumus, Dómine, méntibus nostris infúnde: ut, qui, Ángelo nuntiánte, Christi Fílii tui incarnatiónem cognóvimus; per passiónem ejus et crucem, ad resurrectiónis glóriam perducámur. Per eúmdem Christum Dóminum nóstrum. *Amen.*

De Nativitate

℣. Post partum, Virgo, invioláta permansísti.

℟. Dei Génitrix, intercéde pro nobis.

Marian Anthems   **Daily Office**   Ave, Regina Cælorum

Let us pray.

GOD, who by the fruitful virginity of Blessed Mary hast bestowed upon mankind the reward of eternal salvation: Grant, we beseech thee, that we may know the help of her intercession through whom we have been accounted worthy to receive the Author of our life, Jesus Christ thy Son our Lord. *Amen.*

Orémus.

EUS, qui salútis ætérnæ, beátæ Maríæ virginitáte fecúnda, humáno géneri præmia præstitísti: tríbue, quǽsumus; ut ipsam pro nobis intercédere sentiámus, per quam merúimus auctórem vitæ suscípere, Dóminum nóstrum Jesum Christum Fílium tuum. *Amen.*

AVE, REGINA CÆLORUM

From Compline of the Purification until Compline of Holy Wednesday, inclusive.

UEEN of the heavens, we hail thee,
Hail thee, Lady of all the Angels;
Thou the dawn, the door of morning
Whence the world's true light is risen:

Joy to thee, O Virgin glorious,
Beautiful beyond all other;
Hail and farewell, O most gracious,
Intercede for us alway to Jesus.

℣. Vouchsafe that I may praise thee, O holy Virgin.
℟. Give me strength against thine enemies.

Let us pray.

RANT us, O merciful God, protection in our weakness: that we who celebrate the memory of the holy Mother of God may, through the aid of her intercession, rise again from our sins. Through the same Christ our Lord. *Amen.*

VE, Regína cælórum,
Ave, Dómina Angelórum:
Salve radix, salve porta,
Ex qua mundo lux est orta:

Gaude, Virgo gloriósa,
Super omnes speciósa,
Vale, o valde decóra,
Et pro nobis Christum exóra.

℣. Dignáre me laudáre te, Virgo sacráta.
℟. Da mihi virtútem contra hostes tuos.

Orémus.

ONCÉDE, miséricors Deus, fragilitáti nostræ præsídium; ut, qui sanctæ Dei Genetrícis memóriam ágimus; intercessiónis ejus auxílio, a nostris iniquitátibus resurgámus. Per eúmdem Christum Dóminum nóstrum. *Amen.*

Regina Cæli

From Compline of Holy Saturday until I Evensong of Trinity Sunday, exclusive.

QUEEN of heaven, be joyful, alleluia;
Because he whom so meetly thou barest, alleluia,
Hath arisen, as he promised, alleluia:
Pray for us to the Father, alleluia.

℣. Rejoice and be glad, O Virgin Mary, alleluia.
℟. For the Lord is risen indeed, alleluia.

Let us pray.

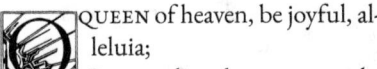GOD, who, by the resurrection of thy Son Jesus Christ didst vouchsafe to give gladness unto the world: Grant, we beseech thee, that we, being holpen by the Virgin Mary, his Mother, may attain unto the joys of everlasting life. Through the same Christ our Lord. *Amen.*

EGÍNA cæli, lætáre, allelúja;
Quia quem meruísti portáre, allelúja,
Resurréxit, sicut dixit, allelúja:
Ora pro nobis Deum, allelúja.

℣. Gaude et lætáre, Virgo María, allelúja.
℟. Quia surréxit Dóminus vere, allelúja.

Orémus.

EUS, qui per resurrectiónem Fílii tui, Dómini nostri Jesu Christi, mundum lætificáre dignátus es: præsta, quæsumus; ut, per eius Genetrícem Vírginem Maríam, perpétuæ capiámus gáudia vitæ. Per eúmdem Christum Dóminum nóstrum. *Amen.*

Salve Regina

From I Evensong of Trinity Sunday until I Evensong of Advent I, exclusive.

ARY, we hail thee, Mother and Queen compassionate;
Mary, our comfort, life and hope, we hail thee.
To thee we exiles, children of Eve, lift our crying.
To thee we are sighing, as mournful and weeping,
We pass through this vale of sorrow.

Turn thou therefore, O our intercessor,
Those thine eyes of pity and lovingkindness upon us sinners.
Hereafter, when our earthly exile shall be ended,
Show us Jesus, the blessed fruit of thy womb.
O gentle, O tender, O gracious Virgin Mary.

℣. Pray for us, O holy Mother of God.
℟. That we may be made worthy of the promises of Christ.
Let us pray.

LMIGHTY and everlasting God, who by the cooperation of the Holy Ghost, didst prepare the body and soul of the glorious Virgin Mother Mary to become a habitation meet for thy Son: Grant that as we rejoice in her commemoration, we may be delivered by her loving intercession from our present evils and from eternal death. Through the same Christ our Lord. *Amen.*

ALVE, Regína, mater misericórdiæ;
Vita, dulcédo et spes nóstra, salve.
Ad te clamámus éxsules fílii Hevæ.
Ad te suspirámus geméntes et flentes
In hac lacrimárum valle.

Eja ergo, advocáta nostra,
Illos tuos misericórdes óculos ad nos convérte.
Et Jesum, benedíctum fructum ventris tui,
Nobis post hoc exsílium osténde.
O clemens, o pia, o dulcis Virgo María.

℣. Ora pro nobis, sancta Dei Génitrix.
℟. Ut digni efficiámur promissiónibus Christi.
Orémus.

MNÍPOTENS sempitérne Deus, qui gloriósæ Vírginis Matris Maríæ corpus et ánimam, ut dignum Fílii tui habitáculum éffici mererétur, Spíritu Sancto cooperánte, præparásti: da, ut, cujus commemoratióne lætámur, ejus pia intercessióne, ab instántibus malis et a morte perpétua liberémur. Per eúmdem Christum Dóminum nóstrum. *Amen.*

Prayers & Thanksgivings

Prayers

Prayers for the United States of America

For the President of the United States, and all in Civil Authority

O LORD, our heavenly Father, the high and mighty Ruler of the universe, who dost from thy throne behold all the dwellers upon earth; Most heartily we beseech thee, with thy favour to behold and bless thy servant THE PRESIDENT OF THE UNITED STATES, and all others in authority; and so replenish them with the grace of thy Holy Spirit, that they may always incline to thy will, and walk in thy way. Endue them plenteously with heavenly gifts; grant them in health and prosperity long to live; and finally, after this life, to attain everlasting joy and felicity; through Jesus Christ our Lord. *Amen.*

For Congress

¶ To be used during their Session.

MOST gracious God, we humbly beseech thee, as for the people of these United States in general, so especially for their Senate and Representatives in Congress assembled; that thou wouldest be pleased to direct and prosper all their consultations, to the advancement of thy glory, the good of thy Church, the safety, honour, and welfare of thy people; that all things may be so ordered and settled by their endeavours, upon the best and surest foundations, that peace and happiness, truth and justice, religion and piety, may be established among us for all generations. These and all other necessaries, for them, for us, and thy whole Church, we humbly beg in the Name and mediation of Jesus Christ, our most blessed Lord and Saviour. *Amen.*

For a State Legislature

O GOD, the fountain of wisdom, whose statutes are good and gracious and whose law is truth; We beseech thee so to guide and bless the Legislature of this *State,* that it may ordain for our governance only such things as please thee, to the glory of thy Name and the welfare of the people; through Jesus Christ, thy Son, our Lord. *Amen.*

For Courts of Justice

ALMIGHTY God, who sittest in the throne judging right; We humbly beseech thee to bless the courts of justice and the magistrates in all this land; and give unto them the spirit of wisdom and understanding, that they may discern the truth and impartially administer the law in the fear of thee alone; through him who shall come to be our judge, thy Son, our Saviour, Jesus Christ. *Amen.*

Prayers

For the Military

O LORD God of Hosts, stretch forth, we pray thee, thine almighty arm to strengthen and protect the Soldiers, Sailors, Marines, Airmen, Coast Guardsmen, and Guardians of our country; Support them in the day of battle, and in the time of peace keep them safe from all evil; endue them with courage and loyalty; and grant that in all things they may serve without reproach; through Jesus Christ our Lord. *Amen.*

¶ or this.

HEAVENLY Father, we commend to thy gracious care and keeping all the men and women in our Armed Forces at home and abroad. Defend them day by day with thy heavenly grace; strengthen them in their trials and temptations; give them courage to face the perils that beset them; and help them to know that none can pluck out of thy hand those who put their trust in thee; through Jesus Christ our Lord. *Amen.*

PRAYERS FOR CANADA & COMMONWEALTH

For the King's Majesty

O LORD, our heavenly Father, high and mighty, King of kings, Lord of lords, the only Ruler of princes, who dost from thy throne behold all the dwellers upon earth: Most heartily we beseech thee with thy favour to behold our most gracious Sovereign Lord, King *CHARLES*; and so replenish him with the grace of thy Holy Spirit, that he may alway incline to thy will, and walk in thy way. Endue him plenteously with heavenly gifts; grant him in health and wealth long to live; strengthen him that he may vanquish and overcome all his enemies; and finally after this life he may attain everlasting joy and felicity; through Jesus Christ our Lord. *Amen.*

For the Royal Family

ALMIGHTY God, the fountain of all goodness, we humbly beseech thee to bless Queen *Camilla*, *William* Prince of Wales, the Princess of Wales, and all the Royal Family: Endue them with thy Holy Spirit; enrich them with thy heavenly grace; prosper them with all happiness; and bring them to thine everlasting kingdom; through Jesus Christ our Lord. *Amen.*

Prayers

For Parliament

Most gracious God, we humbly beseech thee, as for this Commonwealth in general, so especially for the High Court of Parliament, *the Parliament of this Dominion, and the Legislature of this Province,* under our most religious and gracious King at this time assembled: That thou wouldest be pleased to direct and prosper all their consultations to the advancement of thy glory, the good of thy Church, the safety, honour, and welfare of our Sovereign and his Dominions; that all things may be so ordered and settled by their endeavours, upon the best and surest foundations, that peace and happiness, truth and justice, religion and piety, may be established among us for all generations. These and all other necessaries, for them, for us, and thy whole Church, we humbly beg in the Name and Mediation of Jesus Christ our most blessed Lord and Saviour. *Amen.*

For the Forces of the King

O Lord of Hosts, stretch forth, we pray thee, thine Almighty arm to strengthen and protect the forces of our King in every peril of sea, and land, and air; shelter them in the day of battle, and in time of peace keep them safe from all evil; endue them ever with loyalty and courage; and grant that in all things they may serve as seeing thee who art invisible; through Jesus Christ our Lord. *Amen.*

For the Commonwealth

Almighty God, who rulest in the kingdom of men, and hast given to our Sovereign Lord, King *Charles*, a great dominion in all parts of the earth: Draw together, we pray thee, in true fellowship the men of divers races, languages, and customs, who dwell therein, that, bearing one another's burdens, and working together in brotherly concord, they may fulfil the purpose of thy providence, and set forward thy everlasting kingdom. Pardon, we beseech thee our sins and shortcomings: keep far from us all selfishness and pride: and give us grace to employ thy good gifts of order and freedom to thy glory and the welfare of mankind; through Jesus Christ thy Son our Lord, to whom with thee and the Holy Ghost be all glory and dominion, world without end. *Amen.*

Prayers

Prayers for the Church

For the Unity of God's People

O GOD, the Father of our Lord Jesus Christ, our only Saviour, the Prince of Peace; Give us grace seriously to lay to heart the great dangers we are in by our unhappy divisions. Take away all hatred and prejudice, and whatsoever else may hinder us from godly union and concord: that as there is but one Body and one Spirit, and one hope of our calling, one Lord, one Faith, one Baptism, one God and Father of us all, so we may be all of one heart and of one soul, united in one holy bond of truth and peace, of faith and charity, and may with one mind and one mouth glorify thee; through Jesus Christ our Lord. *Amen.*

For those who are to be admitted into Holy Orders

¶ To be used in the Weeks preceding the stated Times of Ordination.

ALMIGHTY God, our heavenly Father, who hast purchased to thyself an universal Church by the precious blood of thy dear Son; Mercifully look upon the same, and at this time so guide and govern the minds of thy servants the Bishops and Pastors of thy flock, that they may lay hands suddenly on no man, but faithfully and wisely make choice of fit persons, to serve in the sacred Ministry of thy Church, And to those who shall be ordained to any holy function, give thy grace and heavenly benediction; that both by their life and doctrine they may show forth thy glory, and set forward the salvation of all men; through Jesus Christ our Lord. *Amen.*

For the Increase of the Ministry

O ALMIGHTY God, look mercifully upon the world which thou hast redeemed by the blood of thy dear Son, and incline the hearts of many to dedicate themselves to the sacred ministry of thy Church; through the same thy Son Jesus Christ our Lord. *Amen.*

For Missions

O GOD, who hast made of one blood all nations of men for to dwell on the face of the whole earth, and didst send thy blessed Son to preach peace to them that are far off and to them that are nigh; Grant that all men everywhere may seek after thee and find thee. Bring the nations into thy fold, and add the heathen to thine inheritance. And we pray thee shortly to accomplish the number of thine elect, and to hasten thy kingdom; through the same Jesus Christ our Lord. *Amen.*

Prayers

Prayers in Times of Illness

In Time of Great Sickness and Mortality

ALMIGHTY God, the Lord of life and death, of sickness and health; Regard our supplications, we humbly beseech thee; and, thou hast thought fit to visit us for our sins with great sickness and mortality, in the midst of thy judgment, O Lord, remember mercy. Have pity upon us miserable sinners, and withdraw from us the grievous sickness with which we are afflicted. May this thy fatherly correction have its due influence upon us, by leading us to consider how frail and uncertain our life is; that we may apply our hearts unto that heavenly wisdom which in the end will bring us to everlasting life; through Jesus Christ our Lord. *Amen.*

For a Sick Person

O FATHER of mercies and God of all comfort, our only help in time of need; We humbly beseech thee to behold, visit, and relieve thy sick *servant N.* for whom our prayers are desired. Look upon *him* with the eyes of thy mercy; comfort *him* with a sense of thy goodness; preserve *him* from the temptations of the enemy; and give *him* patience under *his* affliction. In thy good time, restore *him* to health, and enable *him* to lead the residue of *his* life in thy fear, and to thy glory; and grant that finally *he* may dwell with thee in life everlasting; through Jesus Christ our Lord. *Amen.*

Prayers in Times of Other Necessities

For Fruitful Seasons

¶ To be used on Rogation Sunday and the Rogation Days

ALMIGHTY God, who hast blessed the earth that it should be fruitful and bring forth whatsoever is needful for the life of man, and hast commanded us to work with quietness, and eat our own bread; Bless the labours of the husbandman, and grant such seasonable weather that we may gather in the fruits of the earth, and ever rejoice in thy goodness, to the praise of thy holy Name; through Jesus Christ our Lord. *Amen.*

For Rain

O GOD, heavenly Father, who by thy Son Jesus Christ hast promised to all those who seek thy kingdom, and the righteousness thereof, all things necessary to their bodily sustenance; Send us, we beseech thee, in this our necessity, such moderate rain and showers, that we may receive the fruits of the earth to our comfort, and to thy honour; through Jesus Christ our Lord. *Amen.*

Prayers

For Fair Weather

O LORD God, which for the sin of man didst once drown all the world, except eight persons, and afterward of thy great mercy, didst promise never to destroy it so again: We humbly beseech thee, that although we for our iniquities have worthily deserved this plague of rain and waters, yet, upon our true repentance, thou wilt send us such weather whereby we may receive the fruits of the earth in due season, and learn both by the punishment to amend our lives, and by the granting of our petition to give thee praise and glory: Through Jesu Christ our Lord. *Amen.*

For Every Man in his Work

ALMIGHTY God, our heavenly Father, who declarest thy glory and showest forth thy handiwork in the heavens and in the earth; Deliver us, we beseech thee, in our several callings, from the service of mammon, that we may do the work which thou givest us to do, in truth, in beauty, and in righteousness, with singleness of heart as thy servants, and to the benefit of our fellow men; for the sake of him who came among us as one that serveth, thy Son, Jesus Christ our Lord. *Amen.*

For Christian Justice

ALMIGHTY God, who hast created man in thine own image; Grant us grace fearlessly to contend against evil, and to make no peace with oppression; and, that we may reverently use our freedom, help us to employ it in the maintenance of justice among men and nations, to the glory of thy holy Name; through Jesus Christ our Lord. *Amen.*

In Time of Dearth and Famine

O GOD, heavenly Father, whose gift it is that the rain doth fall, and the earth bring forth her increase; Behold, we beseech thee, the afflictions of thy people; increase the fruits of the earth by thy heavenly benediction; and grant that the scarcity and dearth, which we now most justly suffer for our sins, may, through thy goodness, be mercifully turned into plenty; for the love of Jesus Christ our Lord, to whom, with thee and the Holy Ghost, be all honour and glory, now and for ever. *Amen.*

Prayers

In Time of War and Tumults

ALMIGHTY God, King of all kings, and Governor of all things, whose power no creature is able to resist, to whom it belongeth justly to punish sinners, and to be merciful to those who truly repent; Save and deliver us, we humbly beseech thee, from the hands of our enemies; abate their pride, assuage their malice, and confound their devices; that we, being armed with thy defence, may be preserved evermore from all perils, to glorify thee, who art the only giver of all victory; through the merits of thy Son, Jesus Christ our Lord. *Amen.*

For a Person under Affliction

MERCIFUL God, and heavenly Father, who hast taught us in thy holy Word that thou dost not willingly afflict or grieve the children of men; Look with pity, we beseech thee, upon the sorrows of thy *servant* for whom our prayers are offered. Remember *him*, O Lord, in mercy; endue *his* soul with patience; comfort *him* with a sense of thy goodness; lift up thy countenance upon *him*, and give *him* peace; through Jesus Christ our Lord. *Amen.*

For a Person, or Persons, going to Sea

ETERNAL God, who alone spreadest out the heavens, and rulest the raging of the sea; We commend to thy almighty protection, thy *servant*, for whose preservation on the great deep our prayers are desired. Guard *him*, we beseech thee, from the dangers of the sea, from sickness, from the violence of enemies, and from every evil to which *he* may be exposed. Conduct *him* in safety to the haven where *he* would be, with a grateful sense of thy mercies; through Jesus Christ our Lord. *Amen.*

For Prisoners

GOD, who sparest when we deserve punishment, and in thy wrath rememberest mercy; We humbly beseech thee, of thy goodness, to comfort and succour all prisoners (especially those who are condemned to die). Give them a right understanding of themselves, and of thy promises; that, trusting wholly in thy mercy, they may not place their confidence anywhere but in thee. Relieve the distressed, protect the innocent, awaken the guilty; and forasmuch as thou alone bringest light out of darkness, and good out of evil, grant to these thy servants, that by the power of thy Holy Spirit they may be set free from the chains of sin, and may be brought to newness of life; through Jesus Christ our Lord. *Amen.*

Prayers

¶ or this.

MOST gracious and merciful God, we earnestly beseech thee to have pity and compassion upon these persons recommended to our prayers, who now lie under the sentence of the law and are appointed to die. Visit them, O Lord, with thy mercy and salvation convince them of the miserable condition they are in, by their sins and wickedness; and let thy powerful grace produce in them such a godly sorrow, and sincere repentance, as thou wilt be pleased to accept. Give them a strong and lively faith in thy Son, our blessed Saviour and make it effectual to the salvation of their souls. O Lord, in judgment remember mercy and whatever sufferings they are to endure in this world, yet deliver them, O God, from the bitter pains of eternal death. Pardon their sins, and save their souls, for the sake and merits of thy dear Son, our blessed Saviour and Redeemer. *Amen.*

PRAYERS FOR THE DEAD

For All the Faithful Departed

O GOD, the Creator and Redeemer of all the faithful: grant unto the souls of thy servants and handmaids the remission of all their sins; that through devout supplications they may obtain the pardon they have always desired. Who with God the Father in the unity of the Holy Spirit livest and reignest God, world without end. *Amen.*

On the Day of Burial

ABSOLVE, O Lord, we beseech thee, the soul of thy *servant N.*, that being dead to the world *he* may live unto thee: and whatsoever *he* hath done amiss in *his* earthly conversation through frailty of the flesh, do thou wipe away by the pardon of thy merciful goodness. Through.

For a Priest Departed

O GOD, who hast made thy *servant N.* to flourish among the Ministers of Apostolic Succession in the honourable office of a Priest: grant, we beseech thee, that *he* may also be joined with them in a perpetual fellowship. Through.

Another Collect for a Priest Departed

GRANT, we beseech thee, O Lord: that the soul of thy servant the Priest *N.*, whom while dwelling in this world thou didst adorn with holy gifts, may ever rejoice with glory in the heavenly mansions. Through.

Prayers

For a Father and Mother

O GOD, who hast bidden us to honour our father and mother: of thy mercy have compassion on the *souls* of *my father and mother*; forgive *their* sins, and grant that *I* may behold *them* in the joy of eternal brightness. Through.

For Many Deceased

O GOD, whose nature and property is ever to have mercy and to forgive: have compassion on the souls of thy servants and handmaids, and grant them the remission of all their sins; that being delivered from the bonds of mortality, they may be worthy to pass over into life. Through.

Another Collect for Many Deceased

GRANT, we beseech thee, O Lord, to the souls of thy servants and handmaids thy perpetual mercy: and let it profit them in eternity that they hoped and believed in thee. Through.

For a Man Departed

INCLINE thine ear, O Lord, unto our prayers, wherein we humbly entreat thy mercy: that thou wouldest appoint unto the soul of thy servant *N*., which thou hast bidden to depart out of this world, a place in the land of life and peace; and wouldest make him a partaker with thy Saints. Through.

For a Woman Departed

WE beseech thee, O Lord, of thy loving kindness have mercy upon the soul of thine handmaid *N*.: and now that she is released from the contagion of mortality, do thou restore her portion in everlasting salvation. Through.

Through the Year

O GOD, who hast made thy servants to flourish among the Ministers of Apostolic Succession in the honourable offices of Bishopric and Priesthood: grant, we beseech thee, that they may also be joined with them in a perpetual fellowship.

Prayers

¶ *or this.*

O GOD, the Giver of pardon and the Author of man's salvation: we humbly beseech thy mercy to grant that the *brethren*, kinsfolk, and benefactors of our Congregation who have departed out of this world, blessed Mary ever Virgin and all thy Saints praying for them, may attain to the fellowship of everlasting blessedness.

¶ *or this.*

O GOD, the Creator and Redeemer of all the faithful: grant unto the souls of thy servants and handmaids the remission of all their sins; that through devout supplications they may obtain the pardon they have always desired. Who with God the Father, in the unity of the Holy Spirit, livest and reignest God, world without end. *Amen.*

ADDITIONAL COLLECTS

¶ These Collects are said for the conclusion of Antecommunion. They may be said after the Collects of Morning and Evening Prayer, at the discretion of the Minister.

O LORD Jesus Christ, who saidst unto thine Apostles, Peace I leave with you, my peace I give unto you; Regard not our sins, but the faith of thy Church; and grant to it that peace and unity which is according to thy will, who livest and reignest with the Father and the Holy Ghost, one God, world without end. *Amen.*

ASSIST us mercifully, O Lord, in these our supplications and prayers, and dispose the way of thy servants towards the attainment of everlasting salvation; that, among all the changes and chances of this mortal life, they may ever be defended by thy most gracious and ready help; through Jesus Christ our Lord. *Amen.*

GRANT, we beseech thee, Almighty God, that the words which we have heard this day with our outward ears, may, through thy grace, be so grafted inwardly in our hearts, that they may bring forth in us the fruit of good living, to the honour and praise of thy Name; through Jesus Christ our Lord. *Amen.*

DIRECT us, O Lord, in all our doings, with thy most gracious favour, and further us with thy continual help; that in all our works begun, continued, and ended in thee, we may glorify thy holy Name, and finally, by thy mercy, obtain everlasting life; through Jesus Christ our Lord. *Amen.*

Prayers

ALMIGHTY God, the fountain of all wisdom, who knowest our necessities before we ask, and our ignorance in asking; We beseech thee to have compassion upon our infirmities; and those things which for our unworthiness we dare not, and for our blindness we cannot ask, vouchsafe to give us, for the worthiness of thy Son Jesus Christ our Lord. *Amen.*

ALMIGHTY God, who hast promised to hear the petitions of those who ask in thy Son's Name; We beseech thee mercifully to incline thine ears to us who have now made our prayers and supplications unto thee; and grant that those things which we have faithfully asked according to thy will, may effectually be obtained, to the relief of our necessity, and to the setting forth of thy glory; through Jesus Christ our Lord. *Amen.*

A Bidding Prayer

¶ *To be used to preface Sermons, or on Special Occasions.*

AFTER a laudable custom of our Mother holy Church, ye shall kneel down, moving your hearts unto Almighty God, and making your special prayers for the three estates, concerning all Christian people, that is, for the Spirituality, the Temporality, and the souls departed.

FIRST for all archbishops, and bishops, and in special for my Lord Archbishop of *these United States*, your Metropolitan, and also for my Lord Bishop of this *Diocese*, and in general for all parsons, vicars, and parish priests having cure of souls, with the ministers of Christ's Church, as well monastic as not monastic.

SECONDLY, ye shall pray for the unity and peace of all Christian Realms. And for the noble Realm of *America*, and for *the President of these United States*; that Almighty God may send them grace, so to govern and rule the land, that it may be pleasing unto Almighty God, wealth and profit to the land, and salvation to their souls. Also ye shall pray for all those that have honoured the Church with light, lamp, vestment, or bell, or with any other ornaments, by which the service of Almighty God is the better maintained and kept. Furthermore ye shall pray for all true travellers and tillers of the earth, that truly and duly done their duty to God and holy Church, as they be bound to do.

Also ye shall pray for all manner of fruits that be done upon the ground, or shall be that Almighty God of his great pity and mercy may send such weather, that it may come to the sustenance of man. Ye shall pray also for all those that be in debt or deadly sin, that Almighty God may give them grace to come out thereof, and the sooner by our prayer. Also ye shall pray for all those that be sick or diseased, either in body or in soul, that the Almighty would send them

Prayers

the thing that is most profitable as well bodily as ghostly. Also ye shall pray for all pilgrims, and palmers, that have taken the way to Rome, to Saint James of Jerusalem, or to any other place: that Almighty God may give them grace to go safe, and to come safe, and give us grace to have part of their prayers, and they part of ours. Also ye shall pray for the holy Cross, that is in possession and hands of unrightful people; that God Almighty may send it into the hands of Christian people when it pleaseth him. Furthermore I commit unto your devout prayers, all women that be in our ladies' bonds: that Almighty God may send them grace, the child to receive the Sacrament of Baptism, and the mother purification. Also ye shall pray for the good man and woman, that this day giveth bread to make the holy loaf, and for all those that first began it, and them that longest continue. For these and for all true Christian people, every man and woman say the Lord's Prayer and the Angelic Salutation.

¶ The Priest and the People say,

OUR Father, who art in heaven, Hallowed be thy Name. Thy kingdom come. Thy will be done on earth, As it is in heaven. Give us this day our daily bread. And forgive us our trespasses, As we forgive those who trespass against us. And lead us not into temptation; But deliver us from evil: For thine is the kingdom, and the power, and the glory, for ever and ever. Amen.

HAIL Mary, full of grace; The Lord is with thee; Blessed art thou amongst women, And blessed is the fruit of thy womb, Jesus. Holy Mary, Mother of God, Pray for us sinners, now and at the hour of our death. Amen.

¶ The Priest then says,

YE shall make a special prayer for your fathers' souls, for your mothers' souls, godfathers' souls and godmothers' souls, brothers' souls and sisters' souls, and for all your elders' souls, and for all the souls, that ye or I be bound to pray for, and specially for all the souls whose bones are buried in this Church or in this Churchyard, or in any other holy place, and especially for all the souls that bid the great mercy of Almighty God, that God for his great mercy release them of their pain, if it be his blessed will, and that our prayers may sum what stand them in stead; every man and woman of your charity help them with the Lord's Prayer and the Angelic Salutation.

¶ The Priest and the People then conclude the Bidding of the Bedes by saying the Lord's Prayer and Angelic Salutation once more.

Thanksgivings

A Thanksgiving to Almighty God for the Fruits of the Earth and all the other Blessings of his merciful Providence

Most gracious God, by whose knowledge the depths are broken up, and the clouds drop down the dew; We yield thee unfeigned thanks and praise for the return of seed-time and harvest, for the increase of the ground and the gathering in of the fruits thereof, and for all the other blessings of thy merciful providence bestowed upon this nation and people. And, we beseech thee, give us a just sense of these great mercies; such as may appear in our lives by an humble, holy, and obedient walking before thee all our days; through Jesus Christ our Lord, to whom, with thee and the Holy Ghost, be all glory and honour, world without end. *Amen.*

The Thanksgiving of Women after Child-birth

¶ To be said when any Woman, being present in Church, shall have desired to return thanks to Almighty God for her safe deliverance.

O almighty God, we give thee humble thanks for that thou hast been graciously pleased to preserve, through the great pain and peril of childbirth, this woman, thy handmaid, who desireth now to offer her praises and thanksgivings unto thee. Grant, we beseech thee, most merciful Father, that she, through thy help, may both faithfully live and walk according to thy will in this life present, and also may be partaker of everlasting glory in the life to come; through Jesus Christ our Lord. *Amen.*

For Rain

O God, our heavenly Father, by whose gracious providence the former and the latter rain descend upon the earth, that it may bring forth fruit for the use of man; We give thee humble thanks that it hath pleased thee to send us rain to our great comfort, and to the glory of thy holy Name; through Jesus Christ our Lord. *Amen.*

Thanksgivings

For Fair Weather

LORD God, who hast justly humbled us by thy late visitation of us with immoderate rain and waters, and in thy mercy hast relieved and comforted our souls by this seasonable and blessed change of weather; We praise and glorify thy holy Name for this thy mercy, and will always declare thy loving-kindness from generation to generation; through Jesus Christ our Lord. *Amen.*

For Peace, and Deliverance from our Enemies

ALMIGHTY God, who art a strong tower of defence unto thy servants against the face of their enemies; We yield thee praise and thanksgiving for our deliverance from those great and apparent dangers wherewith we were compassed. We acknowledge in thy goodness that we were not delivered over as a prey unto them; beseeching thee still to continue such thy mercies towards us, that all the world may know that thou art our Saviour and mighty Deliverer; through Jesus Christ our Lord. *Amen.*

For Restoring Public Peace at Home

ETERNAL God, our heavenly Father, who alone makest men to be of one mind in a house, and stillest the outrage of a violent and unruly people; We bless thy holy Name, that it hath pleased thee to appease the seditious tumults which have been lately raised up amongst us; most humbly beseeching thee to grant to all of us grace, that we may henceforth obediently walk in thy holy commandments; and, leading a quiet and peaceable life in all godliness and honesty, may continually offer unto thee our sacrifice of praise and thanksgiving for these thy mercies towards us; through Jesus Christ our Lord. *Amen.*

For Deliverance from great Sickness and Mortality

LORD God, who hast wounded us for our sins, and consumed us for our transgressions, by thy late heavy and dreadful visitation and now, in the midst of judgment remembering mercy, hast redeemed our souls from the jaws of death; We offer unto thy fatherly goodness ourselves, our souls and bodies which thou hast delivered, to be a living sacrifice unto thee, always praising and magnifying thy mercies in the midst of thy Church; through Jesus Christ our Lord. *Amen.*

Thanksgivings

For Recovery from Sickness

O GOD, who art the giver of life, of health, and of safety; We bless thy Name, that thou hast been pleased to deliver from *his* bodily sickness this thy *servant*, who now desireth to return thanks unto thee, in the presence of all thy people. Gracious art thou, O Lord, and full of compassion to the children of men. May *his* heart be duly impressed with a sense of thy merciful goodness, and may *he* devote the residue of *his* days to an humble, holy, and obedient walking before thee; through Jesus Christ our Lord. *Amen.*

For a Child's Recovery from Sickness

ALMIGHTY God and heavenly Father, we give thee humble thanks for that thou hast been graciously pleased to deliver from *his* bodily sickness the child in whose behalf we bless and praise thy Name, in the presence of all thy people. Grant, we beseech thee, O gracious Father, that *he*, through thy help, may both faithfully live in this world according to thy will, and also may be partaker of everlasting glory in the life to come; through Jesus Christ our Lord. *Amen.*

For a Safe Return from a Journey

MOST gracious Lord, whose mercy is over all thy works; We praise thy holy Name that thou hast been pleased to conduct in safety, through the perils of the great deep, (*his* way,) this thy *servant*, who now desireth to return *his* thanks unto thee in thy holy Church. May *he* be duly sensible of thy merciful providence towards *him*, and ever express *his* thankfulness by a holy trust in thee, and obedience to thy laws; through Jesus Christ our Lord. *Amen.*

Litanies & Offices of the Church

Litanies & Offices

Great Litany

⁋ To be used after the Third Collect at Morning or Evening Prayer; or before the Holy Communion; or separately.

GOD the Father, Creator of heaven and earth;
℟. Have mercy upon us.
O God the Son, Redeemer of the world;
℟. Have mercy upon us.
O God the Holy Ghost, Sanctifier of the faithful;
℟. Have mercy upon us.
O holy, blessed, and glorious Trinity, one God;
℟. Have mercy upon us.

HOLY Virgin Mary, Mother of God our Saviour Jesu Christ,
℟. Pray for us.
All holy Angels and Archangels, and all holy orders of blessed spirits.
℟. Pray for us.
All holy Patriarchs and Prophets, Apostles, Martyrs, Confessors and Virgins, and all the blessed company of heaven.
℟. Pray for us.

EMEMBER not, Lord, our offences, nor the offences of our forefathers; neither take thou vengeance of our sins: Spare us, good Lord, spare thy people, whom thou hast redeemed with thy most precious blood, and be not angry with us for ever.
℟. Spare us, good Lord.

From all evil and mischief; from sin; from the crafts and assaults of the devil; from thy wrath, and from everlasting damnation;
℟. Good Lord, deliver us.

From all blindness of heart; from pride, vainglory, and hypocrisy; from envy, hatred, and malice, and all uncharitableness.
℟. Good Lord, deliver us.

From all inordinate and sinful affections; and from all the deceits of the world, the flesh, and the devil,
℟. Good Lord, deliver us.

From lightning and tempest; from earthquake, fire, and flood; from plague, pestilence, and famine; from battle and murder, and from sudden death,
℟. Good Lord, deliver us.

From all sedition, privy conspiracy, and rebellion; from all false doctrine, heresy, and schism; from hardness of heart, and contempt of thy Word and Commandment,
℟. Good Lord, deliver us.

By the mystery of thy holy Incarnation; by thy holy Nativity and Circumcision; by thy Baptism, Fasting, and Temptation,
℞. Good Lord, deliver us.
By thine Agony and Bloody Sweat; by thy Cross and Passion; by thy precious Death and Burial; by thy glorious Resurrection and Ascension; and by the Coming of the Holy Ghost,
℞. Good Lord, deliver us.
In all time of our tribulation; in all time of our prosperity; in the hour of death, and in the day of judgment,
℞. Good Lord, deliver us.

E sinners do beseech thee to hear us, O Lord God; and that it may please thee to rule and govern thy holy Church universal in the right way;
℞. We beseech thee to hear us, good Lord.

¶ *In the United States and its territories, the following is said,*

That it may please thee so to rule the heart of thy servant, The President of the United States, that he may above all things seek thy honour and glory;
℞. We beseech thee to hear us, good Lord.

¶ *In the British Commonwealth, the following is said,*

That it may please thee to keep and strengthen in the true worshipping of thee, in righteousness and holiness of life, thy servant *CHARLES*, our most gracious King and Governor,
℞. We beseech thee to hear us, good Lord.
That it may please thee to rule his heart in thy faith, fear, and love, and that he may evermore have affiance in thee, and ever seek thy honour and glory,
℞. We beseech thee to hear us, good Lord.
That it may please thee to be his defender and keeper, giving him the victory over all his enemies,
℞. We beseech thee to hear us, good Lord.
That it may please thee to bless and preserve Queen *Camilla*, *William* Prince of Wales, the Princess of Wales, and all the Royal Family;
℞. We beseech thee to hear us, good Lord.

That it may please thee to bless and preserve all Christian Rulers and Magistrates; giving them grace to execute justice, and to maintain truth;
℞. We beseech thee to hear us, good Lord.

Great Litany — Litanies & Offices

That it may please thee to bless and illuminate all Bishops, Priests, and Deacons, with true knowledge and understanding of thy Word; and that both by their preaching and living they may set it forth, and show it accordingly;
℟. We beseech thee to hear us, good Lord.

That it may please thee to send forth labourers into thy harvest;
℟. We beseech thee to hear us, good Lord.

That it may please thee to bless and keep all thy people;
℟. We beseech thee to hear us, good Lord.

That it may please thee to give to all nations unity, peace, and concord;
℟. We beseech thee to hear us, good Lord.

That it may please thee to give us an heart to love and fear thee, and diligently to live after thy commandments;
℟. We beseech thee to hear us, good Lord.

That it may please thee to give to all thy people increase of grace to hear meekly thy Word, and to receive it with pure affection, and to bring forth the fruits of the Spirit:
℟. We beseech thee to hear us, good Lord.

That it may please thee to bring into the way of truth all such as have erred, and are deceived;
℟. We beseech thee to hear us, good Lord.

That it may please thee to strengthen such as do stand; and to comfort and help the weak-hearted; and to raise up those who fall; and finally to beat down Satan under our feet;
℟. We beseech thee to hear us, good Lord.

That it may please thee to succour, help, and comfort, all who are in danger, necessity, and tribulation;
℟. We beseech thee to hear us, good Lord.

That it may please thee to preserve all who travel by land, by water, or by air, all women in child-birth, all sick persons, and young children; and to show thy pity upon all prisoners and captives;
℟. We beseech thee to hear us, good Lord.

That it may please thee to defend, and provide for, the fatherless children, and widows, and all who are desolate and oppressed;
℟. We beseech thee to hear us, good Lord.

That it may please thee to have mercy upon all men;
℟. We beseech thee to hear us, good Lord.

That it may please thee to forgive our enemies, persecutors, and slanderers, and to turn their hearts;
℟. We beseech thee to hear us, good Lord.

Litanies & Offices *Great Litany*

That it may please thee to give and preserve to our use the kindly fruits of the earth, so that in due time we may enjoy them;

℟. We beseech thee to hear us, good Lord.

That it may please thee to give us true repentance; to forgive us all our sins, negligences, and ignorances; and to endue us with the grace of thy Holy Spirit to amend our lives according to thy Holy Word;

℟. We beseech thee to hear us, good Lord.

Son of God, we beseech thee to hear us.

℟. Son of God, we beseech thee to hear us.

O Lamb of God, who takest away the sins of the world;

℟. Grant us thy peace.

O Lamb of God, who takest away the sins of the world;

℟. Have mercy upon us.

O Christ, hear us.

℟. O Christ, hear us.

Lord, have mercy upon us.

℟. Lord, have mercy upon us.

Christ, have mercy upon us.

℟. Christ, have mercy upon us.

Lord, have mercy upon us.

℟. Lord, have mercy upon us.

¶ Then shall the Minister, and the People with him, say the Lord's Prayer.

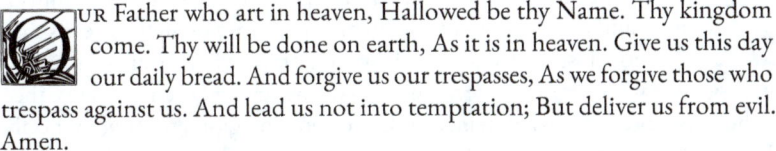OUR Father who art in heaven, Hallowed be thy Name. Thy kingdom come. Thy will be done on earth, As it is in heaven. Give us this day our daily bread. And forgive us our trespasses, As we forgive those who trespass against us. And lead us not into temptation; But deliver us from evil. Amen.

¶ The Minister may, at his discretion, omit all that followeth, to the Prayer, We humbly beseech thee, O Father, etc.

℣. O Lord, deal not with us according to our sins.

℟. Neither reward us according to our iniquities.

℣. Let us pray.

O GOD, merciful Father, who despisest not the sighing of a contrite heart, nor the desire of such as are sorrowful; Mercifully assist our prayers which we make before thee in all our troubles and adversities, whensoever they oppress us; and graciously hear us, that those evils which the craft and subtilty of the devil or man worketh against us, may, by thy good providence, be brought to nought; that we thy servants, being hurt by no persecutions, may

Great Litany   **Litanies & Offices**

evermore give thanks unto thee in thy holy Church; through Jesus Christ our Lord.

℟. O Lord, arise, help us, and deliver us, for thy Name's sake.

GOD, we have heard with our ears, and our fathers have declared unto us, the noble works that thou didst in their days, and in the old time before them.

℟. O Lord, arise, help us, and deliver us, for thine honour.

℣. Glory be to the Father, and to the Son, and to the Holy Ghost;

℟. As it was in the beginning, is now, and ever shall be, world without end. Amen.

℣. From our enemies defend us, O Christ.

℟. Graciously look upon our afflictions.

℣. With pity behold the sorrows of our hearts.

℟. Mercifully forgive the sins of thy people.

℣. Favourably with mercy hear our prayers.

℟. O Son of David, have mercy upon us.

℣. Both now and ever vouchsafe to hear us, O Christ.

℟. Graciously hear us, O Christ; graciously hear us, O Lord Christ.

℣. O Lord, let thy mercy be showed upon us;

℟. As we do put our trust in thee.

℣. Let us pray.

———————

WE humbly beseech thee, O Father, mercifully to look upon our infirmities; and for the glory of thy Name, turn from us all those evils that we most justly have deserved; and grant, that in all our troubles we may put our whole trust and confidence in thy mercy, and evermore serve thee in holiness and pureness of living, to thy honour and glory; through our only Mediator and Advocate, Jesus Christ our Lord. *Amen.*

¶ The Minister may end the Litany here, or at his discretion add other Prayers from this Book.

Litanies & Offices *Penitential Office*

A Penitential Office

¶ On the First Day of Lent, the Penitential Office is read immediately after the Great Litany during Morning Prayer. It may also be used during Evening Prayer or as a separate Office.
¶ The Penitential Office may be read at other times, at the discretion of the Minister.
¶ The Minister and the People kneeling, then shall be said by them this Psalm following.

Psalm 51. *Miserere mei, Deus*

Have mercy upon me, O God, after thy great goodness : according to the multitude of thy mercies do away mine offences.
2 Wash me throughly from my wickedness : and cleanse me from my sin.
3 For I acknowledge my faults : and my sin is ever before me.
4 Against thee only have I sinned, and done this evil in thy sight : that thou mightest be justified in thy saying, and clear when thou art judged.
5 Behold, I was shapen in wickedness : and in sin hath my mother conceived me.
6 But lo, thou requirest truth in the inward parts : and shalt make me to understand wisdom secretly.
7 Thou shalt purge me with hyssop, and I shall be clean : thou shalt wash me, and I shall be whiter than snow.
8 Thou shalt make me hear of joy and gladness : that the bones which thou hast broken may rejoice.
9 Turn thy face from my sins : and put out all my misdeeds.
10 Make me a clean heart, O God : and renew a right spirit within me.
11 Cast me not away from thy presence : and take not thy holy Spirit from me.
12 O give me the comfort of thy help again : and stablish me with thy free Spirit.
13 Then shall I teach thy ways unto the wicked : and sinners shall be converted unto thee.
14 Deliver me from blood-guiltiness, O God, thou that art the God of my health : and my tongue shall sing of thy righteousness.
15 Thou shalt open my lips, O Lord : and my mouth shall shew thy praise.
16 For thou desirest no sacrifice, else would I give it thee : but thou delightest not in burnt-offerings.
17 The sacrifice of God is a troubled spirit : a broken and contrite heart, O God, shalt thou not despise.
18 O be favourable and gracious unto Sion : build thou the walls of Jerusalem.

Penitential Office   # Litanies & Offices

19 Then shalt thou be pleased with the sacrifice of righteousness, with the burnt-offerings and oblations : then shall they offer young bullocks upon thine altar.

℣. Glory be to the Father, and to the Son, and to the Holy Ghost.

℟. As it was in the beginning, is now, and ever shall be, world without end. Amen.

¶ *If the Litany hath been already said, the Minister may pass at once to* O Lord, save thy servants; *etc.*

℣. Lord, have mercy upon us.
℟. Christ, have mercy upon us.
℣. Lord, have mercy upon us.

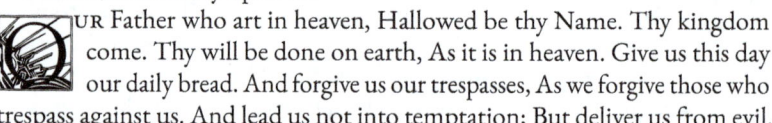OUR Father who art in heaven, Hallowed be thy Name. Thy kingdom come. Thy will be done on earth, As it is in heaven. Give us this day our daily bread. And forgive us our trespasses, As we forgive those who trespass against us. And lead us not into temptation; But deliver us from evil. Amen.

℣. O Lord, save thy servants;
℟. That put their trust in thee.
℣. Send unto them help from above.
℟. And evermore mightily defend them.
℣. Help us, O God our Saviour.
℟. And for the glory of thy Name deliver us; be merciful to us sinners, for thy Name's sake.
℣. O Lord, hear our prayer.
℟. And let our cry come unto thee.

Let us pray.

O LORD, we beseech thee, mercifully hear our prayers, and spare all those who confess their sins unto thee; that they, whose consciences by sin are accused, by thy merciful pardon may be absolved; through Christ our Lord. *Amen.*

O MOST mighty God, and merciful Father, who hast compassion upon all men, and who wouldest not the death of a sinner, but rather that he should turn from his sin, and be saved; Mercifully forgive us our trespasses; receive and comfort us, who are grieved and wearied with the burden of our sins. Thy property is always to have mercy; to thee only it appertaineth to forgive sins. Spare us therefore, good Lord, spare thy people, whom thou hast redeemed; enter not into judgment with thy servants; but so turn thine anger

Litanies & Offices — *Penitential Office*

from us, who meekly acknowledge our transgressions, and truly repent us of our faults, and so make haste to help us in this world, that we may ever live with thee in the world to come; through Jesus Christ our Lord. *Amen.*

¶ Then shall the People say this that followeth, with the Minister.

TURN thou us, O good Lord, and so shall we be turned. Be favourable, O Lord, Be favourable to thy people, Who turn to thee in weeping, fasting, and praying. For thou art a merciful God, Full of compassion, Long-suffering, and of great pity. Thou sparest when we deserve punishment, And in thy wrath thinkest upon mercy. Spare thy people, good Lord, spare them, And let not thine heritage be brought to confusion. Hear us, O Lord, for thy mercy is great, And after the multitude of thy mercies look upon us; Through the merits and mediation of thy blessed Son, Jesus Christ our Lord. *Amen.*

¶ Then the Minister shall say,

O GOD, whose nature and property is ever to have mercy and to forgive; Receive our humble petitions; and though we be tied and bound with the chain of our sins, yet let the pitifulness of thy great mercy loose us; for the honour of Jesus Christ, our Mediator and Advocate. *Amen.*

THE Lord bless us, and keep us. The Lord make his face to shine upon us, and be gracious unto us. The Lord lift up his countenance upon us, and give us peace, both now and evermore. *Amen.*

Baptismal Blessing   # Litanies & Offices

Blessing of Baptismal Waters

❡ The baptismal container being washed and cleaned, it is filled with clean water. The Priest and his clerics (or other Priests) proceed—with a Cross, two candles, and a thurible with incense—and with salt and the phials of Sacred Chrism & the Oil of Catechumens placed nearby, they approach the Font where he says the Litany of Saints (p. 98) after the Seven Penitential Psalms (Psalms 6, 32, 38, 51, 102, 130, & 143).

NOTE, The Priest may instead say the shorter Litany from Holy Saturday in the Prayer Book Hymnal.

❡ Before the That thou wouldest vouchsafe (Ut nos exáudire dignéris,) is said and then repeated: That thou wouldest vouchsafe to ✠ bless and ✠ consecrate this Font for the regeneration unto thee of new offspring. ℟. We beseech thee to hear us. (Ut Fontem istum ad regenerándam tibi novam prolem bene ✠ dícere, et conse ✠ cráre dignéris. ℟. Te rogámus, audi nos.)

❡ After the final Kyrie, eléison, the Priest says the Lord's Prayer (as noted) and the Apostles' Creed, all in a clear voice. He then proceeds with the following.

℣. With thee, O Lord, is the well of life.

℟. And in thy light shall we see light.

℣. O Lord, hear my prayer.

℟. And let my cry come unto thee.

℣. The Lord be with you.

℟. And with thy spirit.

Let us pray.

LMIGHTY and everlasting God, be present at the mysteries, be present at the sacraments of thy great goodness: and send forth the spirit of adoption for the regeneration of the new peoples whom the Font of Baptism doth bring forth unto thee: that what is to be done by our humble ministry, may be effectually fulfilled by thy power. Through.

℟. Amen.

℣. Apud te, Dómine, est fons vitæ.

℟. Et in lúmine tuo vidébimus lumen.

℣. Dómine, exáudi oratiónem meam.

℟. Et clamor meus ad te véniat.

℣. Dóminus vobíscum.

℟. Et cum spíritu tuo.

Orémus.

MNÍPOTENS sempitérne Deus, adésto magnæ pietátis tuæ mystériis, adésto sacraméntis: et ad recreándos novos pópulos, quos tibi fons Baptísmatis párturit, spíritum adoptiónis emítte; ut, quod nostræ humilitátis geréndum est ministério, virtútis tuæ impleátur efféctu. Per Dóminum nostrum.

℟. Amen.

Litanies & Offices *Baptismal Blessing*

Exorcism of Water

I EXORCISE thee, O creature of water, by the living ✠ God, by the true ✠ God, by the holy ✠ God, by God, who in the beginning through his Word divided thee form the dry land: whose Spirit moved upon thee, who commanded thee to flow from paradise.

EXORCÍZO te, creatúra aquæ, per Deum ✠ vivum, per Deum ✠ verum, per Deum ✠ sanctum, per Deum, qui te in princípio verbo separávit ab árida: cujus Spíritus super te ferebátur, qui te de paradíso manáre jussit.

❦ *The Priest divides the waters with his hand and then scatters it beyond the edge of the Font, towards the four quarters of the world, proceeding with the following.*

And commanded thee to water the whole earth with thy four rivers, Who in the desert by wood bestowed upon thee sweetness when thou wast bitter, that men might drink. Who brought thee forth from the rock, that he might refresh the people, wearied with thirst, whom he had delivered out of Egypt. I exorcise thee through Jesus Christ, his only Son, our Lord: who in Cana of Galilee by a wondrous miracle did change thee through his power into wine: who walked upon thee with his feet, and was baptized in thee by John in Jordan. Who brought thee forth together with blood from his wide: and commanded his disciples, that they should baptize in thee them that believe, saying: Go ye, teach all nations, baptizing them in the Name of the Father, and of the Son, and of the Holy Ghost, that thou mayest be made holy water, blessed water, water that washeth away stains and cleanseth sins. I command thee therefore, every unclean spirit, every phantom, every lie, be rooted out, and flee away from this creature of water; that to them who

Et in quátuor flumínibus totam terram rigáre præcépit: qui te in desérto amáram per lignum, dulcem fecit atque potábilem; qui te de petra prodúxit, ut pópulum, quem ex Ægýpto liberáverat, siti fatigátum recreáret. Exorcízo te per Jesum Christum, Fílium ejus únicum, Dóminum nostrum: qui te in Cana Galilǽæ signo admirábili sua poténtia convértit in vinum: qui super te pédibus ambulávit, et a Joánne in Jordáne in te baptizátus est. Qui te una cum sánguine de látere suo prodúxit: et discípulis suis jussit, ut credéntes baptizárent in te, dicens: Ite, docéte omnes gentes, baptizántes eos in nómine Patris, et Fílii, et Spíritus Sancti; ut efficiáris aqua sancta, aqua benedícta, aqua, quæ lavat sordes, et mundat peccáta. Tibi ígitur præcípio, omnis spíritus immúnde, omne phantásma, omne mendácium, eradicáre, et effugáre ab hac creatúra aquæ, ut qui in ipsa baptizándi erunt, fiat eis fons aquæ saliéntis in vitam ætérnam, regénerans eos Deo Patri, et Fílio, et Spírítui Sancto, in nómine ejúsdem Dómini nostri Jesu Christi, qui ventúrus est judicá-

Baptismal Blessing   **Litanies & Offices**

shall be baptized therein, it may become a Font of water springing up unto life eternal, regenerating them unto God the Father, and the Son, and the Holy Ghost, in the Name of the same our Lord Jesus Christ, who shall come to judge the living and the dead, and the world by fire. *Amen.*

Let us pray.

LORD holy, Father almighty, everlasting God, who dost sanctify spiritual waters, we humbly entreat thee: that thou wouldest vouchsafe to look upon this ministry of our humble service, and to send forth upon these waters, made ready for the washing and purifying of men, the Angel of holiness; to the end that, the sins of their former life being washed, and their guilt cleansed, they being regenerate may be worthy to be made a spotless habitation for the Holy Spirit. Through.

℟. Amen.

re vivos et mórtuos, et sǽculum per ignem. *Amen.*

Orémus.

ÓMINE sancte, Pater omnípotens, ætérne Deus, aquárum spirituálium sanctificátor, te supplíciter deprecámur: ut ad hoc ministérium humilitátis nostræ respícere dignéris, et super has aquas, abluéndis et purificándis homínibus præparátas, Angelum sanctitátis emíttas, quo, peccátis vitæ prióris ablútis, reatúque detérso, purum Sancto Spirítui habitáculum regeneráti éffici mereántur. Per Dóminum nostrum.

℟. Amen.

¶ The Priest breathes thrice into the water in the form of a Ψ. Then he places incense in the thurible, blesses it, and censes the Font with three simple swings. He then pours some of the Oil of Catechumens into the water in the form of Cross saying in a clear voice,

AY this Font be sanctified and made fruitful by the Oil of salvation, for such as shall be born again therefrom unto life eternal, in the Name of the ✠ Father, and of the ✠ Son, and of the Holy ✠ Ghost. *Amen.*

ANCTIFICÉTUR, et fecundétur fons iste óleo salútis renascéntibus ex eo in vitam ætérnam, in nómine Pa ✠ tris, et Fí ✠ lii, et Spíritus ✠ Sancti. *Amen.*

Litanies & Offices *Baptismal Blessing*

❡ The Priest then pours in some of the Sacred Chrism in the same mode, saying the following.

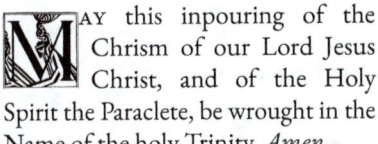AY this inpouring of the Chrism of our Lord Jesus Christ, and of the Holy Spirit the Paraclete, be wrought in the Name of the holy Trinity. *Amen.*

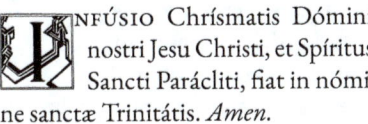NFÚSIO Chrísmatis Dómini nostri Jesu Christi, et Spíritus Sancti Parácliti, fiat in nómine sanctæ Trinitátis. *Amen.*

❡ The Priest then receives both vessels for the Sacred Chrism and the Oil of Catechumens and pours them both in the form of a Cross, saying the following.

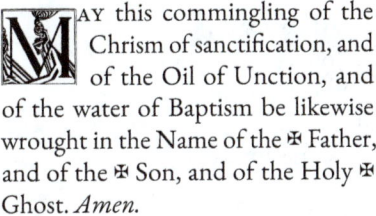AY this commingling of the Chrism of sanctification, and of the Oil of Unction, and of the water of Baptism be likewise wrought in the Name of the ✠ Father, and of the ✠ Son, and of the Holy ✠ Ghost. *Amen.*

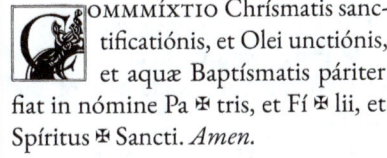OMMMÍXTIO Chrísmatis sanctificatiónis, et Olei unctiónis, et aquæ Baptísmatis páriter fiat in nómine Pa ✠ tris, et Fí ✠ lii, et Spíritus ✠ Sancti. *Amen.*

❡ Then setting down the phials, with his right hand he mingles the holy Oil and the infused Chrism with the Water, and scatters it over the whole Font. Then he wipes his hand with crumbs of bread. And if there are those to be baptised, he baptises them, changing his vestments from violet to white. But if he baptises noöne, then he washes his hands and pours the ablution into the sacrarium.

Litanies & Offices

Litany of Saints

Lord, have mercy upon us.
℟. Lord, have mercy upon us.
Christ, have mercy upon us.
℟. Christ, have mercy upon us.
Lord, have mercy upon us.
℟. Lord, have mercy upon us.
O Christ hear us.
℟. O Christ graciously hear us.
O God the Father of heaven,
℟. Have mercy upon us.
O God the Son, Redeemer of the world,
℟. Have mercy upon us.
O God the Holy Ghost,
℟. Have mercy upon us.
Holy Trinity one God,
℟. Have mercy upon us.
Holy Mary,
℟. Pray for us.
Holy Mother of God,
℟. Pray for us.
Holy Virgin of virgins,
℟. Pray for us.
Holy Michael,
℟. Pray for us.
Holy Gabriel,
℟. Pray for us.
Holy Raphael,
℟. Pray for us.
All ye holy Angels and Archangels,
℟. Pray for us.
All ye holy orders of blessed Spirits,
℟. Pray for us.
St. John Baptist,
℟. Pray for us.
St. Joseph,
℟. Pray for us.
All ye holy Patriarchs and Prophets,
℟. Pray for us.
St. Peter,
℟. Pray for us.
St. Paul,
℟. Pray for us.
St. Andrew,
℟. Pray for us.
St. James,
℟. Pray for us.
St. John,
℟. Pray for us.
St. Thomas,
℟. Pray for us.
St. James,
℟. Pray for us.
St. Philip,
℟. Pray for us.
St. Bartholomew,
℟. Pray for us.
St. Matthew,
℟. Pray for us.
St. Simon,
℟. Pray for us.
St. Jude,
℟. Pray for us.
St. Matthias,
℟. Pray for us.
St. Barnabas,
℟. Pray for us.
St. Luke,
℟. Pray for us.
St. Mark,
℟. Pray for us.
All ye holy Apostles and Evangelists,
℟. Pray for us.
All ye holy Disciples of the Lord,
℟. Pray for us.
All ye holy Innocents,

Litanies & Offices *Litany of Saints*

℟. Pray for us.
St. Stephen,
℟. Pray for us.
St. Lawrence,
℟. Pray for us.
St. Vincent,
℟. Pray for us.
St. Fabian and St. Sebastian,
℟. Pray for us.
St. John and St. Paul,
℟. Pray for us.
St. Cosmas and Damien,
℟. Pray for us.
St. Gervase and St. Protase,
℟. Pray for us.
All ye holy Martyrs,
℟. Pray for us.
St. Sylvester,
℟. Pray for us.
St. Gregory,
℟. Pray for us.
St. Ambrose,
℟. Pray for us.
St. Augustine,
℟. Pray for us.
St. Jerome,
℟. Pray for us.
St. Martin,
℟. Pray for us.
St. Nicholas,
℟. Pray for us.
All ye holy Bishops and Confessors,
℟. Pray for us.
All ye holy Doctors,
℟. Pray for us.
Holy St. Anthony,
℟. Pray for us.
Holy St. Benedict,
℟. Pray for us.
All ye holy Priests and Levites,
℟. Pray for us.
All ye holy Monks and Hermits,
℟. Pray for us.
St. Mary Magdalene,
℟. Pray for us.
St. Agatha,
℟. Pray for us.
St. Lucy,
℟. Pray for us.
St. Agnes,
℟. Pray for us.
St. Cecilia,
℟. Pray for us.
St. Catherine,
℟. Pray for us.
St. Anastasia,
℟. Pray for us.
All ye holy Virgins and Widows,
℟. Pray for us.
All ye Saints of God,
℟. Intercede for us.
Be thou merciful,
℟. Spare us, O Lord.
Be thou merciful,
℟. Hear us, O Lord.
From all evil,
℟. Deliver us, O Lord.
From all sin,
℟. Deliver us, O Lord.
From thy wrath,
℟. Deliver us, O Lord.
From sudden and unprepared death,
℟. Deliver us, O Lord.
From the crafts of the devil,
℟. Deliver us, O Lord.
From anger, hatred, and all uncharitableness,
℟. Deliver us, O Lord.
From the spirit of fornication,
℟. Deliver us, O Lord.

From lightning and tempest,
℞. Deliver us, O Lord.
From the scourge of earthquake,
℞. Deliver us, O Lord.
From pestilence, famine, and war,
℞. Deliver us, O Lord.
From everlasting death,
℞. Deliver us, O Lord.
By the mystery of thy holy Incarnation,
℞. Deliver us, O Lord.
By thine advent,
℞. Deliver us, O Lord.
By thy nativity,
℞. Deliver us, O Lord.
By thy baptism and holy fasting,
℞. Deliver us, O Lord.
By thy cross and passion,
℞. Deliver us, O Lord.
By thy death and burial,
℞. Deliver us, O Lord.
By thy holy resurrection,
℞. Deliver us, O Lord.
By thy wonderful ascension,
℞. Deliver us, O Lord.
By the coming of the Holy Ghost the Paraclete,
℞. Deliver us, O Lord.
In the day of judgment,
℞. Deliver us, O Lord.
We sinners,
℞. Beseech thee, hear us.
That thou wouldest spare us,
℞. We beseech thee, hear us.
That thou wouldest vouchsafe to bring us to true repentance,
℞. We beseech thee, hear us.
That thou wouldest vouchsafe to govern and preserve thy holy Church,
℞. We beseech thee, hear us.
That thou wouldest vouchsafe to preserve our Apostolic lord and all orders of the Church in holy religion,
℞. We beseech thee, hear us.
That thou wouldest vouchsafe to humble the enemies of holy Church,
℞. We beseech thee, hear us.
That thou wouldest vouchsafe to give unto Christian kings and rulers peace and true concord,
℞. We beseech thee, hear us.
That thou wouldest vouchsafe to grant to all the Christian people peace and unity,
℞. We beseech thee, hear us.
That thou wouldest vouchsafe to recall such as do err into the unity of the Church, and to bring all heathen unto the light of the gospel,
℞. We beseech thee, hear us.
That thou wouldest vouchsafe to strengthen, and preserve us in thy holy service,
℞. We beseech thee, hear us.
That thou wouldest vouchsafe to lift up our minds unto heavenly desires,
℞. We beseech thee, hear us.
That thou wouldest vouchsafe to reward all our benefactors with everlasting blessings,
℞. We beseech thee, hear us.
That thou wouldest vouchsafe to deliver our souls, and the souls of our brethren, kinsfolk, and benefactors, from eternal damnation,
℞. We beseech thee, hear us.
That thou wouldest vouchsafe to give and preserve the fruits of the earth,
℞. We beseech thee, hear us.

Litanies & Offices — *Litany of Saints*

That thou wouldest vouchsafe to grant unto all the faithful departed ✠ rest eternal,
℟. We beseech thee, hear us.
That thou wouldest vouchsafe graciously to hear us,
℟. We beseech thee, hear us.
Son of God,
℟. We beseech thee, hear us.
O Lamb of God, who takest away the sins of the world,
℟. Spare us, O Lord, hear us.

O Lamb of God, who takest away the sins of the world,
℟. Graciously hear us, O Lord.
O Lamb of God, who takest away the sins of the world,
℟. Have mercy upon us.
O Christ, hear us.
℟. O Christ, graciously hear us.
Lord, have mercy upon us.
℟. Christ, have mercy upon us.
Lord, have mercy upon us.

¶ *The Lord's Prayer is here said until,*

℣. And lead us not into temptation,
℟. But deliver us from evil.

Psalm 70. *Deus, in adjutorium*

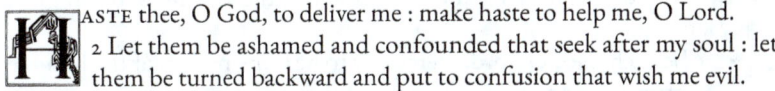
Haste thee, O God, to deliver me : make haste to help me, O Lord.

2 Let them be ashamed and confounded that seek after my soul : let them be turned backward and put to confusion that wish me evil.

3 Let them for their reward be soon brought to shame : that cry over me, There, there.

4 But let all those that seek thee be joyful and glad in thee : and let all such as delight in thy salvation say alway, The Lord be praised.

5 As for me, I am poor and in misery : haste thee unto me, O God.

6 Thou art my helper and my redeemer : O Lord, make no long tarrying.

℣. Glory be to the Father, and to the Son, and to the Holy Ghost.
℟. As it was in the beginning, is now, and ever shall be, world without end. Amen.

℣. Save thy servants.
℟. My God, who put their trust in thee.
℣. Be unto us, O Lord, a strong tower.
℟. From the face of the enemy.
℣. Let the enemy have no advantage over us.
℟. Nor the son of wickedness approach to hurt us.
℣. O Lord, deal not with us after our sins.
℟. Neither reward us after our iniquities.
℣. Let us pray for our *Bishop, N.*
℟. The Lord preserve him and keep

him alive, and make him blessed upon earth, and deliver him not into the hands of his enemies.

℣. Let us pray for our benefactors.

℟. Vouchsafe, O Lord, to reward with eternal life all them that do us good for thy name's sake. Amen.

℣. Let us pray for the faithful departed.

℟. Rest eternal grant unto them, O Lord, and let light perpetual shine upon them.

℣. May they rest in peace.

℟. Amen.

℣. For our absent brethren.

℟. My God, save thy servants who put their trust in thee.

℣. O Lord, send them help from thy holy place.

℟. And strengthen them out of Sion.

℣. O Lord, hear my prayer.

℟. And let my prayer come unto thee.

℣. The Lord be with you.

℟. And with thy spirit.

℣. Let us pray.

Collects

GOD, whose nature and property is ever to have mercy and to forgive: receive our humble petitions; and though we and all thy servants be bound with the chain of our sins, yet let the pitifulness of thy great mercy loose us.

E beseech thee, O Lord, mercifully to hear the prayers of thy humble servants, and to forgive the sins of them that confess the same unto thee: that they may obtain of thy loving-kindness pardon and peace.

RACIOUSLY shew forth upon us, O Lord, thy unspeakable mercy: that thou wouldest both loose us from all our sins, and likewise deliver us from the punishment which for the same we deserve.

GOD, who art wroth with them that sin against thee, and sparest them that are penitent: mercifully look upon the prayers of thy people who call upon thee; and turn away the scourges of thy wrath, which for our sins we justly deserve.

¶ If the Bishoprick be vacant, the following prayer is omitted.

LMIGHTY and everlasting God, have mercy upon thy servant *N.*, our Bishop, and, according to thy great goodness, direct him into the way of everlasting salvation: that, by thy grace, he may desire that which is well pleasing unto thee, and with all his strength perform the same.

Litanies & Offices *Litany of Saints*

GOD, from whom all holy desires, all good counsels, and all just works do proceed: give unto thy servants that peace which the world cannot give; that both our hearts may be set to obey thy commandments, and also, that by thee we being defended from the fear of our enemies may pass our time in rest and quietness.

INDLE, O Lord, with the fire of the Holy Spirit our reins and our hearts: that we may serve thee with a chaste body, and please thee with a clean heart.

GOD, the Creator and Redeemer of all the faithful, grant unto the souls of thy servants and handmaids the remission of all their sins: that through devout supplications they may obtain the pardon which they have alway desired.

REVENT us, O Lord, we beseech thee, in all our doings with thy most gracious favour, and further us with thy continual help: that all our prayer and work may be begun, continued, and ended in thee.

LMIGHTY and everlasting God, who hast dominion both of the living and of the dead, and hast mercy upon all whom thou foreknowest will be thine in faith and works: we humbly beseech thee; that all those for whom we are minded to pour forth our prayers, whether in this present world they still be held in the flesh, or being delivered from the body have passed into that which is to come, may at the intercession of all thy Saints obtain of thy bountiful goodness the remission of all their sins. Through Jesus Christ thy Son, our Lord, who liveth and reigneth with thee, in the unity of the Holy Ghost, God, throughout all ages, world without end.

℟. Amen.

Conclusion

℣. The Lord be with you.
℟. And with thy spirit.
℣. May the almighty and merciful Lord graciously hear us.
℟. Amen.
℣. And may the souls ✠ of the faithful departed, through the mercy of God, rest in peace.
℟. Amen.

OFFICE OF THE DEAD

Vespers

Office of the Dead

Vespers of the Dead

❡ Vespers begins with the Lord's Prayer and Angelic Salutation, unless it should follow the carrying of the body to the Church or Matins & Lauds of the occurrent Office, in which case the Office begins with the Antiphon.

Psalm 116. *Dilexi, quoniam*

Ant. I will walk † before the Lord in the land of the living.

IAM well pleased : that the Lord hath heard the voice of my prayer;
2 That he hath inclined his ear unto me : therefore will I call upon him as long as I live.
3 The snares of death compassed me round about : and the pains of hell gat hold upon me.
4 I shall find trouble and heaviness, and I will call upon the Name of the Lord : O Lord, I beseech thee, deliver my soul.
5 Gracious is the Lord, and righteous : yea, our God is merciful.
6 The Lord preserveth the simple : I was in misery, and he helped me.
7 Turn again then unto thy rest, O my soul : for the Lord hath rewarded thee.
8 And why? thou hast delivered my soul from death : mine eyes from tears, and my feet from falling.
9 I will walk before the Lord : in the land of the living.
℣. Rest eternal * grant unto them, O Lord.
℟. And let light perpetual * shine upon them.
Ant. I will walk before the Lord in the land of the living.

Psalm 120. *Ad Dominum*

Ant. Woe is me † that I am constrained to dwell with Mesech.

WHEN I was in trouble I called upon the Lord : and he heard me.
2 Deliver my soul, O Lord, from lying lips : and from a deceitful tongue.
3 What reward shall be given or done unto thee, thou false tongue : even mighty and sharp arrows, with hot burning coals.
4 Woe is me, that I am constrained to dwell with Mesech : and to have my habitation among the tents of Kedar.
5 My soul hath long dwelt among them : that are enemies unto peace.
6 I labour for peace, but when I speak unto them thereof : they make them ready to battle.
℣. Rest eternal * grant unto them, O Lord.
℟. And let light perpetual * shine upon them.
Ant. Woe is me that I am constrained to dwell with Mesech.

Office of the Dead *Vespers*

PSALM 121. *LEVAVI OCULUS*

Ant. The Lord † shall preserve thee from all evil yea, it is even he that shall keep thy soul.

WILL lift up mine eyes unto the hills : from whence cometh my help.

2 My help cometh even from the Lord : who hath made heaven and earth.

3 He will not suffer thy foot to be moved : and he that keepeth thee will not sleep.

4 Behold, he that keepeth Israel : shall neither slumber nor sleep.

5 The Lord himself is thy keeper : the Lord is thy defence upon thy right hand;

6 So that the sun shall not burn thee by day : neither the moon by night.

7 The Lord shall preserve thee from all evil : yea, it is even he that shall keep thy soul.

8 The Lord shall preserve thy going out, and thy coming in : from this time forth for evermore.

℣. Rest eternal * grant unto them, O Lord.

℟. And let light perpetual * shine upon them.

Ant. The Lord shall preserve thee from all evil yea, it is even he that shall keep thy soul.

PSALM 130. *DE PROFUNDIS*

Ant. If thou, Lord, wilt be extreme † to mark what is done amiss, O Lord, who may abide it?

UT of the deep have I called unto thee, O Lord : Lord, hear my voice.

2 O let thine ears consider well : the voice of my complaint.

3 If thou, Lord, wilt be extreme to mark what is done amiss : O Lord, who may abide it?

4 For there is mercy with thee : therefore shalt thou be feared.

5 I look for the Lord; my soul doth wait for him : in his word is my trust.

6 My soul fleeth unto the Lord : before the morning watch, I say, before the morning watch.

7 O Israel, trust in the Lord, for with the Lord there is mercy : and with him is plenteous redemption.

8 And he shall redeem Israel : from all his sins.

℣. Rest eternal * grant unto them, O Lord.

℟. And let light perpetual * shine upon them.

Ant. If thou, Lord, wilt be extreme to mark what is done amiss, O Lord, who may abide it?

Vespers # Office of the Dead

Psalm 138. *Confitebor tibi*

Ant. Despise not then, † O Lord, the works of thine own hands.

I WILL give thanks unto thee, O Lord, with my whole heart : even before the gods will I sing praise unto thee.

2 I will worship toward thy holy temple, and praise thy Name, because of thy loving-kindness and truth : for thou hast magnified thy Name and thy word above all things.

3 When I called upon thee, thou heardest me : and enduedst my soul with much strength.

4 All the kings of the earth shall praise thee, O Lord : for they have heard the words of thy mouth.

5 Yea, they shall sing in the ways of the Lord : that great is the glory of the Lord.

6 For though the Lord be high, yet hath he respect unto the lowly : as for the proud, he beholdeth them afar off.

7 Though I walk in the midst of trouble, yet shalt thou refresh me : thou shalt stretch forth thy hand upon the furiousness of mine enemies, and thy right hand shall save me.

8 The Lord shall make good his loving-kindness toward me : yea, thy mercy, O Lord, endureth for ever; despise not then the works of thine own hands.

℣. Rest eternal * grant unto them, O Lord.

℟. And let light perpetual * shine upon them.

Ant. Despise not then, O Lord, the works of thine own hands.

℣. I heard a voice from heaven, saying unto me.

℟. Blessed are the dead which die in the Lord.

Magnificat

Ant. All that the Father † giveth me shall come to me; and him that cometh to me, I will in no wise cast out.

MY soul ✠ doth magnify the Lord, * and my spirit hath rejoiced in God my Saviour.

For he hath regarded * the lowliness of his handmaiden.

For behold, from henceforth * all generations shall call me blessed.

For he that is mighty hath magnified me; * and holy is his Name.

And his mercy is on them that fear him * throughout all generations.

He hath showed strength with his arm; * he hath scattered the proud in the imagination of their hearts.

Office of the Dead — *Vespers*

He hath put down the mighty from their seat, * and hath exalted the humble and meek.

He hath filled the hungry with good things; * and the rich he hath sent empty away.

He remembering his mercy hath holpen his servant Israel; * as he promised to our forefathers, Abraham and his seed, for ever.

℣. Rest eternal * grant unto them, O Lord.

℟. And let light perpetual * shine upon them.

Ant. All that the Father giveth me shall come to me; and him that cometh to me, I will in no wise cast out.

Lord's Prayer

¶ The Lord's Prayer is here said, in secret, kneeling, ending with,

℣. And lead us not into temptation.

℟. But deliver us from evil.

Psalm 146. *Lauda, anima mea*

¶ Psalm 146 is not said on All Souls Day, on the day of death or burial, nor at any time when the Office is recited with Double rite.

PRAISE the Lord, O my soul; while I live will I praise the Lord : yea, as long as I have any being, I will sing praises unto my God.

2 O put not your trust in princes, nor in any child of man : for there is no help in them.

3 For when the breath of man goeth forth he shall turn again to his earth : and then all his thoughts perish.

4 Blessed is he that hath the God of Jacob for his help : and whose hope is in the Lord his God;

5 Who made heaven and earth, the sea, and all that therein is : who keepeth his promise for ever;

6 Who helpeth them to right that suffer wrong : who feedeth the hungry.

7 The Lord looseth men out of prison : the Lord giveth sight to the blind.

8 The Lord helpeth them that are fallen : the Lord careth for the righteous.

9 The Lord careth for the strangers, he defendeth the fatherless and widow : as for the way of the ungodly, he turneth it upside down.

10 The Lord thy God, O Sion, shall be King for evermore : and throughout all generations.

℣. Rest eternal * grant unto them, O Lord.

℟. And let light perpetual * shine upon them.

Vespers # Office of the Dead

Responsory

℣. From the gate of hell.
℟. Deliver *his soul*, O Lord.
℣. May *he* rest in peace.
℟. Amen.

Conclusion

℣. O Lord, hear my prayer.
℟. And let my cry come unto thee.
℣. The Lord be with you.
℟. And with thy spirit.
℣. Let us pray.

¶ The appropriate collect is here said (p. 77).

℣. Rest eternal * grant unto them, O Lord.
℟. And let light perpetual * shine upon them.
℣. May they rest in peace.
℟. Amen.

Here endeth the Order of Vespers of the Dead.

Office of the Dead

Matins

Matins of the Dead

℣ Matins begins with the Lord's Prayer, Angelic Salutation, and Apostles' Creed, unless it should follow the carrying of the body to the Church or Matins & Lauds of the occurrent Office, in which case the Office immediately begins with the Invitatory or the Antiphon of the Nocturn.

℣ The following Invitatory is only said when the Office of the Dead is recited with three Nocturns (even when the rite is Semidouble) or when one Nocturn only is said but with Double rite.

℣ The Nocturns placed below, or one Nocturn only, may be said as noted—except on the day of a burial (on which the first Nocturn is always to be said) and in the Commemoration of All the Faithful Departed.

Venite, exultemus

Ant. The King unto whom all live, * O come, let us adore him.

Ant. The King unto whom all live, * O come, let us adore him.

COME, let us sing unto the Lord : let us heartily rejoice in the strength of our salvation.

2 Let us come before his presence with thanksgiving : and shew ourselves glad in him with psalms.

Ant. The King unto whom all live, * O come, let us adore him.

3 For the Lord is a great God : and a great King above all gods.

4 In his hand are all the corners of the earth : and the strength of the hills is his also.

Ant. O come, let us adore him.

5 The sea is his, and he made it : and his hands prepared the dry land.

6 O come, let us worship and fall down : and kneel before the Lord our Maker.

7 For he is the Lord our God : and we are the people of his pasture, and the sheep of his hand.

Ant. The King unto whom all live, * O come, let us adore him.

8 To-day if ye will hear his voice, harden not your hearts : as in the provocation, and as in the day of temptation in the wilderness.

9 When your fathers tempted me : proved me, and saw my works.

Ant. O come, let us adore him.

10 Forty years long was I grieved with this generation, and said : It is a people that do err in their hearts, for they have not known my ways;

11 Unto whom I sware in my wrath : that they should not enter into my rest.

Ant. The King unto whom all live, * O come, let us adore him.

Matins # Office of the Dead

℣. Rest eternal * grant unto them, O Lord.
℞. And let light perpetual * shine upon them.
Ant. O come, let us adore him.
Ant. The King unto whom all live, * O come, let us adore him.

Nocturn I

❧ If only one Nocturn be said, Nocturn I is said on Sunday, Monday, & Thursday.

Psalm 5. Verba mea auribus.

Ant. Make thy way plain, † O Lord my God, before my face.

PONDER my words, O Lord : consider my meditation
2 O hearken thou unto the voice of my calling, my King, and my God : for unto thee will I make my prayer.
3 My voice shalt thou hear betimes, O Lord : early in the morning will I direct my prayer unto thee, and will look up.
4 For thou art the God that hast no pleasure in wickedness : neither shall any evil dwell with thee.
5 Such as be foolish shall not stand in thy sight : for thou hatest all them that work vanity.
6 Thou shalt destroy them that speak leasing : the Lord will abhor both the blood-thirsty and deceitful man.
7 But as for me, I will come into thine house, even upon the multitude of thy mercy : and in thy fear will I worship toward thy holy temple.
8 Lead me, O Lord, in thy righteousness, because of mine enemies : make thy way plain before my face.
9 For there is no faithfulness in his mouth : their inward parts are very wickedness.
10 Their throat is an open sepulchre : they flatter with their tongue.
11 Destroy thou them, O God; let them perish through their own imaginations : cast them out in the multitude of their ungodliness; for they have rebelled against thee.
12 And let all them that put their trust in thee rejoice : they shall ever be giving of thanks, because thou defendest them; they that love thy Name shall be joyful in thee;
13 For thou, Lord, wilt give thy blessing unto the righteous : and with thy favourable kindness wilt thou defend him as with a shield.

℣. Rest eternal * grant unto them, O Lord.
℞. And let light perpetual * shine upon them.
Ant. Make thy way plain, O Lord my God, before my face.

Office of the Dead   *Matins*

Psalm 6. Domine, ne in furore

Ant. Turn thee, † O Lord, and deliver my soul: for in death no man remembereth thee.

O LORD, rebuke me not in thine indignation : neither chasten me in thy displeasure.

2 Have mercy upon me, O Lord, for I am weak : O Lord, heal me, for my bones are vexed.

3 My soul also is sore troubled : but, Lord, how long wilt thou punish me?

4 Turn thee, O Lord, and deliver my soul : O save me for thy mercy's sake.

5 For in death no man remembereth thee : and who will give thee thanks in the pit?

6 I am weary of my groaning; every night wash I my bed : and water my couch with my tears.

7 My beauty is gone for very trouble : and worn away because of all mine enemies.

8 Away from me, all ye that work vanity : for the Lord hath heard the voice of my weeping.

9 The Lord hath heard my petition : the Lord will receive my prayer.

10 All mine enemies shall be confounded, and sore vexed : they shall be turned back, and put to shame suddenly.

℣. Rest eternal * grant unto them, O Lord.

℟. And let light perpetual * shine upon them.

Ant. Turn thee, O Lord, and deliver my soul: for in death no man remembereth thee.

Psalm 7. Domine, Deus meus

Ant. Lest he devour † my soul like a lion, and tear it in pieces, while there is none to help.

O LORD my God, in thee have I put my trust : save me from all them that persecute me, and deliver me;

2 Lest he devour my soul, like a lion, and tear it in pieces : while there is none to help.

3 O Lord my God, if I have done any such thing : or if there be any wickedness in my hands;

4 If I have rewarded evil unto him that dealt friendly with me : yea, I have delivered him that without any cause is mine enemy,

5 Then let mine enemy persecute my soul, and take me : yea, let him tread my life down upon the earth, and lay mine honour in the dust.

Matins — Office of the Dead

6 Stand up, O Lord, in thy wrath, and lift up thyself, because of the indignation of mine enemies : arise up for me in the judgement that thou hast commanded.

7 And so shall the congregation of the people come about thee : for their sakes therefore lift up thyself again.

8 The Lord shall judge the people; give sentence with me, O Lord : according to my righteousness, and according to the innocency that is in me.

9 O let the wickedness of the ungodly come to an end : but guide thou the just.

10 For the righteous God : trieth the very hearts and reins.

11 My help cometh of God : who preserveth them that are true of heart.

12 God is a righteous Judge, strong and patient : and God is provoked every day.

13 If a man will not turn, he will whet his sword : he hath bent his bow, and made it ready.

14 He hath prepared for him the instruments of death : he ordaineth his arrows against the persecutors.

15 Behold, he travaileth with mischief : he hath conceived sorrow, and brought forth ungodliness.

16 He hath graven and digged up a pit : and is fallen on himself into the destruction that he made for other.

17 For his travail shall come upon his own head : and his wickedness shall fall on his own pate.

18 I will give thanks unto the Lord, according to his righteousness : and I will praise the Name of the Lord most High.

℣. Rest eternal * grant unto them, O Lord.

℟. And let light perpetual * shine upon them.

Ant. Lest he devour my soul like a lion, and tear it in pieces, while there is none to help.

℣. From the gate of hell.

℟. Deliver their souls, O Lord.

❡ The Lord's Prayer is said secretly.

Lesson 1. Job 7:16

LET me alone; for my days are vanity. What is man, that thou shouldest magnify him? and that thou shouldest set thine heart upon him? And that thou shouldest visit him every morning, and try him every moment? How long wilt thou not depart from me, nor let me alone till I swallow

Office of the Dead *Matins*

down my spittle? I have sinned; what shall I do unto thee, O thou preserver of men? why hast thou set me as a mark against thee, so that I am a burden to myself? And why dost thou not pardon my transgression, and take away mine iniquity? for now shall I sleep in the dust; and thou shalt seek me in the morning, but I shall not be.

℟. I know † that my Redeemer liveth, and that he shall stand at the latter day upon the earth: * And in my flesh shall I see God my Saviour.

℣. Whom I shall see for myself, and mine eyes shall behold, and not another.

℟. And in my flesh shall I see God my Saviour.

Lesson 2. Job 10:1

My soul is weary of my life; I will leave my complaint upon myself; I will speak in the bitterness of my soul. I will say unto God, Do not condemn me; shew me wherefore thou contendest with me. Is it good unto thee that thou shouldest oppress, that thou shouldest despise the work of thine hands, and shine upon the counsel of the wicked? Hast thou eyes of flesh? or seest thou as man seeth? Are thy days as the days of man? are thy years as man's days, That thou enquirest after mine iniquity, and searchest after my sin? Thou knowest that I am not wicked; and there is none that can deliver out of thine hand.

℟. Thou who didst raise Lazarus † already corrupting from the grave; * Grant them rest, O Lord, and a place of forgiveness.

℣. Thou who shalt come to judge the quick and the dead, and the world by fire.

℟. Grant them rest, O Lord, and a place of forgiveness.

Lesson 3. Job 10:8

Thine hands have made me and fashioned me together round about; yet thou dost destroy me. Remember, I beseech thee, that thou hast made me as the clay; and wilt thou bring me into dust again? Hast thou not poured me out as milk, and curdled me like cheese? Thou hast clothed me with skin and flesh, and hast fenced me with bones and sinews. Thou hast granted me life and favour, and thy visitation hath preserved my spirit.

℟. O Lord, † when thou comest to judge the earth, where shall I hide myself from the wrath of thy countenance? * For I have sinned grievously in my life.

℣. I am afraid of my transgressions, and I am ashamed before thee: when thou comest to judgment, O condemn me not.

℟. For I have sinned grievously in my life.

Office of the Dead

Matins

℣. Rest eternal grant unto them, O Lord: and let light perpetual shine upon them.
℟. For I have sinned grievously in my life.

¶ If only one Nocturn be said, Lauds begins immediately (p. 126).

Nocturn II

Tuesday and Friday

Psalm 23. Dominus regit me.

Ant. He shall feed me † in a green pasture.

THE Lord is my shepherd : therefore can I lack nothing.
2 He shall feed me in a green pasture : and lead me forth beside the waters of comfort.
3 He shall convert my soul : and bring me forth in the paths of righteousness, for his Name's sake.
4 Yea, though I walk through the valley of the shadow of death, I will fear no evil : for thou art with me; thy rod and thy staff comfort me.
5 Thou shalt prepare a table before me against them that trouble me : thou hast anointed my head with oil, and my cup shall be full.
6 But thy loving-kindness and mercy shall follow me all the days of my life : and I will dwell in the house of the Lord for ever.

℣. Rest eternal * grant unto them, O Lord.
℟. And let light perpetual * shine upon them.
Ant. He shall feed me in a green pasture.

Psalm 25. Ad te, Domine, levavi

Ant. Remember not † the sins and offences of my youth, O Lord.

UNTO thee, O Lord, will I lift up my soul; my God, I have put my trust in thee : O let me not be confounded, neither let mine enemies triumph over me.
2 For all they that hope in thee shall not be ashamed : but such as transgress without a cause shall be put to confusion.
3 Shew me thy ways, O Lord : and teach me thy paths.
4 Lead me forth in thy truth, and learn me : for thou art the God of my salvation; in thee hath been my hope all the day long.
5 Call to remembrance, O Lord, thy tender mercies : and thy loving-kindnesses, which have been ever of old.

Office of the Dead — *Matins*

6 O remember not the sins and offences of my youth : but according to thy mercy think thou upon me, O Lord, for thy goodness.

7 Gracious and righteous is the Lord : therefore will he teach sinners in the way.

8 Them that are meek shall he guide in judgement : and such as are gentle, them shall he learn his way.

9 All the paths of the Lord are mercy and truth : unto such as keep his covenant and his testimonies.

10 For thy Name's sake, O Lord : be merciful unto my sin, for it is great.

11 What man is he that feareth the Lord : him shall he teach in the way that he shall choose.

12 His soul shall dwell at ease : and his seed shall inherit the land.

13 The secret of the Lord is among them that fear him : and he will shew them his covenant.

14 Mine eyes are ever looking unto the Lord : for he shall pluck my feet out of the net.

15 Turn thee unto me, and have mercy upon me : for I am desolate and in misery.

16 The sorrows of my heart are enlarged : O bring thou me out of my troubles.

17 Look upon my adversity and misery : and forgive me all my sin.

18 Consider mine enemies, how many they are : and they bear a tyrannous hate against me.

19 O keep my soul, and deliver me : let me not be confounded, for I have put my trust in thee.

20 Let perfectness and righteous dealing wait upon me : for my hope hath been in thee.

21 Deliver Israel, O God : out of all his troubles.

℣. Rest eternal * grant unto them, O Lord.

℟. And let light perpetual * shine upon them.

Ant. Remember not the sins and offences of my youth, O Lord.

Psalm 27. Dominus illuminatio

Ant. I believe † verily to see the goodness of the Lord in the land of the living.

THE Lord is my light and my salvation; whom then shall I fear : the Lord is the strength of my life; of whom then shall I be afraid?

2 When the wicked, even mine enemies and my foes, came upon me to eat up my flesh : they stumbled and fell.

3 Though an host of men were laid against me, yet shall not my heart be afraid : and though there rose up war against me, yet will I put my trust in him.

Matins **Office of the Dead**

4 One thing have I desired of the Lord, which I will require : even that I may dwell in the house of the Lord all the days of my life, to behold the fair beauty of the Lord, and to visit his temple.

5 For in the time of trouble he shall hide me in his tabernacle : yea, in the secret place of his dwelling shall he hide me, and set me up upon a rock of stone.

6 And now shall he lift up mine head : above mine enemies round about me.

7 Therefore will I offer in his dwelling an oblation with great gladness : I will sing, and speak praises unto the Lord.

8 Hearken unto my voice, O Lord, when I cry unto thee : have mercy upon me, and hear me.

9 My heart hath talked of thee, Seek ye my face : Thy face, Lord, will I seek.

10 O hide not thou thy face from me : nor cast thy servant away in displeasure.

11 Thou hast been my succour : leave me not, neither forsake me, O God of my salvation.

12 When my father and my mother forsake me : the Lord taketh me up.

13 Teach me thy way, O Lord : and lead me in the right way, because of mine enemies.

14 Deliver me not over into the will of mine adversaries : for there are false witnesses risen up against me, and such as speak wrong.

15 I should utterly have fainted : but that I believe verily to see the goodness of the Lord in the land of the living.

16 O tarry thou the Lord's leisure : be strong, and he shall comfort thine heart; and put thou thy trust in the Lord.

℣. Rest eternal * grant unto them, O Lord.

℟. And let light perpetual * shine upon them.

Ant. I believe verily to see the goodness of the Lord in the land of the living.

℣. The Lord shall set them with the princes.

℟. Even with the princes of his people.

¶ The Lord's Prayer is said secretly.

Lesson 4. Job 13:22

THEN call thou, and I will answer: or let me speak, and answer thou me. How many are mine iniquities and sins? make me to know my transgression and my sin. Wherefore hidest thou thy face, and holdest me for thine enemy? Wilt thou break a leaf driven to and fro? and wilt thou pursue the dry stubble? For thou writest bitter things against me, and makest me to possess the iniquities of my youth. Thou puttest my feet also in the stocks,

Office of the Dead *Matins*

and lookest narrowly unto all my paths; thou settest a print upon the heels of my feet. And he, as a rotten thing, consumeth, as a garment that is moth eaten.

℟. Remember me, † O God, that my life is wind: * The eye of him that hath seen me shall see me no more.

℣. Out of the deep have I called unto thee, O Lord: Lord, hear my voice.

℟. The eye of him that hath seen me shall see me no more.

Lesson 5. Job 14:1

MAN that is born of a woman is of few days, and full of trouble. He cometh forth like a flower, and is cut down: he fleeth also as a shadow, and continueth not. And dost thou open thine eyes upon such an one, and bringest me into judgment with thee? Who can bring a clean thing out of an unclean? not one. Seeing his days are determined, the number of his months are with thee, thou hast appointed his bounds that he cannot pass; Turn from him, that he may rest, till he shall accomplish, as an hireling, his day.

℟. Woe is me, † O Lord, for I have sinned grievously all the days of my life! O wretched man, what shall I do? Whither shall I flee, but unto thee, O my God? * Have mercy upon me, when thou comest at the day of judgment.

℣. My soul is sore troubled; but, Lord, be thou my helper.

℟. Have mercy upon me, when thou comest at the day of judgment.

Lesson 6. Job 14:13

O THAT thou wouldest hide me in the grave, that thou wouldest keep me secret, until thy wrath be past, that thou wouldest appoint me a set time, and remember me! If a man die, shall he live again? all the days of my appointed time will I wait, till my change come. Thou shalt call, and I will answer thee: thou wilt have a desire to the work of thine hands. For now thou numberest my steps: dost thou not watch over my sin?

℟. Remember not † my trespasses, O Lord, * When thou shalt come to judge the world by fire.

℣. Make thy way plain before my face, O Lord my God.

℟. When thou shalt come to judge the world by fire.

℣. Rest eternal grant unto them, O Lord: and let light perpetual shine upon them.

℟. When thou shalt come to judge the world by fire.

❡ If only one Nocturn be said, Lauds begins immediately (p. 126).

Matins # Office of the Dead

Nocturn III

Wednesday and Saturday

Psalm 40. Expectans expectavi

Ant. O Lord, † let it be thy pleasure to deliver me; make haste, O Lord, to help me.

I WAITED patiently for the Lord : and he inclined unto me, and heard my calling.

2 He brought me also out of the horrible pit, out of the mire and clay : and set my feet upon the rock, and ordered my goings.

3 And he hath put a new song in my mouth : even a thanksgiving unto our God.

4 Many shall see it, and fear : and shall put their trust in the Lord.

5 Blessed is the man that hath set his hope in the Lord : and turned not unto the proud, and to such as go about with lies.

6 O Lord my God, great are the wondrous works which thou hast done, like as be also thy thoughts which are to us-ward : and yet there is no man that ordereth them unto thee:

7 If I should declare them, and speak of them : they should be more than I am able to express.

8 Sacrifice and meat-offering thou wouldest not : but mine ears hast thou opened.

9 Burnt-offerings, and sacrifice for sin, hast thou not required : then said I, Lo, I come,

10 In the volume of the book it is written of me, that I should fulfil thy will, O my God : I am content to do it; yea, thy law is within my heart.

11 I have declared thy righteousness in the great congregation : lo, I will not refrain my lips, O Lord, and that thou knowest.

12 I have not hid thy righteousness within my heart : my talk hath been of thy truth and of thy salvation.

13 I have not kept back thy loving mercy and truth : from the great congregation.

14 Withdraw not thou thy mercy from me, O Lord : let thy loving-kindness and thy truth alway preserve me.

15 For innumerable troubles are come about me; my sins have taken such hold upon me that I am not able to look up : yea, they are more in number than the hairs of my head, and my heart hath failed me.

Office of the Dead *Matins*

16 O Lord, let it be thy pleasure to deliver me : make haste, O Lord, to help me.

17 Let them be ashamed and confounded together, that seek after my soul to destroy it : let them be driven backward and put to rebuke, that wish me evil.

18 Let them be desolate, and rewarded with shame : that say unto me, Fie upon thee, fie upon thee.

19 Let all those that seek thee be joyful and glad in thee : and let such as love thy salvation say alway, The Lord be praised.

20 As for me, I am poor and needy : but the Lord careth for me.

21 Thou art my helper and redeemer : make no long tarrying, O my God.

℣. Rest eternal * grant unto them, O Lord.

℟. And let light perpetual * shine upon them.

Ant. O Lord, let it be thy pleasure to deliver me; make haste, O Lord, to help me.

Psalm 41. Beatus qui intelligit

Ant. Heal my soul, † O Lord, for I have sinned against thee.

BLESSED is he that considereth the poor and needy : the Lord shall deliver him in the time of trouble.

2 The Lord preserve him, and keep him alive, that he may be blessed upon earth : and deliver not thou him into the will of his enemies.

3 The Lord comfort him, when he lieth sick upon his bed : make thou all his bed in his sickness.

4 I said, Lord, be merciful unto me : heal my soul, for I have sinned against thee.

5 Mine enemies speak evil of me : When shall he die, and his name perish?

6 And if he come to see me, he speaketh vanity : and his heart conceiveth falsehood within himself, and when he cometh forth he telleth it.

7 All mine enemies whisper together against me : even against me do they imagine this evil.

8 Let the sentence of guiltiness proceed against him : and now that he lieth, let him rise up no more.

9 Yea, even mine own familiar friend, whom I trusted : who did also eat of my bread, hath laid great wait for me.

10 But be thou merciful unto me, O Lord : raise thou me up again, and I shall reward them.

11 By this I know thou favourest me : that mine enemy doth not triumph against me.

Matins — **Office of the Dead**

12 And when I am in my health, thou upholdest me : and shalt set me before thy face for ever.

13 Blessed be the Lord God of Israel : world without end. Amen.

℣. Rest eternal * grant unto them, O Lord.

℟. And let light perpetual * shine upon them.

Ant. Heal my soul, O Lord, for I have sinned against thee.

Psalm 42. *Quemadmodum*

Ant. My soul is athirst for God, † yea, even for the living God: when shall I come to appear before the presence of the Lord.

LIKE as the hart desireth the water-brooks : so longeth my soul after thee, O God.

2 My soul is athirst for God, yea, even for the living God : when shall I come to appear before the presence of God?

3 My tears have been my meat day and night : while they daily say unto me, Where is now thy God?

4 Now when I think thereupon, I pour out my heart by myself : for I went with the multitude, and brought them forth into the house of God;

5 In the voice of praise and thanksgiving : among such as keep holy-day.

6 Why art thou so full of heaviness, O my soul : and why art thou so disquieted within me?

7 Put thy trust in God : for I will yet give him thanks for the help of his countenance.

8 My God, my soul is vexed within me : therefore will I remember thee concerning the land of Jordan, and the little hill of Hermon.

9 One deep calleth another, because of the noise of the water-pipes : all thy waves and storms are gone over me.

10 The Lord hath granted his loving-kindness in the day-time : and in the night-season did I sing of him, and made my prayer unto the God of my life.

11 I will say unto the God of my strength, Why hast thou forgotten me : why go I thus heavily, while the enemy oppresseth me?

12 My bones are smitten asunder as with a sword : while mine enemies that trouble me cast me in the teeth;

13 Namely, while they say daily unto me : Where is now thy God?

14 Why art thou so vexed, O my soul : and why art thou so disquieted within me?

15 O put thy trust in God : for I will yet thank him, which is the help of my countenance, and my God.

℣. Rest eternal * grant unto them, O Lord.

Office of the Dead — *Matins*

℟. And let light perpetual * shine upon them.
Ant. My soul is athirst for God, yea, even for the living God: when shall I come to appear before the presence of the Lord.

℣. O deliver not the soul of thy turtle-dove unto the multitude of the enemies.
℟. Forget not the congregation of the poor for ever.

¶ The Lord's Prayer is said secretly.

Lesson 7. Job 17:1

My breath is corrupt, my days are extinct, the graves are ready for me. Are there not mockers with me? and doth not mine eye continue in their provocation? Lay down now, put me in a surety with thee; who is he that will strike hands with me? My days are past, my purposes are broken off, even the thoughts of my heart. They change the night into day: the light is short because of darkness. If I wait, the grave is mine house: I have made my bed in the darkness. I have said to corruption, Thou art my father: to the worm, Thou art my mother, and my sister. And where is now my hope? as for my hope, who shall see it?

℟. The while I trespass daily † and have no repentance, the fear of death appalleth me: * Because in hell there is no redemption, have mercy upon me, O God, and save me.
℣. Save me, O God, for thy Name's sake, and deliver me in thy strength.
℟. Because in hell there is no redemption, have mercy upon me, O God, and save me.

Lesson 8. Job 19:20

My bone cleaveth to my skin and to my flesh, and I am escaped with the skin of my teeth. Have pity upon me, have pity upon me, O ye my friends; for the hand of God hath touched me. Why do ye persecute me as God, and are not satisfied with my flesh? Oh that my words were now written! oh that they were printed in a book! That they were graven with an iron pen and lead in the rock for ever! For I know that my redeemer liveth, and that he shall stand at the latter day upon the earth: And though after my skin worms destroy this body, yet in my flesh shall I see God: Whom I shall see for myself, and mine eyes shall behold, and not another; though my reins be consumed within me.

℟. Judge me not, † O Lord, according to my deeds; for I have done nothing worthy in thy sight: wherefore I humbly beseech thy Majesty, * That thou, O God, mayest do away mine offences.

Matins — **Office of the Dead**

℣. Wash me throughly, O Lord, from mine unrighteousness, and cleanse me from my sin.
℟. That thou, O God, mayest do away mine offences.

Lesson 9. Job 10:18

WHEREFORE then hast thou brought me forth out of the womb? Oh that I had given up the ghost, and no eye had seen me! I should have been as though I had not been; I should have been carried from the womb to the grave. Are not my days few? cease then, and let me alone, that I may take comfort a little, Before I go whence I shall not return, even to the land of darkness and the shadow of death; A land of darkness, as darkness itself; and of the shadow of death, without any order, and where the light is as darkness.

Responsory

¶ The following Responsory is said when only the Third Nocturn is said.

℟. Deliver me, O Lord, † from the paths of hell, thou that brakest in pieces the gates of brass; and visitedst hell, and gavest them light, that they might see thee, * Who dwelt in the pains of darkness.
℣. Crying out and saying, Thou art come, O our Redeemer.
℟. Who dwelt in the pains of darkness.
℣. Rest eternal grant unto them, O Lord: and let light perpetual shine upon them.
℟. Who dwelt in the pains of darkness.

¶ If only one Nocturn be said, Lauds begins immediately (p. 126).

¶ The following Responsory is said when three Nocturns are said.

℟. Deliver me, O Lord, † from death eternal in that day of trembling: * When heaven and earth shall be shaken: * When thou shalt come to judge the world by fire.
℣. Trembling taketh hold upon me, and fearfulness, as the sifting draweth on and the wrath to come.
℟. When heaven and earth shall be shaken.
℣. Ah, that day, that day of anger, of calamity and misery; Ah that great day, and exceeding bitter!
℟. When thou shalt come to judge the world by fire.

Office of the Dead — *Matins*

℣. Rest eternal grant unto them, O Lord: and let light perpetual shine upon them.

℟. Deliver me, O Lord, from death eternal in that day of trembling: When heaven and earth shall be shaken: When thou shalt come to judge the world by fire.

Conclusion

¶ The following Conclusion is said when Matins is separated from Lauds.

℣. The Lord be with you.
or, O Lord, hear our prayer.
℟. And with thy spirit.
or, And let our cry come unto thee.

¶ The appropriate collect is here said (p. 77).

℣. Rest eternal * grant unto them, O Lord.
℟. And let light perpetual * shine upon them.
℣. May they rest in peace.
℟. Amen.

Here endeth the Order of Matins of the Dead.

Lauds

Office of the Dead

Lauds of the Dead

❡ Before Lauds—if it be said separately from Matins—the Lord's Prayer and Angelic Salutation are said secretly. Otherwise, the Office begins at once with the Antiphon.

Psalm 51. *Miserere mei, Deus*

Ant. The bones which thou hast broken † shall rejoice in the Lord.

Have mercy upon me, O God, after thy great goodness : according to the multitude of thy mercies do away mine offences.

2 Wash me throughly from my wickedness : and cleanse me from my sin.

3 For I acknowledge my faults : and my sin is ever before me.

4 Against thee only have I sinned, and done this evil in thy sight : that thou mightest be justified in thy saying, and clear when thou art judged.

5 Behold, I was shapen in wickedness : and in sin hath my mother conceived me.

6 But lo, thou requirest truth in the inward parts: and shalt make me to understand wisdom secretly.

7 Thou shalt purge me with hyssop, and I shall be clean : thou shalt wash me, and I shall be whiter than snow.

8 Thou shalt make me hear of joy and gladness : that the bones which thou hast broken may rejoice.

9 Turn thy face from my sins : and put out all my misdeeds.

10 Make me a clean heart, O God : and renew a right spirit within me.

11 Cast me not away from thy presence : and take not thy holy Spirit from me.

12 O give me the comfort of thy help again : and stablish me with thy free Spirit.

13 Then shall I teach thy ways unto the wicked : and sinners shall be converted unto thee.

14 Deliver me from blood-guiltiness, O God, thou that art the God of my health : and my tongue shall sing of thy righteousness.

15 Thou shalt open my lips, O Lord : and my mouth shall shew thy praise.

16 For thou desirest no sacrifice, else would I give it thee : but thou delightest not in burnt-offerings.

17 The sacrifice of God is a troubled spirit : a broken and contrite heart, O God, shalt thou not despise.

18 O be favourable and gracious unto Sion : build thou the walls of Jerusalem.

Office of the Dead *Lauds*

19 Then shalt thou be pleased with the sacrifice of righteousness, with the burnt-offerings and oblations : then shall they offer young bullocks upon thine altar.

℣. Rest eternal * grant unto them, O Lord.

℟. And let light perpetual * shine upon them.

Ant. The bones which thou hast broken shall rejoice in the Lord.

PSALM 65. *TE DECET HYMNUS*

Ant. Thou, O Lord, † that hearest the prayer, unto thee shall all flesh come.

THOU, O God, art praised in Sion : and unto thee shall the vow be performed in Jerusalem.

2 Thou that hearest the prayer : unto thee shall all flesh come.

3 My misdeeds prevail against me : O be thou merciful unto our sins.

4 Blessed is the man whom thou choosest, and receivest unto thee : he shall dwell in thy court, and shall be satisfied with the pleasures of thy house, even of thy holy temple.

5 Thou shalt shew us wonderful things in thy righteousness, O God of our salvation : thou that art the hope of all the ends of the earth, and of them that remain in the broad sea.

6 Who in his strength setteth fast the mountains : and is girded about with power.

7 Who stilleth the raging of the sea : and the noise of his waves, and the madness of the people.

8 They also that dwell in the uttermost parts of the earth shall be afraid at thy tokens : thou that makest the outgoings of the morning and evening to praise thee.

9 Thou visitest the earth, and blessest it : thou makest it very plenteous.

10 The river of God is full of water : thou preparest their corn, for so thou providest for the earth.

11 Thou waterest her furrows, thou sendest rain into the little valleys thereof : thou makest it soft with the drops of rain, and blessest the increase of it.

12 Thou crownest the year with thy goodness : and thy clouds drop fatness.

13 They shall drop upon the dwellings of the wilderness : and the little hills shall rejoice on every side.

14 The folds shall be full of sheep : the valleys also shall stand so thick with corn, that they shall laugh and sing.

℣. Rest eternal * grant unto them, O Lord.

℟. And let light perpetual * shine upon them.

Ant. Thou, O Lord, that hearest the prayer, unto thee shall all flesh come.

Lauds

Office of the Dead

Psalm 63. *Deus, Deus meus*

Ant. Thy right hand † hath upholden me, O Lord.

God, thou art my God : early will I seek thee.

2 My soul thirsteth for thee, my flesh also longeth after thee : in a barren and dry land where no water is.

3 Thus have I looked for thee in holiness : that I might behold thy power and glory.

4 For thy loving-kindness is better than the life itself : my lips shall praise thee.

5 As long as I live will I magnify thee on this manner : and lift up my hands in thy Name.

6 My soul shall be satisfied, even as it were with marrow and fatness : when my mouth praiseth thee with joyful lips.

7 Have I not remembered thee in my bed : and thought upon thee when I was waking?

8 Because thou hast been my helper : therefore under the shadow of thy wings will I rejoice.

9 My soul hangeth upon thee : thy right hand hath upholden me.

10 These also that seek the hurt of my soul : they shall go under the earth.

11 Let them fall upon the edge of the sword : that they may be a portion for foxes.

12 But the King shall rejoice in God; all they also that swear by him shall be commended : for the mouth of them that speak lies shall be stopped.

℣. Rest eternal * grant unto them, O Lord.

℟. And let light perpetual * shine upon them.

Ant. Thy right hand hath upholden me, O Lord.

Ego dixi

Ant. From the gate of hell, † deliver my soul, O Lord.

I said in the cutting off of my days, † I shall go to the gates of the grave: * I am deprived of the residue of my years.

I said, I shall not see the Lord, † even the Lord, in the land of the living: * I shall behold man no more with the inhabitants of the world.

Mine age is departed, * and is removed from me as a shepherd's tent;

I have cut off like a weaver my life: † he will cut me off with pining sickness: * from day even to night wilt thou make an end of me.

I reckoned till morning, † that, as a lion, so will he break all my bones: * from day even to night wilt thou make an end of me.

Like a crane or a swallow, so did I chatter: * I did mourn as a dove.

Office of the Dead *Lauds*

Mine eyes fail with looking upward: * O Lord, I am oppressed; undertake for me.

What shall I say? † he hath both spoken unto me, and himself hath done it: * I shall go softly all my years in the bitterness of my soul.

O Lord, by these things men live, † and in all these things is the life of my spirit: * so wilt thou recover me, and make me to live.

Behold, for peace I had great bitterness: † but thou hast in love to my soul delivered it from the pit of corruption: * for thou hast cast all my sins behind thy back.

For the grave cannot praise thee, † death can not celebrate thee: * they that go down into the pit cannot hope for thy truth.

The living, the living, he shall praise thee, as I do this day: * the father to the children shall make known thy truth.

The Lord was ready to save me: * therefore we will sing my songs to the stringed instruments all the days of our life in the house of the Lord.

℣. Rest eternal * grant unto them, O Lord.

℟. And let light perpetual * shine upon them.

Ant. From the gate of hell, deliver my soul, O Lord.

PSALM 150. *LAUDATE DOMINUM*

Ant. Let everything that hath breath † praise the Lord.

PRAISE God in his holiness : praise him in the firmament of his power.

2 Praise him in his noble acts : praise him according to his excellent greatness.

3 Praise him in the sound of the trumpet : praise him upon the lute and harp.

4 Praise him in the cymbals and dances : praise him upon the strings and pipe.

5 Praise him upon the well-tuned cymbals : praise him upon the loud cymbals.

6 Let every thing that hath breath : praise the Lord.

℣. Rest eternal * grant unto them, O Lord.

℟. And let light perpetual * shine upon them.

Ant. Let everything that hath breath praise the Lord.

℣. I heard a voice from heaven, saying unto me.

℟. Blessed are the dead which die in the Lord.

Lauds # Office of the Dead

Benedictus

Ant. I am the resurrection † and the life: he that believeth in me, though he were dead, yet shall he live: and whosoever liveth and believeth in me, shall never die.

BLESSED ✠ be the Lord God of Israel; * for he hath visited and redeemed his people;

And hath raised up a mighty salvation for us, * in the house of his servant David;

As he spake by the mouth of his holy Prophets, * which have been since the world began;

That we should be saved from our enemies, * and from the hand of all that hate us.

To perform the mercy promised to our forefathers, * and to remember his holy covenant;

To perform the oath which he sware to our forefather Abraham, * that he would give us;

That we being delivered out of the hand of our enemies * might serve him without fear;

In holiness and righteousness before him, * all the days of our life.

And thou, child, shalt be called the prophet of the Highest: * for thou shalt go before the face of the Lord to prepare his ways;

To give knowledge of salvation unto his people * for the remission of their sins,

Through the tender mercy of our God; * whereby the day-spring from on high hath visited us;

To give light to them that sit in darkness, and in the shadow of death, * and to guide our feet into the way of peace.

℣. Rest eternal * grant unto them, O Lord.

℟. And let light perpetual * shine upon them.

Ant. I am the resurrection and the life: he that believeth in me, though he were dead, yet shall he live; and whosoever liveth and believeth in me, shall never die.

Lord's Prayer

❡ The Lord's Prayer is said, in secret, kneeling, ending with,

℣. And lead us not into temptation.

℟. But deliver us from evil.

Office of the Dead — *Lauds*

Psalm 130. *De profundis*

❡ Psalm 130 is not said on All Souls Day, on the day of death or burial, nor at any time when the Office is recited with Double rite.

Out of the deep have I called unto thee, O Lord : Lord, hear my voice.

2 O let thine ears consider well : the voice of my complaint.

3 If thou, Lord, wilt be extreme to mark what is done amiss : O Lord, who may abide it?

4 For there is mercy with thee : therefore shalt thou be feared.

5 I look for the Lord; my soul doth wait for him : in his word is my trust.

6 My soul fleeth unto the Lord : before the morning watch, I say, before the morning watch.

7 O Israel, trust in the Lord, for with the Lord there is mercy : and with him is plenteous redemption.

8 And he shall redeem Israel : from all his sins.

℣. Rest eternal * grant unto them, O Lord.
℟. And let light perpetual * shine upon them.

Responsory

℣. From the gate of hell.
℟. Deliver *his soul*, O Lord.
℣. May *he* rest in peace.
℟. Amen.

Conclusion

℣. O Lord, hear my prayer.
℟. And let my cry come unto thee.
℣. The Lord be with you.
℟. And with thy spirit.

❡ The appropriate collect is here said (p. 77).

℣. Rest eternal * grant unto them, O Lord.
℟. And let light perpetual * shine upon them.
℣. May they rest in peace.
℟. Amen.

Here endeth the Order of Lauds of the Dead.

EUCHARISTIC DEVOTIONS

Benediction — # Eucharistic Devotions

Benediction of the Blessed Sacrament

O Salutaris Hostia

¶ The Priest brings the Sacrament out of the Tabernacle with all kneeling, singing:

SAVING Victim op'ning wide * The Gate of heav'n to man below,
Our foes press on from ev'ry side, * Thine aid supply, thy strength bestow.
All praise and thanks to thee ascend * For evermore, blest One in Three;
O grant us life that shall not end, * In our true native land with thee. Amen.

SALUTÁRIS Hóstia, * Quæ cæli pandis óstium:
Bella premunt hostília, * Da robur, fer auxílium.
Uni trinóque Dómino * Sit sempitérna glória,
Qui vitam sine término * Nobis donet in pátria. Amen.

Tantum Ergo Sacramentum

¶ After a time for silence, the following Hymn is sung:

HEREFORE we, before him bending, * This great Sacrament revere;
Types and shadows have their ending, * For the newer rite is here;
Faith, our outward sense befriending, * Makes our inward vision clear.

Glory let us give and blessing * To the Father and the Son,
Honour, thanks, and praise addressing, * While eternal ages run;
Ever too his love confessing * Who from One with Both is One. Amen.

℣. Thou gavest them bread from heaven. (Alleluia)
℟. Containing in itself all sweetness. (Alleluia)

ÁNTUM ergo Sacraméntum * Venerémur cérnui,
Et antíquum documéntum, * Nóvo cédat rítui,
Præstet fídes suppleméntum * Sénsuum deféctui.

Genitóri, Genitóque, * Laus et jubilátio;
Sálus, hónor, vírtus quoque * Sit et benedíctio.
Procedénti ab unóque * Cómpar sit laudátio. Amen.

℣. Panem de cælis præstitísti eis. (Allelúja.)
℟. Omne delectaméntum in se habéntem. (Allelúja.)

Eucharistic Devotions — *Benediction*

Let us pray.	*Orémus.*
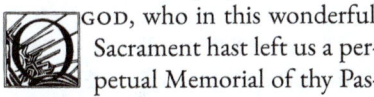GOD, who in this wonderful Sacrament hast left us a perpetual Memorial of thy Passion: Grant us, we beseech thee, so to venerate the Sacred Mysteries of thy Body and Blood, that we may ever perceive within ourselves the fruit of thy redemption; who livest and reignest, world without end. *Amen.*	EUS, qui nobis sub sacraménto mirábili, passiónis tuæ memóriam reliquísti: tríbue, quǽsumus, ita nos córporis et sánguinis tui sacra mystéria venerári, ut redemptiónis tuæ fructum in nobis iúgiter sentiámus. Qui vivis et regnas in sǽcula sæculorum. *Amen.*

Divine Praises

¶ All kneeling, the Priest blesses the People with the Blessed Sacrament. He then places it upon the Altar and says the Divine Praises, as followeth.

Blessed be God.	Benedíctus Deus.
Blessed be his Holy Name.	Benedíctum Nomen Sanctum ejus.
Blessed be Jesus Christ, true God and true Man.	Benedíctus Jesus Christus, verus Deus et verus homo.
Blessed be the Name of Jesus.	Benedíctum Nomen Jesu.
Blessed be Jesus in the Most Holy Sacrament of the Altar.	Benedíctus Jesus in sanctíssimo altáris Sacraménto.
Blessed be God the Holy Ghost, the Comforter.	Benedíctus Sanctus Spíritus, Paraclítus.
Blessed be the Great Mother of God, Mary most Holy.	Benedícta magna Mater Dei, María sanctíssima.
Blessed be the name of Mary, Virgin and Mother.	Benedíctum nomen Maríæ, Vírginis et Matris.
Blessed be Saint Joseph, her most chaste spouse.	Benedíctus sanctus Joseph, ejus castíssimus Sponsus.
Blessed be God in his Angels and in his Saints.	Benedíctus Deus in Angelis suis, et in Sanctis suis.

Benediction # Eucharistic Devotions

Psalm 117. *Laudate Dominum*

❡ The Blessed Sacrament is replaced in the Tabernacle. All stand and pray the following,

Ant. Let us forever adore the Most Holy Sacrament. (Alleluia.)

PRAISE the LORD, all ye heathen : praise him, all ye nations.

For his merciful kindness is ever more and more toward us : and the truth of the LORD endureth for ever. Praise the LORD.

Glory be to the Father, and to the Son, * and to the Holy Ghost:

As it was in the beginning, is now, and ever shall be, * world without end. Amen.

Ant. Let us forever adore the Most Holy Sacrament. (Alleluia.)

Ant. Adorémus in ætérnum Sanctíssimum Sacramentum. (Allelúja.)

AUDÁTE Dóminum, omnes gentes: * laudáte eum, omnes pópuli:

Quóniam confirmáta est super nos misericórdia ejus: * et véritas Dómini manet in ætérnum.

Glória Patri, et Fílio, * et Spirítui Sancto.

Sicut erat in princípio, et nunc, et semper, * et in sǽcula sæculórum. Amen.

Ant. Adorémus in ætérnum Sanctíssimum Sacraméntum. (Allelúja.)

Eucharistic Devotions *Preparation*

Preparation for Holy Communion

Psalms

EMEMBER not, † Lord, our offences, nor the offences of our forefathers; neither take thou vengeance of our sins. (Alleluia.)

E reminiscáris, † Dómine, delícta nostra, vel paréntum nostrórum, neque vindíctam sumas de peccátis nostris. (Allelúja.)

Psalm 84

HOW amiable are thy dwellings : thou Lord of hosts!
2 My soul hath a desire and longing to enter into the courts of the Lord : my heart and my flesh rejoice in the living God.
3 Yea, the sparrow hath found her an house, and the swallow a nest where she may lay her young : even thy altars, O Lord of hosts, my King and my God.
4 Blessed are they that dwell in thy house : they will be alway praising thee.
5 Blessed is the man whose strength is in thee : in whose heart are thy ways.
6 Who going through the vale of misery use it for a well : and the pools are filled with water.
7 They will go from strength to strength : and unto the God of gods appeareth every one of them in Sion.
8 O Lord God of hosts, hear my prayer : hearken, O God of Jacob.
9 Behold, O God our defender : and look upon the face of thine Anointed.
10 For one day in thy courts : is better than a thousand.
11 I had rather be a door-keeper in the house of my God : than to dwell in the tents of ungodliness.

UAM dilécta tabernácula tua, Dómine virtútum: * concupíscit, et déficit ánima mea in átria Dómini.
Cor meum, et caro mea * exsultavérunt in Deum vivum.
Étenim passer invénit sibi domum: * et turtur nidum sibi, ubi ponat pullos suos.
Altária tua, Dómine virtútum: * Rex meus, et Deus meus.
Beáti, qui hábitant in domo tua, Dómine: * in sǽcula sæculórum laudábunt te.
Beátus vir, cujus est auxílium abs te: * ascensiónes in corde suo dispósuit, in valle lacrimárum in loco, quem pósuit.
Étenim benedictiónem dabit legislátor, ibunt de virtúte in virtútem: * vidébitur Deus deórum in Sion.
Dómine, Deus virtútum, exáudi oratiónem meam: * áuribus pércipe, Deus Iacob.
Protéctor noster, áspice, Deus: * et réspice in fáciem Christi tui:
Quia mélior est dies una in átriis tuis, * super míllia.
Elégi abiéctus esse in domo Dei mei: * magis quam habitáre in tabernáculis

Preparation   Eucharistic Devotions

12 For the Lord God is a light and defence : the Lord will give grace and worship, and no good thing shall he withhold from them that live a godly life.

13 O Lord God of hosts : blessed is the man that putteth his trust in thee.

℣. Glory be to the Father, and to the Son, and to the Holy Ghost.

℟. As it was in the beginning, is now, and ever shall be, world without end. Amen.

peccatórum.

Quia misericórdiam, et veritátem díligit Deus: * grátiam et glóriam dabit Dóminus.

Non privábit bonis eos, qui ámbulant in innocéntia: * Dómine virtútum, beátus homo, qui sperat in te.

℣. Glória Patri, et Fílio, * et Spirítui Sancto:

℟. Sicut erat in princípio, et nunc, et semper, * et in sǽcula sæculórum. Amen.

Psalm 85

ORD, thou art become gracious unto thy land : thou hast turned away the captivity of Jacob.

2 Thou hast forgiven the offence of thy people : and covered all their sins.

3 Thou hast taken away all thy displeasure : and turned thyself from thy wrathful indignation.

4 Turn us then, O God our Saviour : and let thine anger cease from us.

5 Wilt thou be displeased at us for ever : and wilt thou stretch out thy wrath from one generation to another?

6 Wilt thou not turn again, and quicken us : that thy people may rejoice in thee?

7 Shew us thy mercy, O Lord : and grant us thy salvation.

8 I will hearken what the Lord God will say concerning me : for he shall speak peace unto his people, and to his saints, that they turn not again.

ENEDIXÍSTI, Dómine, terram tuam: * avertísti captivitátem Iacob.

Remisísti iniquitátem plebis tuæ: * operuísti ómnia peccáta eórum.

Mitigásti omnem iram tuam: * avertísti ab ira indignatiónis tuæ.

Convérte nos, Deus, salutáris noster: * et avérte iram tuam a nobis.

Numquid in ætérnum irascéris nobis? * aut exténdes iram tuam a generatióne in generatiónem?

Deus, tu convérsus vivificábis nos: * et plebs tua lætábitur in te.

Osténde nobis, Dómine, misericórdiam tuam: * et salutáre tuum da nobis.

Áudiam quid loquátur in me Dóminus Deus: * quóniam loquétur pacem in plebem suam.

Et super sanctos suos: * et in eos, qui convertúntur ad cor.

Verúmtamen prope timéntes eum salutáre ipsíus: * ut inhábitet glória in terra nostra.

Eucharistic Devotions — *Preparation*

9 For his salvation is nigh them that fear him : that glory may dwell in our land.

10 Mercy and truth are met together : righteousness and peace have kissed each other.

11 Truth shall flourish out of the earth : and righteousness hath looked down from heaven.

12 Yea, the Lord shall shew lovingkindness : and our land shall give her increase.

13 Righteousness shall go before him : and he shall direct his going in the way.

℣. Glory be to the Father, and to the Son, and to the Holy Ghost.

℟. As it was in the beginning, is now, and ever shall be, world without end. Amen.

Misericórdia, et véritas obviavérunt sibi: * justítia, et pax osculátæ sunt.

Véritas de terra orta est: * et justítia de cælo prospéxit.

Étenim Dóminus dabit benignitátem: * et terra nostra dabit fructum suum.

Justítia ante eum ambulábit: * et ponet in via gressus suos.

℣. Glória Patri, et Fílio, * et Spirítui Sancto:

℟. Sicut erat in princípio, et nunc, et semper, * et in sǽcula sæculórum. Amen.

Psalm 86

ow down thine ear, O Lord, and hear me : for I am poor, and in misery.

2 Preserve thou my soul, for I am holy : my God, save thy servant that putteth his trust in thee.

3 Be merciful unto me, O Lord : for I will call daily upon thee.

4 Comfort the soul of thy servant : for unto thee, O Lord, do I lift up my soul.

5 For thou, Lord, art good and gracious : and of great mercy unto all them that call upon thee.

6 Give ear, Lord, unto my prayer : and ponder the voice of my humble desires.

NCLÍNA, Dómine, aurem tuam, et exáudi me: * quóniam inops, et pauper sum ego.

Custódi ánimam meam, quóniam sanctus sum: * salvum fac servum tuum, Deus meus, sperántem in te.

Miserére mei, Dómine, quóniam ad te clamávi tota die: * lætífica ánimam servi tui, quóniam ad te, Dómine, ánimam meam levávi.

Quóniam tu, Dómine, suávis, et mitis: * et multæ misericórdiæ ómnibus invocántibus te.

Áuribus pércipe, Dómine, oratiónem meam: * et inténde voci deprecatiónis meæ.

Preparation   # Eucharistic Devotions

7 In the time of my trouble I will call upon thee : for thou hearest me.

8 Among the gods there is none like unto thee, O Lord : there is not one that can do as thou doest.

9 All nations whom thou hadst made shall come and worship thee, O Lord : and shall glorify thy Name.

10 For thou art great, and doest wondrous things : thou art God alone.

11 Teach me thy way, O Lord, and I will walk in thy truth : O knit my heart unto thee, that I may fear thy Name.

12 I will thank thee, O Lord my God, with all my heart : and will praise thy Name for evermore.

13 For great is thy mercy toward me : and thou hast delivered my soul from the nethermost hell.

14 O God, the proud are risen against me : and the congregations of naughty men have sought after my soul, and have not set thee before their eyes.

15 But thou, O Lord God, art full of compassion and mercy : long-suffering, plenteous in goodness and truth.

16 O turn thee then unto me, and have mercy upon me : give thy strength unto thy servant, and help the son of thine handmaid.

17 Shew some token upon me for good, that they who hate me may see it and be ashamed : because thou, Lord, hast holpen me and comforted me.

℣. Glory be to the Father, and to the Son, and to the Holy Ghost.

℟. As it was in the beginning, is now, and ever shall be, world without end. Amen.

In die tribulatiónis meæ clamávi ad te: * quia exaudísti me.

Non est símilis tui in diis, Dómine: * et non est secúndum ópera tua.

Omnes gentes quascúmque fecísti, vénient, et adorábunt coram te, Dómine: * et glorificábunt nomen tuum.

Quóniam magnus es tu, et fáciens mirabília: * tu es Deus solus.

Deduc me, Dómine, in via tua, et ingrédiar in veritáte tua: * lætétur cor meum ut tímeat nomen tuum.

Confitébor tibi, Dómine, Deus meus, in toto corde meo, * et glorificábo nomen tuum in ætérnum:

Quia misericórdia tua magna est super me: * et eruísti ánimam meam ex inférno inferióri.

Deus, iníqui insurrexérunt super me, et synagóga poténtium quæsiérunt ánimam meam: * et non proposuérunt te in conspéctu suo.

Et tu, Dómine, Deus miserátor et miséricors, * pátiens, et multæ misericórdiæ, et verax,

Réspice in me, et miserére mei, * da impérium tuum púero tuo: et salvum fac fílium ancíllæ tuæ.

Fac mecum signum in bonum, ut vídeant qui odérunt me, et confundántur: * quóniam tu, Dómine, adjuvísti me, et consolátus es me.

℣. Glória Patri, et Fílio, * et Spirítui Sancto:

℟. Sicut erat in princípio, et nunc, et semper, * et in sǽcula sæculórum. Amen.

Eucharistic Devotions — *Preparation*

Psalm 116:10

I BELIEVED, and therefore will I speak; but I was sore troubled : I said in my haste, All men are liars.

11 What reward shall I give unto the Lord : for all the benefits that he hath done unto me?

12 I will receive the cup of salvation : and call upon the Name of the Lord.

13 I will pay my vows now in the presence of all his people : right dear in the sight of the Lord is the death of his saints.

14 Behold, O Lord, how that I am thy servant : I am thy servant, and the son of thine handmaid; thou hast broken my bonds in sunder.

15 I will offer to thee the sacrifice of thanksgiving : and will call upon the Name of the Lord.

16 I will pay my vows unto the Lord, in the sight of all his people : in the courts of the Lord's house, even in the midst of thee, O Jerusalem. Praise the Lord.

℣. Glory be to the Father, and to the Son, and to the Holy Ghost.

℟. As it was in the beginning, is now, and ever shall be, world without end. Amen.

CRÉDIDI, propter quod locútus sum: * ego autem humiliátus sum nimis.

Ego dixi in excéssu meo: * Omnis homo mendax.

Quid retríbuam Dómino, * pro ómnibus, quæ retríbuit mihi?

Cálicem salutáris accípiam: * et nomen Dómini invocábo.

Vota mea Dómino reddam coram omni pópulo ejus: * pretiósa in conspéctu Dómini mors sanctórum ejus:

O Dómine, quia ego servus tuus: * ego servus tuus, et fílius ancíllæ tuæ.

Dirupísti víncula mea: * tibi sacrificábo hóstiam laudis, et nomen Dómini invocábo.

Vota mea Dómino reddam in conspéctu omnis pópuli ejus: * in átriis domus Dómini, in médio tui, Jerúsalem.

℣. Glória Patri, et Fílio, * et Spirítui Sancto:

℟. Sicut erat in princípio, et nunc, et semper, * et in sǽcula sæculórum. Amen.

Psalm 130

OUT of the deep have I called unto thee, O Lord : Lord, hear my voice.

2 O let thine ears consider well : the voice of my complaint.

DE profúndis clamávi ad te, Dómine: * Dómine, exáudi vocem meam:

Fiant aures tuæ intendéntes, * in vocem deprecatiónis meæ.

Preparation — **Eucharistic Devotions**

3 If thou, Lord, wilt be extreme to mark what is done amiss : O Lord, who may abide it?

4 For there is mercy with thee : therefore shalt thou be feared.

5 I look for the Lord; my soul doth wait for him : in his word is my trust.

6 My soul fleeth unto the Lord : before the morning watch, I say, before the morning watch.

7 O Israel, trust in the Lord, for with the Lord there is mercy : and with him is plenteous redemption.

8 And he shall redeem Israel : from all his sins.

℣. Glory be to the Father, and to the Son, and to the Holy Ghost.

℟. As it was in the beginning, is now, and ever shall be, world without end. Amen.

EMEMBER not, Lord, our offences, nor the offences of our forefathers; neither take thou vengeance of our sins. (Alleluia.)

℣. Lord, have mercy upon us.
℟. Christ, have mercy upon us.
℣. Lord, have mercy upon us.

¶ The Lord's Prayer is said silently until,

℣. And lead us not into temptation.
℟. But deliver us from evil. Amen.
℣. I said, Lord, be merciful unto me.
℟. Heal my soul; for I have sinned against thee.
℣. Turn thee again, O Lord, at the last.
℟. And be gracious unto thy servants.
℣. O Lord, let thy mercy be shewed upon us.

Si iniquitátes observáveris, Dómine: * Dómine, quis sustinébit?

Quia apud te propitiátio est: * et propter legem tuam sustínui te, Dómine.

Sustínuit ánima mea in verbo ejus: * sperávit ánima mea in Dómino.

A custódia matutína usque ad noctem: * speret Israël in Dómino.

Quia apud Dóminum misericórdia: * et copiósa apud eum redémptio.

Et ipse rédimet Israël, * ex ómnibus iniquitátibus ejus.

℣. Glória Patri, et Fílio, * et Spirítui Sancto:

℟. Sicut erat in princípio, et nunc, et semper, * et in sǽcula sæculórum. Amen.

E reminiscáris, Dómine, delícta nostra, vel paréntum nostrórum, neque vindíctam sumas de peccátis nostris. (Allelúja.)

℣. Kýrie, eléison.
℟. Christe, eléison.
℣. Kýrie, eléison.

℣. Et ne nos indúcas in tentatiónem.
℟. Sed líbera nos a malo. Amen.
℣. Ego dixi: Dómine, miserére mei.
℟. Sana ánimam meam, quia peccávi tibi.
℣. Convértere, Dómine, aliquántulum.
℟. Et deprecáre super servos tuos.
℣. Fiat misericórdia tua, Dómine, super nos.

Eucharistic Devotions   *Preparation*

℟. As we do put our trust in thee.
℣. Let thy priests be clothed with righteousness.
℟. And let thy saints sing with joyfulness.
℣. Cleanse me, O Lord, from my secret faults.
℟. Keep thy servant also from presumptuous sins.
℣. O Lord, hear my prayer.
℟. And let my cry come unto thee.
℣. The Lord be with you.
℟. And with thy spirit.

Let us pray.

OST gracious God, incline thy merciful ears unto our prayers and by the grace of the Holy Spirit illumine our hearts, that we may worthily serve at thy holy Mysteries, and love thee with an everlasting love.

GOD, unto whom all hearts are open, all desires known, and from whom no secrets are hid: cleanse the thoughts of our hearts by the inspiration of thy Holy Spirit, that we may perfectly love thee and worthily magnify thy holy Name.

NKINDLE, O Lord, our hearts and minds with the fire of the Holy Spirit: that we may serve thee with a chaste body and please thee with a clean heart.

E beseech thee, O Lord, that the Comforter, who proceedeth from thee, may enlighten our minds: and lead us into all truth, as thy Son hath promised.

℟. Quemádmodum sperávimus in te.
℣. Sacerdótes tui induántur justítiam.
℟. Et Sancti tui exsúltent.
℣. Ab occúltis meis munda me, Dómine.
℟. Et ab aliénis parce servo tuo.
℣. Dómine, exáudi oratiónem meam.
℟. Et clamor meus ad te véniat.
℣. Dóminus vobíscum.
℟. Et cum spíritu tuo.

Orémus.

URES tuæ pietátis, mitíssime Deus, inclína précibus nostris, et grátia Sancti Spíritus illúmina cor nostrum: ut tuis mystériis digne ministráre, teque ætérna caritáte dilígere mereámur.

EUS, cui omne cor patet et omnis volúntas lóquitur, et quem nullum latet secrétum: puríficaper infusiónem Sancti Spíritus cogitatiónes cordis nostri: ut te perfécte dilígere, et digne laudáre mereámur.

RE igne Sancti Spíritus renes nostros et cor nostrum, Dómine: ut tibi casto córpore serviámus, et mundo corde placeámus.

ENTES nostras, quæsumus, Dómine, Paráclitus, qui a te procédit, illúminet: et indúcat in omnem, sicut tuus promísit Fílius, veritátem.

DSIT nobis, quæsumus, Dómine, virtus Spíritus Sancti: quæ et corda nostra cleménter expúrget et ab ómnibus tueátur advérsis.

Preparation # Eucharistic Devotions

ET the power of the Holy Spirit come upon us, O Lord, we beseech thee: that he may both mercifully cleanse our hearts, and defend us from all adversities.

GOD, who didst teach the hearts of thy faithful people, by sending them the light of thy Holy Spirit: grant us by the same Spirit to have a right judgement in all things, and evermore to rejoice in his holy comfort.

URIFY our consciences, we beseech thee, O Lord, by thy visitation: that our Lord Jesus Christ thy Son, when he cometh, may find in us a mansion prepared for himself. Who with thee, in the unity of the Holy Spirit, liveth and reigneth God, world without end. Amen.

EUS, qui corda fidélium Sancti Spíritus illustratióne docuísti: da nobis in eódem Spíritu recta sápere; et de ejus semper consolatióne gaudére.

ONSCIÉNTIAS nostras, quæsumus, Dómine, visitándo puríficá: ut véniens Dóminus noster Jesus Christus, Fílius tuus, parátam sibi in nobis invéniat mansiónem: Qui tecum vivit et regnat.

PRAYER OF ST. AMBROSE

¶ In the following prayers, the sections in parentheses is said, unless he be a Priest preparing to celebrate Mass, in which case he should always say the text in the margin.

Sunday

^a *teach me, thy unworthy servant, whom among thy other gifts, not for my own merit, but only our of the worthiness of thy mercy, thou hast deigned to call to the priestly office;*

^b *handle*

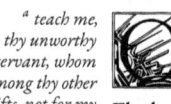SUPREME High Priest and true Chief Bishop, Jesus Christ, who didst offer thyself to God the Father a pure and spotless Victim upon the Altar of the Cross for us miserable sinners, and who didst give us thy Flesh to eat and thy Blood to drink, and didst ordain that Mystery in the power of the Holy Spirit, saying, This do, as often as ye shall do it, in remembrance of me; I pray thee, by that same Blood of thine, the great price of our salvation; I pray thee, by that wonderful and unspeakable love wherewith thou didst vouchsafe to love us, miserable and unworthy, as to wash us from our sins in thy Blood;^a teach me, I pray thee, by thy Holy Spirit, to [approach]^b so great a Mystery with such reverence and honour, with such fear and devotion, as are due and fitting. Make me, through thy grace, always so to believe and understand, so to conceive and firmly hold, so to think and speak of this wondrous Mystery,

Eucharistic Devotions *Preparation*

as shall please thee and benefit my own soul. Let thy good Spirit enter into my heart, there silently to sound, and without clamour of words to speak all truth. For exceeding deep are thy Mysteries, and covered with a sacred veil. Of thy great mercy grant me to [assist at]^c the Solemnity of the Mass with a clean heart and ^c*celebrate* a pure mind. Set free my heart from all unclean and unholy, all vain and hurtful thoughts. Defend me with the loving and faithful guard, the mighty protection of thy blessed Angels, that the enemies of all good may go away ashamed. By the virtue of this great Mystery and by the hand of thy holy Angel drive away from me and from all thy servants the hard spirit of pride and vain-glory, of impurity and uncleanness, of doubting and mistrust. Let them be confounded that persecute us: let them perish that make haste to destroy us.

Monday

O KING of virgins and lover of chastity and innocence, extinguish in my body, by the dew of thy heavenly blessing, whatever may kindle the burning of wanton desire, that so one even purity of soul and body may abide in me. Mortify in my members the incitements of the flesh, and all lustful emotions, and give me true and persevering chastity with thine other gifts which please thee in truth, so that I may with chaste body and pure heart offer unto thee the sacrifice of praise. For with what contrition of heart and flowing of tears, with what reverence and awe, with what chastity of body and purity of soul, should that divine and heavenly Sacrifice be celebrated, wherein thy Flesh is eaten indeed, where thy Blood is drunk indeed, wherein things lowest and highest, earthly and divine, are united, where the holy Angels are present, where thou art in a marvellous and unspeakable manner both Priest and Sacrifice

Tuesday

WHO can worthily [assist at]^d this Sacrifice unless thou, O God, makest him ^d*celebrate* worthy? I know, O Lord, yea, truly do I know, and this do I confess to thy loving-kindness, that I am unworthy to approach so great a Mystery, by reason of my numberless sins and negligences; but I know and truly with my whole heart do I believe, and with my mouth confess, that thou canst make me worthy, who alone canst make clean one conceived of unclean seed, and canst make sinners to be righteous and holy. By this thine almighty power I beseech thee, O my God, to grant that I, a sinner, may [assist at]^e this Sacrifice ^e*celebrate* with fear and trembling, with purity of heart and streams of tears, with spiritual gladness and heavenly joy; may my mind feel the sweetness of thy most blessed Presence, and the guardianship of thy holy Angels round about me.

Preparation # Eucharistic Devotions

Wednesday

For now, O Lord, mindful of thy venerable Passion, I approach thine Altar, to offer thee that Sacrifice which thou hast instituted, and commanded us to offer in remembrance of thee for our salvation. Receive it, I beseech thee, O God Most High, for thy holy Church, and for the people whom thou hast purchased with thy Blood.[f] If thou wilt graciously vouchsafe to behold[g] the tribulations of the people, the perils of the nations, the groans of prisoners, the miseries of orphans, the necessities of strangers, the helplessness of the weak, the depression of the weary, the infirmities of the aged, the aspirations of the young, the vows of virgins, the lamentations of widows.

Thursday

For thou, O Lord, art merciful unto all and hatest nothing that thou hast made. Remember what is our nature, for thou art our Father, thou art our God. Be not angry with us for ever, nor withhold the multitude of thy mercies from us; for it is not in our righteousness that we humbly present our prayers before thy face, but because of thy great compassion. Take away from us our iniquities, and graciously kindle the fire of thy Holy Spirit within us. Take away our hearts of stone, and give us an heart of flesh, which may love thee, prefer thee, delight in thee, follow thee, and enjoy thee. We pray thee of thy mercy, O Lord, vouchsafe to shew the light of thy countenance unto thy family awaiting the service of thy holy Name; and that the good desires of none may be ineffectual, the petitions of none unfruitful, do thou put into our minds such prayers as thou mayest delight graciously to hear and answer.

Friday

We beseech thee also, O Lord, Holy Father, for the souls of the faithful departed; that this great Sacrament of thy love may be unto them health and salvation, joy and refreshment. Grant them this day, O Lord my God, a great and abundant feast of thee, the living Bread, which camest down from heaven, and givest life unto the world; even of thy holy and blessed Flesh, the Lamb without spot, that takest away the sins of the world; even of that Flesh, which was taken from the holy and glorious womb of the blessed Virgin Mary, and conceived of the Holy Ghost; and of that Fountain of mercy which by the soldier's spear flowed from thy most sacred Side; that after being fed and satisfied, refreshed and comforted, they may rejoice in thy praise and glory.

I pray thy mercy, O Lord, that on the bread to be offered unto thee may descend the fulness of thy blessing and the hallowing of thy Godhead. May

---

[f] *And since thou hast willed that I, a sinner, should be in the midst between thee and the same thy people, although thou perceivest in me the evidence of no good works, at least refuse not the service of the ministry which thou hast given me; let not the price of their salvation be wasted through my unworthiness, whose saving Victim and redemption thou didst deign to be.*

[g] *Also I bring before thee, O Lord*

Eucharistic Devotions — *Preparation*

there also descend the invisible and incomprehensible majesty of thy Holy Spirit, as it came down of old on the sacrifices of the fathers; which will both make our oblations thy Body and Blood, and teach us, [thy unworthy servants]^h to treat so great a Mystery with purity of heart and with tears of devotion, with reverence and trembling, so that thou mayest graciously and favourably receive this sacrifice^i for the well-being of all, both living and departed.

[b] *me thy unworthy priest,*
[i] *at my hands*

Saturday

ENTREAT thee also, O Lord, by this most holy mystery of thy Body and Blood, wherewith we are daily fed and given to drink, washed and sanctified in thy Church, and are made partakers of the one supreme Divinity, grant unto me thy holy graces, that fulfilled therewith I may draw near to thine Altar with a good conscience; so that these heavenly Sacraments may be made unto me salvation and life; for thou hast said with thy holy and blessed mouth, 'The bread that I will give is my flesh, which I will give for the life of the world. I am the living bread which came down from heaven. If any man eat of this bread, he shall live for ever.'

O sweetest Bread, heal the palate of my heart, that I may taste the pleasant savour of thy love. Heal it of all infirmities, that I may find sweetness in nothing out of thee. O purest Bread, having all delight and all savour, which ever refreshest us, and never failest, let my heart feed on thee, and may my inmost soul be fulfilled with the sweetness of thy savour. The Angels feed upon thee fully: let the wayfaring man feed on thee according to his measure, that, refreshed with such a Viaticum, he fail not by the way. O holy Bread, O living Bread, O pure Bread, who camest down from heaven, and givest life unto the world, come into my heart, and cleanse me from all defilement of flesh and spirit. Enter into my soul; heal and cleanse me within and without; be the protection and continual health of my soul and body. Drive far from me all foes that lie in wait; Let them flee at the presence of thy power, so that being guarded without and within by thee, I may come to thy kingdom by a straight way: where, not as now in mysteries, but face to face, we shall behold thee: when thou shalt have delivered up the kingdom to God, even the Father, and shalt be God, all in all. Then shalt thou satisfy me with thyself in wondrous fulness, so that I shall never hunger nor thirst any more. Who with the same God the Father and the Holy Ghost livest and reignest, world without end. Amen.

Preparation # Eucharistic Devotions

Another Prayer of St. Ambrose

To the Table of thy most sweet Feast, O loving Lord Jesus Christ, I, a sinner, presuming nothing on my own merits, but trusting in thy mercy and goodness, approach with fear and trembling. For my heart and my body are stained with many and grievous sins, my thoughts and my lips have not been carefully kept. Wherefore, O gracious God, O awful majesty, I, in my misery, being brought into a great strait, turn to thee, the Fountain of mercy, to thee I hasten to be healed, and flee under thy protection: and thee, before whom I cannot stand as my Judge, I long to have as my Saviour. To thee, O Lord, I show my wounds, to thee I discover my shame. I know my sins, many and great, for which I am afraid: but I hope in thy mercies, of which there is no end. Look therefore upon me with the eyes of thy mercy, O Lord Jesus Christ, eternal King, God and Man, crucified for man. Hearken unto me whose trust is in thee: have mercy upon me who am full of misery and sin, thou Fountain of mercy that will never cease to flow. Hail, Victim of Salvation, offered for me and for all mankind upon the Altar of the Cross! Hail, noble and precious Blood, flowing from the wounds of my crucified Lord Jesus Christ, and washing away the sins of the whole world! Remember O Lord, thy creature, whom thou hast redeemed with thine own Blood. It repents me that I have sinned, and I desire to amend what I have done. Take away therefore from me, O most merciful Father, all my sins and iniquities; that being purified both in soul and body, I may be made meet worthily to taste the Holy of Holies; and grant that this holy foretaste of thy Body and Blood, which I, unworthy, purpose to take, may be for the remission of my sins; the perfect cleansing of my faults; the driving away of shameful thoughts, and the renewal of good desires; the healthful performance of works well pleasing unto thee; and the most sure protection of soul and body against the wiles of my enemies. Amen.

A Devotional Prayer of St. Augustine

Against thee only have I sinned, O Lord, for no man is without sin: and therefore against thee only have I sinned, because thou alone art without sin. O Lord, who hast so long spared the guilty, shew forth thy mercy upon the miserable offender. Behold the unhappy, O Unfathomable Piety. Regard the cruel ones, O Mercy of All. As one about to despair, I come unto the Almighty. I run, wounded, unto the Physician. Keep, O Lord, the compassion of thy gentleness, who hast so long stayed the sword of vengeance. Blot out the great number of my crimes by the greatness of thy mercy.

Eucharistic Devotions *Preparation*

Unto thee have I cried, O Lord: and early shall my prayer come before thee. Lord, why abhorrest thou my soul: and hidest thou thy face from me? I am in misery, and like unto him that is at the point to die: even from my youth up thy terrors have I suffered with a troubled mind. Thy wrathful displeasure goeth over me: and the fear of thee hath undone me. They came round about me daily like water: and compassed me together on every side. My lovers and friends hast thou put away from me: and hid mine acquaintance out of my sight.

But thou, O Redeemer of all, ineffable Saviour God, who didst enter hell for us, and wast made free among the dead: hear our morning prayer, and have mercy, O Lord, unto thy family, and deliver us from the most grievous bondage of the lurking enemy. Who livest and reignest with the Father, in the unity of the Holy Ghost, God, throughout all ages, world without end. Amen.

Another Devotional Prayer before Communion

O MOTHER of pity and mercy, Blessed Virgin Mary, I, a miserable and unworthy sinner, flee to thee with my whole heart and affection, and I pray thy most sweet pity, that as thou didst stand by thy most sweet Son hanging upon the Cross, so thou wouldest vouchsafe mercifully to stand by me a miserable offender and all who here and in all the holy Church offer the Most Holy Sacrifice of the Mass this day, that, aided by thy merits and prayers, we may be enabled to offer a worthy and acceptable Victim in the sight of the most high and undivided Trinity. Amen.

Declaration of Intention before Mass

I INTEND to [assist at this celebration of the Mass and at the consecration of]^j the Body and Blood of our Lord Jesus Christ, according to the rite of Holy Church, to the praise of Almighty God, and of the whole Church triumphant; for my own benefit; for the benefit of the whole Church militant and expectant; for all who have commended themselves to my prayers in general and in particular, . . . and for the good estate of the Holy Catholic Church.

 THE Almighty and merciful Lord grant unto us joy with peace, amendment of life, time for true repentance, the grace and comfort of the Holy Ghost, and perseverance in good works. Amen.

^j *celebrate Mass and to consecrate*

Thanksgiving   Eucharistic Devotions

Thanksgiving for Holy Communion

Ant. Let us sing † the song of the three children, which the Saints sang in the furnace of fire, blessing the Lord (Alleluia).

Benedicite

All ye Works of the Lord, bless ye the Lord: * praise him, and magnify him for ever.

O ye Angels of the Lord, bless ye the Lord: * O ye heavens, bless ye the Lord.

O ye waters that be above the firmament, bless ye the Lord: * O all ye powers of the Lord, bless ye the Lord.

O ye sun and moon, bless ye the Lord: * O ye stars of heaven, bless ye the Lord.

O ye showers and dew, bless ye the Lord: * O ye winds of God, bless ye the Lord.

O ye fire and heat, bless ye the Lord: * O ye winter and summer, bless ye the Lord.

O ye dews and frosts, bless ye the Lord: * O ye frost and cold, bless ye the Lord.

O ye ice and snow, bless ye the Lord: * O ye nights and days, bless ye the Lord.

O ye light and darkness, bless ye the Lord: * O ye lightnings and clouds, bless ye the Lord.

Let the earth bless the Lord: yea, let it praise him, and magnify him for ever.

O ye mountains and hills, bless ye the Lord: * O all ye green things upon the earth, bless ye the Lord.

O ye wells, bless ye the Lord: * O ye Seas and Floods, bless ye the Lord.

O ye whales, and all that move in the waters, bless ye the Lord: * O all ye fowls of the air, bless ye the Lord.

O all ye beasts and cattle, bless ye the Lord: * O ye children of men, bless ye the Lord.

Let Israel bless the Lord: * praise him, and magnify him for ever.

O ye priests of the Lord, bless ye the Lord: * O ye servants of the Lord, bless ye the Lord.

O ye spirits and souls of the righteous, bless ye the Lord: * O ye holy and humble men of heart, bless ye the Lord.

O Ananias, Azarias, and Misael, bless ye the Lord: * praise him, and magnify him for ever.

Let us bless the Father and the Son with the Holy Ghost: * let us praise him and magnify him for ever.

Blessed art thou, O Lord, in the firmament of heaven: * and to be praised and glorified and exalted above all for ever.

¶ Here neither **Glory be** nor **Amen** is said.

Eucharistic Devotions *Thanksgiving*

Psalm 150

PRAISE God in his holiness : * praise him in the firmament of his power.

2 Praise him in his noble acts : * praise him according to his excellent greatness.

3 Praise him in the sound of the trumpet : * praise him upon the lute and harp.

4 Praise him in the cymbals and dances : * praise him upon the strings and pipe.

5 Praise him upon the well-tuned cymbals : * praise him upon the loud cymbals.

6 Let every thing that hath breath * praise the Lord.

℣. Glory be to the Father, and to the Son, and to the Holy Ghost.

℟. As it was in the beginning, is now, and ever shall be, world without end. Amen.

Ant. Let us sing the song of the three children, which the Saints sang in the furnace of fire, blessing the Lord (Alleluia).

℣. Lord, have mercy upon us.
℟. Christ, have mercy upon us.
℣. Lord, have mercy upon us.

¶ The Lord's Prayer is here said, in secret, kneeling, ending with,

℣. And lead us not into temptation.
℟. But deliver us from evil.
℣. All thy works praise thee, O Lord.
℟. And thy Saints give thanks unto thee.
℣. Let thy Saints be joyful in glory,
℟. Let them rejoice in their beds.
℣. Not unto us, O Lord, not unto us,
℟. But unto thy name give the praise.
℣. O Lord, hear my prayer.
℟. And let my cry come unto thee.
℣. The Lord be with you.
℟. And with thy spirit.

Let us pray.

GOD, who to the three children didst assuage the flames of fire: mercifully grant; that the flames of sin may not kindle upon thy servants.

REVENT us, O Lord, in all our doings with thy most gracious favour, and further us with thy continual help: that all our prayer and work may be begun, continued, and ended in thee.

RANT to us, we beseech thee, O Lord, that we may quench the flames of our sins: as thou didst enable blessed Lawrence to overcome the fires of his torments. Through Christ, our Lord. *Amen.*

Aspersion

Eucharistic Devotions

Aspersion of the People

Asperges, Me

¶ Having blest the water, the Priest who is going to celebrate, vested in a cope of the colour of the day, proceeds to the Altar. And there kneeling, even in Eastertide, with the ministers below the steps, he receives the aspersorium from the Deacon, and first asperses the Altar thrice, then himself, and, standing up, the ministers, beginning the Antiphon Thou shalt purge me. And the Quire continues: O Lord, with hyssop, etc., as below. Meanwhile the Celebrant asperses the Clergy, and then the People, saying with a low voice with the ministers the Psalm Have mercy upon me, O God.

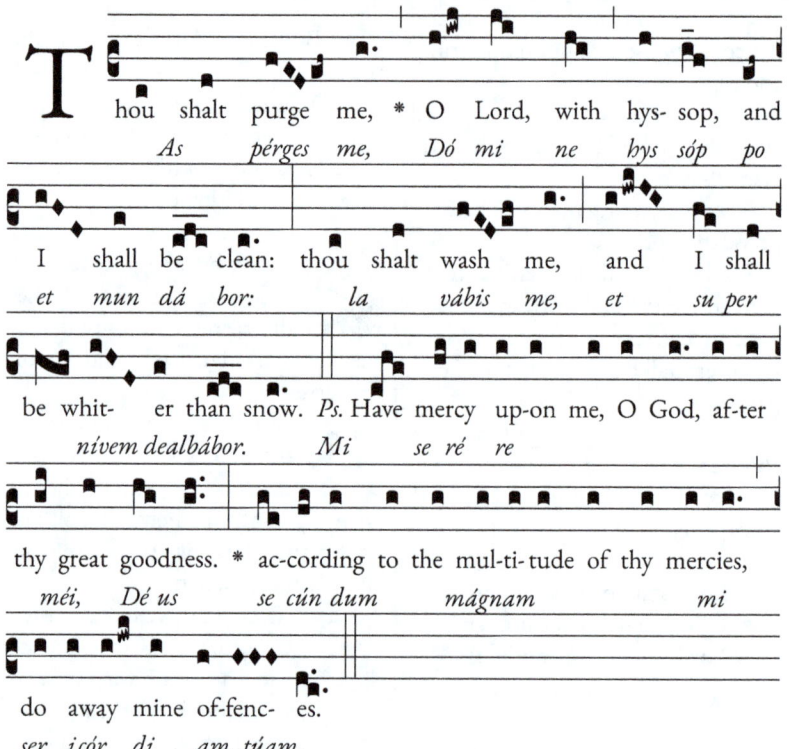

Thou shalt purge me, * O Lord, with hyssop, and I shall be clean: thou shalt wash me, and I shall be whiter than snow. Ps. Have mercy upon me, O God, after thy great goodness. * according to the multitude of thy mercies, do away mine offences.

Aspérges me, Dómine hyssópo, et mundábor: lavábis me, et super nívem dealbábor. Miserére méi, Déus secúndum mágnam misericórdiam túam.

Eucharistic Devotions *Aspersion*

❧ The following **Gloria Patri** is omitted in Passiontide, the psalm simply being repeated.

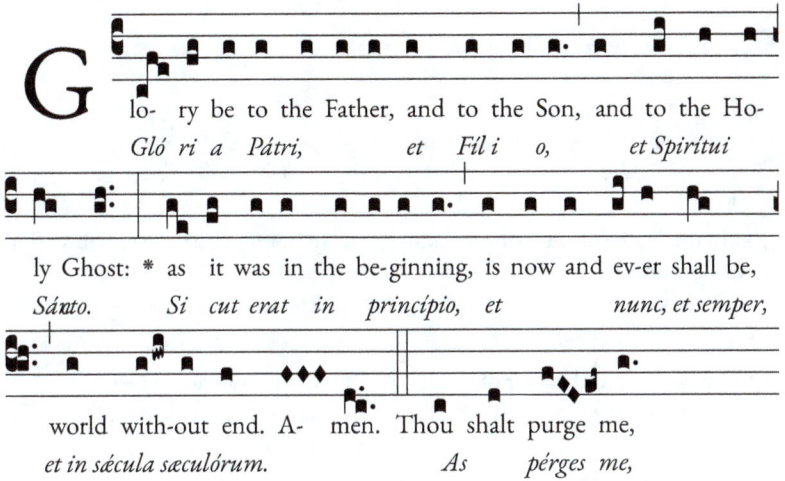

Glory be to the Father, and to the Son, and to the Holy Ghost: * as it was in the beginning, is now and ever shall be, world without end. Amen. Thou shalt purge me,
Glória Patri, et Fílio, et Spirítui Sancto. Sicut erat in princípio, et nunc, et semper, et in sǽcula sæculórum. As pérges me,

Vidi Aquam

❧ The following replaces the **Asperges, me** during Eastertide.

Ant. I beheld water * issuing out from the temple, on the right side, alleluia: and all to whom that water came were saved, and they shall say: alleluia, alleluia.
O give thanks unto the Lord, for he is gracious: because his mercy endureth for ever.
Glory be to the Father, and to the Son, and to the Holy Ghost: * as it was in the beginning, is now and ever shall be, world without end. Amen.
Ant. I beheld water * issuing out from the temple, on the right side, alleluia: and all to whom that water came were saved, and they shall say: alleluia, alleluia.

Ant. Vidi aquam egredientem de templo, * a latere dextro, allelúja: * Et omnes, ad quos pervenit aqua ista, * salvi facti sunt et dicent, allelúja, allelúja.
Confitémini Domino, quoniam bonus: * quoniam in saeculum misericordia ejus.
Glória Patri, et Fílio, et Spirítui Sancto. Sicut erat in princípio, et nunc, et semper: et in sǽcula sæculórum. Amen.
Ant. Vidi aquam egredientem de templo, * a latere dextro, allelúja: * Et omnes, ad quos pervenit aqua ista, * salvi facti sunt et dicent, allelúja, allelúja.

Foot of the Altar # Eucharistic Devotions

Prayers at the Foot of the Altar

❧ A Hymn may be sung during the Prayers at the Foot of the Altar, except in a Low Mass.

❧ After the Rite of Aspersion (or immediately upon processing to the Foot of the Altar if the Rite not occur), the Priest—having vested—approaches the Altar, makes the due reverence, signs himself with the sign of the Cross from forehead to breast, and says in the clear voice:

℣. In the Name of the Father, ✠ and of the Son, and of the Holy Ghost.
℞. Amen.

℣. In nómine Patris, ✠ et Fílii, et Spíritus Sancti.
℞. Amen.

❧ Then, with hands joined before his breast, the Priest begins the Antiphon:

℣. I will go unto the altar of God.
℞. Even unto the God of my joy and gladness.

℣. Introíbo ad altáre Dei.
℞. Ad Deum, qui lætíficat juventútem meam.

❧ In Masses for the Dead, and in Masses of the Season from Passion Sunday to Holy Saturday exclusive, the following Psalm Give sentence is omitted together with Glory be and the repetition of the Antiphon. And the Priest then moves immediately to Our help.

℣. Give sentence with me, O God, and defend my cause against the ungodly people: O deliver me from the deceitful and wicked man.
℞. For thou art the God of my strength; why hast thou put me from thee: and why go I so heavily, while the enemy oppresseth me?
℣. O send out thy light and thy truth, that they may lead me: and bring me unto thy holy hill, and to thy dwelling.
℞. And that I may go unto the altar of God, even the God of my joy and gladness: and upon the harp will I give thanks unto thee, O God, my God.
℣. Why art thou so heavy, O my soul: and why art thou so disquieted within me?

℣. Júdica me, Deus, et discérne causam meam de gente non sancta: ab hómine iníquo et dolóso érue me.
℞. Quia tu es, Deus, fortitúdo mea: quare me repulísti, et quare tristis incédo, dum afflígit me inimícus?
℣. Emítte lucem tuam et veritátem tuam: ipsa me deduxérunt, et adduxérunt in montem sanctum tuum et in tabernácula tua.
℞. Et introíbo ad altáre Dei: ad Deum, qui lætíficat juventútem meam.
℣. Confitébor tibi in cíthara, Deus, Deus meus: quare tristis es, ánima mea, et quare contúrbas me?
℞. Spera in Deo, quóniam adhuc confitébor illi: salutáre vultus mei, et Deus meus.

Eucharistic Devotions *Foot of the Altar*

℟. O put thy trust in God: for I will yet give him thanks, which is the help of my countenance, and my God.

℣. Glory be to the Father, and to the Son: and to the Holy Ghost.

℟. As it was in the beginning, is now, and ever shall be: world without end. Amen.

℣. I will go unto the altar of God:

℟. Even unto the God of my joy and gladness.

℣. Glória Patri, et Fílio, et Spirítui Sancto.

℟. Sicut erat in princípio, et nunc, et semper: et in sǽcula sæculórum. Amen.

℣. Introíbo ad altáre Dei.

℟. Ad Deum, qui lætíficat juventútem meam.

℣. Our help is in the Name ✠ of the Lord:

℟. Who hath made heaven and earth.

℣. Adjutórium nostrum ✠ in nómine Dómini.

℟. Qui fecit cælum et terram.

¶ Then, with hands joined, bowing profoundly, the Priest says,

I CONFESS to Almighty God, to Blessed Mary ever Virgin, to Blessed Michael the Archangel, to Blessed John Baptist, to the Holy Apostles Peter and Paul, to all the Saints, and to you, brethren: that I have sinned exceedingly in thought, word, and deed: *(Strike breast thrice.)* by my fault, my own fault, my own most grievous fault. Wherefore I beg Blessed Mary ever Virgin, Blessed Michael the Archangel, Blessed John Baptist, the Holy Apostles Peter and Paul, all the Saints, and you, brethren, to pray for me to the Lord our God.

℟. Almighty God have mercy upon thee, forgive thee thy sins, and bring thee to everlasting life.

℟. Amen.[a]

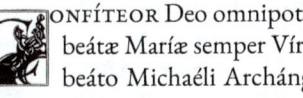

CONFÍTEOR Deo omnipoténti, beátæ Maríæ semper Vírgini, beáto Micháéli Archángelo, beáto Joánni Baptístæ, sanctis Apóstolis Petro et Paulo, ómnibus Sanctis, et vobis, fratres: quia peccávi nimis cogitatióne, verbo et ópere: *(Strike breast thrice.)* mea culpa, mea culpa, mea máxima culpa. Ideo precor beátam Maríam semper Vírginem, beátum Micháélem Archángelum, beátum Joánnem Baptístam, sanctos Apóstolos Petrum et Paulum, omnes Sanctos, et vos, fratres, oráre pro me ad Dóminum, Deum nostrum.

℟. Misereátur tui omnípotens Deus, et, dimíssis peccátis tuis, perdúcat te ad vitam ætérnam.

℟. Amen.[a]

[a] *The Priest rises. The Ministers bow.*

Foot of the Altar   # Eucharistic Devotions

¶ The Ministers, bowing, say,

CONFESS to Almighty God, to Blessed Mary ever Virgin, to Blessed Michael the Archangel, to Blessed John Baptist, to the Holy Apostles Peter and Paul, to all the Saints, and to thee, Father: that I have sinned exceedingly in thought, word, and deed: (Strike breast thrice.) by my fault, my own fault, my own most grievous fault. Wherefore I beg Blessed Mary ever Virgin, Blessed Michael the Archangel, Blessed John Baptist, the Holy Apostles Peter and Paul, all the Saints, and thee, Father, to pray for me to the Lord our God.

℣. Almighty God have mercy upon you, forgive you your sins, and bring you to everlasting life.

℟. Amen.

℣. The Almighty and Merciful Lord grant unto us pardon, ✠ absolution, and remission of our sins.

[b] *Ministers rise.*   ℟. Amen.[b]

℣. Wilt thou not turn again and quicken us, O God?

℟. That thy people may rejoice in thee.

℣. O Lord, show thy mercy upon us.

℟. And grant us thy salvation.

℣. O Lord, hear my prayer.

℟. And let my cry come unto thee.

℣. The Lord be with you.

℟. And with thy spirit.

ONFÍTEOR Deo omnipoténti, beátæ Maríæ semper Vírgini, beáto Michaéli Archángelo, beáto Joánni Baptístæ, sanctis Apóstolis Petro et Paulo, ómnibus Sanctis, et tibi, pater: quia peccávi nimis cogitatióne, verbo et ópere: (Strike breast thrice.) mea culpa, mea culpa, mea máxima culpa. Ideo precor beátam Maríam semper Vírginem, beátum Michaélem Archángelum, beátum Joánnem Baptístam, sanctos Apóstolos Petrum et Paulum, omnes Sanctos, et te, pater, oráre pro me ad Dóminum, Deum nostrum.

℣. Misereátur vestri omnípotens Deus, et, dimíssis peccátis vestris, perdúcat vos ad vitam ætérnam.

℟. Amen.

℣. Indulgéntiam, ✠ absolutiónem et remissiónem peccatórum nostrórum tríbuat nobis omnípotens et miséricors Dóminus.

℟. Amen.[b]

℣. Deus, tu convérsus vivificábis nos?

℟. Et plebs tua lætábitur in te.

℣. Osténde nobis, Dómine, misericórdiam tuam.

℟. Et salutáre tuum da nobis.

℣. Dómine, exáudi oratiónem meam.

℟. Et clamor meus ad te véniat.

℣. Dóminus vobíscum.

℟. Et cum spíritu tuo.

¶ The Priest, extending and joining his hands, says in a loud voice:

℣. Let us pray. | ℣. Orémus.

Holy Mass

Holy Mass

Collect for Purity

¶ The Priest, at the Foot of the Altar, saith the Collect for Purity, as followeth, in an audible voice.

ALMIGHTY God, unto whom all hearts are open, all desires known, and from whom no secrets are hid; Cleanse the thoughts of our hearts by the inspiration of thy Holy Spirit, that we may perfectly love thee, and worthily magnify thy holy Name; through Christ our Lord. *Amen.*

¶ Then shall the Priest, turning to the People, rehearse distinctly—in an audible voice—the Ten Commandments; and the People, still kneeling, shall, after every Commandment, ask God mercy for their transgressions for the time past, and grace to keep the law for the time to come.

¶ And NOTE, that in rehearsing the Ten Commandments, the Priest may omit that part of the Commandment which is inset.

¶ The Ten Commandments may be omitted. When ever it is omitted, the Minister shall say the Summary of the Law, beginning, **Hear what our Lord Jesus Christ saith.**

Ten Commandments

God spake these words, and said:

I am the LORD thy God; Thou shalt have none other gods but me.
Lord, have mercy upon us, and incline our hearts to keep this law.
Thou shalt not make to thyself any graven image, nor the likeness of any thing that is in heaven above, or in the earth beneath, or in the water under the earth; thou shalt not bow down to them, nor worship them:
> for I the Lord thy God am a jealous God, and visit the sins of the fathers upon the children, unto the third and fourth generation of them that hate me; and show mercy unto thousands in them that love me and keep my commandments.

Lord, have mercy upon us, and incline our hearts to keep this law.
Thou shalt not take the Name of the Lord thy God in vain;
> for the Lord will not hold him guiltless, that taketh his Name in vain.

Lord, have mercy upon us, and incline our hearts to keep this law.
Remember that thou keep holy the Sabbath-day.
> Six days shalt thou labour, and do all that thou hast to do; but the seventh day is the Sabbath of the Lord thy God. In it thou shalt do no manner of work; thou, and thy son, and thy daughter, thy man-servant, and thy maid-servant, thy cattle, and the stranger that is within thy gates. For in six days the Lord made heaven and earth, the sea, and all that in them is, and rested the seventh day: wherefore the Lord blessed the seventh day, and hallowed it.

Lord, have mercy upon us, and incline our hearts to keep this law.

Holy Mass

Honour thy father and thy mother;
> that thy days may be long in the land which the Lord thy God giveth thee.
> *Lord, have mercy upon us, and incline our hearts to keep this law.*

Thou shalt do no murder.
> *Lord, have mercy upon us, and incline our hearts to keep this law.*

Thou shalt not commit adultery.
> *Lord, have mercy upon us, and incline our hearts to keep this law.*

Thou shalt not steal.
> *Lord, have mercy upon us, and incline our hearts to keep this law.*

Thou shalt not bear false witness against thy neighbour.
> *Lord, have mercy upon us, and incline our hearts to keep this law.*

Thou shalt not covet.
> thy neighbour's house, thou shalt not covet thy neighbour's wife, nor his servant, nor his maid, nor his ox, nor his ass, nor any thing that is his.
> *Lord, have mercy upon us, and write all these thy laws in our hearts, we beseech thee.*

SUMMARY OF THE LAW

¶ *Then may the Priest say the Summary of the Law, as followeth, in an audible voice.*

HEAR WHAT OUR LORD JESUS CHRIST SAITH.

THOU shalt love the Lord thy God with all thy heart, and with all thy soul, and with all thy mind. This is the first and great commandment. And the second is like unto it; Thou shalt love thy neighbour as thyself. On these two commandments hang all the Law and the Prophets.

ASCENDING THE ALTAR

¶ *Then shall the Priest turn towards the Altar and ascend, saying secretly,*

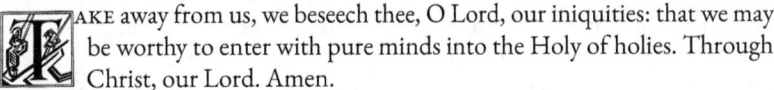
TAKE away from us, we beseech thee, O Lord, our iniquities: that we may be worthy to enter with pure minds into the Holy of holies. Through Christ, our Lord. Amen.

¶ *Then, with hands joined upon the Altar, the Priest saith, bowing (kissing the Altar at the middle),*

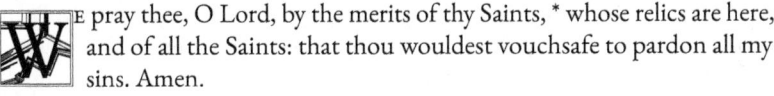
WE pray thee, O Lord, by the merits of thy Saints, * whose relics are here, and of all the Saints: that thou wouldest vouchsafe to pardon all my sins. Amen.

Holy Mass

℣ At a solemn Mass, the Celebrant, before reading the Introit, shall bless the incense saying: Be thou bles ✠ sed by him in whose honour thou shalt be burnt. Amen.

℣ Receiving the thurible from the Deacon, he censeth the Altar, saying nothing. Then the Deacon taketh the thurible from the Celebrant and censeth him only.

℣ Then shall the Priest move to the Epistle side and, signing himself with the sign of the Cross, begin the Introit: which finished, at the middle of the Altar, with joined hands, he saith alternately with the Ministers the Kyrie,

℣. Lord, have mercy upon us.	℣. Kyrie, eléison.
℟. Lord, have mercy upon us.	℟. Kyrie, eléison.
℣. Lord, have mercy upon us.	℣. Kyrie, eléison.
℟. Christ, have mercy upon us.	℟. Christe, eléison.
℣. Christ, have mercy upon us.	℣. Christe, eléison.
℟. Christ, have mercy upon us.	℟. Christe, eléison.
℣. Lord, have mercy upon us.	℣. Kyrie, eléison.
℟. Lord, have mercy upon us.	℟. Kyrie, eléison.
℣. Lord, have mercy upon us.	℣. Kyrie, eléison.

GLORIA IN EXCELSIS

℣ Then the Priest shall, at the middle of the Altar, extend and join his hands and—bowing his head slightly—say, if it is to be said,

GLORY be to God on high, and on earth peace, good will towards men. We praise thee, we bless thee, we worship thee,[a] we glorify thee, we give thanks[b] to thee for thy great glory, O Lord God, heavenly King, God the Father Almighty.

O Lord, the only-begotten Son, Jesus Christ; O Lord God, Lamb of God, Son of the Father, that takest away the sins of the world, have mercy upon us. Thou that takest away the sins of the world, receive our prayer.[c] Thou that sittest at the right hand of God the Father, have mercy upon us.

For thou only art holy; thou only art the Lord; thou only, O Christ, with the Holy Ghost, ✠ art most high in the glory of God the Father. Amen.

GLÓRIA in excélsis Deo. Et in terra pax homínibus bonæ voluntátis. Laudámus te. Benedícimus te. Adorámus te.[a] Glorificámus te. Grátias ágimus tibi[b] propter magnam glóriam tuam. Dómine Deus, Rex cæléstis, Deus Pater omnípotens.

Dómine Fili unigénite, Jesu Christe. Dómine Deus, Agnus Dei, Fílius Patris. Qui tollis peccáta mundi, miserére nobis. Qui tollis peccáta mundi, súscipe deprecatiónem nostram.[c] Qui sedes ad déxteram Patris, miserére nobis.

Quóniam tu solus Sanctus. Tu solus Dóminus. Tu solus Altíssimus, Jesu Christe. Cum Sancto Spíritu ✠ in glória Dei Patris. Amen.

[a] Bow head.
[b] Bow head.
[c] Bow head.

Holy Mass

⁋ Then shall the Priest kiss the Altar in the middle, turn to the People, extend his hands, and say,

℣. The Lord be with you.	℣. Dóminus vobíscum.
℟. And with thy spirit.	℟. Et cum spíritu tuo.
℣. Let us pray.	℣. Orémus.

Collect

⁋ Then shall the Priest move to the Epistle corner of the Altar and pray the Collect(s) of the Day.

Epistle

⁋ The Epistle for the Day shall then be read by the Subdeacon, first saying, **The Epistle is written in the – Chapter of –, beginning at the – Verse.**

⁋ The Epistle ended, he shall say, **Here endeth the Epistle,** the people responding, **Thanks be to God.**

⁋ The Gradual and Alleluia (or Tract) and (if provided) Sequence is here chanted by the Choir.

Gospel

⁋ These being ended, if it be a Solemn Mass, the Deacon shall then place the book of the Gospels on the middle of the Altar, and the Celebrant shall bless the incense with the **Be thou blessed,** as above.

⁋ Then shall the Deacon kneeling before the Altar (or the Priest only bowing in the midst of the Altar) say with joined hands,

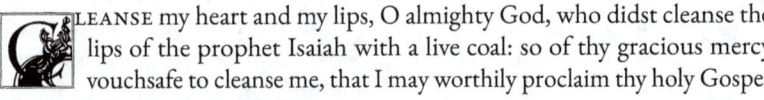LEANSE my heart and my lips, O almighty God, who didst cleanse the lips of the prophet Isaiah with a live coal: so of thy gracious mercy vouchsafe to cleanse me, that I may worthily proclaim thy holy Gospel. Through Christ, our Lord. Amen.

Deacon	Priest
Deacon. Bid, sir, a blessing.	*Priest.* Bid, Lord, a blessing.
Priest. The Lord be in thy heart and on thy lips: that thou mayest worthily and fitly proclaim his Gospel: In the name of the Father, and of the Son, ✠ and of the Holy Ghost. Amen.	*Priest.* The Lord be in my heart and on my lips: that I may worthily and fitly proclaim his Gospel.

Holy Mass

℣ Having received the blessing, the Deacon kisseth the hand of the Celebrant. And going with the other Ministers, with the incense and the lights, to the place of the Gospel, he standeth with joined hands.

℣ Then, the People standing, the Deacon, turning to the Book, saith with joined hands,

℣. The Lord be with you.	℣. Dóminus vobíscum.
℟. And with thy spirit.	℟. Et cum spíritu tuo.
℣. The Beginning (or, Continuation) ✠ of the Holy Gospel according to N.	℣. Inítium (vel, Sequéntia) ✠ sancti Evangélii secúndum N.
℟. Glory be to thee, O Lord.	℟. Glória tibi, Dómine.

℣ Then shall the Deacon sign the book with the thumb of his right hand at the beginning of the Gospel text which he is to read, then himself on the forehead, the mouth, and the breast: and while the Ministers respond, he censeth the book thrice, then readeth the Gospel with joined hands.

℣ At the end of the Gospel, the Ministers respond,

| ℟. Praise be to thee, O Christ. | ℟. Laus tibi, Christe. |

℣ Then shall the Subdeacon carry the book to the Priest, who kisseth the Gospel text, saying: **Through the words of the Gospel may our sins be blotted out.** Then the Priest is censed by the Deacon.

NOTE, In Masses of the Dead, **Cleanse** is said, but a blessing is not asked, lights are not carried, and the Celebrant doth not kiss the book.

℣ Then, in the middle of the Altar, extending, raising, and joining his hands, the Priest shall say, if it is to be said, **I believe in one God,** proceeding with joined hands.

NICENE CREED

d Bow head to Cross.

e Bow head to Cross.

I BELIEVE in one God,[d] the Father Almighty, Maker of heaven and earth, And of all things visible and invisible: And in one Lord Jesus Christ,[e] the only-begotten Son of God; Begotten of his Father before all worlds, God of God, Light of Light, Very God of very God; Begotten, not made; Being of one substance with the Father; By whom all things were made: Who for us men and for our salvation came

REDO in unum Deum,[d] Patrem omnipoténtem, factórem cæli et terræ, visibílium ómnium et invisibílium. Et in unum Dóminum Jesum Christum,[e] Fílium Dei unigénitum. Et ex Patre natum ante ómnia sǽcula. Deum de Deo, lumen de lúmine, Deum verum de Deo vero. Génitum, non factum, consubstantiálem Patri: per quem ómnia facta sunt. Qui propter nos hómines et propter nostram

Holy Mass

down from heaven, (Everyone genuflects.) And was incarnate by the Holy Ghost of the Virgin Mary, And was made man: (Everyone rises.) And was crucified also for us under Pontius Pilate; He suffered and was buried: And the third day he rose again according to the Scriptures: And ascended into heaven, And sitteth on the right hand of the Father: And he shall come again, with glory, to judge both the quick and the dead; Whose kingdom shall have no end.

And I believe in the Holy Ghost, The Lord, and Giver of Life, Who proceedeth from the Father; Who with the Father and the Son together is worshiped[f] and glorified; Who spake by the Prophets: And I believe one, holy, catholic, and apostolic Church: I acknowledge one Baptism for the remission of sins: And I look for the Resurrection of the dead: ✠ And the Life of the world to come. Amen.

salútem descéndit de cælis. (Everyone genuflects.) Et incarnátus est de Spíritu Sancto ex María Vírgine: Et homo factus est. (Everyone rises.) Crucifíxus étiam pro nobis: sub Póntio Piláto passus, et sepúltus est. Et resurréxit tértia die, secúndum Scriptúras. Et ascéndit in cælum: sedet ad déxteram Patris. Et íterum ventúrus est cum glória judicáre vivos et mórtuos: cujus regni non erit finis.

Et in Spíritum Sanctum, Dóminum et vivificántem: qui ex Patre procédit. Qui cum Patre et Fílio simul adorátur[f] et conglorificátur: qui locútus est per Prophétas. Et unam sanctam cathólicam et apostólicam Ecclésiam. Confíteor unum baptísma in remissiónem peccatórum. Et exspécto resurrectiónem mortuórum. ✠ Et vitam ventúri sæculi. Amen.

[f] *Bow head to Cross.*

¶ Then shall be declared unto the People what Holy-days, or Fasting-days, are in the week following to be observed; and (if occasion be) shall Notice be given of the Communion, and of the Banns of Matrimony, and other matters to be published.

¶ Here, or immediately after the Creed, may be said the Bidding Prayer, or other authorized Prayers and intercessions.

¶ Then followeth the Sermon.

¶ Then shall the Priest ascend the Altar, kiss it, turn towards the People, and say,

℣. The Lord be with you.
℟. And with thy spirit.
℣. Let us pray.

℣. Dóminus vobíscum.
℟. Et cum spíritu tuo.
℣. Orémus.

Holy Mass

Offertory

¶ The Priest then saith the Offertory Verse.
   Note, At High Mass, a Hymn may be sung while the Priest prepareth the Oblations in the Offertory, and while the Collection is taken, if there be one.

Offering the Bread

¶ Then shall the Deacon present the Paten with the Bread to the Celebrant, which he then offereth, saying,

Receive, O holy Father, almighty everlasting God, this spotless host, which I, thine unworthy servant, offer unto thee, my living and true God, for my numberless sins, offences, and negligences, and for all who stand around, as also for all faithful Christians, both living and departed: that to me and to them it may avail for salvation unto life eternal. Amen.

¶ Then, making a cross with the same Paten, he shall place the Bread upon the Corporal (or the Paten with the Bread upon the Corporal).

Offering the Wine

¶ Then the Deacon shall minister the Wine, and the Subdeacon the Water into the Cup. The Priest (blessing with the sign of the Cross the Water to be mixed in the Cup, unless it be a Requiem Mass) shall say,

O God, who didst wonderfully create, and yet more wonderfully renew the dignity of man's nature: grant that by the mystery of this water and wine we may be made partakers of his divinity, who vouchsafed to share our humanity, Jesus Christ thy Son our Lord: Who liveth and reigneth with thee in the unity of the Holy Ghost, God: throughout all ages world without end. Amen.

¶ Then shall the Priest receive the Cup and offer it, saying,

We offer unto thee, O Lord, the cup of salvation, humbly beseeching thy mercy: that in the sight of thy divine majesty it may ascend as a sweet-smelling savour for our salvation, and for that of the whole world. Amen.

Holy Mass

Offering the Gifts

¶ Then shall he make the sign of the Cross with the Cup, place it upon the Corporal, and cover it with the Pall. Then, with hands joined upon the Altar, he saith, bowing slightly,

N a humble spirit, and with a contrite heart, may we be accepted of thee, O Lord: and so let our sacrifice be offered in thy sight this day, that it may be pleasing unto thee, O Lord God.

¶ Then shall the Priest—standing upright—extend his hands, raise them, and join them; and lifting his eyes to heaven and lowering them immediately, he saith,

OME, O Sanctifier almighty, everlasting God, and bl ✠ ess this sacrifice, prepared for thy holy name.

Censing the Altar

¶ If he be celebrating solemnly, the Priest blesseth incense, saying,

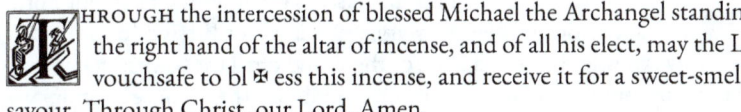HROUGH the intercession of blessed Michael the Archangel standing at the right hand of the altar of incense, and of all his elect, may the Lord vouchsafe to bl ✠ ess this incense, and receive it for a sweet-smelling savour. Through Christ, our Lord. Amen.

¶ Receiving the Thurible from the Deacon, he censeth the Oblations, in the manner prescribed in the traditional manner, saying,

AY this incense which thou hast blessed, ascend unto thee, O Lord: and let thy mercy descend upon us.

¶ Then the Priest censeth the Altar, saying,

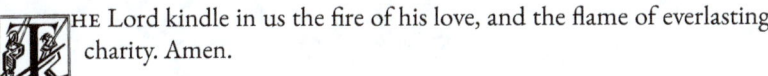ET my prayer, O Lord, be set forth in thy sight as the incense: and let the lifting up of my hands be an evening sacrifice. Set a watch, O Lord, before my mouth, and keep the door of my lips: O let not mine heart be inclined to any evil thing, let me not be occupied in ungodly works.

¶ While he returneth the Thurible to the Deacon, he saith,

HE Lord kindle in us the fire of his love, and the flame of everlasting charity. Amen.

¶ Then the Priest is censed by the Deacon, and afterwards the others in order.

Holy Mass

Washing the Hands

¶ Meanwhile, the Priest washeth his hands, saying,

I WILL wash my hands in innocency, O Lord: and so will I go to thine altar: That I may shew the voice of thanksgiving, and tell of all thy wondrous works. Lord, I have loved the habitation of thy house and the place where thine honour dwelleth. O shut not up my soul with the sinners, nor my life with the blood-thirsty: In whose hands is wickedness: and their right hand is full of gifts. But as for me, I will walk innocently: O deliver me, and be merciful unto me. My foot standeth right: I will praise the Lord in the congregations. Glory be to the Father, and to the Son, and to the Holy Ghost. As it was in the beginning, is now, and ever shall be, world without end. Amen.

Offering the Oblation

¶ Then bowing slightly, in the middle of the Altar with hands joined upon it, he saith,

RECEIVE, O holy Trinity, this oblation which we offer unto thee in memory of the Passion, Resurrection, and Ascension of Jesus Christ, our Lord: and in honour of Blessed Mary ever Virgin, of Blessed John Baptist, of the Holy Apostles Peter and Paul, of these, and of all the Saints: that it may avail to their honour, and for our salvation: and may they, whose memory we celebrate on earth, vouchsafe to intercede for us in heaven. Through the same Christ, our Lord. Amen.

¶ Then shall the Priest kiss the Altar and, turning to the People, extend and join his hands, and say, raising his voice a little,

℣. Pray, brethren: that my sacrifice and yours may be acceptable to God the Father Almighty.	℣. Oráte, fratres: ut meum ac vestrum sacrifícium acceptábile fiat apud Deum Patrem omnipoténtem.
℟. The Lord receive this sacrifice at thy hands, to the praise and glory of his Name, both to our benefit, and that of all his holy Church	℟. Suscípiat Dóminus sacrifícium de mánibus tuis ad laudem et glóriam nominis sui, ad utilitátem quoque nostram, totiúsque Ecclésiæ suæ sanctæ.

¶ The Priest saith in a low voice: **Amen.**

Secret Prayers

¶ Then shall the Priest, with hands extended, immediately (without **Let us pray**), add the Secret Prayers.

NOTE, When these are ended, he saith in a loud voice,

℣. Throughout all ages, world without end.
℟. Amen.

Holy Mass

¶ Then shall the Deacon say,

Let us pray for the whole state of Christ's Church.

¶ The Priest then saith, with hands extended, the following.

ALMIGHTY and everliving God, who by thy holy Apostle hast taught us to make prayers, and supplications, and to give thanks for all men; We humbly beseech thee most mercifully to accept our (alms and) oblations, and to receive these our prayers, which we offer unto thy Divine Majesty; beseeching thee to inspire continually the Universal Church with the spirit of truth, unity, and concord: And grant that all those who do confess thy holy Name may agree in the truth of thy holy Word, and live in unity and godly love.

WE beseech thee also, so to direct and dispose the hearts of all Christian Rulers, that they may truly and impartially administer justice, to the punishment of wickedness and vice, and to the maintenance of thy true religion, and virtue.

GIVE grace, O heavenly Father, to all Bishops and other Ministers, and especially to thy servant *N.* our Metropolitan (and *N.* our Bishop), that *he* may, both by *his* life and doctrine, set forth thy true and lively Word, and rightly and duly administer thy holy Sacraments.

AND to all thy People give thy heavenly grace; and especially to this congregation here present; that, with meek heart and due reverence, they may hear, and receive thy holy Word; truly serving thee in holiness and righteousness all the days of their life.

AND we most humbly beseech thee, of thy goodness, O Lord, to comfort and succour all those who, in this transitory life, are in trouble, sorrow, need, sickness, or any other adversity.

AND we also bless thy holy Name for all thy servants departed this life in thy faith and fear; beseeching thee to grant them continual growth in thy love and service, and to give us grace so to follow their good examples, chiefly the Blessed Virgin Mary, Mother of thy Son Jesus Christ our Lord and God, and the Holy Patriarchs, Prophets, Apostles, and Martyrs, that with them we may be partakers of thy heavenly kingdom.

¶ The Priest placeth both hands upon the Altar, outside the Corporal, and continueth,

Grant this, O Father, for Jesus Christ's sake,

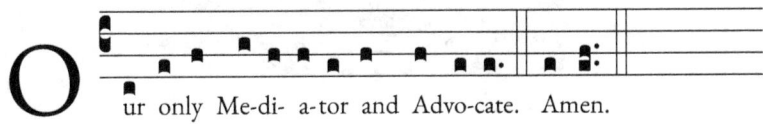

Our only Me-di- a-tor and Advo-cate. Amen.

Holy Mass

Preface

⁋ Then shall the Priest begin the Preface, with both hands placed apart on the Altar.

℣. The Lord be with you.	℣. Dóminus vobíscum.
℟. And with thy spirit.	℟. Et cum spíritu tuo.
℣. Lift up your hearts.^g	℣. Sursum corda.^g
℟. We lift them up unto the Lord.	℟. Habémus ad Dóminum.
℣. Let us give thanks unto our Lord God.^h	℣. Grátias agámus Dómino, Deo nostro.^h
℟. It is meet and right so to do.	℟. Dignum et justum est.

^g *He raises his hands a little.*

^h *He joins his hands before his breast, & bows his head.*

⁋ The Priest separateth his hands and continueth with the following.

T is very meet, right, and our bounden duty, that we should at all times, and in all places, give thanks unto thee, O Lord, Holy Father, Almighty, Everlasting God.

⁋ The Proper Preface is then here said (p. 185)—if there be one—concluding with the following.

HEREFORE with Angels and Archangels, and with all the company of heaven, we laud and magnify thy glorious Name; evermore praising thee, and saying:ⁱ

ⁱ *He joins his hands & bows.*

Sanctus

OLY, HOLY, HOLY, Lord God of hosts, Heaven and earth are full of thy glory: Glory be to thee, O Lord Most High. Blessed^j ✠ is he that cometh in the Name of the Lord. Hosanna in the Highest.

SANCTUS, SANCTUS, SANCTUS, Dóminus, Deus Sábaoth. Pleni sunt cæli et terra glória tua. Glória tibi, Dómine altíssime. Benedíctus,^j✠ qui venit in nómine Dómini. Hosánna in excélsis.

^j *He stands upright & signs himself.*

Holy Mass

Canon of the Mass

¶ The Priest, extending, raising somewhat, and joining his hands, raising his eyes towards heaven, and immediately lowering them, shall begin the Canon, as followeth.

ALL glory be to thee, Almighty God, our heavenly Father, for that thou, of thy tender mercy, didst give thine only Son Jesus Christ to suffer death upon the Cross for our redemption; who (by his own oblation of himself once offered) made a full, perfect, and sufficient sacrifice, oblation, and satisfaction, for the sins of the whole world; and did institute, and in his holy Gospel command us to continue, a perpetual memory of that his precious death and sacrifice, until his coming again:

Words of Institution

FOR in the night in which he was betrayed, *(a)* he took Bread; *(b)* and when he had given ✠ thanks, he brake it, and gave it to his disciples, saying, Take, eat, *(c)*

(a) He takes & holds the Bread.
(b) He looks up to heaven & bows his head.
(c) He holds the Bread between both of his thumbs & forefingers.

**This is my Body, which is given for you;
Do this in remembrance of me.**

¶ Then shall the Priest immediately genuflect, briefly elevate the Bread for the People to see, replace it upon the Corporal (or Paten), genuflect again, and then immediately continue,

Note, From henceforth, the Priest doth not disjoin his forefingers & thumbs until the ablutions.

Likewise, after supper, *(d)* he took the Cup; *(e)* and when he had given ✠ thanks, he gave it to them, saying, Drink ye all of this; for *(f)*

(d) He uncovers the Cup, holds it with both hands, & bows his head.
(e) He holds the Cup in his left hand.
(f) He holds the Cup slightly raised.

This is my Blood of the New Testament, which is shed for you, and for many, for the remission of sins;

¶ Then shall the Priest place the Cup back upon the Corporal and immediately say,

Do this, as oft as ye shall drink it, in remembrance of me.

¶ Then shall the Priest immediately genuflect, briefly elevate the Cup, replace the Cup upon the Corporal, cover it, genuflect again, and continue with hands extended.

Holy Mass

Recollection

HEREFORE O Lord and heavenly Father, according to the institution of thy dearly beloved Son our Saviour Jesus Christ, we, thy humble servants, do celebrate and make here before thy Divine Majesty, with these thy holy ✠ gifts, which we now offer unto thee, the memorial thy Son hath commanded us to make; having in remembrance his blessed passion and precious death, his mighty resurrection and glorious ascension; rendering unto thee most hearty thanks for the innumerable benefits procured unto us by the same.

Invocation

❧ Then shall the Priest uncover the Cup, bow profoundly, join his hands upon the Altar, and continue,

ND we thine unworthy servants beseech thee, most merciful Father, to hear us, *(g)* and to send thy Holy Spirit upon us and upon the ✠ se thy *(g) He stands upright and imposes his hands over the Gifts.*

gifts and creatures of Br ✠ ead and W ✠ ine, that, being blessed and hallowed by his life-giving power, they may become the Bo ✠ dy and Bl ✠ ood of thy most dearly beloved Son, to the end that all who shall receive the same may be sanctified both in body and soul, and preserved unto everlasting life.

❧ Then shall the Priest cover the Cup, genuflect, and continue, with hands extended,

ND we earnestly desire thy fatherly goodness, mercifully to accept this our Sacrifice of Praise and Thanksgiving; most humbly beseeching thee to grant that, by the merits and death of thy Son Jesus Christ, and through faith in his Blood, we, and all thy whole Church, may obtain remission of our sins, and all other benefits of his Passion.

Commemoration for the Departed

REMEMBER also, O Lord, thy servants and handmaids *N.* and *N.*, who have gone before us with the sign of faith, and rest in the sleep of peace.

❧ Then shall the Priest join his hands, pray for the dead he hath in mind, then extend his hands and say,

To them, O Lord, and to all that rest in Christ, we beseech thee to grant a place of refreshing, light, and peace.

Holy Mass

Oblation

AND here we offer and present unto thee, O Lord, our selves, our souls and bodies, to be a reasonable, holy, and living sacrifice unto thee; humbly beseeching thee, (He kisses the Altar) that we, and all others who shall be partakers of this Holy Communion, may worthily receive the most precious Bo ✠ dy and Bl ✠ ood *(h)* of thy Son Jesus Christ, be filled with thy grace and heavenly benediction, and made one body with him, that he may dwell in us, and we in him.

(h) After signing the Gifts, he signs himself.

AND although we are unworthy, through our manifold sins, to offer unto thee any sacrifice; yet we beseech thee to accept this our bounden duty and service; not weighing our merits, but pardoning our offences. (He joins his hands & bows his head profoundly.)

THROUGH Jesus Christ our Lord; *(i)* by ✠ whom, and with wh ✠ om, in the unity of the Holy ✠ Ghost, *(j)* all ho ✠ nour and gl ✠ ory be unto thee,

(i) He genuflects & makes the sign the Cross with the Host over the Cup thrice, from lip to lip.

(j) He makes the sign of the Cross twice with the Host between the Cup & his breast.

¶ The Priest then uncovereth the Cup, elevateth the Host and Cup to the height of his breast then replacing them on the Altar, covereth the Cup, genuflecteth, then joineth his hands.

O Father Almighty, world without end. ℟. Amen.

Lord's Prayer

Let us pray. And now, as our Saviour Christ hath taught us, we are bold to say,

¶ The Priest alone extendeth his hands while the Priest and Congregation say together,

OUR Father, who art in heaven, Hallowed be thy Name. Thy kingdom come. Thy will be done, on earth, As it is in heaven. Give us this day our daily bread. And forgive us our trespasses, As we forgive those who trespass against us. And lead us not into temptation, But deliver us from evil. For thine is the kingdom, and the power, and the glory, for ever and ever. Amen.

Holy Mass

℟ Unless the Priest consecrated on the Paten, he takes the Paten between the fore and middle fingers of his right hand, and holds it upright upon the Altar.

DELIVER us, O Lord, we beseech thee, from all evils, past, present, and to come: and at the intercession of the blessed and glorious ever Virgin Mary, Mother of God, with thy blessed Apostles Peter and Paul, and with Andrew, and all the Saints, (The Priest signs himself—with the Paten, if he consecrated on the Corporal) favourably grant peace in our days: that by the help of thine availing mercy we may ever both be free from sin and safe from all distress.

℟ If the Host be not already on the Paten, the Priest is to slide the Paten underneath the Host. He then shall uncover the Cup, genuflect, and break the Host in half over the Cup, saying,

Through the same Jesus Christ, thy Son our Lord.

℟ The Priest placeth the half in his right hand upon the Paten. He then breaketh a particle off from the half in his left hand, saying,

Who liveth and reigneth with thee in the unity of the Holy Ghost, God.

℟ Then shall the Priest join the other half, which he holdeth in his left hand, to the half laid upon the Paten, and retaining the small particle in his right hand over the Cup, which he holdeth with his left by the knop below the Cup, say in an audible voice, or sing,

Throughout all ages world without end.
 ℟. Amen.

℟ With the same particle, the Priest signs thrice over the Cup, saying,

| ℣. The peace ✠ of the Lord be ✠ alway with ✠ you. | ℣. Pax ✠ Dómini sit ✠ semper vobís ✠ cum. |
| ℟. And with thy spirit. | ℟. Et cum spíritu tuo. |

℟ The Priest, putting the same particle into the Cup, saith, in the secret voice:

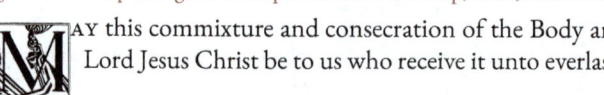

MAY this commixture and consecration of the Body and Blood of our Lord Jesus Christ be to us who receive it unto everlasting life. Amen.

Holy Mass

Agnus Dei

❧ Then shall the Priest cover the Cup, genuflect, and—bowing to the Sacrament—join his hands and strike his breast thrice, saying in an audible voice:

O LAMB of God, that takest away the sins of the world, have mercy upon us.
    O Lamb of God, that takest away the sins of the world, have mercy upon us.
    O Lamb of God, that takest away the sins of the world, grant us thy peace.

AGNUS Dei, qui tollis peccáta mundi: miserére nobis.
    Agnus Dei, qui tollis peccáta mundi: miserére nobis.
    Agnus Dei, qui tollis peccáta mundi: dona nobis pacem.

❧ In Requiem Masses, Have mercy upon us is replaced by grant them rest and grant us thy peace by grant them rest everlasting.

Confession

❧ Then the Deacon turneth to the People and saith to those who come to receive the Holy Communion,

YE who do truly and earnestly repent you of your sins, and are in love and charity with your neighbours, and intend to lead a new life, following the commandments of God, and walking from henceforth in his holy ways; Draw near with faith, and take this holy Sacrament to your comfort; and make your humble confession to Almighty God, devoutly kneeling.

❧ Then shall this General Confession be made, in an audible voice, by the Priest, bowing, and all those who are minded to receive the Holy Communion, humbly kneeling.

ALMIGHTY God, Father of our Lord Jesus Christ, Maker of all things, Judge of all men; We acknowledge and bewail our manifold sins and wickedness, Which we, from time to time, most grievously have committed, By thought, word, and deed, Against thy Divine Majesty, Provoking most justly thy wrath and indignation against us. We do earnestly repent, And are heartily sorry for these our misdoings; The remembrance of them is grievous unto us; The burden of them is intolerable. Have mercy upon us, Have mercy upon us, most merciful Father; For thy Son our Lord Jesus Christ's sake, Forgive us all that is past; And grant that we may ever hereafter Serve and please thee in newness of life, To the honour and glory of thy Name; Through Jesus Christ our Lord. Amen.

Holy Mass

℣ Then shall the Priest (Bishop if he be present) stand up and, turning to the People, say,

ALMIGHTY God, our heavenly Father, who of his great mercy hath promised forgiveness of sins to all those who with hearty repentance and true faith turn unto him; Have mercy upon you; pardon ✠ and deliver you from all your sins; confirm and strengthen you in all goodness; and bring you to everlasting life; through Jesus Christ our Lord.

℟. Amen.

Comfortable Words

℣ Then shall the Priest, facing the People, say,

HEAR WHAT COMFORTABLE WORDS OUR SAVIOUR CHRIST SAITH UNTO ALL WHO TRULY TURN TO HIM.

Come unto me, all ye that travail and are heavy laden, and I will refresh you. (Matt. 11:28)
So God loved the world, that he gave his only-begotten Son, to the end that all that believe in him should not perish, but have everlasting life. (John 3:16)

HEAR ALSO WHAT SAINT PAUL SAITH.

This is a true saying, and worthy of all men to be received, That Christ Jesus came into the world to save sinners. (1 Tim. 1:15)

HEAR ALSO WHAT SAINT JOHN SAITH.

If any man sin, we have an Advocate with the Father, Jesus Christ the righteous; and he is the Propitiation for our sins. (1 John 2:1-2)

℣ Then the Priest, turning to the Altar, bowing with hands joined upon the Altar, saith in the secret voice,

O LORD Jesu Christ, who saidst to thine Apostles: Peace I leave with you, my peace I give unto you: regard not my sins but the faith of thy Church; and vouchsafe to grant her peace and unity according to thy will: Who livest and reignest God, throughout all ages, world without end. Amen.

℣ If the Pax be given, the Priest is to kiss the Altar and—giving the Pax—say: Peace be with thee, with the response And with thy spirit.

Holy Mass

Prayer of Humble Access

¶ The Priest alone then saith, in an audible voice,

WE do not presume to come to this thy Table, O merciful Lord, trusting in our own righteousness, but in thy manifold and great mercies. We are not worthy so much as to gather up the crumbs under thy Table. But thou art the same Lord, whose property is always to have mercy: Grant us therefore, gracious Lord, so to eat the flesh of thy dear Son Jesus Christ, and to drink his blood, that our sinful bodies may be made clean by his Body, and our souls washed through his most precious Blood, and that we may evermore dwell in him, and he in us.

℟. Amen.

Communion of the Priest

¶ Then the Priest shall say that which followeth,

O LORD Jesu Christ, Son of the living God, who by the will of the Father, and the co-operation of the Holy Ghost, hast through thy death given life unto the world: deliver me by this thy most sacred Body and Blood from all mine iniquities, and from every evil: and make me ever to cleave unto thy commandments, and suffer me never to be separated from thee: Who with the same God the Father and the Holy Ghost livest and reignest God, world without end. Amen.

LET the partaking of thy Body, O Lord Jesu Christ, which I, unworthy, presume to receive, turn not to my judgement and condemnation: but of thy goodness let it avail unto me for protection of mind and of body, that I may receive thy healing: Who livest and reignest with God the Father in the unity of the Holy Ghost, God, throughout all ages, world without end. Amen.

¶ He then genuflecteth and saith: **I will receive the bread of heaven, and call upon the name of the Lord.**

¶ Then, bowing slightly, the Priest shall take both parts of the Host between the thumb and forefinger of his left hand, and place the Paten between the same forefinger and middle finger, and striking his breast three times with his right hand, say thrice, devoutly and humbly, raising his voice slightly:

Lord, I am not worthy, (Proceeding in the secret voice:) **that thou shouldest come under my roof: but speak the word only, and my soul shall be healed.**

¶ After signing himself with his right hand with the Host over the Paten, he saith,

The Body of our Lord Jesus Christ preserve my soul unto everlasting life. Amen.

Holy Mass

❧ And bowing, he reverently taketh both parts of the Host. After consuming the Host, he is to place the Paten down upon the Corporal, and raising himself, join his hands, and remain still for a short time in meditation on the Most Holy Sacrament.

❧ Then he shall uncover the Cup, genuflect, collect the fragments (if there be any), and cleanse the Paten over the Cup, saying meanwhile:

What reward shall I give unto the Lord for all the benefits that he hath done unto me? I will receive the cup of salvation, and call upon the Name of the Lord. I will call upon the Lord which is worthy to be praised, so shall I be safe from mine enemies.

❧ Taking the Cup in his right hand and signing himself with it, he saith,

The Blood of our Lord Jesus Christ preserve my soul unto everlasting life. Amen.

❧ Holding the Paten under the Cup with his left hand, the Priest is to reverently receive the Blood with the particle.

❧ Having received, if there be any to be communicated, let him communicate them before he purifieth himself.

COMMUNION OF THE PEOPLE

❧ If there be any to be communicated, the Priest shall genuflect and place the consecrated particles in a Ciborium (or if there are few to be communicated, on the Paten), unless from the beginning they had been placed in a Ciborium.

❧ If the Priest is to administer Communion from the reserved Sacrament, he openeth the Tabernacle, genuflecteth, taketh out the Ciborium, & placeth it upon the Corporal.

❧ Then shall the Priest genuflect, take the Ciborium with his left hand (or the Cup, if he consecrated on the Paten), and take one particle with his right hand takes, which he holdeth between his thumb and forefinger slightly raised above the Ciborium (Cup); and turning to the people in the midst of the Altar, he saith in the clear voice:

℣. Behold the Lamb of God. Behold him who taketh away the sins of the world.	℣. Ecce Agnus Dei, ecce, qui tollit peccáta mundi.
℟. Lord, I am not worthy that thou shouldest come under my roof, but speak the word only, and my soul shall be healed.	℟. Dómine, non sum dignus, ut intres sub tectum meum, sed tantum dic verbo, et sanábitur ánima mea.
℟. Lord, I am not worthy that thou shouldest come under my roof, but speak the word only, and my soul shall be healed.	℟. Dómine, non sum dignus, ut intres sub tectum meum, sed tantum dic verbo, et sanábitur ánima mea.

Holy Mass

℟. Lord, I am not worthy that thou shouldest come under my roof, but speak the word only, and my soul shall be healed.

℟. Dómine, non sum dignus, ut intres sub tectum meum, sed tantum dic verbo, et sanábitur ánima mea.

¶ After the Priest returneth to the Altar, the Pre-Communion Hymn (p. 184) is to then be sung as communicants approach the Altar Rail.

NOTE, The Pre-Communion Hymn may be said or sung any time after the Prayer of Humble Access.

¶ Only Orthodox Christians in good standing and properly disposed may receive the Eucharist.

NOTE, Each communicant shall receive the Communion kneeling.

¶ If they are to communicate, the Priest first communicateth the Sacred Ministers, and then the other Priests and Clerics in choir. (Priest and Deacons shall wear a stole either of white colour or of the same colour as the administering Priest.) And last of all, he proceedeth to communicate the others, beginning with those on the Epistle side.

Distribution of the Body & Blood Separately

¶ If both kinds are to be administered separately, the Priest, when giving the Body, shall make with the Host the sign of the Cross over the Ciborium and place the Host on the tongue of each communicant, while saying:

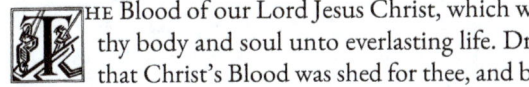HE Body of our Lord Jesus Christ, which was given for thee, preserve thy body and soul unto everlasting life. Take and eat this in remembrance that Christ died for thee, and feed on him in thy heart by faith, with thanksgiving.

¶ And then, while administering the Cup to each communicant, the Priest, keeping hold of the Cup, shall say:

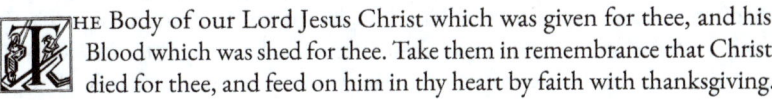HE Blood of our Lord Jesus Christ, which was shed for thee, preserve thy body and soul unto everlasting life. Drink this in remembrance that Christ's Blood was shed for thee, and be thankful.

Distribution of the Body & Blood Together

¶ But if the Body and Blood of Christ are to be administered together by intinction, then the Priest, when giving the Sacrament to each one, intincteth the Host into the Cup; then, making with the Host the sign of the Cross over the Cup, he placeth the Host on the tongue of each communicant, while saying:

HE Body of our Lord Jesus Christ which was given for thee, and his Blood which was shed for thee. Take them in remembrance that Christ died for thee, and feed on him in thy heart by faith with thanksgiving.

Holy Mass

¶ The Communion ended, the Priest shall return to the Altar, saying nothing, nor doth he give the Blessing since he will give it at the end of Mass.

Ablutions

¶ When the faithful have received Holy Communion, the Deacon and Priest return the Blessed Sacrament to the Altar. The Priest shall then consume everything not being reserved.

  Note, When prepared for reservation, the Host shall be touched with the Blood, the Blood then being completely consumed.

¶ Then shall the Priest say,

RANT, O Lord, that what we have taken with our mouths we may receive with a pure heart: and from a temporal gift may it become to us an everlasting remedy.

¶ Meanwhile, he presenteth the Cup to the Minister, who shall pour in a little wine and water, wherewith he purifieth himself. Then he continueth,

ET thy Body, O Lord, which I have taken, and thy Blood which I have drunk, cleave to my members: and grant; that no stain of sin may remain in me, whom thou hast refreshed with pure and holy sacraments: Who livest and reignest, world without end. Amen.

¶ Then shall the Priest wash and wipe his fingers and take the ablution. Then he wipeth his mouth and the Cup.

¶ After folding the Corporal, he is to cover the Cup and place it upon the Altar as before. Then he proceedeth with the Mass.

Thanksgiving

¶ Standing with his hands joined, the Priest shall read the Communion Antiphon. Then, at the Epistle corner, he alone saith the Thanksgiving, in an audible voice.

Let us pray.

LMIGHTY and everliving God, we most heartily thank thee, for that thou dost vouchsafe to feed us who have duly received these holy mysteries with the spiritual food of the most precious Body and Blood of thy Son our Saviour Jesus Christ; and dost assure us thereby of thy favour and goodness towards us; and that we are very members incorporate in the mystical body of thy Son, which is the blessed company of all faithful people; and are also heirs through hope of thy everlasting kingdom, by the merits of his most precious death and passion. And we humbly beseech thee, O heavenly Father, so to assist us with thy grace, that we may continue in that holy fellowship, and do all such

Holy Mass

good works as thou hast prepared for us to walk in; through Jesus Christ our Lord, to whom, with thee and the Holy Ghost, be all honour and glory, world without end.

℟. Amen.

Dismissal

¶ Then, with hands joined before his breast, the Priest shall proceed to the midst of the Altar, kiss the Altar, and turn to the People, with hands extended, saying:

℣. The Lord be with you.　　　℣. Dóminus vobíscum.
℟. And with thy spirit.　　　℟. Et cum spíritu tuo.

¶ Then, turning back to the Book, he saith:

℣. Let us pray.　　　℣. Orémus.

Postcommunion Prayers

¶ The Priest then saith the Postcommunion Prayers in the same manner, number, and order as the Collects at the beginning of Mass.

Final Blessing

¶ After saying the last Prayer, the Priest is to return to the midst of the Altar, kissing it, and turning toward the people, saying:

℣. The Lord be with you.　　　℣. Dóminus vobíscum.
℟. And with thy spirit.　　　℟. Et cum spíritu tuo.

¶ On days when the Gloria in exclesis is said,

℣. Depart in peace.　　　℣. Ite, Missa est.
℟. Thanks be to God.　　　℟. Deo grátias.

¶ On days when the Gloria in excelsis is not said,

℣. Let us bless the Lord.　　　℣. Benedicámus Dómino.
℟. Thanks be to God.　　　℟. Deo grátias.

¶ In Requiem Masses,

℣. May they rest in peace.　　　℣. Requiéscant in pace.
℟. Amen.　　　℟. Amen.

¶ In Eastertide, in Masses of the Season,

℣. Depart in peace, alleluia, alleluia.　　　℣. Ite, Missa est, allelúja, allelúja.
℟. Thanks be to God, alleluia, alleluia.　　　℟. Deo grátias, allelúja, allelúja.

Holy Mass

¶ *Having said the Dismissal, the Priest boweth before the midst of the Altar, and with hands joined thereon, saith in the secret voice,*

ET this my bounden duty and service be pleasing to thee, O holy Trinity: and grant; that the sacrifice, which I unworthy have offered before the eyes of thy majesty, may be acceptable to thee, and through thy mercy obtain thy gracious favour for me and all for whom I have offered it. Through Christ, our Lord. Amen.

¶ *Then—unless it be a Requiem Mass—the Congregation kneeling, the Priest shall kiss the Altar; raise his eyes; extend, raise, and join his hands; bow his head to the Cross; and give the Blessing, saying,*

THE Peace of God, which passeth all understanding, keep your hearts and minds in the knowledge and love of God, and of his Son Jesus Christ our Lord: And the Blessing of God Almighty,[a] the Father, ✠ the Son, and the Holy Ghost, be amongst you, and remain with you always. *Amen.*

[a] *He turns to the people, blessing them once only, even in solemn Masses.*

¶ *In Pontifical Masses, the Blessing is given by the Bishop and is threefold, as ordered in the Pontifical.*

¶ *In Masses of the Dead, the Blessing is not given, but having said* May they rest in peace *and* Let this my bounden duty, *he kisseth the Altar and readeth the Last Gospel.*

Last Gospel

¶ *Unless a proper Last Gospel be provided, the Priest shall conclude the Mass with this Last Gospel, at the Gospel corner and with hands joined:*

℣. The Lord be with you.

℟. And with thy spirit.

℣. The[b] ✠ beginning of the Holy Gospel according to John.

℟. Glory be to thee, O Lord.

In the beginning was the Word, and the Word was with God, and the Word was God. The same was in the beginning with God. All things were made by him; and without him was not any thing made that was made. In him was life; and the life was the light of men. And the light shineth in darkness; and the darkness comprehended it not. There was a man sent from God, whose name was John. The same came for a witness, to bear witness of

[b] *He signs with the sign of the Cross first the Altar or the Book, then himself on the forehead, mouth, & breast.*

℣. Dóminus vobíscum.

℟. Et cum spíritu tuo.

℣. Inítium[b] ✠ sancti Evangélii secúndum Joánnem.

℟. Glória tibi, Dómine.

In princípio erat Verbum, et Verbum erat apud Deum, et Deus erat Verbum. Hoc erat in princípio apud Deum. Omnia per ipsum facta sunt: et sine ipso factum est nihil, quod factum est: in ipso vita erat, et vita erat lux hóminum: et lux in ténebris lucet, et ténebræ eam non comprehendérunt. Fuit homo missus a Deo, cui nomen erat Joánnes. Hic venit in testimónium, ut testimónium perhibéret de lúmine, ut omnes créderent per illum. Non erat

Holy Mass

the Light, that all men through him might believe. He was not that Light, but was sent to bear witness of that Light. That was the true Light, which lighteth every man that cometh into the world. He was in the world, and the world was made by him, and the world knew him not. He came unto his own, and his own received him not. But as many as received him, to them gave he power to become the sons of God, even to them that believe on his name: Which were born, not of blood, nor of the will of the flesh, nor of the will of man, but of God. (Everyone genuflects.) And the Word was made flesh, and dwelt among us, (Everyone rises.) (and we beheld his glory, the glory as of the only begotten of the Father,) full of grace and truth.

℟. Thanks be to God.

ille lux, sed ut testimónium perhibéret de lúmine. Erat lux vera, quæ illúminat omnem hóminem veniéntem in hunc mundum. In mundo erat, et mundus per ipsum factus est, et mundus eum non cognóvit. In própria venit, et sui eum non recepérunt. Quotquot autem recepérunt eum, dedit eis potestátem fílios Dei fíeri, his, qui credunt in nómine ejus: qui non ex sanguínibus, neque ex voluntáte carnis, neque ex voluntáte viri, sed ex Deo nati sunt. (Everyone genuflects.) Et Verbum caro factum est, (Everyone rises.) et habitávit in nobis: et vídimus glóriam ejus, glóriam quasi Unigéniti a Patre, plenum grátiæ et veritátis.

℟. Deo grátias.

¶ At High Mass, a Hymn may be sung while the Priest and ministers leave the sanctuary.

¶ As he departeth from the Altar, the Priest saith for thanksgiving the Antiphon **Let us sing**, with the rest (p. 150).

General Rubrics

¶ It is expedient to have, set upon the Altar, cards with the most common prayers.

¶ The Altar at the Communion-time—having a fair white linen cloth, a cross, and at least two candles upon it—shall stand in the Sanctuary.

¶ The Bread for the Eucharist ought to be provided by the Priest or the members of the Congregation. It must be leavened. That is, before and after being initially baked, it must be made of—and only made of—wheat flour, water, yeast, and salt. The Wine should be made of grapes, without additives or supplements. The Vessels should be made of precious metal.

¶ It is an ancient and laudable rule of the Church to receive this Holy Sacrament fasting. That is, one who desireth to receive the Eucharist must consume neither food nor drink (water excepted) from the midnight before the liturgy until the time of reception. In the case of Masses which occur after noon, it is sufficient that the fasting begin at noon or immediately after one's noon-time meal.

Pre-Communion Hymn # Holy Mass

Pre-Communion Hymn

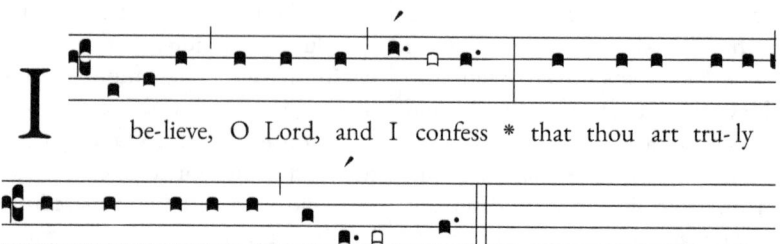

I be-lieve, O Lord, and I confess * that thou art tru-ly the Christ, the Son of the Liv-ing God,

Who didst come into the world to save • sinners, * of whom • I am first.

And I believe that this is truly thine own immaculate • Body, * and that this is truly thine own • precious Blood.

Wherefore I pray thee: have mercy • upon me * and forgive my transgressions both voluntary and in • voluntary,

Of word and of deed, of knowledge and of • ignorance. * And make me worthy to partake without • condemnation

Of thine immaculate • Mysteries, * unto the remission of my sins and unto life ever • lasting. Amen.

OF thy Mystical Supper, O • Son of God, * accept me today as a • communicant;

For I will not speak of thy • Mystery * to thine • enemies,

Neither will I give thee a kiss as • did Judas; * but like the thief will I • confess thee:

Remember • me, * O Lord in • thy Kingdom.

NOT unto judgement, nor unto condemn • ation, * be my partaking of thy holy • Mysteries,

O Lord, but unto • the healing * of soul • and body.

Holy Mass
Prefaces

Prefaces for the Mass

Proper Prefaces without Notation

Advent

℟ Every day in Advent, including Christmas Eve.

HROUGH Jesus Christ our Lord; whom thou, the merciful and faithful God, didst promise as a Saviour to lost mankind; by whose truth the unlearned should be instructed, by whose holiness the ungodly should be justified, by whose power the weak should be holpen. Now, therefore, when the time in which thou shouldest send him draweth near, and now that the day of our deliverance already shineth; trusting in these thy promises, with holy joy we do rejoice.

Christmas

℟ Upon Christmas Day and its Octave, until Epiphany Eve, inclusive, and on the Feast of the Most Holy Body of Christ and its Octave.

ECAUSE thou didst give Jesus Christ, thine only Son, to be born (as at this time) for us; who, by the operation of the Holy Ghost, was made very man, of the substance of the Virgin Mary his mother; and that without spot of sin, to make us clean from all sin.

Epiphany

℟ Upon the Epiphany and its Octave.

HROUGH Jesus Christ our Lord, who, in substance of our mortal flesh, manifested forth his glory; that he might bring us out of darkness into his own glorious light.

Septuagesima Sunday

℟ Optionally upon Septuagesima Sunday.

OR by things seen, we are instructed how we should pursue those things unseen. And so are reminded, as the year leadeth on its course, to pass, from things past unto things to come, from the old man into the newness of life; that, being freed from reliance on earthly goods, we may lay hold upon the excelling richness of the heavenly gift; and by that food, which is preserved for us in every age, we may arrive unto that victorious sustenance which remaineth for ever, even Jesus Christ our Lord.

Sexagesima Sunday

℟ Optionally upon Sexagesima Sunday.

HO deigned to instruct the rational creature by such stewardship, lest he be given over to temporal things and strive not for the everlasting reward. That he may neither withdraw from correction nor become haughty in approbation, but rather overcome all adversities, this being his glorious devotion: Jesus Christ our Lord.

Quinquagesima Sunday

¶ Optionally on **Quinquagesima Sunday**.

ND to entreat thy Majesty by lowly devotion, that thou, beholding the weakness of our mortal nature, accuse us not of our depravity in thy wrath, but rather cleanse, cultivate, and console us by thine immeasurable gentleness. And since we can do no good thing without thee, bestow upon us thy grace alone that we may live in wholesome conversation.

Lent

¶ From **Ash Wednesday** until the Saturday before **Passion Sunday**, inclusive.

HO by bodily fasting dost overcome vice, dost raise the mind, and dost bestow on us virtue and heavenly rewards: through Christ, our Lord.

Holy Rood

¶ From **Passion Sunday** until **Maundy Thursday**, inclusive. And all Masses of the **Holy Rood**, the **Passion of the Lord**, or the **Most Precious Blood**, and within their Octaves, even when celebrated within the Octave of **Christmas**.

HO by the tree of the Cross didst give salvation unto mankind: that whence death arose, thence life might rise again: and that he, who by a tree overcame, might also by a tree be overcome: through Christ our Lord.

Easter

¶ From **Holy Saturday** until **Ascension Eve**, inclusive.

UT chiefly are we bound to praise thee for the glorious Resurrection of thy Son Jesus Christ our Lord: for he is the very Paschal Lamb, which was offered for us, and hath taken away the sin of the world; who by his death hath destroyed death, and by his rising to life again hath restored to us everlasting life.

Ascension

¶ From **Ascension Thursday** until the Friday after its Octave, inclusive. It is also said, even without a Commemoration, on the Friday after the Octave.

HROUGH thy most dearly beloved Son Jesus Christ our Lord; who, after his most glorious Resurrection, manifestly appeared to all his Apostles, and in their sight ascended up into heaven, to prepare a place for us; that where he is, thither we might also ascend, and reign with him in glory.

Holy Ghost

¶ From **Whitsunday Eve** until **Trinity Sunday**, exclusive, in Votive Masses of the Holy Ghost, even when celebrated within the Octave of **Christmas**.

HROUGH Jesus Christ our Lord; according to whose most true promise, the Holy

Ghost came down (as at this time) from heaven, lighting upon the Apostles, to teach them, and to lead them into all truth; giving them boldness with fervent zeal constantly to preach the Gospel unto all nations; whereby we have been brought out of darkness and error into the clear light and true knowledge of thee, and of thy Son Jesus Christ.

Most Holy Trinity

❡ Upon Sundays, from the 3rd Sunday after Trinity until the Sunday Next before Advent, inclusive. And also in Masses of the Most Holy Trinity, even when celebrated within the Octave of Christmas. And on Sundays in Septuagesimatide.

WHO, with thine only-begotten Son, and the Holy Ghost, art one God, one Lord, in Trinity of Persons and in Unity of Substance. For that which we believe of thy glory, O Father, the same we believe of the Son, and of the Holy Ghost, without any difference of inequality.

Compassion of Our Lord

❡ Upon the Feast of the of the Compassion of Our Lord and its Octave Day.

WHO didst will that thine only-begotten Son, as he hung upon the Cross, should be pierced by the soldier's spear: that his Heart thus opened, the shrine of the divine bounty, might pour forth upon us streams of mercy and of grace: that as it never ceased to burn with love for us, so it might be a rest for the godly, and an open refuge of salvation for the penitent.

Christ the King

❡ Masses of Our Lord Jesus Christ the King, even when they are celebrated within the Octave of Christmas.

WHO didst anoint thine only-begotten Son, our Lord Jesus Christ, with the oil of gladness, to be a Priest for ever and the King of all the world: that, offering himself an unspotted sacrifice of peace upon the altar of the cross, he might accomplish the sacrament of the redemption of mankind: and making all creatures subject to his governance, might deliver up to thine infinite Majesty an eternal and universal kingdom. A kingdom of truth and life: a kingdom of sanctity and grace: a kingdom of justice, love, and peace.

All Hallows'

❡ Upon the Feast of All Hallows and its Octave.

WHO, in the multitude of thy saints, hast compassed us about with so great a cloud of witnesses that we, rejoicing in their fellowship, may run with patience the race that is set before us, and together with them may receive the crown of glory that fadeth not away.

Prefaces

Holy Mass

Of Our Lord

¶ Upon the Feasts of the Purification, Annunciation, and Transfiguration.

ECAUSE in the Mystery of the Word made flesh, thou hast caused a new light to shine in our hearts, to give the knowledge of thy glory in the face of thy Son, Jesus Christ our Lord.

Blessed Virgin Mary

¶ In Masses of the Blessed Virgin Mary, and their Octaves.

ND that in the N. of Blessed Mary ever Virgin we should praise, bless, and magnify thee. In that by the overshadowing of the Holy Ghost she conceived thine only-begotten Son: and, the glory of her maidenhood yet abiding, shed forth upon the world the light eternal, Jesus Christ, our Lord.

St. Joseph, Spouse of the Blessed Virgin

¶ In Masses of St. Joseph, and their Octaves.

ND that in the Festivity (Veneration) of blessed Joseph, we should magnify, bless, and glorify thee with worthy praises. Who being a just man was given by thee for a Spouse to the Virgin Mother of God: and, being a faithful and wise servant, was made ruler over thy Household: that in the office of a father he should guard thine only-begotten Son, conceived by the overshadowing of the Holy Ghost, even Jesus Christ our Lord.

Apostles & Evangelists

¶ In Masses of the Apostles or Evangelists and in a Mass of the Election and Enthronement of the Patriarch and their anniversaries.

HAT we, O Lord, should humbly entreat thee, that thou, the everlasting Shepherd, wouldst not forsake thy flock: but through thy blessed Apostles keep it by thy continual protection. That it may be governed by those same rulers, whom in thy stead thou hast appointed for thy work, as shepherds of thy people.

Requiem

¶ In all Masses for the Dead.

HROUGH Christ, our Lord. In whom hath shone forth unto us the hope of a blessed resurrection, that they who bewail the certain condition of their mortality may be consoled by the promise of immortality to come. For to thy faithful people, O Lord, life is changed not taken away: and at the dissolution of the tabernacle of this earthly sojourning a dwelling-place eternal is made ready in the heavens.

Propers of the Church Year

Advent I

Proper of Season

First Sunday of Advent

First Class Semidouble

Introit

UNTO thee lift I up my soul: my God, in thee have I trusted, let me not be confounded: neither let mine enemies triumph over me: for all they that look for thee shall not be ashamed. *Ps.* Shew me thy ways, O Lord; and teach me thy paths.

Collect

ALMIGHTY God, give us grace that we may cast away the works of darkness, and put upon us the armour of light, now in the time of this mortal life, in which thy Son Jesus Christ came to visit us in great humility; that in the last day, when he shall come again in his glorious majesty to judge both the quick and the dead, we may rise to the life immortal, through him who liveth and reigneth with thee and the Holy Ghost, now and ever. *Amen.*

¶ This Collect is to be repeated every day, with the other Collects in Advent, until Christmas Day.

¶ 2nd Collect is of St. Mary in Advent (p. 541) & 3rd Against the Persecutors of the Church (p. 543) or for the Chief Bishop (p. 543).

Epistle. Romans 13:8

BRETHREN: Owe no man any thing, but to love one another: for he that loveth another hath fulfilled the law. For this, Thou shalt not commit adultery, Thou shalt not kill, Thou shalt not steal, Thou shalt not bear false witness, Thou shalt not covet; and if there be any other commandment, it is briefly comprehended in this saying, namely, Thou shalt love thy neighbour as thyself. Love worketh no ill to his neighbour: therefore love is the fulfilling of the law. And that, knowing the time, that now it is high time to awake out of sleep: for now is our salvation nearer than when we believed. The night is far spent, the day is at hand: let us therefore cast off the works of darkness, and let us put on the armour of light. Let us walk honestly, as in the day; not in rioting and drunkenness, not in chambering and wantonness, not in strife and envying. But put ye on the Lord Jesus Christ, and make not provision for the flesh, to fulfil the lusts thereof.

Proper of Season *Advent I*

Gradual. All they that look for thee shall not be ashamed, O Lord. ℣. Shew me thy ways, O Lord; and teach me thy paths.

Alleluia. Alleluia, alleluia. ℣. Shew us thy mercy, O Lord: and grant us thy salvation. Alleluia.

❡ On Ferias in Advent, when during the week the Sunday Mass is resumed, Alleluia is not said, but only the Gradual.

Gospel. Matthew 21:1

AT THAT TIME: When they drew nigh unto Jerusalem, and were come to Bethphage, unto the mount of Olives, then sent Jesus two disciples, Saying unto them, Go into the village over against you, and straightway ye shall find an ass tied, and a colt with her: loose them, and bring them unto me. And if any man say ought unto you, ye shall say, The Lord hath need of them; and straightway he will send them. All this was done, that it might be fulfilled which was spoken by the prophet, saying, Tell ye the daughter of Sion, Behold, thy King cometh unto thee, meek, and sitting upon an ass, and a colt the foal of an ass. And the disciples went, and did as Jesus commanded them, And brought the ass, and the colt, and put on them their clothes, and they set him thereon. And a very great multitude spread their garments in the way; others cut down branches from the trees, and strawed them in the way. And the multitudes that went before, and that followed, cried, saying, Hosanna to the Son of David: Blessed is he that cometh in the name of the Lord; Hosanna in the highest. And when he was come into Jerusalem, all the city was moved, saying, Who is this? And the multitude said, This is Jesus the prophet of Nazareth of Galilee. And Jesus went into the temple of God, and cast out all them that sold and bought in the temple, and overthrew the tables of the moneychangers, and the seats of them that sold doves, And said unto them, It is written, My house shall be called the house of prayer; but ye have made it a den of thieves.

Offertory. Unto thee lift I up my soul: my God in thee have I trusted, let me not be confounded: neither let mine enemies triumph over me: for all they that look for thee shall not be ashamed.

Secret

MAY these sacred mysteries, O Lord, so cleanse us by their mighty power, that growing in purity, we may attain unto thee who art the author of the same. Through.

❡ 2nd Secret is of St. Mary in Advent (p. 541) & 3rd Against the Persecutors of the Church (p. 543) or for the Chief Bishop (p. 543).

Advent II   **Proper of Season**

Communion. The Lord shall shew loving-kindness; and our land shall give her increase.

Postcommunion

RANT, O Lord, that we may so wait for thy loving-kindness in the midst of thy temple; that we may with worthy reverence prevent the coming festival of our redemption. Through.

¶ 2nd Postcommunion is of St. Mary in Advent (p. 541) & 3rd Against the Persecutors of the Church (p. 543) or for the Chief Bishop (p. 543).

SECOND SUNDAY OF ADVENT

Second Class Semidouble

Introit

PEOPLE of Sion, behold the Lord is nigh at hand to redeem the nations: and in the gladness of your heart the Lord shall cause his glorious voice to be heard. *Ps.* Hear, O thou Shepherd of Israel: thou that leadest Joseph like a sheep.

Collect

LESSED Lord, who hast caused all holy Scriptures to be written for our learning; Grant that we may in such wise hear them, read, mark, learn, and inwardly digest them, that by patience and comfort of thy holy Word, we may embrace, and ever hold fast, the blessed hope of everlasting life, which thou hast given us in our Saviour Jesus Christ. Who liveth.

¶ 2nd Collect is of St. Mary in Advent (p. 541) & 3rd Against the Persecutors of the Church (p. 543) or for the Chief Bishop (p. 543).

Epistle. Romans 15:4

BRETHREN: Whatsoever things were written aforetime were written for our learning, that we through patience and comfort of the scriptures might have hope. Now the God of patience and consolation grant you to be likeminded one toward another according to Christ Jesus: That ye may with one mind and one mouth glorify God, even the Father of our Lord Jesus Christ. Wherefore receive ye one another, as Christ also received us to the glory of God. Now I say that Jesus Christ was a minister of the circumcision for the

Proper of Season   *Advent II*

truth of God, to confirm the promises made unto the fathers: And that the Gentiles might glorify God for his mercy; as it is written, For this cause I will confess to thee among the Gentiles, and sing unto thy name. And again he saith, Rejoice, ye Gentiles, with his people. And again, Praise the Lord, all ye Gentiles; and laud him, all ye people. And again, Esaias saith, There shall be a root of Jesse, and he that shall rise to reign over the Gentiles; in him shall the Gentiles trust. Now the God of hope fill you with all joy and peace in believing, that ye may abound in hope, through the power of the Holy Ghost.

Gradual. Out of Sion hath God appeared; in perfect beauty, ℣. Gather my saints together unto me, those that have made a covenant with me with sacrifice.

Alleluia. Alleluia, alleluia. ℣. I was glad when they said unto me: we will go into the house of the Lord. Alleluia.

Gospel. Luke 21:25

AT THAT TIME: Jesus said unto his disciples: There shall be signs in the sun, and in the moon, and in the stars; and upon the earth distress of nations, with perplexity; the sea and the waves roaring; Men's hearts failing them for fear, and for looking after those things which are coming on the earth: for the powers of heaven shall be shaken. And then shall they see the Son of man coming in a cloud with power and great glory. And when these things begin to come to pass, then look up, and lift up your heads; for your redemption draweth nigh. And he spake to them a parable; Behold the fig tree, and all the trees; When they now shoot forth, ye see and know of your own selves that summer is now nigh at hand. So likewise ye, when ye see these things come to pass, know ye that the kingdom of God is nigh at hand. Verily I say unto you, This generation shall not pass away, till all be fulfilled. Heaven and earth shall pass away: but my words shall not pass away.

Offertory. Wilt not thou turn again, O God, and quicken us, that thy people may rejoice in thee; shew us thy mercy, O Lord, and grant us thy salvation.

Secret

WE beseech thee, O Lord, mercifully to accept the prayers and sacrifices of thy humble servants: that we, who cannot of our own prayers and merits help ourselves may be defended by thy succour. Through.

¶ 2ⁿᵈ Secret is of St. Mary in Advent (p. 541) & 3ʳᵈ Against the Persecutors of the Church (p. 543) or for the Chief Bishop (p. 543).

Advent III   # Proper of Season

Communion. Arise, O Jerusalem, and stand on high, and behold the joy that cometh unto thee from thy God.

Postcommunion

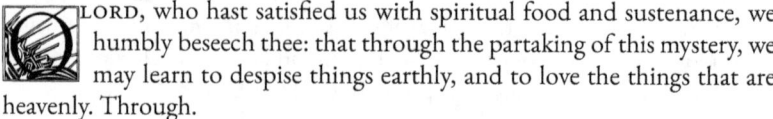LORD, who hast satisfied us with spiritual food and sustenance, we humbly beseech thee: that through the partaking of this mystery, we may learn to despise things earthly, and to love the things that are heavenly. Through.

¶ 2nd Postcommunion is of St. Mary in Advent (p. 541) & 3rd Against the Persecutors of the Church (p. 543) or for the Chief Bishop (p. 543).

Third Sunday of Advent

Second Class Semidouble

Introit

REJOICE in the Lord alway: and again I say, rejoice. Let your moderation be known unto all men: for the Lord is at hand. Be careful for nothing; but in all things by prayer let your requests be made known unto God. *Ps.* Lord, thou art become gracious unto thy land; thou hast turned away the captivity of Jacob.

Collect

O LORD Jesus Christ, who at thy first coming didst send thy messenger to prepare thy way before thee; Grant that the ministers and stewards of thy mysteries may likewise so prepare and make ready thy way, by turning the hearts of the disobedient to the wisdom of the just, that at thy second coming to judge the world we may be found an acceptable people in thy sight, who livest and reignest with the Father and the Holy Spirit ever one God, world without end. *Amen.*

¶ 2nd Collect is of St. Mary in Advent (p. 541) & 3rd Against the Persecutors of the Church (p. 543) or for the Chief Bishop (p. 543).

Epistle. 1 Corinthians 4:1

BRETHREN: Let a man so account of us, as of the ministers of Christ, and stewards of the mysteries of God. Moreover it is required in stewards, that a man be found faithful. But with me it is a very small thing that

Proper of Season *Advent III*

I should be judged of you, or of man's judgment: yea, I judge not mine own self. For I know nothing by myself; yet am I not hereby justified: but he that judgeth me is the Lord. Therefore judge nothing before the time, until the Lord come, who both will bring to light the hidden things of darkness, and will make manifest the counsels of the hearts: and then shall every man have praise of God.

Gradual. O Lord, thou that sittest upon the Cherubim, stir up thy strength and come. ℣. Hear, O thou Shepherd of Israel: thou that leadest Joseph like a sheep.

Alleluia. Alleluia, alleluia. ℣. Stir up thy strength, O Lord, and come and help us. Alleluia.

Gospel. Matthew 11:2

T THAT TIME: When John had heard in the prison the works of Christ, he sent two of his disciples, And said unto him, Art thou he that should come, or do we look for another? Jesus answered and said unto them, Go and shew John again those things which ye do hear and see: The blind receive their sight, and the lame walk, the lepers are cleansed, and the deaf hear, the dead are raised up, and the poor have the gospel preached to them. And blessed is he, whosoever shall not be offended in me. And as they departed, Jesus began to say unto the multitudes concerning John, What went ye out into the wilderness to see? A reed shaken with the wind? But what went ye out for to see? A man clothed in soft raiment? behold, they that wear soft clothing are in kings' houses. But what went ye out for to see? A prophet? yea, I say unto you, and more than a prophet. For this is he, of whom it is written, Behold, I send my messenger before thy face, which shall prepare thy way before thee.

Offertory. O Lord, thou art become gracious unto thy land: thou hast turned away the captivity of Jacob: thou hast forgiven the offence of thy people.

Secret

E beseech thee, O Lord, that the continual offering of this sacrifice of our devotion may fulfil thine institution of this sacred mystery and may accomplish in us the wondrous work of thy salvation. Through.

¶ 2ⁿᵈ Secret is of St. Mary in Advent (p. 541) & 3ʳᵈ Against the Persecutors of the Church (p. 543) or for the Chief Bishop (p. 543).

Communion. Say to them that are of a fearful heart: be strong, fear not: behold, our God will come and save us.

Advent Emberday   # Proper of Season   Ember Wednesday

Postcommunion

E entreat, O Lord, thy mercy: that these means of heavenly grace may so cleanse us from our sins, that we may be made ready for thy coming festival. Through.

¶ 2nd Postcommunion is of St. Mary in Advent (p. 541) & 3rd Against the Persecutors of the Church (p. 543) or for the Chief Bishop (p. 543).

EMBER WEDNESDAY IN ADVENT

Second Class Feria

Introit

ROP down, ye heavens, from above, and let the skies pour down justice: let the earth open, and bring forth a Saviour. *Ps.* The heavens declare the glory of God: and the firmament sheweth his handywork.

¶ After the Kyrie,

℣. Let us pray.	℣. Orémus.
℣. Let us bow the knee.	℣. Flectámus génua.
℣. Arise.	℣. Leváte.

Collect

RANT, we beseech thee, Almighty God: that the coming solemnity of our redemption may bestow on us thy succour in this present life, and win for us the rewards of everlasting blessedness. Through.

¶ 2nd Collect is of St. Mary in Advent (p. 541) & 3rd Against the Persecutors of the Church (p. 543) or for the Chief Bishop (p. 543).

Epistle. Isaiah 2:2

IN THOSE DAYS: Said Isaiah the Prophet: And it shall come to pass in the last days, that the mountain of the LORD's house shall be established in the top of the mountains, and shall be exalted above the hills; and all nations shall flow unto it. And many people shall go and say, Come ye, and let us go up to the mountain of the LORD, to the house of the God of Jacob; and he will teach us of his ways, and we will walk in his paths: for out of Zion shall go forth the law, and the word of the LORD from Jerusalem. And he shall judge among the nations, and shall rebuke many people: and they shall beat

Ember Wednesday — Proper of Season — Advent Emberday

their swords into plowshares, and their spears into pruninghooks: nation shall not lift up sword against nation, neither shall they learn war any more. O house of Jacob, come ye, and let us walk in the light of the LORD our God.

Gradual. Lift up your heads, O ye gates: and be ye lift up, ye everlasting doors: and the King of glory shall come in, ℣. Who shall ascend into the hill of the Lord? or who shall rise up in his holy place? Even he that hath clean hands and a pure heart.

℣. The Lord be with you.	℣. Dóminus vobíscum.
R̲. And with thy spirit.	R̲. Et cum spíritu tuo.
℣. Let us pray.	℣. Orémus.

Collect

O LORD, make haste, we pray thee, and delay not to bestow upon us the assistance of thy heavenly might: that they who put their confidence in thy mercy may be succoured by the consolations of thine advent. Who livest.

Epistle. Isaiah 7:10

IN THOSE DAYS: The LORD spake unto Ahaz, saying, Ask thee a sign of the LORD thy God; ask it either in the depth, or in the height above. But Ahaz said, I will not ask, neither will I tempt the LORD. And he said, Hear ye now, O house of David; Is it a small thing for you to weary men, but will ye weary my God also? Therefore the Lord himself shall give you a sign; Behold, a virgin shall conceive, and bear a son, and shall call his name Immanuel. Butter and honey shall he eat, that he may know to refuse the evil, and choose the good.

Gradual. The Lord is nigh unto all them that call upon him: yea all such as call upon him faithfully. ℣. My mouth shall speak the praise of the Lord: and let all flesh give thanks unto his holy name.

Gospel. Luke 1:26

AT THAT TIME: The angel Gabriel was sent from God unto a city of Galilee, named Nazareth, To a virgin espoused to a man whose name was Joseph, of the house of David; and the virgin's name was Mary. And the angel came in unto her, and said, Hail, thou that art highly favoured, the Lord is with thee: blessed art thou among women. And when she saw him,

Advent Emberday   **Proper of Season**   Ember Wednesday

she was troubled at his saying, and cast in her mind what manner of salutation this should be. And the angel said unto her, Fear not, Mary: for thou hast found favour with God. And, behold, thou shalt conceive in thy womb, and bring forth a son, and shalt call his name JESUS. He shall be great, and shall be called the Son of the Highest: and the Lord God shall give unto him the throne of his father David: And he shall reign over the house of Jacob for ever; and of his kingdom there shall be no end. Then said Mary unto the angel, How shall this be, seeing I know not a man? And the angel answered and said unto her, The Holy Ghost shall come upon thee, and the power of the Highest shall overshadow thee: therefore also that holy thing which shall be born of thee shall be called the Son of God. And, behold, thy cousin Elisabeth, she hath also conceived a son in her old age: and this is the sixth month with her, who was called barren. For with God nothing shall be impossible. And Mary said, Behold the handmaid of the Lord; be it unto me according to thy word.

Offertory. Be strong, fear not: behold, our God will come with vengeance, even God with a recompence: he will come and save us.

Secret

E beseech thee, O Lord, that these our fasts may be acceptable in thy sight: that we, being cleansed thereby and made worthy of thy grace, may be brought unto thine everlasting promises. Through.

¶ 2nd Secret is of St. Mary in Advent (p. 541) & 3rd Against the Persecutors of the Church (p. 543) or for the Chief Bishop (p. 543).

Communion. Behold, a Virgin shall conceive, and bear a son: and shall call his name Immanuel.

Postcommunion

LORD, who hast satisfied us with the gift of thy salvation, we humbly beseech thee: that as we joyfully taste thereof, so we may effectually be renewed by the same. Through.

¶ 2nd Postcommunion is of St. Mary in Advent (p. 541) & 3rd Against the Persecutors of the Church (p. 543) or for the Chief Bishop (p. 543).

Ember Friday — **Proper of Season** — *Advent Emberday*

EMBER FRIDAY IN ADVENT

Second Class Feria

Introit

Be thou nigh at hand, O Lord, for all thy commandments are true: as concerning thy testimonies, I have known long since, that thou art from everlasting. *Ps.* Blessed are those that are undefiled in the way: and walk in the law of the Lord.

Collect

Stir up, we beseech thee, O Lord, thy power, and come among us: that they who put their confidence in thy goodness may speedily be delivered from all adversity. Who livest.

¶ 2nd Collect is of St. Mary in Advent (p. 541) & 3rd Against the Persecutors of the Church (p. 543) or for the Chief Bishop (p. 543).

Epistle. Isaiah 11:1

Thus saith the Lord God: There shall come forth a rod out of the stem of Jesse, and a Branch shall grow out of his roots: And the spirit of the LORD shall rest upon him, the spirit of wisdom and understanding, the spirit of counsel and might, the spirit of knowledge and of the fear of the LORD; And shall make him of quick understanding in the fear of the LORD: and he shall not judge after the sight of his eyes, neither reprove after the hearing of his ears: But with righteousness shall he judge the poor, and reprove with equity for the meek of the earth: and he shall smite the earth with the rod of his mouth, and with the breath of his lips shall he slay the wicked. And righteousness shall be the girdle of his loins, and faithfulness the girdle of his reins.

Gradual. Shew us thy mercy, O Lord: and grant us thy salvation. ℣. Lord, thou art become gracious unto thy land: thou hast turned away the captivity of Jacob.

Gospel. Luke 1:39

At that time: Mary arose, and went into the hill country with haste, into a city of Juda; And entered into the house of Zacharias, and saluted Elisabeth. And it came to pass, that, when Elisabeth heard the salutation of Mary, the babe leaped in her womb; and Elisabeth was filled with the Holy Ghost: And she spake out with a loud voice, and said, Blessed art thou among women, and blessed is the fruit of thy womb. And whence is this to me, that the mother of my Lord should come to me? For, lo, as soon as the voice of thy salutation sounded in mine ears, the babe leaped in my womb for joy. And blessed is she that believed: for there shall be a performance of those things which were told her from the Lord. And Mary said, My soul doth magnify the Lord, And my spirit hath rejoiced in God my Saviour.

Offertory. Wilt thou not turn again, O God, and quicken us, that thy people may rejoice in thee: shew us thy mercy, O Lord, and grant us thy salvation.

Secret

E beseech thee, O Lord, to accept our prayers and oblations: and graciously hearken unto us, whom thou dost cleanse by thy heavenly mysteries. Through.

¶ 2ⁿᵈ Secret is of St. Mary in Advent (p. 541) & 3ʳᵈ Against the Persecutors of the Church (p. 543) or for the Chief Bishop (p. 543).

Communion. Behold, the Lord shall come, and all his Saints with him: and in that day there shall be a great light.

Postcommunion

AY the holy partaking of thy sacrament, O Lord, in such wise restore us: that we, being cleansed from our former nature, may enter into the fellowship of this saving mystery. Through.

¶ 2ⁿᵈ Postcommunion is of St. Mary in Advent (p. 541) & 3ʳᵈ Against the Persecutors of the Church (p. 543) or for the Chief Bishop (p. 543).

Ember Saturday in Advent

Second Class Feria

Introit

OME and shew us the light of thy countenance, O Lord, that sittest upon the Cherubim: and we shall be whole. *Ps.* Hear, O thou Shepherd of Israel: thou that leadest Joseph like a sheep.

Ember Saturday — Proper of Season — *Advent Emberday*

¶ After the Kyrie,

℣. Let us pray.
℣. Let us bow the knee.
℣. Arise.

℣. Orémus.
℣. Flectámus génua.
℣. Leváte.

Collect

O GOD, who seest us that we are afflicted by reason of our iniquity: mercifully grant; that we may be comforted by thy visitation. Who livest.

Epistle. Isaiah 19:20

IN THOSE DAYS: They shall cry unto the LORD because of the oppressors, and he shall send them a saviour, and a great one, and he shall deliver them. And the LORD shall be known to Egypt, and the Egyptians shall know the LORD in that day, and shall do sacrifice and oblation; yea, they shall vow a vow unto the LORD, and perform it. And the LORD shall smite Egypt: he shall smite and heal it: and they shall return even to the LORD, and he shall be intreated of them, and shall heal them, the Lord our God.

Gradual. He goeth forth from the uttermost part of the heaven; and runneth about unto the end of it again. ℣. The heavens declare the glory of God; and the firmament sheweth his handy-work.

℣. Let us pray.
℣. Let us bow the knee.
℣. Arise.

℣. Orémus.
℣. Flectámus génua.
℣. Leváte.

Collect

GRANT, we beseech thee, Almighty God: that, whereas through our ancient bondage we are bowed down beneath the yoke of sin; the new birth of thine only-begotten Son which we await may be for our deliverance. Who liveth.

Epistle. Isaiah 35:1

THUS SAITH THE LORD: The wilderness and the solitary place shall be glad for them; and the desert shall rejoice, and blossom as the rose. It shall blossom abundantly, and rejoice even with joy and singing: the glory of Lebanon shall be given unto it, the excellency of Carmel and Sharon, they shall see the glory of the LORD, and the excellency of our God. Strengthen

Advent Emberday   **Proper of Season**   Ember Saturday

ye the weak hands, and confirm the feeble knees. Say to them that are of a fearful heart, Be strong, fear not: behold, your God will come with vengeance, even God with a recompence; he will come and save you. Then the eyes of the blind shall be opened, and the ears of the deaf shall be unstopped. Then shall the lame man leap as an hart, and the tongue of the dumb sing: for in the wilderness shall waters break out, and streams in the desert. And the parched ground shall become a pool, and the thirsty land springs of water: saith the Lord Almighty.

Gradual. He hath set his tabernacle in the sun: and he cometh forth as a bridegroom out of his chamber. ℣. He goeth forth from the uttermost part of the heaven: and runneth about unto the end of it again.

℣. Let us pray.	℣. Orémus.
℣. Let us bow the knee.	℣. Flectámus génua.
℣. Arise.	℣. Leváte.

Collect

O LORD, we pray thee, that we thine unworthy servants, who now bewail the guilt of our misdeeds, may be gladdened by the advent of thy onlybegotten Son. Who liveth.

Epistle. Isaiah 40:9

THUS SAITH THE LORD: O Zion, that bringest good tidings, get thee up into the high mountain; O Jerusalem, that bringest good tidings, lift up thy voice with strength; lift it up, be not afraid; say unto the cities of Judah, Behold your God! Behold, the Lord GOD will come with strong hand, and his arm shall rule for him: behold, his reward is with him, and his work before him. He shall feed his flock like a shepherd: he shall gather the lambs with his arm, and carry them in his bosom, the Lord our God.

Gradual. Turn us again, O Lord God of hosts: shew the light of thy countenance, and we shall be whole. ℣. Stir up thy strength, O Lord, and come, and save us.

℣. Let us pray.	℣. Orémus.
℣. Let us bow the knee.	℣. Flectámus génua.
℣. Arise.	℣. Leváte.

Ember Saturday   **Proper of Season**   *Advent Emberday*

Collect

RANT, we beseech thee, Almighty God: that the coming solemnity of thy Son may bestow upon us healing in this present life, and obtain for us everlasting rewards. Through the same.

Epistle. Isaiah 45:1

THUS saith the LORD to his anointed, to Cyrus, whose right hand I have holden, to subdue nations before him; and I will loose the loins of kings, to open before him the two leaved gates; and the gates shall not be shut; I will go before thee, and make the crooked places straight: I will break in pieces the gates of brass, and cut in sunder the bars of iron: And I will give thee the treasures of darkness, and hidden riches of secret places, that thou mayest know that I, the LORD, which call thee by thy name, am the God of Israel. For Jacob my servant's sake, and Israel mine elect, I have even called thee by thy name: I have surnamed thee, though thou hast not known me. I am the LORD, and there is none else, there is no God beside me: I girded thee, though thou hast not known me: That they may know from the rising of the sun, and from the west, that there is none beside me. I am the LORD, and there is none else. I form the light, and create darkness: I make peace, and create evil: I the LORD do all these things. Drop down, ye heavens, from above, and let the skies pour down righteousness: let the earth open, and let them bring forth salvation, and let righteousness spring up together; I the LORD have created it.

Gradual. Stir up, O Lord, thy strength, and come, and save us. ℣. Hear, O thou Shepherd of Israel: thou that leadest Joseph like a sheep: shew thyself, thou that sittest upon the Cherubim, before Ephraim, Benjamin, and Manasses.

℣. Let us pray.	℣. Orémus.
℣. Let us bow the knee.	℣. Flectámus génua.
℣. Arise.	℣. Leváte.

Collect

LORD, we beseech thee favourably to hear the prayers of thy people: that we, who are justly punished for our offences, may be comforted by the visitation of thy mercy. Who livest.

Advent Emberday **Proper of Season** Ember Saturday

Epistle. Song of the Three Young Men 26

IN THOSE DAYS: The angel of the Lord came down into the oven together with Azarias and his fellows, and smote the flame of the fire out of the oven; And made the midst of the furnace as it had been a moist whistling wind, so that the fire touched them not at all, neither hurt nor troubled them. Then the three, as out of one mouth, praised, glorified, and blessed, God in the furnace, saying,

¶ Here the response Thanks be to God, is not made.

Hymn

BLESSED art thou, O Lord God of our fathers. And worthy to be praised and glorious for ever.
And blessed is the name of thy glory, which is holy. And worthy to be praised and glorious for ever.
Blessed art thou in the holy temple of thy glory. And worthy to be praised and glorious for ever.
Blessed art thou on the holy throne of thy kingdom. And worthy to be praised and glorious for ever.
Blessed art thou in the sceptre of thy Godhead. And worthy to be praised and glorious for ever.
Blessed art thou that sittest upon the Cherubim, and beholdest the depths. And worthy to be praised and glorious for ever.
Blessed art thou that walkest on the wings of the winds and on the waves of the sea. And worthy to be praised and glorious for ever.
Let all thine Angels and Saints bless thee. And let them praise thee and glorify thee for ever.
Let the heavens, the earth, the sea, and all that in them is bless thee. And let them praise thee and glorify thee for ever.
Glory be to the Father, and to the Son, and to the Holy Ghost. And worthy to be praised and glorious for ever.
As it was in the beginning, is now, and ever shall be: world without end. Amen. And worthy to be praised and glorious for ever.
Blessed art thou, O Lord God of our fathers. And worthy to be praised and glorious for ever.

℣. The Lord be with you.	℣. Dóminus vobíscum.
℟. And with thy spirit.	℟. Et cum spíritu tuo.

Ember Saturday   **Proper of Season**   Advent Emberday

℣. Let us pray. | ℣. Orémus.

Collect

O GOD, who to the three children didst assuage the flames of fire: mercifully grant; that the flames of sin may not kindle upon us thy servants. Through.

¶ 2nd Collect is of St. Mary in Advent (p. 541) & 3rd Against the Persecutors of the Church (p. 543) or For the Chief Bishop (p. 543).

Epistle. 2 Thessalonians 2:1

BRETHREN: We beseech you, by the coming of our Lord Jesus Christ, and by our gathering together unto him, That ye be not soon shaken in mind, or be troubled, neither by spirit, nor by word, nor by letter as from us, as that the day of Christ is at hand. Let no man deceive you by any means: for that day shall not come, except there come a falling away first, and that man of sin be revealed, the son of perdition; Who opposeth and exalteth himself above all that is called God, or that is worshipped; so that he as God sitteth in the temple of God, shewing himself that he is God. Remember ye not, that, when I was yet with you, I told you these things? And now ye know what withholdeth that he might be revealed in his time. For the mystery of iniquity doth already work: only he who now letteth will let, until he be taken out of the way. And then shall that Wicked be revealed, whom the Lord shall consume with the spirit of his mouth, and shall destroy with the brightness of his coming.

Tract. Hear, O thou Shepherd of Israel: thou that leadest Joseph like a sheep, ℣. Thou that sittest upon the Cherubim, shew thyself before Ephraim, Benjamin, and Manasses. ℣. Stir up thy strength, O Lord, and come, and save us.

Gospel. Luke 3:1

IN the fifteenth year of the reign of Tiberius Caesar, Pontius Pilate being governor of Judaea, and Herod being tetrarch of Galilee, and his brother Philip tetrarch of Ituraea and of the region of Trachonitis, and Lysanias the tetrarch of Abilene, Annas and Caiaphas being the high priests, the word of God came unto John the son of Zacharias in the wilderness. And he came into all the country about Jordan, preaching the baptism of repentance for the remission of sins; As it is written in the book of the words of Esaias the prophet, saying, The voice of one crying in the wilderness, Prepare ye the way of the Lord, make his paths straight. Every valley shall be filled, and every

Advent IV

mountain and hill shall be brought low; and the crooked shall be made straight, and the rough ways shall be made smooth; And all flesh shall see the salvation of God.

Offertory. Rejoice greatly, O daughter of Zion, shout aloud, O daughter of Jerusalem: behold, thy King cometh to thee, he is just and having salvation.

Secret

E beseech thee, O Lord, mercifully to have respect unto these our sacrifices: that they may increase our devotion, and set forward our salvation. Through.

¶ 2nd Secret is of St. Mary in Advent (p. 541) & 3rd Against the Persecutors of the Church (p. 543) or For the Chief Bishop (p. 543).

Communion. He rejoiceth as a giant to run his course: he goeth forth from the uttermost part of the heaven, and runneth about unto the end of it again.

Postcommunion

E beseech thee, O Lord our God: that these holy mysteries which thou hast given to us for the assurance of our redemption; may be for our healing both in this life and in that which is to come. Through.

¶ 2nd Postcommunion is of St. Mary in Advent (p. 541) & 3rd Against the Persecutors of the Church (p. 543) or For the Chief Bishop (p. 543).

Fourth Sunday of Advent

Second Class Semidouble

Introit

ROP down, ye heavens, from above, and let the skies pour down justice: let the earth open, and bring forth a Saviour. *Ps.* The heavens declare the glory of God: and the firmament sheweth his handywork.

Collect

LORD, raise up, we pray thee, thy power, and come among us, and with great might succour us; that whereas, through our sins and wickedness, we are sore let and hindered in running the race that is set before us, thy bountiful grace and mercy may speedily help and deliver us; through the

Proper of Season *Advent IV*

satisfaction of thy Son our Lord, to whom, with thee and the Holy Ghost, be honour and glory, world without end. *Amen.*

¶ 2ⁿᵈ Collect is of St. Mary in Advent (p. 541) & 3ʳᵈ Against the Persecutors of the Church (p. 543) or for the Chief Bishop (p. 543).

Epistle. Philippians 4:4

BRETHREN: Rejoice in the Lord alway: and again I say, Rejoice. Let your moderation be known unto all men. The Lord is at hand. Be careful for nothing; but in every thing by prayer and supplication with thanksgiving let your requests be made known unto God. And the peace of God, which passeth all understanding, shall keep your hearts and minds through Christ Jesus our Lord.

Gradual. The Lord is nigh unto all them that call upon him: yea, all such as call upon him faithfully. ℣. My mouth shall speak the praise of the Lord: and let all flesh give thanks unto his holy name.

Alleluia. Alleluia, alleluia. ℣. Come, O Lord, and tarry not: forgive the misdeeds of thy people Israel. Alleluia.

Gospel. John 1:19

THIS IS THE RECORD OF JOHN: The Jews sent priests and Levites from Jerusalem to ask him, Who art thou? And he confessed, and denied not; but confessed, I am not the Christ. And they asked him, What then? Art thou Elias? And he saith, I am not. Art thou that prophet? And he answered, No. Then said they unto him, Who art thou? that we may give an answer to them that sent us. What sayest thou of thyself? He said, I am the voice of one crying in the wilderness, Make straight the way of the Lord, as said the prophet Esaias. And they which were sent were of the Pharisees. And they asked him, and said unto him, Why baptizest thou then, if thou be not that Christ, nor Elias, neither that prophet? John answered them, saying, I baptize with water: but there standeth one among you, whom ye know not; He it is, who coming after me is preferred before me, whose shoe's latchet I am not worthy to unloose. These things were done in Bethabara beyond Jordan, where John was baptizing.

Offertory. Hail, Mary, full of grace; the Lord is with thee: blessed art thou among women, and blessed is the fruit of thy womb.

Christmas Eve

Proper of Season

Secret

E beseech thee, O Lord, mercifully to have respect unto these our sacrifices: that they may increase our devotion and set forward our salvation. Through.

¶ 2ⁿᵈ Secret is of St. Mary in Advent (p. 541) & 3ʳᵈ Against the Persecutors of the Church (p. 543) or for the Chief Bishop (p. 543).

Communion. Behold, a Virgin shall conceive, and bear a son: and his name shall be called Immanuel.

Postcommunion

E beseech thee, O Lord: that as we have now received thy gifts, so, continually drawing near to this mystery, we may set forward the work of our salvation. Through.

¶ 2ⁿᵈ Postcommunion is of St. Mary in Advent (p. 541) & 3ʳᵈ Against the Persecutors of the Church (p. 543) or for the Chief Bishop (p. 543).

VIGIL OF THE NATIVITY OF OUR LORD

First Class Vigil

Opening Sentence. To-morrow shall the wickedness of the earth be done away. And the Saviour of the world shall be King over us.

¶ If the Vigil of the Nativity fall on a Sunday, the whole Office of the Mass is of the Vigil, with commemoration of the Sunday, but its Gospel is not read at the end.

Introit

O-DAY shall ye know that the Lord will come to deliver us: and in the morning shall ye behold his glory. *Ps.* The earth is the Lord's, and all that therein is; the compass of the world, and they that dwell therein.

Collect

GOD, who makest us glad with the yearly expectation of our redemption: vouchsafe; that as we joyfully receive thine Only-begotten Son for our Redeemer, so we may with sure confidence behold him when he shall come to be our judge, even Jesus Christ thy Son our Lord. Who liveth.

Proper of Season *Christmas Eve*

Epistle. Romans 1:1

PAUL, a servant of Jesus Christ, called to be an apostle, separated unto the gospel of God, (Which he had promised afore by his prophets in the holy scriptures,) Concerning his Son Jesus Christ our Lord, which was made of the seed of David according to the flesh; And declared to be the Son of God with power, according to the spirit of holiness, by the resurrection from the dead: By whom we have received grace and apostleship, for obedience to the faith among all nations, for his name: Among whom are ye also the called of Jesus Christ our Lord.

Gradual. To-day shall ye know that the Lord will come to deliver us: and in the morning shall ye behold his glory. ℣. Hear, O thou Shepherd of Israel: thou that leadest Joseph like a sheep: thou that sittest upon the Cherubim, shew thyself before Ephraim, Benjamin, and Manasses.

¶ The Alleluia Verse is not said unless the Vigil fall on a Sunday.

Alleluia. Alleluia, alleluia. ℣. On the morrow the iniquity of the earth shall be blotted out: and the Saviour of the world shall reign over us. Alleluia.

Gospel. Matthew 1:18

WHEN as Mary the Mother of Jesus was espoused to Joseph, before they came together, she was found with child of the Holy Ghost. Then Joseph her husband, being a just man, and not willing to make her a publick example, was minded to put her away privily. But while he thought on these things, behold, the angel of the Lord appeared unto him in a dream, saying, Joseph, thou son of David, fear not to take unto thee Mary thy wife: for that which is conceived in her is of the Holy Ghost. And she shall bring forth a son, and thou shalt call his name JESUS: for he shall save his people from their sins.

Offertory. Lift up your heads, O ye gates: and be ye lift up, ye everlasting doors, and the King of glory shall come in.

Secret

GRANT to us, we beseech thee, almighty God: that like as we do prevent the feast of the adorable Birth of thy Son, so we may joyfully receive his everlasting gifts. Who with thee liveth.

Communion. The glory of the Lord shall be revealed: and all flesh shall see the salvation of our God.

Christmas   **Proper of Season**   First Mass at Night

Postcommunion

RANT to us, we beseech thee, O Lord: that like as we do eat and drink of the heavenly mystery of thine only begotten Son; so we may be renewed by the remembrance of his birth. Through the same.

Nativity of Our Lord

First Class Double, Third Class Octave

(The First Mass at Night)

Introit

HE Lord hath said unto me: Thou art my Son, this day have I begotten thee. *Ps.* Why do the heathen so furiously rage together: and why do the people imagine a vain thing?

Collect

GOD, who makest us glad with the yearly remembrance of the birth of thine only Son Jesus Christ; Grant that as we joyfully receive him for our Redeemer, so we may with sure confidence behold him when he shall come to be our Judge, who liveth and reigneth with thee and the Holy Ghost, one God, world without end. *Amen.*

Epistle. Titus 2:11

DEARLY BELOVED: The grace of God that bringeth salvation hath appeared to all men, Teaching us that, denying ungodliness and worldly lusts, we should live soberly, righteously, and godly, in this present world; Looking for that blessed hope, and the glorious appearing of the great God and our Saviour Jesus Christ; Who gave himself for us, that he might redeem us from all iniquity, and purify unto himself a peculiar people, zealous of good works. These things speak, and exhort: in Christ Jesus our Lord.

Gradual. In the day of thy power shall the people offer thee free-will offerings with an holy worship: the dew of thy birth is of the womb of the morning. ℣. The Lord said unto my Lord: Sit thou on my right hand: until I make thine enemies thy footstool.

Alleluia. Alleluia, alleluia. ℣. The Lord hath said unto me: Thou art my Son, this day have I begotten thee. Alleluia.

First Mass at Night   **Proper of Season**   *Christmas*

Gospel. Luke 2:1

AT THAT TIME: There went out a decree from Caesar Augustus, that all the world should be taxed. (And this taxing was first made when Cyrenius was governor of Syria.) And all went to be taxed, every one into his own city. And Joseph also went up from Galilee, out of the city of Nazareth, into Judaea, unto the city of David, which is called Bethlehem; (because he was of the house and lineage of David:) To be taxed with Mary his espoused wife, being great with child. And so it was, that, while they were there, the days were accomplished that she should be delivered. And she brought forth her firstborn son, and wrapped him in swaddling clothes, and laid him in a manger; because there was no room for them in the inn. And there were in the same country shepherds abiding in the field, keeping watch over their flock by night. And, lo, the angel of the Lord came upon them, and the glory of the Lord shone round about them: and they were sore afraid. And the angel said unto them, Fear not: for, behold, I bring you good tidings of great joy, which shall be to all people. For unto you is born this day in the city of David a Saviour, which is Christ the Lord. And this shall be a sign unto you; Ye shall find the babe wrapped in swaddling clothes, lying in a manger. And suddenly there was with the angel a multitude of the heavenly host praising God, and saying, Glory to God in the highest, and on earth peace, good will toward men.

Offertory. Let the heavens rejoice, and let the earth be glad before the Lord: for he is come.

Secret

WE beseech thee, O Lord, that the oblation of this day's festival may be acceptable unto thee: that by thy bountiful grace we may, through this holy communion, be found in the likeness of him in whom our substance is united unto thee. Who liveth.

Communion. With an holy worship, the dew of thy birth is of the womb of the morning.

Postcommunion

GRANT, to us, we beseech thee, O Lord our God, that we who in these mysteries draw near with gladness unto the Nativity of Jesus Christ our Lord; may by godly conversation be found worthy to attain unto his fellowship. Who liveth.

Christmas 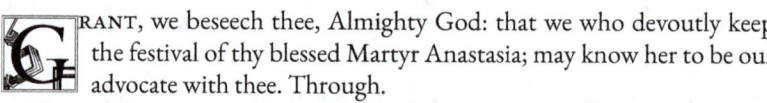 Second Mass at Dawn

NATIVITY OF OUR LORD

(The Second Mass at Dawn)

Introit

LIGHT shall shine upon us to-day: for unto us the Lord is born: and he shall be called Wonderful, God, the Prince of Peace, Father of the world to come: of whose kingdom there shall be no end. *Ps.* The Lord is King, and hath put on glorious apparel: the Lord hath put on his apparel, and girded himself with strength.

Collect

GRANT, to us, we beseech thee, Almighty God: that as thou dost pour forth on us the new light of thine incarnate Word; so he, who doth illuminate our minds by faith, may likewise in our works shew forth his brightness. Through the same.

¶ Commemoration of St. Anastasia, as followeth,

GRANT, we beseech thee, Almighty God: that we who devoutly keep the festival of thy blessed Martyr Anastasia; may know her to be our advocate with thee. Through.

Epistle. Titus 3:4

DEARLY BELOVED: The kindness and love of God our Saviour toward man appeared, Not by works of righteousness which we have done, but according to his mercy he saved us, by the washing of regeneration, and renewing of the Holy Ghost; Which he shed on us abundantly through Jesus Christ our Saviour; That being justified by his grace, we should be made heirs according to the hope of eternal life: in Christ Jesus our Lord.

Gradual. Blessed is he that cometh in the name of the Lord: God is the Lord who hath shewed us light. ℣. This is the Lord's doing: and it is marvellous in our eyes.

Alleluia. Alleluia, alleluia. ℣. The Lord is King, and hath put on glorious apparel: the Lord hath put on his apparel, and girded himself with strength. Alleluia.

Second Mass at Dawn **Proper of Season** *Christmas*

Gospel. Luke 2:15

T THAT TIME: The shepherds said one to another, Let us now go even unto Bethlehem, and see this thing which is come to pass, which the Lord hath made known unto us. And they came with haste, and found Mary, and Joseph, and the babe lying in a manger. And when they had seen it, they made known abroad the saying which was told them concerning this child. And all they that heard it wondered at those things which were told them by the shepherds. But Mary kept all these things, and pondered them in her heart. And the shepherds returned, glorifying and praising God for all the things that they had heard and seen, as it was told unto them.

Offertory. God hath made the round world so sure, that it cannot be moved: ever since the world began, hath thy seat, O God, been prepared, thou art from everlasting.

Secret

E beseech thee, O Lord, that these our gifts may be worthy of the mysteries of this day's Nativity, and may evermore shed forth thy peace upon us: that even as he who was born in our manhood did shew forth therein the glory of the Godhead, so we in these thy earthly creatures may be made partakers of that which is heavenly. Through the same.

¶ Commemoration of St. Anastasia, as followeth,

CCEPT, we beseech thee, O Lord, the gifts which we duly offer: that, by the merits and intercession of blessed Anastasia thy Martyr, they may be profitable to the advancement of our salvation. Through.

Communion. Rejoice greatly, O daughter of Zion, shout, O daughter of Jerusalem: behold, thy King cometh, the holy one and the Saviour of the world.

Postcommunion

LORD, who by the wondrous Birth of thy Son hast put away the old nature of our manhood: grant that by this sacrament of his Nativity we may be restored unto newness of life. Through the same.

¶ Commemoration of St. Anastasia, as followeth,

LORD, who hast satisfied thy family with sacred gifts: we beseech thee, that we may at all times be comforted by the intercession of her whose festival we celebrate. Through.

Christmas   # Proper of Season Third Mass during Day

NATIVITY OF OUR LORD

(The Third Mass during the Day)

Introit

UNTO us a child is born, unto us a son is given: and the government shall be upon his shoulder: and his name shall be called, Angel of mighty counsel. *Ps.* O sing unto the Lord a new song, for he hath done marvellous things.

Collect

ALMIGHTY God, who hast given us thy only begotten Son to take our nature upon him, and as at this time to be born of a Holy Virgin; Grant that we being regenerate, and made thy children by adoption and grace, may daily be renewed by thy holy Spirit; through the same our Lord Jesus Christ, who liveth and reigneth with thee and the same Spirit ever, one God, world without end. *Amen.*

Epistle. Hebrews 1:1

GOD, who at sundry times and in divers manners spake in time past unto the fathers by the prophets, Hath in these last days spoken unto us by his Son, whom he hath appointed heir of all things, by whom also he made the worlds; Who being the brightness of his glory, and the express image of his person, and upholding all things by the word of his power, when he had by himself purged our sins, sat down on the right hand of the Majesty on high; Being made so much better than the angels, as he hath by inheritance obtained a more excellent name than they. For unto which of the angels said he at any time, Thou art my Son, this day have I begotten thee? And again, I will be to him a Father, and he shall be to me a Son? And again, when he bringeth in the firstbegotten into the world, he saith, And let all the angels of God worship him. And of the angels he saith, Who maketh his angels spirits, and his ministers a flame of fire. But unto the Son he saith, Thy throne, O God, is for ever and ever: a sceptre of righteousness is the sceptre of thy kingdom. Thou hast loved righteousness, and hated iniquity; therefore God, even thy God, hath anointed thee with the oil of gladness above thy fellows. And, Thou, Lord, in the beginning hast laid the foundation of the earth; and the heavens are the works of thine hands: They shall perish; but thou remainest; and they all shall wax old as doth a garment; And as a vesture shalt thou fold them up, and they shall be changed: but thou art the same, and thy years shall not fail.

Third Mass during Day Proper of Season *Christmas*

Gradual. All the ends of the earth have seen the salvation of our God: O be joyful in God, all ye lands. ℣. The Lord hath declared his salvation : in the sight of the heathen hath he openly shewed his righteousness.

Alleluia. Alleluia, alleluia. ℣. A hallowed day hath dawned upon us: come, ye nations, and worship the Lord: for on this day a great light hath descended upon the earth. Alleluia.

Gospel. John 1:1

IN the beginning was the Word, and the Word was with God, and the Word was God. The same was in the beginning with God. All things were made by him; and without him was not any thing made that was made. In him was life; and the life was the light of men. And the light shineth in darkness; and the darkness comprehended it not. There was a man sent from God, whose name was John. The same came for a witness, to bear witness of the Light, that all men through him might believe. He was not that Light, but was sent to bear witness of that Light. That was the true Light, which lighteth every man that cometh into the world. He was in the world, and the world was made by him, and the world knew him not. He came unto his own, and his own received him not. But as many as received him, to them gave he power to become the sons of God, even to them that believe on his name: Which were born, not of blood, nor of the will of the flesh, nor of the will of man, but of God. (Here Genuflect.) And the Word was made flesh, and dwelt among us, (and we beheld his glory, the glory as of the only begotten of the Father,) full of grace and truth.

Offertory. The heavens are thine, the earth also is thine: thou hast laid the foundation of the round world, and all that therein is: righteousness and equity are the habitation of thy seat.

Secret

SANCTIFY, O Lord, by the new Birth of thine only-begotten Son, the gifts which we offer: and cleanse us from the defilements of our iniquities. Through the same.

Communion. All the ends of the world have seen the salvation of our God.

Postcommunion

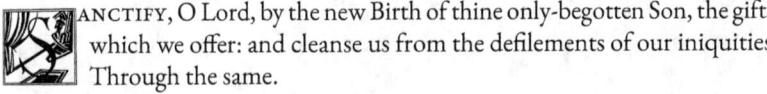

GRANT, we beseech thee, almighty God: that as he who was born this day the Saviour of the world is the author of our heavenly birth; so he may likewise bestow on us the gift of everlasting life. Who liveth.

Christmas   **Proper of Season** Third Mass during Day

Last Gospel. Matthew 2:1

WHEN Jesus was born in Bethlehem of Judæa in the days of Herod the king, behold, there came wise men from the east to Jerusalem, Saying, Where is he that is born King of the Jews? for we have seen his star in the east, and are come to worship him. When Herod the king had heard these things, he was troubled, and all Jerusalem with him. And when he had gathered all the chief priests and scribes of the people together, he demanded of them where Christ should be born. And they said unto him, In Bethlehem of Judaea: for thus it is written by the prophet, And thou Bethlehem, in the land of Juda, art not the least among the princes of Juda: for out of thee shall come a Governor, that shall rule my people Israel. Then Herod, when he had privily called the wise men, enquired of them diligently what time the star appeared. And he sent them to Bethlehem, and said, Go and search diligently for the young child; and when ye have found him, bring me word again, that I may come and worship him also. When they had heard the king, they departed; and, lo, the star, which they saw in the east, went before them, till it came and stood over where the young child was. When they saw the star, they rejoiced with exceeding great joy. And when they were come into the house, they saw the young child with Mary his mother, and fell down, and worshipped him: and when they had opened their treasures, they presented unto him gifts; gold, and frankincense, and myrrh. And being warned of God in a dream that they should not return to Herod, they departed into their own country another way.

St. Stephen

26 December
Second Class Double, Simple Octave

Opening Sentence. The righteous shall flourish like a palm-tree: and shall spread abroad like a cedar in Libanus. (Ps. 92:11)

Introit

PRINCES did sit, and speak against me, and the wicked persecuted me: help me, O Lord my God, for thy servant is occupied in thy commandments. *Ps.* Blessed are those that are undefiled in the way, and walk in the law of the Lord.

Collect

GRANT, O Lord, that, in all our sufferings here upon earth for the testimony of thy truth, we may stedfastly look up to heaven, and by faith behold the glory that shall be revealed; and, being filled with the Holy Ghost, may learn to love and bless our persecutors by the example of thy first Martyr Saint Stephen, who prayed for his murderers to thee, O blessed Jesus, who standest at the right hand of God to succour all those who suffer for thee, our only Mediator and Advocate. *Amen.*

❡ Commemoration is made of the Nativity from the Third Mass (p. 214).

Epistle. Acts 7:55

IN THOSE DAYS: Stephen, being full of the Holy Ghost, looked up stedfastly into heaven, and saw the glory of God, and Jesus standing on the right hand of God, and said, Behold, I see the heavens opened, and the Son of man standing on the right hand of God. Then they cried out with a loud voice, and stopped their ears, and ran upon him with one accord, and cast him out of the city, and stoned him: and the witnesses laid down their clothes at a young man's feet, whose name was Saul. And they stoned Stephen, calling upon God, and saying, Lord Jesus, receive my spirit. And he kneeled down, and cried with a loud voice, Lord, lay not this sin to their charge. And when he had said this, he fell asleep.

Gradual. Princes did sit and speak against me; and the wicked persecuted me. ℣. Help me, O Lord my God: save me for thy mercy's sake.

Alleluia. Alleluia, alleluia. ℣. I see the heavens opened, and Jesus standing on the right hand of the power of God. Alleluia.

Gospel. Matthew 23:34

T THAT TIME: Jesus said unto the scribes and Pharisees: Behold, I send unto you prophets, and wise men, and scribes: and some of them ye shall kill and crucify; and some of them shall ye scourge in your synagogues, and persecute them from city to city: That upon you may come all the righteous blood shed upon the earth, from the blood of righteous Abel unto the blood of Zacharias son of Barachias, whom ye slew between the temple and the altar. Verily I say unto you, All these things shall come upon this generation. O Jerusalem, Jerusalem, thou that killest the prophets, and stonest them which are sent unto thee, how often would I have gathered thy children together, even as a hen gathereth her chickens under her wings, and ye would not! Behold, your house is left unto you desolate. For I say unto you, Ye shall not see me henceforth, till ye shall say, Blessed is he that cometh in the name of the Lord.

Offertory. The Apostles chose Stephen the Levite, a man full of faith and of the Holy Ghost: whom the Jews stoned as he prayed, saying: Lord Jesus, receive my spirit, alleluia.

Secret

CCEPT, O Lord, these gifts for the commemoration of thy Saints: that like as their passion hath raised them to glory; so our devotion may lead us to innocency of life. Through.

¶ Commemoration is made of the Nativity from the Third Mass (p. 215).

Communion. I see the heavens opened, and Jesus standing on the tight hand of the power of God: O Lord Jesus, receive my spirit, and lay not this sin to their charge.

Postcommunion

MAY the mysteries which we have received be for our help, O Lord: and at the intercession of blessed Stephen thy Martyr, may they stablish us with thine everlasting protection. Through.

¶ Commemoration is made of the Nativity from the Third Mass (p. 215).

ST. JOHN

27 December
Second Class Double, Simple Octave

Opening Sentence. Greatly to be had in honour is blessed John. For he leaned on the Lord's bosom at Supper.

Introit

IN the midst of the Church he opened his mouth: and the Lord filled him with the spirit of wisdom and understanding: in a robe of glory he arrayed him. *Ps.* It is a good thing to give thanks unto the Lord: and to sing praises unto thy name, O most Highest.

Collect

MERCIFUL Lord, we beseech thee to cast thy bright beams of light upon thy Church, that it, being illumined by the doctrine of thy blessed Apostle and Evangelist Saint John, may so walk in the light of thy truth, that it may at length attain to life everlasting. Through.

℣ Commemoration is made of the Nativity from the Third Mass (p. 214).

Epistle. 1 John 1:1

THAT which was from the beginning, which we have heard, which we have seen with our eyes, which we have looked upon, and our hands have handled, of the Word of life; (For the life was manifested, and we have seen it, and bear witness, and shew unto you that eternal life, which was with the Father, and was manifested unto us;) That which we have seen and heard declare we unto you, that ye also may have fellowship with us: and truly our fellowship is with the Father, and with his Son Jesus Christ. And these things write we unto you, that your joy may be full. This then is the message which we have heard of him, and declare unto you, that God is light, and in him is no darkness at all. If we say that we have fellowship with him, and walk in darkness, we lie, and do not the truth: But if we walk in the light, as he is in the light, we have fellowship one with another, and the blood of Jesus Christ his Son cleanseth us from all sin. If we say that we have no sin, we deceive ourselves, and the truth is not in us. If we confess our sins, he is faithful and just to forgive us our sins, and to cleanse us from all unrighteousness. If we say that we have not sinned, we make him a liar, and his word is not in us.

St. John — **Proper of Season** — 27 December

Gradual. Then went this saying abroad among the brethren: That that disciple should not die: yet Jesus said not: He shall not die. ℣. But: If I will that he tarry till I come: follow thou me.

Alleluia. Alleluia, alleluia. ℣. This is the disciple which testifieth of these things: and we know that his testimony is true. Alleluia.

Gospel. John 21:19

T THAT TIME: Jesus said unto Peter: Follow me. Then Peter, turning about, seeth the disciple whom Jesus loved following; which also leaned on his breast at supper, and said, Lord, which is he that betrayeth thee? Peter seeing him saith to Jesus, Lord, and what shall this man do? Jesus saith unto him, If I will that he tarry till I come, what is that to thee? follow thou me. Then went this saying abroad among the brethren, that that disciple should not die: yet Jesus said not unto him, He shall not die; but, If I will that he tarry till I come, what is that to thee? This is the disciple which testifieth of these things, and wrote these things: and we know that his testimony is true. And there are also many other things which Jesus did, the which, if they should be written every one, I suppose that even the world itself could not contain the books that should be written.

Offertory. The just shall flourish like a palm-tree: and shall spread abroad like a cedar in Libanus.

Secret

ECEIVE, O Lord, the gifts which we offer unto thee on the solemnity (commemoration) of him, in whose advocacy we trust for deliverance. Through.

❡ Commemoration is made of the Nativity from the Third Mass (p. 215).

Communion. Then went abroad this saying among the brethren, that that disciple should not die: yet Jesus said not: He shall not die; but: If I will that he tarry till I come.

Postcommunion

GOD, who hast refreshed us with heavenly meat and drink, we humbly beseech thee: that we may be defended by the prayers of him, in whose memory we have received the same. Through.

❡ Commemoration is made of the Nativity from the Third Mass (p. 215).

Proper of Season

28 December — *Holy Innocents*

HOLY INNOCENTS

28 December
Second Class Double, Simple Octave

Opening Sentence. The righteous live for evermore. Their reward also is with the Lord.

Introit

OUT of the mouths of babes, O God, and of sucklings, hast thou perfected praise because of thine adversaries. *Ps.* O Lord our Governor: how excellent is thy name in all the world.

❡ Gloria in excelsis is not said, nor Alleluia, nor Ite, Missa est, unless this Feast falls on a Sunday, or enjoys the rite of a 1st Double; but on the Octave Day they are always said.

Collect

ALMIGHTY God, who out of the mouths of babes and sucklings hast ordained strength, and madest infants to glorify thee by their deaths: Mortify and kill all vices in us, and so strengthen us by thy grace, that by the innocency of our lives, and constancy of our faith even unto death, we may glorify thy holy Name. Through.

❡ Commemoration is made of the Nativity from the Third Mass (p. 214).

Epistle. Revelation 14:1

IN THOSE DAYS: I looked, and, lo, a Lamb stood on the mount Zion, and with him an hundred forty and four thousand, having his Father's name written in their foreheads. And I heard a voice from heaven, as the voice of many waters, and as the voice of a great thunder: and I heard the voice of harpers harping with their harps: And they sung as it were a new song before the throne, and before the four beasts, and the elders: and no man could learn that song but the hundred and forty and four thousand, which were redeemed from the earth. These are they which were not defiled with women; for they are virgins. These are they which follow the Lamb whithersoever he goeth. These were redeemed from among men, being the firstfruits unto God and to the Lamb. And in their mouth was found no guile: for they are without fault before the throne of God.

Gradual. Our soul is escaped, even as a bird, out of the snare of the fowler. ℣. The snare is broken, and we are delivered: our help standeth in the name of the Lord, who hath made heaven and earth.

Holy Innocents   # Proper of Season   28 December

¶ The Tract is not said when the Alleluia is said.

Tract. The blood of the Saints have they shed like water on every side of Jerusalem. ℣. And there was no man to bury them. ℣. Avenge, O Lord, the blood of thy Saints, that is shed upon the earth.

¶ The following Alleluia is said when this Feast falls on Sunday or enjoys the rite of a 1ˢᵗ Double: but on the Octave Day it is always said, as also in Votive Masses before Septuagesima or after Pentecost.

Alleluia. Alleluia, alleluia. ℣. Praise the Lord, ye children: O praise the name of the Lord. Alleluia.

Gospel. Matthew 2:13

AT THAT TIME: the angel of the Lord appeareth to Joseph in a dream, saying, Arise, and take the young child and his mother, and flee into Egypt, and be thou there until I bring thee word: for Herod will seek the young child to destroy him. When he arose, he took the young child and his mother by night, and departed into Egypt: And was there until the death of Herod: that it might be fulfilled which was spoken of the Lord by the prophet, saying, Out of Egypt have I called my son. Then Herod, when he saw that he was mocked of the wise men, was exceeding wroth, and sent forth, and slew all the children that were in Bethlehem, and in all the coasts thereof, from two years old and under, according to the time which he had diligently enquired of the wise men. Then was fulfilled that which was spoken by Jeremy the prophet, saying, In Rama was there a voice heard, lamentation, and weeping, and great mourning, Rachel weeping for her children, and would not be comforted, because they are not.

Offertory. Our soul is escaped, even as a bird out of the snare of the fowler: the snare is broken, and we are delivered.

Secret

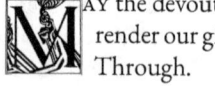MAY the devout prayers of thy Saints never fail us, O Lord: that they may render our gifts acceptable unto thee, and ever obtain for us thy pardon. Through.

¶ Commemoration is made of the Nativity from the Third Mass (p. 215).

Communion. In Rama, a voice was heard, lamentation and mourning: Rachel weeping for her children, and would not be comforted, because they are not.

Proper of Season *Christmas I*

Postcommunion

E beseech thee, O Lord: that the gifts, which we have offered and received, may through the prayers of thy Saints effectually avail for our succour both in this life and in that which is to come. Through.

☞ Commemoration is made of the Nativity from the Third Mass (p. 215).

SUNDAY WITHIN THE NATIVITY OCTAVE

Semidouble

Introit

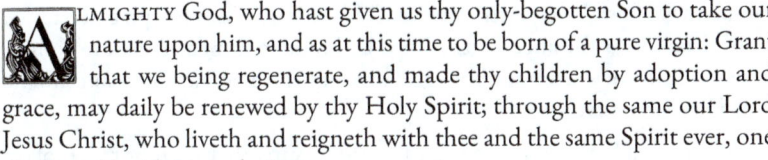HILE all things were in quiet silence, and night was in the midst of her swift course, thine almighty Word, O Lord, leaped down from heaven out of thy royal throne. *Ps.* The Lord is King, and hath put on glorious apparel: the Lord hath put on his apparel, and girded himself with strength.

Collect

LMIGHTY God, who hast given us thy only-begotten Son to take our nature upon him, and as at this time to be born of a pure virgin: Grant that we being regenerate, and made thy children by adoption and grace, may daily be renewed by thy Holy Spirit; through the same our Lord Jesus Christ, who liveth and reigneth with thee and the same Spirit ever, one God, world without end. *Amen.*

RANT, we beseech thee, Almighty God: that we, who through our ancient bondage are held beneath the yoke of sin; may by the new Birth of thy only-begotten Son in the flesh obtain deliverance. Through the same.

Epistle. Galatians 4:1

RETHREN: The heir, as long as he is a child, differeth nothing from a servant, though he be lord of all; But is under tutors and governors until the time appointed of the father. Even so we, when we were children, were in bondage under the elements of the world: But when the fulness of the time was come, God sent forth his Son, made of a woman, made under the law, To redeem them that were under the law, that we might receive the adoption of sons. And because ye are sons, God hath sent forth the Spirit of his Son into your hearts, crying, Abba, Father. Wherefore thou art no more a servant, but a son; and if a son, then an heir of God through Christ.

Christmas I # Proper of Season

Gradual. Thou art fairer than the children of men: full of grace are thy lips. ℣. My heart is inditing of a good matter, I speak of the things which I have made unto the King: my tongue is the pen of a ready writer.

Alleluia. Alleluia, alleluia. ℣. The Lord is King, and hath put on glorious apparel: the Lord hath put on his apparel, and girded himself with strength. Alleluia.

Gospel. Matthew 1:18

THE birth of Jesus Christ was on this wise: When as his mother Mary was espoused to Joseph, before they came together, she was found with child of the Holy Ghost. Then Joseph her husband, being a just man, and not willing to make her a publick example, was minded to put her away privily. But while he thought on these things, behold, the angel of the Lord appeared unto him in a dream, saying, Joseph, thou son of David, fear not to take unto thee Mary thy wife: for that which is conceived in her is of the Holy Ghost. And she shall bring forth a son, and thou shalt call his name JESUS: for he shall save his people from their sins. Now all this was done, that it might be fulfilled which was spoken of the Lord by the prophet, saying, Behold, a virgin shall be with child, and shall bring forth a son, and they shall call his name Emmanuel, which being interpreted is, God with us. Then Joseph being raised from sleep did as the angel of the Lord had bidden him, and took unto him his wife: And knew her not till she had brought forth her firstborn son: and he called his name JESUS.

Offertory. God hath made the round world so sure, that it cannot be moved: ever since the world began hath thy seat, O God, been prepared, thou art from everlasting.

Secret

GRANT, we beseech thee, Almighty God: that the gift which we offer in the sight of thy majesty, may obtain for us grace to serve thee with all godliness, and bring us in the end to everlasting felicity. Through.

¶ Commemoration is made of the Nativity from the Third Mass (p. 215).

Communion. Take the young Child and his Mother, and go into the land of Israel: for they are dead which sought the young Child's life.

Postcommunion

MAY the operation of this mystery, O Lord, avail for the cleansing of our sins, and for the fulfilment of our godly desires. Through.

¶ Commemoration is made of the Nativity from the Third Mass (p. 215).

Proper of Season

CIRCUMCISION OF OUR LORD

1 January
Second Class Double

Opening Sentence. The Word was made flesh and dwelt among us. Alleluia.

Introit

UNTO us a Child is born, unto us a son is given; and the government shall be upon his shoulder: and his name shall be called Angel of mighty counsel. *Ps.* O sing unto the Lord a new song: for he hath done marvellous things.

Collect

ALMIGHTY God, who madest thy blessed Son to be circumcised, and obedient to the law for man; Grant us the true circumcision of the Spirit; that, our hearts, and all our members, being mortified from all worldly and carnal lusts, we may in all things obey thy blessed will; through the same thy Son Jesus Christ our Lord. Who liveth.

Epistle. Romans 4:8

BRETHREN: Blessed is the man to whom the Lord will not impute sin. Cometh this blessedness then upon the circumcision only, or upon the uncircumcision also? for we say that faith was reckoned to Abraham for righteousness. How was it then reckoned? when he was in circumcision, or in uncircumcision? Not in circumcision, but in uncircumcision. And he received the sign of circumcision, a seal of the righteousness of the faith which he had yet being uncircumcised: that he might be the father of all them that believe, though they be not circumcised; that righteousness might be imputed unto them also: And the father of circumcision to them who are not of the circumcision only, but who also walk in the steps of that faith of our father Abraham, which he had being yet uncircumcised. For the promise, that he should be the heir of the world, was not to Abraham, or to his seed, through the law, but through the righteousness of faith. For if they which are of the law be heirs, faith is made void, and the promise made of none effect.

Gradual. All the ends of the earth have seen the salvation of our God: O be joyful in God, all ye lands. ℣. The Lord declared his salvation: his righteousness hath he shewed in the sight of the heathen.

Circumcision — **Proper of Season** — 1 January

Alleluia. Alleluia, alleluia. ℣. God, who at sundry times spake in time past unto the fathers by the Prophets, hath in these last days spoken unto us by his Son. Alleluia.

Gospel. Luke 2:15

T THAT TIME: It came to pass, as the angels were gone away from them into heaven, the shepherds said one to another, Let us now go even unto Bethlehem, and see this thing which is come to pass, which the Lord hath made known unto us. And they came with haste, and found Mary, and Joseph, and the babe lying in a manger. And when they had seen it, they made known abroad the saying which was told them concerning this child. And all they that heard it wondered at those things which were told them by the shepherds. But Mary kept all these things, and pondered them in her heart. And the shepherds returned, glorifying and praising God for all the things that they had heard and seen, as it was told unto them. And when eight days were accomplished for the circumcising of the child, his name was called JESUS, which was so named of the angel before he was conceived in the womb.

Offertory. The heavens are thine, the earth also is thine: thou hast laid the foundation of the round world, and all that therein is: righteousness and equity are the habitation of thy seat.

Secret

E beseech thee, O Lord, to accept our prayers and oblations: and graciously hearken unto us, whom thou dost cleanse by thy heavenly mysteries. Through.

Communion. All the ends of the world have seen the salvation of our God.

Postcommunion

AY this communion, O Lord, cleanse us from guilt: and at the intercession of blessed Mary the Virgin Mother of God, make us partakers of thy heavenly healing. Through the same.

¶ The same Collect, Epistle, and Gospel shall serve for every day after unto the Epiphany.

Most Holy Name of Jesus

2 January
Second Class Double

Opening Sentence. Our help is in the Name of the Lord who hath made heaven and earth. (Ps. 124:8)

Introit

AT the name of Jesus every knee should bow, of things in heaven, and things in earth, and things under the earth: and every tongue should confess that Jesus Christ is Lord, to the glory of God the Father. *Ps.* O Lord our Governor, how excellent is thy name in all the world.

Collect

O GOD, who didst appoint thine only-begotten Son to be the Saviour of mankind, and didst command that he should be called JESUS: mercifully grant; that as we venerate his holy name on earth, so we may rejoice to behold him in heaven. Through the same.

¶ Commemoration of the Octave Day of St. Stephen, as followeth,

ALMIGHTY and everlasting God, who, in the blood of the blessed Levite Stephen, didst consecrate the first-fruits of the Martyrs: grant, we beseech thee; that he may intercede for us, who prayed even for his persecutors to our Lord Jesus Christ, thy Son. Who liveth and reigneth with thee.

Epistle. Acts 4:8

IN THOSE DAYS: Peter, filled with the Holy Ghost, said unto them, Ye rulers of the people, and elders of Israel, If we this day be examined of the good deed done to the impotent man, by what means he is made whole; Be it known unto you all, and to all the people of Israel, that by the name of Jesus Christ of Nazareth, whom ye crucified, whom God raised from the dead, even by him doth this man stand here before you whole. This is the stone which was set at nought of you builders, which is become the head of the corner. Neither is there salvation in any other: for there is none other name under heaven given among men, whereby we must be saved.

Gradual. Deliver us, O Lord our God, and gather us from among the heathen: that we may give thanks unto thy holy name, and make our boast of thy praise. ℣. Thou, O Lord, art our Father, our Redeemer: thy name is from everlasting.

Most Holy Name   **Proper of Season**   2 January

Alleluia. Alleluia, alleluia. ℣. My mouth shall speak the praise of the Lord: and let all flesh give thanks unto his holy name. Alleluia.

Gospel. Luke 2:21

T THAT TIME: When eight days were accomplished for the circumcising of the child, his name was called JESUS, which was so named of the angel before he was conceived in the womb.

Offertory. I will thank thee, O Lord my God, with all my heart, and will praise thy name for evermore: for thou, Lord, art good and gracious: and of great mercy unto all them that call upon thee, alleluia.

Secret

E beseech thee, most merciful God, that thy benediction, whereby all created things are sustained, may sanctify this our sacrifice, which we offer unto thee to the glory of the name of thy Son Jesus Christ our Lord: that it may be acceptable for the praise of thy majesty, and profitable for our salvation. Through the same.

¶ Commemoration of the Octave Day of St. Stephen, as followeth,

CCEPT, O Lord, these gifts for the commemoration of thy Saints: that like as their passion hath raised them to glory; so our devotion may lead us to innocency of life. Through.

Communion. All nations whom thou hast made shall come and worship thee, O Lord, and shall glorify thy name: for thou art great, and doest wondrous things: thou art God alone, alleluia.

Postcommunion

LMIGHTY and everlasting God, our Creator and Redeemer, mercifully regard our prayers: and vouchsafe to receive with favourable and gracious countenance the sacrifice of the saving victim, which we have offered to thy majesty; in honour of the name of thy Son Jesus Christ our Lord; that we, being fulfilled with thy grace, may rejoice that our names are written in heaven beneath the glorious name of Jesus, in the book of everlasting predestination. Through the same.

¶ Commemoration of the Octave Day of St. Stephen, as followeth,

AY the mysteries which we have received be for our help, O Lord: and at the intercession of blessed Stephen thy Martyr, may they stablish us with thine everlasting protection. Through.

Proper of Season *Christmas II*

Second Sunday after Nativity

The Sunday between Circumcision & Epiphany, if there be one.
Semidouble

Introit

UNTO us a Child is born, unto us a son is given; and the government shall be upon his shoulder: and his name shall be called Angel of mighty counsel. *Ps.* O sing unto the Lord a new song: for he hath done marvellous things.

Collect

ALMIGHTY God, who hast poured upon us the new light of thine incarnate Word; Grant that the same light enkindled in our hearts may shine forth in our lives. Through.

Epistle. Isaiah 61:1

THE Spirit of the Lord GOD is upon me; because the LORD hath anointed me to preach good tidings unto the meek; he hath sent me to bind up the brokenhearted, to proclaim liberty to the captives, and the opening of the prison to them that are bound; To proclaim the acceptable year of the LORD, and the day of vengeance of our God; to comfort all that mourn; To appoint unto them that mourn in Zion, to give unto them beauty for ashes, the oil of joy for mourning, the garment of praise for the spirit of heaviness; that they might be called trees of righteousness, the planting of the LORD, that he might be glorified.

Gradual. All the ends of the earth have seen the salvation of our God: O be joyful in God, all ye lands. ℣. The Lord declared his salvation: his righteousness hath he shewed in the sight of the heathen.

Alleluia. Alleluia, alleluia. ℣. God, who at sundry times spake in time past unto the fathers by the Prophets, hath in these last days spoken unto us by his Son. Alleluia.

Gospel. Matthew 2:19

AT THAT TIME: When Herod was dead, behold, an angel of the Lord appeareth in a dream to Joseph in Egypt, Saying, Arise, and take the young child and his mother, and go into the land of Israel: for they are dead which sought the young child's life. And he arose, and took the young child and his mother, and came into the land of Israel. But when he heard that Archelaus did reign in Judaea in the room of his father Herod, he was afraid to go thither: notwithstanding, being warned of God in a dream, he turned aside into the parts of Galilee: And he came and dwelt in a city called Nazareth: that it might be fulfilled which was spoken by the prophets, He shall be called a Nazarene.

Offertory. The heavens are thine, the earth also is thine: thou hast laid the foundation of the round world, and all that therein is: righteousness and equity are the habitation of thy seat.

Secret

E beseech thee, O Lord, to accept our prayers and oblations: and graciously hearken unto us, whom thou dost cleanse by thy heavenly mysteries. Through.

Communion. All the ends of the world have seen the salvation of our God.

Postcommunion

AY this communion, O Lord, cleanse us from guilt: and at the intercession of blessed Mary the Virgin Mother of God, make us partakers of thy heavenly healing. Through the same.

EPIPHANY OF OUR LORD

First Class Double, Second Class Octave

Introit

EHOLD, the Lord the ruler is come: and in his hand the kingdom, and power, and dominion. *Ps.* Give the King thy judgments, O God: and thy righteousness unto the King's Son.

Collect

GOD, who by the leading of a star didst manifest thy only-begotten Son to the Gentiles; Mercifully grant that we, who know thee now by faith, may after this life have the fruition of thy glorious Godhead. Through the same.

¶ This Collect to be said daily throughout the Octave.

6 January   **Proper of Season**   *Epiphany*

Epistle. Ephesians 3:1

BRETHREN: For this cause I Paul, the prisoner of Jesus Christ for you Gentiles, If ye have heard of the dispensation of the grace of God which is given me to you-ward: How that by revelation he made known unto me the mystery; (as I wrote afore in few words, Whereby, when ye read, ye may understand my knowledge in the mystery of Christ) Which in other ages was not made known unto the sons of men, as it is now revealed unto his holy apostles and prophets by the Spirit; That the Gentiles should be fellowheirs, and of the same body, and partakers of his promise in Christ by the gospel: Whereof I was made a minister, according to the gift of the grace of God given unto me by the effectual working of his power. Unto me, who am less than the least of all saints, is this grace given, that I should preach among the Gentiles the unsearchable riches of Christ; And to make all men see what is the fellowship of the mystery, which from the beginning of the world hath been hid in God, who created all things by Jesus Christ: To the intent that now unto the principalities and powers in heavenly places might be known by the church the manifold wisdom of God, According to the eternal purpose which he purposed in Christ Jesus our Lord: In whom we have boldness and access with confidence by the faith of him.

Gradual. All they from Saba shall come, bringing gold and incense, and shall shew forth the praises of the Lord. ℣. Arise and shine, O Jerusalem: for the glory of the Lord is risen upon thee.

Alleluia. Alleluia, alleluia. ℣. We have seen his star in the East: and are come with gifts to worship the Lord. Alleluia.

Gospel. Matthew 2:1

WHEN Jesus was born in Bethlehem of Judæa in the days of Herod the king, behold, there came wise men from the east to Jerusalem, Saying, Where is he that is born King of the Jews? for we have seen his star in the east, and are come to worship him. When Herod the king had heard these things, he was troubled, and all Jerusalem with him. And when he had gathered all the chief priests and scribes of the people together, he demanded of them where Christ should be born. And they said unto him, In Bethlehem of Judæa: for thus it is written by the prophet, And thou Bethlehem, in the land of Juda, art not the least among the princes of Juda: for out of thee shall come a Governor, that shall rule my people Israel. Then Herod, when he had privily called the wise men, enquired of them diligently what time the star appeared. And he sent them to Bethlehem, and said, Go and search diligently for the young

Epiphany   **Proper of Season**   6 January

child; and when ye have found him, bring me word again, that I may come and worship him also. When they had heard the king, they departed; and, lo, the star, which they saw in the east, went before them, till it came and stood over where the young child was. When they saw the star, they rejoiced with exceeding great joy. And when they were come into the house, they saw the young child with Mary his mother, (Genuflect here.) and fell down, and worshipped him: and when they had opened their treasures, they presented unto him gifts; gold, and frankincense, and myrrh. And being warned of God in a dream that they should not return to Herod, they departed into their own country another way.

Offertory. The kings of Tharsis and of the isles shall give presents: the kings of Arabia and Saba shall bring gifts: all kings shall fall down before him, all nations shall do him service.

Secret

WE beseech thee, O Lord, mercifully to look upon the gifts of thy Church: wherein no longer offering gold and frankincense and myrrh; we sacrifice and receive him who by those gifts was signified, even Jesus Christ thy Son our Lord; Who liveth and reigneth with thee.

Communion. We have seen his star in the East, and are come with gifts to worship the Lord.

Postcommunion

GRANT, we beseech thee, almighty God: that those things which we celebrate in solemn worship, we may attain in pureness of mind and understanding. Through.

¶ Within the Octave, Mass is said as on the Feast. The 2nd Prayer of St. Mary after Christmas (p. 541), and 3rd Against the Persecutors of the Church (p. 543), or, for the Chief Bishop (p. 543).

Proper of Season *Epiphany I*

SUNDAY WITHIN THE OCTAVE OF THE EPIPHANY

Semidouble

Introit

ON a throne exalted I beheld a man sitting, whom a multitude of Angels worship, singing together: behold him, the name of whose empire is for everlasting. *Ps.* O be joyful in the Lord, all ye lands: serve the Lord with gladness.

Collect

O LORD, we beseech thee mercifully to receive the prayers of thy people who call upon thee: and grant that they may both perceive and know what things they ought to do, and also may have grace and power faithfully to fulfil the same. Through.

¶ Commemoration is made of the Epiphany (p. 230).

Epistle. Romans 12:1

BRETHREN: I beseech you, by the mercies of God, that ye present your bodies a living sacrifice, holy, acceptable unto God, which is your reasonable service. And be not conformed to this world: but be ye transformed by the renewing of your mind, that ye may prove what is that good, and acceptable, and perfect, will of God. For I say, through the grace given unto me, to every man that is among you, not to think of himself more highly than he ought to think; but to think soberly, according as God hath dealt to every man the measure of faith. For as we have many members in one body, and all members have not the same office: So we, being many, are one body in Christ, and every one members one of another.

Gradual. Blessed be the Lord, even the God of Israel, which only doeth wondrous things from the beginning. ℣. The mountains shall bring peace, and the little hills righteousness unto thy people.

Alleluia. Alleluia, alleluia. ℣. O be joyful in the Lord, all ye lands: serve the Lord with gladness. Alleluia.

Epiphany I # Proper of Season

Gospel. Luke 2:41

ow Jesus' parents went to Jerusalem every year at the feast of the passover. And when he was twelve years old, they went up to Jerusalem after the custom of the feast. And when they had fulfilled the days, as they returned, the child Jesus tarried behind in Jerusalem; and Joseph and his mother knew not of it. But they, supposing him to have been in the company, went a day's journey; and they sought him among their kinsfolk and acquaintance. And when they found him not, they turned back again to Jerusalem, seeking him. And it came to pass, that after three days they found him in the temple, sitting in the midst of the doctors, both hearing them, and asking them questions. And all that heard him were astonished at his understanding and answers. And when they saw him, they were amazed: and his mother said unto him, Son, why hast thou thus dealt with us? behold, thy father and I have sought thee sorrowing. And he said unto them, How is it that ye sought me? wist ye not that I must be about my Father's business? And they understood not the saying which he spake unto them. And he went down with them, and came to Nazareth, and was subject unto them: but his mother kept all these sayings in her heart. And Jesus increased in wisdom and stature, and in favour with God and man.

Offertory. O be joyful in the Lord, all ye lands, serve the Lord with gladness: and come before his presence with a song: for the Lord he is God.

Secret

ay the sacrifice which we offer unto thee, O Lord, evermore quicken and defend us. Through.

¶ Commemoration is made of the Epiphany (p. 232).

Communion. Son, why hast thou thus dealt with us? behold, thy father and I have sought thee sorrowing. And how is it that ye sought me? wist ye not that I must be about my Father's business?

Postcommunion

We humbly beseech thee, almighty God: that as thou dost refresh us with thy sacraments, so thou wouldest vouchsafe unto us to do thee worthy and acceptable service. Through.

¶ Commemoration is made of the Epiphany (p. 232).

Proper of Season — *Baptism of Our Lord*

BAPTISM OF OUR LORD

(Octave Day of the Epiphany)
Greater Double

Introit

EHOLD, the Lord the ruler is come: and in his hand the kingdom, and power, and dominion. *Ps.* Give the King thy judgements, O God: and thy righteousness unto the King's Son.

Collect

GOD, whose only-begotten Son hath been made manifest in substance of our flesh: grant, we beseech thee; that, as we have known him after the fashion of our outward likeness, so through him we may be made worthy inwardly to be renewed. Who liveth.

Epistle. Isaiah 60:1

ARISE, shine; for thy light is come, and the glory of the LORD is risen upon thee. For, behold, the darkness shall cover the earth, and gross darkness the people: but the LORD shall arise upon thee, and his glory shall be seen upon thee. And the Gentiles shall come to thy light, and kings to the brightness of thy rising. Lift up thine eyes round about, and see: all they gather themselves together, they come to thee: thy sons shall come from far, and thy daughters shall be nursed at thy side. Then thou shalt see, and flow together, and thine heart shall fear, and be enlarged; because the abundance of the sea shall be converted unto thee, the forces of the Gentiles shall come unto thee. The multitude of camels shall cover thee, the dromedaries of Midian and Ephah; all they from Sheba shall come: they shall bring gold and incense; and they shall shew forth the praises of the LORD.

Gradual. All they from Saba shall come, bringing gold and incense, and shall shew forth the praise of the Lord. ℣. Arise and shine, O Jerusalem: for the glory of the Lord is risen upon thee.

Alleluia. Alleluia, alleluia. ℣. We have seen his star in the East, and are come with gifts to worship the Lord. Alleluia.

Baptism of Our Lord   ## Proper of Season

Gospel. John 1:29

AT THAT TIME: John seeth Jesus coming unto him, and saith, Behold the Lamb of God, which taketh away the sin of the world. This is he of whom I said, After me cometh a man which is preferred before me: for he was before me. And I knew him not: but that he should be made manifest to Israel, therefore am I come baptizing with water. And John bare record, saying, I saw the Spirit descending from heaven like a dove, and it abode upon him. And I knew him not: but he that sent me to baptize with water, the same said unto me, Upon whom thou shalt see the Spirit descending, and remaining on him, the same is he which baptizeth with the Holy Ghost. And I saw, and bare record that this is the Son of God.

Offertory. The Kings of Tharsis and of the isles shall give presents: the Kings of Arabia and Saba shall bring gifts: all Kings shall fall down before him, all nations shall do him service.

Secret

WE offer our sacrifices unto thee, O Lord, in remembrance of the manifestation of thy new-born Son, humbly beseeching thee: that like as he is the author of our gifts, so he may also mercifully receive the same, even Jesus Christ our Lord. Who liveth.

Communion. We have seen his star in the East, and are come with gifts to worship the Lord.

Postcommunion

PREVENT us, O Lord, we beseech thee, at all times and in all places with thy heavenly light: that as thou hast vouchsafed to make us partakers of this mystery, so we may understand it aright in purity of heart, and receive it with worthy affection. Through.

Proper of Season *Epiphany II*

Second Sunday after Epiphany

Semidouble

Introit

ALL the earth shall worship thee, O God, and sing of thee: they shall sing praise unto thy name, O thou most Highest. *Ps.* O be joyful in God, all ye lands: sing praises unto the honour of his name: make his praise to be glorious.

Collect

ALMIGHTY and everlasting God, who dost govern all things in heaven and earth; Mercifully hear the supplications of thy people, and grant us thy peace all the days of our life. Through.

¶ 2nd Collect is of St. Mary after Christmas (p. 541) & 3rd Collect is Against the Persecutors of the Church (p. 543) or for the Chief Bishop (p. 543).

Epistle. Romans 12:6

BRETHREN: Having then gifts differing according to the grace that is given to us, whether prophecy, let us prophesy according to the proportion of faith; Or ministry, let us wait on our ministering: or he that teacheth, on teaching; Or he that exhorteth, on exhortation: he that giveth, let him do it with simplicity; he that ruleth, with diligence; he that sheweth mercy, with cheerfulness. Let love be without dissimulation. Abhor that which is evil; cleave to that which is good. Be kindly affectioned one to another with brotherly love; in honour preferring one another; Not slothful in business; fervent in spirit; serving the Lord; Rejoicing in hope; patient in tribulation; continuing instant in prayer; Distributing to the necessity of saints; given to hospitality Bless them which persecute you: bless, and curse not. Rejoice with them that do rejoice, and weep with them that weep. Be of the same mind one toward another. Mind not high things, but condescend to men of low estate.

Gradual. The Lord sent his word, and healed them: and they were saved from their destruction. ℣. O that men would therefore praise the Lord for his goodness: and declare the wonders that he doeth for the children of men.

Alleluia. Alleluia, alleluia. ℣. Praise the Lord, all ye Angels of his: praise him, all his hosts. Alleluia.

Epiphany II # Proper of Season

Gospel. John 2:1

AT THAT TIME: The third day there was a marriage in Cana of Galilee; and the mother of Jesus was there: And both Jesus was called, and his disciples, to the marriage. And when they wanted wine, the mother of Jesus saith unto him, They have no wine. Jesus saith unto her, Woman, what have I to do with thee? mine hour is not yet come. His mother saith unto the servants, Whatsoever he saith unto you, do it. And there were set there six waterpots of stone, after the manner of the purifying of the Jews, containing two or three firkins apiece. Jesus saith unto them, Fill the waterpots with water. And they filled them up to the brim. And he saith unto them, Draw out now, and bear unto the governor of the feast. And they bare it. When the ruler of the feast had tasted the water that was made wine, and knew not whence it was: (but the servants which drew the water knew;) the governor of the feast called the bridegroom, And saith unto him, Every man at the beginning doth set forth good wine; and when men have well drunk, then that which is worse: but thou hast kept the good wine until now. This beginning of miracles did Jesus in Cana of Galilee, and manifested forth his glory; and his disciples believed on him.

Offertory. O be joyful in God, all ye lands : sing praises unto the honour of his name: O come hither and hearken, all ye that fear God, and I will tell you what the Lord hath done for my soul, alleluia.

Secret

SANCTIFY, O Lord, the gifts which we offer; and cleanse us from the defilements of our iniquities. Through.

¶ 2ⁿᵈ Secret is of St. Mary after Christmas (p. 541) & 3ʳᵈ Secret is Against the Persecutors of the Church (p. 543) or for the Chief Bishop (p. 543).

Communion. The Lord saith: Fill the water-pots with water, and bear unto the governor of the feast. When the ruler of the feast had tasted the water that was made wine, he saith unto the bridegroom: Thou hast kept the good wine until now. This beginning of miracles did Jesus before his disciples.

Postcommunion

INCREASE in us, O Lord, we beseech thee, the operation of thy power: that we, whom thou hast quickened with divine sacraments, may by thy bounty be made ready to receive the promises of the same. Through.

¶ 2ⁿᵈ Postcommunion is of St. Mary after Christmas (p. 541) & 3ʳᵈ Postcommunion is Against the Persecutors of the Church (p. 543) or for the Chief Bishop (p. 543).

Proper of Season *Epiphany III*

Third Sunday after Epiphany

Semidouble

Introit

ORSHIP God, all ye Angels of his: Sion heard, and rejoiced: and the daughters of Judah were glad *Ps.* The Lord is King, the earth may be glad thereof: yea, the multitude of the isles may be glad thereof.

Collect

LMIGHTY and everlasting God, mercifully look upon our infirmities, and in all our dangers and necessities stretch forth thy right hand to help and defend us. Through.

¶ 2nd Collect is of St. Mary after Christmas (p. 541) & 3rd Collect is Against the Persecutors of the Church (p. 543) or for the Chief Bishop (p. 543).

Epistle. Romans 12:16

RETHREN: Be not wise in your own conceits. Recompense to no man evil for evil. Provide things honest in the sight of all men. If it be possible, as much as lieth in you, live peaceably with all men. Dearly beloved, avenge not yourselves, but rather give place unto wrath: for it is written, Vengeance is mine; I will repay, saith the Lord. Therefore if thine enemy hunger, feed him; if he thirst, give him drink: for in so doing thou shalt heap coals of fire on his head. Be not overcome of evil, but overcome evil with good.

Gradual. The heathen shall fear thy name, O Lord, and all the kings of the earth thy majesty. ℣. When the Lord shall build up Sion, and when his glory shall appear.

Alleluia. Alleluia, alleluia. ℣. The Lord is King, the earth may be glad thereof: yea, the multitude of the isles may be glad thereof. Alleluia.

Gospel. Matthew 8:1

T THAT TIME: When Jesus was come down from the mountain, great multitudes followed him. And, behold, there came a leper and worshipped him, saying, Lord, if thou wilt, thou canst make me clean. And Jesus put forth his hand, and touched him, saying, I will; be thou clean. And immediately his leprosy was cleansed. And Jesus saith unto him, See thou tell

Epiphany III # Proper of Season

no man; but go thy way, shew thyself to the priest, and offer the gift that Moses commanded, for a testimony unto them. And when Jesus was entered into Capernaum, there came unto him a centurion, beseeching him, And saying, Lord, my servant lieth at home sick of the palsy, grievously tormented. And Jesus saith unto him, I will come and heal him. The centurion answered and said, Lord, I am not worthy that thou shouldest come under my roof: but speak the word only, and my servant shall be healed. For I am a man under authority, having soldiers under me: and I say to this man, Go, and he goeth; and to another, Come, and he cometh; and to my servant, Do this, and he doeth it. When Jesus heard it, he marvelled, and said to them that followed, Verily I say unto you, I have not found so great faith, no, not in Israel And I say unto you, That many shall come from the east and west, and shall sit down with Abraham, and Isaac, and Jacob, in the kingdom of heaven. But the children of the kingdom shall be cast out into outer darkness: there shall be weeping and gnashing of teeth. And Jesus said unto the centurion, Go thy way; and as thou hast believed, so be it done unto thee. And his servant was healed in the selfsame hour.

Offertory. The right hand of the Lord bringeth mighty things to pass, the right hand of the Lord hath exalted me: I shall not die, but live, and declare the works of the Lord.

Secret

E beseech thee, O Lord, that this oblation may cleanse us from our sins: and sanctify thy servants both in body and mind for the celebration of this sacrifice. Through.

¶ 2nd Secret is of St. Mary after Christmas (p. 541) & 3rd Secret is Against the Persecutors of the Church (p. 543) or for the Chief Bishop (p. 543).

Communion. All wondered at the gracious words which proceeded out of the mouth of God.

Postcommunion

LORD, who dost suffer us to be made partakers of these great mysteries: we beseech thee; that thou wouldest vouchsafe to render us worthy to obtain the benefits of the same. Through.

¶ 2nd Postcommunion is of St. Mary after Christmas (p. 541) & 3rd Postcommunion is Against the Persecutors of the Church (p. 543) or for the Chief Bishop (p. 543).

Proper of Season *Epiphany IV*

Fourth Sunday after Epiphany

Semidouble

Introit

ORSHIP God, all ye Angels of his: Sion heard, and rejoiced: and the daughters of Judah were glad *Ps.* The Lord is King, the earth may be glad thereof: yea, the multitude of the isles may be glad thereof.

Collect

GOD, who knowest us to be set in the midst of so many and great dangers, that by reason of the frailty of our nature we cannot always stand upright; Grant to us such strength and protection, as may support us in all dangers, and carry us through all temptations. Through.

¶ If it be after 2 February, 2nd Collect is of the Saints (p. 542) & 3rd is ad libitum.

¶ Otherwise, 2nd Collect is of St. Mary after Christmas (p. 541) & 3rd Collect is Against the Persecutors of the Church (p. 543) or for the Chief Bishop (p. 543).

Epistle. Romans 13:1

BRETHREN: Let every soul be subject unto the higher powers. For there is no power but of God: the powers that be are ordained of God. Whosoever therefore resisteth the power, resisteth the ordinance of God: and they that resist shall receive to themselves damnation. For rulers are not a terror to good works, but to the evil. Wilt thou then not be afraid of the power? do that which is good, and thou shalt have praise of the same: For he is the minister of God to thee for good. But if thou do that which is evil, be afraid; for he beareth not the sword in vain: for he is the minister of God, a revenger to execute wrath upon him that doeth evil. Wherefore ye must needs be subject, not only for wrath, but also for conscience sake. For for this cause pay ye tribute also: for they are God's ministers, attending continually upon this very thing. Render therefore to all their dues: tribute to whom tribute is due; custom to whom custom; fear to whom fear; honour to whom honour.

Gradual. The heathen shall fear thy name, O Lord, and all the kings of the earth thy majesty. ℣. When the Lord shall build up Sion, and when his glory shall appear.

Alleluia. Alleluia, alleluia. ℣. The Lord is King, the earth may be glad thereof: yea, the multitude of the isles may be glad thereof. Alleluia.

Epiphany IV   # Proper of Season

Gospel. Matthew 8:23

AT THAT TIME: When Jesus was entered into a ship, his disciples followed him. And, behold, there arose a great tempest in the sea, insomuch that the ship was covered with the waves: but he was asleep. And his disciples came to him, and awoke him, saying, Lord, save us: we perish. And he saith unto them, Why are ye fearful, O ye of little faith? Then he arose, and rebuked the winds and the sea; and there was a great calm. But the men marvelled, saying, What manner of man is this, that even the winds and the sea obey him! And when he was come to the other side into the country of the Gergesenes, there met him two possessed with devils, coming out of the tombs, exceeding fierce, so that no man might pass by that way. And, behold, they cried out, saying, What have we to do with thee, Jesus, thou Son of God? art thou come hither to torment us before the time? And there was a good way off from them an herd of many swine feeding. So the devils besought him, saying, If thou cast us out, suffer us to go away into the herd of swine. And he said unto them, Go. And when they were come out, they went into the herd of swine: and, behold, the whole herd of swine ran violently down a steep place into the sea, and perished in the waters. And they that kept them fled, and went their ways into the city, and told every thing, and what was befallen to the possessed of the devils. And, behold, the whole city came out to meet Jesus: and when they saw him, they besought him that he would depart out of their coasts.

Offertory. The right hand of the Lord bringeth mighty things to pass, the right hand of the Lord hath exalted me: I shall not die, but live, and declare the works of the Lord.

Secret

RANT, we beseech thee, almighty God: that the gift now offered in this sacrifice may cleanse our frailty from all evil and evermore defend us. Through.

¶ If it be after 2 February, 2nd Secret is of the Saints (p. 542) & 3rd is ad libitum.

¶ Otherwise, 2nd Secret is of St. Mary after Christmas (p. 541) & 3rd Secret is Against the Persecutors of the Church (p. 543) or for the Chief Bishop (p. 543).

Communion. All wondered at the gracious words which proceeded out of the mouth of God.

Proper of Season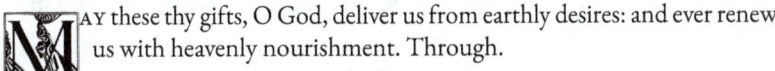

Postcommunion

MAY these thy gifts, O God, deliver us from earthly desires: and ever renew us with heavenly nourishment. Through.

❡ If it be after 2 February, 2nd Postcommunion is of the Saints (p. 542) & 3rd is ad libitum.

❡ Otherwise, 2nd Postcommunion is of St. Mary after Christmas (p. 541) & 3rd Postcommunion is Against the Persecutors of the Church (p. 543) or for the Chief Bishop (p. 543).

Fifth Sunday after Epiphany

Semidouble

Introit

WORSHIP God, all ye Angels of his: Sion heard, and rejoiced: and the daughters of Judah were glad *Ps.* The Lord is King, the earth may be glad thereof: yea, the multitude of the isles may be glad thereof.

Collect

O LORD, we beseech thee to keep thy Church and household continually in thy true religion; that they who do lean only upon the hope of thy heavenly grace may evermore be defended by thy mighty power. Through.

❡ 2nd Collect is of the Saints (p. 542) & 3rd is ad libitum.

Epistle. Colossians 3:12

BRETHREN: Put on therefore, as the elect of God, holy and beloved, bowels of mercies, kindness, humbleness of mind, meekness, longsuffering; Forbearing one another, and forgiving one another, if any man have a quarrel against any: even as Christ forgave you, so also do ye. And above all these things put on charity, which is the bond of perfectness. And let the peace of God rule in your hearts, to the which also ye are called in one body; and be ye thankful. Let the word of Christ dwell in you richly in all wisdom; teaching and admonishing one another in psalms and hymns and spiritual songs, singing with grace in your hearts to the Lord. And whatsoever ye do in word or deed, do all in the name of the Lord Jesus, giving thanks to God and the Father by Our Lord Jesus Christ.

Epiphany V   # Proper of Season

Gradual. The heathen shall fear thy name, O Lord, and all the kings of the earth thy majesty. ℣. When the Lord shall build up Sion, and when his glory shall appear.

Alleluia. Alleluia, alleluia. ℣. The Lord is King, the earth may be glad thereof: yea, the multitude of the isles may be glad thereof. Alleluia.

Gospel. Matthew 13:24

T THAT TIME: Jesus spake this parable unto the crowds: The kingdom of heaven is likened unto a man which sowed good seed in his field: But while men slept, his enemy came and sowed tares among the wheat, and went his way. But when the blade was sprung up, and brought forth fruit, then appeared the tares also. So the servants of the householder came and said unto him, Sir, didst not thou sow good seed in thy field? from whence then hath it tares? He said unto them, An enemy hath done this. The servants said unto him, Wilt thou then that we go and gather them up? But he said, Nay; lest while ye gather up the tares, ye root up also the wheat with them. Let both grow together until the harvest: and in the time of harvest I will say to the reapers, Gather ye together first the tares, and bind them in bundles to burn them: but gather the wheat into my barn.

Offertory. The right hand of the Lord bringeth mighty things to pass, the right hand of the Lord hath exalted me: I shall not die, but live, and declare the works of the Lord.

Secret

E offer unto thee, O Lord, sacrifices of propitiation: that thou wouldest mercifully absolve our offences and thyself direct the hearts of those that go astray. Through.

¶ 2ⁿᵈ Secret is of the Saints (p. 542) & 3ʳᵈ is ad libitum.

Communion. All wondered at the gracious words which proceeded out of the mouth of God.

Postcommunion

E beseech thee, almighty God: that as in these mysteries we have received the pledge of our salvation, so we may be brought unto the fulfilment of the same. Through.

¶ 2ⁿᵈ Postcommunion is of the Saints (p. 542) & 3ʳᵈ is ad libitum.

Proper of Season *Epiphany VI*

Sixth Sunday after Epiphany

Semidouble

Introit

WORSHIP God, all ye Angels of his: Sion heard, and rejoiced: and the daughters of Judah were glad *Ps.* The Lord is King, the earth may be glad thereof: yea, the multitude of the isles may be glad thereof.

Collect

O GOD, whose blessed Son was manifested that he might destroy the works of the devil, and make us the sons of God, and heirs of eternal life; Grant us, we beseech thee, that, having this hope, we may purify ourselves, even as he is pure; that, when he shall appear again with power and great glory, we may be made like unto him in his eternal and glorious kingdom; where with thee, O Father, and thee, O Holy Ghost, he liveth and reigneth ever, one God, world without end. *Amen.*

¶ 2nd Collect is of the Saints (p. 542) & 3rd is ad libitum.

Epistle. 1 John 3:1

DEARLY BELOVED: Behold, what manner of love the Father hath bestowed upon us, that we should be called the sons of God: therefore the world knoweth us not, because it knew him not. Beloved, now are we the sons of God, and it doth not yet appear what we shall be: but we know that, when he shall appear, we shall be like him; for we shall see him as he is. And every man that hath this hope in him purifieth himself, even as he is pure. Whosoever committeth sin transgresseth also the law: for sin is the transgression of the law. And ye know that he was manifested to take away our sins; and in him is no sin. Whosoever abideth in him sinneth not: whosoever sinneth hath not seen him, neither known him. Little children, let no man deceive you: he that doeth righteousness is righteous, even as he is righteous. He that committeth sin is of the devil; for the devil sinneth from the beginning. For this purpose the Son of God was manifested, that he might destroy the works of the devil.

Gradual. The heathen shall fear thy name, Lord, and all the kings of the earth thy majesty. ℣. When the Lord shall build up Sion, and when his glory shall appear.

Alleluia. Alleluia, alleluia. ℣. The Lord is King, the earth may be glad thereof: yea, the multitude of the isles may be glad thereof. Alleluia.

Epiphany VI # Proper of Season

Gospel. Matthew 24:23

AT THAT TIME: Jesus spake unto his disciples: If any man shall say unto you, Lo, here is Christ, or there; believe it not. For there shall arise false Christs, and false prophets, and shall shew great signs and wonders; insomuch that, if it were possible, they shall deceive the very elect. Behold, I have told you before. Wherefore if they shall say unto you, Behold, he is in the desert; go not forth: behold, he is in the secret chambers; believe it not. For as the lightning cometh out of the east, and shineth even unto the west; so shall also the coming of the Son of man be. For wheresoever the carcase is, there will the eagles be gathered together. Immediately after the tribulation of those days shall the sun be darkened, and the moon shall not give her light, and the stars shall fall from heaven, and the powers of the heavens shall be shaken: And then shall appear the sign of the Son of man in heaven: and then shall all the tribes of the earth mourn, and they shall see the Son of man coming in the clouds of heaven with power and great glory. And he shall send his angels with a great sound of a trumpet, and they shall gather together his elect from the four winds, from one end of heaven to the other.

Offertory. The right hand of the Lord bringeth mighty things to pass, the right hand of the Lord hath exalted me: I shall not die, but live, and declare the works of the Lord.

Secret

GOD, we pray thee, that this oblation may cleanse and regenerate, govern, and defend us. Through.

¶ 2nd Secret is of the Saints (p. 542) & 3rd is ad libitum.

Communion. All wondered at the gracious words which proceeded out of the mouth of God.

Postcommunion

LORD, who hast fulfilled us with thy heavenly delights: we beseech thee; that we may ever earnestly seek after those things whereby we truly live. Through.

¶ 2nd Postcommunion is of the Saints (p. 542) & 3rd is ad libitum.

¶ If there be more than six Sundays of Epiphany before Septuagesima, then the upcoming unused Sundays after Trinity (p. 402) are used, the Introit, Gradual, Alleluia, Offertory, and Communion being of Epiphany VI.

Proper of Season *Septuagesima*

Septuagesima Sunday

Second Class Semidouble

Introit

THE sorrows of death compassed me, the pains of hell came about me: and in my tribulation I called upon the Lord, and he heard my voice out of his holy temple. *Ps.* I will love thee, O Lord, my strength: the Lord is my stony rock, my fortress, and my saviour.

¶ Gloria in excelsis is not said in Masses of the Season from this Sunday until Wednesday in Holy Week, inclusive, either on Sundays or week-days.

Collect

O LORD, we beseech thee favourably to hear the prayers of thy people; that we, who are justly punished for our offences, may be mercifully delivered by thy goodness, for the glory of thy Name; through Jesus Christ our Saviour, who liveth and reigneth with thee and the Holy Ghost ever, one God, world without end. *Amen.*

¶ 2nd Collect is of the Saints (p. 542) & 3rd is ad libitum.

Epistle. 1 Corinthians 9:24

BRETHREN: Know ye not that they which run in a race run all, but one receiveth the prize? So run, that ye may obtain. And every man that striveth for the mastery is temperate in all things. Now they do it to obtain a corruptible crown; but we an incorruptible. I therefore so run, not as uncertainly; so fight I, not as one that beateth the air: But I keep under my body, and bring it into subjection: lest that by any means, when I have preached to others, I myself should be a castaway.

Gradual. A refuge in due time of trouble: they that know thee will put their trust in thee: for thou, Lord, never failest them that seek thee. ℣. For the poor shall not alway be forgotten: the patient abiding of the meek shall not perish for ever: up, Lord, and let not man have the upper hand.

¶ From Septuagesima until the Tuesday after Quinquagesima Sunday inclusive, when the Sunday Mass is resumed on week-days, the Tract is not said, but only the Gradual.

Tract. Out of the deep have I called unto thee, O Lord: Lord, hear my voice. ℣. O let thine ears consider well the prayer of thy servant. ℣. If thou, Lord, wilt be extreme to mark what is done amiss: O Lord, who may abide it? ℣. For there is mercy with thee, and because of thy law, I have waited for thee, O Lord.

Septuagesima # Proper of Season

Gospel. Matthew 20:1

AT THAT TIME: Jesus spake unto his disciples this parable: The kingdom of heaven is like unto a man that is an householder, which went out early in the morning to hire labourers into his vineyard. And when he had agreed with the labourers for a penny a day, he sent them into his vineyard. And he went out about the third hour, and saw others standing idle in the marketplace, And said unto them; Go ye also into the vineyard, and whatsoever is right I will give you. And they went their way. Again he went out about the sixth and ninth hour, and did likewise. And about the eleventh hour he went out, and found others standing idle, and saith unto them, Why stand ye here all the day idle? They say unto him, Because no man hath hired us. He saith unto them, Go ye also into the vineyard; and whatsoever is right, that shall ye receive. So when even was come, the lord of the vineyard saith unto his steward, Call the labourers, and give them their hire, beginning from the last unto the first. And when they came that were hired about the eleventh hour, they received every man a penny. But when the first came, they supposed that they should have received more; and they likewise received every man a penny. And when they had received it, they murmured against the goodman of the house, Saying, These last have wrought but one hour, and thou hast made them equal unto us, which have borne the burden and heat of the day. But he answered one of them, and said, Friend, I do thee no wrong: didst not thou agree with me for a penny? Take that thine is, and go thy way: I will give unto this last, even as unto thee. Is it not lawful for me to do what I will with mine own? Is thine eye evil, because I am good? So the last shall be first, and the first last: for many be called, but few chosen.

Offertory. It is a good thing to give thanks unto the Lord, and to sing praises unto thy name, O most Highest.

Secret

WE beseech thee, O Lord, to accept our prayers and oblations: and graciously hearken unto us, whom thou dost cleanse by thy heavenly mysteries. Through.

¶ 2nd Secret is of the Saints (p. 542) & 3rd is ad libitum.

Communion. Shew thy servant the light of thy countenance, and save me for thy mercy's sake: let me not be confounded, O Lord, for I have called upon thee.

Proper of Season *Sexagesima*

Postcommunion

MAY thy faithful people, O God, be strengthened by thy gifts: that they receiving the same may seek them the more, and seeking them may obtain them everlastingly. Through.

¶ 2nd Postcommunion is of the Saints (p. 542) & 3rd is ad libitum.

SEXAGESIMA SUNDAY

Second Class Semidouble

Introit

ARISE, O Lord, wherefore sleepest thou? Awake, and cast us not away for ever: wherefore hidest thou thy countenance, and forgettest our trouble? Our belly cleaveth unto the ground: arise, O Lord, help us, and deliver us. *Ps.* O God, we have heard with our ears: our fathers have told us.

Collect

O GOD, who seest that we put not our trust in any thing that we do: mercifully grant; that by the protection of the Doctor of the Gentiles we may be defended against all adversity. Through.

¶ 2nd Collect is of the Saints (p. 542) & 3rd is ad libitum.

Epistle. 2 Corinthians 11:19

BRETHREN: Ye suffer fools gladly, seeing ye yourselves are wise. For ye suffer, if a man bring you into bondage, if a man devour you, if a man take of you, if a man exalt himself, if a man smite you on the face. I speak as concerning reproach, as though we had been weak. Howbeit whereinsoever any is bold, (I speak foolishly,) I am bold also. Are they Hebrews? so am I. Are they Israelites? so am I. Are they the seed of Abraham? so am I. Are they ministers of Christ? (I speak as a fool) I am more; in labours more abundant, in stripes above measure, in prisons more frequent, in deaths oft. Of the Jews five times received I forty stripes save one. Thrice was I beaten with rods, once was I stoned, thrice I suffered shipwreck, a night and a day I have been in the deep; In journeyings often, in perils of waters, in perils of robbers, in perils by mine own countrymen, in perils by the heathen, in perils in the city, in perils in the wilderness, in perils in the sea, in perils among false brethren; In weariness and painfulness, in watchings often, in hunger and thirst, in fastings often, in cold and nakedness. Beside those things that are without, that which cometh upon me daily, the care of all the churches. Who is weak, and I am not weak? who is offended, and I burn not? If I must needs glory, I will glory of the things which concern mine infirmities. The God and Father of our Lord Jesus Christ, which is blessed for evermore, knoweth that I lie not.

Gradual. Let the nations know that thou, whose name is Jehovah: art only the Most Highest over all the earth. ℣. O my God, make them like unto a wheel, and as the stubble before the wind.

Tract. Thou hast moved the land, O Lord, and divided it. ℣. Heal the sores thereof, for it shaketh. ℣. That they may triumph because of the truth: that thy beloved may be delivered.

Gospel. Luke 8:4

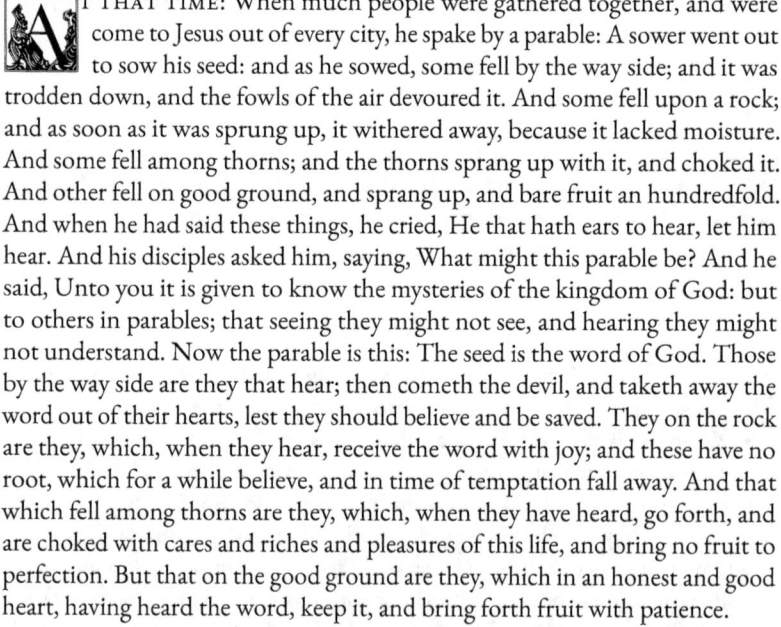
AT THAT TIME: When much people were gathered together, and were come to Jesus out of every city, he spake by a parable: A sower went out to sow his seed: and as he sowed, some fell by the way side; and it was trodden down, and the fowls of the air devoured it. And some fell upon a rock; and as soon as it was sprung up, it withered away, because it lacked moisture. And some fell among thorns; and the thorns sprang up with it, and choked it. And other fell on good ground, and sprang up, and bare fruit an hundredfold. And when he had said these things, he cried, He that hath ears to hear, let him hear. And his disciples asked him, saying, What might this parable be? And he said, Unto you it is given to know the mysteries of the kingdom of God: but to others in parables; that seeing they might not see, and hearing they might not understand. Now the parable is this: The seed is the word of God. Those by the way side are they that hear; then cometh the devil, and taketh away the word out of their hearts, lest they should believe and be saved. They on the rock are they, which, when they hear, receive the word with joy; and these have no root, which for a while believe, and in time of temptation fall away. And that which fell among thorns are they, which, when they have heard, go forth, and are choked with cares and riches and pleasures of this life, and bring no fruit to perfection. But that on the good ground are they, which in an honest and good heart, having heard the word, keep it, and bring forth fruit with patience.

Offertory. O hold thou up my goings in thy paths, that my footsteps slip not: incline thine ear to me, and hearken unto my words: shew thy marvellous loving-kindness, O Lord, thou that art the Saviour of them which put their trust in thee.

Proper of Season *Quinquagesima*

Secret

AY the sacrifice which we offer unto thee, O Lord, evermore quicken and defend us. Through.

℣ 2nd Secret is of the Saints (p. 542) & 3rd is ad libitum.

Communion. I will go unto the altar of God, even unto the God of my joy and gladness.

Postcommunion

E humbly beseech thee, almighty God: that as thou dost refresh us with thy sacraments, so thou wouldest vouchsafe unto us to do thee worthy and acceptable service. Through.

℣ 2nd Postcommunion is of the Saints (p. 542) & 3rd is ad libitum.

Quinquagesima Sunday

Second Class Semidouble

Introit

BE thou my strong rock, and house of defence, that thou mayest save me: for thou art my strong rock, and my castle: be thou also my guide, and lead me for thy name's sake. *Ps.* In thee, O Lord, have I put my trust, let me never be put to confusion: deliver me in thy righteousness and save me.

Collect

O LORD, who hast taught us that all our doings without charity are nothing worth; Send thy Holy Ghost, and pour into our hearts that most excellent gift of charity, the very bond of peace and of all virtues, without which whosoever liveth is counted dead before thee. Grant this for thine only Son Jesus Christ's sake. Who liveth.

℣ 2nd Collect is of the Saints (p. 542) & 3rd is ad libitum.

Quinquagesima # Proper of Season

Epistle. 1 Corinthians 13:1

BRETHREN: Though I speak with the tongues of men and of angels, and have not charity, I am become as sounding brass, or a tinkling cymbal. And though I have the gift of prophecy, and understand all mysteries, and all knowledge; and though I have all faith, so that I could remove mountains, and have not charity, I am nothing. And though I bestow all my goods to feed the poor, and though I give my body to be burned, and have not charity, it profiteth me nothing. Charity suffereth long, and is kind; charity envieth not; charity vaunteth not itself, is not puffed up, Doth not behave itself unseemly, seeketh not her own, is not easily provoked, thinketh no evil; Rejoiceth not in iniquity, but rejoiceth in the truth; Beareth all things, believeth all things, hopeth all things, endureth all things. Charity never faileth: but whether there be prophecies, they shall fail; whether there be tongues, they shall cease; whether there be knowledge, it shall vanish away. For we know in part, and we prophesy in part. But when that which is perfect is come, then that which is in part shall be done away. When I was a child, I spake as a child, I understood as a child, I thought as a child: but when I became a man, I put away childish things. For now we see through a glass, darkly; but then face to face: now I know in part; but then shall I know even as also I am known. And now abideth faith, hope, charity, these three; but the greatest of these is charity.

Gradual. Thou art the God that only doeth wonders: and hast declared thy power among the people. ℣. Thou hast mightily delivered thy people, even the sons of Jacob and Joseph.

Tract. O be joyful in the Lord, all ye lands: serve the Lord with gladness. ℣. Come before his presence with a song: be ye sure that the Lord he is God. ℣. It is he that hath made us, and not we ourselves: we are his people, and the sheep of his pasture.

Gospel. Luke 18:31

AT THAT TIME: Jesus took unto him the twelve, and said unto them, Behold, we go up to Jerusalem, and all things that are written by the prophets concerning the Son of man shall be accomplished. For he shall be delivered unto the Gentiles, and shall be mocked, and spitefully entreated, and spitted on: And they shall scourge him, and put him to death: and the third day he shall rise again. And they understood none of these things: and this saying was hid from them, neither knew they the things which were spoken. And it came to pass, that as he was come nigh unto Jericho, a certain blind man sat by the way side begging: And hearing the multitude pass by, he asked what

Proper of Season *Quinquagesima*

it meant. And they told him, that Jesus of Nazareth passeth by. And he cried, saying, Jesus, thou Son of David, have mercy on me. And they which went before rebuked him, that he should hold his peace: but he cried so much the more, Thou Son of David, have mercy on me. And Jesus stood, and commanded him to be brought unto him: and when he was come near, he asked him, Saying, What wilt thou that I shall do unto thee? And he said, Lord, that I may receive my sight. And Jesus said unto him, Receive thy sight: thy faith hath saved thee. And immediately he received his sight, and followed him, glorifying God: and all the people, when they saw it, gave praise unto God.

Offertory. Blessed art thou, O Lord, O teach me thy statutes: with my lips have I been telling of all the judgments of thy mouth.

Secret

E beseech thee, O Lord, that this oblation may cleanse us from our sins: and sanctify thy servants both in body and mind for the celebration of this sacrifice. Through.

¶ 2nd Secret is of the Saints (p. 542) & 3rd is ad libitum.

Communion. They did eat, and were well filled, for the Lord gave them the own desire: they were not disappointed of their lust.

Postcommunion

E beseech thee, Almighty God: that we who have received this heavenly food, may be thereby defended against all adversities. Through.

¶ 2nd Postcommunion is of the Saints (p. 542) & 3rd is ad libitum.

Ash Wednesday   # Proper of Season

Ash Wednesday

First Class Feria

℣ On Ash Wednesday, during the Order of Morning Prayer, the **Great Litany** (p. 86) should said in its appropriate place after the Third Collect followed by **A Penitential Office** (p. 91).

Rite of Ashes

℣ Before Mass, ashes prepared from the branches of olive or other trees blessed the year before are blessed, as followeth.

℣ Mattins being ended, the Priest vested in a violet cope, or without a chasuble, accompanied by the Ministers similarly vested, proceeds to bless ashes placed in some vessel on the Altar. And first the following Antiphon is sung by the choir, akin to the Introit.

EAR us, O Lord, for thy loving-kindness is comfortable: turn thee unto us, O Lord, according to the multitude of thy mercies. *Ps.* Save me, O God: for the waters are come in, even unto my soul.

℣ Then the Priest at the Epistle corner, without turning to the people or disjoining his bands (which rule of joined hands holds in the Prayers of all benedictions), says:

| ℣. The Lord be with you. | ℣. Dóminus vobíscum. |
| ℞. And with thy spirit. | ℞. Et cum spíritu tuo. |

Let us pray.

LMIGHTY and everlasting God, spare them that are penitent, be favourable to them that call upon thee: and vouchsafe to send thy holy Angel from heaven, to bl ✠ ess, and sanc ✠ tify these ashes, that they may be a wholesome medicine to all who humbly call upon thy holy name, who in their consciences by sin are accused, who in the sight of thy divine compassion bewail their faults, and earnestly and meekly implore thy most gracious lovingkindness: and grant that, by the invocation of thy most holy name; all who are sprinkled therewith for the redemption of their transgressions may receive healing of body and protection of soul. Through Christ, our Lord. *Amen.*

Let us pray.

GOD, who wouldest not the death of a sinner, but rather that he should repent: mercifully look upon the frailty of our mortal nature: and of thy goodness vouchsafe to bl ✠ ess these ashes which we purpose to have set upon our heads for the increase of humility, and the meriting of pardon: that we, acknowledging that we are but ashes, and that by reason of our vileness unto dust we shall return; may through thy mercy be found meet to receive forgiveness of all our sins and the rewards which thou hast promised to them that are penitent. Through Christ, our Lord. *Amen.*

Proper of Season *Ash Wednesday*

Let us pray.

O GOD, who dost turn unto them that abase themselves, and art favourable unto them that make satisfaction: incline thy merciful ear to our prayers; and graciously pour forth upon the heads of thy servants now to be sprinkled with these ashes the grace of thy benediction: that thou wouldest fill them with the spirit of contrition, and grant that those things which they have asked rightly they may obtain effectually; that those things which thou dost bestow may by thine appointment remain constant and unchanged for evermore. Through Christ, our Lord. *Amen.*

Let us pray.

ALMIGHTY and everlasting God, who upon the people of Nineveh, repenting in sackcloth and ashes, didst bestow the healing of thy pardon: mercifully grant; that we may so imitate them in outward fashion that we may be made like unto them in the obtaining of thy forgiveness. Through.

¶ The Celebrant after putting incense into the thurible, thrice sprinkles the ashes with holy water, saying the Antiphon, **Thou shalt purge me,** without singing and without the Psalm, and then thrice censes them.

¶ The senior Priest amongst the Clergy approaches the Altar, and puts ashes on the bead of the Celebrant, who does not kneel. If there be no other Priest present, the Celebrant, turning to the Altar, puts ashes upon his own head, saying nothing, and forthwith the Choir sings the Antiphon,

LET us change our raiment for sackcloth and ashes: let us fast and mourn before the Lord; for our God is exceedingly merciful to forgive us our sins.

or,

LET the priests, the ministers of the Lord, weep between the porch and the altar, and let them say: Spare, O Lord, spare thy people: and shut not up, Lord, the mouths of them that praise thee.

¶ The Responsory follows.

LET us amend the sins that in our ignorance we have committed: lest the day of death come suddenly upon us, and we find no place for repentance, though we seek it.

℟. Hear, O Lord, and have mercy: for we have sinned against thee.

℣. Help us, O God of our salvation: and for the glory of thy name deliver us, O Lord.

℟. Hear, O Lord, and have mercy: for we have sinned against thee.

℣. Glory be to the Father, and to the Son, and to the Holy Ghost.

℟. Hear, O Lord, and have mercy: for we have sinned against thee.

Ash Wednesday # Proper of Season

¶ While the Antiphons and Responsory are being sung, the Priest with uncovered head first puts ashes on the senior Priest from whom he has received them, and then on the Ministers being vested and kneeling before the Altar, saying:

REMEMBER, O MAN, THAT DUST THOU ART, AND UNTO DUST SHALT THOU RETURN.

¶ Then come the others, first the Clergy in order then the people: and kneeling before the Altar receive the ashes severally from the Priest, as has been said of the Ministers.

¶ The imposition of ashes being finished, the Priest says:

℣. The Lord be with you.
℟. And with thy spirit.

℣. Dóminus vobíscum.
℟. Et cum spíritu tuo.

Let us pray.

GRANT to us, O Lord, to put on the armour of our Christian warfare with holy fastings: that we who are about to fight against all spiritual wickedness, may be defended by the power of abstinence. Through Christ, our Lord. *Amen.*

¶ The Mass is then said.

Introit

THOU hast mercy upon all, O Lord, and hatest nothing that thou hast created: and winkest at the sins of men, because they should amend, and sparest them: for thou art the Lord our God. *Ps.* Be merciful unto me, O God, be merciful unto me: for my soul trusteth in thee.

Collect

ALMIGHTY and everlasting God, who hatest nothing that thou hast made, and dost forgive the sins of all those who are penitent; Create and make in us new and contrite hearts, that we, worthily lamenting our sins and acknowledging our wretchedness, may obtain of thee, the God of all mercy, perfect remission and forgiveness. Through.

¶ This Collect is to be said every day in Lent, after the Collect appointed for the day, until Palm Sunday.

¶ 2nd Collect is of the Saints (p. 542) & 3rd for the Living and Departed (p. 544).

Proper of Season *Ash Wednesday*

Epistle. Joel 2:12

THUS saith the Lord: Turn ye even to me with all your heart, and with fasting, and with weeping, and with mourning: And rend your heart, and not your garments, and turn unto the LORD your God: for he is gracious and merciful, slow to anger, and of great kindness, and repenteth him of the evil. Who knoweth if he will return and repent, and leave a blessing behind him; even a meat offering and a drink offering unto the LORD your God? Blow the trumpet in Zion, sanctify a fast, call a solemn assembly: Gather the people, sanctify the congregation, assemble the elders, gather the children, and those that suck the breasts: let the bridegroom go forth of his chamber, and the bride out of her closet. Let the priests, the ministers of the LORD, weep between the porch and the altar, and let them say, Spare thy people, O LORD, and give not thine heritage to reproach, that the heathen should rule over them: wherefore should they say among the people, Where is their God?

Gradual. Be merciful unto me, O God, be merciful unto me: for my soul trusteth in thee. ℣. He shall send from heaven, and save me from the reproof of him that would eat me up.

¶ The following Tract is said in the Masses of Monday, Wednesday, and Friday—up to Monday in Holy Week, inclusive—except on Ember Wednesday.

Tract. O Lord, deal not with us after our sins: nor reward us according to our wickednesses. ℣. O Lord, remember not our old sins: but have mercy upon us, and that soon, for we are come to great misery. (Here genuflect.) ℣. Help us, O God of our salvation: and for the glory of thy name, O Lord, deliver us: and be merciful unto our sins, for thy name's sake.

Gospel. Matthew 6:16

AT THAT TIME: Jesus spake unto his disciples: When ye fast, be not, as the hypocrites, of a sad countenance: for they disfigure their faces, that they may appear unto men to fast. Verily I say unto you, They have their reward. But thou, when thou fastest, anoint thine head, and wash thy face; That thou appear not unto men to fast, but unto thy Father which is in secret: and thy Father, which seeth in secret, shall reward thee openly. Lay not up for yourselves treasures upon earth, where moth and rust doth corrupt, and where thieves break through and steal: But lay up for yourselves treasures in heaven, where neither moth nor rust doth corrupt, and where thieves do not break through nor steal: For where your treasure is, there will your heart be also.

Ash Wednesday # Proper of Season

Offertory. I will magnify thee, O Lord, for thou hast set me up, and not made my foes to triumph over me: O Lord, I cried unto thee, and thou hast healed me.

Secret

RANT, we beseech thee, O Lord, that like as we by these our gifts do celebrate the institution of this venerable sacrament: so we may by thee be enabled worthily to offer the same. Through.

¶ 2nd Secret is of the Saints (p. 542) & 3rd for the Living and Departed (p. 544).

Communion. He who doth meditate on the law of the Lord day and night, will bring forth his fruit in due season.

Postcommunion

ET the sacraments, O Lord, which we have received, avail for our succour: that these our fasts may be acceptable unto thee, and profitable unto us for our healing. Through.

¶ 2nd Postcommunion is of the Saints (p. 542) & 3rd for the Living and Departed (p. 544).

PRIEST. Let us pray.
DEACON. Humble your heads before God.

¶ The Priest then prays the following:

OOK down in mercy, O Lord, upon those who bow before thy majesty: that they who have been refreshed by the divine gift, may evermore be nourished by thy heavenly succour. Through.

¶ This manner of saying the Prayer over the people is observed in Masses of the Feria only until the Wednesday in Holy Week inclusive.

¶ The Propers of Ash Wednesday shall serve for every day after, unto the next Sunday, except upon a Feast Day.

Proper of Season   *Lent I*

First Sunday of Lent

First Class Semidouble

Introit

HE shall call upon me, and I will hearken unto him: I will deliver him, and bring him to honour: with length of days will I satisfy him. *Ps.* Whoso dwelleth under the defence of the most High, shall abide under the shadow of the Almighty.

Collect

O LORD, who for our sake didst fast forty days and forty nights; Give us grace to use such abstinence, that, our flesh being subdued to the Spirit, we may ever obey thy godly motions in righteousness, and true holiness, to thy honour and glory, who livest and reignest with the Father and the Holy Ghost, one God, world without end. *Amen.*

¶ 2nd Collect is of the Saints (p. 542) & 3rd for the Living and Departed (p. 544).

Epistle. 2 Corinthians 6:1

BRETHREN: We then, as workers together with him, beseech you also that ye receive not the grace of God in vain. (For he saith, I have heard thee in a time accepted, and in the day of salvation have I succoured thee: behold, now is the accepted time; behold, now is the day of salvation.) Giving no offence in any thing, that the ministry be not blamed: But in all things approving ourselves as the ministers of God, in much patience, in afflictions, in necessities, in distresses, In stripes, in imprisonments, in tumults, in labours, in watchings, in fastings; By pureness, by knowledge, by longsuffering, by kindness, by the Holy Ghost, by love unfeigned, By the word of truth, by the power of God, by the armour of righteousness on the right hand and on the left, By honour and dishonour, by evil report and good report: as deceivers, and yet true; As unknown, and yet well known; as dying, and, behold, we live; as chastened, and not killed; As sorrowful, yet alway rejoicing; as poor, yet making many rich; as having nothing, and yet possessing all things.

Gradual. God shall give his Angels charge over thee, to keep thee in all thy ways. ℣. They shall bear thee in their hands, that thou hurt not thy foot against a stone.

Proper of Season

Lent I

Tract. Whoso dwelleth under the defence of the most High, shall abide under the shadow of the Almighty. ℣. I will say unto the Lord: Thou art my hope and my stronghold: my God, in him will I trust. ℣. For he shall deliver thee from the snare of the hunter, and from the noisome pestilence. ℣. He shall defend thee under his wings, and thou shalt be safe under his feathers. ℣. His faithfulness and truth shall be thy shield and buckler: thou shalt not be afraid for any terror by night. ℣. Nor for the arrow that flieth by day, for the pestilence that walketh in darkness, nor for the sickness that destroyeth in the noon-day. ℣. A thousand shall fall beside thee, and ten thousand at thy right hand: but it shall not come nigh thee. ℣. For he shall give his Angels charge over thee, to keep thee in all thy ways. ℣. They shall bear thee in their hands: that thou hurt not thy foot against a stone. ℣. Thou shalt go upon the lion and adder, the young lion and the dragon shalt thou tread under thy feet. ℣. Because he hath set his love upon me, therefore will I deliver him: I will set him up, because he hath known my name. ℣. He shall call upon me, and I will hear him: yea, I am with him in trouble. ℣. I will deliver him and bring him to honour: with long life will I satisfy him, and shew him my salvation.

Gospel. Matthew 4:1

AT THAT TIME: Jesus was led up of the Spirit into the wilderness to be tempted of the devil. And when he had fasted forty days and forty nights, he was afterward an hungered. And when the tempter came to him, he said, If thou be the Son of God, command that these stones be made bread. But he answered and said, It is written, Man shall not live by bread alone, but by every word that proceedeth out of the mouth of God. Then the devil taketh him up into the holy city, and setteth him on a pinnacle of the temple, And saith unto him, If thou be the Son of God, cast thyself down: for it is written, He shall give his angels charge concerning thee: and in their hands they shall bear thee up, lest at any time thou dash thy foot against a stone. Jesus said unto him, It is written again, Thou shalt not tempt the Lord thy God. Again, the devil taketh him up into an exceeding high mountain, and sheweth him all the kingdoms of the world, and the glory of them; And saith unto him, All these things will I give thee, if thou wilt fall down and worship me. Then saith Jesus unto him, Get thee hence, Satan: for it is written, Thou shalt worship the Lord thy God, and him only shalt thou serve. Then the devil leaveth him, and, behold, angels came and ministered unto him.

Offertory. The Lord shall defend thee under his wings, and thou shalt be safe under his feathers: his faithfulness and truth shall be thy shield and buckler.

Ember Wednesday   **Proper of Season**   *Lenten Emberday*

Secret

E solemnly offer unto thee, O Lord, this sacrifice in the beginning of Lent, beseeching thee: that, while we abstain from carnal feastings, we may likewise refrain from hurtful pleasures. Through.

¶ 2ⁿᵈ Secret is of the Saints (p. 542) & 3ʳᵈ for the Living and Departed (p. 544).

Communion. The Lord shall defend thee under his wings, and thou shalt be safe under his feathers: his faithfulness and truth shall be thy shield and buckler.

Postcommunion

AY the holy partaking of thy sacrament, O Lord, in such wise restore us: that we, being cleansed from our former nature, may enter into the fellowship of this saving mystery. Through.

¶ 2ⁿᵈ Postcommunion is of the Saints (p. 542) & 3ʳᵈ for the Living and Departed (p. 544).

EMBER WEDNESDAY IN LENT

Second Class Feria

Introit

ALL to remembrance thy tender mercies, O Lord, and thy loving kindnesses, which have been ever of old: neither let our enemies triumph over us: deliver us, O God of Israel, out of all our troubles. *Ps.* Unto thee, O Lord, will I lift up my soul: my God, I have put my trust in thee, O let me not be confounded.

¶ After the Kyrie,

℣. Let us pray.   ℣. Orémus.
℣. Let us bow the knee.   ℣. Flectámus génua.
℣. Arise.   ℣. Leváte.

Collect

E beseech thee, O Lord, mercifully hear our prayers: and stretch forth the right hand of thy majesty to be our defence against all things that may hurt us. Through.

Lenten Emberday   **Proper of Season**   Ember Wednesday

Epistle. Exodus 24:12

IN THOSE DAYS: The LORD said unto Moses, Come up to me into the mount, and be there: and I will give thee tables of stone, and a law, and commandments which I have written; that thou mayest teach them. And Moses rose up, and his minister Joshua: and Moses went up into the mount of God. And he said unto the elders, Tarry ye here for us, until we come again unto you: and, behold, Aaron and Hur are with you: if any man have any matters to do, let him come unto them. And Moses went up into the mount, and a cloud covered the mount. And the glory of the LORD abode upon mount Sinai, and the cloud covered it six days: and the seventh day he called unto Moses out of the midst of the cloud. And the sight of the glory of the LORD was like devouring fire on the top of the mount in the eyes of the children of Israel. And Moses went into the midst of the cloud, and gat him up into the mount: and Moses was in the mount forty days and forty nights.

Gradual. The sorrows of my heart are enlarged: O Lord, bring thou me out of my troubles. ℣. Look upon my adversity and misery: and forgive me all my sin.

℣. The Lord be with you.   ℣. Dóminus vobíscum.
℞. And with thy spirit.   ℞. Et cum spíritu tuo.

Let us pray.

WE beseech thee, O Lord, graciously to regard the devout prayers of thy people: that they who by abstinence do mortify the body, may in their minds be refreshed by the fruit of good works. Through.

¶ 2ⁿᵈ Collect is of the Saints (p. 542) & 3ʳᵈ for the Living and Departed (p. 544).

Epistle. 1 Kings 19:3

IN THOSE DAYS: Elijah came to Beersheba, which belongeth to Judah, and left his servant there. But he himself went a day's journey into the wilderness, and came and sat down under a juniper tree: and he requested for himself that he might die; and said, It is enough; now, O LORD, take away my life; for I am not better than my fathers. And as he lay and slept under a juniper tree, behold, then an angel touched him, and said unto him, Arise and eat. And he looked, and, behold, there was a cake baken on the coals, and a cruse of water at his head. And he did eat and drink, and laid him down again. And the angel of the LORD came again the second time, and touched him, and said, Arise and eat; because the journey is too great for thee. And he arose, and did eat and drink, and went in the strength of that meat forty days and forty nights unto Horeb the mount of God.

Ember Wednesday   Proper of Season   *Lenten Emberday*

Tract. O Lord, bring thou me out of my troubles: look upon my adversity and misery: and forgive me all my sin. ℣. Unto thee, O Lord, will I lift up my soul: my God, I have put my trust in thee: O let me not be confounded: neither let mine enemies triumph over me. ℣. For all they that hope in thee shall not be ashamed: but such as transgress without a cause shall be put to confusion.

Gospel. Matthew 12:38

AT THAT TIME: Certain of the scribes and of the Pharisees answered Jesus, saying, Master, we would see a sign from thee. But he answered and said unto them, An evil and adulterous generation seeketh after a sign; and there shall no sign be given to it, but the sign of the prophet Jonas: For as Jonas was three days and three nights in the whale's belly; so shall the Son of man be three days and three nights in the heart of the earth. The men of Nineveh shall rise in judgment with this generation, and shall condemn it: because they repented at the preaching of Jonas; and, behold, a greater than Jonas is here. The queen of the south shall rise up in the judgment with this generation, and shall condemn it: for she came from the uttermost parts of the earth to hear the wisdom of Solomon; and, behold, a greater than Solomon is here. When the unclean spirit is gone out of a man, he walketh through dry places, seeking rest, and findeth none. Then he saith, I will return into my house from whence I came out; and when he is come, he findeth it empty, swept, and garnished. Then goeth he, and taketh with himself seven other spirits more wicked than himself, and they enter in and dwell there: and the last state of that man is worse than the first. Even so shall it be also unto this wicked generation. While he yet talked to the people, behold, his mother and his brethren stood without, desiring to speak with him. Then one said unto him, Behold, thy mother and thy brethren stand without, desiring to speak with thee. But he answered and said unto him that told him, Who is my mother? and who are my brethren? And he stretched forth his hand toward his disciples, and said, Behold my mother and my brethren! For whosoever shall do the will of my Father which is in heaven, the same is my brother, and sister, and mother.

Offertory. My delight shall be in thy commandments, which I have loved exceedingly: my hand also will I lift up to thy commandments which I have loved.

Secret

WE offer unto thee, O Lord, sacrifices of propitation: that thou wouldest mercifully absolve our offences, and thyself direct the hearts of them that go astray. Through.

¶ 2nd Secret is of the Saints (p. 542) & 3rd for the Living and Departed (p. 544).

Communion. Consider my meditation: O hearken thou unto the voice of my calling, my King, and my God: for unto thee, O Lord, will I make my prayer.

Postcommunion

LORD, let the partaking of thy sacrament both cleanse us from our secret faults; and deliver us from the snares of our enemies. Through.

¶ 2ⁿᵈ Postcommunion is of the Saints (p. 542) & 3ʳᵈ for the Living and Departed (p. 544).

PRIEST. Let us pray.
DEACON. Humble your heads before God.

LORD, we beseech thee, illumine our minds with the light of thy brightness: that we may be able to perceive those things which we ought to do; and have strength to do those things which be right. Through.

EMBER FRIDAY IN LENT

Second Class Feria

Introit

LORD, bring thou me out of my troubles: look upon my adversity and misery, and forgive me all my sin. *Ps.* Unto thee, O Lord, will I lift up my soul; my God, I have put my trust in thee, O let me not be confounded.

Collect

BE favourable, O Lord, to thy people: and mercifully comfort with thy gracious help those whom thou dost make to do thee godly service. Through.

¶ 2ⁿᵈ Collect is of the Saints (p. 542) & 3ʳᵈ for the Living and Departed (p. 544).

Epistle. Ezekiel 18:20

THUS SAITH THE LORD GOD: The soul that sinneth, it shall die. The son shall not bear the iniquity of the father, neither shall the father bear the iniquity of the son: the righteousness of the righteous shall be upon him, and the wickedness of the wicked shall be upon him. But if the wicked will turn from all his sins that he hath committed, and keep all my statutes, and do that which is lawful and right, he shall surely live, he shall not die. All his

Ember Friday — **Proper of Season** — *Lenten Emberday*

transgressions that he hath committed, they shall not be mentioned unto him: in his righteousness that he hath done he shall live. Have I any pleasure at all that the wicked should die? saith the Lord GOD: and not that he should return from his ways, and live? But when the righteous turneth away from his righteousness, and committeth iniquity, and doeth according to all the abominations that the wicked man doeth, shall he live? All his righteousness that he hath done shall not be mentioned: in his trespass that he hath trespassed, and in his sin that he hath sinned, in them shall he die. Yet ye say, The way of the Lord is not equal. Hear now, O house of Israel; Is not my way equal? are not your ways unequal? When a righteous man turneth away from his righteousness, and committeth iniquity, and dieth in them; for his iniquity that he hath done shall he die. Again, when the wicked man turneth away from his wickedness that he hath committed, and doeth that which is lawful and right, he shall save his soul alive. Because he considereth, and turneth away from all his transgressions that he hath committed, he shall surely live, he shall not die, saith the Lord almighty.

Gradual. My God, save thy servant that putteth his trust in thee. ℣. Give ear, Lord, unto my prayer.

Tract. O Lord, deal not with us after our sins: nor reward us according to our wickednesses. ℣. O Lord, remember not our old sins: but have mercy upon us, and that soon, for we are come to great misery. (Here genuflect) ℣. Help us, O God of our salvation: and for the glory of thy name, O Lord, deliver us: and be merciful unto our sins, for thy name's sake.

Gospel. John 5:1

AT THAT TIME: There was a feast of the Jews; and Jesus went up to Jerusalem. Now there is at Jerusalem by the sheep market a pool, which is called in the Hebrew tongue Bethesda, having five porches. In these lay a great multitude of impotent folk, of blind, halt, withered, waiting for the moving of the water. For an angel went down at a certain season into the pool, and troubled the water: whosoever then first after the troubling of the water stepped in was made whole of whatsoever disease he had. And a certain man was there, which had an infirmity thirty and eight years. When Jesus saw him lie, and knew that he had been now a long time in that case, he saith unto him, Wilt thou be made whole? The impotent man answered him, Sir, I have no man, when the water is troubled, to put me into the pool: but while I am coming, another steppeth down before me. Jesus saith unto him, Rise, take up thy bed, and walk. And immediately the man was made whole, and took up his bed, and walked: and on the same day was the sabbath. The Jews therefore said unto him

Lenten Emberday — **Proper of Season** — Ember Friday

that was cured, It is the sabbath day: it is not lawful for thee to carry thy bed. He answered them, He that made me whole, the same said unto me, Take up thy bed, and walk. Then asked they him, What man is that which said unto thee, Take up thy bed, and walk? And he that was healed wist not who it was: for Jesus had conveyed himself away, a multitude being in that place. Afterward Jesus findeth him in the temple, and said unto him, Behold, thou art made whole: sin no more, lest a worse thing come unto thee. The man departed, and told the Jews that it was Jesus, which had made him whole.

Offertory. Praise the Lord, O my soul, and forget not all his benefits: who maketh thee young and lusty as an eagle.

Secret

CCEPT, O Lord, we pray thee, these oblations of our humble service: and graciously sanctify these thy gifts. Through.

¶ 2ⁿᵈ Secret is of the Saints (p. 542) & 3ʳᵈ for the Living and Departed (p. 544).

Communion. All mine enemies shall be confounded, and sore vexed: they shall be turned back, and put to shame suddenly.

Postcommunion

AY the operation of this mystery, O Lord, avail for the cleansing of our sins, and for the fulfilment of our godly desires. Through.

¶ 2ⁿᵈ Postcommunion is of the Saints (p. 542) & 3ʳᵈ for the Living and Departed (p. 544).

PRIEST. Let us pray.
DEACON. Humble your heads before God.

RACIOUSLY hear us, O merciful God: and shew forth in our hearts the light of thy grace. Through.

Ember Saturday in Lent

Second Class Feria

Introit

LET my prayer enter into thy presence: incline thine ear, O Lord, unto my calling. *Ps.* O Lord God of my salvation: I have cried day and night before thee.

¶ After the Kyrie,

℣. Let us pray.
℣. Let us bow the knee.
℣. Arise.

℣. Orémus.
℣. Flectámus génua.
℣. Leváte.

Collect

E beseech thee, O Lord, graciously look upon thy people: and mercifully turn away from them the scourges of thy wrath. Through.

Epistle. Deuteronomy 26:12

IN THOSE DAYS: Spake Moses unto the people saying: When thou hast made an end of tithing all the tithes of thine increase the third year, which is the year of tithing, and hast given it unto the Levite, the stranger, the fatherless, and the widow, that they may eat within thy gates, and be filled; Then thou shalt say before the LORD thy God, I have brought away the hallowed things out of mine house, and also have given them unto the Levite, and unto the stranger, to the fatherless, and to the widow, according to all thy commandments which thou hast commanded me: I have not transgressed thy commandments, neither have I forgotten them: I have not eaten thereof in my mourning, neither have I taken away ought thereof for any unclean use, nor given ought thereof for the dead: but I have hearkened to the voice of the LORD my God, and have done according to all that thou hast commanded me. Look down from thy holy habitation, from heaven, and bless thy people Israel, and the land which thou hast given us, as thou swarest unto our fathers, a land that floweth with milk and honey. This day the LORD thy God hath commanded thee to do these statutes and judgments: thou shalt therefore keep and do them with all thine heart, and with all thy soul. Thou hast avouched the LORD this day to be thy God, and to walk in his ways, and to keep his statutes, and his commandments, and his judgments, and to hearken unto his voice: And the

Lenten Emberday   **Proper of Season**   Ember Saturday

LORD hath avouched thee this day to be his peculiar people, as he hath promised thee, and that thou shouldest keep all his commandments; And to make thee high above all nations which he hath made, in praise, and in name, and in honour; and that thou mayest be an holy people unto the LORD thy God, as he hath spoken.

Gradual. Be merciful, O Lord, unto our sins: wherefore do the heathen say: Where is now their God? ℣. Help us, O God of our salvation: and for the glory of thy name, O Lord, deliver us.

℣. Let us pray.	℣. Orémus.
℣. Let us bow the knee.	℣. Flectámus génua.
℣. Arise.	℣. Leváte.

Collect

EHOLD, O God our defender: that we, who are oppressed by the weight of our misdeeds, may through the obtaining of thy mercy serve thee in freedom of spirit. Through.

Epistle. Deuteronomy 11:22

IN THOSE DAYS: Moses said unto the children of Israel: If ye shall diligently keep all these commandments which I command you, to do them, to love the LORD your God, to walk in all his ways, and to cleave unto him; Then will the LORD drive out all these nations from before you, and ye shall possess greater nations and mightier than yourselves. Every place whereon the soles of your feet shall tread shall be yours: from the wilderness and Lebanon, from the river, the river Euphrates, even unto the uttermost sea shall your coast be. There shall no man be able to stand before you: for the LORD your God shall lay the fear of you and the dread of you upon all the land that ye shall tread upon, as he hath said unto you, the Lord your God.

Gradual. Behold, O God our defender, and look upon thy servants. ℣. O Lord God of hosts, hear the prayers of thy servants.

℣. Let us pray.	℣. Orémus.
℣. Let us bow the knee.	℣. Flectámus génua.
℣. Arise.	℣. Leváte.

Ember Saturday   **Proper of Season**   *Lenten Emberday*

Collect

ssist us, O Lord, we beseech thee, in these our supplications: that by thy goodness we may be found worthy to be humble in prosperity and tranquil in adversity. Through.

Epistle. 1 Maccabees 2:23

IN THOSE DAYS: The priests made a prayer whilst the sacrifice was consuming, I say, both the priests, and all the rest, Jonathan beginning, and the rest answering thereunto, as Neemias did. And the prayer was after this manner; O Lord, Lord God, Creator of all things, who art fearful and strong, and righteous, and merciful, and the only and gracious King, The only giver of all things, the only just, almighty, and everlasting, thou that deliverest Israel from all trouble, and didst choose the fathers, and sanctify them: Receive the sacrifice for thy whole people Israel, and preserve thine own portion, and sanctify it. Gather those together that are scattered from us, deliver them that serve among the heathen, look upon them that are despised and abhorred, and let the heathen know that thou art our God.

Gradual. Turn thee again, O Lord, at the last, and be gracious unto thy servants. ℣. Lord, thou hast been our refuge, from one generation to another.

℣. Let us pray.	℣. Orémus.
℣. Let us bow the knee.	℣. Flectámus génua.
℣. Arise.	℣. Leváte.

Collect

LORD, we beseech thee favourably to hear the prayers of thy people: that we, who are justly punished for our offences, may be mercifully delivered for the glory of thy name. Through.

Epistle. Ecclesiasticus 36:1

HAVE mercy upon us, O Lord the God of all, and behold; And send thy fear upon all the nations: Lift up thy hand against the strange nations; And let them see thy mighty power. As thou wast sanctified in us before them, So be thou magnified in them before us. And let them know thee, as we also have known thee, That there is no God but only thou, O God. Shew new signs, and work divers wonders; Glorify thy hand and thy right arm. Raise up indignation, and pour out wrath; Take away the adversary, and destroy the

Lenten Emberday — **Proper of Season** — Ember Saturday

enemy. Hasten the time, and remember the oath; And let them declare thy mighty works.

Gradual. Let my prayer be set forth in thy sight, O Lord, as the incense. ℣. Let the lifting up of my hands be an evening sacrifice.

℣. Let us pray.
℣. Let us bow the knee.
℣. Arise.

℣. Orémus.
℣. Flectámus génua.
℣. Leváte.

Collect

PREVENT us, O Lord, we beseech thee, in all our doings with thy most gracious favour, and further us with thy continual help: that all our prayers and works may be begun, continued, and ended in thee. Through.

Epistle. Song of the Three Children 26

IN THOSE DAYS: The angel of the Lord came down into the oven together with Azarias and his fellows, and smote the flame of the fire out of the oven; And made the midst of the furnace as it had been a moist whistling wind, so that the fire touched them not at all, neither hurt nor troubled them. Then the three, as out of one mouth, praised, glorified, and blessed, God in the furnace, saying,

¶ Here the response Thanks be to God, is not made.

Hymn

BLESSED art thou, O Lord God of our fathers. And worthy to be praised and glorious for ever.
And blessed is the name of thy glory, which is holy. And worthy to be praised and glorious for ever.
Blessed art thou in the holy temple of thy glory. And worthy to be praised and glorious for ever.
Blessed art thou on the holy throne of thy kingdom. And worthy to be praised and glorious for ever.
Blessed art thou in the sceptre of thy Godhead. And worthy to be praised and glorious for ever.
Blessed art thou that sittest upon the Cherubim, and beholdest the depths. And worthy to be praised and glorious for ever.

Ember Saturday — **Proper of Season** — *Lenten Emberday*

Blessed art thou that walkest on the wings of the winds and on the waves of the sea. And worthy to be praised and glorious for ever.

Let all thine Angels and Saints bless thee. And let them praise thee and glorify thee for ever.

Let the heavens, the earth, the sea, and all that in them is bless thee. And let them praise thee and glorify thee for ever.

Glory be to the Father, and to the Son, and to the Holy Ghost. And worthy to be praised and glorious for ever.

As it was in the beginning, is now, and ever shall be: world without end. Amen. And worthy to be praised and glorious for ever.

| ℣. The Lord be with you. | ℣. Dóminus vobíscum. |
| R. And with thy spirit. | R. Et cum spíritu tuo. |

Let us pray.

GOD, who to the three children didst assuage the flames of fire: mercifully grant; that the flames of sin may not kindle upon us thy servants. Through.

¶ 2nd Collect is of the Saints (p. 542) & 3rd for the Living and Departed (p. 544).

Epistle. 1 Thessalonians 5:14

RETHREN: We exhort you, brethren, warn them that are unruly, comfort the feebleminded, support the weak, be patient toward all men. See that none render evil for evil unto any man; but ever follow that which is good, both among yourselves, and to all men. Rejoice evermore. Pray without ceasing. In every thing give thanks: for this is the will of God in Christ Jesus concerning you. Quench not the Spirit. Despise not prophesyings. Prove all things; hold fast that which is good. Abstain from all appearance of evil. And the very God of peace sanctify you wholly; and I pray God your whole spirit and soul and body be preserved blameless unto the coming of our Lord Jesus Christ.

Tract. O praise the Lord all ye heathen: praise him, all ye nations. ℣. For his merciful kindness is ever more and more towards us: and the truth of the Lord endureth for ever.

Gospel. Matthew 17:1

T THAT TIME: Jesus taketh Peter, James, and John his brother, and bringeth them up into an high mountain apart, And was transfigured before them: and his face did shine as the sun, and his raiment was white as the light. And, behold, there appeared unto them Moses and Elias talking with him. Then answered Peter, and said unto Jesus, Lord, it is good for us to be here: if thou wilt, let us make here three tabernacles; one for thee, and one for Moses, and one for Elias. While he yet spake, behold, a bright cloud overshadowed them: and behold a voice out of the cloud, which said, This is my beloved Son, in whom I am well pleased; hear ye him. And when the disciples heard it, they fell on their face, and were sore afraid. And Jesus came and touched them, and said, Arise, and be not afraid. And when they had lifted up their eyes, they saw no man, save Jesus only. And as they came down from the mountain, Jesus charged them, saying, Tell the vision to no man, until the Son of man be risen again from the dead.

Offertory. O Lord God of my salvation, I have cried day and night before thee: let my prayer enter into thy presence, O Lord.

Secret

ANCTIFY, we beseech thee, O Lord, our fasts by these present sacrifices: that those things, which our observance outwardly shews forth, it may inwardly effect. Through.

¶ 2ⁿᵈ Secret is of the Saints (p. 542) & 3ʳᵈ for the Living and Departed (p. 544).

Communion. O Lord my God, in thee have I put my trust: save me from all them that persecute me, and deliver me.

Postcommunion

LMIGHTY God, let thy holy mysteries both heal our vices, and bestow upon us everlasting remedies. Through.

¶ 2ⁿᵈ Postcommunion is of the Saints (p. 542) & 3ʳᵈ for the Living and Departed (p. 544).

PRIEST. Let us pray.
DEACON. Humble your heads before God.

AY thy faithful people, O God, be strengthened by the blessing which they desire: that they may never turn aside from thy will, and may evermore rejoice in thy bountiful goodness. Through.

Proper of Season *Lent II*

Second Sunday of Lent

First Class Semidouble

Introit

CALL to remembrance thy tender mercies, O Lord, and thy loving kindnesses, which have been ever of old: neither let our enemies triumph over us: deliver us, O God of Israel, out of all our troubles. *Ps.* Unto thee, O Lord, do I lift up my soul: my God, in thee have I trusted, let me not be confounded.

Collect

ALMIGHTY God, who seest that we have no power of ourselves to help ourselves; Keep us both outwardly in our bodies, and inwardly in our souls; that we may be defended from all adversities which may happen to the body, and from all evil thoughts which may assault and hurt the soul. Through.

¶ 2nd Collect is of the Saints (p. 542) & 3rd for the Living and Departed (p. 544).

Epistle. 1 Thessalonians 4:1

BRETHREN: we beseech you, and exhort you by the Lord Jesus, that as ye have received of us how ye ought to walk and to please God, so ye would abound more and more. For ye know what commandments we gave you by the Lord Jesus. For this is the will of God, even your sanctification, that ye should abstain from fornication: That every one of you should know how to possess his vessel in sanctification and honour; Not in the lust of concupiscence, even as the Gentiles which know not God That no man go beyond and defraud his brother in any matter: because that the Lord is the avenger of all such, as we also have forewarned you and testified. For God hath not called us unto uncleanness, but unto holiness. He therefore that despiseth, despiseth not man, but God, who hath also given unto us his holy Spirit.

Gradual. The sorrows of my heart are enlarged: O bring thou me out of my troubles, O Lord. ℣. Look upon my adversity and misery: and forgive me all my sin.

Tract. O give thanks unto the Lord, for he is gracious: and his mercy endureth for ever. ℣. Who can express the noble acts of the Lord: or shew forth all his praise? ℣. Blessed are they that alway keep judgment, and do righteousness. ℣. Remember us, O Lord, according to the favour that thou bearest unto thy people: O visit us with thy salvation.

Lent II

Proper of Season

Gospel. Matthew 15:21

T THAT TIME: Jesus went thence, and departed into the coasts of Tyre and Sidon. And, behold, a woman of Canaan came out of the same coasts, and cried unto him, saying, Have mercy on me, O Lord, thou Son of David; my daughter is grievously vexed with a devil. But he answered her not a word. And his disciples came and besought him, saying, Send her away; for she crieth after us. But he answered and said, I am not sent but unto the lost sheep of the house of Israel. Then came she and worshipped him, saying, Lord, help me. But he answered and said, It is not meet to take the children's bread, and to cast it to dogs. And she said, Truth, Lord: yet the dogs eat of the crumbs which fall from their masters' table. Then Jesus answered and said unto her, O woman, great is thy faith: be it unto thee even as thou wilt. And her daughter was made whole from that very hour.

Offertory. My delight shall be in thy commandments, which I have loved exceedingly: my hands also will I lift up unto thy commandments, which I have loved.

Secret

E beseech thee, O Lord, mercifully to have respect unto these our sacrifices: that they may increase our devotion and set forward our salvation. Through.

❡ 2ⁿᵈ Secret is of the Saints (p. 542) & 3ʳᵈ for the Living and Departed (p. 544).

Communion. Consider my meditation: O hearken thou unto the voice of my calling, my King and my God: for unto thee will I make my prayer, O Lord.

Postcommunion

E humbly beseech thee, almighty God: that as thou dost refresh us with thy sacraments, so thou wouldest vouchsafe unto us to do thee worthy and acceptable service. Through.

❡ 2ⁿᵈ Postcommunion is of the Saints (p. 542) & 3ʳᵈ for the Living and Departed (p. 544).

Proper of Season *Lent III*

Third Sunday of Lent

First Class Semidouble

Introit

MINE eyes are ever looking unto the Lord: for he shall pluck my feet out of the net: look thou upon me and have mercy upon me, for I am desolate, and in misery. *Ps.* Unto thee, O Lord, do I lift up my soul; my God, in thee have I trusted: let me not be confounded.

Collect

WE beseech thee, Almighty God, look upon the hearty desires of thy humble servants, and stretch forth the right hand of thy Majesty, to be our defence against all our enemies. Through.

¶ 2ⁿᵈ Collect is of the Saints (p. 542) & 3ʳᵈ for the Living and Departed (p. 544).

Epistle. Ephesians 5:1

BRETHREN: Be ye therefore followers of God, as dear children; And walk in love, as Christ also hath loved us, and hath given himself for us an offering and a sacrifice to God for a sweetsmelling savour. But fornication, and all uncleanness, or covetousness, let it not be once named among you, as becometh saints; Neither filthiness, nor foolish talking, nor jesting, which are not convenient: but rather giving of thanks. For this ye know, that no whoremonger, nor unclean person, nor covetous man, who is an idolater, hath any inheritance in the kingdom of Christ and of God. Let no man deceive you with vain words: for because of these things cometh the wrath of God upon the children of disobedience. Be not ye therefore partakers with them. For ye were sometimes darkness, but now are ye light in the Lord: walk as children of light: (For the fruit of the Spirit is in all goodness and righteousness and truth;) Proving what is acceptable unto the Lord. And have no fellowship with the unfruitful works of darkness, but rather reprove them. For it is a shame even to speak of those things which are done of them in secret. But all things that are reproved are made manifest by the light: for whatsoever doth make manifest is light. Wherefore he saith, Awake thou that sleepest, and arise from the dead, and Christ shall give thee light.

Gradual. Up, Lord, and let not man have the upper hand: let the heathen be judged in thy sight. ℣. While mine enemies are driven back: they shall fall and perish at thy presence.

Lent III   # Proper of Season

Tract. Unto thee lift I up mine eyes: O thou that dwellest in the heavens. ℣. Behold, even as the eyes of servants: look unto the hand of their masters. ℣. And as the eyes of a maiden unto the hand of her mistress: even so our eyes wait upon the Lord our God, until he have mercy upon us. ℣. Have mercy upon us, O Lord: have mercy upon us.

Gospel. Luke 11:14

T THAT TIME: Jesus was casting out a devil, and it was dumb. And it came to pass, when the devil was gone out, the dumb spake; and the people wondered. But some of them said, He casteth out devils through Beelzebub the chief of the devils. And others, tempting him, sought of him a sign from heaven. But he, knowing their thoughts, said unto them, Every kingdom divided against itself is brought to desolation; and a house divided against a house falleth. If Satan also be divided against himself, how shall his kingdom stand? because ye say that I cast out devils through Beelzebub. And if I by Beelzebub cast out devils, by whom do your sons cast them out? therefore shall they be your judges. But if I with the finger of God cast out devils, no doubt the kingdom of God is come upon you. When a strong man armed keepeth his palace, his goods are in peace: But when a stronger than he shall come upon him, and overcome him, he taketh from him all his armour wherein he trusted, and divideth his spoils. He that is not with me is against me: and he that gathereth not with me scattereth. When the unclean spirit is gone out of a man, he walketh through dry places, seeking rest; and finding none, he saith, I will return unto my house whence I came out. And when he cometh, he findeth it swept and garnished Then goeth he, and taketh to him seven other spirits more wicked than himself; and they enter in, and dwell there: and the last state of that man is worse than the first. And it came to pass, as he spake these things, a certain woman of the company lifted up her voice, and said unto him, Blessed is the womb that bare thee, and the paps which thou hast sucked. But he said, Yea rather, blessed are they that hear the word of God, and keep it.

Offertory. The statutes of the Lord are right, and rejoice the heart; his judgments also are sweeter than honey and the honey-comb: moreover, thy servant keepeth them.

Secret

E beseech thee, O Lord, that this oblation may cleanse us from our sins: and sanctify thy servants both in body and mind for the celebration of this sacrifice. Through.

¶ 2nd Secret is of the Saints (p. 542) & 3rd for the Living and Departed (p. 544).

Proper of Season *Lent IV*

Communion. The sparrow hath found her an house, and the swallow a nest, where she may lay her young : even thy altars, O Lord of hosts, my King and my God: blessed are they that dwell in thy house: they will be alway praising thee.

Postcommunion

O LORD, who sufferest us to be made partakers of so great a mystery: we beseech thee, that by thy mercy we may be delivered from all perils and iniquities. Through.

¶ 2nd Postcommunion is of the Saints (p. 542) & 3rd for the Living and Departed (p. 544).

Fourth Sunday of Lent

First Class Semidouble

Introit

REJOICE, O Jerusalem, and come together, all ye that love her; rejoice for joy, all ye that have mourned: that ye may be glad, and be satisfied with the breasts of your consolation. *Ps.* I was glad when they said unto me: We will go into the house of the Lord.

Collect

GRANT, we beseech thee, Almighty God, that we, who for our evil deeds do worthily deserve to be punished, by the comfort of thy grace may mercifully be relieved; through our Lord and Saviour Jesus Christ. Who liveth.

¶ 2nd Collect is of the Saints (p. 542) & 3rd for the Living and Departed (p. 544).

Epistle. Galatians 4:21

BRETHREN: tell me, ye that desire to be under the law, do ye not hear the law? For it is written, that Abraham had two sons, the one by a bondmaid, the other by a freewoman. But he who was of the bondwoman was born after the flesh; but he of the freewoman was by promise. Which things are an allegory: for these are the two covenants; the one from the mount Sinai, which gendereth to bondage, which is Agar. For this Agar is mount Sinai in Arabia, and answereth to Jerusalem which now is, and is in bondage with her children. But Jerusalem which is above is free, which is the mother of us all. For it is written, Rejoice, thou barren that bearest not; break forth and cry, thou that travailest not: for the desolate hath many more children than she which hath an husband. Now we, brethren, as Isaac was, are the children of promise. But as then he that was born after the flesh persecuted him that was born after the Spirit, even so it is now. Nevertheless what saith the scripture? Cast out the bondwoman and her son: for the son of the bondwoman shall not be heir with the son of the freewoman. So then, brethren, we are not children of the bondwoman, but of the free.

Gradual. I was glad when they said unto me: We will go into the house of the Lord. ℣. Peace be within thy walls: and plenteousness within thy palaces.

Tract. They that put their trust in the Lord shall be even as the mount Sion: which may not be removed, but standeth fast for ever. ℣. The hills stand about Jerusalem: even so standeth the Lord round about his people, from this time forth for evermore.

Gospel. John 6:1

AT THAT TIME: Jesus went over the sea of Galilee, which is the sea of Tiberias. And a great multitude followed him, because they saw his miracles which he did on them that were diseased. And Jesus went up into a mountain, and there he sat with his disciples. And the passover, a feast of the Jews, was nigh. When Jesus then lifted up his eyes, and saw a great company come unto him, he saith unto Philip, Whence shall we buy bread, that these may eat? And this he said to prove him: for he himself knew what he would do. Philip answered him, Two hundred pennyworth of bread is not sufficient for them, that every one of them may take a little. One of his disciples, Andrew, Simon Peter's brother, saith unto him, There is a lad here, which hath five barley loaves, and two small fishes: but what are they among so many? And Jesus said, Make the men sit down. Now there was much grass in the place. So the men sat down, in number about five thousand. And Jesus took the loaves; and when he had given thanks, he distributed to the disciples, and the disciples to them that were set down; and likewise of the fishes as much as they would. When they were filled, he said unto his disciples, Gather up the fragments that remain, that nothing be lost. Therefore they gathered them together, and filled twelve baskets with the fragments of the five barley loaves, which remained over and above unto them that had eaten. Then those men, when they had seen the miracle that Jesus did, said, This is of a truth that prophet that should come into the world.

Offertory. O praise the Lord, for he is gracious: O sing praises unto his name, for he is lovely: whatsoever he pleased, that did he in heaven, and in earth.

Proper of Season *Passion Sunday*

Secret

E beseech thee, O Lord, mercifully to have respect unto these our sacrifices: that they may increase our devotion and set forward our salvation. Through.

¶ 2nd Secret is of the Saints (p. 542) & 3rd for the Living and Departed (p. 544).

Communion. Jerusalem is built as a city, that is at unity in itself: for thither the tribes go up, even the tribes of the Lord, to give thanks unto thy name, O Lord.

Postcommunion

MERCIFUL God, who never failest to fulfil us with thy holy mysteries: grant to us, we beseech thee, that we may ever approach them in lowliness and sincerity, and receive them in faithfulness of heart. Through.

¶ 2nd Postcommunion is of the Saints (p. 542) & 3rd for the Living and Departed (p. 544).

Passion Sunday

First Class Semidouble

¶ From this Sunday until Maundy Thursday, inclusive, in Masses of the Season the Psalm, Give sentence, is not said before the Confession nor Glory be at the Introit and after the Psalm Lavabo.

Introit

IVE sentence with me, O God, and defend my cause against the ungodly people: O deliver me from the deceitful and wicked man: for thou art the God of my strength. *Ps.* O send out thy light and thy truth: that they may lead me and bring me unto thy holy hill, and to thy dwelling.

Collect

WE beseech thee, Almighty God, mercifully to look upon thy people; that by thy great goodness they may be governed and preserved evermore, both in body and soul. Through.

¶ From today until Saturday before Low Sunday inclusive, after the Collect of the Day is said the Collect Against the Persecutors of the Church (p. 543) or for the Chief Bishop (p. 543).

Passion Sunday # Proper of Season

Epistle. Hebrews 9:11

BRETHREN: Christ being come an high priest of good things to come, by a greater and more perfect tabernacle, not made with hands, that is to say, not of this building; Neither by the blood of goats and calves, but by his own blood he entered in once into the holy place, having obtained eternal redemption for us. For if the blood of bulls and of goats, and the ashes of an heifer sprinkling the unclean, sanctifieth to the purifying of the flesh: How much more shall the blood of Christ, who through the eternal Spirit offered himself without spot to God, purge your conscience from dead works to serve the living God? And for this cause he is the mediator of the new testament, that by means of death, for the redemption of the transgressions that were under the first testament, they which are called might receive the promise of eternal inheritance, in Christ Jesus our Lord.

Gradual. Deliver me, O Lord, from mine enemies: teach me to do the thing that pleaseth thee. ℣. It is thou, Lord, that deliverest me from my cruel enemies: and settest me up above mine adversaries: thou shalt rid me from the wicked man.

Tract. Many a time have they fought against me from my youth up. ℣. May Israel now say: yea, many a time have they vexed me from my youth up. ℣. But they have not prevailed against me: the plowers plowed upon my back. ℣. And made long furrows: but the righteous Lord hath hewn the snares of the ungodly in pieces.

Gospel. John 8:46

AT THAT TIME: Jesus said unto the multitudes of the Jews: Which of you convinceth me of sin? And if I say the truth, why do ye not believe me? He that is of God heareth God's words: ye therefore hear them not, because ye are not of God. Then answered the Jews, and said unto him, Say we not well that thou art a Samaritan, and hast a devil? Jesus answered, I have not a devil; but I honour my Father, and ye do dishonour me. And I seek not mine own glory: there is one that seeketh and judgeth. Verily, verily, I say unto you, If a man keep my saying, he shall never see death. Then said the Jews unto him, Now we know that thou hast a devil. Abraham is dead, and the prophets; and thou sayest, If a man keep my saying, he shall never taste of death. Art thou greater than our father Abraham, which is dead? and the prophets are dead: whom makest thou thyself? Jesus answered, If I honour myself, my honour is nothing: it is my Father that honoureth me; of whom ye say, that he is your God: Yet ye have not known him; but I know him: and if I should say, I know

Proper of Season — *Passion Sunday*

him not, I shall be a liar like unto you: but I know him, and keep his saying. Your father Abraham rejoiced to see my day: and he saw it, and was glad. Then said the Jews unto him, Thou art not yet fifty years old, and hast thou seen Abraham? Jesus said unto them, Verily, verily, I say unto you, Before Abraham was, I AM. Then took they up stones to cast at him: but Jesus hid himself, and went out of the temple.

Offertory. I will give thanks unto thee, O Lord, with my whole heart: O do well unto thy servant, that I may live, and keep thy word: quicken thou me, O Lord, according to thy word.

Secret

E beseech thee, O Lord, that these our oblations may both loose the bonds of our iniquity, and obtain for us the gifts of thy loving kindness. Through.

¶ The Secret Against the Persecutors of the Church (p. 543) or for the Chief Bishop (p. 543) is said.

Communion. This is my body, which is given for you: this cup is the new Testament in my blood, saith the Lord: this do ye, as oft as ye drink it, in remembrance of me.

Postcommunion

SSIST us, O Lord our God: that we, whom thou hast here refreshed with thy mysteries, may be defended by thy perpetual succour. Through.

¶ The Postcommunion Against the Persecutors of the Church (p. 543) or for the Chief Bishop (p. 543) is said.

Palm Sunday

Proper of Season

Palm Sunday

First Class Semidouble

Blessing of Palms

¶ In Choir, Mattins having been said, the sprinkling of water is performed in the usual manner. Then the Priest, vested in a violet Cope, or without the Chasuble, with the Ministers vested in like manner, proceeds to bless branches of palm and olive or other trees placed in the midst before the Altar, or at the Epistle corner. And first the Choir sing the Antiphon:

Ant. Hosanna to the Son of David: blessed is he that cometh in the name of the Lord. O King of Israel: Hosanna in the Highest.

¶ Then the Priest standing at the Epistle corner, without turning toward the people, sings with joined hands in the tone of the Ferial Collect:

℣. The Lord be with you. | ℣. Dóminus vobíscum.
℟. And with thy spirit. | ℟. Et cum spíritu tuo.

Let us pray.

O GOD, whose love and service is our justice, multiply upon us the gifts of thy unspeakable grace: and like as by the death of thy Son thou hast given unto us the hope of our faith; so grant that by his resurrection we may be brought unto the country which we seek. Who liveth and reigneth with thee.

¶ Then the Subdeacon in the accustomed place sings the following Lesson in the tone of the Epistle, and at the end kisses the hand of the Priest.

Lesson. Exodus 15:27

IN THOSE DAYS: The children of Israel came to Elim, where were twelve wells of water, and threescore and ten palm trees: and they encamped there by the waters. And they took their journey from Elim, and all the congregation of the children of Israel came unto the wilderness of Sin, which is between Elim and Sinai, on the fifteenth day of the second month after their departing out of the land of Egypt. And the whole congregation of the children of Israel murmured against Moses and Aaron in the wilderness: And the children of Israel said unto them, Would to God we had died by the hand of the LORD in the land of Egypt, when we sat by the flesh pots, and when we did eat bread to the full; for ye have brought us forth into this wilderness, to kill this whole assembly with hunger. Then said the LORD unto Moses, Behold, I will rain bread from heaven for you; and the people shall go out and gather a certain rate every day, that I may prove them, whether they will walk in my law, or no.

Proper of Season *Palm Sunday*

And it shall come to pass, that on the sixth day they shall prepare that which they bring in; and it shall be twice as much as they gather daily. And Moses and Aaron said unto all the children of Israel, At even, then ye shall know that the LORD hath brought you out from the land of Egypt: And in the morning, then ye shall see the glory of the LORD.

Gradual. The chief priests and the Pharisees gathered a council, and said: What do we, for this man doeth many miracles? If we let him thus alone, all men will believe on him: * And the Romans shall come, and take away both our place and nation. ℟. And one of them named Caiaphas, being the high priest that same year, prophesied saying: It is expedient for us, that one man should die for the people, and that the whole nation perish not. Then from that day forth they took counsel together to put him to death, saying. * And the Romans shall come, and take away both our place and nation. ℟. On the Mount of Olives he prayed to his Father; Father, if it be possible, let this cup pass from me. * The spirit indeed is willing, but the flesh is weak; thy will be done. ℣. Watch and pray, that ye enter not into temptation. * The spirit indeed is willing, but the flesh is weak; thy will be done.

※ During the singing of the ℟., the Deacon places the Book of the Gospels on the Altar: and the Priest, the Deacon ministering the incense-boat, places incense in the censer. Then the Deacon says: **Cleanse my heart,** takes the Book from the Altar, and asks a blessing from the Priest: then, while the Subdeacon holds the Book, he stands between two Acolytes holding lighted candles, signs the book and censes it, and sings the Gospel, as below, in the usual way: after which the Subdeacon carries the Book to be kissed by the Priest, who is censed by the Deacon.

Gospel. Matthew 21:1

AT THAT TIME: When Jesus drew nigh unto Jerusalem, and was come to Bethphage, unto the mount of Olives, then sent he two disciples, Saying unto them, Go into the village over against you, and straightway ye shall find an ass tied, and a colt with her: loose them, and bring them unto me. And if any man say ought unto you, ye shall say, The Lord hath need of them; and straightway he will send them. All this was done, that it might be fulfilled which was spoken by the prophet, saying, Tell ye the daughter of Sion, Behold, thy King cometh unto thee, meek, and sitting upon an ass, and a colt the foal of an ass. And the disciples went, and did as Jesus commanded them, And brought the ass, and the colt, and put on them their clothes, and they set him thereon. And a very great multitude spread their garments in the way; others cut down branches from the trees, and strawed them in the way. And the multitudes that went before, and that followed, cried, saying, Hosanna to the Son of David: Blessed is he that cometh in the name of the Lord.

Palm Sunday # Proper of Season

⁋ After this the branches are blessed. The Priest, standing at the same Epistle corner, says in the tone of the Ferial Collect,

| ℣. The Lord be with you. | ℣. Dóminus vobíscum. |
| ℟. And with thy spirit. | ℟. Et cum spíritu tuo. |

Let us pray.

INCREASE, O God, the faith of them that put their trust in thee, and graciously hear the prayers of thy humble servants; let thy manifold mercies descend upon us: and let these branches of palm or olive be ble ✠ ssed : and, as in a figure of the Church thou didst multiply Noah going forth from the ark, and Moses when he went out of Egypt with the children of Israel: so may we, bearing palms and branches of olive, go forth with good works to meet Christ: and through him enter into everlasting joy: Who liveth and reigneth with thee in the unity of the Holy Ghost, God: throughout all ages, world without end. *Amen.*

℣. The Lord be with you.	℣. Dóminus vobíscum.
℟. And with thy spirit.	℟. Et cum spíritu tuo.
℣. Lift up your hearts.	℣. Sursum corda.
℟. We lift them up unto the Lord.	℟. Habémus ad Dóminum.
℣. Let us give thanks unto our Lord God.	℣. Grátias agámus Dómino, Deo nostro.
℟. It is meet and right so to do.	℟. Dignum et justum est.

It is very meet, right, and our bounden duty, that we should at all times, and in all places, give thanks unto thee: O Lord holy Father almighty, everlasting God: Who art glorified in the council of thy Saints. For thee thy creatures serve: and acknowledge thee their only maker and their God, and thee all thy works do praise, and thee thy Saints do bless. For with fearless voice, before the kings and rulers of this world, they confess the great name of thine only begotten Son. Before whom Angels and Archangels, Thrones and Dominations stand: and with all the host of the heavenly army, do sing the hymn of thy glory, evermore saying:

⁋ And the **Sanctus** is sung by the Choir,

HOLY, HOLY, HOLY, Lord God of hosts, Heaven and earth are full of thy glory: Glory be to thee, O Lord Most High. Blessed ✠ is he that cometh in the Name of the Lord. Hosanna in the Highest.

SANCTUS, SANCTUS, SANCTUS, Dóminus, Deus Sábaoth. Pleni sunt cæli et terra glória tua. Glória tibi, Dómine altíssime. Benedíctus, ✠ qui venit in nómine Dómini. Hosánna in excélsis.

Proper of Season *Palm Sunday*

| ℣. The Lord be with you. | ℣. Dóminus vobíscum. |
| ℟. And with thy spirit. | ℟. Et cum spíritu tuo. |

Let us pray.

WE beseech thee, O Lord holy Father almighty, everlasting God: that thou wouldest vouchsafe to bl ✠ ess and sanc ✠ tify this creature of olive, which thou hast bidden to spring from the wood of the tree, which likewise the dove, returning to the ark, did bear in her mouth: that all who shall receive thereof, may obtain for themselves protection both in body and soul: and let it be, O Lord, a remedy for our salvation, a sacrament of thy grace. Through.

Let us pray.

O GOD, who dost gather together the things which are dispersed abroad, and dost preserve that which thou dost gather: who didst bless the people when they went forth bearing branches to meet Jesus: bl ✠ ess also these branches of palm and olive which thy servants receive with faith to the honour of thy name; that into whatsoever place they shall be brought, the dwellers in that place may obtain thy blessing: that all adversity being put to flight, thy right hand may protect those who are redeemed by Jesus Christ thy Son our Lord. Who liveth and reigneth with thee.

Let us pray.

O GOD, who by a wonderful order of thy providence wast pleased, even by means of things insensible, to shew forth the dispensation of our salvation: grant, we beseech thee; that the devout hearts of thy faithful people may profitably understand what is mystically signified by that deed when, on this day, the multitude, inspired by the heavenly light, went forth to meet the Redeemer, and strawed branches of palm and olive beneath his feet. The branches, then, of palm foreshadow his triumph over the prince of death; and the boughs of olive in a manner proclaim that the anointing of the Spirit is come. For the multitude rejoiced to know that even then it was prefigured: that our Redeemer, having compassion on the misery of mankind, was about to battle with the prince of death, and by his death to triumph. And therefore obediently they laid before him such things as should signify in him both the triumphs of his victory and the abundance of his mercy. Wherefore we likewise with sure faith, having in memory both the deed and the signification of the same, humbly beseech thee, O Lord holy Father almighty, everlasting God, through the same Jesus Christ our Lord: that in him and through him, whose members thou hast been pleased to make us, we may win the victory over the empire of death, and be found worthy to be partakers of his glorious resurrection. Who liveth and reigneth with thee.

Palm Sunday # Proper of Season

Let us pray.

GOD, who by an olive-branch didst command the dove to proclaim peace on earth: vouchsafe, we beseech thee; to sanctify with thy heavenly bless ✠ ing these branches of olive and other trees; that for all thy people they may be profitable unto salvation. Through Christ, our Lord. *Amen.*

Let us pray.

L ✠ ESS, we beseech thee, O Lord, these branches of palm or olive: and grant; that as thy people on this day do outwardly perform these things to thy honour, so they, spiritually fulfilling the same with pure devotion, may win the victory over the enemy, and cleave steadfastly to every work of mercy. Through.

℣ Then the Celebrant, after putting incense into the thurible, thrice sprinkles the boughs with holy water, saying the Antiphon, Thou shalt purge me, without note and without the Psalm: and then thrice incenses them. Then he says:

| ℣. The Lord be with you. | ℣. Dóminus vobíscum. |
| ℟. And with thy spirit. | ℟. Et cum spíritu tuo. |

Let us pray.

GOD, who didst send forth thy Son, Jesus Christ our Lord, into the world for our salvation, that he might humble himself to be made like unto us, and call us back to thee: before whom, at his coming to Jerusalem for the fulfilling of the Scriptures, the multitude of the people that believed with faithful devotion strawed their raiment and palm branches in the way: grant, we beseech thee; that we may so prepare for him the way of faith, that, every stone of stumbling and rock of offence being done away, our works may blossom before thee with branches of righteousness: and that we may be found worthy to follow in his footsteps. Who liveth and reigneth with thee.

℣ The blessing being completed, the senior of the Clergy goes up to the Altar and presents a blessed branch to the Celebrant, who does not genuflect, nor kiss the hand of him who gives it. Then the Celebrant, standing before the Altar, turns to the people and distributes the branches, first to the senior from whom he received his, then to the Deacon and Subdeacon vested, and to the other clergy severally in order, last of all to the laity: all genuflecting and kissing the branch and the hand of the Celebrant, except Prelates, if they are present. And when he begins to distribute, the Choir sings the following Antiphons:

Ant. The children of the Hebrews bearing branches of olive, went out to meet the Lord, crying out and saying: Hosanna in the highest.

Another Ant. The children of the Hebrews spread their garments in the way and cried out, saying: Hosanna to the Son of David; blessed is he that cometh in the name of the Lord.

Proper of Season *Palm Sunday*

℣ If these be not sufficient, they are repeated until the distribution is finished. Then the Priest says:

℣. The Lord be with you. ℣. Dóminus vobíscum.
℟. And with thy spirit. ℟. Et cum spíritu tuo.

Let us pray.

ALMIGHTY and everlasting God, who didst ordain that our Lord Jesus Christ should ride upon the foal of an ass, and didst teach the multitudes of the people to straw in his way their raiment and branches of trees, and likewise to sing Hosanna in his praise: grant, we beseech thee; that we may by thee be enabled to follow their innocency, and be partakers of their merit. Through the same Christ, our Lord. *Amen.*

℣ Then the Procession is made. And first the Celebrant puts incense in the censer: and the Deacon, turning to the people, says: Let us proceed in peace, and the Choir responds: In the name of Christ. Amen.

℣ The Thurifer goes first with the smoking censer: then the Subdeacon vested, carrying the Cross, between two Acolytes with lighted candles: the Clergy follow in order, and last of all the Celebrant with the Deacon on his left, all with branches in their hands: and the following Antiphons are sung, either all, or some, so long as the Procession lasts.

Ant. When the Lord drew nigh unto Jerusalem, he sent two of his disciples, saying: Go into the village over against you: and ye shall find the colt of an ass tied, whereon never man sat: loose him, and bring him unto me. If any man say ought unto you, ye shall say: The Lord hath need of him. They loose him and bring him to Jesus: and put on him their clothes, and set him thereon: some spread their garments in the way: others strawed branches from the trees: and they that followed, cried: Hosanna, blessed is he that cometh in the name of the Lord: blessed is the kingdom of our father David: Hosanna in the highest: Son of David, have mercy upon us.

Another Ant. When the people heard that Jesus was coming to Jerusalem, they took branches of palm-trees: and went forth to meet him, and the children cried saying: This is he that should come for the salvation of the people. This is our salvation and the redemption of Israel. How great is he whom Thrones and Dominations go forth to meet! Fear not, daughter of Sion: behold thy King cometh to thee, sitting upon an ass' colt, as it is written. Hail, O King, Creator of the world, who art come to redeem us.

Another Ant. Six days before the solemnity of the Passover, when the Lord came into the city of Jerusalem, the children went forth to meet him: and in their hands carried branches of palm trees, and cried with a loud voice, saying: Hosanna in the highest: blessed art thou, that art come in the multitude of thy mercies: Hosanna in the highest.

Palm Sunday # Proper of Season

Another Ant. The multitudes with flowers and palms go forth to meet the Redeemer: and render worthy homage to the triumphant conqueror: the Gentiles with their lips proclaim the Son of God: and in the praise of Christ their voices thunder through the skies: Hosanna in the highest.

Another Ant. With the Angels and the children may we be found faithful, crying unto the vanquisher of death: Hosanna in the highest.

Another Ant. A great multitude, that were come together to the feast, cried unto the Lord: Blessed is he that cometh in the name of the Lord: Hosanna in the highest.

¶ As the Procession turns back, two or four Cantors enter the church, and the door being shut, with their faces toward the Procession, sing the first verse of the following hymn, Gloria laus, etc.; which verse is repeated by the Priest and others outside the church. Then those within sing the other verses which follow; either all or a part, as shall seem good: and those who are without respond to each verse: Gloria laus, as at the ℣. at the beginning.

GLORY and honour and praise be to thee, our King and Redeemer, Christ, to whom children of old loved their Hosannas to raise. ℟. Glory and honour.

Israel's Monarch art thou, and the glorious Offspring of David,

Thou that approachest, a King, blest in the Name of the Lord. ℟. Glory and honour.

Glory to thee in the highest, the heavenly armies are singing: Glory to thee upon earth, man and creation reply. ℟. Glory and honour.

Met thee with palms in their hands that day the folk of the Hebrews,

We with our prayers and our hymns now to thy presence approach. ℟. Glory and honour.

They to thee proffered their praise for to herald thy dolorous Passion;

We to the King on his throne utter the jubilant hymn. ℟. Glory and honour.

They were then pleasing to thee, unto thee our devotion be pleasing;

Merciful King, kind King, who in all goodness art pleased. ℟. Glory and honour.

or,

ALL glory, laud, and honour To thee, Redeemer, King, To whom the lips of children Made sweet hosannas ring. ℟. All glory, laud.

Thou art the King of Israel, Thou David's royal Son, Who in the Lord's name comest, The King and blessed One. ℟. All glory, laud.

The company of Angels Are praising thee on high, And mortal men and all things Created make reply. ℟. All glory, laud.

Proper of Season *Palm Sunday*

The people of the Hebrews With palms before thee went; Our praise and prayer and anthems Before thee we present. ℟. All glory, laud.

To thee before thy passion They sang their hymns of praise; To thee now high exalted Our melody we raise. ℟. All glory, laud.

Thou didst accept their praises, Accept the prayers we bring, Who in all good delightest, Thou good and gracious King. ℟. All glory, laud.

¶ Then the Subdeacon with the foot of the Cross knocks at the door, which being straightway opened, the Procession enters the church singing:

℟. When the Lord entered the holy city, the children of the Hebrews, foretelling the resurrection of life, * With branches of palm cried: Hosanna in the highest. ℣. When the people heard that Jesus was coming to Jerusaiem, they went forth to meet him. With branches of palm cried: Hosanna in the highest.

¶ Then Mass is celebrated, and branches are held in the hands, while the Passion and Gospel are sung only.

Introit

BE not thou far from me, O Lord, thou art my succour, haste thee to help me: save me from the lion's mouth, thou hast heard me also from among the horns of the unicorns. *Ps.* My God, my God, look upon me, why hast thou forsaken me: and art so far from my health, and from the words of my complaint?

Collect

ALMIGHTY and everlasting God, who of thy tender love towards mankind, hast sent thy Son, our Saviour Jesus Christ, to take upon him our flesh, and to suffer death upon the cross, that all mankind should follow the example of his great humility; Mercifully grant, that we may both follow the example of his patience, and also be made partakers of his resurrection. Through the same.

¶ This Collect only is said, even if a Commemoration has been made in the Office.

¶ This Collect is to be said every day, after the Collect appointed for the day, until Good Friday.

Palm Sunday # Proper of Season

Epistle. Philippians 2:5

BRETHREN: Let this mind be in you, which was also in Christ Jesus: Who, being in the form of God, thought it not robbery to be equal with God: But made himself of no reputation, and took upon him the form of a servant, and was made in the likeness of men: And being found in fashion as a man, he humbled himself, and became obedient unto death, even the death of the cross. Wherefore God also hath highly exalted him, and given him a name which is above every name: (Genuflect.) That at the name of Jesus every knee should bow, of things in heaven, and things in earth, and things under the earth; And that every tongue should confess that Jesus Christ is Lord, to the glory of God the Father.

Gradual. Thou hast holden me by my right hand; thou shalt guide me with thy counsel: and after that receive me with glory. ℣. Truly God is loving unto Israel, even unto such as are of a clean heart; nevertheless, my feet were almost gone; my treadings had well nigh slipt: and why? I was grieved at the wicked, I do also see the ungodly in such prosperity.

Tract. My God, my God, look upon me: why hast thou forsaken me? ℣. And art so far from my health, and from the words of my complaint? ℣. O my God, I cry in the daytime, but thou hearest not: and in the night season also I take no rest. ℣. And thou continuest holy, O thou worship of Israel. ℣. Our fathers hoped in thee: they trusted in thee, and thou didst deliver them. ℣. They called upon thee, and were holpen: they put their trust in thee, and were not confounded. ℣. But as for me, I am a worm, and no man: a very scorn of men, and the outcast of the people. ℣. All they that see me laugh me to scorn: they shoot out their lips, and shake their head, saying: ℣.He trusted in God that he would deliver him: let him deliver him, if he will have him. ℣. They stand staring and looking upon me: they part my garments among them, and cast lots upon my vesture. ℣. Save me from the lion's mouth: thou hast heard me also from among the horns of the unicorns. ℣. O praise the Lord, ye that fear him: magnify him, all ye of the seed of Jacob. ℣. They shall be counted unto the Lord for a generation: they shall come, and the heavens shall declare his righteousness. ℣. Unto a people that shall be born, whom the Lord hath made.

¶ The Passion begins at once: **Cleanse my heart** is not said, nor is a blessing asked, and lights and incense are not carried; neither is **The Lord be with you** said, nor the response, **Glory be to thee, O Lord,** and the Celebrant or Deacon, while be announces The Passion of our Lord, does not sign the book nor himself. Which is observed likewise on other days, when the Passion is read.

Proper of Season   *Palm Sunday*

Gospel. Matthew 26:1

AT THAT TIME: Jesus said unto his disciples: ✠ Ye know that after two days is the feast of the passover, and the Son of man is betrayed to be crucified. *C.* Then assembled together the chief priests, and the scribes, and the elders of the people, unto the palace of the high priest, who was called Caiaphas, and consulted that they might take Jesus by subtilty, and kill him. But they said, *S.* Not on the feast day, lest there be an uproar among the people.

C. Now when Jesus was in Bethany, in the house of Simon the leper, there came unto him a woman having an alabaster box of very precious ointment, and poured it on his head, as he sat at meat. But when his disciples saw it, they had indignation, saying, *S.* To what purpose is this waste? For this ointment might have been sold for much, and given to the poor. *C.* When Jesus understood it, he said unto them, ✠ Why trouble ye the woman? for she hath wrought a good work upon me. For ye have the poor always with you; but me ye have not always. For in that she hath poured this ointment on my body, she did it for my burial. Verily I say unto you, Wheresoever this gospel shall be preached in the whole world, there shall also this, that this woman hath done, be told for a memorial of her.

C. Then one of the twelve, called Judas Iscariot, went unto the chief priests, and said unto them, *S.* What will ye give me, and I will deliver him unto you? *C.* And they covenanted with him for thirty pieces of silver. And from that time he sought opportunity to betray him.

Now the first day of the feast of unleavened bread the disciples came to Jesus, saying unto him, *S.* Where wilt thou that we prepare for thee to eat the passover? *C.* And he said, ✠ Go into the city to such a man, and say unto him, The Master saith, My time is at hand; I will keep the passover at thy house with my disciples. *C.* And the disciples did as Jesus had appointed them; and they made ready the passover.

Now when the even was come, he sat down with the twelve. And as they did eat, he said, ✠ Verily I say unto you, that one of you shall betray me. *C.* And they were exceeding sorrowful, and began every one of them to say unto him, *S.* Lord, is it I? *C.* And he answered and said, ✠ He that dippeth his hand with me in the dish, the same shall betray me. The Son of man goeth as it is written of him: but woe unto that man by whom the Son of man is betrayed! it had been good for that man if he had not been born. *C.* Then Judas, which betrayed him, answered and said, *S.* Master, is it I? *C.* He said unto him, ✠ Thou hast said.

C. And as they were eating, Jesus took bread, and blessed it, and brake it, and gave it to the disciples, and said, ✠ Take, eat; this is my body. *C.* And he took the cup, and gave thanks, and gave it to them, saying, ✠ Drink ye all of it; for

Palm Sunday

Proper of Season

this is my blood of the new testament, which is shed for many for the remission of sins. But I say unto you, I will not drink henceforth of this fruit of the vine, until that day when I drink it new with you in my Father's kingdom.

C. And when they had sung an hymn, they went out into the mount of Olives. Then saith Jesus unto them, ✠ All ye shall be offended because of me this night: for it is written, I will smite the shepherd, and the sheep of the flock shall be scattered abroad. But after I am risen again, I will go before you into Galilee. *C.* Peter answered and said unto him, *S.* Though all men shall be offended because of thee, yet will I never be offended. *C.* Jesus said unto him, ✠ Verily I say unto thee, That this night, before the cock crow, thou shalt deny me thrice. *C.* Peter said unto him, *S.* Though I should die with thee, yet will I not deny thee. *C.* Likewise also said all the disciples.

Then cometh Jesus with them unto a place called Gethsemane, and saith unto the disciples, ✠ Sit ye here, while I go and pray yonder. *C.* And he took with him Peter and the two sons of Zebedee, and began to be sorrowful and very heavy. Then saith he unto them, ✠ My soul is exceeding sorrowful, even unto death: tarry ye here, and watch with me. *C.* And he went a little further, and fell on his face, and prayed, saying, ✠ O my Father, if it be possible, let this cup pass from me: nevertheless not as I will, but as thou wilt.

C. And he cometh unto the disciples, and findeth them asleep, and saith unto Peter, ✠ What, could ye not watch with me one hour? Watch and pray, that ye enter not into temptation: the spirit indeed is willing, but the flesh is weak.

C. He went away again the second time, and prayed, saying, ✠ O my Father, if this cup may not pass away from me, except I drink it, thy will be done. *C.* And he came and found them asleep again: for their eyes were heavy. And he left them, and went away again, and prayed the third time, saying the same words.

Then cometh he to his disciples, and saith unto them, ✠ Sleep on now, and take your rest: behold, the hour is at hand, and the Son of man is betrayed into the hands of sinners. Rise, let us be going: behold, he is at hand that doth betray me.

C. And while he yet spake, lo, Judas, one of the twelve, came, and with him a great multitude with swords and staves, from the chief priests and elders of the people. Now he that betrayed him gave them a sign, saying, *S.* Whomsoever I shall kiss, that same is he: hold him fast. *C.* And forthwith he came to Jesus, and said, *S.* Hail, master; *C.* and kissed him. And Jesus said unto him, ✠ Friend, wherefore art thou come? *C.* Then came they, and laid hands on Jesus, and took him.

And, behold, one of them which were with Jesus stretched out his hand, and drew his sword, and struck a servant of the high priest's, and smote off his ear. Then said Jesus unto him, ✠ Put up again thy sword into his place: for all they

Proper of Season *Palm Sunday*

that take the sword shall perish with the sword. Thinkest thou that I cannot now pray to my Father, and he shall presently give me more than twelve legions of angels? But how then shall the scriptures be fulfilled, that thus it must be?

C. In that same hour said Jesus to the multitudes, ✠ Are ye come out as against a thief with swords and staves for to take me? I sat daily with you teaching in the temple, and ye laid no hold on me. But all this was done, that the scriptures of the prophets might be fulfilled. *C.* Then all the disciples forsook him, and fled.

And they that had laid hold on Jesus led him away to Caiaphas the high priest, where the scribes and the elders were assembled. But Peter followed him afar off unto the high priest's palace, and went in, and sat with the servants, to see the end. Now the chief priests, and elders, and all the council, sought false witness against Jesus, to put him to death; but found none: yea, though many false witnesses came, yet found they none. At the last came two false witnesses, and said, *S.* This fellow said, I am able to destroy the temple of God, and to build it in three days. *C.* And the high priest arose, and said unto him, *S.* Answerest thou nothing? what is it which these witness against thee? *C.* But Jesus held his peace. And the high priest answered and said unto him, *S.* I adjure thee by the living God, that thou tell us whether thou be the Christ, the Son of God. *C.* Jesus saith unto him, ✠ Thou hast said: nevertheless I say unto you, Hereafter shall ye see the Son of man sitting on the right hand of power, and coming in the clouds of heaven. *C.* Then the high priest rent his clothes, saying, *S.* He hath spoken blasphemy; what further need have we of witnesses? behold, now ye have heard his blasphemy. What think ye? *C.* They answered and said, *S.* He is guilty of death.

C. Then did they spit in his face, and buffeted him; and others smote him with the palms of their hands, saying, *S.* Prophesy unto us, thou Christ, Who is he that smote thee?

C. Now Peter sat without in the palace: and a damsel came unto him, saying, *S.* Thou also wast with Jesus of Galilee. *C.* But he denied before them all, saying, *S.* I know not what thou sayest. *C.* And when he was gone out into the porch, another maid saw him, and said unto them that were there, *S.* This fellow was also with Jesus of Nazareth. *C.* And again he denied with an oath, *S.* I do not know the man. *C.* And after a while came unto him they that stood by, and said to Peter, *S.* Surely thou also art one of them; for thy speech bewrayeth thee. *C.* Then began he to curse and to swear, saying, *S.* I know not the man. *C.* And immediately the cock crew. And Peter remembered the word of Jesus, which said unto him, ✠ Before the cock crow, thou shalt deny me thrice. *C.* And he went out, and wept bitterly.

When the morning was come, all the chief priests and elders of the people took counsel against Jesus to put him to death: and when they had bound him,

Palm Sunday   **Proper of Season**

they led him away, and delivered him to Pontius Pilate the governor.

Then Judas, which had betrayed him, when he saw that he was condemned, repented himself, and brought again the thirty pieces of silver to the chief priests and elders, saying, *S.* I have sinned in that I have betrayed the innocent blood. *C.* And they said, *S.* What is that to us? see thou to that. *C.* And he cast down the pieces of silver in the temple, and departed, and went and hanged himself. And the chief priests took the silver pieces, and said, *S.* It is not lawful for to put them into the treasury, because it is the price of blood. *C.* And they took counsel, and bought with them the potter's field, to bury strangers in. Wherefore that field was called, The field of blood, unto this day. Then was fulfilled that which was spoken by Jeremy the prophet, saying, And they took the thirty pieces of silver, the price of him that was valued, whom they of the children of Israel did value; and gave them for the potter's field, as the Lord appointed me.

And Jesus stood before the governor: and the governor asked him, saying, *S.* Art thou the King of the Jews? *C.* And Jesus said unto him, ✠ Thou sayest. *C.* And when he was accused of the chief priests and elders, he answered nothing. Then said Pilate unto him, *S.* Hearest thou not how many things they witness against thee? *C.* And he answered him to never a word; insomuch that the governor marvelled greatly.

Now at that feast the governor was wont to release unto the people a prisoner, whom they would. And they had then a notable prisoner, called Barabbas. Therefore when they were gathered together, Pilate said unto them, *S.* Whom will ye that I release unto you? Barabbas, or Jesus which is called Christ? *C.* For he knew that for envy they had delivered him.

When he was set down on the judgment seat, his wife sent unto him, saying, *S.* Have thou nothing to do with that just man: for I have suffered many things this day in a dream because of him. *C.* But the chief priests and elders persuaded the multitude that they should ask Barabbas, and destroy Jesus. The governor answered and said unto them, *S.* Whether of the twain will ye that I release unto you? *C.* They said, *S.* Barabbas. *C.* Pilate saith unto them, *S.* What shall I do then with Jesus which is called Christ? *C.* They all say unto him, *S.* Let him be crucified. *C.* And the governor said, *S.* Why, what evil hath he done? *C.* But they cried out the more, saying, *S.* Let him be crucified.

C. When Pilate saw that he could prevail nothing, but that rather a tumult was made, he took water, and washed his hands before the multitude, saying, *S.* I am innocent of the blood of this just person: see ye to it. *C.* Then answered all the people, and said, *S.* His blood be on us, and on our children. *C.* Then released he Barabbas unto them: and when he had scourged Jesus, he delivered him to be crucified.

Then the soldiers of the governor took Jesus into the common hall, and

Proper of Season *Palm Sunday*

gathered unto him the whole band of soldiers. And they stripped him, and put on him a scarlet robe. And when they had platted a crown of thorns, they put it upon his head, and a reed in his right hand: and they bowed the knee before him, and mocked him, saying, *S.* Hail, King of the Jews! *C.* And they spit upon him, and took the reed, and smote him on the head. And after that they had mocked him, they took the robe off from him, and put his own raiment on him, and led him away to crucify him. And as they came out, they found a man of Cyrene, Simon by name: him they compelled to bear his cross.

And when they were come unto a place called Golgotha, that is to say, a place of a skull, they gave him vinegar to drink mingled with gall: and when he had tasted thereof, he would not drink. And they crucified him, and parted his garments, casting lots: that it might be fulfilled which was spoken by the prophet, They parted my garments among them, and upon my vesture did they cast lots. And sitting down they watched him there; and set up over his head his accusation written, THIS IS JESUS THE KING OF THE JEWS. Then were there two thieves crucified with him, one on the right hand, and another on the left.

And they that passed by reviled him, wagging their heads, and saying, *S.* Thou that destroyest the temple, and buildest it in three days, save thyself. If thou be the Son of God, come down from the cross. *C.* Likewise also the chief priests mocking him, with the scribes and elders, said, *S.* He saved others; himself he cannot save. If he be the King of Israel, let him now come down from the cross, and we will believe him. He trusted in God; let him deliver him now, if he will have him: for he said, I am the Son of God. *C.* The thieves also, which were crucified with him, cast the same in his teeth.

Now from the sixth hour there was darkness over all the land unto the ninth hour. And about the ninth hour Jesus cried with a loud voice, saying, ✠ Eli, Eli, lama sabachthani? *C.* that is to say, ✠ My God, my God, why hast thou forsaken me? *C.* Some of them that stood there, when they heard that, said, *S.* This man calleth for Elias. *C.* And straightway one of them ran, and took a spunge, and filled it with vinegar, and put it on a reed, and gave him to drink. The rest said, *S.* Let be, let us see whether Elias will come to save him.

C. Jesus, when he had cried again with a loud voice, yielded up the ghost. (Here genuflect and pause awhile.) And, behold, the veil of the temple was rent in twain from the top to the bottom; and the earth did quake, and the rocks rent; and the graves were opened; and many bodies of the saints which slept arose, and came out of the graves after his resurrection, and went into the holy city, and appeared unto many. Now when the centurion, and they that were with him, watching Jesus, saw the earthquake, and those things that were done, they feared greatly, saying, *S.* Truly this was the Son of God.

C. And many women were there beholding afar off, which followed Jesus

Palm Sunday # Proper of Season

from Galilee, ministering unto him: among which was Mary Magdalene, and Mary the mother of James and Joses, and the mother of Zebedee's children.

When the even was come, there came a rich man of Arimathæa, named Joseph, who also himself was Jesus' disciple: he went to Pilate, and begged the body of Jesus. Then Pilate commanded the body to be delivered. And when Joseph had taken the body, he wrapped it in a clean linen cloth, and laid it in his own new tomb, which he had hewn out in the rock: and he rolled a great stone to the door of the sepulchre, and departed. And there was Mary Magdalene, and the other Mary, sitting over against the sepulchre.

¶ Here **Cleanse my heart** is said, a blessing is asked, incense is carried without lights, and the book is censed: **The Lord be with you** is not said, and the Celebrant or Deacon does not sign the Book nor himself: and what follows is sung in the tone of the Gospel: at the conclusion of which the Celebrant kisses the Book and is censed. All of which is observed in the other Passions except on Good Friday.

Now the next day, that followed the day of the preparation, the chief priests and Pharisees came together unto Pilate, saying, Sir, we remember that that deceiver said, while he was yet alive, After three days I will rise again. Command therefore that the sepulchre be made sure until the third day, lest his disciples come by night, and steal him away, and say unto the people, He is risen from the dead: so the last error shall be worse than the first. Pilate said unto them, Ye have a watch: go your way, make it as sure as ye can. So they went, and made the sepulchre sure, sealing the stone, and setting a watch.

Offertory. Thy rebuke hath broken my heart; I am full of heaviness: I looked for some to have pity on me, but there was no man, neither found I any to comfort me: they gave me gall to eat: and when I was thirsty they gave me vinegar to drink.

Secret

RANT, we beseech thee, O God: that the gift which we offer in the sight of thy majesty may obtain for us grace to serve thee with devotion, and bring us in the end to everlasting felicity. Through

Communion. Father, if this cup may not pass away from me, except I drink it: thy will be done.

Postcommunion

AY the operation of this mystery, O Lord: avail for the cleansing of our sins, and for the fulfilment of our godly desires. Through.

Proper of Season — Holy Week

Holy Week

Holy Monday

ALMIGHTY God, whose most dear Son went not up to joy but first he suffered pain, and entered not into glory before he was crucified; Mercifully grant that we, walking in the way of the cross, may find it none other than the way of life and peace. *Through the same.*

Holy Tuesday

O LORD God, whose blessed Son, our Saviour, gave his back to the smiters and hid not his face from shame; Grant us grace to take joyfully the sufferings of the present time, in full assurance of the glory that shall be revealed. *Through the same.*

Spy Wednesday

ASSIST us mercifully with thy help, O Lord God of our salvation; that we may enter with joy upon the meditation of those mighty acts, whereby thou hast given unto us life and immortality. *Through.*

Maundy Thursday

ALMIGHTY Father, whose dear Son, on the night before he suffered, did institute the Sacrament of his Body and Blood; Mercifully grant that we may thankfully receive the same in remembrance of him, who in these holy mysteries giveth us a pledge of life eternal; through the same thy Son Jesus Christ our Lord, who now liveth and reigneth with thee and the Holy Spirit ever, one God, world without end. *Amen.*

Good Friday

ALMIGHTY God, we beseech thee graciously to behold this thy family, for which our Lord Jesus Christ was contented to be betrayed and given up into the hands of wicked men, and to suffer death upon the cross; who now liveth and reigneth with thee and the Holy Ghost ever, one God, world without end. *Amen.*

ALMIGHTY and everlasting God, by whose Spirit the whole body of the Church is governed and sanctified; Receive our supplications and prayers, which we offer before thee for all estates of men in thy holy Church, that every member of the same, in his vocation and ministry, may truly and godly serve thee. *Through.*

Easter Day # Proper of Season

MERCIFUL God, who hast made all men, and hatest nothing that thou hast made, nor desirest the death of a sinner, but rather that he should be converted and live; Have mercy upon all Jews, Turks, infidels, and heretics; and take from them all ignorance, hardness of heart, and contempt of thy Word; and so fetch them home, blessed Lord, to thy flock, that they may be saved among the remnant of the true Israelites, and be made one fold under one shepherd, Jesus Christ our Lord, who liveth and reigneth with thee and the Holy Spirit, one God, world without end. *Amen.*

Easter Even

RANT, O Lord, that as we are baptized into the death of thy blessed Son, our Saviour Jesus Christ, so by continual mortifying our corrupt affections we may be buried with him; and that through the grave, and gate of death, we may pass to our joyful resurrection; for his merits, who died, and was buried, and rose again for us, the same thy Son Jesus Christ our Lord. Who with thee.

Easter Day

First Class Double, First Class Octave

Pascha Nostrum

¶ At Morning Prayer, instead of the **Venite,** the following shall be said, and may be said throughout the Octave.

HRIST our Passover is sacrificed for us : therefore let us keep the feast, Not with old leaven, neither with the leaven of malice and wickedness : but with the unleavened bread of sincerity and truth. (1 Cor. 5:7)

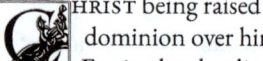HRIST being raised from the dead dieth no more : death hath no more dominion over him.
For in that he died, he died unto sin once : but in that he liveth, he liveth unto God.
Likewise reckon ye also yourselves to be dead indeed unto sin : but alive unto God through Jesus Christ our Lord. (Rom. 6:9)

HRIST is risen from the dead : and become the firstfruits of them that slept.
For since by man came death : by man came also the resurrection of the dead.
For as in Adam all die : even so in Christ shall all be made alive. (1 Cor. 15:20)

Proper of Season — *Easter Day*

℣. Glory be to the Father, and to the Son : and to the Holy Ghost;
℟. As it was in the beginning, is now, and ever shall be: world without end. Amen.

Introit

I AM risen, and am still with thee, alleluia: thou hast laid thine hand upon me, alleluia: thy knowledge is too wonderful, alleluia, alleluia. *Ps.* O Lord, thou hast searched me out, and known me: thou knowest my down-sitting, and mine uprising.

Collect

ALMIGHTY God, who through thine only-begotten Son Jesus Christ hast overcome death, and opened unto us the gate of everlasting life; We humbly beseech thee that, as by thy special grace preventing us thou dost put into our minds good desires, so by thy continual help we may bring the same to good effect; through the same Jesus Christ our Lord, who liveth and reigneth with thee and the Holy Ghost ever, one God, world without end. *Amen.*

❡ This Collect is to be said daily throughout the Easter Octave.

Epistle. Colossians 3:1

BRETHREN: If ye then be risen with Christ, seek those things which are above, where Christ sitteth on the right hand of God. Set your affection on things above, not on things on the earth. For ye are dead, and your life is hid with Christ in God. When Christ, who is our life, shall appear, then shall ye also appear with him in glory. Mortify therefore your members which are upon the earth; fornication, uncleanness, inordinate affection, evil concupiscence, and covetousness, which is idolatry: For which things' sake the wrath of God cometh on the children of disobedience: In the which ye also walked some time, when ye lived in them.

Gradual. This is the day which the Lord hath made: we will rejoice and be glad in it. ℣. O give thanks unto the Lord, for he is gracious: and his mercy endureth for ever.

Alleluia. Alleluia, alleluia. ℣. Christ our Passover is sacrificed for us.

Easter Day   # Proper of Season

Sequence

CHRISTIANS, to the Paschal Victim offer your thankful praises.
A Lamb the sheep redeemeth: Christ, who only is sinless, reconcileth sinners to the Father.

Death and life have contended in that combat stupendous: the prince of life, who died, reigns immortal.

Speak, Mary, declaring what thou sawest wayfaring:

The tomb of Christ, who is living. The glory of Jesu's Resurrection;

Bright angels attesting, the shroud and napkin resting.

Yea, Christ my hope is arisen: to Galilee he goes before you.

Happy they who hear the witness, Mary's word believing above the tales of Jewry deceiving.

Christ indeed from death is risen, our new life obtaining: have mercy, victor King, ever reigning. Amen. Alleluia.

¶ The Sequence is said until Saturday before Low Sunday, inclusive.

Gospel. John 20:1

AT THAT TIME: On the first day of the week cometh Mary Magdalene early, when it was yet dark, unto the sepulchre, and seeth the stone taken away from the sepulchre. Then she runneth, and cometh to Simon Peter, and to the other disciple, whom Jesus loved, and saith unto them, They have taken away the Lord out of the sepulchre, and we know not where they have laid him. Peter therefore went forth, and that other disciple, and came to the sepulchre. So they ran both together: and the other disciple did outrun Peter, and came first to the sepulchre. And he stooping down, and looking in, saw the linen clothes lying; yet went he not in. Then cometh Simon Peter following him, and went into the sepulchre, and seeth the linen clothes lie, And the napkin, that was about his head, not lying with the linen clothes, but wrapped together in a place by itself. Then went in also that other disciple, which came first to the sepulchre, and he saw, and believed. For as yet they knew not the scripture, that he must rise again from the dead. Then the disciples went away again unto their own home.

Offertory. The earth trembled and was still, when God arose to judgment, alleluia.

Proper of Season *Easter Monday*

Secret

RECEIVE, we beseech thee, O Lord, the prayers of thy people together with the offering of these sacrifices: that those things which we have begun in these paschal mysteries may, by thine operation, be profitable for our healing in eternity. Through.

Communion. Christ our Passover is sacrificed for us, alleluia: therefore let us keep the feast with the unleavened bread of sincerity and truth, alleluia, alleluia, alleluia.

Postcommunion

POUR forth upon us, O Lord, the Spirit of thy charity: that as thou hast fulfilled us with these paschal sacraments, so of thy goodness thou wouldest make us to be of one heart and mind. Through.

EASTER MONDAY

First Class Double

Introit

THE Lord hath brought you into a land flowing with milk and honey, alleluia: that the law of the Lord may alway be in your mouth, alleluia, alleluia. *Ps.* O give thanks unto the Lord, and call upon his name: tell the people what things he hath done.

Collect

O GOD, who by the paschal solemnity hast bestowed healing upon the world: prosper, we beseech thee, thy people with thy heavenly gift; that they may be worthy to attain unto perfect freedom, and may likewise be profited unto everlasting life. Through.

¶ 2nd Collect is of Easter Day (p. 299).

Epistle. Acts 10:34

IN THOSE DAYS: Peter opened his mouth, and said, Of a truth I perceive that God is no respecter of persons: But in every nation he that feareth him, and worketh righteousness, is accepted with him. The word which God sent unto the children of Israel, preaching peace by Jesus Christ: (he is

Easter Monday   **Proper of Season**

Lord of all:) That word, I say, ye know, which was published throughout all Judaea, and began from Galilee, after the baptism which John preached; How God anointed Jesus of Nazareth with the Holy Ghost and with power: who went about doing good, and healing all that were oppressed of the devil; for God was with him. And we are witnesses of all things which he did both in the land of the Jews, and in Jerusalem; whom they slew and hanged on a tree: Him God raised up the third day, and shewed him openly; Not to all the people, but unto witnesses chosen before of God, even to us, who did eat and drink with him after he rose from the dead. And he commanded us to preach unto the people, and to testify that it is he which was ordained of God to be the Judge of quick and dead. To him give all the prophets witness, that through his name whosoever believeth in him shall receive remission of sins.

Gradual. This is the day which the Lord hath made: we will rejoice and be glad in it. ℣. Let Israel now confess, that he is gracious: and that his mercy endureth for ever.

Alleluia. Alleluia, alleluia. ℣. The Angel of the Lord descended from heaven: and came and roiled back the stone and sat upon it.

¶ Sequence as on Easter Day (p. 300).

Gospel. Luke 24:13

AT THAT TIME: Behold, two of Jesus' disciples went that same day to a village called Emmaus, which was from Jerusalem about threescore furlongs. And they talked together of all these things which had happened. And it came to pass, that, while they communed together and reasoned, Jesus himself drew near, and went with them. But their eyes were holden that they should not know him. And he said unto them, What manner of communications are these that ye have one to another, as ye walk, and are sad? And the one of them, whose name was Cleopas, answering said unto him, Art thou only a stranger in Jerusalem, and hast not known the things which are come to pass there in these days? And he said unto them, What things? And they said unto him, Concerning Jesus of Nazareth, which was a prophet mighty in deed and word before God and all the people: And how the chief priests and our rulers delivered him to be condemned to death, and have crucified him. But we trusted that it had been he which should have redeemed Israel: and beside all this, to day is the third day since these things were done. Yea, and certain women also of our company made us astonished, which were early at the sepulchre; And when they found not his body, they came, saying, that they had also seen a vision of angels, which said that he was alive. And certain of them which were with us

Proper of Season *Easter Monday*

went to the sepulchre, and found it even so as the women had said: but him they saw not. Then he said unto them, O fools, and slow of heart to believe all that the prophets have spoken: Ought not Christ to have suffered these things, and to enter into his glory? And beginning at Moses and all the prophets, he expounded unto them in all the scriptures the things concerning himself. And they drew nigh unto the village, whither they went: and he made as though he would have gone further. But they constrained him, saying, Abide with us: for it is toward evening, and the day is far spent. And he went in to tarry with them. And it came to pass, as he sat at meat with them, he took bread, and blessed it, and brake, and gave to them. And their eyes were opened, and they knew him; and he vanished out of their sight. And they said one to another, Did not our heart burn within us, while he talked with us by the way, and while he opened to us the scriptures? And they rose up the same hour, and returned to Jerusalem, and found the eleven gathered together, and them that were with them Saying, The Lord is risen indeed, and hath appeared to Simon. And they told what things were done in the way, and how he was known of them in breaking of bread.

Offertory. The Angel of the Lord descended from heaven, and said unto the women: He whom ye seek is risen as he said, alleluia.

Secret

RECEIVE, we beseech thee, O Lord, the prayers of thy people together with the offering of these sacrifices; that those things which we have begun in these paschal mysteries may, by thine operation, be profitable for our healing in eternity. Through.

¶ 2nd Secret is of Easter Day (p. 301).

Communion. The Lord is risen, and hath appeared to Peter, alleluia.

Postcommunion

POUR forth upon us, O Lord, the Spirit of thy charity: that as thou hast fulfilled us with these paschal sacraments, so of thy goodness thou wouldest make us to be of one heart and mind. Through ... in the unity of the same.

¶ 2nd Postcommunion is of Easter Day (p. 301).

Easter Tuesday   **Proper of Season**

Easter Tuesday

First Class Double

Introit

HE water of wisdom hath he given them to drink, alleluia; he shall be stayed upon them, and shall not be moved, alleluia: and he shall exalt them for ever, alleluia, alleluia. *Ps.* O give thanks unto the Lord, and call upon his name: tell the people what things he hath done.

Collect

O GOD, who dost ever multiply thy Church with new offspring; grant unto thy servants; that they may hold fast in their lives the sacrament which by faith they have received. Through.

¶ 2nd Collect is of Easter Day (p. 299).

Epistle. Acts 13:26

IN THOSE DAYS: Paul stood up, and beckoning with his hand said, Men of Israel, and ye that fear God, give audience. Men and brethren, children of the stock of Abraham, and whosoever among you feareth God, to you is the word of this salvation sent. For they that dwell at Jerusalem, and their rulers, because they knew him not, nor yet the voices of the prophets which are read every sabbath day, they have fulfilled them in condemning him. And though they found no cause of death in him, yet desired they Pilate that he should be slain. And when they had fulfilled all that was written of him, they took him down from the tree, and laid him in a sepulchre. But God raised him from the dead: And he was seen many days of them which came up with him from Galilee to Jerusalem, who are his witnesses unto the people. And we declare unto you glad tidings, how that the promise which was made unto the fathers, God hath fulfilled the same unto us their children, in that he hath raised up Jesus again; as it is also written in the second psalm, Thou art my Son, this day have I begotten thee. And as concerning that he raised him up from the dead, now no more to return to corruption, he said on this wise, I will give you the sure mercies of David. Wherefore he saith also in another psalm, Thou shalt not suffer thine Holy One to see corruption. For David, after he had served his own generation by the will of God, fell on sleep, and was laid unto his fathers, and saw corruption: But he, whom God raised again, saw no corruption. Be it known unto you therefore, men and brethren, that through this man is preached unto you the forgiveness of sins: And by him all that believe are justified from all things, from which ye could not be justified by the law of Moses. Beware therefore, lest that come upon you, which is spoken of in the prophets; Behold, ye despisers, and wonder, and perish: for I work a work in your days, a work which ye shall in no wise believe, though a man declare it unto you.

Gradual. This is the day which the Lord hath made: we will rejoice and be glad in it. ℣. Let them now give thanks whom the Lord hath redeemed: and delivered from the hand of the enemy, and gathered them out of the lands.

Alleluia. Alleluia, alleluia. ℣. The Lord is risen from the tomb, who for us hung upon the tree.

¶ Sequence as on Easter Day (p. 300).

Gospel. Luke 24:36

AT THAT TIME: Jesus stood in the midst of his disciples, and saith unto them, Peace be unto you. But they were terrified and affrighted, and supposed that they had seen a spirit. And he said unto them, Why are ye troubled? and why do thoughts arise in your hearts? Behold my hands and my feet, that it is I myself: handle me, and see; for a spirit hath not flesh and bones, as ye see me have. And when he had thus spoken, he shewed them his hands and his feet. And while they yet believed not for joy, and wondered, he said unto them, Have ye here any meat? And they gave him a piece of a broiled fish, and of an honeycomb. And he took it, and did eat before them. And he said unto them, These are the words which I spake unto you, while I was yet with you, that all things must be fulfilled, which were written in the law of Moses, and in the prophets, and in the psalms, concerning me. Then opened he their understanding, that they might understand the scriptures, And said unto them, Thus it is written, and thus it behoved Christ to suffer, and to rise from the dead the third day: And that repentance and remission of sins should be preached in his name among all nations, beginning at Jerusalem. And ye are witnesses of these things.

Offertory. The Lord thundered out of heaven: and the Highest gave his thunder: and the springs of waters were seen, alleluia.

Easter Wednesday   # Proper of Season

Secret

ECEIVE, O Lord, the prayers of thy faithful people, together with the offering of these sacrifices: that through these observances of our bounden devotion we may attain unto heavenly glory. Through.

¶ 2nd Secret is of Easter Day (p. 301).

Communion. If ye be risen with Christ, seek those things which are above, where Christ sitteth on the right hand of God, alleluia: set your affection on things above, alleluia.

Postcommunion

RANT, we beseech thee, almighty God: that the paschal sacrament, which we have received, may continually abide in our hearts. Through.

¶ 2nd Postcommunion is of Easter Day (p. 301).

Easter Wednesday

Semidouble

Introit

OME, ye blessed of my Father, inherit the kingdom, alleluia: which hath been prepared for you from the foundation of the world, alleluia, alleluia, alleluia. *Ps.* O sing unto the Lord a new song: sing unto the Lord, all the whole earth.

Collect

GOD, who dost gladden us with the yearly solemnity of the Resurrection of the Lord: mercifully grant; that through this temporal feast which we observe, we may be found worthy to attain unto everlasting joys. Through the same.

¶ 2nd Collect is of Easter Day (p. 299) & 3rd Against the Persecutors of the Church (p. 543) or for the Chief Bishop (p. 543).

Proper of Season *Easter Wednesday*

Epistle. Acts 3:12

IN THOSE DAYS: Peter opened his mouth and said: Ye men of Israel, and ye that fear God, hearken. The God of Abraham, and of Isaac, and of Jacob, the God of our fathers, hath glorified his Son Jesus; whom ye delivered up, and denied him in the presence of Pilate, when he was determined to let him go. But ye denied the Holy One and the Just, and desired a murderer to be granted unto you; And killed the Prince of life, whom God hath raised from the dead; whereof we are witnesses. And his name through faith in his name hath made this man strong, whom ye see and know: yea, the faith which is by him hath given him this perfect soundness in the presence of you all. And now, brethren, I wot that through ignorance ye did it, as did also your rulers. But those things, which God before had shewed by the mouth of all his prophets, that Christ should suffer, he hath so fulfilled. Repent ye therefore, and be converted, that your sins may be blotted out.

Gradual. This is the day which the Lord hath made: we will rejoice and be glad in it. ℣. The right hand of the Lord bringeth mighty things to pass, the right hand of the Lord hath exalted me.

Alleluia. Alleluia, alleluia. ℣. The Lord is risen indeed: and hath appeared to Peter.

¶ Sequence as on Easter Day (p. 300).

Gospel. John 21:1

AT THAT TIME: Jesus shewed himself again to the disciples at the sea of Tiberius. And on this wise shewed he himself. There were together Simon Peter, and Thomas called Didymus, and Nathanael of Cana in Galilee, and the sons of Zebedee, and two other of his disciples. Simon Peter saith unto them, I go a fishing. They say unto him, We also go with thee. They went forth, and entered into a ship immediately; and that night they caught nothing. But when the morning was now come, Jesus stood on the shore: but the disciples knew not that it was Jesus. Then Jesus saith unto them, Children, have ye any meat? They answered him, No. And he said unto them, Cast the net on the right side of the ship, and ye shall find. They cast therefore, and now they were not able to draw it for the multitude of fishes. Therefore that disciple whom Jesus loved saith unto Peter, It is the Lord. Now when Simon Peter heard that it was the Lord, he girt his fisher's coat unto him, (for he was naked,) and did cast himself into the sea. And the other disciples came in a little ship; (for they were not far from land, but as it were two hundred cubits,) dragging the net with fishes. As soon then as they were come to land, they saw a fire of coals

Easter Thursday

Proper of Season

there, and fish laid thereon, and bread. Jesus saith unto them, Bring of the fish which ye have now caught. Simon Peter went up, and drew the net to land full of great fishes, an hundred and fifty and three: and for all there were so many, yet was not the net broken. Jesus saith unto them, Come and dine. And none of the disciples durst ask him, Who art thou? knowing that it was the Lord. Jesus then cometh, and taketh bread, and giveth them, and fish likewise. This is now the third time that Jesus shewed himself to his disciples, after that he was risen from the dead.

Offertory. The Lord opened the doors of heaven: and rained down manna upon them for to eat: he gave them food from heaven: so man did eat Angels' food, alleluia.

Secret

E offer unto thee, O Lord, the sacrifices of our paschal gladness: whereby thou dost wondrously both feed and sustain thy Church. Through.

¶ 2nd Secret is of Easter Day (p. 301) & 3rd Against the Persecutors of the Church (p. 543) or for the Chief Bishop (p. 543).

Communion. Christ being raised from the dead, dieth no more, alleluia: death hath no more dominion over him, alleluia, alleluia.

Postcommunion

E beseech thee, O Lord, that we, being cleansed from all our former nature: may by the devout receiving of thy sacrament be transformed into a new creature. Who livest.

¶ 2nd Postcommunion is of Easter Day (p. 301) & 3rd Against the Persecutors of the Church (p. 543) or for the Chief Bishop (p. 543).

Easter Thursday

Semidouble

Introit

HY victorious hand, O Lord, have they magnified, with one accord, alleluia: for wisdom hath opened the mouth of the dumb, and made eloquent the tongues of them that cannot speak, alleluia, alleluia. *Ps.* O sing unto the Lord a new song: for he hath done marvellous things.

Proper of Season *Easter Thursday*

Collect

GOD, who hast united the diversity of nations in the confession of thy name: grant that they who are born again in the font of Baptism may agree in unity of faith and in godliness of conversation. Through.

¶ 2nd Collect is of Easter Day (p. 299) & 3rd Against the Persecutors of the Church (p. 543) or for the Chief Bishop (p. 543).

Epistle. Acts 8:26

IN THOSE DAYS: The Angel of the Lord spake unto Philip, saying: Arise, and go toward the south unto the way that goeth down from Jerusalem unto Gaza, which is desert. And he arose and went: and, behold, a man of Ethiopia, an eunuch of great authority under Candace queen of the Ethiopians, who had the charge of all her treasure, and had come to Jerusalem for to worship, Was returning, and sitting in his chariot read Esaias the prophet. Then the Spirit said unto Philip, Go near, and join thyself to this chariot. And Philip ran thither to him, and heard him read the prophet Esaias, and said, Understandest thou what thou readest? And he said, How can I, except some man should guide me? And he desired Philip that he would come up and sit with him. The place of the scripture which he read was this, He was led as a sheep to the slaughter; and like a lamb dumb before his shearer, so opened he not his mouth: In his humiliation his judgment was taken away: and who shall declare his generation? for his life is taken from the earth. And the eunuch answered Philip, and said, I pray thee, of whom speaketh the prophet this? of himself, or of some other man? Then Philip opened his mouth, and began at the same scripture, and preached unto him Jesus. And as they went on their way, they came unto a certain water: and the eunuch said, See, here is water; what doth hinder me to be baptized? And Philip said, If thou believest with all thine heart, thou mayest. And he answered and said, I believe that Jesus Christ is the Son of God. And he commanded the chariot to stand still: and they went down both into the water, both Philip and the eunuch; and he baptized him. And when they were come up out of the water, the Spirit of the Lord caught away Philip, that the eunuch saw him no more: and he went on his way rejoicing. But Philip was found at Azotus: and passing through he preached in all the cities, till he came to Caesarea.

Gradual. This is the day which the Lord hath made: we will rejoice and be glad in it. ℣. The same stone, which the builders refused, is become the head-stone in the corner: this is the Lord's doing, and it is marvellous in our eyes.

Easter Thursday # Proper of Season

Alleluia. Alleluia, alleluia. ℣. Christ, who created all things, is risen: and he hath had compassion on mankind.

⁋ Sequence as on Easter Day (p. 300).

Gospel. John 20:11

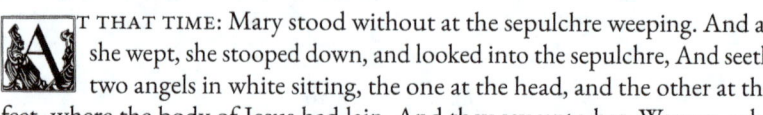T THAT TIME: Mary stood without at the sepulchre weeping. And as she wept, she stooped down, and looked into the sepulchre, And seeth two angels in white sitting, the one at the head, and the other at the feet, where the body of Jesus had lain. And they say unto her, Woman, why weepest thou? She saith unto them, Because they have taken away my Lord, and I know not where they have laid him. And when she had thus said, she turned herself back, and saw Jesus standing, and knew not that it was Jesus. Jesus saith unto her, Woman, why weepest thou? whom seekest thou? She, supposing him to be the gardener, saith unto him, Sir, if thou have borne him hence, tell me where thou hast laid him, and I will take him away. Jesus saith unto her, Mary. She turned herself, and saith unto him, Rabboni; which is to say, Master. Jesus saith unto her, Touch me not; for I am not yet ascended to my Father: but go to my brethren, and say unto them, I ascend unto my Father, and your Father; and to my God, and your God. Mary Magdalene came and told the disciples that she had seen the Lord, and that he had spoken these things unto her.

Offertory. In the day of your solemnity, saith the Lord, I will bring you into a land flowing with milk and honey, alleluia.

Secret

E beseech thee, O Lord, mercifully to accept the oblations of thy people: that being made regenerate by the confession of thy name, and by baptism, they may attain to everlasting blessedness. Through.

⁋ 2ⁿᵈ Secret is of Easter Day (p. 301) & 3ʳᵈ Against the Persecutors of the Church (p. 543) or for the Chief Bishop (p. 543).

Communion. Ye are a peculiar people, shew ye forth the praises of him, alleluia: who hath called you out of darkness into his marvellous light, alleluia.

Postcommunion

RACIOUSLY hear our prayers, O Lord: that this holy communion of our redemption may both bestow on us thy succour in this present life, and obtain for us everlasting joys. Through.

⁋ 2ⁿᵈ Postcommunion is of Easter Day (p. 301) & 3ʳᵈ Against the Persecutors of the Church (p. 543) or for the Chief Bishop (p. 543).

Proper of Season *Easter Friday*

Easter Friday

Semidouble

Introit

HE Lord hath brought them out safely, alleluia: and overwhelmed their enemies with the sea, alleluia, alleluia, alleluia. *Ps.* Hear my law, O my people: incline your ears unto the words of my mouth.

Collect

LMIGHTY and everlasting God, who hast bestowed the paschal sacrament for a pledge of man's reconciliation: grant unto our hearts; that what we celebrate in outward profession we may effectually fulfil. Through.

¶ 2nd Collect is of Easter Day (p. 299) & 3rd Against the Persecutors of the Church (p. 543) or for the Chief Bishop (p. 543).

Epistle. 1 Peter 3:18

DEARLY BELOVED: Christ hath once suffered for sins, the just for the unjust, that he might bring us to God, being put to death in the flesh, but quickened by the Spirit: By which also he went and preached unto the spirits in prison; Which sometime were disobedient, when once the longsuffering of God waited in the days of Noah, while the ark was a preparing, wherein few, that is, eight souls were saved by water. The like figure whereunto even baptism doth also now save us (not the putting away of the filth of the flesh, but the answer of a good conscience toward God,) by the resurrection of Jesus Christ: Who is gone into heaven, and is on the right hand of God.

Gradual. This is the day which the Lord hath made: we will rejoice and be glad in it. ℣. Blessed is he that cometh in the name of the Lord: God is the Lord who hath shewed us light.

Alleluia. Alleluia, alleluia. ℣. Tell it out among the heathen: that the Lord hath reigned from the tree.

¶ Sequence as on Easter Day (p. 300).

Easter Friday # Proper of Season

Gospel. Matthew 28:16

AT THAT TIME: The eleven disciples went away into Galilee, into a mountain where Jesus had appointed them. And when they saw him, they worshipped him: but some doubted. And Jesus came and spake unto them, saying, All power is given unto me in heaven and in earth. Go ye therefore, and teach all nations, baptizing them in the name of the Father, and of the Son, and of the Holy Ghost: Teaching them to observe all things whatsoever I have commanded you: and, lo, I am with you alway, even unto the end of the world.

Offertory. This day shall be unto you for a memorial, alleluia: and ye shall keep it a feast to the Lord throughout your generations: ye shall keep it a feast by an ordinance for ever, alleluia, alleluia, alleluia.

Secret

WE beseech thee, O Lord, mercifully to accept our oblations: which we offer unto thee for the expiation of the sins of them that are born again, and for the speedy attaining of thy heavenly succour. Through.

¶ 2nd Secret is of Easter Day (p. 301) & 3rd Against the Persecutors of the Church (p. 543) or for the Chief Bishop (p. 543).

Communion. All power is given to me in heaven and in earth, alleluia: go ye, and teach all nations, baptizing them in the name of the Father, and of the Son, and of the Holy Ghost, alleluia, alleluia.

Postcommunion

WE beseech thee, O Lord, look upon thy people: and as thou hast vouchsafed to renew them with thine eternal mysteries, so of thy goodness deliver them from temporal guilt. Through.

¶ 2nd Postcommunion is of Easter Day (p. 301) & 3rd Against the Persecutors of the Church (p. 543) or for the Chief Bishop (p. 543).

Proper of Season *Easter Saturday*

EASTER SATURDAY

Semidouble

Introit

THE Lord hath brought forth his people with joy, alleluia: and his chosen with gladness, alleluia, alleluia. *Ps.* O give thanks unto the Lord, and call upon his name: tell the people what things he hath done.

Collect

GRANT, we beseech thee, almighty God: that we who have devoutly kept this paschal festival may thereby be found worthy to attain to everlasting joys. Through.

¶ 2nd Collect is of Easter Day (p. 299) & 3rd Against the Persecutors of the Church (p. 543) or for the Chief Bishop (p. 543).

Epistle. 1 Peter 2:1

DEARLY BELOVED: Laying aside therefore all malice, and all guile, and hypocrisies, and envies, and all evil speakings, As newborn babes, desire the sincere milk of the word, that ye may grow thereby: If so be ye have tasted that the Lord is gracious. To whom coming, as unto a living stone, disallowed indeed of men, but chosen of God, and precious, Ye also, as lively stones, are built up a spiritual house, an holy priesthood, to offer up spiritual sacrifices, acceptable to God by Jesus Christ. Wherefore also it is contained in the scripture, Behold, I lay in Sion a chief corner stone, elect, precious: and he that believeth on him shall not be confounded. Unto you therefore which believe he is precious: but unto them which be disobedient, the stone which the builders disallowed, the same is made the head of the corner, And a stone of stumbling, and a rock of offence, even to them which stumble at the word, being disobedient: whereunto also they were appointed. But ye are a chosen generation, a royal priesthood, an holy nation, a peculiar people; that ye should shew forth the praises of him who hath called you out of darkness into his marvellous light: Which in time past were not a people, but are now the people of God: which had not obtained mercy, but now have obtained mercy.

¶ From this day until Ember Saturday in Whitsun Week, inclusive, in all Masses, the Gradual is not said, but the Greater Alleluia.

Easter Saturday   # Proper of Season

Alleluia. Alleluia, alleluia. ℣. This is the day which the Lord hath made: we will rejoice and be glad in it. Alleluia. ℣. Praise the Lord, ye servants, O praise the name of the Lord.

¶ Sequence as on Easter Day (p. 300).

Gospel. John 20:1

T THAT TIME: On the first day of the week cometh Mary Magdalene early, when it was yet dark, unto the sepulchre, and seeth the stone taken away from the sepulchre. Then she runneth, and cometh to Simon Peter, and to the other disciple, whom Jesus loved, and saith unto them, They have taken away the Lord out of the sepulchre, and we know not where they have laid him. Peter therefore went forth, and that other disciple, and came to the sepulchre. So they ran both together: and the other disciple did outrun Peter, and came first to the sepulchre. And he stooping down, and looking in, saw the linen clothes lying; yet went he not in. Then cometh Simon Peter following him, and went into the sepulchre, and seeth the linen clothes lie, And the napkin, that was about his head, not lying with the linen clothes, but wrapped together in a place by itself. Then went in also that other disciple, which came first to the sepulchre, and he saw, and believed. For as yet they knew not the scripture, that he must rise again from the dead.

Offertory. Blessed is he that cometh in the name of the Lord: we have wished you good luck, ye that are of the house of the Lord: God is the Lord who hath shewed us light, alleluia, alleluia.

Secret

RANT us, we beseech thee, O Lord, alway to rejoice in these paschal mysteries: that the continual working of our redemption may be to us the cause of everlasting gladness. Through.

¶ 2nd Secret is of **Easter Day** (p. 301) & 3rd **Against the Persecutors of the Church** (p. 543) or for the **Chief Bishop** (p. 543).

Communion. As many of you as have been baptized into Christ have put on Christ, alleluia.

Postcommunion

LORD, who hast quickened us with the gift of our redemption, we beseech thee: that this aid to everlasting salvation may avail for our advancement in the true faith. Through.

¶ 2nd Postcommunion is of **Easter Day** (p. 301) & 3rd **Against the Persecutors of the Church** (p. 543) or for the **Chief Bishop** (p. 543).

Proper of Season *Easter I*

Low Sunday

First Class Double, Octave Day of Easter

Introit

s new-born babes, alleluia: desire ye the guileless milk of the spirit, alleluia, alleluia, alleluia. *Ps.* Sing we merrily unto God our helper: make a cheerful noise unto the God of Jacob.

¶ **Gloria in excelsis** is said on this and the following Sundays after Easter, even when on week-days the Mass of the preceding Sunday is resumed.

Collect

LMIGHTY Father, who hast given thine only Son to die for our sins, and to rise again for our justification; Grant us so to put away the leaven of malice and wickedness, that we may always serve thee in pureness of living and truth; through the merits of the same thy Son Jesus Christ our Lord. Who with.

Epistle. 1 John 5:4

EARLY BELOVED: Whatsoever is born of God overcometh the world: and this is the victory that overcometh the world, even our faith. Who is he that overcometh the world, but he that believeth that Jesus is the Son of God? This is he that came by water and blood, even Jesus Christ; not by water only, but by water and blood. And it is the Spirit that beareth witness, because the Spirit is truth. For there are three that bear witness, the Spirit, and the water, and the blood: and these three agree in one. If we receive the witness of men, the witness of God is greater: for this is the witness of God which he hath testified of his Son. He that believeth on the Son of God hath the witness in himself: he that believeth not God hath made him a liar; because he believeth not the record that God gave of his Son. And this is the record, that God hath given to us eternal life, and this life is in his Son. He that hath the Son hath life; and he that hath not the Son hath not life.

Alleluia. Alleluia, alleluia. ℣. In the day of my resurrection, saith the Lord, I will go before you into Galilee. Alleluia. ℣. After eight days, when the doors were shut, Jesus stood in the midst of his disciples, and said: Peace be unto you. Alleluia.

Easter I   # Proper of Season

Gospel. John 20:19

A T THAT TIME: The same day at evening, being the first day of the week, when the doors were shut where the disciples were assembled for fear of the Jews, came Jesus and stood in the midst, and saith unto them, Peace be unto you. And when he had so said, he shewed unto them his hands and his side. Then were the disciples glad, when they saw the Lord. Then said Jesus to them again, Peace be unto you: as my Father hath sent me, even so send I you. And when he had said this, he breathed on them, and saith unto them, Receive ye the Holy Ghost: Whose soever sins ye remit, they are remitted unto them; and whose soever sins ye retain, they are retained.

Offertory. The Angel of the Lord descended from heaven, and saith unto the women: He whom ye seek is risen, as he said, alleluia.

Secret

ECEIVE, we beseech thee, O Lord, the offerings of thy Church exultant: and grant unto her, on whom thou hast bestowed cause for so great joy, the fruit of perpetual gladness. Through.

Communion. Reach hither thy hand, and behold the print of the nails, alleluia: and be not faithless, but believing, alleluia, alleluia.

Postcommunion

W E beseech thee, O Lord our God: that these holy mysteries which thou hast given us for the assurance of our redemption; may avail for our healing both in this life and in that which is to come. Through.

Proper of Season *Easter II*

Second Sunday after Easter

Semidouble

Introit

THE loving-kindness of the Lord filleth the whole world, alleluia: by the word of the Lord the heavens were stablished, alleluia, alleluia. *Ps.* Rejoice in the Lord, O ye righteous: for it becometh well the just to be thankful.

Collect

ALMIGHTY GOD, who hast given thine only Son to be unto us both a sacrifice for sin, and also an ensample of godly life; Give us grace that we may always most thankfully receive that his inestimable benefit, and also daily endeavour ourselves to follow the blessed steps of his most holy life. Through the same.

¶ 2nd Collect is of St. Mary in Eastertide (p. 542) & 3rd Against the Persecutors of the Church (p. 543) or for the Chief Bishop (p. 543).

Epistle. 1 Peter 2:19

DEARLY BELOVED: This is thankworthy, if a man for conscience toward God endure grief, suffering wrongfully. For what glory is it, if, when ye be buffeted for your faults, ye shall take it patiently? but if, when ye do well, and suffer for it, ye take it patiently, this is acceptable with God. For even hereunto were ye called: because Christ also suffered for us, leaving us an example, that ye should follow his steps: Who did no sin, neither was guile found in his mouth: Who, when he was reviled, reviled not again; when he suffered, he threatened not; but committed himself to him that judgeth righteously: Who his own self bare our sins in his own body on the tree, that we, being dead to sins, should live unto righteousness: by whose stripes ye were healed. For ye were as sheep going astray; but are now returned unto the Shepherd and Bishop of your souls.

Alleluia. Alleluia, alleluia. ℣. The disciples knew the Lord Jesus in the breaking of bread. Alleluia. ℣. I am the good shepherd: and know my sheep, and am known of mine. Alleluia.

Easter II # Proper of Season

Gospel. John 10:11

AT THAT TIME: Jesus said unto the Pharisees: I am the good shepherd: the good shepherd giveth his life for the sheep. But he that is an hireling, and not the shepherd, whose own the sheep are not, seeth the wolf coming, and leaveth the sheep, and fleeth: and the wolf catcheth them, and scattereth the sheep. The hireling fleeth, because he is an hireling, and careth not for the sheep. I am the good shepherd, and know my sheep, and am known of mine. As the Father knoweth me, even so know I the Father: and I lay down my life for the sheep. And other sheep I have, which are not of this fold: them also I must bring, and they shall hear my voice; and there shall be one fold, and one shepherd.

Offertory. O God, thou art my God, early will I seek thee: and lift up my hands in thy name, alleluia.

Secret

MAY this sacred oblation, O Lord, ever bestow upon us thy saving benediction: that what is performed in a mystery may in power be fulfilled. Through.

¶ 2ⁿᵈ Secret is of St. Mary in Eastertide (p. 542) & 3ʳᵈ Against the Persecutors of the Church (p. 543) or for the Chief Bishop (p. 543).

Communion. I am the good shepherd, alleluia: and know my sheep, and am known of mine, alleluia, alleluia.

Postcommunion

GRANT to us, we beseech thee, almighty God: that we, receiving the quickening of thy grace, may ever glory in thy gift. Through.

¶ 2ⁿᵈ Postcommunion is of St. Mary in Eastertide (p. 542) & 3ʳᵈ Against the Persecutors of the Church (p. 543) or for the Chief Bishop (p. 543).

Proper of Season — *Patronage of St. Joseph*

Patronage of St. Joseph

Wednesday after the Second Sunday after Easter
First Class Double, Simple Octave

Opening Sentence. He made him lord also of his house : and ruler of all his substance.

Introit

THE Lord is our help, and our shield: our heart shall rejoice in him, because we have hoped in his holy name, alleluia, alleluia. *Ps.* Hear, O thou Shepherd of Israel: thou that leadest Joseph like a sheep.

Collect

O GOD, who by thy ineffable providence didst vouchsafe to choose blessed Joseph to be the spouse of thy most holy Mother: grant, we beseech thee; that we, who venerate him as a protector on earth, may be found worthy to have him as an intercessor in heaven. Who livest.

Epistle. Genesis 49:22

JOSEPH is a fruitful bough, even a fruitful bough by a well; whose branches run over the wall: The archers have sorely grieved him, and shot at him, and hated him: But his bow abode in strength, and the arms of his hands were made strong by the hands of the mighty God of Jacob; (from thence is the shepherd, the stone of Israel:) Even by the God of thy father, who shall help thee; and by the Almighty, who shall bless thee with blessings of heaven above, blessings of the deep that lieth under, blessings of the breasts, and of the womb: The blessings of thy father have prevailed above the blessings of my progenitors unto the utmost bound of the everlasting hills: they shall be on the head of Joseph, and on the crown of the head of him that was separate from his brethren.

Alleluia. Alleluia, alleluia, ℣. From whatsoever tribulation they shall cry unto me, I will hear them, and I will be their defender for ever. Alleluia. ℣. Grant us, O Joseph, to lead an innocent life: and may it ever be safe beneath thy care. Alleluia.

Patronage of St. Joseph # Proper of Season

Gospel. Luke 3:21

AT THAT TIME: When all the people were baptized, it came to pass, that Jesus also being baptized, and praying, the heaven was opened, And the Holy Ghost descended in a bodily shape like a dove upon him, and a voice came from heaven, which said, Thou art my beloved Son; in thee I am well pleased. And Jesus himself began to be about thirty years of age, being (as was supposed) the son of Joseph.

Offertory. Praise the Lord, O Jerusalem: for he hath made fast the bars of thy gates, and hath blessed thy children within thee, alleluia, alleluia.

Secret

O LORD, forasmuch as we put our trust in the advocacy of the spouse of thy most holy Mother, we entreat thy mercy: that thou wouldest make our hearts to despise all earthly things, and to love thee the true God with perfect charity. Who livest.

Communion. And Jacob begat Joseph the husband of Mary, of whom was born Jesus, who is called Christ, alleluia, alleluia.

Postcommunion

WE beseech thee, O Lord our God: that we whom thou hast refreshed with the fountain of the divine gift, may by thee be enabled so to rejoice in the protection of blessed Joseph: that, by his merits and intercession, we may be made partakers of thy heavenly glory. Through.

Proper of Season *Easter III*

Third Sunday after Easter

Semidouble

Introit

BE joyful in God, all ye lands, alleluia: sing ye praises unto the honour of his name, alleluia: make his praise to be exceeding glorious, alleluia, alleluia, alleluia. *Ps.* Say unto God, O how wonderful art thou in thy works, O Lord! through the greatness of thy power shall thine enemies be found liars unto thee.

Collect

ALMIGHTY God, who showest to them that are in error the light of thy truth, to the intent that they may return into the way of righteousness; Grant unto all those who are admitted into the fellowship of Christ's Religion, that they may avoid those things that are contrary to their profession, and follow all such things as are agreeable to the same. Through.

¶ 2nd Collect is of St. Mary in Eastertide (p. 542) & 3rd Against the Persecutors of the Church (p. 543) or for the Chief Bishop (p. 543).

Epistle. 1 Peter 2:11

DEARLY BELOVED: I beseech you as strangers and pilgrims, abstain from fleshly lusts, which war against the soul; Having your conversation honest among the Gentiles: that, whereas they speak against you as evildoers, they may by your good works, which they shall behold, glorify God in the day of visitation. Submit yourselves to every ordinance of man for the Lord's sake: whether it be to the king, as supreme; Or unto governors, as unto them that are sent by him for the punishment of evildoers, and for the praise of them that do well. For so is the will of God, that with well doing ye may put to silence the ignorance of foolish men: As free, and not using your liberty for a cloke of maliciousness, but as the servants of God. Honour all men. Love the brotherhood. Fear God. Honour the king.

Alleluia. Alleluia, alleluia. ℣. The Lord hath sent redemption unto his people. Alleluia. ℣. It behoved Christ to suffer, and to rise from the dead: and so to enter into his glory. Alleluia.

Easter III # Proper of Season

Gospel. John 16:16

AT THAT TIME: Jesus said to his disciples: A little while, and ye shall not see me: and again, a little while, and ye shall see me, because I go to the Father. Then said some of his disciples among themselves, What is this that he saith unto us, A little while, and ye shall not see me: and again, a little while, and ye shall see me: and, Because I go to the Father? They said therefore, What is this that he saith, A little while? we cannot tell what he saith. Now Jesus knew that they were desirous to ask him, and said unto them, Do ye enquire among yourselves of that I said, A little while, and ye shall not see me: and again, a little while, and ye shall see me? Verily, verily, I say unto you, That ye shall weep and lament, but the world shall rejoice: and ye shall be sorrowful, but your sorrow shall be turned into joy. A woman when she is in travail hath sorrow, because her hour is come: but as soon as she is delivered of the child, she remembereth no more the anguish, for joy that a man is born into the world. And ye now therefore have sorrow: but I will see you again, and your heart shall rejoice, and your joy no man taketh from you.

Offertory. Praise the Lord, O my soul: while I live will I praise the Lord: yea, as long as I have any being, I will sing praises unto my God, alleluia.

Secret

RANT to us, O Lord, that through these mysteries we may so assuage our earthly desires, that we may learn to love things heavenly. Through.

¶ 2ⁿᵈ Secret is of St. Mary in Eastertide (p. 542) & 3ʳᵈ Against the Persecutors of the Church (p. 543) or for the Chief Bishop (p. 543).

Communion. A little while, and ye shall not see me, alleluia: and again, a little while and ye shall see me, because I go to the Father, alleluia, alleluia.

Postcommunion

AY the sacraments which we have received, we beseech thee, O Lord: both renew us with spiritual sustenance, and defend us with bodily succour. Through.

¶ 2ⁿᵈ Postcommunion is of St. Mary in Eastertide (p. 542) & 3ʳᵈ Against the Persecutors of the Church (p. 543) or for the Chief Bishop (p. 543).

Proper of Season *Easter IV*

Fourth Sunday after Easter

Semidouble

Introit

SING unto the Lord a new song, alleluia: for the Lord hath done marvellous things, alleluia: in the sight of the nations hath he shewed his righteousness, alleluia, alleluia, alleluia. *Ps.* With his own right hand, and with his holy arm: hath he gotten himself the victory.

Collect

ALMIGHTY God, who alone canst order the unruly wills and affections of sinful men; Grant unto thy people, that they may love the thing which thou commandest, and desire that which thou dost promise; that so, among the sundry and manifold changes of the world, our hearts may surely there be fixed, where true joys are to be found. Through.

¶ 2nd Collect is of St. Mary in Eastertide (p. 542) & 3rd Against the Persecutors of the Church (p. 543) or for the Chief Bishop (p. 543).

Epistle. James 1:17

DEARLY BELOVED: Every good gift and every perfect gift is from above, and cometh down from the Father of lights, with whom is no variableness, neither shadow of turning. Of his own will begat he us with the word of truth, that we should be a kind of firstfruits of his creatures. Wherefore, my beloved brethren, let every man be swift to hear, slow to speak, slow to wrath: For the wrath of man worketh not the righteousness of God. Wherefore lay apart all filthiness and superfluity of naughtiness, and receive with meekness the engrafted word, which is able to save your souls.

Alleluia. Alleluia, alleluia, ℣. The right hand of the Lord bringeth mighty things to pass: the right hand of the Lord hath exalted me. Alleluia. ℣. Christ being raised from the dead dieth no more: death hath no more dominion over him. Alleluia.

Gospel. John 16:5

AT THAT TIME: Jesus said unto his disciples: I go my way to him that sent me; and none of you asketh me, Whither goest thou? But because I have said these things unto you, sorrow hath filled your heart. Nevertheless

Easter IV # Proper of Season

I tell you the truth; It is expedient for you that I go away: for if I go not away, the Comforter will not come unto you; but if I depart, I will send him unto you. And when he is come, he will reprove the world of sin, and of righteousness, and of judgment: Of sin, because they believe not on me; Of righteousness, because I go to my Father, and ye see me no more; Of judgment, because the prince of this world is judged. I have yet many things to say unto you, but ye cannot bear them now. Howbeit when he, the Spirit of truth, is come, he will guide you into all truth: for he shall not speak of himself; but whatsoever he shall hear, that shall he speak: and he will shew you things to come. He shall glorify me: for he shall receive of mine, and shall shew it unto you. All things that the Father hath are mine: therefore said I, that he shall take of mine, and shall shew it unto you.

Offertory. O be joyful in God, all ye lands, sing praises unto the honour of his name: O come hither and hearken, all ye that fear God, and I will tell you what the Lord hath done for my soul, alleluia.

Secret

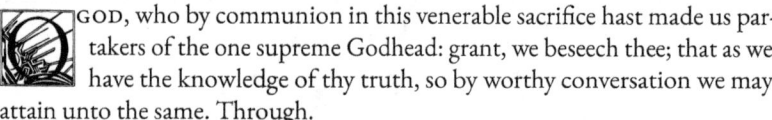GOD, who by communion in this venerable sacrifice hast made us partakers of the one supreme Godhead: grant, we beseech thee; that as we have the knowledge of thy truth, so by worthy conversation we may attain unto the same. Through.

¶ 2nd Secret is of St. Mary in Eastertide (p. 542) & 3rd Against the Persecutors of the Church (p. 543) or for the Chief Bishop (p. 543).

Communion. When the Comforter, the Spirit of Truth, is come, he will reprove the world of sin, and of righteousness, and of judgment, alleluia, alleluia.

Postcommunion

SSIST us, O Lord our God: that by these things, which we have faithfully received, we may both be purged from sin, and delivered from all dangers. Through.

¶ 2nd Postcommunion is of St. Mary in Eastertide (p. 542) & 3rd Against the Persecutors of the Church (p. 543) or for the Chief Bishop (p. 543).

Proper of Season *Rogation Sunday*

ROGATION SUNDAY

Semidouble

Introit

ITH a voice of singing declare ye this, and let it be heard, alleluia: utter it even unto the end of the earth: the Lord hath delivered his people, alleluia, alleluia. *Ps.* O be joyful in God, all ye lands, sing praises unto the honour of his name: make his praise to be glorious.

Collect

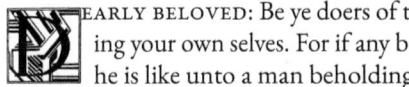LORD, from whom all good things do come; Grant to us thy humble servants, that by thy holy inspiration we may think those things that are good, and by thy merciful guiding may perform the same. Through.

¶ 2nd Collect is of St. Mary in Eastertide (p. 542) & 3rd Against the Persecutors of the Church (p. 543) or for the Chief Bishop (p. 543).

Epistle. James 1:22

EARLY BELOVED: Be ye doers of the word, and not hearers only, deceiving your own selves. For if any be a hearer of the word, and not a doer, he is like unto a man beholding his natural face in a glass: For he beholdeth himself, and goeth his way, and straightway forgetteth what manner of man he was. But whoso looketh into the perfect law of liberty, and continueth therein, he being not a forgetful hearer, but a doer of the work, this man shall be blessed in his deed. If any man among you seem to be religious, and bridleth not his tongue, but deceiveth his own heart, this man's religion is vain. Pure religion and undefiled before God and the Father is this, To visit the fatherless and widows in their affliction, and to keep himself unspotted from the world.

Alleluia. Alleluia, alleluia, ℣. Christ is risen, and hath shewed light unto us, whom he hath redeemed with his blood. Alleluia. ℣. I came forth from the Father, and am come into the world: again, I leave the world, and go to the Father. Alleluia.

Gospel. John 16:23

T THAT TIME: Jesus said unto his disciples: Verily, verily, I say unto you, Whatsoever ye shall ask the Father in my name, he will give it you. Hitherto have ye asked nothing in my name: ask, and ye shall receive,

Rogation Sunday   **Proper of Season**

that your joy may be full. These things have I spoken unto you in proverbs: but the time cometh, when I shall no more speak unto you in proverbs, but I shall shew you plainly of the Father. At that day ye shall ask in my name: and I say not unto you, that I will pray the Father for you: For the Father himself loveth you, because ye have loved me, and have believed that I came out from God. I came forth from the Father, and am come into the world: again, I leave the world, and go to the Father. His disciples said unto him, Lo, now speakest thou plainly, and speakest no proverb. Now are we sure that thou knowest all things, and needest not that any man should ask thee: by this we believe that thou camest forth from God. Jesus answered them, Do ye now believe? Behold, the hour cometh, yea, is now come, that ye shall be scattered, every man to his own, and shall leave me alone: and yet I am not alone, because the Father is with me. These things I have spoken unto you, that in me ye might have peace. In the world ye shall have tribulation: but be of good cheer; I have overcome the world.

Offertory. O praise the Lord our God, ye people, and make the voice of his praise to be heard: who holdeth our soul in life, and suffereth not our feet to slip: praised be the Lord who hath not cast out my prayer, nor turned his mercy from me, alleluia.

Secret

ECEIVE, O Lord, the prayers of thy faithful people, together with the offering of these sacrifices: that through these observances of our bounden devotion we may attain unto heavenly glory. Through.

¶ 2nd Secret is of St. Mary in Eastertide (p. 542) & 3rd Against the Persecutors of the Church (p. 543) or for the Chief Bishop (p. 543).

Communion. O sing unto the Lord, alleluia: sing unto the Lord, and praise his name, be telling of his salvation from day to day, alleluia, alleluia.

Postcommunion

RANT unto us, O Lord: that we who have been fulfilled with the strength of thy heavenly table: may both desire those things which be right, and obtain those things which we desire. Through.

¶ 2nd Postcommunion is of St. Mary in Eastertide (p. 542) & 3rd Against the Persecutors of the Church (p. 543) or for the Chief Bishop (p. 543).

Proper of Season — *Rogation Days*

ROGATION DAYS

¶ Rogation Monday is a Second Class Feria. Rogation Tuesday is a Feria.

Introit

HE hath heard my voice out of his holy temple, alleluia: and my complaint hath come before him, it hath entered even into his ears, alleluia, alleluia. *Ps.* I will love thee, O Lord, my strength: the Lord is my stony rock, my fortress, and my saviour.

¶ In this Mass, **Gloria in excelsis** is not said, nor the Creed.

Collect

ALMIGHTY God, Lord of heaven and earth; We beseech thee to pour forth thy blessing upon this land, and to give us a fruitful season; that we, constantly receiving thy bounty, may evermore give thanks unto thee in thy holy Church. Through.

¶ 2nd Collect is of St. Mary in Eastertide (p. 542) & 3rd Against the Persecutors of the Church (p. 543) or for the Chief Bishop (p. 543).

Epistle. Ezekiel 34:25

I WILL make with them a covenant of peace, and will cause the evil beasts to cease out of the land: and they shall dwell safely in the wilderness, and sleep in the woods. And I will make them and the places round about my hill a blessing; and I will cause the shower to come down in his season; there shall be showers of blessing. And the tree of the field shall yield her fruit, and the earth shall yield her increase, and they shall be safe in their land, and shall know that I am the LORD, when I have broken the bands of their yoke, and delivered them out of the hand of those that served themselves of them. And they shall no more be a prey to the heathen, neither shall the beast of the land devour them; but they shall dwell safely, and none shall make them afraid. And I will raise up for them a plant of renown, and they shall be no more consumed with hunger in the land, neither bear the shame of the heathen any more. Thus shall they know that I the LORD their God am with them, and that they, even the house of Israel, are my people, saith the Lord GOD. And ye my flock, the flock of my pasture, are men, and I am your God, saith the Lord GOD.

Alleluia. Alleluia, ℣. O give thanks unto the Lord, for he is gracious: and his mercy endureth for ever.

Rogation Days # Proper of Season

Gospel. Luke 11:5

AT THAT TIME: Jesus said unto his disciples: And he said unto them, Which of you shall have a friend, and shall go unto him at midnight, and say unto him, Friend, lend me three loaves; For a friend of mine in his journey is come to me, and I have nothing to set before him? And he from within shall answer and say, Trouble me not: the door is now shut, and my children are with me in bed; I cannot rise and give thee. I say unto you, Though he will not rise and give him, because he is his friend, yet because of his importunity he will rise and give him as many as he needeth. And I say unto you, Ask, and it shall be given you; seek, and ye shall find; knock, and it shall be opened unto you. For every one that asketh receiveth; and he that seeketh findeth; and to him that knocketh it shall be opened. If a son shall ask bread of any of you that is a father, will he give him a stone? or if he ask a fish, will he for a fish give him a serpent? Or if he shall ask an egg, will he offer him a scorpion? If ye then, being evil, know how to give good gifts unto your children: how much more shall your heavenly Father give the Holy Spirit to them that ask him?

Offertory. I will give great thanks unto the Lord with my mouth: and praise him among the multitude, for he shall stand at the right hand of the poor: to save his soul from unrighteous judges, alleluia.

Secret

E beseech thee, O Lord, that these our oblations may both loose the bonds of our iniquity, and obtain for us the gifts of thy loving-kindness. Through.

¶ 2nd Secret is of St. Mary in Eastertide (p. 542) & 3rd Against the Persecutors of the Church (p. 543) or for the Chief Bishop (p. 543).

Communion. Ask, and ye shall receive : seek, and ye shall find: knock, and it shall be opened unto you: for every one that asketh receiveth; and he that seeketh findeth: and to him that knocketh it shall be opened, alleluia.

Postcommunion

E beseech thee, O Lord, to further with thy gracious favour these our supplications: that we, receiving thy gifts in our tribulation, may increase in thy love by the consolation of the same. Through.

¶ 2nd Postcommunion is of St. Mary in Eastertide (p. 542) & 3rd Against the Persecutors of the Church (p. 543) or for the Chief Bishop (p. 543).

Proper of Season *Ascension Eve*

Vigil of Ascension

Introit

WITH a voice of singing declare ye this, and let it be heard, alleluia: utter it even unto the end of the earth: the Lord hath delivered his people, alleluia, alleluia. *Ps.* O be joyful in God, all ye lands: sing praises unto his name, make his praise to be glorious.

Collect

O LORD, from whom all good things do come, grant to us thy humble servants: that by thy holy inspiration we may think those things that be good; and by thy merciful guiding may perform the same. Through.

GRANT, we beseech thee, Almighty God: that we, who in our affliction do put our trust in thy mercy; may ever be defended by thy protection against all adversities. (Through.)

¶ 3rd Collect is of St. Mary in Eastertide (p. 542).

Epistle. Ephesians 4:7

BRETHREN: Unto every one of us is given grace according to the measure of the gift of Christ. Wherefore he saith, When he ascended up on high, he led captivity captive, and gave gifts unto men. (Now that he ascended, what is it but that he also descended first into the lower parts of the earth? He that descended is the same also that ascended up far above all heavens, that he might fill all things.) And he gave some, apostles; and some, prophets; and some, evangelists; and some, pastors and teachers; For the perfecting of the saints, for the work of the ministry, for the edifying of the body of Christ: Till we all come in the unity of the faith, and of the knowledge of the Son of God, unto a perfect man, unto the measure of the stature of the fulness of Christ.

Alleluia. Alleluia, alleluia. ℣. Christ is risen, and hath shewed light unto us, whom he hath redeemed with his blood. Alleluia. ℣. I came forth from the Father, and am come into the world: again I leave the world, and go to the Father. Alleluia.

Gospel. John 17:1

AT THAT TIME: Jesus lifted up his eyes to heaven, and said: Father, the hour is come; glorify thy Son, that thy Son also may glorify thee: As thou hast given him power over all flesh, that he should give eternal life to as many as thou hast given him. And this is life eternal, that they might know

Ascension Eve   # Proper of Season

thee the only true God, and Jesus Christ, whom thou hast sent. I have glorified thee on the earth: I have finished the work which thou gavest me to do. And now, O Father, glorify thou me with thine own self with the glory which I had with thee before the world was. I have manifested thy name unto the men which thou gavest me out of the world: thine they were, and thou gavest them me; and they have kept thy word. Now they have known that all things whatsoever thou hast given me are of thee. For I have given unto them the words which thou gavest me; and they have received them, and have known surely that I came out from thee, and they have believed that thou didst send me. I pray for them: I pray not for the world, but for them which thou hast given me; for they are thine. And all mine are thine, and thine are mine; and I am glorified in them. And now I am no more in the world, but these are in the world, and I come to thee.

Offertory. O praise the Lord our God, ye people, and make the voice of his praise to be heard: who holdeth our soul in life, and suffereth not out feet to slip: praised be the Lord, who hath not cast out my prayer, nor turned his mercy from me, alleluia.

Secret

ECEIVE, O Lord, the prayers of thy faithful people, together with the offering of these sacrifices: that through these observances of our bounden devotion, we may attain unto heavenly glory. Through.

E beseech thee, O Lord, that these our oblations may both loose the bonds of our iniquity, and obtain for us the gifts of thy loving-kindness. (Through.)

¶ 3rd Secret is of St. Mary in Eastertide (p. 542).

Communion. O sing unto the Lord, alleluia: sing unto the Lord, and praise his name: be telling of his salvation from day to day, alleluia, alleluia.

Postcommunion

RANT unto us, O Lord, that we who have been fulfilled with the strength of thy heavenly table: may both desire those things which be right and obtain those things which we desire. Through.

E beseech thee, O Lord, to further with thy gracious favour these our supplications: that we, receiving thy gifts in our tribulation, may increase in thy love by the consolation of the same. (Through.)

¶ 3rd Postcommunion is of St. Mary in Eastertide (p. 542).

Proper of Season *Ascension Thursday*

Ascension Thursday

First Class Double, Third Class Octave

Introit

YE men of Galilee, why marvel ye gazing up into heaven? alleluia: in like manner as ye have seen him going up into heaven, so shall he come again, alleluia, alleluia, alleluia. *Ps.* O clap your hands together, all ye people: O sing unto God with the voice of melody,

Collect

GRANT, we beseech thee, Almighty God, that like as we do believe thy only-begotten Son our Lord Jesus Christ to have ascended into the heavens; so we may also in heart and mind thither ascend, and with him continually dwell, who liveth and reigneth with thee and the Holy Ghost, one God, world without end. *Amen.*

Epistle. Acts 1:1

THE former treatise have I made, O Theophilus, of all that Jesus began both to do and teach, Until the day in which he was taken up, after that he through the Holy Ghost had given commandments unto the apostles whom he had chosen: To whom also he shewed himself alive after his passion by many infallible proofs, being seen of them forty days, and speaking of the things pertaining to the kingdom of God: And, being assembled together with them, commanded them that they should not depart from Jerusalem, but wait for the promise of the Father, which, saith he, ye have heard of me. For John truly baptized with water; but ye shall be baptized with the Holy Ghost not many days hence. When they therefore were come together, they asked of him, saying, Lord, wilt thou at this time restore again the kingdom to Israel? And he said unto them, It is not for you to know the times or the seasons, which the Father hath put in his own power. But ye shall receive power, after that the Holy Ghost is come upon you: and ye shall be witnesses unto me both in Jerusalem, and in all Judaea, and in Samaria, and unto the uttermost part of the earth. And when he had spoken these things, while they beheld, he was taken up; and a cloud received him out of their sight. And while they looked stedfastly toward heaven as he went up, behold, two men stood by them in white apparel; Which also said, Ye men of Galilee, why stand ye gazing up into heaven? this same Jesus,

Ascension Thursday # Proper of Season

which is taken up from you into heaven, shall so come in like manner as ye have seen him go into heaven.

Alleluia. Alleluia, alleluia. ℣. God is gone up with a merry noise, and the Lord with the sound of the trumpet. Alleluia. ℣. The Lord in the holy place of Sinai, ascending up on high, hath led captivity captive. Alleluia.

Gospel. Mark 16:14

T THAT TIME: Jesus appeared unto the eleven as they sat at meat, and upbraided them with their unbelief and hardness of heart, because they believed not them which had seen him after he was risen. And he said unto them, Go ye into all the world, and preach the gospel to every creature. He that believeth and is baptized shall be saved; but he that believeth not shall be damned. And these signs shall follow them that believe; In my name shall they cast out devils; they shall speak with new tongues; They shall take up serpents; and if they drink any deadly thing, it shall not hurt them; they shall lay hands on the sick, and they shall recover. So then after the Lord had spoken unto them, he was received up into heaven, and sat on the right hand of God. And they went forth, and preached every where, the Lord working with them, and confirming the word with signs following.

Offertory. God is gone up with a merry noise: and the Lord with the sound of the trumpet, alleluia.

Secret

ECEIVE, O Lord, the gifts which we offer for the glorious Ascension of thy Son: and mercifully grant: that we may be delivered from present dangers, and attain to everlasting life. Through the same.

Communion. Sing ye to the Lord, who ascended above the heaven of heavens, to the Sunrising, alleluia.

Postcommunion

RANT to us, we beseech thee, almighty and merciful God: that those things which we have known to be received in visible mysteries we may obtain in invisible effect. Through.

¶ During the Octave, the Mass is said as on the Feast, and after the Prayers of the Day are added the Seasonal Propers for Easter II (p. 317).

Proper of Season *Ascension Sunday*

SUNDAY WITHIN THE ASCENSION OCTAVE

Semidouble

Introit

HEARKEN unto my voice, O Lord, when I cry unto thee, alleluia: unto thee my heart hath said, Thy face have I sought, thy face, Lord, will I seek: O hide not thou thy face from me, alleluia, alleluia. *Ps.* The Lord is my light, and my salvation: whom then shall I fear?

Collect

O GOD, the King of glory, who hast exalted thine only Son Jesus Christ with great triumph unto thy kingdom in heaven; We beseech thee, leave us not comfortless; but send to us thine Holy Ghost to comfort us, and exalt us unto the same place whither our Saviour Christ is gone before, who liveth and reigneth with thee and the Holy Ghost, one God, world without end. *Amen.*

¶ Commemoration is made of Ascension Thursday (p. 331).

Epistle. 1 Peter 4:7

DEARLY BELOVED: The end of all things is at hand: be ye therefore sober, and watch unto prayer. And above all things have fervent charity among yourselves: for charity shall cover the multitude of sins. Use hospitality one to another without grudging. As every man hath received the gift, even so minister the same one to another, as good stewards of the manifold grace of God. If any man speak, let him speak as the oracles of God; if any man minister, let him do it as of the ability which God giveth: that God in all things may be glorified through Jesus Christ, to whom be praise and dominion for ever and ever. Amen.

Alleluia. Alleluia, alleluia, ℣. The Lord reigneth over all the heathen: God sitteth upon his holy seat. Alleluia. ℣. I will not leave you comfortless: I go away and come again unto you, and your heart shall rejoice. Alleluia.

Gospel. John 15:26

AT THAT TIME: Jesus said unto his disciples: When the Comforter is come, whom I will send unto you from the Father, even the Spirit of truth, which proceedeth from the Father, he shall testify of me: And ye

Ascension Sunday — **Proper of Season**

also shall bear witness, because ye have been with me from the beginning. These things have I spoken unto you, that ye should not be offended. They shall put you out of the synagogues: yea, the time cometh, that whosoever killeth you will think that he doeth God service. And these things will they do unto you, because they have not known the Father, nor me. But these things have I told you, that when the time shall come, ye may remember that I told you of them.

Offertory. God is gone up with a merry noise: and the Lord with the sound of the trump, alleluia.

Secret

AY these spotless sacrifices purify us, O Lord: and give unto our souls the strength of thy heavenly grace. Through.

⁋ Commemoration is made of Ascension Thursday (p. 332).

Communion. Father, while I was with them, I kept those that thou gavest me, alleluia: and now I come to thee: I pray not that thou shouldest take them out of the world; but that thou shouldest keep them from the evil, alleluia, alleluia.

Postcommunion

RANT, we beseech thee, O Lord: that we, being filled with thy sacred gifts; may ever continue in thanksgiving for the same. Through.

⁋ Commemoration is made of Ascension Thursday (p. 332).

⁋ On the Octave Day of the Ascension (Greater Double), Mass is said as on the Feast.

⁋ On the Friday after the Octave (Semidouble), Mass of the preceding Sunday said, with **Gloria in excelsis**; 2nd Collect of **St. Mary in Eastertide** (p. 542) & 3rd **Against the Persecutors of the Church** (p. 543) or for the **Chief Bishop** (p. 543); and Preface of the Ascension, which is to be said even in Masses of the Saints, or Votives—which have no proper preface—according to the Rubrics: but the Creed is omitted.

⁋ If on the preceding Sunday a 1st or 2nd Double should have been celebrated, on this Feria private votive Masses and daily read Masses of the Dead are prohibited.

Proper of Season *Whitsunday*

WHITSUNDAY

First Class Double, First Class Octave

Introit

THE Spirit of the Lord hath filled the whole world, alleluia: and that which containeth all things hath knowledge of the voice, alleluia, alleluia, alleluia. *Ps.* Let God arise, and let his enemies be scattered: let them also that hate him flee before him.

Collect

O GOD, who as at this time didst teach the hearts of thy faithful people, by sending to them the light of thy Holy Spirit; Grant us by the same Spirit to have a right judgment in all things, and evermore to rejoice in his holy comfort. Through.

Epistle. Acts 2:1

WHEN the day of Pentecost was fully come, they were all with one accord in one place. And suddenly there came a sound from heaven as of a rushing mighty wind, and it filled all the house where they were sitting. And there appeared unto them cloven tongues like as of fire, and it sat upon each of them. And they were all filled with the Holy Ghost, and began to speak with other tongues, as the Spirit gave them utterance. And there were dwelling at Jerusalem Jews, devout men, out of every nation under heaven. Now when this was noised abroad, the multitude came together, and were confounded, because that every man heard them speak in his own language. And they were all amazed and marvelled, saying one to another, Behold, are not all these which speak Galilaeans? And how hear we every man in our own tongue, wherein we were born? Parthians, and Medes, and Elamites, and the dwellers in Mesopotamia, and in Judaea, and Cappadocia, in Pontus, and Asia, Phrygia, and Pamphylia, in Egypt, and in the parts of Libya about Cyrene, and strangers of Rome, Jews and proselytes, Cretes and Arabians, we do hear them speak in our tongues the wonderful works of God.

Alleluia. Alleluia, alleluia. ℣. O send forth thy Spirit and they shall be made, and thou shalt renew the face of the earth. Alleluia. (Here genuflect.) ℣. Come, Holy Ghost, fill the hearts of thy faithful: and kindle in them the fire of thy love.

Whitsunday # Proper of Season

Sequence

COME, thou Holy Spirit, come, and from thy celestial home send thy light and brilliancy.

Come, thou Father of the poor; come thou source of all our store; come, the soul's true radiancy.

Thou of comforters the best, of the soul the sweetest guest, come in toil refreshingly.

In our labour rest most sweet, grateful shadow from the heat, comfort in adversity.

O thou light most pure and blest, shine within the inmost breast of thy faithful company.

Where thou art not, man hath nought, every holy deed and thought comes from thy divinity.

What is soiled, make thou pure, what is wounded, work its cure, water what is parched and dry.

What is rigid, gently bend, what is frozen, warmly tend, strengthen what goes erringly.

Fill thy faithful, who confide in thy power to guard and guide, with thy sevenfold mystery.

Here thy grace and virtue send, grant salvation in the end, and in heaven felicity. Amen. Alleluia.

Gospel. John 14:15

AT THAT TIME: Jesus said unto his disciples: If ye love me, keep my commandments. And I will pray the Father, and he shall give you another Comforter, that he may abide with you for ever; Even the Spirit of truth; whom the world cannot receive, because it seeth him not, neither knoweth him: but ye know him; for he dwelleth with you, and shall be in you. I will not leave you comfortless: I will come to you. Yet a little while, and the world seeth me no more; but ye see me: because I live, ye shall live also. At that day ye shall know that I am in my Father, and ye in me, and I in you. He that hath my commandments, and keepeth them, he it is that loveth me: and he that loveth me shall be loved of my Father, and I will love him, and will manifest myself to him. Judas saith unto him, not Iscariot, Lord, how is it that thou wilt manifest thyself unto us, and not unto the world? Jesus answered and said unto him, If a man love me, he will keep my words: and my Father will love him, and we will come unto him, and make our abode with him. He that loveth me not keepeth not my sayings: and the word which ye hear is not mine, but the Father's which

Proper of Season — *Whitsunday*

sent me. These things have I spoken unto you, being yet present with you. But the Comforter, which is the Holy Ghost, whom the Father will send in my name, he shall teach you all things, and bring all things to your remembrance, whatsoever I have said unto you. Peace I leave with you, my peace I give unto you: not as the world giveth, give I unto you. Let not your heart be troubled, neither let it be afraid. Ye have heard how I said unto you, I go away, and come again unto you. If ye loved me, ye would rejoice, because I said, I go unto the Father: for my Father is greater than I. And now I have told you before it come to pass, that, when it is come to pass, ye might believe. Hereafter I will not talk much with you: for the prince of this world cometh, and hath nothing in me. But that the world may know that I love the Father; and as the Father gave me commandment, even so I do.

Offertory. Stablish the thing, O God, that thou hast wrought in us: for thy temple's sake at Jerusalem shall kings bring presents unto thee, alleluia.

Secret

ANCTIFY, we beseech thee, O Lord, the gifts which we offer: and cleanse our hearts by the enlightening of the Holy Spirit. Through.

Communion. Suddenly there came a sound from heaven as of a rushing mighty wind, where they were sitting, alleluia: and they were all filled with the Holy Ghost, speaking the wonderful works of God, alleluia, alleluia.

Postcommunion

OUR thy Holy Spirit upon us, O Lord, and cleanse our hearts: that they may be made fruitful by the inward sprinkling of his dew. Through ... in the unity of the same Holy Spirit.

Whit-Monday

Proper of Season

WHIT-MONDAY

First Class Double

Introit

HE fed them with the finest wheat-flour, alleluia: and with honey out of the stony rock hath he satisfied them, alleluia, alleluia. *Ps.* Sing we merrily unto God our strength: make a cheerful noise unto the God of Jacob.

Collect

SEND, we beseech thee, Almighty God, thy Holy Spirit into our hearts, that he may direct and rule us according to thy will, comfort us in all our afflictions, defend us from all error, and lead us into all truth; through Jesus Christ our Lord, who with thee and the same Holy Spirit liveth and reigneth, one God, world without end. *Amen.*

Epistle. Acts 10:34

IN THOSE DAYS: Peter opened his mouth, and said, Of a truth I perceive that God is no respecter of persons: But in every nation he that feareth him, and worketh righteousness, is accepted with him. The word which God sent unto the children of Israel, preaching peace by Jesus Christ: (he is Lord of all:) That word, I say, ye know, which was published throughout all Judaea, and began from Galilee, after the baptism which John preached; How God anointed Jesus of Nazareth with the Holy Ghost and with power: who went about doing good, and healing all that were oppressed of the devil; for God was with him. And we are witnesses of all things which he did both in the land of the Jews, and in Jerusalem; whom they slew and hanged on a tree: Him God raised up the third day, and shewed him openly; Not to all the people, but unto witnesses chosen before of God, even to us, who did eat and drink with him after he rose from the dead. And he commanded us to preach unto the people, and to testify that it is he which was ordained of God to be the Judge of quick and dead. To him give all the prophets witness, that through his name whosoever believeth in him shall receive remission of sins. While Peter yet spake these words, the Holy Ghost fell on all them which heard the word. And they of the circumcision which believed were astonished, as many as came with Peter, because that on the Gentiles also was poured out the gift of the Holy Ghost. For they heard them speak with tongues, and magnify God. Then answered

Proper of Season — *Whit-Monday*

Peter, Can any man forbid water, that these should not be baptized, which have received the Holy Ghost as well as we? And he commanded them to be baptized in the name of the Lord. Then prayed they him to tarry certain days.

Alleluia. Alleluia, alleluia. ℣. The Apostles spake with other tongues the wonderful works of God, alleluia. (Here genuflect.) ℣. Come, Holy Ghost, fill the hearts of thy faithful: and kindle in them the fire of thy love.

¶ The Sequence as on Whit-Sunday (p. 336)

Gospel. John 3:16

T THAT TIME: Jesus said unto Nicodemus: God so loved the world, that he gave his only begotten Son, that whosoever believeth in him should not perish, but have everlasting life. For God sent not his Son into the world to condemn the world; but that the world through him might be saved. He that believeth on him is not condemned: but he that believeth not is condemned already, because he hath not believed in the name of the only begotten Son of God. And this is the condemnation, that light is come into the world, and men loved darkness rather than light, because their deeds were evil. For every one that doeth evil hateth the light, neither cometh to the light, lest his deeds should be reproved. But he that doeth truth cometh to the light, that his deeds may be made manifest, that they are wrought in God.

Offertory. The Lord thundered out of heaven, and the Highest gave forth his voice: and the springs of waters were seen, alleluia.

Secret

E beseech thee, O Lord, graciously to sanctify these gifts: and by the acceptable offering of our spiritual sacrifice, render us ourselves an everlasting oblation unto thee. Through.

Communion. The Holy Ghost shall teach you, alleluia: whatsoever I have said unto you, alleluia, alleluia.

Postcommunion

SSIST, O Lord, we beseech thee, thy people: and defend from the fury of their enemies those whom thou hast fulfilled with heavenly mysteries. Through.

Whit-Tuesday

Proper of Season

WHIT-TUESDAY

First Class Double

Introit

RECEIVE the joyfulness of your glory, alleluia: giving thanks unto God, alleluia: who hath called you to the heavenly kingdom, alleluia, alleluia, alleluia. *Ps.* Hear my law, O my people: incline your ears unto the words of my mouth.

Collect

GRANT, we beseech thee, merciful God, that thy Church, being gathered together in unity by thy Holy Spirit, may manifest thy power among all peoples, to the glory of thy Name; through Jesus Christ our Lord, who liveth and reigneth with thee and the same Spirit, one God, world without end. *Amen.*

Epistle. Acts 8:14

IN THOSE DAYS: When the apostles which were at Jerusalem heard that Samaria had received the word of God, they sent unto them Peter and John: Who, when they were come down, prayed for them, that they might receive the Holy Ghost: (For as yet he was fallen upon none of them: only they were baptized in the name of the Lord Jesus.) Then laid they their hands on them, and they received the Holy Ghost.

Alleluia. Alleluia, alleluia, ℣. The Holy Ghost shall teach you, whatsoever I have said unto you. Alleluia. (Here genuflect.) ℣. Come, Holy Ghost, fill the hearts of thy faithful: and kindle in them the fire of thy love.

❡ The Sequence as on Whit-Sunday (p. 336)

Gospel. John 10:1

AT THAT TIME: Jesus said unto the Pharisees: Verily, verily, I say unto you, He that entereth not by the door into the sheepfold, but climbeth up some other way, the same is a thief and a robber. But he that entereth in by the door is the shepherd of the sheep. To him the porter openeth; and the sheep hear his voice: and he calleth his own sheep by name, and leadeth them out. And when he putteth forth his own sheep, he goeth before them, and the sheep follow him: for they know his voice. And a stranger will they not follow, but will flee from him: for they know not the voice of strangers. This parable spake Jesus unto them: but they understood not what things they were which he spake unto them. Then said Jesus unto them again, Verily, verily, I say unto you, I am the door of the sheep. All that ever came before me are thieves and robbers: but the sheep did not hear them. I am the door: by me if any man enter in, he shall be saved, and shall go in and out, and find pasture. The thief cometh not, but for to steal, and to kill, and to destroy: I am come that they might have life, and that they might have it more abundantly.

Offertory. The Lord opened the doors of heaven: he rained down manna also upon them for to eat: he gave them food from heaven, so man did eat Angels' food, alleluia.

Secret

AY the offering of this gift purify us, we beseech thee, O Lord: and render us worthy to partake of holy things. Through.

Communion. The Spirit which proceedeth from the Father, alleluia: he shall glorify me, alleluia, alleluia.

Postcommunion

E beseech thee, O Lord, that the Holy Ghost may renew our minds by divine sacraments: forasmuch as he is himself the remission of all sins. Through.

EMBER WEDNESDAY IN WHITSUNTIDE

Semidouble

Introit

 GOD, when thou wentest forth before the people, journeying and dwelling with them, alleluia: the earth shook, and the heavens dropped, alleluia, alleluia. *Ps.* Let God arise, and let his enemies be scattered: let them also that hate him flee before him.

Collect

E beseech thee, O Lord, that the Paraclete, who proceedeth from thee, may enlighten our minds: and lead us, as thy Son hath promised, into all truth; Who liveth.

Whitsun Emberday   Proper of Season   Ember Wednesday

Epistle. Acts 2:14

IN THOSE DAYS: Peter, standing up with the eleven, lifted up his voice, and said unto them, Ye men of Judaea, and all ye that dwell at Jerusalem, be this known unto you, and hearken to my words: For these are not drunken, as ye suppose, seeing it is but the third hour of the day. But this is that which was spoken by the prophet Joel; And it shall come to pass in the last days, saith God, I will pour out of my Spirit upon all flesh: and your sons and your daughters shall prophesy, and your young men shall see visions, and your old men shall dream dreams: And on my servants and on my handmaidens I will pour out in those days of my Spirit; and they shall prophesy: And I will shew wonders in heaven above, and signs in the earth beneath; blood, and fire, and vapour of smoke: The sun shall be turned into darkness, and the moon into blood, before that great and notable day of the Lord come: And it shall come to pass, that whosoever shall call on the name of the Lord shall be saved.

Alleluia. Alleluia. ℣. By the word of the Lord were the heavens made, and all the hosts of them by the breath of his mouth.

Collect

GRANT, we beseech thee, almighty and merciful God: that the Holy Ghost descending on us may by his gracious indwelling render us a temple of his glory. Through.

¶ From this day until the Saturday following, inclusive, after the Collect of the Day is said the 2nd Against the Persecutors of the Church (p. 543) or for the Chief Bishop (p. 543).

Epistle. Acts 5:12

IN THOSE DAYS: By the hands of the apostles were many signs and wonders wrought among the people; (and they were all with one accord in Solomon's porch. And of the rest durst no man join himself to them: but the people magnified them. And believers were the more added to the Lord, multitudes both of men and women.) Insomuch that they brought forth the sick into the streets, and laid them on beds and couches, that at the least the shadow of Peter passing by might overshadow some of them. There came also a multitude out of the cities round about unto Jerusalem, bringing sick folks, and them which were vexed with unclean spirits: and they were healed every one.

Ember Wednesday   Proper of Season   *Whitsun Emberday*

Alleluia. Alleluia, alleluia. (Here genuflect.) ℣. Come, Holy Ghost, fill the hearts of thy faithful: and kindle in them the fire of thy love.

❡ The Sequence as on Whit-Sunday (p. 336)

Gospel. John 6:44

AT THAT TIME: Jesus said to the multitudes of the Jews: No man can come to me, except the Father which hath sent me draw him: and I will raise him up at the last day. It is written in the prophets, And they shall be all taught of God. Every man therefore that hath heard, and hath learned of the Father, cometh unto me. Not that any man hath seen the Father, save he which is of God, he hath seen the Father. Verily, verily, I say unto you, He that believeth on me hath everlasting life. I am that bread of life. Your fathers did eat manna in the wilderness, and are dead. This is the bread which cometh down from heaven, that a man may eat thereof, and not die. I am the living bread which came down from heaven: if any man eat of this bread, he shall live for ever: and the bread that I will give is my flesh, which I will give for the life of the world.

Offertory. My delight shall be in thy commandments, which I have loved exceedingly: my hands also will I lift up unto thy commandments, which I have loved, alleluia.

Secret

ACCEPT, we beseech thee, O Lord, the gift which we offer: and vouchsafe so to work, that what we perform in a mystery, we may celebrate with godly devotion. Through.

❡ 2nd Secret is Against the Persecutors of the Church (p. 543) or for the Chief Bishop (p. 543).

Communion. Peace I leave with you, alleluia: my peace I give unto you, alleluia, alleluia.

Postcommunion

WE, O Lord, who receive the heavenly sacraments, beseech thy mercy: that by those things which we perform in this life we may attain unto everlasting joys. Through.

❡ 2nd Postcommunion is Against the Persecutors of the Church (p. 543) or for the Chief Bishop (p. 543).

Whit-Thursday

Semidouble

Introit

THE Spirit of the Lord hath filled the whole world, alleluia: and that which containeth all things hath knowledge of the voice, alleluia, alleluia, alleluia. *Ps.* Let God arise, and let his enemies be scattered: let them also that hate him flee before him.

Collect

GOD, who as at this time didst teach the hearts of thy faithful people, by sending to them the light of thy Holy Spirit; grant us by the same Spirit to have a right judgment in all things, and evermore to rejoice in his holy comfort. Through.

¶ 2ⁿᵈ Collect is Against the Persecutors of the Church (p. 543) or for the Chief Bishop (p. 543).

Epistle. Acts 8:5

IN THOSE DAYS: Philip went down to the city of Samaria, and preached Christ unto them. And the people with one accord gave heed unto those things which Philip spake, hearing and seeing the miracles which he did. For unclean spirits, crying with loud voice, came out of many that were possessed with them: and many taken with palsies, and that were lame, were healed. And there was great joy in that city.

Alleluia. Alleluia, alleluia, ℣. O send forth thy Spirit, and they shall be made: and thou shalt renew the face of the earth. Alleluia. (Here genuflect.) ℣. Come, Holy Ghost, fill the hearts of thy faithful: and kindle in them the fire of thy love.
¶ The Sequence as on Whit-Sunday (p. 336)

Gospel. Luke 9:1

AT THAT TIME: Jesus called his twelve disciples together, and gave them power and authority over all devils, and to cure diseases. And he sent them to preach the kingdom of God, and to heal the sick. And he said unto them, Take nothing for your journey, neither staves, nor scrip, neither bread, neither money; neither have two coats apiece. And whatsoever house ye

Proper of Season   *Whit-Thursday*

enter into, there abide, and thence depart. And whosoever will not receive you, when ye go out of that city, shake off the very dust from your feet for a testimony against them. And they departed, and went through the towns, preaching the gospel, and healing every where.

Offertory. Stablish the thing, O God, that thou hast wrought in us: for thy temple's sake at Jerusalem shall kings bring presents unto thee, alleluia.

Secret

ANCTIFY, we beseech thee, O Lord, the gifts which we offer: and cleanse our hearts by the enlightening of the Holy Spirit. Through.

¶ 2nd Secret is Against the Persecutors of the Church (p. 543) or for the Chief Bishop (p. 543).

Communion. Suddenly there came a sound from heaven, as of a rushing mighty wind, where they were sitting, alleluia: and they were all filled with the Holy Ghost speaking the wonderful works of God, alleluia, alleluia.

Postcommunion

OUR thy Holy Spirit upon us, O Lord, and cleanse our hearts: that they may be made fruitful by the inward sprinkling of his dew. Through.

¶ 2nd Postcommunion is Against the Persecutors of the Church (p. 543) or for the Chief Bishop (p. 543).

Ember Friday in Whitsuntide

Semidouble

Introit

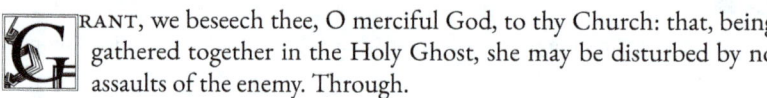LET my mouth be filled with thy praise, alleluia: that I may sing, alleluia: my lips will be fain when I sing unto thee, alleluia, alleluia. *Ps.* In thee, O Lord, have I put my trust, let me never be put to confusion: but rid me, and deliver me in thy righteousness.

Collect

GRANT, we beseech thee, O merciful God, to thy Church: that, being gathered together in the Holy Ghost, she may be disturbed by no assaults of the enemy. Through.

¶ 2nd Collect is Against the Persecutors of the Church (p. 543) or for the Chief Bishop (p. 543).

Epistle. Joel 2:23

THUS SAITH THE LORD GOD: Be glad then, ye children of Zion, and rejoice in the LORD your God: for he hath given you the former rain moderately, and he will cause to come down for you the rain, the former rain, and the latter rain in the first month. And the floors shall be full of wheat, and the fats shall overflow with wine and oil. And I will restore to you the years that the locust hath eaten, the cankerworm, and the caterpiller, and the palmerworm, my great army which I sent among you. And ye shall eat in plenty, and be satisfied, and praise the name of the LORD your God, that hath dealt wondrously with you: and my people shall never be ashamed. And ye shall know that I am in the midst of Israel, and that I am the LORD your God, and none else: and my people shall never be ashamed, saith the Lord Almighty.

Alleluia. Alleluia, alleluia. ℣. O how good and sweet, O Lord, is thy Spirit within us. Alleluia. (Here genuflect.) ℣. Come, Holy Ghost, fill the hearts of thy faithful: and kindle in them the fire of thy love.

¶ The Sequence as on Whit-Sunday (p. 336)

Gospel. Luke 5:17

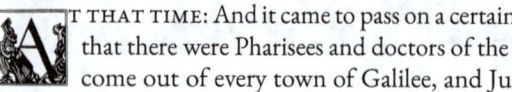T THAT TIME: And it came to pass on a certain day, as Jesus was teaching, that there were Pharisees and doctors of the law sitting by, which were come out of every town of Galilee, and Judaea, and Jerusalem: and

Ember Friday — Proper of Season — Whitsun Emberday

the power of the Lord was present to heal them. And, behold, men brought in a bed a man which was taken with a palsy: and they sought means to bring him in, and to lay him before him. And when they could not find by what way they might bring him in because of the multitude, they went upon the housetop, and let him down through the tiling with his couch into the midst before Jesus. And when he saw their faith, he said unto him, Man, thy sins are forgiven thee. And the scribes and the Pharisees began to reason, saying, Who is this which speaketh blasphemies? Who can forgive sins, but God alone? But when Jesus perceived their thoughts, he answering said unto them, What reason ye in your hearts? Whether is easier, to say, Thy sins be forgiven thee; or to say, Rise up and walk? But that ye may know that the Son of man hath power upon earth to forgive sins, (he said unto the sick of the palsy,) I say unto thee, Arise, and take up thy couch, and go into thine house. And immediately he rose up before them, and took up that whereon he lay, and departed to his own house, glorifying God. And they were all amazed, and they glorified God, and were filled with fear, saying, We have seen strange things to day.

Offertory. Praise the Lord, O my soul: while I live will I praise the Lord: yea, as long as I have any being, I will sing praises unto my God, alleluia.

Secret

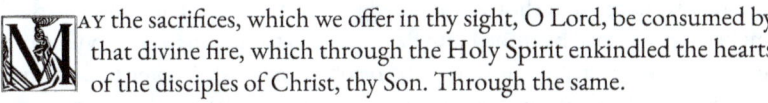AY the sacrifices, which we offer in thy sight, O Lord, be consumed by that divine fire, which through the Holy Spirit enkindled the hearts of the disciples of Christ, thy Son. Through the same.

¶ 2ⁿᵈ Secret is Against the Persecutors of the Church (p. 543) or for the Chief Bishop (p. 543).

Communion. I will not leave you comfortless: I will come to you again, alleluia: and your heart shall rejoice, alleluia.

Postcommunion

We have received, O Lord, the gifts of thy sacred mystery: humbly beseeching thee; that those things which thou hast commanded us to do in remembrance of thee, may be profitable to the succour of our infirmity. Who livest.

¶ 2ⁿᵈ Postcommunion is Against the Persecutors of the Church (p. 543) or for the Chief Bishop (p. 543).

Ember Saturday in Whitsuntide

Semidouble

Introit

HE love of God is shed abroad in our hearts, alleluia: by the Holy Ghost which dwelleth in us, alleluia, alleluia. *Ps.* Praise the Lord, O my soul: and all that is within me, praise his holy name.

Collect

E beseech thee, O Lord, graciously pour the Holy Ghost into our hearts: by whose wisdom we were created, and by whose providence we are governed. Through.

Epistle. Joel 2:28

HUS SAITH THE LORD GOD: I will pour out my spirit upon all flesh; and your sons and your daughters shall prophesy, your old men shall dream dreams, your young men shall see visions: And also upon the servants and upon the handmaids in those days will I pour out my spirit. And I will shew wonders in the heavens and in the earth, blood, and fire, and pillars of smoke. The sun shall be turned into darkness, and the moon into blood, before the great and the terrible day of the LORD come. And it shall come to pass, that whosoever shall call on the name of the LORD shall be delivered.

Alleluia. Alleluia. ℣. It is the spirit that quickeneth: the flesh profiteth nothing.

Collect

E beseech thee, O Lord, that the Holy Ghost may inflame us with that fire: which our Lord Jesus Christ sent upon earth, and willed that it should be kindled exceedingly. Who liveth.

Epistle. Leviticus 23:9

IN THOSE DAYS: The LORD spake unto Moses, saying, Speak unto the children of Israel, and say unto them, When ye be come into the land which I give unto you, and shall reap the harvest thereof, then ye shall bring a sheaf of the firstfruits of your harvest unto the priest: And he shall wave the sheaf before the LORD, to be accepted for you: on the morrow after the

Ember Saturday — Proper of Season — Whitsun Emberday

sabbath the priest shall wave it. And ye shall offer that day when ye wave the sheaf an he lamb without blemish of the first year for a burnt offering unto the LORD. And the meat offering thereof shall be two tenth deals of fine flour mingled with oil, an offering made by fire unto the LORD for a sweet savour: and the drink offering thereof shall be of wine, the fourth part of an hin. And ye shall eat neither bread, nor parched corn, nor green ears, until the selfsame day that ye have brought an offering unto your God: it shall be a statute for ever throughout your generations in all your dwellings. And ye shall count unto you from the morrow after the sabbath, from the day that ye brought the sheaf of the wave offering; seven sabbaths shall be complete: Even unto the morrow after the seventh sabbath shall ye number fifty days; and ye shall offer a new meat offering unto the LORD. Ye shall bring out of your habitations two wave loaves of two tenth deals: they shall be of fine flour; they shall be baken with leaven; they are the firstfruits unto the LORD. And ye shall offer with the bread seven lambs without blemish of the first year, and one young bullock, and two rams: they shall be for a burnt offering unto the LORD, with their meat offering, and their drink offerings, even an offering made by fire, of sweet savour unto the LORD. Then ye shall sacrifice one kid of the goats for a sin offering, and two lambs of the first year for a sacrifice of peace offerings. And the priest shall wave them with the bread of the firstfruits for a wave offering before the LORD, with the two lambs: they shall be holy to the LORD for the priest. And ye shall proclaim on the selfsame day, that it may be an holy convocation unto you: ye shall do no servile work therein: it shall be a statute for ever in all your dwellings throughout your generations, saith the Lord almighty.

Alleluia. Alleluia. ℣. By his Spirit he hath garnished the heavens.

Collect

O GOD, who for the healing of our souls hast commanded us to chasten our bodies with godly fasting: mercifully grant unto us: that we may ever serve thee both in body and soul. Through.

Epistle. Deuteronomy 26:1

IN THOSE DAYS: Moses said to the children of Israel: Hear, O Israel, what I command thee this day. When thou art come in unto the land which the LORD thy God giveth thee for an inheritance, and possessest it, and dwellest therein; That thou shalt take of the first of all the fruit of the earth, which thou shalt bring of thy land that the LORD thy God giveth thee, and shalt put it in a basket, and shalt go unto the place which the LORD thy God shall

Whitsun Emberday   **Proper of Season**   Ember Saturday

choose to place his name there. And thou shalt go unto the priest that shall be in those days, and say unto him, I profess this day unto the LORD thy God, that I am come unto the country which the LORD sware unto our fathers for to give us. And the priest shall take the basket out of thine hand, and set it down before the altar of the LORD thy God. And thou shalt speak and say before the LORD thy God, A Syrian ready to perish was my father, and he went down into Egypt, and sojourned there with a few, and became there a nation, great, mighty, and populous: And the Egyptians evil entreated us, and afflicted us, and laid upon us hard bondage: And when we cried unto the LORD God of our fathers, the LORD heard our voice, and looked on our affliction, and our labour, and our oppression: And the LORD brought us forth out of Egypt with a mighty hand, and with an outstretched arm, and with great terribleness, and with signs, and with wonders: And he hath brought us into this place, and hath given us this land, even a land that floweth with milk and honey. And now, behold, I have brought the firstfruits of the land, which thou, O LORD, hast given me. And thou shalt set it before the LORD thy God, and worship before the LORD thy God: And thou shalt rejoice in every good thing which the LORD thy God hath given unto thee

Alleluia. Alleluia. ℣. When the day of Pentecost was fully come, they were all sitting with one accord.

Collect

RANT, we beseech thee, almighty God: that we, being taught by these saving fasts, and likewise abstaining from all vices, may more readily obtain thy pardon. Through.

Epistle. Leviticus 26:3

IN THOSE DAYS: The Lord said unto Moses: Speak unto the children of Israel, and say unto them: If ye walk in my statutes, and keep my commandments, and do them; Then I will give you rain in due season, and the land shall yield her increase, and the trees of the field shall yield their fruit. And your threshing shall reach unto the vintage, and the vintage shall reach unto the sowing time: and ye shall eat your bread to the full, and dwell in your land safely. And I will give peace in the land, and ye shall lie down, and none shall make you afraid: and I will rid evil beasts out of the land, neither shall the sword go through your land. And ye shall chase your enemies, and they shall fall before you by the sword. And five of you shall chase an hundred, and an hundred of you shall put ten thousand to flight: and your enemies shall fall

Ember Saturday — Proper of Season — *Whitsun Emberday*

before you by the sword. For I will have respect unto you, and make you fruitful, and multiply you, and establish my covenant with you. And ye shall eat old store, and bring forth the old because of the new. And I will set my tabernacle among you: and my soul shall not abhor you. And I will walk among you, and will be your God, and ye shall be my people, saith the Lord Almighty.

Alleluia. Alleluia. (Here genuflect.) ℣. Come, Holy Ghost, fill the hearts of thy faithful: and kindle in them the fire of thy love.

Collect

GRANT, we beseech thee, Almighty God: that we may so abstain from carnal feasting; that we may likewise fast from the vices which beset us. Through.

Epistle. Song of the Three Children 26

IN THOSE DAYS: The Angel of the Lord came down into the oven together with Azarias and his fellows, and smote the flame of the fire out of the oven; And made the midst of the furnace as it had been a moist whistling wind, so that the fire touched them not at all, neither hurt nor troubled them. Then the three, as out of one mouth, praised, glorified, and blessed, God in the furnace, saying,

¶ Here the response Thanks be to God, is not made.

Alleluia. Alleluia. ℣. Blessed art thou, O Lord, God of our Fathers, and worthy to be praised for ever.

Collect

O GOD, who to the three children didst assuage the flames of fire; mercifully grant; that the flames of sin may not kindle upon us thy servants. Through.

¶ 2nd Collect is Against the Persecutors of the Church (p. 543) or for the Chief Bishop (p. 543).

Epistle. Romans 5:1

BRETHREN: Being justified by faith, we have peace with God through our Lord Jesus Christ: By whom also we have access by faith into this grace wherein we stand, and rejoice in hope of the glory of God. And not only so, but we glory in tribulations also: knowing that tribulation worketh

Whitsun Emberday **Proper of Season** Ember Saturday

patience; And patience, experience; and experience, hope: And hope maketh not ashamed; because the love of God is shed abroad in our hearts by the Holy Ghost which is given unto us.

Tract. O praise the Lord, all ye heathen: praise him, all ye nations, ℣. For his merciful kindness is ever more and more towards us: and the truth of the Lord endureth for ever.

❡ The Sequence as on Whit-Sunday (p. 336)

❡ Note, At the end, Alleluia is not said.

Gospel. Luke 4:38

AT THAT TIME: Jesus arose out of the synagogue, and entered into Simon's house. And Simon's wife's mother was taken with a great fever; and they besought him for her. And he stood over her, and rebuked the fever; and it left her: and immediately she arose and ministered unto them. Now when the sun was setting, all they that had any sick with divers diseases brought them unto him; and he laid his hands on every one of them, and healed them. And devils also came out of many, crying out, and saying, Thou art Christ the Son of God. And he rebuking them suffered them not to speak: for they knew that he was Christ. And when it was day, he departed and went into a desert place: and the people sought him, and came unto him, and stayed him, that he should not depart from them. And he said unto them, I must preach the kingdom of God to other cities also: for therefore am I sent. And he preached in the synagogues of Galilee.

Offertory. O Lord God of my salvation, I have cried day and night before thee: let my prayer enter into thy presence, O Lord, alleluia.

Secret

THAT our fasts may be acceptable to thee, O Lord: grant us, we beseech thee: by the gift of this sacrament to offer unto thee a purified heart. Through.

❡ 2ⁿᵈ Secret is Against the Persecutors of the Church (p. 543) or for the Chief Bishop (p. 543).

Communion. The Spirit bloweth where it listeth; and thou hearest the sound thereof, alleluia, alleluia: but canst not tell whence it cometh and whither it goeth, alleluia, alleluia, alleluia.

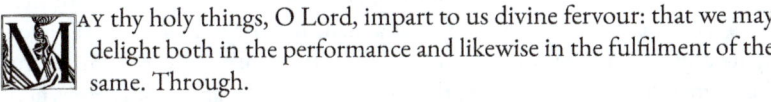
Proper of Season *Trinity Sunday*

Postcommunion

MAY thy holy things, O Lord, impart to us divine fervour: that we may delight both in the performance and likewise in the fulfilment of the same. Through.

¶ 2ⁿᵈ Postcommunion is Against the Persecutors of the Church (p. 543) or for the Chief Bishop (p. 543).

Trinity Sunday

First Class Double

Introit

BLESSED be the holy Trinity, and the undivided Unity: we will praise and glorify him, because he hath showed his mercy upon us. *Ps.* O Lord our governor: how excellent is thy name in all the world!

Collect

ALMIGHTY and everlasting God, who hast given unto us thy servants grace by the confession of a true faith to acknowledge the glory of the eternal Trinity, and in the power of the Divine Majesty to worship the Unity: We beseech thee; that thou wouldest keep us stedfast in this faith, and evermore defend us from all adversities. Who livest and reignest, one God, world without end. *Amen.*

Epistle. Revelation 4:1

IN THOSE DAYS: I looked, and, behold, a door was opened in heaven: and the first voice which I heard was as it were of a trumpet talking with me; which said, Come up hither, and I will shew thee things which must be hereafter. And immediately I was in the spirit: and, behold, a throne was set in heaven, and one sat on the throne. And he that sat was to look upon like a jasper and a sardine stone: and there was a rainbow round about the throne, in sight like unto an emerald. And round about the throne were four and twenty seats: and upon the seats I saw four and twenty elders sitting, clothed in white raiment; and they had on their heads crowns of gold. And out of the throne proceeded lightnings and thunderings and voices: and there were seven lamps of fire burning before the throne, which are the seven Spirits of God. And before the throne there was a sea of glass like unto crystal: and in the

Trinity Sunday

midst of the throne, and round about the throne, were four beasts full of eyes before and behind. And the first beast was like a lion, and the second beast like a calf, and the third beast had a face as a man, and the fourth beast was like a flying eagle. And the four beasts had each of them six wings about him; and they were full of eyes within: and they rest not day and night, saying, Holy, holy, holy, Lord God Almighty, which was, and is, and is to come. And when those beasts give glory and honour and thanks to him that sat on the throne, who liveth for ever and ever, The four and twenty elders fall down before him that sat on the throne, and worship him that liveth for ever and ever, and cast their crowns before the throne, saying, Thou art worthy, O Lord, to receive glory and honour and power: for thou hast created all things, and for thy pleasure they are and were created.

Gradual. Blessed art thou, O Lord, that beholdest the depths, and sittest upon the Cherubim. ℣. Blessed art thou, O Lord, in the firmament of heaven, and worthy to be praised for ever.

Alleluia. Alleluia, alleluia. ℣. Blessed art thou, O Lord God of our fathers, and worthy to be praised for evermore. Alleluia.

Gospel. John 3:1

AT THAT TIME: There was a man of the Pharisees, named Nicodemus, a ruler of the Jews: The same came to Jesus by night, and said unto him, Rabbi, we know that thou art a teacher come from God: for no man can do these miracles that thou doest, except God be with him. Jesus answered and said unto him, Verily, verily, I say unto thee, Except a man be born again, he cannot see the kingdom of God. Nicodemus saith unto him, How can a man be born when he is old? can he enter the second time into his mother's womb, and be born? Jesus answered, Verily, verily, I say unto thee, Except a man be born of water and of the Spirit, he cannot enter into the kingdom of God. That which is born of the flesh is flesh; and that which is born of the Spirit is spirit. Marvel not that I said unto thee, Ye must be born again. The wind bloweth where it listeth, and thou hearest the sound thereof, but canst not tell whence it cometh, and whither it goeth: so is every one that is born of the Spirit. Nicodemus answered and said unto him, How can these things be? Jesus answered and said unto him, Art thou a master of Israel, and knowest not these things? Verily, verily, I say unto thee, We speak that we do know, and testify that we have seen; and ye receive not our witness. If I have told you earthly things, and ye believe not, how shall ye believe, if I tell you of heavenly things? And no man hath ascended up to heaven, but he that came down from heaven, even the Son of man which is in heaven. And as Moses lifted up the serpent in the wilderness, even so must the Son of man be lifted up: That whosoever believeth in him should not perish, but have eternal life.

Offertory. Blessed be God the Father, and the only-begotten Son of God, and the Holy Spirit: because he hath showed his mercy upon us.

Secret

ANCTIFY, we beseech thee, O Lord our God, the sacrifice which we here offer by the invocation of thy holy name: that through the same we may ourselves be made a perfect gift unto thee for evermore. Through.

Communion. We bless the God of heaven, and will praise him in the sight of all that live: because he hath showed his mercy upon us.

Postcommunion

RANT, O Lord our God: that we who receive this sacrament and who acknowledge the holy and everlasting Trinity, and likewise the undivided Unity: may be profited thereby unto salvation of body and soul. Through.

THE MOST HOLY BODY OF CHRIST

Thursday after Trinity Sunday
First Class Double, Second Class Octave

Opening Sentence. Thou gavest them Bread from heaven. Containing in itself all sweetness. (Wis. 16:20)

Introit

E fed them with the finest wheat-flour, alleluia: and with honey out of the stony rock hath he satisfied them, alleluia, alleluia, alleluia. *Ps.* Sing we merrily unto God, our strength: make a cheerful noise unto the God of Jacob.

Collect

 GOD, who under a wonderful sacrament hast left unto us a memorial of thy Passion: grant us, we beseech thee, so to venerate the sacred mysteries of thy Body and Blood; that we may ever perceive within ourselves the fruit of thy redemption. Who livest and reignest with God the Father.

Corpus Christi # Proper of Season

Epistle. 1 Corinthians 11:23

BRETHREN: I have received of the Lord that which also I delivered unto you, That the Lord Jesus the same night in which he was betrayed took bread: and when he had given thanks, he brake it, and said, Take, eat: this is my body, which is broken for you: this do in remembrance of me. After the same manner also he took the cup, when he had supped, saying, This cup is the new testament in my blood: this do ye, as oft as ye drink it, in remembrance of me. For as often as ye eat this bread, and drink this cup, ye do shew the Lord's death till he come. Wherefore whosoever shall eat this bread, and drink this cup of the Lord, unworthily, shall be guilty of the body and blood of the Lord. But let a man examine himself, and so let him eat of that bread, and drink of that cup. For he that eateth and drinketh unworthily, eateth and drinketh damnation to himself, not discerning the Lord's body.

Gradual. The eyes of all wait upon thee, O Lord: and thou givest them their meat in due season. ℣. Thou openest thine hand: and fillest all things living with plenteousness.

Alleluia. Alleluia, alleluia. ℣. My flesh is meat indeed, and my blood is drink indeed: he that eateth my flesh and drinketh my blood, dwelleth in me, and I in him.

Sequence

LAUD, O Sion, thy salvation, laud with hymns of exultation Christ, thy King and Shepherd true.

Spend thyself, his honour raising: who surpasseth all thy praising, never canst thou reach his due.

Sing to-day, the mystery shewing of the living, life-bestowing bread from heaven before thee set.

E'en the same of old provided, where the twelve, divinely guided, at the holy table met.

Full and clear ring out thy chanting, joy nor sweetest grace be wanting to thy heart and soul today.

When we gather up the measure of that supper and its treasure, keeping feast in glad array.

Lo, the new King's table gracing, this new Passover of blessing hath fulfilled the elder rite.

Now the new the old effaceth, truth revealed the shadow chaseth, day is breaking on the night.

Proper of Season   *Corpus Christi*

What he did at supper seated, Christ ordained to be repeated, his memorial ne'er to cease.

And, his word for guidance taking, bread and wine we hallow, making thus our sacrifice of peace.

This the truth to Christians given–bread becomes his flesh from heaven, wine becomes his holy blood.

Doth it pass thy comprehending? yet by faith, thy sight transcending, wondrous things are understood.

Yea, beneath these sign are hidden glorious things to sight forbidden, signs, not things, are all we see.

Wine is poured and bread is broken: but in either sacred token Christ entire we know to be.

Whoso of this food partaketh rendeth not the Lord nor breaketh: Christ is whole to all that taste.

Thousands are, as one, receivers: one, as thousands of believers, takes the Food that cannot waste.

Good and evil men are sharing one repast: a doom preparing varied as the heart of man.

Doom of life or death awarded: as their days shall be recorded which from one beginning ran.

When the Sacrament is broken, doubt not in each severed token, hallowed by the word once spoken, resteth all the true content.

Nought the precious gift divideth: breaking but the sign betideth: he himself the same abideth, nothing of his fulness spent.

Lo! the Angels' Food is given to the pilgrim who hath striven: see the children's Bread from heaven, which to dogs may not be cast.

Truth the ancient types fulfilling, Isaac bound, a Victim willing: Paschal Lamb, its life-blood spilling: Manna sent in ages past.

Very Bread, Good Shepherd, tend us: Jesu, of thy love befriend us: thou refresh us, thou defend us: thine eternal goodness send us in the land of life to see.

Thou who all things canst and knowest: who on earth such food bestowest: grant us with thy Saints, though lowest, where the heavenly feast thou showest, fellow-heirs and guests to be. Amen. Alleluia.

Corpus Christi # Proper of Season

Gospel. John 6:55

AT THAT TIME: Jesus said to the multitudes of the Jews: My flesh is meat indeed, and my blood is drink indeed. He that eateth my flesh, and drinketh my blood, dwelleth in me, and I in him. As the living Father hath sent me, and I live by the Father, so he that eateth me, even he shall live by me. This is that bread which came down from heaven; not as your fathers did eat manna and are dead; he that eateth of this bread shall live for ever.

Offertory. The priests of the Lord offer incense and bread unto God: and therefore shall they be holy unto their God, and shall not profane his name, alleluia.

Secret

GRACIOUSLY grant, we beseech thee, O Lord, unto thy Church the gifts of unity and peace: which are shewn forth in a mystery in the gifts we offer. Through.

Communion. As often as ye eat this bread, and drink this cup, ye do show the Lord's death till he come: wherefore whosoever shall eat this bread or drink this cup of the Lord, unworthily, shall be guilty of the body and blood of the Lord, alleluia.

Postcommunion

WE beseech thee, O Lord: that like as the receiving of thy precious Body and Blood in this life doth foreshadow the everlasting fruition of thy Godhead, so thou wouldest vouchsafe unto us to be fulfilled with the same. Who livest.

¶ Within the Octave (Semidouble) and on the Octave Day (Greater Double), Mass is said as on the Feast.

¶ Within the Octave are added, according to the Rubrics, the Seasonal Prayers, 2nd of St. Mary in Eastertide (p. 542) & 3rd Against the Persecutors of the Church (p. 543) or for the Chief Bishop (p. 543).

Proper of Season *Trinity I*

SUNDAY IN THE OCTAVE OF CORPUS CHRISTI

(First Sunday after Trinity)
Semidouble

Introit

O LORD, in thy loving-kindness have I trusted: and my heart is joyful in thy salvation: I will sing unto the Lord, because he hath dealt so lovingly with me. *Ps.* How long wilt thou forget me, O Lord, for ever? How long wilt thou hide thy face from me?

¶ Gloria in excelsis is said on all Sundays after Trinity. But it is not said on Ferial Days, when the Mass of the preceding Sunday is resumed.

Collect

O GOD, the strength of all those who put their trust in thee, mercifully accept our prayers: and because through the weakness of our mortal nature we can do no good thing without thee, grant us the help of thy grace; that in keeping thy commandments we may please thee, both in will and deed. Through.

O GOD, who under a wonderful sacrament hast left unto us a memorial of thy Passion: grant us, we beseech thee, so to venerate the sacred mysteries of thy Body and Blood; that we may ever perceive within ourselves the fruit of thy redemption. Who livest and reignest with God the Father.

Epistle. 1 John 4:7

DEARLY BELOVED: Let us love one another: for love is of God; and every one that loveth is born of God, and knoweth God. He that loveth not knoweth not God; for God is love. In this was manifested the love of God toward us, because that God sent his only begotten Son into the world, that we might live through him. Herein is love, not that we loved God, but that he loved us, and sent his Son to be the propitiation for our sins. Beloved, if God so loved us, we ought also to love one another. No man hath seen God at any time. If we love one another, God dwelleth in us, and his love is perfected in us. Hereby know we that we dwell in him, and he in us, because he hath given us of his Spirit. And we have seen and do testify that the Father sent the Son to be the Saviour of the world. Whosoever shall confess that Jesus is the Son of God, God dwelleth in him, and he in God. And we have known and believed the love that God hath to us. God is love; and he that dwelleth in love dwelleth in God, and God in him. Herein is our love made perfect, that we may have boldness in the day of judgment: because as he is, so are we in this world. There is no fear in love; but perfect love casteth out fear: because fear hath torment. He that feareth is not made perfect in love. We love him, because he first loved us. If a man say, I love God, and hateth his brother, he is a liar: for he that loveth not his brother whom he hath seen, how can he love God whom he hath not seen? And this commandment have we from him, That he who loveth God love his brother also.

Gradual. I said, Lord, be merciful unto me: heal my soul, for I have sinned against thee. ℣. Blessed is he that considereth the poor and needy: the Lord shall deliver him in the time of trouble.

Alleluia. Alleluia, alleluia. ℣. Ponder my words, O Lord: consider my meditation. Alleluia.

Gospel. Luke 16:19

AT THAT TIME: Jesus said unto his disciples: There was a certain rich man, which was clothed in purple and fine linen, and fared sumptuously every day: and there was a certain beggar named Lazarus, which was laid at his gate, full of sores, and desiring to be fed with the crumbs which fell from the rich man's table: moreover the dogs came and licked his sores. And it came to pass, that the beggar died, and was carried by the angels into Abraham's bosom: the rich man also died, and was buried; and in hell he lift up his eyes, being in torments, and seeth Abraham afar off, and Lazarus in his bosom. And he cried and said, Father Abraham, have mercy on me, and send Lazarus, that he may dip the tip of his finger in water, and cool my tongue; for I am tormented in this flame. But Abraham said, Son, remember that thou in thy lifetime receivedst thy good things, and likewise Lazarus evil things: but now he is comforted, and thou art tormented. And beside all this, between us and you there is a great gulf fixed: so that they which would pass from hence to you cannot; neither can they pass to us, that would come from thence. Then he said, I pray thee therefore, father, that thou wouldest send him to my father's house: for I have five brethren; that he may testify unto them, lest they also come into this place of torment. Abraham saith unto him, They have Moses and the prophets; let them hear them. And he said, Nay, father Abraham: but if one went unto them from the dead, they will repent. And he said unto him, If they hear not Moses and the prophets, neither will they be persuaded, though one rose from the dead.

Proper of Season *Divine Compassion*

¶ The Creed is said on all Sundays after Trinity. But it is not said on Ferial Days, when the Mass of the preceding Sunday is resumed.

Offertory. O hearken thou unto the voice of my calling, my King and my God: for unto thee, O Lord, will I make my prayer.

Secret

O thou, we beseech thee, O Lord, graciously accept the offerings which have been dedicated unto thee: and grant that they may become to us an abiding source of strength. Through.

RACIOUSLY grant, we beseech thee, O Lord, unto thy Church the gifts of unity and peace: which are shewn forth in a mystery in the gifts we offer. Through.

Communion. I will speak of all thy marvellous works: I will be glad and rejoice in thee: yea, my songs will I make of thy name, O Most Highest.

Postcommunion

LORD, who hast filled us with such great gifts: grant, we beseech thee; that we may both receive these saving gifts, and never cease from thy praise. Through.

E beseech thee, O Lord: that like as the receiving of thy precious Body and Blood in this life doth foreshadow the everlasting fruition of thy Godhead, so thou wouldest vouchsafe unto us to be fulfilled with the same. Who livest.

COMPASSION OF OUR LORD JESUS CHRIST

Friday after Trinity I
Second Class Double, Simple Octave

Opening Sentence. The Lord is full of compassion and mercy: long-suffering, and of great goodness.

Introit

HE thoughts of his Heart are from generation to generation: to deliver their soul from death, and to feed them in time of dearth (Alleluia, alleluia). *Ps.* Rejoice in the Lord, O ye righteous: for it becometh well the just to be thankful.

Divine Compassion # Proper of Season

Collect

O GOD, who in the Heart of thy Son, wounded by our sins, dost vouchsafe mercifully to bestow upon us the infinite treasures of love: grant, we beseech thee; that we, giving him the homage of our devotion and piety, may likewise perform the duty of worthy satisfaction. Through the same.

Epistle. Ephesians 3:8

BRETHREN: Unto me, who am less than the least of all saints, is this grace given, that I should preach among the Gentiles the unsearchable riches of Christ, and to make all men see what is the fellowship of the mystery, which from the beginning of the world hath been hid in God, who created all things by Jesus Christ: to the intent that now unto the principalities and powers in heavenly places might be known by the church the manifold wisdom of God, according to the eternal purpose which he purposed in Christ Jesus our Lord, in whom we have boldness and access with confidence by the faith of him. For this cause I bow my knees unto the Father of our Lord Jesus Christ, of whom the whole family in heaven and earth is named, that he would grant you, according to the riches of his glory, to be strengthened with might by his Spirit in the inner man; that Christ may dwell in your hearts by faith; that ye, being rooted and grounded in love, may be able to comprehend with all saints what is the breadth, and length, and depth, and height; and to know the love of Christ, which passeth knowledge, that ye might be filled with all the fulness of God.

Gradual. Gracious and righteous is the Lord: therefore will he teach sinners in the way. ℣. Them that are meek shall he guide in judgment, and such as are gentle, them shall he learn his way.

Alleluia. Alleluia, alleluia. ℣. Take my yoke upon you and learn of me, for I am meek and lowly in heart, and ye shall find rest unto your souls. Alleluia.

¶ In Septuagesimatide or Lent, replacing the Alleluia:

Tract. The Lord is full of compassion and mercy, long suffering and of great goodness. ℣. He will not always be chiding, neither keepeth he his anger for ever. ℣. He hath not dealt with us after our sins, nor rewarded us according to our wickedness.

¶ In Eastertide, replacing the Lesser Alleluia:

Alleluia. Alleluia, alleluia. ℣. Take my yoke upon you and learn of me, for I am meek and lowly in heart, and ye shall find rest unto your souls. Alleluia. ℣. Come unto me all ye that labor and are heavy laden, and I will refresh you. Alleluia.

Proper of Season *Divine Compassion*

Gospel. John 19:31

AT THAT TIME: The Jews, because it was the Preparation, that the bodies should not remain upon the cross on the sabbath day, (for that sabbath day was an high day,) besought Pilate that their legs might be broken, and that they might be taken away. Then came the soldiers, and brake the legs of the first, and of the other which was crucified with him. But when they came to Jesus, and saw that he was dead already, they brake not his legs, but one of the soldiers with a spear pierced his side, and forthwith came there out blood and water. And he that saw it bare record, and his record is true: and he knoweth that he saith true, that ye might believe. For these things were done, that the scripture should be fulfilled, A bone of him shall not be broken. And again another scripture saith, They shall look on him whom they pierced.

Offertory. Thy rebuke hath broken my heart, I am full of heaviness: I looked for some to have pity upon me, but there was no man: neither found I any to comfort me. Burnt offerings and sacrifice for sin hast thou not required: then said I: Lo I come. In the volume of the book it is written of me that I should fulfill thy will, O my God: I am content to do it, yea thy law is within my heart, alleluia.

Secret

REGARD, we beseech thee, O Lord, the ineffable charity of the Heart of thy beloved Son: that the gift which we offer may be acceptable unto thee, and avail for the expiation of our offences. Through the same.

Communion. One of the soldiers with a spear pierced his side, and forthwith came there out blood and water. If any man thirst, let him come to me and drink, alleluia, alleluia.

Postcommunion

MAY thy holy gifts, O Lord Jesu, endue us with divine fervour: that we, having tasted thereby the delights of thy most sweet Heart, may learn to despise things earthly, and to love things of heaven. Who livest.

¶ On the Octave Day of the Compassion of Our Lord (Simple), Mass is said as on the Feast.

Trinity II

Proper of Season

Second Sunday after Trinity

Semidouble

Introit

HE Lord was my upholder, he brought me forth also into a place of liberty: he delivered me because he delighted in me. *Ps.* I will love thee, O Lord, my strength: the Lord is my rock, my defence, and my saviour.

Collect

LORD, who never failest to help and govern those whom thou dost bring up in thy stedfast fear and love; Keep us, we beseech thee, under the protection of thy good providence, and make us to have a perpetual fear and love of thy holy Name. Through.

Epistle. 1 John 3:13

EARLY BELOVED: Marvel not, my brethren, if the world hate you. We know that we have passed from death unto life, because we love the brethren. He that loveth not his brother abideth in death. Whosoever hateth his brother is a murderer: and ye know that no murderer hath eternal life abiding in him. Hereby perceive we the love of God, because he laid down his life for us: and we ought to lay down our lives for the brethren. But whoso hath this world's good, and seeth his brother have need, and shutteth up his bowels of compassion from him, how dwelleth the love of God in him? My little children, let us not love in word, neither in tongue; but in deed and in truth. And hereby we know that we are of the truth, and shall assure our hearts before him. For if our heart condemn us, God is greater than our heart, and knoweth all things. Beloved, if our heart condemn us not, then have we confidence toward God. And whatsoever we ask, we receive of him, because we keep his commandments, and do those things that are pleasing in his sight. And this is his commandment, That we should believe on the name of his Son Jesus Christ, and love one another, as he gave us commandment. And he that keepeth his commandments dwelleth in him, and he in him. And hereby we know that he abideth in us, by the Spirit which he hath given us.

Gradual. When I was in trouble I called upon the Lord, and he heard me. ℣. Deliver my soul, O Lord, from lying lips, and from a deceitful tongue.

Alleluia. Alleluia, alleluia. ℣. O Lord my God, in thee have I put my trust: save me from them that persecute me, and deliver me. Alleluia.

Proper of Season *Trinity II*

Gospel. Luke 14:16

AT THAT TIME: Jesus spake this parable unto the Pharisees: A certain man made a great supper, and bade many: And sent his servant at supper time to say to them that were bidden, Come; for all things are now ready. And they all with one consent began to make excuse. The first said unto him, I have bought a piece of ground, and I must needs go and see it: I pray thee have me excused. And another said, I have bought five yoke of oxen, and I go to prove them: I pray thee have me excused. And another said, I have married a wife, and therefore I cannot come. So that servant came, and shewed his lord these things. Then the master of the house being angry said to his servant, Go out quickly into the streets and lanes of the city, and bring in hither the poor, and the maimed, and the halt, and the blind. And the servant said, Lord, it is done as thou hast commanded, and yet there is room. And the lord said unto the servant, Go out into the highways and hedges, and compel them to come in, that my house may be filled. For I say unto you, That none of those men which were bidden shall taste of my supper.

Offertory. Turn thee, O Lord, and deliver my soul: O save me for thy mercy's sake.

Secret

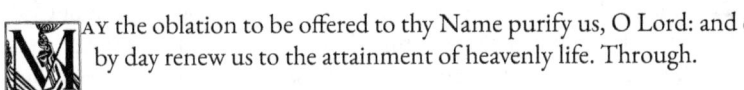**M**AY the oblation to be offered to thy Name purify us, O Lord: and day by day renew us to the attainment of heavenly life. Through.

Communion. I will sing of the Lord, because he hath dealt so lovingly with me: yea, I will praise the name of the Lord Most Highest.

Postcommunion

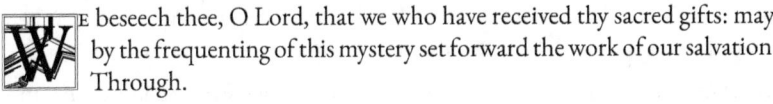**W**E beseech thee, O Lord, that we who have received thy sacred gifts: may by the frequenting of this mystery set forward the work of our salvation. Through.

Trinity III

Proper of Season

Third Sunday after Trinity

Semidouble

Introt

URN thee unto me, and have mercy upon me, O Lord: for I am desolate and in misery: look thou on mine affliction and my travail: and forgive me all mine iniquities, O my God. *Ps.* Unto thee, O Lord, do I lift up my soul: my God, in thee have I trusted, let me not be confounded.

Collect

LORD, we beseech thee mercifully to hear us; and grant that we, to whom thou hast given an hearty desire to pray, may, by thy mighty aid, be defended and comforted in all dangers and adversities. Through.

¶ 2nd Collect is of the Saints (p. 542) & 3rd is ad libitum.

Epistle. 1 Peter 5:5

Dearly beloved: All of you be subject one to another, and be clothed with humility: for God resisteth the proud, and giveth grace to the humble. Humble yourselves therefore under the mighty hand of God, that he may exalt you in due time: casting all your care upon him; for he careth for you. Be sober, be vigilant; because your adversary the devil, as a roaring lion, walketh about, seeking whom he may devour: whom resist stedfast in the faith, knowing that the same afflictions are accomplished in your brethren that are in the world. But the God of all grace, who hath called us unto his eternal glory by Christ Jesus, after that ye have suffered a while, make you perfect, stablish, strengthen, settle you. To him be glory and dominion for ever and ever. Amen.

Gradual. O cast thy burden upon the Lord: and he shall nourish thee. ℣. When I called upon the Lord, he heard my voice from the battle that was against me.

Alleluia. Alleluia, alleluia. ℣. God is a righteous Judge, strong and patient, and God is provoked every day. Alleluia.

Proper of Season *Trinity III*

Gospel. Luke 15:1

AT THAT TIME: There drew near unto Jesus all the publicans and sinners for to hear him. And the Pharisees and scribes murmured, saying, This man receiveth sinners, and eateth with them. And he spake this parable unto them saying, What man of you, having an hundred sheep, if he lose one of them, doth not leave the ninety and nine in the wilderness, and go after that which is lost, until he find it? And when he hath found it, he layeth it on his shoulders, rejoicing. And when he cometh home, he calleth together his friends and neighbours, saying unto them, Rejoice with me; for I have found my sheep which was lost. I say unto you, that likewise joy shall be in heaven over one sinner that repenteth, more than over ninety and nine just persons, which need no repentance. Either what woman having ten pieces of silver, if she lose one piece, doth not light a candle, and sweep the house, and seek diligently till she find it? And when she hath found it, she calleth her friends and her neighbours together, saying, Rejoice with me; for I have found the piece which I had lost. Likewise, I say unto you, there is joy in the presence of the angels of God over one sinner that repenteth.

Offertory. They that know thy name will put their trust in thee: for thou, Lord, hast never failed them that seek thee: O praise the Lord which dwelleth in Sion: for he forgetteth not the complaint of the poor.

Secret

SANCTIFY, O Lord, we beseech thee, the gifts which we offer unto thee: that they may be made unto us the Body and Blood of thine only-begotten Son. Who liveth.

¶ 2nd Secret is of the Saints (p. 542) & 3rd is ad libitum.

Communion. I say unto you: There is joy in the presence of the Angels of God over one sinner that repenteth.

Postcommunion

O LORD, through whom we have received these sacred gifts: we beseech thee; that by the power of the same, thou wouldest both cleanse us from all vices, and evermore fulfil us with the gifts of thy grace. Through.

¶ 2nd Postcommunion is of the Saints (p. 542) & 3rd is ad libitum.

Trinity IV

Proper of Season

Fourth Sunday after Trinity

Semidouble

Introit

THE Lord is my light, and my salvation, whom then shall I fear? The Lord is the stronghold of my life, of whom shall I be afraid? When mine enemies pressed sore against me, they stumbled and fell. *Ps.* Though an host of men were laid against me, yet shall not my heart be afraid.

Collect

O GOD, the protector of all that trust in thee, without whom nothing is strong, nothing is holy; Increase and multiply upon us thy mercy; that, thou being our ruler and guide, we may so pass through things temporal, that we finally lose not the things eternal. Grant this, O heavenly Father, for the sake of Jesus Christ our Lord. Who liveth.

¶ 2nd Collect is of the Saints (p. 542) & 3rd is ad libitum.

Epistle. Romans 8:18

BRETHREN: I reckon that the sufferings of this present time are not worthy to be compared with the glory which shall be revealed in us. For the earnest expectation of the creature waiteth for the manifestation of the sons of God. For the creature was made subject to vanity, not willingly, but by reason of him who hath subjected the same in hope, because the creature itself also shall be delivered from the bondage of corruption into the glorious liberty of the children of God. For we know that the whole creation groaneth and travaileth in pain together until now. And not only they, but ourselves also, which have the firstfruits of the Spirit, even we ourselves groan within ourselves, waiting for the adoption, to wit, the redemption of our body: in Christ Jesus our Lord.

Gradual. Be merciful, O Lord, unto our sins: wherefore do the heathen say: Where is now their God? ℣. Help us, O God of our salvation: and for the glory of thy name, O Lord, deliver us.

Alleluia. Alleluia, alleluia. ℣. O God, who art set in the throne and judgest right: be thou the refuge of the oppressed in time of trouble. Alleluia.

Proper of Season *Trinity IV*

Gospel. Luke 6:36

AT THAT TIME: Jesus said unto his disciples: Be ye therefore merciful, as your Father also is merciful. Judge not, and ye shall not be judged: condemn not, and ye shall not be condemned: forgive, and ye shall be forgiven: give, and it shall be given unto you; good measure, pressed down, and shaken together, and running over, shall men give into your bosom. For with the same measure that ye mete withal it shall be measured to you again. And he spake a parable unto them, Can the blind lead the blind? shall they not both fall into the ditch? The disciple is not above his master: but every one that is perfect shall be as his master. And why beholdest thou the mote that is in thy brother's eye, but perceivest not the beam that is in thine own eye? Either how canst thou say to thy brother, Brother, let me pull out the mote that is in thine eye, when thou thyself beholdest not the beam that is in thine own eye? Thou hypocrite, cast out first the beam out of thine own eye, and then shalt thou see clearly to pull out the mote that is in thy brother's eye.

Offertory. Lighten mine eyes, that I sleep not in death: lest mine enemies says: I have prevailed against him.

Secret

REGARD, O Lord, the gifts of thy suppliant Church: and grant that the partaking thereof may avail for the salvation and continual sanctification of them that believe. Through.

¶ 2nd Secret is of the Saints (p. 542) & 3rd is ad libitum.

Communion. The Lord is my strong rock and my defence, my saviour, my God, and my might.

Postcommunion

MAY the holy things, which we have received, quicken us, O Lord: that we being cleansed thereby may be made ready for thine everlasting mercy. Through.

¶ 2nd Postcommunion is of the Saints (p. 542) & 3rd is ad libitum.

Proper of Season

Trinity V

Fifth Sunday after Trinity

Semidouble

Introit

EARKEN unto my voice, O Lord, when I cry unto thee: be thou my succour, O cast me not away, neither forsake me, O God of my salvation. *Ps.* The Lord is my light and my salvation, whom then shall I fear?

Collect

RANT, O Lord, we beseech thee, that the course of this world may be so peaceably ordered by thy governance, that thy Church may joyfully serve thee in all godly quietness. Through.

¶ 2nd Collect is of the Saints (p. 542) & 3rd is ad libitum.

Epistle. 1 Peter 3:8

EARLY BELOVED: Be ye all of one mind, having compassion one of another, love as brethren, be pitiful, be courteous: Not rendering evil for evil, or railing for railing: but contrariwise blessing; knowing that ye are thereunto called, that ye should inherit a blessing. For he that will love life, and see good days, let him refrain his tongue from evil, and his lips that they speak no guile: Let him eschew evil, and do good; let him seek peace, and ensue it. For the eyes of the Lord are over the righteous, and his ears are open unto their prayers: but the face of the Lord is against them that do evil. And who is he that will harm you, if ye be followers of that which is good? But and if ye suffer for righteousness' sake, happy are ye: and be not afraid of their terror, neither be troubled; But sanctify the Lord God in your hearts.

Gradual. Behold, O God, our defender: and look upon thy servants. ℣. O Lord God of hosts, hear the prayer of thy servants.

Alleluia. Alleluia, alleluia. ℣. The king shall rejoice in thy strength, O Lord: exceeding glad shall he be of thy salvation. Alleluia.

Proper of Season   *Trinity V*

Gospel. Luke 5:1

AT THAT TIME: It came to pass, that, as the people pressed upon Jesus to hear the word of God, he stood by the lake of Gennesaret, and saw two ships standing by the lake: but the fishermen were gone out of them, and were washing their nets. And he entered into one of the ships, which was Simon's, and prayed him that he would thrust out a little from the land. And he sat down, and taught the people out of the ship. Now when he had left speaking, he said unto Simon, Launch out into the deep, and let down your nets for a draught. And Simon answering said unto him, Master, we have toiled all the night, and have taken nothing: nevertheless at thy word I will let down the net. And when they had this done, they inclosed a great multitude of fishes: and their net brake. And they beckoned unto their partners, which were in the other ship, that they should come and help them. And they came, and filled both the ships, so that they began to sink. When Simon Peter saw it, he fell down at Jesus' knees, saying, Depart from me; for I am a sinful man, O Lord. For he was astonished, and all that were with him, at the draught of the fishes which they had taken: and so was also James, and John, the sons of Zebedee, which were partners with Simon. And Jesus said unto Simon, Fear not; from henceforth thou shalt catch men. And when they had brought their ships to land, they forsook all, and followed him.

Offertory. I will bless the Lord who hath given me counsel: I have set God always before me: for he is on my right hand, therefore I shall not fall.

Secret

O LORD, we beseech thee mercifully to receive our oblations: and graciously turn our rebel wills to thee. Through.

❡ 2nd Secret is of the Saints (p. 542) & 3rd is ad libitum.

Communion. One thing have I desired of the Lord, which I will require: even that I may dwell in the house of the Lord all the days of my life.

Postcommunion

WE beseech thee, O Lord: that the mysteries which we have received may purify us: and defend us by the gift which they bestow. Through.

❡ 2nd Postcommunion is of the Saints (p. 542) & 3rd is ad libitum.

Trinity VI — **Proper of Season**

Sixth Sunday after Trinity

Semidouble

Introit

THE Lord is the strength of his people, and a stronghold of salvation to his Anointed: O Lord, save thy people, and give thy blessing unto thine inheritance: O feed them also for ever. *Ps.* Unto thee will I cry, O Lord my God, be not silent unto me: lest, if thou make as though thou hearest not, I become like them that go down into the pit.

Collect

O GOD, who hast prepared for them that love thee such good things as pass man's understanding: pour into our hearts such love toward thee: that we, loving thee above all things, may obtain thy promises, which exceed all that we can desire. Through.

¶ 2nd Collect is of the Saints (p. 542) & 3rd is ad libitum.

Epistle. Romans 6:3

BRETHREN: Know ye not, that so many of us as were baptized into Jesus Christ were baptized into his death? Therefore we are buried with him by baptism into death: that like as Christ was raised up from the dead by the glory of the Father, even so we also should walk in newness of life. For if we have been planted together in the likeness of his death, we shall be also in the likeness of his resurrection: Knowing this, that our old man is crucified with him, that the body of sin might be destroyed, that henceforth we should not serve sin. For he that is dead is freed from sin. Now if we be dead with Christ, we believe that we shall also live with him: Knowing that Christ being raised from the dead dieth no more; death hath no more dominion over him. For in that he died, he died unto sin once: but in that he liveth, he liveth unto God. Likewise reckon ye also yourselves to be dead indeed unto sin, but alive unto God through Jesus Christ our Lord.

Gradual. Turn thee again, O Lord, at the last, and be gracious unto thy servants. ℣. Lord, thou hast been our refuge, from one generation to another.

Alleluia. Alleluia, alleluia. ℣. In thee, O Lord, have I put my trust, let me never be put to confusion: rid me and deliver me in thy righteousness: bow down thine ear to me, make haste to deliver me. Alleluia.

Proper of Season *Trinity VI*

Gospel. Matthew 5:20

T THAT TIME: Jesus said unto his disciples, Except your righteousness shall exceed the righteousness of the scribes and Pharisees, ye shall in no case enter into the kingdom of heaven. Ye have heard that it was said of them of old time, Thou shalt not kill; and whosoever shall kill shall be in danger of the judgment: But I say unto you, That whosoever is angry with his brother without a cause shall be in danger of the judgment: and whosoever shall say to his brother, Raca, shall be in danger of the council: but whosoever shall say, Thou fool, shall be in danger of hell fire. Therefore if thou bring thy gift to the altar, and there rememberest that thy brother hath ought against thee; Leave there thy gift before the altar, and go thy way; first be reconciled to thy brother, and then come and offer thy gift. Agree with thine adversary quickly, whiles thou art in the way with him; lest at any time the adversary deliver thee to the judge, and the judge deliver thee to the officer, and thou be cast into prison. Verily I say unto thee, Thou shalt by no means come out thence, till thou hast paid the uttermost farthing.

Offertory. O hold thou my goings in thy paths, that my footsteps slip not: incline thine ear unto me, and hearken unto my words: shew thy marvellous lovingkindness, thou that art the Saviour of them which put their trust in thee, O Lord.

Secret

E merciful, O Lord, unto our supplications: and graciously receive these oblations of thy servants and handmaids; that those things which each hath offered to the honour of thy name may be profitable unto all for their salvation. Through.

❡ 2nd Secret is of the Saints (p. 542) & 3rd is ad libitum.

Communion. I will offer in his dwelling an oblation with great gladness: I will sing, and speak praises unto the Lord.

Postcommunion

O LORD who hast satisfied us with thy heavenly gift: grant, we beseech thee; that we may be cleansed from our secret faults, and delivered from the snares of our enemies. Through.

❡ 2nd Postcommunion is of the Saints (p. 542) & 3rd is ad libitum.

Trinity VII

Proper of Season

Seventh Sunday after Trinity

Semidouble

Introit

CLAP your hands together, all ye people: O sing unto God with the voice of melody. *Ps.* For the Lord is high, and to be feared: he is the great King upon all the earth.

Collect

ORD of all power and might, who art the author and giver of all good things; Graft in our hearts the love of thy Name, increase in us true religion, nourish us with all goodness, and of thy great mercy keep us in the same. Through.

¶ 2ⁿᵈ Collect is of the Saints (p. 542) & 3ʳᵈ is ad libitum.

Epistle. Romans 6:19

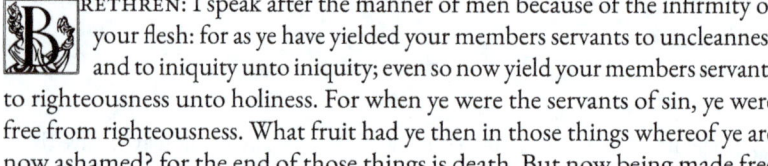RETHREN: I speak after the manner of men because of the infirmity of your flesh: for as ye have yielded your members servants to uncleanness and to iniquity unto iniquity; even so now yield your members servants to righteousness unto holiness. For when ye were the servants of sin, ye were free from righteousness. What fruit had ye then in those things whereof ye are now ashamed? for the end of those things is death. But now being made free from sin, and become servants to God, ye have your fruit unto holiness, and the end everlasting life. For the wages of sin is death; but the gift of God is eternal life, in Christ Jesus our Lord.

Gradual. Come ye children, and hearken unto me: I will teach you the fear of the Lord. ℣. They had an eye unto him and were enlightened: and their faces were not ashamed.

Alleluia. Alleluia, alleluia. ℣. O clap your hands together, all ye people: O sing unto God with the voice of melody. Alleluia.

Proper of Season *Trinity VII*

Gospel. Mark 8:1

IN THOSE DAYS: The multitude being very great, and having nothing to eat, Jesus called his disciples unto him, and saith unto them, I have compassion on the multitude, because they have now been with me three days, and have nothing to eat: And if I send them away fasting to their own houses, they will faint by the way: for divers of them came from far. And his disciples answered him, From whence can a man satisfy these men with bread here in the wilderness? And he asked them, How many loaves have ye? And they said, Seven. And he commanded the people to sit down on the ground: and he took the seven loaves, and gave thanks, and brake, and gave to his disciples to set before them; and they did set them before the people. And they had a few small fishes: and he blessed, and commanded to set them also before them. So they did eat, and were filled: and they took up of the broken meat that was left seven baskets. And they that had eaten were about four thousand: and he sent them away.

Offertory. Like as in the burnt offerings of rams and bullocks, and like as in ten thousands of fat lambs: so let our sacrifice be in thy sight this day, that it may please thee: for they shall not be confounded that put their trust in thee, O Lord.

Secret

BE merciful, O Lord, unto our supplications, and graciously receive these oblations of thy people: and that none may pray amiss or fail in his petition, grant; that what we ask faithfully, we may obtain effectually. Through.

¶ 2nd Secret is of the Saints (p. 542) & 3rd is ad libitum.

Communion. Bow down thine ear, make haste to deliver me.

Postcommunion

WE have been fulfilled with thy gifts, O Lord: grant, we beseech thee; that we may both be cleansed by their operation, and defended by their succour. Through.

¶ 2nd Postcommunion is of the Saints (p. 542) & 3rd is ad libitum.

Trinity VIII

Proper of Season

EIGHTH SUNDAY AFTER TRINITY

Semidouble

Introit

WE have waited, O God, thy loving kindness in the midst of thy temple: according to thy name, O God, so is thy praise unto the world's end: thy right hand is full of righteousness. *Ps.* Great is the Lord, and highly to be praised: in the city of our God, even upon his holy hill.

Collect

O GOD, whose never-failing providence ordereth all things both in heaven and earth; We humbly beseech thee to put away from us all hurtful things, and to give us those things which are profitable for us. Through.

¶ 2nd Collect is of the Saints (p. 542) & 3rd is ad libitum.

Epistle. Romans 6:19

BRETHREN: We are debtors, not to the flesh, to live after the flesh. For if ye live after the flesh, ye shall die: but if ye through the Spirit do mortify the deeds of the body, ye shall live. For as many as are led by the Spirit of God, they are the sons of God. For ye have not received the spirit of bondage again to fear; but ye have received the Spirit of adoption, whereby we cry, Abba, Father. The Spirit itself beareth witness with our spirit, that we are the children of God: And if children, then heirs; heirs of God, and joint-heirs with Christ; if so be that we suffer with him, that we may be also glorified together.

Gradual. Be thou my strong rock and house of defence, that thou mayest save me. ℣. In thee, O God, have I put my trust: let me never be put to confusion, O Lord.

Alleluia. Alleluia, alleluia. ℣. Great is the Lord, and highly to be praised, in the city of our God, even upon his holy hill. Alleluia.

Proper of Season — *Trinity VIII*

Gospel. Matthew 7:15

T THAT TIME: Jesus said unto his disciples: Beware of false prophets, which come to you in sheep's clothing, but inwardly they are ravening wolves. Ye shall know them by their fruits. Do men gather grapes of thorns, or figs of thistles? Even so every good tree bringeth forth good fruit; but a corrupt tree bringeth forth evil fruit. A good tree cannot bring forth evil fruit, neither can a corrupt tree bring forth good fruit. Every tree that bringeth not forth good fruit is hewn down, and cast into the fire. Wherefore by their fruits ye shall know them. Not every one that saith unto me, Lord, Lord, shall enter into the kingdom of heaven; but he that doeth the will of my Father which is in heaven.

Offertory. Thou shalt save the people that are in adversity, O Lord, and shalt bring down the high looks of the proud: for who is God, but thou, O Lord?

Secret

GOD who by the one perfect sacrifice didst ratify the divers offerings of the law: accept the sacrifice of thy bounden servants, and sanctify it with that blessing wherewith thou didst bless the gifts of Abel: that what each hath offered to the honour of thy majesty may be profitable unto all for their salvation. Through.

¶ 2nd Secret is of the Saints (p. 542) & 3rd is ad libitum.

Communion. O taste, and see, how gracious the Lord is: blessed is the man that trusteth in him.

Postcommunion

ET the operation of thy healing, O Lord, both mercifully set us free from our perversities; and lead us to the things that be right. Through.

¶ 2nd Postcommunion is of the Saints (p. 542) & 3rd is ad libitum.

Trinity IX # Proper of Season

NINTH SUNDAY AFTER TRINITY

Semidouble

Introit

EHOLD, God is my helper: the Lord is he that upholdeth my soul: he shall reward evil unto mine enemies: destroy thou them in thy truth, O Lord, my defender. *Ps.* Save me, O God, for thy name's sake: and avenge me in thy strength.

Collect

GRANT to us, Lord, we beseech thee, the spirit to think and do always such things as be rightful: that we, who cannot exist without thee; may by thee be enabled to live according to thy will. Through.

¶ 2nd Collect is of the Saints (p. 542) & 3rd is ad libitum.

Epistle. 1 Corinthians 10:1

BRETHREN: I would not that ye should be ignorant, how that all our fathers were under the cloud, and all passed through the sea; And were all baptized unto Moses in the cloud and in the sea; And did all eat the same spiritual meat; And did all drink the same spiritual drink: for they drank of that spiritual Rock that followed them: and that Rock was Christ. But with many of them God was not well pleased: for they were overthrown in the wilderness. Now these things were our examples, to the intent we should not lust after evil things, as they also lusted. Neither be ye idolaters, as were some of them; as it is written, The people sat down to eat and drink, and rose up to play. Neither let us commit fornication, as some of them committed, and fell in one day three and twenty thousand. Neither let us tempt Christ, as some of them also tempted, and were destroyed of serpents. Neither murmur ye, as some of them also murmured, and were destroyed of the destroyer. Now all these things happened unto them for ensamples: and they are written for our admonition, upon whom the ends of the world are come. Wherefore let him that thinketh he standeth take heed lest he fall. There hath no temptation taken you but such as is common to man: but God is faithful, who will not suffer you to be tempted above that ye are able; but will with the temptation also make a way to escape, that ye may be able to bear it.

Gradual. O Lord our governor: how excellent is thy name in all the world! ℣. Thou that hast set thy glory above the heavens.

Alleluia. Alleluia, alleluia. ℣. Deliver me from mine enemies, O God: defend me from them that rise up against me. Alleluia.

Proper of Season

Trinity IX

Gospel. Luke 16:1

AT THAT TIME: Jesus spake this parable unto his disciples: There was a certain rich man, which had a steward; and the same was accused unto him that he had wasted his goods. And he called him, and said unto him, How is it that I hear this of thee? give an account of thy stewardship; for thou mayest be no longer steward. Then the steward said within himself, What shall I do? for my lord taketh away from me the stewardship: I cannot dig; to beg I am ashamed. I am resolved what to do, that, when I am put out of the stewardship, they may receive me into their houses. So he called every one of his lord's debtors unto him, and said unto the first, How much owest thou unto my lord? And he said, An hundred measures of oil. And he said unto him, Take thy bill, and sit down quickly, and write fifty. Then said he to another, And how much owest thou? And he said, An hundred measures of wheat. And he said unto him, Take thy bill, and write fourscore. And the lord commended the unjust steward, because he had done wisely: for the children of this world are in their generation wiser than the children of light. And I say unto you, Make to yourselves friends of the mammon of unrighteousness; that, when ye fail, they may receive you into everlasting habitations.

Offertory. The statutes of the Lord are right, and rejoice the heart, his judgments are sweeter than honey, and the honey-comb: moreover by them is thy servant taught.

Secret

ACCEPT, we beseech thee, O Lord, the gifts which of thine own bounty we offer unto thee: that, by the mighty working of thy grace, these most sacred mysteries may both sanctify our conversation in this life, and bring us to everlasting joys. Through.

¶ 2nd Secret is of the Saints (p. 542) & 3rd is ad libitum.

Communion. He that eateth my flesh and drinketh my blood, dwelleth in me, and I in him, saith the Lord.

Postcommunion

MAY this heavenly mystery be unto us, O Lord, the renewing both of mind and of body: that like as we do offer unto thee our worship, so we may perceive the benefit of the same. Through.

¶ 2nd Postcommunion is of the Saints (p. 542) & 3rd is ad libitum.

Proper of Season

Tenth Sunday after Trinity

Semidouble

Introit

WHEN I called upon the Lord, he heard my voice from the battle that was against me: and he hath brought them down, even he that is of old, and endureth for ever: O cast thy burden upon the Lord, and he shall nourish thee. *Ps.* Hear my prayer, O Lord, and hide not thyself from my petition: take heed unto me, and hear me.

Collect

LET thy merciful ears, O Lord, be open to the prayers of thy humble servants; and that they may obtain their petitions make them to ask such things as shall please thee. Through.

¶ 2nd Collect is of the Saints (p. 542) & 3rd is ad libitum.

Epistle. 1 Corinthians 12:1

BRETHREN: Concerning spiritual gifts, I would not have you ignorant. Ye know that ye were Gentiles, carried away unto these dumb idols, even as ye were led. Wherefore I give you to understand, that no man speaking by the Spirit of God calleth Jesus accursed: and that no man can say that Jesus is the Lord, but by the Holy Ghost. Now there are diversities of gifts, but the same Spirit. And there are differences of administrations, but the same Lord. And there are diversities of operations, but it is the same God which worketh all in all. But the manifestation of the Spirit is given to every man to profit withal. For to one is given by the Spirit the word of wisdom; to another the word of knowledge by the same Spirit; To another faith by the same Spirit; to another the gifts of healing by the same Spirit; To another the working of miracles; to another prophecy; to another discerning of spirits; to another divers kinds of tongues; to another the interpretation of tongues: But all these worketh that one and the selfsame Spirit, dividing to every man severally as he will.

Gradual. Keep me O Lord, as the apple of an eye: hide me under the shadow of thy wings. ℣. Let my sentence come forth from thy presence: and let thine eyes look upon the thing that is equal.

Alleluia. Alleluia, alleluia. ℣. Thou, O God, art praised in Sion: and unto thee shall the vow be performed in Jerusalem. Alleluia.

Proper of Season *Trinity X*

Gospel. Luke 19:41

AT THAT TIME: When Jesus was come near to Jerusalem, he beheld the city, and wept over it, Saying, If thou hadst known, even thou, at least in this thy day, the things which belong unto thy peace! but now they are hid from thine eyes. For the days shall come upon thee, that thine enemies shall cast a trench about thee, and compass thee round, and keep thee in on every side, And shall lay thee even with the ground, and thy children within thee; and they shall not leave in thee one stone upon another; because thou knewest not the time of thy visitation. And he went into the temple, and began to cast out them that sold therein, and them that bought; Saying unto them, It is written, My house is the house of prayer: but ye have made it a den of thieves. And he taught daily in the temple.

Offertory. Unto thee, O Lord, lift I up my soul: O my God, in thee have I trusted, let me not be confounded: neither let mine enemies triumph over me: for all they that hope for thee shall not be ashamed.

Secret

GRANT to us, we beseech thee, O Lord, worthily to frequent these mysteries: for as oft as the commemoration of this victim is celebrated, the work of our redemption is performed. Through.

¶ 2nd Secret is of the Saints (p. 542) & 3rd is ad libitum.

Communion. Thou shalt be pleased with the sacrifice of righteousness, with the burnt offerings and oblations, upon thine altar, O Lord.

Postcommunion

WE beseech thee, O Lord, that the communion of thy sacrament may both bestow upon us purification, and grant us purity. Through.

¶ 2nd Postcommunion is of the Saints (p. 542) & 3rd is ad libitum.

Trinity XI # Proper of Season

Eleventh Sunday after Trinity

Semidouble

Introit

GOD is in his holy habitation: he is the God that maketh men to be of one mind in an house: he will give strength and power unto his people. *Ps.* Let God arise, and let his enemies be scattered: let them also that hate him flee before him.

Collect

O GOD, who declarest thy almighty power chiefly in showing mercy and pity; Mercifully grant unto us such a measure of thy grace, that we, running the way of thy commandments, may obtain thy gracious promises, and be made partakers of thy heavenly treasure. Through.

¶ 2nd Collect is of the Saints (p. 542) & 3rd is ad libitum.

Epistle. 1 Corinthians 15:1

BRETHREN: I declare unto you the gospel which I preached unto you, which also ye have received, and wherein ye stand; By which also ye are saved, if ye keep in memory what I preached unto you, unless ye have believed in vain. For I delivered unto you first of all that which I also received, how that Christ died for our sins according to the scriptures; And that he was buried, and that he rose again the third day according to the scriptures: And that he was seen of Cephas, then of the twelve: After that, he was seen of above five hundred brethren at once; of whom the greater part remain unto this present, but some are fallen asleep. After that, he was seen of James; then of all the apostles. And last of all he was seen of me also, as of one born out of due time. For I am the least of the apostles, that am not meet to be called an apostle, because I persecuted the church of God. But by the grace of God I am what I am: and his grace which was bestowed upon me was not in vain; but I laboured more abundantly than they all: yet not I, but the grace of God which was with me. Therefore whether it were I or they, so we preach, and so ye believed.

Gradual. My heart hath trusted in God, and I am helped: therefore my heart danceth for joy and in my song will I praise him. ℣. Unto thee will I cry, O Lord: be not silent, O my God, nor depart from me.

Proper of Season *Trinity XI*

Alleluia. Alleluia, alleluia. ℣. Sing we merrily unto God our strength, make a cheerful noise unto the God of Jacob: take the merry psalm, with the lute. Alleluia.

Gospel. Luke 18:9

AT THAT TIME: Jesus spake this parable unto certain which trusted in themselves that they were righteous, and despised others: Two men went up into the temple to pray; the one a Pharisee, and the other a publican. The Pharisee stood and prayed thus with himself, God, I thank thee, that I am not as other men are, extortioners, unjust, adulterers, or even as this publican. I fast twice in the week, I give tithes of all that I possess. And the publican, standing afar off, would not lift up so much as his eyes unto heaven, but smote upon his breast, saying, God be merciful to me a sinner. I tell you, this man went down to his house justified rather than the other: for every one that exalteth himself shall be abased; and he that humbleth himself shall be exalted.

Offertory. I will magnify thee, O Lord, for thou hast set me up, and not made my foes to triumph over me: O Lord, I cried unto thee, and thou hast healed me.

Secret

LET the sacrifices which we dedicate be offered unto thee, O Lord: which thou hast granted us so to present for the honour of thy name, that they may also be for our healing. Through.

¶ 2nd Secret is of the Saints (p. 542) & 3rd is ad libitum.

Communion. Honour the Lord with thy substance, and with the first-fruits of all thine increase: so shall thy barns be filled with plenty, and thy presses shall burst out with new wine.

Postcommunion

WE beseech thee, O Lord our God: that as thou failest not to renew us with thy divine sacraments, so thou wouldest not leave us destitute of thy gracious help. Through.

¶ 2nd Postcommunion is of the Saints (p. 542) & 3rd is ad libitum.

Proper of Season

Trinity XII

Twelfth Sunday after Trinity

Semidouble

Introit

HASTE thee, O God, unto my rescue: O Lord make haste to my deliverance: let mine enemies be ashamed and confounded that seek after my soul. *Ps.* Let them be turned backward and put to confusion: that wish me evil.

Collect

ALMIGHTY and everlasting God, who art always more ready to hear than we to pray, and art wont to give more than either we desire or deserve; Pour down upon us the abundance of thy mercy; forgiving us those things whereof our conscience is afraid, and giving us those good things which we are not worthy to ask, but through the merits and mediation of Jesus Christ, thy Son, our Lord. Who liveth.

¶ 2nd Collect is of the Saints (p. 542) & 3rd is ad libitum.

Epistle. 2 Corinthians 3:4

BRETHREN: Such trust have we through Christ to God-ward: Not that we are sufficient of ourselves to think any thing as of ourselves; but our sufficiency is of God; Who also hath made us able ministers of the new testament; not of the letter, but of the spirit: for the letter killeth, but the spirit giveth life. But if the ministration of death, written and engraven in stones, was glorious, so that the children of Israel could not stedfastly behold the face of Moses for the glory of his countenance; which glory was to be done away: How shall not the ministration of the spirit be rather glorious? For if the ministration of condemnation be glory, much more doth the ministration of righteousness exceed in glory.

Gradual. I will alway give thanks unto the Lord: his praise shall ever be in my mouth. ℣. My soul shall make her boast in the Lord: the humble shall hear thereof, and be glad.

Alleluia. Alleluia, alleluia. ℣. O Lord God of my salvation, I have cried day and night before thee. Alleluia.

Proper of Season *Trinity XII*

Gospel. **Mark 7:31**

AT THAT TIME: Jesus, departing from the coasts of Tyre and Sidon, came unto the sea of Galilee, through the midst of the coasts of Decapolis. And they bring unto him one that was deaf, and had an impediment in his speech; and they beseech him to put his hand upon him. And he took him aside from the multitude, and put his fingers into his ears, and he spit, and touched his tongue; And looking up to heaven, he sighed, and saith unto him, Ephphatha, that is, Be opened. And straightway his ears were opened, and the string of his tongue was loosed, and he spake plain. And he charged them that they should tell no man: but the more he charged them, so much the more a great deal they published it; And were beyond measure astonished, saying, He hath done all things well: he maketh both the deaf to hear, and the dumb to speak.

Offertory. Moses besought the Lord his God, and said: Why, O Lord, doth thy wrath wax hot against thy people? Turn from thy fierce wrath: remember Abraham, Isaac, and Jacob, to whom thou swarest to give a land flowing with milk and honey. And the Lord repented of the evil which he thought to do unto his people.

Secret

LOOK favourably, O Lord, we beseech thee, on this our service: that the gift which we offer may be acceptable to thee, and avail for the succour of our frailty. Through.

❡ 2nd Secret is of the Saints (p. 542) & 3rd is ad libitum.

Communion. The earth, O Lord, is filled with the fruit of thy works: that thou mayest bring food out of the earth, and wine that maketh glad the heart of man: and oil to make him a cheerful countenance, and bread to strengthen man's heart.

Postcommunion

WE beseech thee, O Lord, that we who have received thy sacrament may in such wise feel the succour of the same: that being preserved both in body and soul, we may glory in the fulness of thy heavenly healing. Through.

❡ 2nd Postcommunion is of the Saints (p. 542) & 3rd is ad libitum.

Proper of Season

Trinity XIII

Thirteenth Sunday after Trinity

Semidouble

Introit

Look, O Lord, upon thy covenant, and forsake not the congregation of the poor for ever: arise, O Lord, maintain thine own cause, and be not unmindful of the voices of them that seek thee. *Ps.* O God, wherefore art thou absent from us so long: why is thy wrath so hot against the sheep of thy pasture?

Collect

Almighty and merciful God, of whose only gift it cometh that thy faithful people do unto thee true and laudable service; Grant, we beseech thee, that we may so faithfully serve thee in this life, that we fail not finally to attain thy heavenly promises. Through.

¶ 2nd Collect is of the Saints (p. 542) & 3rd is ad libitum.

Epistle. Galatians 3:16

Brethren: To Abraham and his seed were the promises made. He saith not, And to seeds, as of many; but as of one, And to thy seed, which is Christ. And this I say, that the covenant, that was confirmed before of God in Christ, the law, which was four hundred and thirty years after, cannot disannul, that it should make the promise of none effect. For if the inheritance be of the law, it is no more of promise: but God gave it to Abraham by promise. Wherefore then serveth the law? It was added because of transgressions, till the seed should come to whom the promise was made; and it was ordained by angels in the hand of a mediator. Now a mediator is not a mediator of one, but God is one. Is the law then against the promises of God? God forbid: for if there had been a law given which could have given life, verily righteousness should have been by the law. But the scripture hath concluded all under sin, that the promise by faith of Jesus Christ might be given to them that believe.

Gradual. Look upon thy covenant, O Lord, and forget not the congregation of the poor for ever. ℣. Arise, O Lord, maintain thine own cause: remember the rebuke that thy servants have.

Alleluia. Alleluia, alleluia. ℣. Lord, thou hast been our refuge: from one generation to another. Alleluia.

Proper of Season   *Trinity XIII*

Gospel. Luke 10:23

AT THAT TIME: Jesus said unto his disciples: Blessed are the eyes which see the things that ye see: For I tell you, that many prophets and kings have desired to see those things which ye see, and have not seen them; and to hear those things which ye hear, and have not heard them. And, behold, a certain lawyer stood up, and tempted him, saying, Master, what shall I do to inherit eternal life? He said unto him, What is written in the law? how readest thou? And he answering said, Thou shalt love the Lord thy God with all thy heart, and with all thy soul, and with all thy strength, and with all thy mind; and thy neighbour as thyself. And he said unto him, Thou hast answered right: this do, and thou shalt live. But he, willing to justify himself, said unto Jesus, And who is my neighbour? And Jesus answering said, A certain man went down from Jerusalem to Jericho, and fell among thieves, which stripped him of his raiment, and wounded him, and departed, leaving him half dead. And by chance there came down a certain priest that way: and when he saw him, he passed by on the other side. And likewise a Levite, when he was at the place, came and looked on him, and passed by on the other side. But a certain Samaritan, as he journeyed, came where he was: and when he saw him, he had compassion on him, And went to him, and bound up his wounds, pouring in oil and wine, and set him on his own beast, and brought him to an inn, and took care of him. And on the morrow when he departed, he took out two pence, and gave them to the host, and said unto him, Take care of him; and whatsoever thou spendest more, when I come again, I will repay thee. Which now of these three, thinkest thou, was neighbour unto him that fell among the thieves? And he said, He that shewed mercy on him. Then said Jesus unto him, Go, and do thou likewise.

Offertory. My hope hath been in thee, O Lord; I have said: Thou art my God, my time is in thy hand.

Secret

MERCIFULLY look, we beseech thee, O Lord, upon the sacrifices which we present on thy sacred altars: that while they do bring us pardon, they may minister unto the honour of thy name. Through.

¶ 2ⁿᵈ Secret is of the Saints (p. 542) & 3ʳᵈ is ad libitum.

Communion. Thou hast given us bread from heaven, O Lord, having every delight, and every taste of sweetness.

Trinity XIV # Proper of Season

Postcommunion

UICKEN us, O Lord, we pray thee, who have received these holy mysteries: that they may obtain for us both pardon and protection. Through.

¶ 2ⁿᵈ Postcommunion is of the Saints (p. 542) & 3ʳᵈ is ad libitum.

Fourteenth Sunday after Trinity

Semidouble

Introit

EHOLD, O God, our defender, and look upon the face of thine Anointed: for one day in thy courts is better than a thousand. *Ps.* O how amiable are thy dwellings, thou Lord of hosts! My soul hath a desire and longing to enter into the courts of the Lord.

Collect

LMIGHTY and everlasting God, give unto us the increase of faith, hope, and charity; and, that we may obtain that which thou dost promise, make us to love that which thou dost command. Through.

¶ 2ⁿᵈ Collect is of the Saints (p. 542) & 3ʳᵈ is ad libitum.

Epistle. Galatians 5:16

BRETHREN: Walk in the Spirit, and ye shall not fulfil the lust of the flesh. For the flesh lusteth against the Spirit, and the Spirit against the flesh: and these are contrary the one to the other: so that ye cannot do the things that ye would. But if ye be led of the Spirit, ye are not under the law. Now the works of the flesh are manifest, which are these; Adultery, fornication, uncleanness, lasciviousness, Idolatry, witchcraft, hatred, variance, emulations, wrath, strife, seditions, heresies, Envyings, murders, drunkenness, revellings, and such like: of the which I tell you before, as I have also told you in time past, that they which do such things shall not inherit the kingdom of God. But the fruit of the Spirit is love, joy, peace, longsuffering, gentleness, goodness, faith, Meekness, temperance: against such there is no law. And they that are Christ's have crucified the flesh with the affections and lusts.

Gradual. It is better to trust in the Lord, than to put any confidence in man. ℣. It is better to trust in the Lord, than to put any confidence in princes.

Proper of Season *Trinity XIV*

Alleluia. Alleluia, alleluia. ℣. O come let us sing unto the Lord: let us heartily rejoice in the strength of our salvation. Alleluia.

Gospel. Luke 17:11

T THAT TIME: As Jesus went to Jerusalem, he passed through the midst of Samaria and Galilee. And as he entered into a certain village, there met him ten men that were lepers, which stood afar off: And they lifted up their voices, and said, Jesus, Master, have mercy on us. And when he saw them, he said unto them, Go shew yourselves unto the priests. And it came to pass, that, as they went, they were cleansed. And one of them, when he saw that he was healed, turned back, and with a loud voice glorified God, And fell down on his face at his feet, giving him thanks: and he was a Samaritan. And Jesus answering said, Were there not ten cleansed? but where are the nine? There are not found that returned to give glory to God, save this stranger. And he said unto him, Arise, go thy way: thy faith hath made thee whole.

Offertory. The Angel of the Lord tarrieth round about them that fear him, and delivereth them: O taste, and see, how gracious the Lord is.

Secret

E favourable, O Lord, to thy people, be favourable unto their offerings: that, being well-pleased with this oblation, thou mayest both bestow upon us pardon and grant us our petitions. Through.

❡ 2nd Secret is of the Saints (p. 542) & 3rd is ad libitum.

Communion. Seek ye first the kingdom of God, and all things shall be added unto you, saith the Lord.

Postcommunion

E beseech thee, O Lord, that we who have received thy heavenly sacraments, may thereby grow in grace to the attainment of eternal redemption. Through.

❡ 2nd Postcommunion is of the Saints (p. 542) & 3rd is ad libitum.

Trinity XV # Proper of Season

Fifteenth Sunday after Trinity

Semidouble

Introit

Bow down, O Lord, thine ear to me, and hear me: O my God, save thy servant, that trusteth in thee: have mercy upon me, O Lord, for I have called daily upon thee. *Ps.* Comfort the soul of thy servant: for unto thee, O Lord, do I lift up my soul.

Collect

Keep, we beseech thee, O Lord, thy Church with thy perpetual mercy; and, because the frailty of man without thee cannot but fall, keep us ever by thy help from all things hurtful, and lead us to all things profitable to our salvation. Through.

¶ 2nd Collect is of the Saints (p. 542) & 3rd is ad libitum.

Epistle. Galatians 6:11

Brethren: Ye see how large a letter I have written unto you with mine own hand. As many as desire to make a fair shew in the flesh, they constrain you to be circumcised; only lest they should suffer persecution for the cross of Christ. For neither they themselves who are circumcised keep the law; but desire to have you circumcised, that they may glory in your flesh. But God forbid that I should glory, save in the cross of our Lord Jesus Christ, by whom the world is crucified unto me, and I unto the world. For in Christ Jesus neither circumcision availeth any thing, nor uncircumcision, but a new creature. And as many as walk according to this rule, peace be on them, and mercy, and upon the Israel of God. From henceforth let no man trouble me: for I bear in my body the marks of the Lord Jesus. Brethren, the grace of our Lord Jesus Christ be with your spirit. Amen.

Gradual. It is a good thing to give thanks unto the Lord: and to sing praises unto thy name, O most Highest. ℣. To tell of thy loving-kindness early in the morning, and of thy truth in the night-season.

Alleluia. Alleluia, alleluia. ℣. For the Lord is a great God, and the great King upon all the earth. Alleluia.

Proper of Season *Trinity XV*

Gospel. Matthew 6:24

AT THAT TIME: Jesus said unto his disciples: No man can serve two masters: for either he will hate the one, and love the other; or else he will hold to the one, and despise the other. Ye cannot serve God and mammon. Therefore I say unto you, Take no thought for your life, what ye shall eat, or what ye shall drink; nor yet for your body, what ye shall put on. Is not the life more than meat, and the body than raiment? Behold the fowls of the air: for they sow not, neither do they reap, nor gather into barns; yet your heavenly Father feedeth them. Are ye not much better than they? Which of you by taking thought can add one cubit unto his stature? And why take ye thought for raiment? Consider the lilies of the field, how they grow; they toil not, neither do they spin: And yet I say unto you, That even Solomon in all his glory was not arrayed like one of these. Wherefore, if God so clothe the grass of the field, which to day is, and to morrow is cast into the oven, shall he not much more clothe you, O ye of little faith? Therefore take no thought, saying, What shall we eat? or, What shall we drink? or, Wherewithal shall we be clothed? (For after all these things do the Gentiles seek:) for your heavenly Father knoweth that ye have need of all these things. But seek ye first the kingdom of God, and his righteousness; and all these things shall be added unto you. Take therefore no thought for the morrow: for the morrow shall take thought for the things of itself. Sufficient unto the day is the evil thereof.

Offertory. I waited patiently for the Lord, and he inclined unto me: he heard my calling: and hath put a new song in my mouth, even a thanksgiving unto our God.

Secret

GRANT to us, O Lord, we beseech thee, that this saving victim may avail, both for the cleansing of our offences, and for the propitiation of thy power. Through.

❡ 2nd Secret is of the Saints (p. 542) & 3rd is ad libitum.

Communion. The bread that I will give is my flesh, which I will give for the life of the world.

Postcommunion

MAY thy sacraments, O God, evermore cleanse and defend us: and bring us to the attainment of eternal salvation. Through.

❡ 2nd Postcommunion is of the Saints (p. 542) & 3rd is ad libitum.

Trinity XVI # Proper of Season

Sixteenth Sunday after Trinity

Semidouble

Introit

AVE mercy upon me, O Lord, for I have called daily upon thee: for thou, O Lord, art gracious and merciful, and plenteous in thy loving kindness toward all them that call upon thee. *Ps.* Bow down thine ear to me, O Lord, and hear me: for I am poor and in misery.

Collect

LORD, we beseech thee, let thy continual pity cleanse and defend thy Church; and, because it cannot continue in safety without thy succour, preserve it evermore by thy help and goodness. Through.

¶ 2nd Collect is of the Saints (p. 542) & 3rd is ad libitum.

Epistle. Ephesians 3:13

BRETHREN: I desire that ye faint not at my tribulations for you, which is your glory. For this cause I bow my knees unto the Father of our Lord Jesus Christ, Of whom the whole family in heaven and earth is named, That he would grant you, according to the riches of his glory, to be strengthened with might by his Spirit in the inner man; That Christ may dwell in your hearts by faith; that ye, being rooted and grounded in love, May be able to comprehend with all saints what is the breadth, and length, and depth, and height; And to know the love of Christ, which passeth knowledge, that ye might be filled with all the fulness of God. Now unto him that is able to do exceeding abundantly above all that we ask or think, according to the power that worketh in us, Unto him be glory in the church by Christ Jesus throughout all ages, world without end. Amen.

Gradual. The heathen shall fear thy name, O Lord, and all the kings of the earth thy majesty. ℣. When the Lord shall build up Sion, and when his glory shall appear.

Alleluia. Alleluia, alleluia. ℣. O sing unto the Lord a new song: for the Lord hath done marvellous things. Alleluia.

Proper of Season *Trinity XVI*

Gospel. Luke 7:11

AT THAT TIME: Jesus went into a city called Nain; and many of his disciples went with him, and much people. Now when he came nigh to the gate of the city, behold, there was a dead man carried out, the only son of his mother, and she was a widow: and much people of the city was with her. And when the Lord saw her, he had compassion on her, and said unto her, Weep not. And he came and touched the bier: and they that bare him stood still. And he said, Young man, I say unto thee, Arise. And he that was dead sat up, and began to speak. And he delivered him to his mother. And there came a fear on all: and they glorified God, saying, That a great prophet is risen up among us; and, That God hath visited his people. And this rumour of him went forth throughout all Judaea, and throughout all the region round about.

Offertory. Look down, O Lord, to help me: let them be ashamed, and confounded that seek after my soul to destroy it: look down, O Lord, to help me.

Secret

MAY thy sacraments guard us, O Lord: and ever protect us against the assaults of the devil. Through.

¶ 2nd Secret is of the Saints (p. 542) & 3rd is ad libitum.

Communion. O Lord, I will make mention of thy righteousness only: thou, O God, hast taught me from my youth up until now: forsake me not, O God, in mine old age, when I am gray-headed.

Postcommunion

WE beseech thee, O Lord, that the operation of thy heavenly gift may so possess our souls and bodies: that not our own desires, but the effectual working of the same may ever prevail within us. Through.

¶ 2nd Postcommunion is of the Saints (p. 542) & 3rd is ad libitum.

Trinity XVII

Proper of Season

Seventeenth Sunday after Trinity

Semidouble

Introit

IGHTEOUS art thou, O Lord, and true is thy judgement: O deal with thy servant according unto thy merciful kindness. *Ps.* Blessed are those that are undefiled in the way: and walk in the law of the Lord.

Collect

ORD, we pray thee that thy grace may always prevent and follow us, and make us continually to be given to all good works. Through.

❡ 2nd Collect is of the Saints (p. 542) & 3rd is ad libitum.

Epistle. Ephesians 4:1

RETHREN: I, the prisoner of the Lord, beseech you that ye walk worthy of the vocation wherewith ye are called, With all lowliness and meekness, with longsuffering, forbearing one another in love; Endeavouring to keep the unity of the Spirit in the bond of peace. There is one body, and one Spirit, even as ye are called in one hope of your calling; One Lord, one faith, one baptism, One God and Father of all, who is above all, and through all, and in you all. Who is blessed for ever and ever. Amen.

Gradual. Blessed are the people whose God is the Lord: and blessed are the folk that he hath chosen to him to be his inheritance. ℣. By the word of the Lord were the heavens made: and all the hosts of them by the breath of his mouth.

Alleluia. Alleluia, alleluia. ℣. Hear my prayer, O Lord, and let my cry come unto thee. Alleluia.

Gospel. Luke 14:1

T THAT TIME: When Jesus went into the house of one of the chief Pharisees to eat bread on the sabbath day, that they watched him. And, behold, there was a certain man before him which had the dropsy. And Jesus answering spake unto the lawyers and Pharisees, saying, Is it lawful to heal on the sabbath day? And they held their peace. And he took him, and healed him, and let him go; And answered them, saying, Which of you shall have an ass

Proper of Season *Trinity XVII*

or an ox fallen into a pit, and will not straightway pull him out on the sabbath day? And they could not answer him again to these things. And he put forth a parable to those which were bidden, when he marked how they chose out the chief rooms; saying unto them, When thou art bidden of any man to a wedding, sit not down in the highest room; lest a more honourable man than thou be bidden of him; And he that bade thee and him come and say to thee, Give this man place; and thou begin with shame to take the lowest room. But when thou art bidden, go and sit down in the lowest room; that when he that bade thee cometh, he may say unto thee, Friend, go up higher: then shalt thou have worship in the presence of them that sit at meat with thee. For whosoever exalteth himself shall be abased; and he that humbleth himself shall be exalted.

Offertory. I, Daniel, prayed unto my God, and said: Hear, O Lord, the prayers of thy servant: cause thy face to shine upon thy sanctuary: and behold, O God, this thy people, who are called by thy name.

Secret

LEANSE us, O Lord, we pray thee, by the effectual working of this our sacrifice: and so accomplish in us the work of thy mercy; that we may be found worthy to be made partakers of the same. Through.

¶ 2nd Secret is of the Saints (p. 542) & 3rd is ad libitum.

Communion. Promise unto the Lord your God, and keep it, all ye that are round about him, bring presents unto him that ought to be feared: he shall refrain the spirit of princes: and is wonderful among all the kings of the earth.

Postcommunion

LORD, we beseech thee, mercifully to purify our minds and renew them with thy heavenly sacraments: that we may thereby have help also for our bodies both now and for evermore. Through.

¶ 2nd Postcommunion is of the Saints (p. 542) & 3rd is ad libitum.

Trinity XVIII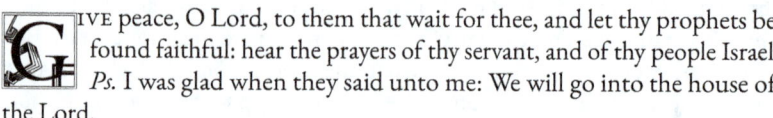

Eighteenth Sunday after Trinity

Semidouble

Introit

IVE peace, O Lord, to them that wait for thee, and let thy prophets be found faithful: hear the prayers of thy servant, and of thy people Israel. *Ps.* I was glad when they said unto me: We will go into the house of the Lord.

Collect

ORD, we beseech thee, grant thy people grace to withstand the temptations of the world, the flesh, and the devil; and with pure hearts and minds to follow thee, the only God. Through.

¶ 2nd Collect is of the Saints (p. 542) & 3rd is ad libitum.

Epistle. 1 Corinthians 1:4

RETHREN: I thank my God always on your behalf, for the grace of God which is given you by Jesus Christ; That in every thing ye are enriched by him, in all utterance, and in all knowledge; Even as the testimony of Christ was confirmed in you: So that ye come behind in no gift; waiting for the coming of our Lord Jesus Christ: Who shall also confirm you unto the end, that ye may be blameless in the day of our Lord Jesus Christ.

Gradual. I was glad when they said unto me: We will go into the house of the Lord. ℣. Peace be within thy walls: and plenteousness within thy palaces.

Alleluia. Alleluia, alleluia. ℣. The heathen shall fear thy name, O Lord, and all the kings of the earth thy majesty. Alleluia.

Gospel. Matthew 22:34

AT THAT TIME: When the Pharisees had heard that Jesus had put the Sadduces to silence, they were gathered together. Then one of them, which was a lawyer, asked him a question, tempting him, and saying, Master, which is the great commandment in the law? Jesus said unto him, Thou shalt love the Lord thy God with all thy heart, and with all thy soul, and with all thy mind. This is the first and great commandment. And the second is like unto it, Thou shalt love thy neighbour as thyself. On these two commandments hang all the law and the prophets. While the Pharisees were gathered together, Jesus asked them, Saying, What think ye of Christ? whose son is he? They say unto him, The Son of David. He saith unto them, How then doth David in spirit call him Lord, saying, The LORD said unto my Lord, Sit thou on my right hand, till I make thine enemies thy footstool? If David then call him Lord, how is he his son? And no man was able to answer him a word, neither durst any man from that day forth ask him any more questions.

Offertory. Moses consecrated an altar unto the Lord, offering burnt offerings upon it, and sacrificing peace offerings: and he made an evening sacrifice for a sweet-smelling savour unto the Lord God, in the sight of the children of Israel.

Secret

E humbly entreat thy majesty, O Lord: that these holy mysteries which we perform may deliver us both from past and future transgressions. Through.

¶ 2nd Secret is of the Saints (p. 542) & 3rd is ad libitum.

Communion. Bring offerings and come into his courts: O worship the Lord in the beauty of holiness.

Postcommunion

LMIGHTY God, let thy holy mysteries both heal our vices, and bestow upon us everlasting remedies. Through.

¶ 2nd Postcommunion is of the Saints (p. 542) & 3rd is ad libitum.

Nineteenth Sunday after Trinity

Semidouble

Introit

I AM the saving health of the people, saith the Lord: out of whatsoever tribulation they shall cry to me, I will hear them: and I will be their Lord for ever. *Ps.* Hear my law, O my people: incline your ears unto the words of my mouth.

Collect

O GOD, forasmuch as without thee we are not able to please thee; Mercifully grant that thy Holy Spirit may in all things direct and rule our hearts. Through.

¶ 2nd Collect is of the Saints (p. 542) & 3rd is ad libitum.

Epistle. Ephesians 4:17

B RETHREN: This I say therefore, and testify in the Lord, that ye henceforth walk not as other Gentiles walk, in the vanity of their mind, Having the understanding darkened, being alienated from the life of God through the ignorance that is in them, because of the blindness of their heart: Who being past feeling have given themselves over unto lasciviousness, to work all uncleanness with greediness. But ye have not so learned Christ; If so be that ye have heard him, and have been taught by him, as the truth is in Jesus: That ye put off concerning the former conversation the old man, which is corrupt according to the deceitful lusts; Be renewed in the spirit of your mind; And that ye put on the new man, which after God is created in righteousness and true holiness. Wherefore putting away lying, speak every man truth with his neighbour: for we are members one of another. Be ye angry, and sin not: let not the sun go down upon your wrath: Neither give place to the devil. Let him that stole steal no more: but rather let him labour, working with his hands the thing which is good, that he may have to give to him that needeth. Let no corrupt communication proceed out of your mouth, but that which is good to the use of edifying, that it may minister grace unto the hearers. And grieve not the holy Spirit of God, whereby ye are sealed unto the day of redemption. Let all bitterness, and wrath, and anger, and clamour, and evil speaking, be put away from you, with all malice: And be ye kind one to another, tenderhearted, forgiving one another, even as God for Christ's sake hath forgiven you.

Proper of Season *Trinity XIX*

Gradual. Let my prayer be set forth in thy sight, O Lord, as the incense. ℣. Let the lifting up of my hands be an evening sacrifice.

Alleluia. Alleluia, alleluia. ℣. O give thanks unto the Lord, and call upon his name: tell the people what things he hath done. Alleluia.

Gospel. Matthew 9:1

AT THAT TIME: Jesus entered into a ship, and passed over, and came into his own city. And, behold, they brought to him a man sick of the palsy, lying on a bed: and Jesus seeing their faith said unto the sick of the palsy; Son, be of good cheer; thy sins be forgiven thee. And, behold, certain of the scribes said within themselves, This man blasphemeth. And Jesus knowing their thoughts said, Wherefore think ye evil in your hearts? For whether is easier, to say, Thy sins be forgiven thee; or to say, Arise, and walk? But that ye may know that the Son of man hath power on earth to forgive sins, (then saith he to the sick of the palsy,) Arise, take up thy bed, and go unto thine house. And he arose, and departed to his house. But when the multitudes saw it, they marvelled, and glorified God, which had given such power unto men.

Offertory. Though I walk in the midst of trouble, yet shalt thou refresh me, O Lord: thou shalt stretch forth thy hand upon the furiousness of mine enemies, and thy right hand shall save me.

Secret

O GOD, who, by communion in this venerable sacrifice, hast made us partakers of the one supreme Godhead: grant, we beseech thee; that as we have the knowledge of thy truth, so by worthy conversation we may attain unto the same. Through.

¶ 2nd Secret is of the Saints (p. 542) & 3rd is ad libitum.

Communion. Thou hast charged that we shall diligently keep thy commandments: O that my ways were made so direct, that I might keep thy statutes.

Postcommunion

WE render thanks unto thee, O Lord, for that thou hast quickened us with thy sacred gift: humbly beseeching thy mercy; that thou wouldest make us worthy partakers of the same. Through.

¶ 2nd Postcommunion is of the Saints (p. 542) & 3rd is ad libitum.

Proper of Season

Twentieth Sunday after Trinity

Semidouble

Introit

EVERYTHING that thou hast done to us, O Lord, thou hast done in true judgment: for we have sinned and have not obeyed thy commandments: but give glory to thy name, and deal with us according to the multitude of thy mercies. *Ps.* Blessed are those that are undefiled in the way: and walk in the law of the Lord.

Collect

OALMIGHTY and most merciful God, of thy bountiful goodness keep us, we beseech thee, from all things that may hurt us; that we, being ready both in body and soul, may cheerfully accomplish those things which thou commandest. Through.

¶ 2nd Collect is of the Saints (p. 542) & 3rd is ad libitum.

Epistle. Ephesians 5:15

BRETHREN: See that ye walk circumspectly, not as fools, but as wise, Redeeming the time, because the days are evil. Wherefore be ye not unwise, but understanding what the will of the Lord is. And be not drunk with wine, wherein is excess; but be filled with the Spirit; Speaking to yourselves in psalms and hymns and spiritual songs, singing and making melody in your heart to the Lord; Giving thanks always for all things unto God and the Father in the name of our Lord Jesus Christ; Submitting yourselves one to another in the fear of God.

Gradual. The eyes of all wait upon thee, O Lord: and thou givest them their meat in due season. ℣. Thou openest thine hand: and fillest all things living with plenteousness.

Alleluia. Alleluia, alleluia. ℣. O God, my heart is ready, my heart is ready: I will sing and give praise unto thee, my glory. Alleluia.

Proper of Season *Trinity XX*

Gospel. Matthew 22:1

T THAT TIME: Jesus spake unto the chief priests and Pharisees in parables, saying: The kingdom of heaven is like unto a certain king, which made a marriage for his son, And sent forth his servants to call them that were bidden to the wedding: and they would not come. Again, he sent forth other servants, saying, Tell them which are bidden, Behold, I have prepared my dinner: my oxen and my fatlings are killed, and all things are ready: come unto the marriage. But they made light of it, and went their ways, one to his farm, another to his merchandise: And the remnant took his servants, and entreated them spitefully, and slew them. But when the king heard thereof, he was wroth: and he sent forth his armies, and destroyed those murderers, and burned up their city. Then saith he to his servants, The wedding is ready, but they which were bidden were not worthy. Go ye therefore into the highways, and as many as ye shall find, bid to the marriage. So those servants went out into the highways, and gathered together all as many as they found, both bad and good: and the wedding was furnished with guests. And when the king came in to see the guests, he saw there a man which had not on a wedding garment: And he saith unto him, Friend, how camest thou in hither not having a wedding garment? And he was speechless. Then said the king to the servants, Bind him hand and foot, and take him away, and cast him into outer darkness; there shall be weeping and gnashing of teeth. For many are called, but few are chosen.

Offertory. By the waters of Babylon we sat down and wept: when we remembered thee, O Sion.

Secret

RANT, we beseech thee, O Lord, that these gifts which we offer in the sight of thy majesty, may be for our salvation. Through.

❡ 2nd Secret is of the Saints (p. 542) & 3rd is ad libitum.

Communion. Remember thy word unto thy servant, O Lord, wherein thou hast caused me to put my trust: the same is my comfort in my affliction.

Postcommunion

MAY the operation of thy healing, O Lord, both mercifully cleanse us from our perversities, and make us ever to cleave unto thy commandments. Through.

❡ 2nd Postcommunion is of the Saints (p. 542) & 3rd is ad libitum.

Trinity XXI # Proper of Season

Twenty-First Sunday after Trinity

Semidouble

Introit

LORD, everything is in subjection to thy will, and there is no man that is able to resist thy power: for thou hast created everything, heaven and earth, and all the wonders which under heaven's vault are contained: thou art the Lord of all things. *Ps.* Blessed are those that are undefiled in the way: and walk in the law of the Lord.

Collect

RANT, we beseech thee, merciful Lord, to thy faithful people pardon and peace, that they may be cleansed from all their sins, and serve thee with a quiet mind. Through.

¶ 2nd Collect is of the Saints (p. 542) & 3rd is ad libitum.

Epistle. Ephesians 6:10

BRETHREN: Be strong in the Lord, and in the power of his might. Put on the whole armour of God, that ye may be able to stand against the wiles of the devil. For we wrestle not against flesh and blood, but against principalities, against powers, against the rulers of the darkness of this world, against spiritual wickedness in high places. Wherefore take unto you the whole armour of God, that ye may be able to withstand in the evil day, and having done all, to stand. Stand therefore, having your loins girt about with truth, and having on the breastplate of righteousness; And your feet shod with the preparation of the gospel of peace; Above all, taking the shield of faith, wherewith ye shall be able to quench all the fiery darts of the wicked. And take the helmet of salvation, and the sword of the Spirit, which is the word of God: Praying always with all prayer and supplication in the Spirit, and watching thereunto with all perseverance and supplication for all saints; And for me, that utterance may be given unto me, that I may open my mouth boldly, to make known the mystery of the gospel, For which I am an ambassador in bonds: that therein I may speak boldly, as I ought to speak.

Gradual. Lord, thou hast been our refuge, from one generation to another. ℣. Before the mountains were brought forth, or ever the earth and the world were made: thou art God from everlasting, and world without end.

Proper of Season — *Trinity XXI*

Alleluia. Alleluia, alleluia. ℣. When Israel came out of Egypt, and the house of Jacob from among the strange people. Alleluia.

Gospel. John 4:46

AT THAT TIME: There was a certain nobleman, whose son was sick at Capernaum. When he heard that Jesus was come out of Judaea into Galilee, he went unto him, and besought him that he would come down, and heal his son: for he was at the point of death. Then said Jesus unto him, Except ye see signs and wonders, ye will not believe. The nobleman saith unto him, Sir, come down ere my child die. Jesus saith unto him, Go thy way; thy son liveth. And the man believed the word that Jesus had spoken unto him, and he went his way. And as he was now going down, his servants met him, and told him, saying, Thy son liveth. Then enquired he of them the hour when he began to amend. And they said unto him, Yesterday at the seventh hour the fever left him. So the father knew that it was at the same hour, in the which Jesus said unto him, Thy son liveth: and himself believed, and his whole house. This is again the second miracle that Jesus did, when he was come out of Judæa into Galilee.

Offertory. There was a man in the land of Uz, whose name was Job: perfect and upright, and one that feared God: and Satan sought to tempt him: and power was given him by the Lord over his possessions and over his flesh: and he destroyed all his substance and his sons: and he smote his flesh with sore boils.

Secret

WE beseech thee, O Lord, that these mysteries may bestow upon us thy heavenly healing: and purge away the vices of our hearts. Through.

❡ 2ⁿᵈ Secret is of the Saints (p. 542) & 3ʳᵈ is ad libitum.

Communion. My soul hath longed for thy salvation, and I have a good hope in thy word: when wilt thou be avenged of them that persecute me? They persecuted me falsely, O be thou my help, O Lord my God.

Postcommunion

WE beseech thee, O Lord, make us ever to obey thy commandments: that we may be rendered worthy of thy sacred gifts. Through.

❡ 2ⁿᵈ Postcommunion is of the Saints (p. 542) & 3ʳᵈ is ad libitum.

Trinity XXII

Proper of Season

Twenty-Second Sunday after Trinity

Semidouble

Introit

F thou, O Lord, wilt be extreme to mark iniquities: O Lord, who may abide it? for there is mercy with thee, O God of Israel. *Ps.* Out of the deep have I called unto thee, O Lord: Lord, hear my voice.

Collect

ORD, we beseech thee to keep thy household the Church in continual godliness; that through thy protection it may be free from all adversities, and devoutly given to serve thee in good works, to the glory of thy Name. Through.

¶ 2nd Collect is of the Saints (p. 542) & 3rd is ad libitum.

Epistle. Philippians 1:3

BRETHREN: I thank my God upon every remembrance of you, Always in every prayer of mine for you all making request with joy, For your fellowship in the gospel from the first day until now; Being confident of this very thing, that he which hath begun a good work in you will perform it until the day of Jesus Christ: Even as it is meet for me to think this of you all, because I have you in my heart; inasmuch as both in my bonds, and in the defence and confirmation of the gospel, ye all are partakers of my grace. For God is my record, how greatly I long after you all in the bowels of Jesus Christ. And this I pray, that your love may abound yet more and more in knowledge and in all judgment; That ye may approve things that are excellent; that ye may be sincere and without offence till the day of Christ; Being filled with the fruits of righteousness, which are by Jesus Christ, unto the glory and praise of God.

Gradual. Behold, how good and joyful a thing it is, brethren, to dwell together in unity. ℣. It is like the precious ointment upon the head, that ran down unto the beard, even unto Aaron's beard.

Alleluia. Alleluia, alleluia. ℣. Ye that fear the Lord, put your trust in him: he is their helper and defender. Alleluia.

Proper of Season *Trinity XXII*

Gospel. Matthew 18:21

AT THAT TIME: Peter came to Jesus, and said, Lord, how oft shall my brother sin against me, and I forgive him? till seven times? Jesus saith unto him, I say not unto thee, Until seven times: but, Until seventy times seven. Therefore is the kingdom of heaven likened unto a certain king, which would take account of his servants. And when he had begun to reckon, one was brought unto him, which owed him ten thousand talents. But forasmuch as he had not to pay, his lord commanded him to be sold, and his wife, and children, and all that he had, and payment to be made. The servant therefore fell down, and worshipped him, saying, Lord, have patience with me, and I will pay thee all. Then the lord of that servant was moved with compassion, and loosed him, and forgave him the debt. But the same servant went out, and found one of his fellowservants, which owed him an hundred pence: and he laid hands on him, and took him by the throat, saying, Pay me that thou owest. And his fellowservant fell down at his feet, and besought him, saying, Have patience with me, and I will pay thee all. And he would not: but went and cast him into prison, till he should pay the debt. So when his fellowservants saw what was done, they were very sorry, and came and told unto their lord all that was done. Then his lord, after that he had called him, said unto him, O thou wicked servant, I forgave thee all that debt, because thou desiredst me: Shouldest not thou also have had compassion on thy fellowservant, even as I had pity on thee? And his lord was wroth, and delivered him to the tormentors, till he should pay all that was due unto him. So likewise shall my heavenly Father do also unto you, if ye from your hearts forgive not every one his brother their trespasses.

Offertory. Remember me, O Lord, King of all power: and put a well-ordered speech in my mouth, that my words may be pleasing in the sight of the prince.

Secret

MERCIFULLY receive, O Lord, these offerings: wherewith thou hast willed that atonement should be made unto thee, and that salvation should be restored to us by the power of thy loving kindness. Through.

¶ 2nd Secret is of the Saints (p. 542) & 3rd is ad libitum.

Communion. I have called upon thee, O God, for thou hast heard me: incline thine ear, and hearken unto my words.

Trinity XXIII # Proper of Season

Postcommunion

LORD, who hast bestowed upon us the food of immortality, we beseech thee: that those things which we have taken with our lips we may seek after in purity of heart. *Through.*

❡ 2ⁿᵈ Postcommunion is of the Saints (p. 542) & 3ʳᵈ is ad libitum.

Twenty-Third Sunday after Trinity

Semidouble

Introit

THUS saith the Lord: I think thoughts of peace, and not of affliction: ye shall call upon me, and I will hearken unto you, and I will bring again your captivity from all places. *Ps.* Lord, thou art become gracious unto thy land: thou hast turned away the captivity of Jacob.

Collect

GOD, our refuge and strength, who art the author of all godliness; Be ready, we beseech thee, to hear the devout prayers of thy Church; and grant that those things which we ask faithfully we may obtain effectually. *Through.*

❡ 2ⁿᵈ Collect is of the Saints (p. 542) & 3ʳᵈ is ad libitum.

Epistle. Philippians 3:17

BRETHREN: Be followers together of me, and mark them which walk so as ye have us for an ensample. (For many walk, of whom I have told you often, and now tell you even weeping, that they are the enemies of the cross of Christ: Whose end is destruction, whose God is their belly, and whose glory is in their shame, who mind earthly things.) For our conversation is in heaven; from whence also we look for the Saviour, the Lord Jesus Christ: Who shall change our vile body, that it may be fashioned like unto his glorious body, according to the working whereby he is able even to subdue all things unto himself.

Gradual. It is thou, O Lord, that savest us from our enemies: and puttest them to confusion that hate us. ℣. We make our boast of God all day long, and will praise thy name for ever.

Proper of Season   *Trinity XXIII*

Alleluia. Alleluia, alleluia. ℣. Out of the deep have I called unto thee, O Lord: Lord, hear my prayer. Alleluia.

Gospel. Matthew 22:15

AT THAT TIME: The Pharisees went, and took counsel how they might entangle Jesus in his talk. And they sent out unto him their disciples with the Herodians, saying, Master, we know that thou art true, and teachest the way of God in truth, neither carest thou for any man: for thou regardest not the person of men. Tell us therefore, What thinkest thou? Is it lawful to give tribute unto Caesar, or not? But Jesus perceived their wickedness, and said, Why tempt ye me, ye hypocrites? Shew me the tribute money. And they brought unto him a penny. And he saith unto them, Whose is this image and superscription? They say unto him, Caesar's. Then saith he unto them, Render therefore unto Caesar the things which are Caesar's; and unto God the things that are God's. When they had heard these words, they marvelled, and left him, and went their way.

Offertory. Out of the deep have I called unto thee, O Lord: Lord, hear my prayer: out of the deep have I called unto thee, O Lord.

Secret

GRANT, O merciful God: that this saving oblation may ever free us from our sins, and shield us from all adversities. Through.

¶ 2nd Secret is of the Saints (p. 542) & 3rd is ad libitum.

Communion. Verily I say unto you, what things soever ye desire, when ye pray, believe that ye receive them, and it shall be done unto you.

Postcommunion

WE have received, O Lord, the gifts of thy sacred mystery, humbly beseeching thee: that those things, which thou hast commanded us to do in remembrance of thee, may be profitable to the succour of our infirmity. Who livest.

¶ 2nd Postcommunion is of the Saints (p. 542) & 3rd is ad libitum.

Trinity XXIV # Proper of Season

Twenty-Fourth Sunday after Trinity

Semidouble

¶ If this Sunday be hindered by the Sunday Next before Advent, it is anticipated on Saturday with all the privileges proper to a Sunday occurring, and in it are said Gloria in excelsis, the Nicene Creed, Preface of the Trinity, and Ite, Missa est.

Introit

THUS saith the Lord: I think thoughts of peace, and not of affliction: ye shall call upon me, and I will hearken unto you: and will bring again your captivity from all places. *Ps.* Lord, thou art become gracious unto thy land: thou hast turned away the captivity of Jacob.

Collect

O LORD, we beseech thee, absolve thy people from their offences; that through thy bountiful goodness we may all be delivered from the bands of those sins, which by our frailty we have committed. Through.

¶ 2nd Collect is of the Saints (p. 542) & 3rd is ad libitum.

Epistle. Colossians 1:3

BRETHREN: We give thanks to God and the Father of our Lord Jesus Christ, praying always for you, Since we heard of your faith in Christ Jesus, and of the love which ye have to all the saints, For the hope which is laid up for you in heaven, whereof ye heard before in the word of the truth of the gospel; Which is come unto you, as it is in all the world; and bringeth forth fruit, as it doth also in you, since the day ye heard of it, and knew the grace of God in truth: As ye also learned of Epaphras our dear fellowservant, who is for you a faithful minister of Christ; Who also declared unto us your love in the Spirit. For this cause we also, since the day we heard it, do not cease to pray for you, and to desire that ye might be filled with the knowledge of his will in all wisdom and spiritual understanding; That ye might walk worthy of the Lord unto all pleasing, being fruitful in every good work, and increasing in the knowledge of God; Strengthened with all might, according to his glorious power, unto all patience and longsuffering with joyfulness; Giving thanks unto the Father, which hath made us meet to be partakers of the inheritance of the saints in light.

Proper of Season *Trinity XXIV*

Gradual. It is thou, O Lord, that savest us from our enemies: and puttest them to confusion that hate us. ℣. We make our boast of God all day long, and will praise thy name for ever.

Alleluia. Alleluia, alleluia. ℣. Out of the deep have I called unto thee, O Lord: Lord, hear my prayer. Alleluia.

Gospel. Matthew 9:18

AT THAT TIME: While Jesus spake these things unto John's disciples: Behold, there came a certain ruler, and worshipped him, saying, My daughter is even now dead: but come and lay thy hand upon her, and she shall live. And Jesus arose, and followed him, and so did his disciples. And, behold, a woman, which was diseased with an issue of blood twelve years, came behind him, and touched the hem of his garment: For she said within herself, If I may but touch his garment, I shall be whole. But Jesus turned him about, and when he saw her, he said, Daughter, be of good comfort; thy faith hath made thee whole. And the woman was made whole from that hour. And when Jesus came into the ruler's house, and saw the minstrels and the people making a noise, He said unto them, Give place: for the maid is not dead, but sleepeth. And they laughed him to scorn. But when the people were put forth, he went in, and took her by the hand, and the maid arose. And the fame hereof went abroad into all that land.

Offertory. Out of the deep have I called unto thee, O Lord: Lord, hear my prayer: out of the deep have I called unto thee, O Lord.

Secret

WE offer thee, O Lord, this sacrifice of praise for the increase of our dutiful service: that thou wouldest mercifully accomplish that which thou hast bestowed upon us beyond our deserving. Through.

¶ 2nd Secret is of the Saints (p. 542) & 3rd is ad libitum.

Communion. Verily I say unto you, What things soever ye desire, when ye pray, believe that ye receive them, and it shall be done unto you.

Postcommunion

WE beseech thee, almighty God: that we, whom thou makest to rejoice in the partaking of heavenly things, may by thee be defended against all earthly perils. Through.

¶ 2nd Postcommunion is of the Saints (p. 542) & 3rd is ad libitum.

Sunday before Advent # Proper of Season

Sunday Next before Advent

Semidouble

Introit

THUS saith the Lord: I think thoughts of peace, and not of affliction: ye shall call upon me, and I will hearken unto you: and will bring again your captivity from all places. *Ps.* Lord, thou art become gracious unto thy land: thou hast turned away the captivity of Jacob.

Collect

STIR up, we beseech thee, O Lord, the wills of thy faithful people; that they, plenteously bringing forth the fruit of good works, may by thee be plenteously rewarded. Through.

¶ 2nd Collect is of the Saints (p. 542) & 3rd is ad libitum.

Epistle. Jeremiah 23:5

IN THOSE DAYS: Jeremiah the Prophet spake, saying: Behold, the days come, saith the LORD, that I will raise unto David a righteous Branch, and a King shall reign and prosper, and shall execute judgment and justice in the earth. In his days Judah shall be saved, and Israel shall dwell safely: and this is his name whereby he shall be called, THE LORD OUR RIGHTEOUSNESS. Therefore, behold, the days come, saith the LORD, that they shall no more say, The LORD liveth, which brought up the children of Israel out of the land of Egypt; But, The LORD liveth, which brought up and which led the seed of the house of Israel out of the north country, and from all countries whither I had driven them; and they shall dwell in their own land.

Gradual. It is thou, O Lord, that savest us from our enemies: and puttest them to confusion that hate us. ℣. We make our boast of God all day long, and will praise thy name for ever.

Alleluia. Alleluia, alleluia. ℣. Out of the deep have I called unto thee, O Lord: Lord, hear my prayer. Alleluia.

Proper of Season *Sunday before Advent*

Gospel. John 6:5

AT THAT TIME: When Jesus then lifted up his eyes, and saw a great company come unto him, he saith unto Philip, Whence shall we buy bread, that these may eat? And this he said to prove him: for he himself knew what he would do. Philip answered him, Two hundred pennyworth of bread is not sufficient for them, that every one of them may take a little. One of his disciples, Andrew, Simon Peter's brother, saith unto him, There is a lad here, which hath five barley loaves, and two small fishes: but what are they among so many? And Jesus said, Make the men sit down. Now there was much grass in the place. So the men sat down, in number about five thousand. And Jesus took the loaves; and when he had given thanks, he distributed to the disciples, and the disciples to them that were set down; and likewise of the fishes as much as they would. When they were filled, he said unto his disciples, Gather up the fragments that remain, that nothing be lost. Therefore they gathered them together, and filled twelve baskets with the fragments of the five barley loaves, which remained over and above unto them that had eaten. Then those men, when they had seen the miracle that Jesus did, said, This is of a truth that prophet that should come into the world.

Offertory. Out of the deep have I called unto thee, O Lord: Lord, hear my prayer: out of the deep have I called unto thee, O Lord.

Secret

BE favourable, O Lord, to our supplications: and, accepting the offerings and prayers of us thy people, turn the hearts of all to thee; that we, being delivered from earthly lusts, may turn to heavenly desires. Through.

¶ 2nd Secret is of the Saints (p. 542) & 3rd is ad libitum.

Communion. Verily I say unto you, what things soever ye desire, when ye pray, believe that ye receive them, and it shall be done unto you.

Postcommunion

GRANT to us, we beseech thee, O Lord: that through these sacraments, which we have received, whatsoever is corrupt in our minds may be made whole by the healing power of the same. Through.

¶ 2nd Postcommunion is of the Saints (p. 542) & 3rd is ad libitum.

St. Andrew — Proper of Saints — 30 November

St. Andrew

Second Class Double
30 November

Opening Sentence. The Lord loved Andrew in the odour of sweetness.

Introit

IGHT honourable are thy friends unto me, O God: right well is their princedom established. *Ps.* O Lord, thou hast searched me out, and known me: thou knowest my down-sitting, and mine uprising.

Collect

E humbly entreat thy Majesty, O Lord: that as blessed Andrew the Apostle was to thy Church a preacher and governor; so he may be a perpetual intercessor for us in thy sight. Through.

¶ In Advent, Commemoration is made of the Feria.

Epistle. Romans 10:9

BRETHREN: If thou shalt confess with thy mouth the Lord Jesus, and shalt believe in thine heart that God hath raised him from the dead, thou shalt be saved. For with the heart man believeth unto righteousness; and with the mouth confession is made unto salvation. For the scripture saith, Whosoever believeth on him shall not be ashamed. For there is no difference between the Jew and the Greek: for the same Lord over all is rich unto all that call upon him. For whosoever shall call upon the name of the Lord shall be saved. How then shall they call on him in whom they have not believed? and how shall they believe in him of whom they have not heard? and how shall they hear without a preacher? And how shall they preach, except they be sent? as it is written, How beautiful are the feet of them that preach the gospel of peace, and bring glad tidings of good things! But they have not all obeyed the gospel. For Esaias saith, Lord, who hath believed our report? So then faith cometh by hearing, and hearing by the word of God. But I say, Have they not heard? Yes verily, their sound went into all the earth, and their words unto the ends of the world. But I say, Did not Israel know? First Moses saith, I will provoke you to jealousy by them that are no people, and by a foolish nation I will anger you. But Esaias is very bold, and saith, I was found of them that sought me not; I was made manifest unto them that asked not after me. But to Israel he saith, All day long I have stretched forth my hands unto a disobedient and gainsaying people.

Proper of Saints

30 November — *St. Andrew*

Gradual. Thou shalt make them princes in all lands: they shall remember thy name, O Lord. ℣. Instead of thy fathers thou shalt have children: therefore shall the people give thanks unto thee.

Alleluia. Alleluia, alleluia. ℣. The Lord loved Andrew as a sweet savour. Alleluia.

Gospel. Matthew 4:18

AT THAT TIME: Jesus, walking by the sea of Galilee, saw two brethren, Simon called Peter, and Andrew his brother, casting a net into the sea: for they were fishers. And he saith unto them, Follow me, and I will make you fishers of men. And they straightway left their nets, and followed him. And going on from thence, he saw other two brethren, James the son of Zebedee, and John his brother, in a ship with Zebedee their father, mending their nets; and he called them. And they immediately left the ship and their father, and followed him.

Offertory. Right honourable are thy friends unto me, O God: right well is their princedom established.

Secret

O LORD, we beseech thee that the holy prayer of thy blessed Apostle Andrew may commend our sacrifice unto thee: that it may be rendered acceptable by the merits of him in whose honour it is solemnly shewn forth. Through.

¶ In Advent, Commemoration is made of the Feria.

Communion. Follow me: I will make you fishers of men: and they straightway left their nets, and followed the Lord.

Postcommunion

WE beseech thee, O Lord, that these divine mysteries, which we have joyfully received on the festivity (commemoration) of blessed Andrew thine Apostle: may effectually avail for the glory of thy Saints, and likewise for our pardon. Through.

¶ In Advent, Commemoration is made of the Feria.

Conception of BVM   # Proper of Saints   8 December

Conception of the Blessed Virgin Mary

Second Class Double with a Common Octave
8 December

Introit

LET us all rejoice in the Lord, and celebrate this feast in honour of the Virgin Mary, at whose Conception Angels rejoice and praise the Son of God. *Ps.* My heart is inditing of a good matter: I speak of the things which I have made unto the King.

Collect

O GOD, mercifully hear the supplication of thy servants; that we who are assembled together on the Conception of the Virgin Mother of God, may at her intercession be delivered by thee from the dangers which beset us. Through.

¶ In Advent, Commemoration is made of the Feria.

Epistle. Ecclesiasticus 24:17

AS the vine I put forth grace; And my flowers are the fruit of glory and riches. Come unto me, ye that are desirous of me, And be ye filled with my produce. For my memorial is sweeter than honey, And mine inheritance than the honeycomb. They that eat me shall yet be hungry; And they that drink me shall yet be thirsty. He that obeyeth me shall not be ashamed; And they that work in me shall not do amiss.

Gradual. Hearken, O daughter, and consider: incline thine ear. So shall the king have pleasure in thy beauty. ℣. According to thy worship and renown, good luck have thou with thine honour: ride on, because of the word of truth, of meekness, and righteousness; and thy right hand shall teach thee terrible things.

Alleluia. Alleluia, alleluia. ℣. The Conception of the glorious Virgin Mary who sprang from the seed of Abraham, of the tribe of Judah, of the root of David. Alleluia.

8 December   Proper of Saints   *Conception of BVM*

Sequence

Let us celebrate this day
Whereon piously we say
Mary was conceived.
Begotten is the Mother Maid,
Conceived, created, channel made
Of pardon to the world.
Adam's primeval banishment
Joachim's childless discontent
There find a remedy.

This the Prophets have foreshown,
This was to the Patriarchs known:
The Virgin whence a flower should spring,
The Star which forth the Sun should bring,
On this day is conceived;
The flower which from the rod should bloom,
The Sun which of the Star should come,
Is Christ interpreted.

O how happy, O how fair!
Sweet to us, to God how dear,
Hath this Conception been!
Misery now is at an end,
Mercy doth on earth descend,
For sorrow joy is seen.
A Mother new new offspring bears,
From a new Star new Sun appears,
New grace doth all inspire;
The Mother bears the Generator,
The Creature brings forth the Creator,
The Daughter bears the Sire:

O unexampled novelty!
O new, unheard of dignity!
The Mother's holy chastity
The Son's Conception shows.
Rejoice, O gracious Virgin mild!
Fair rod with blossoms undefiled,
Mother ennobled by her Child,
Such grace no other knows.

That which lay hid, in figure sealed,
By clouds mysterious concealed,
The future Mother hath revealed:
For once a Virgin pure and good
Reversed the laws of Motherhood:
Nature, surprised, beheld a flood
Of Deity outpoured.

Triste fuit in Eva ve,
Sed ex Eva formans Ave,
Versa vice, sed non prave
Intus ferens in conclave
Verbum bonum et suave
Nobis, Mater Virgo, fave
Tua frui gratia.

Whoe'r thou art, without delay
Open thy lips, her praises pay;
Offer her homage, to her pray
At every hour, on every day.
With swelling voice, with spirit sage,
By supplicating prayer engage
A portion in her patronage.

Thou of the sad art comfort sure,
True Mother of the orphans poor,
Of the opprest the help secure,
Thou of the sick the healing cure,
All things to all thou givest.
With one consent we ask of thee,
Whom praise awaits especially,
Conduct us wanderers o'er this sea
Unto salvation's port, where we
By grace may be at rest. Amen.

Proper of Saints

Conception of BVM — 8 December

Gospel. Matthew 1:1

THE book of the generation of Jesus Christ, the son of David, the son of Abraham. Abraham begat Isaac; and Isaac begat Jacob; and Jacob begat Judas and his brethren; And Judas begat Phares and Zara of Thamar; and Phares begat Esrom; and Esrom begat Aram; And Aram begat Aminadab; and Aminadab begat Naasson; and Naasson begat Salmon; And Salmon begat Booz of Rachab; and Booz begat Obed of Ruth; and Obed begat Jesse; And Jesse begat David the king; and David the king begat Solomon of her that had been the wife of Urias; And Solomon begat Roboam; and Roboam begat Abia; and Abia begat Asa; And Asa begat Josaphat; and Josaphat begat Joram; and Joram begat Ozias; And Ozias begat Joatham; and Joatham begat Achaz; and Achaz begat Ezekias; And Ezekias begat Manasses; and Manasses begat Amon; and Amon begat Josias; And Josias begat Jechonias and his brethren, about the time they were carried away to Babylon: And after they were brought to Babylon, Jechonias begat Salathiel; and Salathiel begat Zorobabel; And Zorobabel begat Abiud; and Abiud begat Eliakim; and Eliakim begat Azor; And Azor begat Sadoc; and Sadoc begat Achim; and Achim begat Eliud; And Eliud begat Eleazar; and Eleazar begat Matthan; and Matthan begat Jacob; And Jacob begat Joseph the husband of Mary, of whom was born Jesus, who is called Christ.

Offertory. Full of grace are thy lips, because God hath blessed thee for ever.

Secret

O LORD, let the human nature of thine only-begotten succour us, that he, who being born of a Virgin diminished not but sanctified the chastity of his Mother, may put away our offences from us on the feast of her Conception, and make our oblations acceptable to himself, even Jesus Christ our Lord. Who liveth.

¶ In Advent, Commemoration is made of the Feria.

Communion. Thy Son's true faith hath cleansed the world of sin. Immaculate thy virginity abideth.

Postcommunion

GRANT, we beseech thee, O Lord, that the sacrament which we have received of our bounden duty on this yearly celebration, may, at the intercession of blessed Mary ever-Virgin, afford us relief in this present life and in the world to come. Through.

¶ In Advent, Commemoration is made of the Feria.

St. Thomas

Second Class Double
21 December

Introot

IGHT honourable are thy friends unto me, O God: right well is their princedom established. *Ps.* O Lord, thou hast searched me out, and known me: thou knowest my down-sitting, and mine uprising.

Collect

RANT us, we beseech thee, O Lord, to glory in the solemnity of thy blessed Apostle Thomas: that we may ever be succoured by his protection; and follow his faith with worthy devotion. Through.

¶ Commemoration of the Feria.

Epistle. Ephesians 2:19

RETHREN: Ye are no more strangers and foreigners, but fellowcitizens with the saints, and of the household of God; and are built upon the foundation of the apostles and prophets, Jesus Christ himself being the chief corner stone; in whom all the building fitly framed together groweth unto an holy temple in the Lord: in whom ye also are builded together for an habitation of God through the Spirit.

Gradual. Right honourable are thy friends, O God: right well is their princedom established. ℣. If I tell them, they are more in number than the sand.

Alleluia. Alleluia, alleluia. ℣. Rejoice in the Lord, O ye righteous: for it becometh well the just to be thankful. Alleluia.

Gospel. John 20:24

T THAT TIME: Thomas, one of the twelve, called Didymus, was not with them when Jesus came. The other disciples therefore said unto him, We have seen the Lord. But he said unto them, Except I shall see in his hands the print of the nails, and put my finger into the print of the nails, and thrust my hand into his side, I will not believe. And after eight days again his disciples were within, and Thomas with them: then came Jesus, the doors being shut, and stood in the midst, and said, Peace be unto you. Then saith he to Thomas, Reach hither thy finger, and behold my hands; and reach hither thy hand, and thrust it into my side: and be not faithless, but believing. And Thomas answered and said unto him, My Lord and my God. Jesus saith unto him, Thomas, because thou hast seen me, thou hast believed: blessed are they that have not seen, and yet have believed. And many other signs truly did Jesus in the presence of his disciples, which are not written in this book: But these are written, that ye might believe that Jesus is the Christ, the Son of God; and that believing ye might have life through his name.

Offertory. Their sound is gone out into all lands: and their words into the ends of the world.

Secret

E render unto thee, O Lord, this duty of our bounden service, humbly beseeching thee: that like as we do offer unto thee this sacrifice of praise in honour of the confession of blessed Thomas the Apostle, so by his prayers thou wouldest preserve thy gifts within us. Through.

¶ Commemoration of the Feria.

Communion. Reach hither thy hand, and behold the print of the nails: and be not faithless, but believing.

Postcommunion

SSIST us, O merciful God: and, at the intercession of blessed Thomas the Apostle on our behalf, continue towards us the gifts of thy loving-kindness. Through.

¶ Commemoration of the Feria.

¶ The Last Gospel is read of the Ember Day, if one occur.

25 January   **Proper of Saints**   *Conversion of St. Paul*

CONVERSION OF ST. PAUL

Greater Double
25 January

Opening Sentence. Thou hast given an heritage unto those that fear thy Name, O Lord. (Ps. 61:5)

Introit

I KNOW whom I have believed, and am persuaded that he is able to keep that which I have committed unto him against that day, a just judge. *Ps.* O Lord, thou hast searched me out, and known me: thou knowest, my down-sitting, and mine up-rising.

Collect

O GOD, who, through the preaching of the blessed Apostle Saint Paul, hast caused the light of the Gospel to shine throughout the world; Grant, we beseech thee, that we, having his wonderful conversion in remembrance, may show forth our thankfulness unto thee for the same, by following the holy doctrine which he taught. Through.

O GOD, who didst bestow upon thy blessed Apostle Peter the keys of the kingdom of heaven, and didst appoint unto him the high priesthood of binding and loosing: vouchsafe; that by the help of his intercession we may be delivered from the bonds of our iniquities. Who livest.

Epistle. Acts 9:1

IN THOSE DAYS: Saul, yet breathing out threatenings and slaughter against the disciples of the Lord, went unto the high priest, And desired of him letters to Damascus to the synagogues, that if he found any of this way, whether they were men or women, he might bring them bound unto Jerusalem. And as he journeyed, he came near Damascus: and suddenly there shined round about him a light from heaven: And he fell to the earth, and heard a voice saying unto him, Saul, Saul, why persecutest thou me? And he said, Who art thou, Lord? And the Lord said, I am Jesus whom thou persecutest: it is hard for thee to kick against the pricks. And he trembling and astonished said, Lord, what wilt thou have me to do? And the Lord said unto him, Arise, and go into the city, and it shall be told thee what thou must do. And the men which journeyed with him stood speechless, hearing a voice, but seeing no man. And Saul arose from the earth; and when his eyes were opened, he saw no man:

Conversion of St. Paul   Proper of Saints   25 January

but they led him by the hand, and brought him into Damascus. And he was three days without sight, and neither did eat nor drink. And there was a certain disciple at Damascus, named Ananias; and to him said the Lord in a vision, Ananias. And he said, Behold, I am here, Lord. And the Lord said unto him, Arise, and go into the street which is called Straight, and enquire in the house of Judas for one called Saul, of Tarsus: for, behold, he prayeth, And hath seen in a vision a man named Ananias coming in, and putting his hand on him, that he might receive his sight. Then Ananias answered, Lord, I have heard by many of this man, how much evil he hath done to thy saints at Jerusalem: And here he hath authority from the chief priests to bind all that call on thy name. But the Lord said unto him, Go thy way: for he is a chosen vessel unto me, to bear my name before the Gentiles, and kings, and the children of Israel: For I will shew him how great things he must suffer for my name's sake. And Ananias went his way, and entered into the house; and putting his hands on him said, Brother Saul, the Lord, even Jesus, that appeared unto thee in the way as thou camest, hath sent me, that thou mightest receive thy sight, and be filled with the Holy Ghost. And immediately there fell from his eyes as it had been scales: and he received sight forthwith, and arose, and was baptized. And when he had received meat, he was strengthened. Then was Saul certain days with the disciples which were at Damascus. And straightway he preached Christ in the synagogues, that he is the Son of God. But all that heard him were amazed, and said; Is not this he that destroyed them which called on this name in Jerusalem, and came hither for that intent, that he might bring them bound unto the chief priests? But Saul increased the more in strength, and confounded the Jews which dwelt at Damascus, proving that this is very Christ.

Gradual. He that wrought effectually in Peter to the apostleship, the same was mighty in me toward the Gentiles: and they perceived the grace that was given unto me. ℣. The grace of God which was bestowed upon me was not in vain: but his grace ever abideth in me.

Alleluia. Alleluia, alleluia. ℣. Great and holy is Paul, a chosen vessel, meet indeed to be glorified, who also was worthy to possess the twelfth throne. Alleluia.

25 January — Proper of Saints — Conversion of St. Paul

Gospel. Matthew 19:27

AT THAT TIME: Peter said unto Jesus: Behold, we have forsaken all, and followed thee; what shall we have therefore? And Jesus said unto them, Verily I say unto you, That ye which have followed me, in the regeneration when the Son of man shall sit in the throne of his glory, ye also shall sit upon twelve thrones, judging the twelve tribes of Israel. And every one that hath forsaken houses, or brethren, or sisters, or father, or mother, or wife, or children, or lands, for my name's sake, shall receive an hundredfold, and shall inherit everlasting life. But many that are first shall be last; and the last shall be first.

Offertory. Right honourable are thy friends unto me, O God: right well is their princedom established.

Secret

SANCTIFY, O Lord, through the prayers of thine Apostle Paul, the gifts of thy people: that those things, which by thine institution are pleasing unto thee, may be made more pleasing by his prayer and advocacy. Through.

WE beseech thee, O Lord, that the intercession of blessed Peter the Apostle may commend unto thee the prayers and sacrifices of thy Church: that those things which we celebrate for his glory may avail for our pardon. Through.

Communion. Verily, I say unto you: that ye which have forsaken all and followed me, shall receive an hundredfold, and shall inherit everlasting life.

Postcommunion

O LORD, who hast sanctified us with this saving mystery: we beseech thee; that he, whom thou hast given to be our advocate and guide, may never fail in prayer for us. Through.

MAY the gift, O Lord, which we have offered make us to rejoice: that as we proclaim thy wonders in thine Apostle Peter; so through him we may receive the abundance of thy loving-kindness. Through.

Proper of Saints

Candlemas   2 February

Purification of the Blessed Virgin Mary

Second Class Double
2 February

¶ If it happen that this Feast be transferred, only the Blessing and Distribution of the Candles and the Procession take place today. Mass is said of the Office occurring, and in it lighted Candles are not held in the hands.

Opening Sentence. It was revealed unto Simeon by the Holy Ghost, that he should not see death, until he had seen the Lord's Christ.

¶ Mattins (or, Terce) being ended, the Priest vested in a violet Cope, or without a Chasuble, with the Ministers vested in like manner, proceeds to bless the Candles, which are placed in the midst before the Altar or at the Epistle corner, and he himself, standing in the same place facing the Altar, says with joined hands in the tone of the Collect of the Ferial Mass:

℣. The Lord be with you. | ℣. Dóminus vobíscum.
℞. And with thy spirit. | ℞. Et cum spíritu tuo.

Let us pray.

O LORD Holy Father Almighty, everlasting God, who hast created all things out of nothing, and by thy command hast caused this liquid through the labour of bees to come to the perfection of wax: and who on this day didst fulfil the petition of Simeon the just: we humbly entreat thee; that through the invocation of thy most holy name and the intercession of blessed Mary ever Virgin, whose festival we this day devoutly celebrate, and through the prayers of all thy Saints, thou wouldest vouchsafe to bl ✠ ess and sanc ✠ tify these candles for the use of men, and the health of their bodies and souls, whether on land or on water: and that from thy holy heaven, and from the seat of thy Majesty, thou wouldest hearken to the voices of this thy people, who desire to bear them in their hands to thine honour and to sing thy praises: and that thou wouldest be gracious to all that cry unto thee, whom thou hast redeemed with the precious Blood of thy Son: Who liveth and reigneth with thee. *Amen.*

Let us pray.

ALMIGHTY and everlasting God, who on this day didst present thine only-begotten Son in thy holy temple, to be received in the arms of Saint Simeon: we humbly entreat thy mercy; that thou wouldest vouchsafe to bl ✠ ess, sanc ✠ tify, and kindle with the light of thy heavenly benediction these candles, which we thy servants, receiving to the glory of thy name, desire to kindle and bear forth: to the intent that we, being made worthy by the offering

Proper of Saints

2 February — *Candlemas*

of them unto thee, the Lord our God, and being enkindled with the holy fire of thy most sweet charity, may be found meet to be presented in the holy temple of thy glory. Through the same. *Amen.*

Let us pray.

O LORD Jesu Christ, the true light, that lightenest every man that cometh into this world: pour forth thy bles ✠ sing upon these candles, and sanc ✠ tify them with the light of thy grace, and mercifully grant; that even as these lights, kindled with visible fire, do scatter the darkness of night; so our hearts, illumined by invisible fire, that is, by the brightness of the Holy Spirit, may be free from the blindness of every iniquity: that, the eyes of our minds being purified, we may be enabled to discern such things as are pleasing unto thee and profitable for our salvation; to the end that after the darkness and dangers of this world, we may be found meet to attain unto the light unfailing. Through thee, Christ Jesu, Saviour of the world who in the perfect Trinity livest and reignest God. *Amen.*

Let us pray.

ALMIGHTY and everlasting God, who through thy servant Moses didst command the purest liquid of oil to be prepared for the lamps to burn continually before thy face: mercifully pour upon these candles the grace of thy bles ✠ sing; that they may so outwardly shed forth light, that, by thy gift, the light of thy Spirit may not inwardly be wanting to our souls. Through . . . in the unity of the same. *Amen.*

Let us pray.

O LORD Jesu Christ, who on this day appearing among men in the substance of our flesh wast presented by thy parents in the temple: whom the old man, the venerable Simeon, illumined by the light of thy Spirit, acknowledged, received, and blessed: mercifully grant; that we, being enlightened and instructed by the grace of the same Holy Spirit, may truly acknowledge and faithfully love thee: Who livest and reignest with God the Father in the unity of the same Holy Spirit, God. *Amen.*

¶ The Prayers being ended, the Celebrant sets incense in the thurible; and thrice sprinkles the Candles with holy water, saying the Antiphon, **Thou shalt purge me,** without chant and without the Psalm: and then thrice incenses them.

¶ Then the senior of the Clergy approaches the Altar, and from him the Celebrant receives a Candle without genuflecting or kissing his hand. Then the Celebrant, standing in the midst before the Altar and turning to the people, distributes candles first to the senior, from whom he himself received; then to the Deacon and Subdeacon vested, and to the rest of the Clergy, one by one in order, lastly to the laity: all kneeling and kissing the Candle and the Celebrant's hand, with the exception of Prelates, if they be present. And when he begins to distribute the Candles the Choir sings:

Proper of Saints

Candlemas — 2 February

Ant. A light to lighten the Gentiles and the glory of thy people Israel.

Ant. Lord, now lettest thou thy servant depart in peace, according to thy word.

¶ Then is repeated the whole Antiphon, A light to lighten the Gentiles, which is likewise repeated after each Verse.

Ant. For mine eyes have seen thy salvation. (Antiphon.)

Ant. Which thou hast prepared before the face of all people. (Antiphon.)

Ant. Glory be to the Father, and to the Son, and to the Holy Ghost. (Antiphon.)

Ant. As it was in the beginning, is now, and ever shall be, world without end. Amen. (Antiphon.)

¶ These being ended, shall be sung:

Ant. O Lord, arise, help us: and deliver us for thy name's sake. *Ps.* O God, we have heard with our ears: our fathers have declared unto us. ℣. Glory be . . .

Ant. O Lord, arise, help us: and deliver us for thy name's sake.

| ℣. Let us pray. | ℣. Orémus. |

¶ If it be after Septuagesima, and not a Sunday, the Deacon says the following versicle.

| ℣. Let us bow the knee. | ℣. Flectámus génua. |
| ℣. Arise. | ℣. Leváte. |

WE beseech thee, O Lord, hearken unto thy people: and grant, that by the light of thy grace we may inwardly attain to those things, which in this yearly devotion thou dost suffer us outwardly to venerate. Through Christ, our Lord. *Amen.*

¶ Then follows the Procession. And first the Celebrant sets incense in the censer: then the Deacon, turning himself to the people, says: Let us proceed in peace. And the Choir answers: In the name of Christ. Amen.

¶ The Thurifer goes first, with smoking thurible: then the Subdeacon vested, carrying the Cross, in the midst between two Acolytes with lighted candles: the Clergy follow in order, last of all the Celebrant with the Deacon on his left, all with lighted Candles in their hands: and the following Antiphons are sung:

Ant. O Sion, adorn thy bride-chamber, and receive Christ the King: greet Mary, who is the gate of heaven: for she beareth the King of the glory of the new light: she remaineth a Virgin, yet beareth in her hands a Son begotten before the morning star: whom Simeon took into his arms, declaring to the nations that he is the Lord of life and death, and Saviour of the world.

Another Ant. It was revealed unto Simeon by the Holy Ghost, that he should not see death, before he had seen the Lord's Christ: and when they brought the Child into the temple, then took he him up in his arms, and blessed God, and said: Lord, now lettest thou thy servant depart in peace. ℣. When his parents brought in the Child Jesus, to do for him according to the custom of the law, then took he him up in his arms.

¶ As they enter the Church, the following is sung:

℣. They offered for him unto the Lord a pair of turtle doves or two young pigeons: As it is written in the law of the Lord.

℣. When the days of Mary's purification according to the law of Moses were accomplished, they brought Jesus to Jerusalem, to present him to the Lord. As it is written in the law of the Lord.

℣. Glory be to the Father, and to the Son, and to the Holy Ghost. As it is written in the law of the Lord.

¶ The Procession being ended, the Celebrant and Ministers lay aside their violet vestments, and put on white for the Mass. And Candles are held in the hands lighted, while the Gospel is read, and again from the beginning of the Canon to the end of the Communion.

¶ Today any Votive Mass, even solemn, of Christ the Lord, is forbidden.

¶ The Mass is then said.

Introit

WE have waited, O God, for thy loving-kindness in the midst of thy temple: according to thy name, O God, so is thy praise unto the world's end: thy right hand is full of righteousness. *Ps.* Great is the Lord, and highly to be praised: in the city of our God, even upon his holy hill.

Collect

ALMIGHTY and everliving God, we humbly beseech thy Majesty, that, as thy only-begotten Son was this day presented in the temple in substance of our flesh, so we may be presented unto thee with pure and clean hearts. By the same thy Son Jesus Christ our Lord. Who liveth.

Epistle. Malachi 3:1

BEHOLD, I will send my messenger, and he shall prepare the way before me: and the Lord, whom ye seek, shall suddenly come to his temple, even the messenger of the covenant, whom ye delight in: behold, he shall come, saith the LORD of hosts. But who may abide the day of his coming? and who shall stand when he appeareth? for he is like a refiner's fire, and like fullers' soap: And he shall sit as a refiner and purifier of silver: and he shall purify the sons of Levi, and purge them as gold and silver, that they may offer unto

Candlemas — **Proper of Saints** — 2 February

the Lord an offering in righteousness. Then shall the offering of Judah and Jerusalem be pleasant unto the Lord, as in the days of old, and as in former years. And I will come near to you to judgment; and I will be a swift witness against the sorcerers, and against the adulterers, and against false swearers, and against those that oppress the hireling in his wages, the widow, and the fatherless, and that turn aside the stranger from his right, and fear not me, saith the Lord of hosts.

Gradual. We have waited, O God, for thy loving-kindness in the midst of thy temple: according to thy name, O God, so is thy praise unto the world's end. ℣. Like as we have heard, so have we seen, in the city of our God, even upon his holy hill.

Alleluia. Alleluia, alleluia. ℣. The old man carried the Child: but the Child was the old man's King. Alleluia.

¶ In Septuagesimatide or Lent, replacing the Alleluia:

Tract. Lord, now lettest thou thy servant depart in peace, according to thy word. ℣. For mine eyes have seen thy salvation. ℣. Which thou hast prepared before the face of all people. ℣. A light to lighten the Gentiles and the glory of thy people Israel.

Gospel. Luke 2:22

AT THAT TIME: When the days of her purification according to the law of Moses were accomplished, they brought him to Jerusalem, to present him to the Lord; (As it is written in the law of the Lord, Every male that openeth the womb shall be called holy to the Lord;) And to offer a sacrifice according to that which is said in the law of the Lord, A pair of turtledoves, or two young pigeons. And, behold, there was a man in Jerusalem, whose name was Simeon; and the same man was just and devout, waiting for the consolation of Israel: and the Holy Ghost was upon him. And it was revealed unto him by the Holy Ghost, that he should not see death, before he had seen the Lord's Christ. And he came by the Spirit into the temple: and when the parents brought in the child Jesus, to do for him after the custom of the law, Then took he him up in his arms, and blessed God, and said, Lord, now lettest thou thy servant depart in peace, according to thy word: For mine eyes have seen thy salvation, Which thou hast prepared before the face of all people; A light to lighten the Gentiles, and the glory of thy people Israel. And Joseph and his mother marvelled at those things which were spoken of him. And Simeon blessed them, and said unto Mary his mother, Behold, this child is set for the fall and rising again of many in Israel; and for a sign which shall be spoken against; (Yea, a sword shall pierce

2 February — Proper of Saints — *Candlemas*

through thy own soul also,) that the thoughts of many hearts may be revealed. And there was one Anna, a prophetess, the daughter of Phanuel, of the tribe of Aser: she was of a great age, and had lived with an husband seven years from her virginity; And she was a widow of about fourscore and four years, which departed not from the temple, but served God with fastings and prayers night and day. And she coming in that instant gave thanks likewise unto the Lord, and spake of him to all them that looked for redemption in Jerusalem. And when they had performed all things according to the law of the Lord, they returned into Galilee, to their own city Nazareth. And the child grew, and waxed strong in spirit, filled with wisdom: and the grace of God was upon him.

Offertory. Full of grace are thy lips: because God hath blessed thee for ever and ever.

Secret

GRACIOUSLY hear our prayers, O Lord: and, that the gifts which we offer before the eyes of thy Majesty may be worthy, do thou bestow upon us the succour of thy loving-kindness. Through.

Communion. It was revealed unto Simeon by the Holy Ghost, that he should not see death, before he had seen the Lord's Christ.

Postcommunion

WE beseech thee, O Lord our God: that these holy mysteries, which thou hast given to us for the assurance of our redemption, may, by the intercession of blessed Mary ever Virgin, be for our healing both in this life and that which is to come. Through.

St. Scholastica

Second Class Double
10 February

Introit

HOW beautiful is the chaste generation with glory: for the memory thereof is immortal: because it is known both with God and with men. *Ps.* My heart and my flesh rejoice in the living God.

Collect

GOD, who didst reveal in a vision the soul of blessed Scholastica thy Virgin entering heaven in the likeness of a dove, that thou mightest shew the way of the undefiled: grant us by the aid of her merits and prayers so innocently to live, that we may worthily attain unto joys eternal. Through.

Epistle. Song of Songs 2:10

Y beloved spake, and said unto me, Rise up, my love, my fair one, and come away. For, lo, the winter is past, the rain is over and gone; The flowers appear on the earth; the time of the singing of birds is come, and the voice of the turtle is heard in our land; The fig tree putteth forth her green figs, and the vines with the tender grape give a good smell. Arise, my love, my fair one, and come away. O my dove, that art in the clefts of the rock, in the secret places of the stairs, let me see thy countenance, let me hear thy voice; for sweet is thy voice, and thy countenance is comely.

Gradual. Whom have I in heaven but thee: and there is none upon earth that I desire in comparison of thee. ℣. My flesh and my heart faileth: but God is the strength of my heart, and my portion for ever.

Alleluia. Alleluia, alleluia. ℣. They are virgins. These are they which follow the Lamb whithersoever he goeth. And in their mouth was found no guile: for they are without fault before the throne of God. Alleluia.

¶ In Septuagesimatide or Lent, replacing the Alleluia:

Tract. Blessed are those that are undefiled in the way: and walk in the law of the Lord. ℣. Blessed are they that keep his testimonies: and seek him with their whole heart. ℣. O that my ways were made so direct: that I might keep thy statutes!

Proper of Saints

10 February — *St. Scholastica*

Gospel. Matthew 19:3

AT THAT TIME: The Pharisees came unto Jesus, tempting him, and saying unto him: Is it lawful for a man to put away his wife for every cause? And he answered and said unto them, Have ye not read, that he which made them at the beginning made them male and female, And said, For this cause shall a man leave father and mother, and shall cleave to his wife: and they twain shall be one flesh? Wherefore they are no more twain, but one flesh. What therefore God hath joined together, let not man put asunder. They say unto him, Why did Moses then command to give a writing of divorcement, and to put her away? He saith unto them, Moses because of the hardness of your hearts suffered you to put away your wives: but from the beginning it was not so. And I say unto you, Whosoever shall put away his wife, except it be for fornication, and shall marry another, committeth adultery: and whoso marrieth her which is put away doth commit adultery. His disciples say unto him, If the case of the man be so with his wife, it is not good to marry. But he said unto them, All men cannot receive this saying, save they to whom it is given. For there are some eunuchs, which were so born from their mother's womb: and there are some eunuchs, which were made eunuchs of men: and there be eunuchs, which have made themselves eunuchs for the kingdom of heaven's sake. He that is able to receive it, let him receive it.

Offertory. The virgins that be her fellows shall bear her company, and shall be brought unto thee. With joy and gladness shall they be brought, and shall enter into the King's palace.

Secret

RECEIVE, O Lord, through the intercession of blessed Scholastica thy Virgin, our humble obedience; and, through the immaculate Victim, cleanse us from every stain of the passions, that we may ever burn with pure and holy love in thy sight. Through.

Communion. For how great is his goodness, and how great is his beauty! corn shall make the young men cheerful, and new wine the virgins.

Postcommunion

WE beseech thee, O Lord, that, refreshed by the sweetness of thine ineffable Sacraments, and assisted by the suffrages of the blessed Virgin Scholastica, we may never be hindered by any earthly things from following thee, the Maker of all good things. Through.

Chair of St. Peter at Antioch

Second Class Double
22 February

Opening Sentence. That they would exalt him also in the congregation of the people : and praise him in the seat of the elders! (Ps. 107:32)

Introit

HE Lord hath established a covenant of peace with him, and made him a prince: that he should have the dignity of the priesthood for ever. *Ps.* Lord, remember David: and all his trouble.

Collect

GOD, who didst bestow upon thy blessed Apostle Peter the keys of the kingdom of heaven, and didst appoint unto him the high priesthood of binding and loosing: vouchsafe; that by the help of his intercession we may be delivered from the bonds of our iniquities. Who livest.

GOD, who by the preaching of the blessed Apostle Paul didst teach the multitude of the Gentiles: grant to us, we beseech thee; that we who celebrate his commemoration may know him to be our advocate with thee. (Through.)

¶ In Lent, Commemoration is made of the Feria.

¶ If this Feast fall on a Saturday—not in a Leap Year—the following Commemoration is made of the Vigil of St. Matthias.

RANT, we beseech thee, Almighty God: that the venerable solemnity of blessed Matthias thine Apostle, which we here prevent, may increase our devotion and set forward our salvation. Through.

Epistle. 1 Peter 1:1

PETER, an apostle of Jesus Christ, to the strangers scattered throughout Pontus, Galatia, Cappadocia, Asia, and Bithynia, Elect according to the foreknowledge of God the Father, through sanctification of the Spirit, unto obedience and sprinkling of the blood of Jesus Christ: Grace unto you, and peace, be multiplied. Blessed be the God and Father of our Lord Jesus Christ, which according to his abundant mercy hath begotten us again unto a lively hope by the resurrection of Jesus Christ from the dead, To an inheritance incorruptible, and undefiled, and that fadeth not away, reserved in heaven for you, Who are kept by the power of God through faith unto salvation ready to be revealed in the last time. Wherein ye greatly rejoice, though now for a season, if need be, ye are in heaviness through manifold temptations: That the trial of your faith, being much more precious than of gold that perisheth, though it be tried with fire, might be found unto praise and honour and glory at the appearing of Jesus Christ our Lord.

Gradual. Let them exalt him in the congregation of the people: and praise him in the seat of the elders. ℣. O that men would praise the Lord for his goodness, and declare the wonder that he doeth for the children of men.

Alleluia. Alleluia, alleluia. ℣. Thou art Peter, and upon this rock I will build my Church. Alleluia.

℣ In Septuagesimatide or Lent, replacing the Alleluia:

Tract. Thou art Peter, and upon this rock I will build my Church. ℣. And the gates of hell shall not prevail against it: and I will give unto thee the keys of the kingdom of heaven. ℣. Whatsoever thou shalt bind on earth shall be bound in heaven. ℣. And whatsoever thou shalt loose on earth shall be loosed in heaven.

Gospel. Matthew 16:13

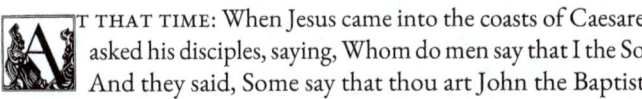T THAT TIME: When Jesus came into the coasts of Caesarea Philippi, he asked his disciples, saying, Whom do men say that I the Son of man am? And they said, Some say that thou art John the Baptist: some, Elias; and others, Jeremias, or one of the prophets. He saith unto them, But whom say ye that I am? And Simon Peter answered and said, Thou art the Christ, the Son of the living God. And Jesus answered and said unto him, Blessed art thou, Simon Barjona: for flesh and blood hath not revealed it unto thee, but my Father which is in heaven. And I say also unto thee, That thou art Peter, and upon this rock I will build my church; and the gates of hell shall not prevail against it. And I will give unto thee the keys of the kingdom of heaven: and whatsoever thou shalt bind on earth shall be bound in heaven: and whatsoever thou shalt loose on earth shall be loosed in heaven.

Offertory. Thou art Peter, and upon this rock I will build my Church: and the gates of hell shall not prevail against it: and I will give unto thee the keys of the kingdom of heaven.

Chair St. Peter Antioch **Proper of Saints** 22 February

Secret

E beseech thee, O Lord, that the intercession of blessed Peter the Apostle may commend unto thee the prayers and sacrifices of thy Church: that those things which we celebrate for his glory may avail for our pardon. Through.

ANCTIFY, O Lord, through the prayers of thine Apostle Paul, the gifts of thy people: that those things, which by thine institution are pleasing unto thee, may be made more pleasing by his prayer and advocacy. (Through.)

¶ In Lent, Commemoration is made of the Feria.

¶ If this Feast fall on a Saturday—not in a Leap Year—the following Commemoration is made of the Vigil of St. Matthias.

 LORD, who didst exalt blessed Matthias to be numbered among thine Apostles: grant that we thy people, who on this day, preventing his heavenly birth, do offer unto thee these holy mysteries, may be assisted by his intercession both in the making of our supplications before thee, and in the obtaining of all that we desire. Through.

Communion. Thou art Peter, and upon this rock I will build my Church.

Postcommunion

AY the gift, O Lord, which we have offered, make us to rejoice: that as we proclaim thy wonders in thine Apostle Peter; so through him we may receive the abundance of thy loving-kindness. Through.

 LORD, who hast sanctified us with this saving mystery: we beseech thee; that he whom thou hast given to be our advocate and guide may never fail in prayer for us. (Through.)

¶ In Lent, Commemoration is made of the Feria.

¶ If this Feast fall on a Saturday—not in a Leap Year—the following Commemoration is made of the Vigil of St. Matthias.

E beseech thee, O Lord, mercifully to hear the supplication of thy holy Apostle Matthias: that thou wouldest vouchsafe unto us thy pardon, and grant us thy everlasting healing. Through.

¶ In Lent, the Last Gospel is of the Feria.

St. Matthias

Second Class Double
24 February (25 February in a Leap Year)

Introit

IGHT honourable are thy friends unto me, O God: right well is their princedom established. *Ps.* O Lord, thou hast searched me out, and known me: thou knowest my down-sitting, and mine up-rising.

Collect

GOD, who didst join blessed Matthias to the college of thine Apostles: grant, we beseech thee; that through his mediation we may ever perceive thy tender mercy towards us. Through.

¶ In Lent, Commemoration is made of the Feria.

Epistle. Acts 1:15

IN THOSE DAYS: Peter stood up in the midst of the disciples, and said, (the number of names together were about an hundred and twenty,) Men and brethren, this scripture must needs have been fulfilled, which the Holy Ghost by the mouth of David spake before concerning Judas, which was guide to them that took Jesus. For he was numbered with us, and had obtained part of this ministry. Now this man purchased a field with the reward of iniquity; and falling headlong, he burst asunder in the midst, and all his bowels gushed out. And it was known unto all the dwellers at Jerusalem; insomuch as that field is called in their proper tongue, Aceldama, that is to say, The field of blood. For it is written in the book of Psalms, Let his habitation be desolate, and let no man dwell therein: and his bishoprick let another take. Wherefore of these men which have companied with us all the time that the Lord Jesus went in and out among us, Beginning from the baptism of John, unto that same day that he was taken up from us, must one be ordained to be a witness with us of his resurrection. And they appointed two, Joseph called Barsabas, who was surnamed Justus, and Matthias. And they prayed, and said, Thou, Lord, which knowest the hearts of all men, shew whether of these two thou hast chosen, That he may take part of this ministry and apostleship, from which Judas by transgression fell, that he might go to his own place. And they gave forth their lots; and the lot fell upon Matthias; and he was numbered with the eleven apostles.

Gradual. Right honourable are thy friends, O God: right well is their princedom established. ℣. If I tell them, they are more in number than the sand.

Alleluia. Alleluia, alleluia. ℣. Right honourable are thy friends unto me, O God: right well is their princedom established. Alleluia.

¶ In Septuagesimatide or Lent, replacing the Alleluia:

Tract. Thou hast given him his heart's desire: and hast not denied him the request of his lips. ℣. For thou hast prevented him with the blessings of goodness: ℣. Thou hast set a crown of pure gold upon his head.

Gospel. Matthew 11:25

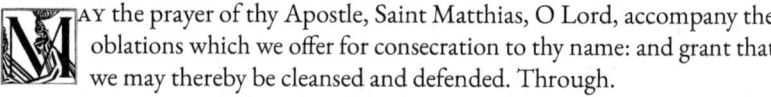T THAT TIME: Jesus answered and said, I thank thee, O Father, Lord of heaven and earth, because thou hast hid these things from the wise and prudent, and hast revealed them unto babes. Even so, Father: for so it seemed good in thy sight. All things are delivered unto me of my Father: and no man knoweth the Son, but the Father; neither knoweth any man the Father, save the Son, and he to whomsoever the Son will reveal him. Come unto me, all ye that labour and are heavy laden, and I will give you rest. Take my yoke upon you, and learn of me; for I am meek and lowly in heart: and ye shall find rest unto your souls. For my yoke is easy, and my burden is light.

Offertory. Thou shalt make them princes in all lands: they shall remember thy name, O Lord, from one generation to another.

Secret

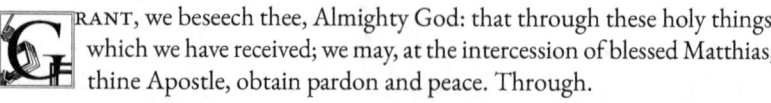AY the prayer of thy Apostle, Saint Matthias, O Lord, accompany the oblations which we offer for consecration to thy name: and grant that we may thereby be cleansed and defended. Through.

¶ In Lent, Commemoration is made of the Feria.

Communion. Ye which have followed me, shall sit upon thrones, judging the twelve tribes of Israel.

Postcommunion

GRANT, we beseech thee, Almighty God: that through these holy things which we have received; we may, at the intercession of blessed Matthias, thine Apostle, obtain pardon and peace. Through.

¶ In Lent, Commemoration is made of the Feria & Last Gospel is of the Feria.

Proper of Saints

12 March — Pope St. Gregory

Pope St. Gregory

Second Class Double
12 March

Introit

YE priests of the Lord, bless ye the Lord: O ye holy and humble men of heart, bless ye the Lord. *Cant.* O all ye works of the Lord, bless ye the Lord: praise him, and magnify him for ever.

Collect

GOD, who on the soul of thy servant Gregory, hast bestowed the rewards of everlasting bliss: mercifully grant; that we, who are oppressed by the burden of our sins, may by his prayers before thee be relieved. Through.

¶ In Lent, Commemoration is made of the Feria.

Epistle. 2 Timothy 4:1

EARLY BELOVED: I charge thee therefore before God, and the Lord Jesus Christ, who shall judge the quick and the dead at his appearing and his kingdom; Preach the word; be instant in season, out of season; reprove, rebuke, exhort with all longsuffering and doctrine. For the time will come when they will not endure sound doctrine; but after their own lusts shall they heap to themselves teachers, having itching ears; And they shall turn away their ears from the truth, and shall be turned unto fables. But watch thou in all things, endure afflictions, do the work of an evangelist, make full proof of thy ministry. For I am now ready to be offered, and the time of my departure is at hand. I have fought a good fight, I have finished my course, I have kept the faith: Henceforth there is laid up for me a crown of righteousness, which the Lord, the righteous judge, shall give me at that day: and not to me only, but unto all them also that love his appearing.

Gradual. The Lord sware, and will not repent: Thou art a priest for ever after the order of Melchisedech. ℣. The Lord said unto my Lord: Sit thou on my right hand.

Tract. Blessed is the man that feareth the Lord: he hath great delight in his commandments. ℣. His seed shall be mighty upon earth: the generation of the faithful shall be blessed. ℣. Riches and plenteousness shall be in his house: and his righteousness endureth for ever.

Pope St. Gregory — **Proper of Saints** — 12 March

Gospel. Matthew 5:13

AT THAT TIME: Jesus said unto his disciples: Ye are the salt of the earth: but if the salt have lost his savour, wherewith shall it be salted? it is thenceforth good for nothing, but to be cast out, and to be trodden under foot of men. Ye are the light of the world. A city that is set on an hill cannot be hid. Neither do men light a candle, and put it under a bushel, but on a candlestick; and it giveth light unto all that are in the house. Let your light so shine before men, that they may see your good works, and glorify your Father which is in heaven. Think not that I am come to destroy the law, or the prophets: I am not come to destroy, but to fulfil. For verily I say unto you, Till heaven and earth pass, one jot or one tittle shall in no wise pass from the law, till all be fulfilled. Whosoever therefore shall break one of these least commandments, and shall teach men so, he shall be called the least in the kingdom of heaven: but whosoever shall do and teach them, the same shall be called great in the kingdom of heaven.

Offertory. My truth and my mercy shall be with him: and in my name shall his horn be exalted.

Secret

GRANT to us, we beseech thee, O Lord: that by the intercession of blessed Gregory this oblation, by the offering of which thou hast bestowed remission of sins on the whole world, may be profitable unto us. Through.

❧ In Lent, Commemoration is made of the Feria.

Communion. A faithful and wise servant, whom the lord hath made ruler over his household: to give them their portion of meat in due season.

Postcommunion

O GOD, who didst make the blessed Bishop Gregory by his merits the equal of thy Saints: mercifully grant; that we, who celebrate the festival of his commemoration, may likewise follow the example of his life. Through.

❧ In Lent, Commemoration is made of the Feria & Last Gospel is of the Feria.

St. Joseph, Spouse of the Blessed Virgin Mary

First Class Double
19 March

Introit

THE just shall flourish like a palm-tree, and shall spread abroad like a cedar in Libanus: planted in the house of the Lord: in the courts of the house of our God. *Ps.* It is a good thing to give thanks unto the Lord: and to sing praises unto thy name, O most Highest.

Collect

WE beseech thee, O Lord, that we may be aided through the merits of the Spouse of thy most holy Mother: that those things, which by our own power we cannot obtain, may through his intercession be granted unto us. Who livest.

¶ In Lent, Commemoration is made of the Feria.

Epistle. Ecclesiasticus 45:1

BELOVED of God and men, even Moses, Whose memorial is blessed. He made him like to the glory of the saints, And magnified him in the fears of his enemies. By his words he caused the wonders to cease; He glorified him in the sight of kings; He gave him commandment for his people, And shewed him part of his glory. He sanctified him in his faithfulness and meekness; He chose him out of all flesh. He made him to hear his voice, And led him into the thick darkness, And gave him commandments face to face, Even the law of life and knowledge.

Gradual. Thou hast prevented him, O Lord, with the blessings of goodness: thou hast set a crown of pure gold upon his head. ℣. He asked life of thee, and thou gavest him a long life, even for ever and ever.

Tract. Blessed is the man that feareth the Lord: he hath great delight in his commandments. ℣. His seed shall be mighty upon earth: the generation of the faithful shall be blessed. ℣. Riches and plenteousness shall be in his house: and his righteousness endureth for ever.

Proper of Saints

St. Joseph Spouse — 19 March

Gospel. Matthew 1:18

WHEN Mary the Mother of Jesus was espoused to Joseph, before they came together, she was found with child of the Holy Ghost. Then Joseph her husband, being a just man, and not willing to make her a publick example, was minded to put her away privily. But while he thought on these things, behold, the angel of the Lord appeared unto him in a dream, saying, Joseph, thou son of David, fear not to take unto thee Mary thy wife: for that which is conceived in her is of the Holy Ghost. And she shall bring forth a son, and thou shalt call his name JESUS: for he shall save his people from their sins.

Offertory. My truth and my mercy shall be with him: and in my name shall his horn be exalted.

Secret

WE render unto thee, O Lord, this duty of our bounden service, humbly beseeching thee: that like as we do offer unto thee this sacrifice of praise in honour of the venerable festivity of blessed Joseph, the Spouse of the Mother of thy Son Jesus Christ our Lord, so by his prayers thou wouldest preserve thy gifts within us. Through the same.

¶ In Lent, Commemoration is made of the Feria.

Communion. Joseph, thou son of David, fear not to take unto thee Mary thy wife: for that which is conceived in her is of the Holy Ghost.

Postcommunion

ASSIST us, we beseech thee, O merciful God: and at the intercession of blessed Joseph, thy Confessor on our behalf, continue towards us the gifts of thy loving-kindness. Through.

¶ In Lent, Commemoration is made of the Feria & Last Gospel is of the Feria.

St. Benedict

Second Class Double
21 March

Introit

THE mouth of the righteous is exercised in wisdom: and his tongue will be talking of judgment. The law of his God is in his heart. *Ps.* Fret not thyself because of the ungodly: neither be thou envious against the evil doers.

Collect

ALMIGHTY and everlasting God, who on this day didst release thy most blessed Confessor Benedict from the bondage of the flesh and take him up to heaven, grant, we beseech thee, to us thy servants who celebrate this feast pardon of all our sins, that we who with joyful hearts take pleasure in his renown may for his sake, and at his intercession, have fellowship with him. Through.

¶ In Lent, Commemoration is made of the Feria.

Epistle. Ecclesiasticus 39:5

HE will apply his heart to resort early to the Lord that made him, And will make supplication before the Most High, And will open his mouth in prayer, And will make supplication for his sins. If the great Lord will, He shall be filled with the spirit of understanding: He shall pour forth the words of his wisdom, And in prayer give thanks unto the Lord. He shall direct his counsel and knowledge, And in his secrets shall he meditate. He shall shew forth the instruction which he hath been taught, And shall glory in the law of the covenant of the Lord. Many shall commend his understanding; And so long as the world endureth, it shall not be blotted out: His memorial shall not depart, And his name shall live from generation to generation.

Gradual. The mouth of the righteous is exercised in wisdom: and his tongue will be talking of judgment. ℣. The law of his God is in his heart, and his goings shall not slide.

Tract. They that sow in tears: shall reap in joy. ℣. He that now goeth on his way weeping, and beareth forth good seed, ℣. Shall doubtless come again with joy, and bring his sheaves with him.

St. Benedict — **Proper of Saints** — 21 March

Sequence

The festive day is come
Which brings to us great joy,

When Holy Church gives thanks acceptable to God.
This day the Heavenly Host sings, Glory in the highest,
With voice and symphony melodious.
This day the holy armies of the heavens
Unite with us in praise of God our King,

Christ, of the holy Virgin Mary born.

Hail, great Confessor Benedict, thou flower of saints
With stedfast faith, Christ's footsteps following,
Thou hast attained the everlasting Kingdom;

Already to their courts the blessed welcome thee.
To thee unitedly our suit we make,
Our frail life by thy blest protection aid.

Praise, glory to thee, blessed, holy Benedict
Entreat for us, O blessed, holy Benedict,

That in the heavenly Temple we may stand,
Fulness of joy beholding in thy presence.
Praise, honour, and thanksgiving pure
Be unto God, who doth for evermore endure.

Let all things say, Amen.

Gospel. Luke 11:33

AT THAT TIME: Jesus said to his disciples: No man, when he hath lighted a candle, putteth it in a secret place, neither under a bushel, but on a candlestick, that they which come in may see the light. The light of the body is the eye: therefore when thine eye is single, thy whole body also is full of light; but when thine eye is evil, thy body also is full of darkness. Take heed therefore that the light which is in thee be not darkness. If thy whole body therefore be full of light, having no part dark, the whole shall be full of light, as when the bright shining of a candle doth give thee light.

Offertory. Thou hast given him his heart's desire, O Lord, and hast not denied him the request of his lips: Thou hast set a crown of pure gold upon his head.

Secret

LORD, let the gifts offered in honour of Saint Benedict, thy Confessor and Abbot, be pleasing unto thee; and, at his intercession, grant us pardon of all our sins. Through.

℣ In Lent, Commemoration is made of the Feria.

Communion. Blessed is that servant whom his lord, when he cometh, shall find watching.

Postcommunion

ET the receiving of thy Sacrament, O Lord, at the intercession of Saint Benedict, thy Confessor and Abbot, lead us to follow the example of his conversation, and also to attain unto his reward. Through.

℣ In Lent, Commemoration is made of the Feria & Last Gospel is of the Feria.

Annunciation of the Blessed Virgin Mary

First Class Double
25 March

Opening Sentence. Send, O Lord, the Lamb, the Ruler of the land. From the rock of the wilderness unto the mountain of the daughter of Sion. (Is. 16:1)

Introit

LL the rich among the people shall make their supplication before thee: the Virgins that be her fellows shall be brought unto the King: they that bear her company shall be brought unto thee with joy and gladness. *Ps.* My heart is inditing of a good matter: I speak of the things which I have made unto the King.

Collect

GOD, who wast pleased that thy Word should take flesh of the womb of the Blessed Virgin Mary at the message of an Angel: grant to thy humble servants; that we who believe her to be truly the Mother of God may be aided by her intercession in thy sight. Through the same.

℣ In Lent, Commemoration is made of the Feria.

Epistle. Isaiah 7:10

IN THOSE DAYS: The LORD spake again unto Ahaz, saying, Ask thee a sign of the LORD thy God; ask it either in the depth, or in the height above. But Ahaz said, I will not ask, neither will I tempt the LORD. And he said, Hear ye now, O house of David; Is it a small thing for you to weary men, but will ye weary my God also? Therefore the Lord himself shall give you a sign; Behold, a virgin shall conceive, and bear a son, and shall call his name Immanuel. Butter and honey shall he eat, that he may know to refuse the evil, and choose the good.

Gradual. Full of grace are thy lips: because God hath blessed thee for ever. ℣. Because of the word of truth, of meekness, and righteousness: and thy right hand shall teach thee terrible things.

Tract. Hearken, O daughter, and consider, incline thine ear: so shall the King have pleasure in thy beauty. ℣. The rich among the people shall make their supplication before thee: kings' daughters were among thy honourable women. ℣. The Virgins that be her fellows shall be brought unto the King: they that bear her company shall be brought unto thee. ℣. With joy and gladness shall they be brought: and shall enter into the King's palace.

Gospel. Luke 1:26

AT THAT TIME: In the sixth month the angel Gabriel was sent from God unto a city of Galilee, named Nazareth, To a virgin espoused to a man whose name was Joseph, of the house of David; and the virgin's name was Mary. And the angel came in unto her, and said, Hail, thou that art highly favoured, the Lord is with thee: blessed art thou among women. And when she saw him, she was troubled at his saying, and cast in her mind what manner of salutation this should be. And the angel said unto her, Fear not, Mary: for thou hast found favour with God. And, behold, thou shalt conceive in thy womb, and bring forth a son, and shalt call his name JESUS. He shall be great, and shall be called the Son of the Highest: and the Lord God shall give unto him the throne of his father David: And he shall reign over the house of Jacob for ever; and of his kingdom there shall be no end. Then said Mary unto the angel, How shall this be, seeing I know not a man? And the angel answered and said unto her, The Holy Ghost shall come upon thee, and the power of the Highest shall overshadow thee: therefore also that holy thing which shall be born of thee shall be called the Son of God. And, behold, thy cousin Elisabeth, she hath also conceived a son in her old age: and this is the sixth month with her, who was called barren. For with God nothing shall be impossible. And Mary said, Behold the handmaid of the Lord; be it unto me according to thy word. And the angel departed from her.

Offertory. Hail, Mary, full of grace; the Lord is with thee: blessed art thou among women, and blessed is the fruit of thy womb.

Secret

ESTABLISH in our hearts, we beseech thee, O Lord, the mysteries of the true faith: that like as we acknowledge thy Son conceived of a Virgin to be very God and very man; so by the power of his life giving Resurrection, we may be found worthy to attain unto everlasting gladness. Through the same.

¶ In Lent, Commemoration is made of the Feria.

Communion. Behold, a Virgin shall conceive, and bear a son: and shall call his name Immanuel.

Postcommunion

WE beseech thee, O Lord, pour thy grace into our hearts; that, as we have known the incarnation of thy Son Jesus Christ by the message of an Angel, so by his cross and passion we may be brought unto the glory of his resurrection. Through the same.

¶ In Lent, Commemoration is made of the Feria & Last Gospel is of the Feria.

¶ If any Feast fall during Holy Week or the Easter Octave, it is transferred to the next available day.

St. Tikhon of Moscow

First Class Double with a Common Octave

7 April

Introit

THE Lord hath established a covenant of peace with him, and made him a prince: that he should have the dignity of the priesthood for ever (alleluia, alleluia). *Ps.* Lord, remember David: and all his trouble.

Collect

GRANT, we beseech thee, Almighty God: that the venerable solemnity of blessed Tikhon, thy Confessor and Bishop may increase our devotion and set forward our salvation. Through.

¶ In Lent, Commemoration is made of the Feria.

St. Tikhon Moscow   **Proper of Saints**   7 April

Epistle. Ecclesiasticus 44:16

ENOCH pleased the Lord, and was translated, Being an example of repentance to all generations. Noah was found perfect and righteous; In the season of wrath he was taken in exchange for the world; Therefore was there left a remnant unto the earth, When the flood came. Everlasting covenants were made with him, That all flesh should no more be blotted out by a flood. Abraham was a great father of a multitude of nations; And there was none found like him in glory; Who kept the law of the Most High, And was taken into covenant with him: In his flesh he established the covenant; And when he was proved, he was found faithful. Therefore he assured him by an oath, That the nations should be blessed in his seed; That he would multiply him as the dust of the earth, And exalt his seed as the stars, And cause them to inherit from sea to sea, And from the River unto the utmost part of the earth. In Isaac also did he establish likewise, for Abraham his father's sake, The blessing of all men, and the covenant: And he made it rest upon the head of Jacob; He acknowledged him in his blessings, And gave to him by inheritance, And divided his portions; Among twelve tribes did he part them. And he brought out of him a man of mercy, Which found favour in the sight of all flesh.

Gradual. Behold, a great priest, who in his days pleased God. ℣. There was none found like unto him who kept the law of the Most High.

Tract. Blessed is the man that feareth the Lord: he hath great delight in his commandments. ℣. His seed shall be mighty upon earth: the generation of the faithful shall be blessed. ℣. Riches and plenteousness shall be in his house: and his righteousness endureth for ever.

¶ In Eastertide, replacing the Gradual & Tract:

Alleluia. Alleluia, alleluia. ℣. Thou art a priest for ever after the order of Melchisedech. Alleluia. ℣. This is a priest whom the Lord hath crowned. Alleluia.

Gospel. Matthew 25:14

AT THAT TIME: Jesus spake this parable unto his disciples: A man travelling into a far country, called his own servants, and delivered unto them his goods. And unto one he gave five talents, to another two, and to another one; to every man according to his several ability; and straightway took his journey. Then he that had received the five talents went and traded with the same, and made them other five talents. And likewise he that had received two, he also gained other two. But he that had received one went and digged in the earth, and hid his lord's money. After a long time the lord of those servants cometh, and reckoneth with them. And so he that had received five talents came and brought other five talents, saying, Lord, thou deliveredst unto me five talents: behold, I have gained beside them five talents more. His lord said unto him, Well done, thou good and faithful servant: thou hast been faithful over a few things, I will make thee ruler over many things: enter thou into the joy of thy lord. He also that had received two talents came and said, Lord, thou deliveredst unto me two talents: behold, I have gained two other talents beside them. His lord said unto him, Well done, good and faithful servant; thou hast been faithful over a few things, I will make thee ruler over many things: enter thou into the joy of thy lord.

Offertory. I have found David my servant, with my holy oil have I anointed them; my hand shall hold him fast, and my arm shall strengthen him (alleluia).

Secret

E beseech thee, O Lord, that we, remembering with gladness the merits of thy Saints, may in all places feel the succour of their intercession. Through.

¶ In Lent, Commemoration is made of the Feria.

Communion. A faithful and wise steward, whom the lord hath made ruler over his household: to give them their portion of meat in due season (alleluia).

Postcommunion

RANT, we beseech thee, Almighty God: that we, shewing forth our thankfulness for the gifts which we have received, may, at the intercession of blessed Tikhon, thy Confessor and Bishop, obtain yet more abundant mercies. Through.

¶ In Lent, Commemoration is made of the Feria & Last Gospel is of the Feria.

St. George

First Class Double with a Common Octave
23 April

Introit

Lent

THE righteous shall rejoice in thy strength, O Lord: exceeding glad shall he be of thy salvation: thou hast given him his heart's desire. *Ps.* For thou hast prevented him with the blessings of goodness: and hast set a crown of pure gold upon his head.

Eastertide

THOU hast hidden me, O God, from the gathering together of the froward, alleluia: and from the insurrection of wicked doers, alleluia, alleluia. *Ps.* Hear my voice, O God, in my prayer: preserve my life from fear of the enemy.

Collect

O GOD, who causest us to rejoice in the good deeds and intercession of Saint George, thy Martyr, mercifully grant that, by the gift of thy grace, we may obtain the benefits we ask of him. Through.

¶ In Lent, Commemoration is made of the Feria.

Epistle. James 1:2

BELOVED: Count it all joy when ye fall into divers temptations; Knowing this, that the trying of your faith worketh patience. But let patience have her perfect work, that ye may be perfect and entire, wanting nothing. If any of you lack wisdom, let him ask of God, that giveth to all men liberally, and upbraideth not; and it shall be given him. But let him ask in faith, nothing wavering. For he that wavereth is like a wave of the sea driven with the wind and tossed. For let not that man think that he shall receive any thing of the Lord. A double minded man is unstable in all his ways. Let the brother of low degree rejoice in that he is exalted: But the rich, in that he is made low: because as the flower of the grass he shall pass away. For the sun is no sooner risen with a burning heat, but it withereth the grass, and the flower thereof falleth, and the grace of the fashion of it perisheth: so also shall the rich man fade away in his ways. Blessed is the man that endureth temptation: for when he is tried, he shall receive the crown of life, which the Lord hath promised to them that love him.

Proper of Saints

23 April — *St. George*

Gradual. The righteous shall not be cast away: for the Lord upholdeth him with his hand. ℣. He is ever merciful, and lendeth: and his seed is blessed.

Tract. Thou hast given him his heart's desire, and hast not denied him the request of his lips. ℣. For thou shalt prevent him with the blessing of goodness. ℣. Thou shalt set a crown of pure gold upon his head.

¶ In Eastertide, replacing the Gradual & Tract:

Alleluia. Alleluia, alleluia. ℣. Blessed is the man that feareth the Lord: he hath great delight in his commandments. Alleluia.

Sequence

Now let us sing, with instruments well tuned,
The feast of George, in divers kinds of voice,
Praying our due thanksgivings to the Lord,
Much to be had in reverence of His saints,
Whom, with high gifts and virtues manifold,
He doth adorn and richly beautify.
In them, as though in instruments of music,
Faith doth with her own finger touch the strings,
Discoursing high of virtues excellent—
As on each single string she lays her hand
She blends it in the fourfold melody
Which she, that mother of all grace, evokes;
Composing thus harmonious symphony;
Without whom all is dissonant,
Yea, trifling, poor, and vain;
With whom all is unisonant,
Yea fraught with endless gain;
Aided by whom the just, in holy lives
Seeking to climb the heights of starry heaven,
Sing forth new songs, and tune their harps in gladness.
May we who keep their feast be counted meet
To hold with them in heaven communion sweet.

St. George   **Proper of Saints**   23 April

Gospel. John 15:1

AT THAT TIME: Jesus said to his disciples: I am the true vine, and my Father is the husbandman. Every branch in me that beareth not fruit he taketh away: and every branch that beareth fruit, he purgeth it, that it may bring forth more fruit. Now ye are clean through the word which I have spoken unto you. Abide in me, and I in you. As the branch cannot bear fruit of itself, except it abide in the vine; no more can ye, except ye abide in me. I am the vine, ye are the branches: He that abideth in me, and I in him, the same bringeth forth much fruit: for without me ye can do nothing. If a man abide not in me, he is cast forth as a branch, and is withered; and men gather them, and cast them into the fire, and they are burned. If ye abide in me, and my words abide in you, ye shall ask what ye will, and it shall be done unto you.

Offertory. O Lord, the very heavens shall praise thy wondrous works: and thy truth in the congregation of the saints, (alleluia, alleluia.)

Secret

WE offer unto thee, O Lord, the wonted Sacrifice of the death of thy Martyr, Saint George, entreating of thy mercy that through these holy Mysteries we may, in thy victory, overcome the temptations of the old enemy, and of thy bounty obtain an everlasting recompense of reward. Through.

℣ In Lent, Commemoration is made of the Feria.

Communion. The righteous shall rejoice in the Lord, and put his trust in him : and all they that are true of heart shall be glad, (alleluia, alleluia.)

Postcommunion

WE humbly pray thee, Almighty Father, that we who are satisfied with the sweetness of the heavenly Table, may at the intercession of thy Martyr, Saint George, also be partakers of his resurrection by whose death we are redeemed. Through.

℣ In Lent, Commemoration is made of the Feria & Last Gospel is of the Feria.

Proper of Saints

St. Mark

25 April

ST. MARK

Second Class Double
25 April

Introit

THOU hast hidden me, O God, from the gathering together of the froward, (alleluia): and from the insurrection of wicked doers, (alleluia, alleluia). *Ps.* Hear my voice, O God, in my prayer: preserve my life from fear of the enemy.

Collect

O GOD, who hast exalted blessed Mark thine Evangelist by the grace of the preaching of the Gospel: grant, we beseech thee; that we may ever both profit by his learning, and be defended by his prayer. Through.

¶ In Lent, Commemoration is made of the Feria.

Epistle. Ephesians 4:7

BRETHREN: Unto every one of us is given grace according to the measure of the gift of Christ. Wherefore he saith, When he ascended up on high, he led captivity captive, and gave gifts unto men. (Now that he ascended, what is it but that he also descended first into the lower parts of the earth? He that descended is the same also that ascended up far above all heavens, that he might fill all things.) And he gave some, apostles; and some, prophets; and some, evangelists; and some, pastors and teachers; For the perfecting of the saints, for the work of the ministry, for the edifying of the body of Christ: Till we all come in the unity of the faith, and of the knowledge of the Son of God, unto a perfect man, unto the measure of the stature of the fulness of Christ: That we henceforth be no more children, tossed to and fro, and carried about with every wind of doctrine, by the sleight of men, and cunning craftiness, whereby they lie in wait to deceive; But speaking the truth in love, may grow up into him in all things, which is the head, even Christ: From whom the whole body fitly joined together and compacted by that which every joint supplieth, according to the effectual working in the measure of every part, maketh increase of the body unto the edifying of itself in love.

Gradual. Thou shalt make them princes in all lands: they shall remember thy name, O Lord. ℣. Instead of thy fathers thou shalt have children: therefore shall the people give thanks unto thee.

Tract. They that sow in tears, shall reap in joy. ℣. He that now goeth on his way weeping, and beareth forth good seed. ℣. Shall doubtless come again with joy, and bring his sheaves with him.

¶ In Eastertide, replacing the Gradual & Tract:

Alleluia. Alleluia, alleluia. ℣. O Lord, the very heavens shall praise thy wondrous works: and thy truth in the congregation of the saints. Alleluia. ℣. Thou hast set, O Lord, a crown of pure gold upon his head. Alleluia.

Gospel. John 15:1

AT THAT TIME: Jesus said unto his disciples: I am the true vine, and my Father is the husbandman. Every branch in me that beareth not fruit he taketh away: and every branch that beareth fruit, he purgeth it, that it may bring forth more fruit. Now ye are clean through the word which I have spoken unto you. Abide in me, and I in you. As the branch cannot bear fruit of itself, except it abide in the vine; no more can ye, except ye abide in me. I am the vine, ye are the branches: He that abideth in me, and I in him, the same bringeth forth much fruit: for without me ye can do nothing. If a man abide not in me, he is cast forth as a branch, and is withered; and men gather them, and cast them into the fire, and they are burned. If ye abide in me, and my words abide in you, ye shall ask what ye will, and it shall be done unto you. Herein is my Father glorified, that ye bear much fruit; so shall ye be my disciples. As the Father hath loved me, so have I loved you: continue ye in my love. If ye keep my commandments, ye shall abide in my love; even as I have kept my Father's commandments, and abide in his love. These things have I spoken unto you, that my joy might remain in you, and that your joy might be full.

Offertory. O Lord, the very heavens shall praise thy wondrous works: and thy truth in the congregation of the saints, (alleluia, alleluia.)

Secret

WE offer unto thee our gifts on the solemnity of blessed Mark, thine Evangelist, beseeching thee, O Lord: that as the preaching of the Gospel made him glorious; so his intercession may render us both in word and deed acceptable unto thee. Through.

¶ In Lent, Commemoration is made of the Feria.

Communion. The righteous shall rejoice in the Lord, and put his trust in him: and all they that are true of heart shall be glad, (alleluia, alleluia.)

Proper of Saints

1 May — *Sts. Philip & James*

Postcommunion

E beseech thee, O Lord, that thy holy mysteries may give unto us continual protection: and through the prayers of blessed Mark thine Evangelist ever defend us from all adversities. Through.

¶ In Lent, Commemoration is made of the Feria & Last Gospel is of the Feria.

STS. PHILIP & JAMES

Second Class Double
1 May

Opening Sentence. He was known of them in breaking of bread. Alleluia.

Introit

HEY cried unto thee, O Lord, in the time of their trouble: and thou didst hear them from heaven, alleluia, alleluia. *Ps.* Rejoice in the Lord, O ye righteous: for it becometh well the just to be thankful.

Collect

ALMIGHTY God, whom truly to know is everlasting life; Grant us perfectly to know thy Son Jesus Christ to be the way, the truth, and the life; that, following the steps of thy holy Apostles, Saint Philip and Saint James, we may stedfastly walk in the way that leadeth to eternal life through the same thy Son Jesus Christ our Lord. Who liveth.

Epistle. James 1:1

JAMES, a servant of God and of the Lord Jesus Christ, to the twelve tribes which are scattered abroad, greeting. My brethren, count it all joy when ye fall into divers temptations; Knowing this, that the trying of your faith worketh patience. But let patience have her perfect work, that ye may be perfect and entire, wanting nothing. If any of you lack wisdom, let him ask of God, that giveth to all men liberally, and upbraideth not; and it shall be given him. But let him ask in faith, nothing wavering. For he that wavereth is like a wave of the sea driven with the wind and tossed. For let not that man think that he shall receive any thing of the Lord. A double minded man is unstable in all his ways. Let the brother of low degree rejoice in that he is exalted: But the rich, in that he is made low: because as the flower of the grass he shall pass away. For the sun is no sooner risen with a burning heat, but it withereth the grass, and the flower thereof falleth, and the grace of the fashion of it perisheth: so also shall the rich man fade away in his ways. Blessed is the man that endureth temptation: for when he is tried, he shall receive the crown of life, which the Lord hath promised to them that love him.

Alleluia. Alleluia, alleluia. ℣. O Lord, the very heavens shall praise thy wondrous works: and thy truth in the congregation of the saints. Alleluia. ℣. Have I been so long time with you, and yet hast thou not known me, Philip? He that hath seen me hath seen my Father also. Alleluia.

Gospel. John 14:1

AT THAT TIME: Jesus said unto his disciples: Let not your heart be troubled: ye believe in God, believe also in me. In my Father's house are many mansions: if it were not so, I would have told you. I go to prepare a place for you. And if I go and prepare a place for you, I will come again, and receive you unto myself; that where I am, there ye may be also. And whither I go ye know, and the way ye know. Thomas saith unto him, Lord, we know not whither thou goest; and how can we know the way? Jesus saith unto him, I am the way, the truth, and the life: no man cometh unto the Father, but by me. If ye had known me, ye should have known my Father also: and from henceforth ye know him, and have seen him. Philip saith unto him, Lord, shew us the Father, and it sufficeth us. Jesus saith unto him, Have I been so long time with you, and yet hast thou not known me, Philip? he that hath seen me hath seen the Father; and how sayest thou then, Shew us the Father? Believest thou not that I am in the Father, and the Father in me? the words that I speak unto you I speak not of myself: but the Father that dwelleth in me, he doeth the works. Believe me that I am in the Father, and the Father in me: or else believe me for the very works' sake. Verily, verily, I say unto you, He that believeth on me, the works that I do shall he do also; and greater works than these shall he do; because I go unto my Father. And whatsoever ye shall ask in my name, that will I do, that the Father may be glorified in the Son. If ye shall ask any thing in my name, I will do it.

Offertory. O Lord, the very heavens shall praise thy wondrous works: and thy truth in the congregation of the saints, alleluia, alleluia.

Secret

GRACIOUSLY receive, O Lord, the gifts which we bring for the solemnity of thine Apostles Philip and James: and turn aside all the evils which we deserve. Through.

Communion. Have I been so long time with you, and yet hast thou not known me, Philip? He that hath seen me hath seen my Father also, alleluia: believest thou not that I am in the Father, and the Father in me? Alleluia, alleluia.

Postcommunion

O LORD, who hast fulfilled us with saving mysteries: we beseech thee that we may be aided by the prayers of those whose festival we celebrate. Through.

Invention of the Holy Cross

Second Class Double
3 May

Opening Sentence. Tell it out among the nations that the Lord reigneth from the tree.

Introit

BUT it behoveth us to glory in the Cross of our Lord Jesus Christ: in whom is our salvation, life and resurrection: by whom we are saved and set free, alleluia, alleluia. *Ps.* God be merciful unto us, and bless us: and shew us the light of his countenance, and be merciful unto us.

Collect

O GOD, who in the wondrous Finding of the Cross of salvation didst renew the miracles of thy Passion: vouchsafe; that by the ransom of the tree of life we may attain thy succour unto life eternal. Who livest.

¶ On 3 May, Commemoration of Sts. Alexander, Eventius, Theodulus, & Juvenalis, as followeth,

GRANT, we beseech thee, Almighty God: that we, who devoutly celebrate the birthday of thy Saints Alexander, Eventius, Theodulus, and Juvenal; may, by their intercession, be delivered from all evils that beset us. Through.

Invention of the Cross   Proper of Saints   3 May

Epistle. Philippians 2:5

BRETHREN: Let this mind be in you, which was also in Christ Jesus: Who, being in the form of God, thought it not robbery to be equal with God: But made himself of no reputation, and took upon him the form of a servant, and was made in the likeness of men: And being found in fashion as a man, he humbled himself, and became obedient unto death, even the death of the cross. Wherefore God also hath highly exalted him, and given him a name which is above every name: That at the name of Jesus every knee should bow, of things in heaven, and things in earth, and things under the earth; And that every tongue should confess that Jesus Christ is Lord, to the glory of God the Father.

Alleluia. Alleluia, alleluia. ℣. Tell it out among the heathen that the Lord hath reigned from the tree. Alleluia. ℣. Sweetest wood, and sweetest iron, sweetest weight is hung on thee: thou alone wast worthy to bear the King of heaven, and its Lord. Alleluia.

Gospel. John 3:1

AT THAT TIME: There was a man of the Pharisees, named Nicodemus, a ruler of the Jews: The same came to Jesus by night, and said unto him, Rabbi, we know that thou art a teacher come from God: for no man can do these miracles that thou doest, except God be with him. Jesus answered and said unto him, Verily, verily, I say unto thee, Except a man be born again, he cannot see the kingdom of God. Nicodemus saith unto him, How can a man be born when he is old? can he enter the second time into his mother's womb, and be born? Jesus answered, Verily, verily, I say unto thee, Except a man be born of water and of the Spirit, he cannot enter into the kingdom of God. That which is born of the flesh is flesh; and that which is born of the Spirit is spirit. Marvel not that I said unto thee, Ye must be born again. The wind bloweth where it listeth, and thou hearest the sound thereof, but canst not tell whence it cometh, and whither it goeth: so is every one that is born of the Spirit. Nicodemus answered and said unto him, How can these things be? Jesus answered and said unto him, Art thou a master of Israel, and knowest not these things? Verily, verily, I say unto thee, We speak that we do know, and testify that we have seen; and ye receive not our witness. If I have told you earthly things, and ye believe not, how shall ye believe, if I tell you of heavenly things? And no man hath ascended up to heaven, but he that came down from heaven, even the Son of man which is in heaven. And as Moses lifted up the serpent in the wilderness, even so must the Son of man be lifted up: That whosoever believeth in him should not perish, but have eternal life.

Proper of Saints — *Invention of the Cross*

3 May

Offertory. The right hand of the Lord bringeth mighty things to pass, the right hand of the Lord hath exalted me: I shall not die, but live and declare the works of the Lord, alleluia.

Secret

MERCIFULLY give heed to the sacrifice which we offer unto thee, O Lord: that we, being preserved from all the wickedness of war, may through the standard of the holy Cross of thy Son ever be stablished with the protection of thy sure defence, that we may destroy the snares of the power of the enemy. Through the same.

¶ On 3 May, Commemoration of Sts. Alexander, Eventius, Theodulus, & Juvenalis, as followeth,

LET thy plenteous benediction, we beseech thee, O Lord, come down upon these sacrifices: that it may mercifully work out our sanctification, and make us to rejoice in the solemnity of thy Saints. Through.

Communion. By the sign of the Cross deliver us from our enemies, O our God, alleluia.

Postcommunion

ALMIGHTY God, who hast fulfilled us with heavenly meat, and refreshed us with spiritual drink, we beseech thee: that as thou hast bidden us to triumph by the wood of the holy Cross of thy Son, the armour of righteousness for the salvation of the world, so thou wouldest defend us from the malicious enemy. Through the same.

¶ On 3 May, Commemoration of Sts. Alexander, Eventius, Theodulus, & Juvenalis, as followeth,

WE beseech thee, O Lord our God, that like as we whom thou hast refreshed by the partaking of thy sacred gift do offer unto thee our worship: so, by the intercession of thy Saints, Alexander, Eventius, Theodulus, and Juvenal, we may perceive the benefit of the same. Through.

St. John Latin Gate   **Proper of Saints**   6 May

St. John before the Latin Gate

Greater Double
6 May

Introit

THOU hast hidden me, O God, from the gathering together of the froward, alleluia: and from the insurrection of wicked doers, alleluia, alleluia. *Ps.* Hear my voice, O God, in my prayer: preserve my life from fear of the enemy.

Collect

O GOD, who seest that we are beset by evils on every side: grant, we beseech thee; that the glorious intercession of blessed John, thine Apostle and Evangelist, may protect us. Through.

Epistle. Wisdom 5:1

THE righteous man shall stand in great boldness before the face of such as have afflicted him, and made no account of his labours. When they see it, they shall be troubled with terrible fear, and shall be amazed at the strangeness of his salvation, so far beyond all that they looked for. And they repenting and groaning for anguish of spirit shall say within themselves, This was he, whom we had sometimes in derision, and a proverb of reproach: We fools accounted his life madness, and his end to be without honour: How is he numbered among the children of God, and his lot is among the saints!

Alleluia. Alleluia, alleluia. ℣. The righteous shall flourish like a palm tree: and shall spread abroad like a cedar in Libanus. Alleluia. ℣. The righteous shall grow as the lily: and shall flourish for ever before the Lord. Alleluia.

Gospel. Matthew 20:20

AT THAT TIME: There came unto Jesus the mother of Zebedee's children with her sons, worshipping him, and desiring a certain thing of him. And he said unto her, What wilt thou? She saith unto him, Grant that these my two sons may sit, the one on thy right hand, and the other on the left, in thy kingdom. But Jesus answered and said, Ye know not what ye ask. Are ye able to drink of the cup that I shall drink of, and to be baptized with the baptism that I am baptized with? They say unto him, We are able. And he saith unto them, Ye shall drink indeed of my cup, and be baptized with the baptism that I am baptized with: but to sit on my right hand, and on my left, is not mine to give, but it shall be given to them for whom it is prepared of my Father.

Offertory. O Lord, the very heavens shall praise thy wondrous works: and thy truth in the congregation of the saints, alleluia, alleluia.

Secret

E beseech thee, O Lord, to accept our prayers and oblations: and graciously hearken unto us whom thou dost cleanse by thy heavenly mysteries. Through.

Communion. The just shall rejoice in the Lord, and put his trust in him: and all they that are true of heart shall be glad, alleluia, alleluia.

Postcommunion

E beseech thee, O Lord: that we, who have been refreshed with heavenly bread, may be nourished unto life eternal. Through.

St. Barnabas

Greater Double
11 June

Introit

IGHT honourable are thy friends unto me, O God: right well is their princedom established. *Ps.* O Lord, thou hast searched me out, and known me: thou knowest my down-sitting, and mine uprising.

Collect

E beseech thee, O Lord, let the prayers of thy Apostle, Saint Barnabas, commend thy Church to thee, and let him continue to intercede for her whom by his doctrine and death he doth glorify. Through.

Proper of Saints

St. Barnabas — 11 June

Epistle. Acts 11:21

IN THOSE DAYS: Tidings of these things came unto the ears of the church which was in Jerusalem: and they sent forth Barnabas, that he should go as far as Antioch. Who, when he came, and had seen the grace of God, was glad, and exhorted them all, that with purpose of heart they would cleave unto the Lord. For he was a good man, and full of the Holy Ghost and of faith: and much people was added unto the Lord. Then departed Barnabas to Tarsus, for to seek Saul. And when he had found him, he brought him unto Antioch. And it came to pass that a whole year they assembled themselves with the church, and taught much people. And the disciples were called Christians first in Antioch. And in these days came prophets from Jerusalem unto Antioch. And there stood up one of them named Agabus, and signified by the spirit that there should be great dearth throughout all the world: which came to pass in the days of Claudius Cæsar. Then the disciples, every man according to his ability, determined to send relief unto the brethren which dwelt in Judæa: which also they did, and sent it to the elders by the hands of Barnabas and Saul.

Gradual. Their sound is gone out into all lands: and their words into the ends of the world. ℣. The heavens declare the glory of God: and the firmament sheweth his handy-work.

Alleluia. Alleluia, alleluia. ℣. I have chosen you out of the world, that ye should go and bring forth fruit: and that your fruit should remain. Alleluia.

❡ In Eastertide, replacing the Gradual & Alleluia:

Alleluia. Alleluia, alleluia. ℣. O Lord, the very heavens shall praise thy wondrous work: and thy truth in the congregation of the saints. Alleluia. ℣. Thou hast set, O Lord, a crown of pure gold upon his head. Alleluia.

Gospel. John 15:12

AT THAT TIME: Jesus said unto his disciples: This is my commandment, That ye love one another, as I have loved you. Greater love hath no man than this, that a man lay down his life for his friends. Ye are my friends, if ye do whatsoever I command you. Henceforth I call you not servants; for the servant knoweth not what his lord doeth: but I have called you friends; for all things that I have heard of my Father I have made known unto you. Ye have not chosen me, but I have chosen you, and ordained you, that ye should go and bring forth fruit, and that your fruit should remain: that whatsoever ye shall ask of the Father in my name, he may give it you.

Offertory. Thou shalt make them princes in all lands: they shall remember thy name, O Lord, from one generation to another.

Secret

SANCTIFY, O Lord, the gifts which we offer: and, at the intercession of blessed Barnabas, thine Apostle, cleanse us thereby from the defilements of our iniquities. Through.

Communion. Ye which have followed me shall sit upon thrones, judging the twelve tribes of Israel.

Postcommunion

WE humbly beseech thee, Almighty God: that as thou dost refresh us with thy sacraments, so, at the intercession of blessed Barnabas, thine Apostle, thou wouldest vouchsafe unto us to do thee worthy and acceptable service. Through.

ST. JOHN BAPTIST

First Class Double with a Common Octave
24 June

Opening Sentence. There was a man sent from God whose name was John.

Introit

FROM the womb of my mother the Lord hath called me by my name: and hath made my mouth as it were a sharp sword: beneath the shadow of his hand hath he hid me, and hath made me like to a polished arrow.
Ps. It is a good thing to give thanks unto the Lord: and to sing praises unto thy name, O most Highest.

Collect

ALMIGHTY God, by whose providence thy servant John Baptist was wonderfully born, and sent to prepare the way of thy Son our Saviour by preaching repentance; Make us so to follow his doctrine and holy life, that we may truly repent according to his preaching; and after his example constantly speak the truth, boldly rebuke vice, and patiently suffer for the truth's sake. Through the same.

St. John Baptist — **Proper of Saints** — 24 June

Epistle. Isaiah 40:1

COMFORT ye, comfort ye my people, saith your God. Speak ye comfortably to Jerusalem, and cry unto her, that her warfare is accomplished, that her iniquity is pardoned: for she hath received of the LORD's hand double for all her sins. The voice of him that crieth in the wilderness, Prepare ye the way of the LORD, make straight in the desert a highway for our God. Every valley shall be exalted, and every mountain and hill shall be made low: and the crooked shall be made straight, and the rough places plain: And the glory of the LORD shall be revealed, and all flesh shall see it together: for the mouth of the LORD hath spoken it. The voice said, Cry. And he said, What shall I cry? All flesh is grass, and all the goodliness thereof is as the flower of the field: The grass withereth, the flower fadeth: because the spirit of the LORD bloweth upon it: surely the people is grass. The grass withereth, the flower fadeth: but the word of our God shall stand for ever. O Zion, that bringest good tidings, get thee up into the high mountain; O Jerusalem, that bringest good tidings, lift up thy voice with strength; lift it up, be not afraid; say unto the cities of Judah, Behold your God! Behold, the Lord GOD will come with strong hand, and his arm shall rule for him: behold, his reward is with him, and his work before him. He shall feed his flock like a shepherd: he shall gather the lambs with his arm, and carry them in his bosom, and shall gently lead those that are with young.

Gradual. Before I formed thee in the belly I knew thee: and before thou camest forth out of the womb I sanctified thee. ℣. The Lord put forth his hand, and touched my mouth, and said unto me.

Alleluia. Alleluia, alleluia. ℣. Thou, child, shalt be called the Prophet of the Highest: thou shalt go before the face of the Lord, to prepare his ways. Alleluia.

Gospel. Luke 1:57

ELISABETH's full time came that she should be delivered; and she brought forth a son. And her neighbours and her cousins heard how the Lord had shewed great mercy upon her; and they rejoiced with her. And it came to pass, that on the eighth day they came to circumcise the child; and they called him Zacharias, after the name of his father. And his mother answered and said, Not so; but he shall be called John. And they said unto her, There is none of thy kindred that is called by this name. And they made signs to his father, how he would have him called. And he asked for a writing table, and wrote, saying, His name is John. And they marvelled all. And his mouth was opened immediately, and his tongue loosed, and he spake, and praised God. And fear came on all that dwelt round about them: and all these sayings were noised abroad throughout all the hill country of Judaea. And all they that heard them laid them up in their hearts, saying, What manner of child shall this be! And the hand of the Lord was with him. And his father Zacharias was filled with the Holy Ghost, and prophesied, saying, Blessed be the Lord God of Israel; for he hath visited and redeemed his people, And hath raised up an horn of salvation for us in the house of his servant David; As he spake by the mouth of his holy prophets, which have been since the world began: That we should be saved from our enemies, and from the hand of all that hate us; To perform the mercy promised to our fathers, and to remember his holy covenant; The oath which he sware to our father Abraham, That he would grant unto us, that we being delivered out of the hand of our enemies might serve him without fear, In holiness and righteousness before him, all the days of our life. And thou, child, shalt be called the prophet of the Highest: for thou shalt go before the face of the Lord to prepare his ways; To give knowledge of salvation unto his people by the remission of their sins, Through the tender mercy of our God; whereby the dayspring from on high hath visited us, To give light to them that sit in darkness and in the shadow of death, to guide our feet into the way of peace. And the child grew, and waxed strong in spirit, and was in the deserts till the day of his shewing unto Israel.

Offertory. The righteous shall flourish like a palm tree: and shall spread abroad like a cedar in Libanus.

Secret

WE set upon thine altars, O Lord, these gifts: celebrating with due honour the nativity of him, who sang of the coming and proclaimed the presence of the Saviour of the world, Jesus Christ thy Son our Lord. Who liveth.

Communion. Thou, child, shalt be called the Prophet of the Highest: for thou shalt go before the face of the lord to prepare his ways.

Postcommunion

LET thy Church, O God, rejoice at the birth of blessed John Baptist: through whom she hath known the author of her new birth, Jesus Christ thy Son our Lord. Who liveth.

¶ Within the Octave, Mass is said as on the Feast, with 2nd Collect of St. Mary in Eastertide (p. 542) & 3rd Against the Persecutors of the Church (p. 543) or for the Chief Bishop (p. 543).

Proper of Saints

Sts. Peter & Paul · 29 June

STS. PETER & PAUL
(St. Peter)
First Class Double with a Common Octave
29 June

Opening Sentence. Thou art Peter and upon this rock I will build my Church. (Mt. 16:18)

Introit

NOW I know of a surety that the Lord hath sent his Angel: and hath delivered me out of the hand of Herod, and from all the expectation of the people of the Jews. *Ps.* O Lord, thou hast searched me out, and known me: thou knowest my down-sitting, and mine uprising.

Collect

O GOD, who hast hallowed this day by the martyrdom of thine Apostles Peter and Paul: grant unto thy Church in all things to follow the commandment of those; through whom she received the beginning of religion. Through.

ALMIGHTY God, who by thy Son Jesus Christ didst give to thy Apostle Saint Peter many excellent gifts, and commandedst him earnestly to feed thy flock; Make, we beseech thee, all Bishops and Pastors diligently to preach thy holy Word, and the people obediently to follow the same, that they may receive the crown of everlasting glory. Through the same.

Epistle. Acts 12:1

IN THOSE DAYS: Herod the king stretched forth his hands to vex certain of the church. And he killed James the brother of John with the sword. And because he saw it pleased the Jews, he proceeded further to take Peter also. (Then were the days of unleavened bread.) And when he had apprehended him, he put him in prison, and delivered him to four quaternions of soldiers to keep him; intending after Easter to bring him forth to the people. Peter therefore was kept in prison: but prayer was made without ceasing of the church unto God for him. And when Herod would have brought him forth, the same night Peter was sleeping between two soldiers, bound with two chains: and the keepers before the door kept the prison. And, behold, the angel of the Lord came upon him, and a light shined in the prison: and he smote Peter on the side, and raised him up, saying, Arise up quickly. And his chains fell off from his hands. And the angel said unto him, Gird thyself, and bind on thy sandals. And so he did. And he saith unto him, Cast thy garment about thee, and follow me. And he went out, and followed him; and wist not that it was true which was done by the angel; but thought he saw a vision. When they were past the first and the second ward, they came unto the iron gate that leadeth unto the city; which opened to them of his own accord: and they went out, and passed on through one street; and forthwith the angel departed from him. And when Peter was come to himself, he said, Now I know of a surety, that the Lord hath sent his angel, and hath delivered me out of the hand of Herod, and from all the expectation of the people of the Jews.

Gradual. Thou shalt make them princes in all lands: they shall remember thy name, O Lord. ℣. Instead of thy fathers thou shalt have children: therefore shall the people give thanks unto thee.

Alleluia. Alleluia, alleluia. ℣. Thou art Peter, and upon this rock I will build my Church. Alleluia.

Gospel. Matthew 16:13

AT THAT TIME: When Jesus came into the coasts of Caesarea Philippi, he asked his disciples, saying, Whom do men say that I the Son of man am? And they said, Some say that thou art John the Baptist: some, Elias; and others, Jeremias, or one of the prophets. He saith unto them, But whom say ye that I am? And Simon Peter answered and said, Thou art the Christ, the Son of the living God. And Jesus answered and said unto him, Blessed art thou, Simon Barjona: for flesh and blood hath not revealed it unto thee, but my Father which is in heaven. And I say also unto thee, That thou art Peter, and upon this rock I will build my church; and the gates of hell shall not prevail against it. And I will give unto thee the keys of the kingdom of heaven: and whatsoever thou shalt bind on earth shall be bound in heaven: and whatsoever thou shalt loose on earth shall be loosed in heaven.

Offertory. Thou shalt make them princes in all lands: they shall remember thy name, O Lord, from one generation to another.

Secret

MAY the prayers of thine Apostles, O Lord, accompany the oblations which we offer for consecration to thy name: and grant that we may thereby be cleansed and defended. Through.

Communion. Thou art Peter, and upon this rock I will build my Church.

St. Paul   **Proper of Saints**   30 June

Postcommunion

LORD, who hast satisfied us with heavenly food: defend us by the intercession of thine Apostles against all adversity. Through.

COMMEMORATION OF ST. PAUL THE APOSTLE

Greater Double
30 June

Introit

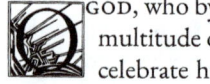KNOW whom I have believed, and am persuaded that he is able to keep that which I have committed unto him against that day, a just judge. *Ps.* O Lord, thou hast searched me out, and known me: thou knowest my down-sitting, and mine up-rising.

Collect

GOD, who by the preaching of the blessed Apostle Paul didst teach the multitude of the Gentiles: grant to us, we beseech thee; that we who celebrate his birthday (commemoration) may know him to be our advocate with thee. Through.

¶ Commemoration of St. Peter is made before all other Commemorations.

GOD, who didst bestow upon thy blessed Apostle Peter the keys of the kingdom of heaven, and didst appoint unto him the high priesthood of binding and loosing: vouchsafe; that by the help of his intercession we may be delivered from the bonds of our iniquities. (Who livest.)

¶ Commemoration is also made of the Octave of St. John (p. 459).

Epistle. Galatians 1:11

BRETHREN: I certify you that the gospel which was preached of me is not after man. For I neither received it of man, neither was I taught it, but by the revelation of Jesus Christ. For ye have heard of my conversation in time past in the Jews' religion, how that beyond measure I persecuted the church of God, and wasted it: and profited in the Jews' religion above many my equals in mine own nation, being more exceedingly zealous of the traditions of my fathers. But when it pleased God, who separated me from my mother's womb, and called me by his grace, to reveal his Son in me, that I might preach him among the heathen; immediately I conferred not with flesh and blood: neither went I up to Jerusalem to them which were apostles before me; but I went into Arabia, and returned again unto Damascus. Then after three years I went up to Jerusalem to see Peter, and abode with him fifteen days. But other of the apostles saw I none, save James the Lord's brother. Now the things which I write unto you, behold, before God, I lie not.

Gradual. He that wrought effectually in Peter to the apostleship, the same was mighty in me toward the Gentiles: and they perceived the grace of God that was given unto me. ℣. The grace of God which was bestowed upon me was not in vain: but his grace ever abideth in me.

Alleluia. Alleluia, alleluia. ℣. Holy Paul Apostle, preacher of truth and teacher of the Gentiles, intercede for us. Alleluia.

Gospel. Matthew 10:16

T THAT TIME: Jesus said unto his disciples: Behold, I send you forth as sheep in the midst of wolves: be ye therefore wise as serpents, and harmless as doves. But beware of men: for they will deliver you up to the councils, and they will scourge you in their synagogues; and ye shall be brought before governors and kings for my sake, for a testimony against them and the Gentiles. But when they deliver you up, take no thought how or what ye shall speak: for it shall be given you in that same hour what ye shall speak. For it is not ye that speak, but the Spirit of your Father which speaketh in you. And the brother shall deliver up the brother to death, and the father the child: and the children shall rise up against their parents, and cause them to be put to death. And ye shall be hated of all men for my name's sake: but he that endureth to the end shall be saved.

Offertory. Right honourable are thy friends unto me, O God: right well is their princedom established.

Secret

SANCTIFY, O Lord, through the prayers of thine Apostle Paul the gifts of thy people: that those things, which by thine institution are pleasing unto thee, may be made more pleasing by his prayer and advocacy. Through.

E beseech thee, O Lord, that the intercession of blessed Peter the Apostle may commend unto thee the prayers and sacrifices of thy Church: that those things which we celebrate for his glory may avail for our pardon. (Through.)

¶ Commemoration is also made of the Octave of St. John (p. 461).

Communion. Verily I say unto you: That ye which have forsaken all and followed me, shall receive an hundredfold, and shall inherit everlasting life.

Postcommunion

O LORD, who hast made us partakers of thy sacrament: we entreat thee; that at the intercession of thy Blessed Apostle Paul, those things which we have celebrated for his glory may be profitable for our healing. Through.

MAY the gift, O Lord, which we have offered make us to rejoice: that as we proclaim thy wonders in thine Apostle Peter; so through him we may receive the abundance of thy loving-kindness. (Through).

☞ Commemoration is also made of the Octave of St. John (p. 461).

THE MOST PRECIOUS BLOOD OF OUR LORD JESUS CHRIST

Second Class Double
1 July

Opening Sentence. We therefore pray thee, help thy servants, whom thou hast redeemed with thy precious blood.

Introit

THOU hast redeemed us, O Lord, by thy blood, out of every kindred, and tongue, and people, and nation: and hast made us a kingdom for our God. *Ps.* My song shall be alway of the loving-kindness of the Lord: with my mouth will I ever be shewing thy truth from one generation to another.

Collect

ALMIGHTY and everlasting God, who didst appoint thine only-begotten Son to be the Redeemer of the world, and hast vouchsafed to be reconciled to us by his Blood: grant us, we beseech thee, so to venerate with solemn worship the price of our salvation, that by its power we may be defended from the evils of this present life on earth; and may rejoice in the everlasting fruit thereof in heaven. Through.

☞ Commemoration is made of the Octave Day of St. John Baptist (p. 459).

1 July — **Proper of Saints** — *Precious Blood*

Epistle. Hebrews 9:11

BRETHREN: Christ being come an high priest of good things to come, by a greater and more perfect tabernacle, not made with hands, that is to say, not of this building; Neither by the blood of goats and calves, but by his own blood he entered in once into the holy place, having obtained eternal redemption for us. For if the blood of bulls and of goats, and the ashes of an heifer sprinkling the unclean, sanctifieth to the purifying of the flesh: How much more shall the blood of Christ, who through the eternal Spirit offered himself without spot to God, purge your conscience from dead works to serve the living God? And for this cause he is the mediator of the new testament, that by means of death, for the redemption of the transgressions that were under the first testament, they which are called might receive the promise of eternal inheritance, in Christ Jesus our Lord.

Gradual. This is he that came by water and blood, even Jesus Christ: not by water only, but by water and blood. ℣. There are three that bear record in heaven: the Father, the Word, and the Holy Ghost; and these three are one. And there are three that bear witness in earth: the spirit, and the water, and the blood: and these three agree in one.

Alleluia. Alleluia, alleluia. ℣. If we receive the witness of men, the witness of God is greater. Alleluia.

Gospel. John 19:30

AT THAT TIME: When Jesus had received the vinegar, he said, It is finished: and he bowed his head, and gave up the ghost. The Jews therefore, because it was the preparation, that the bodies should not remain upon the cross on the sabbath day, (for that sabbath day was an high day,) besought Pilate that their legs might be broken, and that they might be taken away. Then came the soldiers, and brake the legs of the first, and of the other which was crucified with him. But when they came to Jesus, and saw that he was dead already, they brake not his legs: But one of the soldiers with a spear pierced his side, and forthwith came there out blood and water. And he that saw it bare record, and his record is true.

Offertory. The cup of blessing which we bless, is it not the communion of the blood of Christ? the bread which we break, is it not the communion of the body of Christ?

Visitation   **Proper of Saints**   2 July

Secret

WE beseech thee, that through these divine mysteries we may draw near unto Jesus, the mediator of the new Testament: and renew upon thine altars, O Lord of Hosts, the sprinkling of the blood that speaketh better things than that of Abel. Through the same.

¶ Commemoration is made of the Octave Day of St. John Baptist (p. 461).

Communion. Christ was once offered to bear the sins of many: and unto them that look for him shall he appear the second time without sin unto salvation.

Postcommunion

O LORD, who hast suffered us to approach thy holy table, and with joy to draw water out of the wells of the Saviour: we beseech thee, that his blood may be to us a well of water springing up unto life eternal. Who liveth.

¶ Commemoration is made of the Octave Day of St. John Baptist (p. 461).

VISITATION OF THE BLESSED VIRGIN MARY

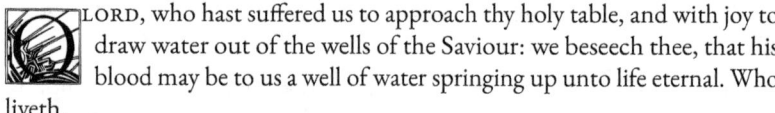

Second Class Double
2 July

Introit

HAIL, O Mother most holy, who in child-birth didst bring forth the Monarch: him who o'er heaven and earth reigneth for ever and ever. *Ps.* My heart is inditing of a good matter: I speak of the things which I have made unto the King.

Collect

WE beseech thee, O Lord, to grant unto us thy servants the gift of heavenly grace: that as the child-bearing of the blessed Virgin was unto us the beginning of salvation; so the devout observance of her Visitation may bestow on us an increase of peace. Through.

¶ On 2 July, Commemoration of St. John of San Francisco, as followeth,

WE beseech thee, O Lord, graciously to hear the prayers which we offer unto thee on the solemnity of blessed John, thy Confessor and Bishop: that, like as he was found worthy to do thee faithful service, so by his merits and intercession we may be absolved from all our sins. Through.

Proper of Saints

2 July — *Visitation*

¶ On 2 July, Commemoration of Sts. Processus and Martinian, as followeth,

GOD, who dost encompass and protect us by the glorious confession of thy holy Martyrs Processus and Martinian: grant us both to profit by their example, and to rejoice in their intercession. Through.

Epistle. Song of Songs 2:8

EHOLD, he cometh leaping upon the mountains, skipping upon the hills. My beloved is like a roe or a young hart: behold, he standeth behind our wall, he looketh forth at the windows, shewing himself through the lattice. My beloved spake, and said unto me, Rise up, my love, my fair one, and come away. For, lo, the winter is past, the rain is over and gone; The flowers appear on the earth; the time of the singing of birds is come, and the voice of the turtle is heard in our land; The fig tree putteth forth her green figs, and the vines with the tender grape give a good smell. Arise, my love, my fair one, and come away. O my dove, that art in the clefts of the rock, in the secret places of the stairs, let me see thy countenance, let me hear thy voice; for sweet is thy voice, and thy countenance is comely.

Gradual. Blessed and venerable art thou, O Virgin Mary: who without spot wast found the Mother of the Saviour. ℣. Virgin, Mother of God, he whom the whole world containeth not, being made man hid in thy womb.

Alleluia. Alleluia, alleluia. ℣. Happy art thou, O sacred Virgin Mary, and most worthy of all praise: for our of thee hath arisen the sun of righteousness, Christ our God. Alleluia.

Gospel. Luke 1:39

T THAT TIME: Mary arose and went into the hill country with haste, into a city of Juda; And entered into the house of Zacharias, and saluted Elisabeth. And it came to pass, that, when Elisabeth heard the salutation of Mary, the babe leaped in her womb; and Elisabeth was filled with the Holy Ghost: And she spake out with a loud voice, and said, Blessed art thou among women, and blessed is the fruit of thy womb. And whence is this to me, that the mother of my Lord should come to me? For, lo, as soon as the voice of thy salutation sounded in mine ears, the babe leaped in my womb for joy. And blessed is she that believed: for there shall be a performance of those things which were told her from the Lord. And Mary said, My soul doth magnify the Lord, And my spirit hath rejoiced in God my Saviour.

Visitation 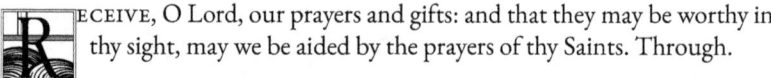 **Proper of Saints** 2 July

Offertory. Blessed art thou, O Virgin Mary, who didst bear the Creator of all things: thou broughtest forth him who made thee, and for ever remainest a Virgin.

Secret

MAY the manhood of thine only-begotten Son, O Lord, avail for our succour: that even as he, being born of a Virgin, destroyed not but hallowed the innocence of his Mother; so on this feast of her Visitation, he may deliver us from our offences, and render us an oblation acceptable unto thee, even Jesus Christ our Lord. Who liveth.

¶ On 2 July, Commemoration of St. John of San Francisco, as followeth,

WE beseech thee, O Lord, that our devout observance of the yearly solemnity of blessed John, thy Confessor and Bishop, may render us acceptable unto thy loving-kindness: that this service of propitiation, which we duly offer, may be profitable unto him for the reward of blessedness, and obtain for us the gifts of thy grace. Through.

¶ On 2 July, Commemoration of Sts. Processus and Martinian, as followeth,

RECEIVE, O Lord, our prayers and gifts: and that they may be worthy in thy sight, may we be aided by the prayers of thy Saints. Through.

Communion. Blessed is the womb of the Virgin Mary, that bore the Son of the everlasting Father.

Postcommunion

GRANT, we beseech thee, O Lord: that the sacrament which we have received in the observance of this yearly festival; may both in this life and in that which is to come be profitable for our healing. Through.

¶ On 2 July, Commemoration of St. John of San Francisco, as followeth,

O GOD, who rewardest the souls of them that put their trust in thee: vouchsafe; that we who keep the solemn festival of blessed John, thy Confessor and Bishop, may by his prayers obtain thy merciful pardon. Through.

¶ On 2 July, Commemoration of Sts. Processus and Martinian, as followeth,

O LORD our God, who hast fulfilled us with the partaking of the sacred Body and the precious Blood, we beseech thee: that those things which we perform with godly devotion we may attain in the assurance of our redemption. Through the same.

Proper of Saints

22 July — *St. Mary Magdalene*

St. Mary Magdalene, Penitent

Greater Double
22 July

Opening Sentence. Mary hath chosen that good part, which shall not be taken away from her. (Lk. 10:42)

Introit

THE ungodly laid wait for me to destroy me: O Lord, I will consider thy testimonies: I see that all things come to an end: but thy commandment is exceeding broad. *Ps.* Blessed are those that are undefiled in the way: and walk in the law of the Lord.

Collect

GRANT us, most merciful Father, like as St. Mary Magdalene, by loving thy Only Begotten Son above all things, obtained forgiveness of her sins, so she may procure for us in thy compassionate presence everlasting blessedness. Through.

Epistle. Proverbs 31:10

WHO can find a virtuous woman? for her price is far above rubies. The heart of her husband doth safely trust in her, so that he shall have no need of spoil. She will do him good and not evil all the days of her life. She seeketh wool, and flax, and worketh willingly with her hands. She is like the merchants' ships; she bringeth her food from afar. She riseth also while it is yet night, and giveth meat to her household, and a portion to her maidens. She considereth a field, and buyeth it: with the fruit of her hands she planteth a vineyard. She girdeth her loins with strength, and strengtheneth her arms. She perceiveth that her merchandise is good: her candle goeth not out by night. She layeth her hands to the spindle, and her hands hold the distaff. She stretcheth out her hand to the poor; yea, she reacheth forth her hands to the needy. She is not afraid of the snow for her household: for all her household are clothed with scarlet. She maketh herself coverings of tapestry; her clothing is silk and purple. Her husband is known in the gates, when he sitteth among the elders of the land. She maketh fine linen, and selleth it; and delivereth girdles unto the merchant. Strength and honour are her clothing; and she shall rejoice in time to come. She openeth her mouth with wisdom; and in her tongue is the law of kindness. She looketh well to the ways of her household, and eateth not the

St. Mary Magdalene — Proper of Saints — 22 July

bread of idleness. Her children arise up, and call her blessed; her husband also, and he praiseth her. Many daughters have done virtuously, but thou excellest them all. Favour is deceitful, and beauty is vain: but a woman that feareth the LORD, she shall be praised. Give her of the fruit of her hands; and let her own works praise her in the gates.

Gradual. Thou hast loved righteousness and hated iniquity. ℣. Wherefore God, even thy God, hath anointed thee with the oil of gladness.

Alleluia. Alleluia, alleluia. ℣. Full of grace are thy lips: because God hath blessed thee for ever. Alleluia.

Gospel. Luke 7:36

AT THAT TIME: One of the Pharisees desired Jesus that he would eat with him. And he went into the Pharisee's house, and sat down to meat. And, behold, a woman in the city, which was a sinner, when she knew that Jesus sat at meat in the Pharisee's house, brought an alabaster box of ointment, And stood at his feet behind him weeping, and began to wash his feet with tears, and did wipe them with the hairs of her head, and kissed his feet, and anointed them with the ointment. Now when the Pharisee which had bidden him saw it, he spake within himself, saying, This man, if he were a prophet, would have known who and what manner of woman this is that toucheth him: for she is a sinner. And Jesus answering said unto him, Simon, I have somewhat to say unto thee. And he saith, Master, say on. There was a certain creditor which had two debtors: the one owed five hundred pence, and the other fifty. And when they had nothing to pay, he frankly forgave them both. Tell me therefore, which of them will love him most? Simon answered and said, I suppose that he, to whom he forgave most. And he said unto him, Thou hast rightly judged. And he turned to the woman, and said unto Simon, Seest thou this woman? I entered into thine house, thou gavest me no water for my feet: but she hath washed my feet with tears, and wiped them with the hairs of her head. Thou gavest me no kiss: but this woman since the time I came in hath not ceased to kiss my feet. My head with oil thou didst not anoint: but this woman hath anointed my feet with ointment. Wherefore I say unto thee, Her sins, which are many, are forgiven; for she loved much: but to whom little is forgiven, the same loveth little. And he said unto her, Thy sins are forgiven. And they that sat at meat with him began to say within themselves, Who is this that forgiveth sins also? And he said to the woman, Thy faith hath saved thee; go in peace.

25 July   **Proper of Saints**   *St. James*

Offertory. Kings' daughters were among thy honourable women, upon thy right hand did stand the queen in a vesture of gold, wrought about with divers colours.

Secret

E beseech thee, O Lord, that the glorious merits of blessed Mary Magdalene may render our gifts pleasing unto thee: even as the oblation of her devout obedience was mercifully accepted by thine only-begotten Son. Who liveth.

Communion. I deal with the thing that is lawful and right, O Lord, let the proud do me no wrong: I hold straight all thy commandments, and all false ways I utterly abhor.

Postcommunion

E beseech thee, O Lord, that we who have received the only and saving remedy, thy precious Body and Blood: may by the protection of Saint Mary Magdalene be delivered from all evils. Who livest.

St. James

Second Class Double
25 July

Introit

IGHT honourable are thy friends unto me, O God: right well is their princedom established. *Ps.* O Lord, thou hast searched me out, and known me: thou knowest my down-sitting and mine up-rising.

Collect

E thou, O Lord, the sanctifier and guardian of thy people, that under the protection of thy Apostle, James, they may please thee in their conversation, and serve thee in all quietness. Through.

❡ On 25 July, Commemoration of St. Christopher, as followeth,

RANT, we beseech thee, Almighty God: that we, who devoutly celebrate the birthday of blessed Christopher, thy Martyr, may by his intercession be stablished in the love of thy name. Through.

St. James   **Proper of Saints**   25 July

Epistle. Acts 11:27

IN THOSE DAYS: Came prophets from Jerusalem unto Antioch. And there stood up one of them named Agabus, and signified by the Spirit that there should be great dearth throughout all the world: which came to pass in the days of Claudius Caesar. Then the disciples, every man according to his ability, determined to send relief unto the brethren which dwelt in Judaea: Which also they did, and sent it to the elders by the hands of Barnabas and Saul. Now about that time Herod the king stretched forth his hands to vex certain of the church. And he killed James the brother of John with the sword. And because he saw it pleased the Jews, he proceeded further to take Peter also.

Gradual. Thou shalt make them princes in all lands: they shall remember thy name, O Lord. ℣. Instead of thy fathers thou shalt have children: therefore shall the people give thanks unto thee.

Alleluia. Alleluia, alleluia. ℣. I have chosen you out of the world, that ye should go and bring forth fruit: and that your fruit should remain. Alleluia.

Gospel. Matthew 20:20

AT THAT TIME: There came unto Jesus the mother of Zebedee's children with her sons, worshipping him, and desiring a certain thing of him. And he said unto her, What wilt thou? She saith unto him, Grant that these my two sons may sit, the one on thy right hand, and the other on the left, in thy kingdom. But Jesus answered and said, Ye know not what ye ask. Are ye able to drink of the cup that I shall drink of, and to be baptized with the baptism that I am baptized with? They say unto him, We are able. And he saith unto them, Ye shall drink indeed of my cup, and be baptized with the baptism that I am baptized with: but to sit on my right hand, and on my left, is not mine to give, but it shall be given to them for whom it is prepared of my Father. And when the ten heard it, they were moved with indignation against the two brethren. But Jesus called them unto him, and said, Ye know that the princes of the Gentiles exercise dominion over them, and they that are great exercise authority upon them. But it shall not be so among you: but whosoever will be great among you, let him be your minister; And whosoever will be chief among you, let him be your servant: Even as the Son of man came not to be ministered unto, but to minister, and to give his life a ransom for many.

Offertory. Their sound is gone out into all lands: and their words into the ends of the world.

Secret

WE beseech thee, O Lord, that the blessed passion of blessed James thy Apostle may commend unto thee the oblations of thy people: that whereas they are not worthy through our merits, they may by his prayers be made acceptable unto thee. Through.

¶ On 25 July, Commemoration of St. Christopher, as followeth,

WE beseech thee, O Lord, to accept our prayers and oblations: and graciously hearken unto us, whom thou dost cleanse by thy heavenly mysteries. Through.

Communion. Ye, which have followed me, shall sit upon thrones, judging the twelve tribes of Israel.

Postcommunion

WE beseech thee, O Lord, that we who on this feast of thy blessed Apostle James, have joyfully received thy holy mysteries: may by his intercession obtain thy succour. Through.

¶ On 25 July, Commemoration of St. Christopher, as followeth,

GRANT, we beseech thee, O Lord our God: that like as we in this life do gladly honour the memory of thy saints; so we may rejoice to behold them for ever. Through.

ST. ANNE

Second Class Double
26 July

Introit

REJOICE we all in the Lord, keeping feast day in honour of blessed Anne: in whose solemnity the Angels rejoice and glorify the Son of God. *Ps.* My heart is inditing of a good matter: I speak of the things which I have made unto the King.

Collect

O GOD, who on blessed Anne didst vouchsafe to bestow grace, that she might be made worthy to become the mother of her who bore thine only-begotten Son: mercifully grant; that we, who celebrate her festival (commemoration) may be aided by her intercession with thee. Through the same.

St. Anne **Proper of Saints** 26 July

Epistle. Proverbs 31:10

WHO can find a virtuous woman? for her price is far above rubies. The heart of her husband doth safely trust in her, so that he shall have no need of spoil. She will do him good and not evil all the days of her life. She seeketh wool, and flax, and worketh willingly with her hands. She is like the merchants' ships; she bringeth her food from afar. She riseth also while it is yet night, and giveth meat to her household, and a portion to her maidens. She considereth a field, and buyeth it: with the fruit of her hands she planteth a vineyard. She girdeth her loins with strength, and strengtheneth her arms. She perceiveth that her merchandise is good: her candle goeth not out by night. She layeth her hands to the spindle, and her hands hold the distaff. She stretcheth out her hand to the poor; yea, she reacheth forth her hands to the needy. She is not afraid of the snow for her household: for all her household are clothed with scarlet. She maketh herself coverings of tapestry; her clothing is silk and purple. Her husband is known in the gates, when he sitteth among the elders of the land. She maketh fine linen, and selleth it; and delivereth girdles unto the merchant. Strength and honour are her clothing; and she shall rejoice in time to come. She openeth her mouth with wisdom; and in her tongue is the law of kindness. She looketh well to the ways of her household, and eateth not the bread of idleness. Her children arise up, and call her blessed; her husband also, and he praiseth her. Many daughters have done virtuously, but thou excellest them all. Favour is deceitful, and beauty is vain: but a woman that feareth the Lord, she shall be praised. Give her of the fruit of her hands; and let her own works praise her in the gates.

Gradual. Thou hast loved righteousness and hated iniquity. ℣. Wherefore God, even thy God, hath anointed thee with the oil of gladness.

Alleluia. Alleluia, alleluia. ℣. Full of grace are thy lips: because God hath blessed thee for ever. Alleluia.

Gospel. Matthew 13:44

AT THAT TIME: Jesus spoke this parable unto his disciples: The kingdom of heaven is like unto treasure hid in a field; the which when a man hath found, he hideth, and for joy thereof goeth and selleth all that he hath, and buyeth that field. Again, the kingdom of heaven is like unto a merchant man, seeking goodly pearls: who, when he had found one pearl of great price, went and sold all that he had, and bought it. Again, the kingdom of heaven is like unto a net, that was cast into the sea, and gathered of every kind: which, when it was full, they drew to shore, and sat down, and gathered the good into vessels, but cast the bad away. So shall it be at the end of the world: the angels shall come forth, and sever the wicked from among the just, and shall cast them into the furnace of fire: there shall be wailing and gnashing of teeth. Jesus saith unto them, Have ye understood all these things? They say unto him, Yea, Lord. Then said he unto them, Therefore every scribe which is instructed unto the kingdom of heaven is like unto a man that is an householder, which bringeth forth out of his treasure things new and old.

Offertory. Kings' daughters were among thy honourable women, upon thy right hand did stand the queen in a vesture of gold, wrought about with divers colours.

Secret

WE beseech thee, O Lord, mercifully to have respect unto these our sacrifices: that through the intercession of blessed Anne, who brought forth the Mother of thy Son, our Lord Jesus Christ, they may increase our devotion and set forward our salvation. Through the same.

Communion. Full of grace are thy lips: because God hath blessed thee for ever, and world without end.

Postcommunion

WE beseech thee, O Lord our God: that by the intercession of blessed Anne, whom thou didst choose to bring forth the Mother of thy Son, we, being quickened with these heavenly sacraments may be found worthy to attain to everlasting salvation. Through the same.

St. Peter in Chains

Greater Double
1 August

Opening Sentence. I will call upon the Lord, which is worthy to be praised. So shall I be saved from mine enemies. (2 Sam. 22:4)

Introit

NOW I know of a surety, that the Lord hath sent his Angel, and hath delivered me out of the hand of Herod, and from all the expectation of the people of the Jews. *Ps.* O Lord, thou hast searched me out, and known me: thou knowest my down-sitting, and mine up-rising.

Lammas # Proper of Saints 1 August

Collect

GOD, who didst deliver blessed Peter the Apostle from his chains, and didst cause him to depart unhurt: loose, we beseech thee, the chains of our sins; and graciously keep from us all evils. Through.

❡ Commemoration of St. Paul, as followeth,

GOD, who by the preaching of the blessed Apostle Paul didst teach the multitude of the Gentiles: grant to us, we beseech thee; that we who celebrate his commemoration may know him to be our advocate with thee. (Through.)

❡ Commemoration of the Holy Maccabees, as followeth,

LORD, let the crown of the brethren, thy Martyrs, cause us to rejoice: that we may thereby be strengthened and increased in our faith; and comforted by their manifold intercession. Through.

Epistle. Acts 12:1

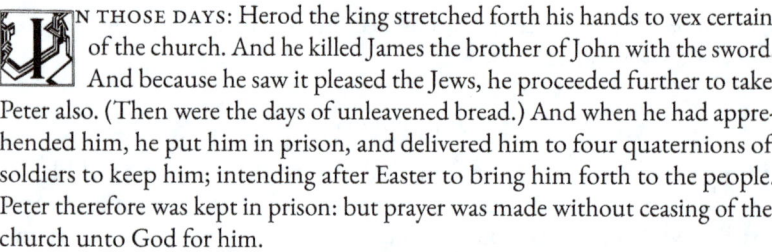N THOSE DAYS: Herod the king stretched forth his hands to vex certain of the church. And he killed James the brother of John with the sword. And because he saw it pleased the Jews, he proceeded further to take Peter also. (Then were the days of unleavened bread.) And when he had apprehended him, he put him in prison, and delivered him to four quaternions of soldiers to keep him; intending after Easter to bring him forth to the people. Peter therefore was kept in prison: but prayer was made without ceasing of the church unto God for him.

And when Herod would have brought him forth, the same night Peter was sleeping between two soldiers, bound with two chains: and the keepers before the door kept the prison. And, behold, the angel of the Lord came upon him, and a light shined in the prison: and he smote Peter on the side, and raised him up, saying, Arise up quickly. And his chains fell off from his hands. And the angel said unto him, Gird thyself, and bind on thy sandals. And so he did. And he saith unto him, Cast thy garment about thee, and follow me. And he went out, and followed him; and wist not that it was true which was done by the angel; but thought he saw a vision. When they were past the first and the second ward, they came unto the iron gate that leadeth unto the city; which opened to them of his own accord: and they went out, and passed on through one street; and forthwith the angel departed from him. And when Peter was come to himself, he said, Now I know of a surety, that the Lord hath sent his angel, and hath delivered me out of the hand of Herod, and from all the expectation of the people of the Jews.

Proper of Saints

1 August — *Lammas*

Gradual. Thou shalt make them princes in all lands: they shall remember thy name, O Lord. ℣. Instead of thy fathers thou shalt have children: therefore shall the people give thanks unto thee.

Alleluia. Alleluia, alleluia. ℣. Loosen at God's command, O Peter, the chains of earth's bondage: thou who dost make to lie open the heavenly realms to the blessed. Alleluia.

Gospel. Matthew 16:13

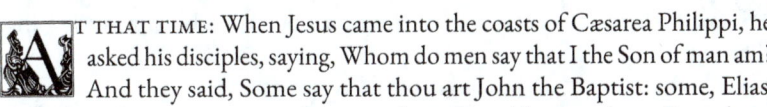T THAT TIME: When Jesus came into the coasts of Cæsarea Philippi, he asked his disciples, saying, Whom do men say that I the Son of man am? And they said, Some say that thou art John the Baptist: some, Elias; and others, Jeremias, or one of the prophets. He saith unto them, But whom say ye that I am? And Simon Peter answered and said, Thou art the Christ, the Son of the living God. And Jesus answered and said unto him, Blessed art thou, Simon Bar-jona: for flesh and blood hath not revealed it unto thee, but my Father which is in heaven. And I say also unto thee, That thou art Peter, and upon this rock I will build my church; and the gates of hell shall not prevail against it. And I will give unto thee the keys of the kingdom of heaven: and whatsoever thou shalt bind on earth shall be bound in heaven: and whatsoever thou shalt loose on earth shall be loosed in heaven.

Offertory. Thou shalt make them princes in all lands: they shall remember thy name, O Lord, from one generation to another.

Secret

MAY the sacrifice which we offer unto thee, O Lord, through the intercession of blessed Peter thine Apostle, evermore quicken and defend us. Through.

¶ Commemoration of St. Paul, as followeth,

SANCTIFY, O Lord, through the prayers of thine Apostle Paul, the gifts of thy people: that those things which, by thine institution, are pleasing unto thee, may be made more pleasing by his prayer and advocacy. (Through.)

¶ Commemoration of the Holy Maccabees, as followeth,

RANT, O Lord, that we may with devout hearts celebrate thy mysteries in honour of thy holy Martyrs: and thereby obtain an increase both of protection and joy. Through.

Communion. Thou art Peter, and upon this rock I will build my Church.

Postcommunion

LORD our God, who hast fulfilled us with the partaking of the sacred Body and the precious Blood, we beseech thee: that, those things which we perform with godly devotion, we may attain in the assurance of our redemption. Through the same.

❡ Commemoration of St. Paul, as followeth,

LORD, who hast made us partakers of thy sacrament: we entreat thee; that at the intercession of thy holy Apostle Paul, those things which we have celebrated for his glory may be profitable for our healing. (Through.)

❡ Commemoration of the Holy Maccabees, as followeth,

RANT, we beseech thee, Almighty God: that growing in virtue we may follow the faith of them whose memory we recall by the partaking of this sacrament. Through.

Transfiguration of Our Lord Jesus Christ

Second Class Double
6 August

Opening Sentence. Let us worship the Father, the Son, and the Holy Ghost, reigning in his Majesty. (Ps. 93:1)

Introit

OME and shew the light of thy countenance, O Lord, thou that sittest upon the cherubims, and we shall be whole. *Ps.* Hear, O thou Shepherd of Israel, thou that leadest Joseph like a sheep.

Collect

GOD, who on this day didst reveal from heaven thine only-begotten Son, transfigured in a wonderful manner, to the fathers of both testaments, grant unto us, we beseech thee, that by actions acceptable unto thee we may attain unto the perpetual contemplation of his glory in whom thou hast testified that thou, the Father, wast well pleased. Through the same.

❡ On 6 August, Commemoration of Sts. Sixtus II, Felicissimus, & Agapitus, as followeth,

GOD, who vouchsafest unto us to celebrate the birthday of thy holy Martyrs Sixtus, Felicissimus, and Agapitus: grant that we may rejoice in the everlasting felicity of their fellowship. Through.

6 August — Proper of Saints — *Transfiguration*

Epistle. 2 Peter 1:13

DEARLY BELOVED: I think it meet, as long as I am in this tabernacle, to stir you up by putting you in remembrance; knowing that shortly I must put off this my tabernacle, even as our Lord Jesus Christ hath shewed me. Moreover I will endeavour that ye may be able after my decease to have these things always in remembrance. We have not followed cunningly devised fables, when we made known unto you the power and coming of our Lord Jesus Christ, but were eyewitnesses of his majesty. For he received from God the Father honour and glory, when there came such a voice to him from the excellent glory, This is my beloved Son, in whom I am well pleased. And this voice which came from heaven we heard, when we were with him in the holy mount.

Gradual. In the day of thy power shall the people offer thee free-will offerings with an holy worship. The dew of thy birth is of the womb of the morning. ℣. The Lord said unto my Lord, Sit thou on my right hand until I make thy enemies thy footstool.

Alleluia. Alleluia, alleluia. ℣. The hallowed day hath lightened upon us; come ye nations and adore the Lord, for a great light hath this day descended upon the earth.

Gospel. Luke 9:28

AT THAT TIME: it came to pass about an eight days after these sayings, he took Peter and John and James, and went up into a mountain to pray. And as he prayed, the fashion of his countenance war altered, and his raiment was white and glistering. And, behold, there talked with him two men, which were Moses and Elias: who appeared in glory, and spake of his decease, which he should accomplish at Jerusalem. But Peter and they that were with him were heavy with sleep: and when they were awake, they saw his glory, and the two men that stood with him. And it came to pass, as they departed from him, Peter said unto Jesus, Master, it is good for us to be here: and let us make three tabernacles; one for thee, and one for Moses, and one for Elias: not knowing what he said. While he thus spake, there came a cloud, and overshadowed them: and they feared as they entered into the cloud. And there came a voice out of the cloud, saying, This is my beloved Son: hear him. And when the voice was past, Jesus was found alone. And they kept it close, and told no man in those days any of those things which they had seen.

Offertory. God hath made the round world so sure that it cannot be moved. Ever since the world began hath thy seat been prepared, O God; thou art from everlasting.

Secret

LORD, Heavenly Father, Almighty, Everlasting God, receive, we beseech thee, the gifts which we present on the glorious Transfiguration of thy Son; and mercifully grant that by them we may be delivered from the disquietude of this world, and may be knit together in happiness eternal. Through the same.

¶ On 6 August, Commemoration of Sts. Sixtus II, Felicissimus, & Agapitus, as followeth,

E beseech thee, O Lord, that the gifts which we offer unto thee of our bounden duty and service may be acceptable unto thee for the honour of thy Just ones: and by thy mercy profitable unto us for our salvation. Through.

Communion. The dew of thy birth is of the womb of the morning.

Postcommunion

GOD, who hast hallowed this day by the Transfiguration of thine Incarnate Word, and by the voice of thee, the Father, sent down to him, grant, we beseech thee, that we who have been fed with the Bread of Heaven, may be found meet to become members of him who gave commandment that this should be done in remembrance of him, Jesus Christ, thy Son, our Lord. Who.

¶ On 6 August, Commemoration of Sts. Sixtus II, Felicissimus, & Agapitus, as followeth,

RANT to us, we beseech thee, O Lord: at the intercession of thy holy Martyrs Sixtus, Felicissimus, and Agapitus; that those things which we touch with our mouths we may receive in purity of heart. Through.

Most Holy Name of Jesus Christ

Second Class Double
7 August

¶ The propers are the same as on the Christmastide Feast Day of the same name (p. 227).

St. Lawrence

Second Class Double with a Simple Octave
10 August

Opening Sentence. He hath dispersed abroad, and given to the poor : and his righteousness remaineth for ever. (Ps. 112:9)

Introit

LORY and worship are before him: power and honour are in his sanctuary. *Ps.* O sing unto the Lord a new song: sing unto the lord, all the whole earth.

Collect

RANT to us, we beseech thee, Almighty God: that we may quench the flames of our sins; as thou didst enable blessed Lawrence to overcome the fires of his torments. Through.

Epistle. 2 Corinthians 9:6

BRETHREN: He which soweth sparingly shall reap also sparingly; and he which soweth bountifully shall reap also bountifully. Every man according as he purposeth in his heart, so let him give; not grudgingly, or of necessity: for God loveth a cheerful giver. And God is able to make all grace abound toward you; that ye, always having all sufficiency in all things, may abound to every good work: (As it is written, He hath dispersed abroad; he hath given to the poor: his righteousness remaineth for ever. Now he that ministereth seed to the sower both minister bread for your food, and multiply your seed sown, and increase the fruits of your righteousness;)

Gradual. Thou hast proved and visited mine heart, O Lord, in the night-season. ℣. Thou hast tried me with fire, and hast found no wickedness in me.

Alleluia. Alleluia, alleluia. ℣. The Levite Lawrence wrought a good work: who by the sign of the cross gave light to the blind. Alleluia.

Gospel. John 12:24

T THAT TIME: Jesus said unto his disciples: Verily, verily, I say unto you, Except a corn of wheat fall into the ground and die, it abideth alone: but if it die, it bringeth forth much fruit. He that loveth his life shall lose it; and he that hateth his life in this world shall keep it unto life eternal. If any man serve me, let him follow me; and where I am, there shall also my servant be: if any man serve me, him will my Father honour.

Offertory. Glory and worship are before him; power and honour are in his sanctuary.

Secret

ccept, we beseech thee, O Lord, the gifts which we duly offer: that by the merits and intercession of blessed Lawrence, thy Martyr, they may be profitable to the advancement of our salvation. Through.

Communion. He that serveth me, let him follow me: and where I am there shall also my servant be.

Postcommunion

  lord, who hast satisfied us with this sacred gift, we humbly beseech thee: that, we who celebrate the service of our bounden duty may, at the intercession of blessed Lawrence thy Martyr perceive the increase of thy saving grace. Through.

Assumption of the Blessed Virgin Mary

First Class Double with a Common Octave
15 August

Introit

ejoice we all in the Lord, keeping feast day in honour of the blessed Virgin Mary: in whose Assumption the Angels rejoice and glorify the Son of God. *Ps.* My heart is inditing of a good matter: I speak of the things which I have made unto the King.

Collect

e beseech thee, O Lord, let us be continually aided by the sacred feast of this day, whereon the holy Mother of God underwent death in this world, and yet could not be holden by the chains of death: who did bring forth thy Son our Lord. Who liveth.

Epistle. Ecclesiasticus 24:7

WITH all these I sought rest; And in whose inheritance shall I lodge? Then the Creator of all things gave me a commandment; And he that created me made my tabernacle to rest, And said, Let thy tabernacle be in Jacob, And thine inheritance in Israel. He created me from the beginning before the world; And to the end I shall not fail. In the holy tabernacle I ministered before him; And so was I established in Sion. In the beloved city likewise he gave me rest; And in Jerusalem was my authority. And I took root in a people that was glorified, Even in the portion of the Lord's own inheritance. I was exalted like a cedar in Libanus, And as a cypress tree on the mountains of Hermon. I was exalted like a palm tree on the sea shore, And as rose plants in Jericho, And as a fair olive tree in the plain; And I was exalted as a plane tree. As cinnamon and aspalathus, I have given a scent of perfumes; And as choice myrrh, I spread abroad a pleasant odour.

Gradual. Because of the word of truth, of meekness, and righteousness, and thy right hand shall teach thee terrible things. ℣. Hearken, O daughter, and consider, incline thine ear: so shall the King have pleasure in thy beauty.

Alleluia. Alleluia, alleluia. ℣. This day the Virgin Mary entered heaven: rejoice, for she reigneth with Christ for ever. Alleluia.

Sequence

From our first Mother Eva's sickly branch
Mary the blooming rose proceeded forth;
Bright as amidst the stars the Morning Star,
And fair in beauty as the moon she came;

Sweet beyond balsam, ointments, frankincense;
As violet glowing, dewy as the rose,
White as the lily, she who was preferred
To bear the highest Father's holy Child,

That of a Virgin's flesh immaculate
He might upon him take flesh hallowed.
Great Gabriel brings the message of new joy,
Th' arising of the eternal King on earth,

And to his Mother thus gives salutation:
Blessed art thou, Queen of the universe!
Blessed art thou, Queen of the universe!
Blessed art thou, Queen of the universe!

Thou shalt bring forth the Everlasting King.
She answered, How can I fruitful be,

Seeing a man I know not, from my birth
Ever a Virgin chaste continuing?
Fear not (the Angel answered), upon thee,
Chaste as thou art, the Holy Ghost shall come,

Whereby thou shalt bear God and Man in one.
O truly holy, truly to be loved!
Of whom redemption hath for us arisen,
Salvation of the world, and our true life.

Mother of God, accept our prayers this day,
Whereon to heaven's portals thou wast borne.
Dear to the Father, Jesus' Mother

pure,
The Holy Spirit's temple thou wast made.

Fair Spouse of God, thou Christ the King hast borne:
Lady thou art in heaven and in earth.
This day hosts met thee from the court of heaven,
And to the starry palace led thee up.

Jesus himself, to welcome thee his Mother,
Came with the angels forth, and set thee up
With him for ever in his Father's seat.
With God now reigning, mercifully pardon

Our evil deeds, and ask for us all good.
O gracious Mediatrix, next to God
Our only hope, commend us to thy Son,
That we in highest heaven may Alleluias sing.

Gospel. Luke 10:38

AT THAT TIME: It came to pass, as they went, that Jesus entered into a certain village: and a certain woman named Martha received him into her house. And she had a sister called Mary, which also sat at Jesus' feet, and heard his word. But Martha was cumbered about much serving, and came to him, and said, Lord, dost thou not care that my sister hath left me to serve alone? bid her therefore that she help me. And Jesus answered and said unto her, Martha, Martha, thou art careful and troubled about many things: but one thing is needful: and Mary hath chosen that good part, which shall not be taken away from her.

Offertory. Full of grace are thy lips, because God hath blessed thee for ever.

16 August   **Proper of Saints**   *St. Joachim*

Secret

WE beseech thee, O Lord, that the prayers of the Blessed Mother of God may make our gifts acceptable to thee, that albeit we know her to have departed this life in respect of this flesh we may perceive her prayers for us continually in the glory of heaven. Through.

Communion. Blessed is the womb of the Virgin Mary, which bare the Son of the everlasting Father.

Postcommunion

WE that have partaken of thy heavenly table implore thy mercy, O Lord our God, that we who keep the feast of the Mother of God may at her intercession be delivered from all evils which beset us. Through.

¶ Within the Octave, Mass is said as on the Feast. And the 2nd Collect is of the Holy Ghost (p. 544) & 3rd Against the Persecutors of the Church (p. 543) or for the Chief Bishop (p. 543).

¶ The following Alleluia is said daily, except on the Sunday in the Octave and the Octave Day.

Alleluia. Alleluia, alleluia. ℣. Mary is taken up into heaven: angels rejoice, praise, and bless the Lord.

St. Joachim, Father of the Blessed Virgin Mary

Second Class Double
16 August

Introit

HE hath dispersed abroad, and given to the poor his righteousness remaineth for ever: his horn shall be exalted with honour. *Ps.* Blessed is the man that feareth the Lord he hath great delight in his commandments.

Collect

O GOD, who from amongst all thy Saints didst choose blessed Joachim to be the father of the Mother of thy Son: grant, we beseech thee; that we who venerate his festival may also continually perceive his advocacy. Through the same.

St. Joachim   **Proper of Saints**   16 August

Epistle. Ecclesiasticus 31:8

BLESSED is the rich that is found without blemish, And that goeth not after gold. Who is he? and we will call him blessed: For wonderful things hath he done among his people. Who hath been tried thereby, and found perfect? Then let him glory. Who hath had the power to transgress, and hath not transgressed? And to do evil, and hath not done it? His goods shall be made sure, And the congregation shall declare his alms.

Gradual. He hath dispersed abroad, and given to the poor: his righteousness remaineth for ever. ℣. His seed shall be mighty upon earth: the generation of the faithful shall be blessed.

Alleluia. Alleluia, alleluia. ℣. Joachim, spouse of Saint Anne, of the gracious Virgin the father, here to thy servants bring safety and aid from on high. Alleluia.

Gospel. Matthew 1:1

THE book of the generation of Jesus Christ, the son of David, the son of Abraham. Abraham begat Isaac; and Isaac begat Jacob; and Jacob begat Judas and his brethren; And Judas begat Phares and Zara of Thamar; and Phares begat Esrom; and Esrom begat Aram; And Aram begat Aminadab; and Aminadab begat Naasson; and Naasson begat Salmon; And Salmon begat Booz of Rachab; and Booz begat Obed of Ruth; and Obed begat Jesse; And Jesse begat David the king; and David the king begat Solomon of her that had been the wife of Urias; And Solomon begat Roboam; and Roboam begat Abia; and Abia begat Asa; And Asa begat Josaphat; and Josaphat begat Joram; and Joram begat Ozias; And Ozias begat Joatham; and Joatham begat Achaz; and Achaz begat Ezekias; And Ezekias begat Manasses; and Manasses begat Amon; and Amon begat Josias; And Josias begat Jechonias and his brethren, about the time they were carried away to Babylon: And after they were brought to Babylon, Jechonias begat Salathiel; and Salathiel begat Zorobabel; And Zorobabel begat Abiud; and Abiud begat Eliakim; and Eliakim begat Azor; And Azor begat Sadoc; and Sadoc begat Achim; and Achim begat Eliud; And Eliud begat Eleazar; and Eleazar begat Matthan; and Matthan begat Jacob; And Jacob begat Joseph the husband of Mary, of whom was born Jesus, who is called Christ.

Offertory. Thou hast crowned him with glory and worship: and hast made him to have dominion of the works of thy hands, O Lord.

Proper of Saints

24 August — *St. Bartholomew*

Secret

RECEIVE, most merciful God, the sacrifice which we offer to thy Majesty, in honour of the holy Patriarch Joachim, father of the Virgin Mary: and grant that, he with his wife and their most blessed offspring interceding for us, we may be counted worthy to receive perfect remission of sins and everlasting glory. Through the same.

Communion. A faithful and wise servant, whom the lord hath made ruler over his household: to give them their portion of meat in due season.

Postcommunion

WE beseech thee, Almighty God: that through these sacraments which we have received, with the pleading of the merits and prayers of blessed Joachim, father of the Mother of thy beloved Son Jesus Christ our Lord, we may be found worthy to be made partakers of thy grace in this life and of eternal glory in the life to come. Through the same.

St. Bartholomew

Second Class Double
24 August

Introit

RIGHT honourable are thy friends unto me, O God: right well is their princedom established. *Ps.* O Lord, thou hast searched me out, and known me: thou knowest my down-sitting and mine up-rising.

Collect

O ALMIGHTY and Everlasting God, who didst give to thine Apostle Bartholomew grace truly to believe and to preach thy Word; Grant, we beseech thee, unto thy Church to love that Word which he believed, and both to preach and receive the same. Through.

Epistle. Acts 5:12

IN THOSE DAYS: By the hands of the apostles were many signs and wonders wrought among the people; (and they were all with one accord in Solomon's porch. And of the rest durst no man join himself to them: but the people magnified them. And believers were the more added to the Lord, multitudes both of men and women.) Insomuch that they brought forth the

St. Bartholomew   **Proper of Saints**   24 August

sick into the streets, and laid them on beds and couches, that at the least the shadow of Peter passing by might overshadow some of them. There came also a multitude out of the cities round about unto Jerusalem, bringing sick folks, and them which were vexed with unclean spirits: and they were healed every one.

Gradual. Thou shalt make them princes in all lands: they shall remember thy name, O Lord. ℣. Instead of thy fathers thou shalt have children: therefore shall the people give thanks unto thee.

Alleluia. Alleluia, alleluia. ℣. The glorious company of the Apostles praise thee, O Lord. Alleluia.

Gospel. Luke 22:24

T THAT TIME: There was a strife among the disciples, which of them should be accounted the greatest. And he said unto them, The kings of the Gentiles exercise lordship over them; and they that exercise authority upon them are called benefactors. But ye shall not be so: but he that is greatest among you, let him be as the younger; and he that is chief, as he that doth serve. For whether is greater, he that sitteth at meat, or he that serveth? is not he that sitteth at meat? but I am among you as he that serveth. Ye are they which have continued with me in my temptations. And I appoint unto you a kingdom, as my Father hath appointed unto me; That ye may eat and drink at my table in my kingdom, and sit on thrones judging the twelve tribes of Israel.

Offertory. Right honourable are thy friends unto me, O God: right well is their princedom established.

Secret

E beseech thee, O Lord, that we, who celebrate the festival of thy blessed Apostle Bartholomew: may, by the succour of him in whose honour we offer thee these sacrifices of praise, receive thy benefits. Through.

Communion. Ye which have followed me shall sit upon thrones, judging the twelve tribes of Israel, saith the Lord.

Postcommunion

LORD, through whom we have received the pledge of eternal redemption: we beseech thee; that at the intercession of blessed Bartholomew, thine Apostle, it may avail for our succour both in this life and that which is to come. Through.

Proper of Saints

Decollation of St. John Baptist

Greater Double
29 August

Introit

I WILL speak of thy testimonies, even before kings, and will not be ashamed: and my delight shall be in thy commandments, which I have loved exceedingly. *Ps.* It is a good thing to give thanks unto the Lord: and to sing praises unto thy name, O most Highest.

Collect

WE beseech thee, O Lord: that the venerable festival of thy Forerunner and Martyr, Saint John Baptist, may effectually bestow upon us thy succour unto our salvation. Who livest.

¶ Commemoration of St. Sabina, as followeth,

O GOD, who among the manifold works of thy power hast bestowed even upon the weakness of women the victory of martyrdom: mercifully grant; that we, who celebrate the birthday of blessed Sabina, thy Virgin and Martyr, may by her example be drawn nearer unto thee. Through.

Epistle. Jeremiah 1:17

IN THOSE DAYS: The word of the Lord came unto me, saying: Gird up thy loins, and arise, and speak unto Judah all that I command thee: be not dismayed at their faces, lest I confound thee before them. For, behold, I have made thee this day a defenced city, and an iron pillar, and brasen walls against the whole land, against the kings of Judah, against the princes thereof, against the priests thereof, and against the people of the land. And they shall fight against thee; but they shall not prevail against thee; for I am with thee, saith the Lord, to deliver thee.

Gradual. The righteous shall flourish like a palm-tree: and shall spread abroad like a cedar in Libanus in the house of the Lord. ℣. To tell of thy loving-kindness early in the morning, and of thy truth in the night-season.

Alleluia. Alleluia, alleluia. ℣. The righteous shall grow as the lily: and shall flourish for ever before the Lord. Alleluia.

Decollation   # Proper of Saints   29 August

Gospel. Mark 6:17

AT THAT TIME: Herod sent forth and laid hold upon John, and bound him in prison for Herodias' sake, his brother Philip's wife: for he had married her. For John had said unto Herod, It is not lawful for thee to have thy brother's wife. Therefore Herodias had a quarrel against him, and would have killed him; but she could not: for Herod feared John, knowing that he was a just man and an holy, and observed him; and when he heard him, he did many things, and heard him gladly. And when a convenient day was come, that Herod on his birthday made a supper to his lords, high captains, and chief estates of Galilee; and when the daughter of the said Herodias came in, and danced, and pleased Herod and them that sat with him, the king said unto the damsel, Ask of me whatsoever thou wilt, and I will give it thee. And he sware unto her, Whatsoever thou shalt ask of me, I will give it thee, unto the half of my kingdom. And she went forth, and said unto her mother, What shall I ask? And she said, The head of John the Baptist. And she came in straightway with haste unto the king, and asked, saying, I will that thou give me by and by in a charger the head of John the Baptist. And the king was exceeding sorry; yet for his oath's sake, and for their sakes which sat with him, he would not reject her. And immediately the king sent an executioner, and commanded his head to be brought: and he went and beheaded him in the prison, and brought his head in a charger, and gave it to the damsel: and the damsel gave it to her mother. And when his disciples heard of it, they came and took up his corpse, and laid it in a tomb.

Offertory. The just shall rejoice in thy strength, O Lord, exceeding glad shall he be of thy salvation: thou hast given him his heart's desire.

Secret

WE beseech thee, O Lord, that the gifts which we offer unto thee for the passion of thy holy Martyr John Baptist: may through his intercession be profitable for our salvation. Through.

¶ Commemoration of St. Sabina, as followeth,

GRACIOUSLY receive, O Lord, through the merits of blessed Sabina, thy Virgin and Martyr, the sacrifices which we offer unto thee: and grant that they may avail for our continual help. Through.

Communion. Thou hast set, O Lord, a crown of pure gold upon his head.

Postcommunion

LET the solemnity, of Saint John Baptist enable us, O Lord: both to reverence those things which are signified in the wondrous sacraments which we have received, and to rejoice abundantly in the fruits that they bring forth in us. Through.

¶ Commemoration of St. Sabina, as followeth,

O LORD our God, who hast fulfilled us with the bounty of thy heavenly gift; we beseech thee, that, at the intercession of blessed Sabina, thy Virgin and Martyr, we may ever live by the partaking of the same. Through.

NATIVITY OF THE BLESSED VIRGIN MARY

Second Class Double with a Simple Octave
8 September

Opening Sentence. The Lord shall come down like the rain into a fleece of wool. Even as the drops that water the earth. (Judg. 6:37)

Introit

HAIL, O Mother most holy, who in childbirth didst bring forth the Monarch: him who o'er heaven and earth reigneth for ever and ever. *Ps.* My heart is inditing of a good matter: I speak of the things which I have made unto the King.

Collect

WE beseech thee, O Lord, to grant unto us thy servants the gift of heavenly grace: that as the childbearing of the blessed Virgin was unto us the beginning of salvation; so the devout observance of her Nativity may bestow an increase of peace. Through.

Epistle. Proverbs 8:22

THE LORD possessed me in the beginning of his way, before his works of old. I was set up from everlasting, from the beginning, or ever the earth was. When there were no depths, I was brought forth; when there were no fountains abounding with water. Before the mountains were settled, before the hills was I brought forth: While as yet he had not made the earth, nor the fields, nor the highest part of the dust of the world. When he prepared the heavens, I was there: when he set a compass upon the face of the depth: When he established the clouds above: when he strengthened the fountains of the deep: When he gave to the sea his decree, that the waters should not pass his commandment: when he appointed the foundations of the earth: Then I was by him, as one brought up with him: and I was daily his delight, rejoicing always before him; Rejoicing in the habitable part of his earth; and my delights were with the sons of men. Now therefore hearken unto me, O ye children: for blessed are they that keep my ways. Hear instruction, and be wise, and refuse it not. Blessed is the man that heareth me, watching daily at my gates, waiting at the posts of my doors. For whoso findeth me findeth life, and shall obtain favour of the LORD.

Gradual. Blessed and venerable art thou, O Virgin Mary: who without spot wast found Mother of the Saviour. ℣. Virgin, Mother of God, he, whom the whole world containeth not, being made man lay hid in thy womb.

Alleluia. Alleluia, alleluia, ℣. Happy art thou, O sacred Virgin Mary, and most worthy of all praise: for out of thee hath arisen the son of righteousness, Christ our God. Alleluia.

Gospel. Matthew 1:1

THE book of the generation of Jesus Christ, the son of David, the son of Abraham. Abraham begat Isaac; and Isaac begat Jacob; and Jacob begat Judas and his brethren; And Judas begat Phares and Zara of Thamar; and Phares begat Esrom; and Esrom begat Aram; And Aram begat Aminadab; and Aminadab begat Naasson; and Naasson begat Salmon; And Salmon begat Booz of Rachab; and Booz begat Obed of Ruth; and Obed begat Jesse; And Jesse begat David the king; and David the king begat Solomon of her that had been the wife of Urias; And Solomon begat Roboam; and Roboam begat Abia; and Abia begat Asa; And Asa begat Josaphat; and Josaphat begat Joram; and Joram begat Ozias; And Ozias begat Joatham; and Joatham begat Achaz; and Achaz begat Ezekias; And Ezekias begat Manasses; and Manasses begat Amon; and Amon begat Josias; And Josias begat Jechonias and his brethren, about the time they were carried away to Babylon: And after they were brought to Babylon, Jechonias begat Salathiel; and Salathiel begat Zorobabel; And Zorobabel begat Abiud; and Abiud begat Eliakim; and Eliakim begat Azor; And Azor begat Sadoc; and Sadoc begat Achim; and Achim begat Eliud; And Eliud begat Eleazar; and Eleazar begat Matthan; and Matthan begat Jacob; And Jacob begat Joseph the husband of Mary, of whom was born Jesus, who is called Christ.

14 September · **Proper of Saints** · *Roodmas*

Offertory. Blessed art thou, O Virgin Mary, who didst bear the Creator of all things: thou broughtest forth him who made thee, and for ever remainest a Virgin.

Secret

MAY the manhood of thine only-begotten Son, O Lord, avail for our succour: that, even as he, being born of a Virgin, destroyed not but hallowed the innocence of his Mother; so on this feast of her Nativity, he may deliver us from out offences, and render us an oblation acceptable unto thee, even Jesus Christ our Lord. Who liveth.

Communion. Blessed is the womb of the Virgin Mary, that bore the Son of the everlasting Father.

Postcommunion

GRANT, we beseech thee, O Lord: that the sacraments which we have received in the observance of this yearly festival; may both in this life and that which is to come be profitable for our healing. Through.

¶ Within the Octave, nothing is said of it; but Votive Masses of the Blessed Virgin Mary and her Mass on Saturday are said as on the Feast, with Gloria in excelsis, 2ⁿᵈ Collect of the Holy Ghost (p. 544) & 3ʳᵈ Against the Persecutors of the Church (p. 543) or for the Chief Bishop (p. 543), and the Creed is omitted.

¶ Also, if by reason of another Octave celebrated in any place the 2ⁿᵈ or 3ʳᵈ Collect is to be said of St. Mary, it is said of the Nativity, as above.

Exaltation of the Holy Cross

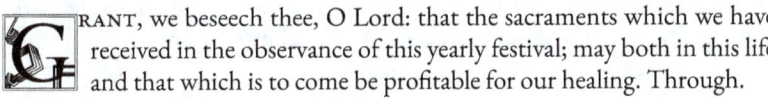

Greater Double
14 September

Introit

BUT it behoveth us to glory in the Cross of our Lord Jesus Christ: in whom is our salvation, life, and resurrection: by whom we are saved and set free. *Ps.* God be merciful unto us, and bless us: and shew us the light of his countenance, and be merciful unto us.

Roodmas   # Proper of Saints   *14 September*

Collect

O GOD, who on this day dost gladden us with the yearly solemnity of the exaltation of the holy Cross: grant, we beseech thee; that as we have known the mystery of thy Son on earth, so we may attain unto the rewards of his redemption in heaven. Through the same

Epistle. Philippians 2:5

BRETHREN: Let this mind be in you, which was also in Christ Jesus: who, being in the form of God, thought it not robbery to be equal with God: but made himself of no reputation, and took upon him the form of a servant, and was made in the likeness of men: and being found in fashion as a man, he humbled himself, and became obedient unto death, even the death of the cross. Wherefore God also hath highly exalted him, and given him a name which is above every name: (Here genuflect.) that at the name of Jesus every knee should bow, of things in heaven, and things in earth, and things under the earth; and that every tongue should confess that Jesus Christ is Lord, to the glory of God the Father.

Gradual. Christ for us became obedient unto death even the death of the cross. ℣. Wherefore God also hath highly exalted him, and given him a name which is above every name.

Alleluia. Alleluia, alleluia. ℣. Sweetest wood, sweetest iron, sweetest weight is hung on thee: thou alone wast counted worthy to bear the King of heaven and its Lord. Alleluia.

Gospel. John 12:31

AT THAT TIME: Jesus said unto the multitudes of the Jews: Now is the judgment of this world: now shall the prince of this world be cast out. And I, if I be lifted up from the earth, will draw all men unto me. This he said, signifying what death he should die. The people answered him, We have heard out of the law that Christ abideth for ever: and how sayest thou, The Son of man must be lifted up? who is this Son of man? Then Jesus said unto them, Yet a little while is the light with you. Walk while ye have the light, lest darkness come upon you: for he that walketh in darkness knoweth not whither he goeth. While ye have light, believe in the light, that ye may be the children of light.

Offertory. Protect, O Lord, thy people, by the sign of the holy Cross, from all the snares of every enemy: that we may render thee pleasing service, and that our sacrifice may be acceptable unto thee, alleluia.

Proper of Saints

15 September — *Seven Sorrows*

Secret

O LORD, our God, who dost fulfil us with the Body and Blood of Jesus Christ our Lord, through whom thou hast sanctified the standard of the Cross: we beseech thee; that as we have been counted worthy to venerate that Cross, so we may effectually be made partakers of its glory unto everlasting salvation. Through the same.

Communion. By the sign of the cross deliver us from our enemies, O our God.

Postcommunion

ASSIST us, O Lord our God: and as thou dost vouchsafe unto us to rejoice in honouring the holy Cross, so defend us by the perpetual succour of the same. Through.

SEVEN SORROWS OF THE BLESSED VIRGIN MARY

Second Class Double
15 September

Introit

THERE stood by the Cross of Jesus his Mother, and his Mother's sister, Mary the wife of Cleophas, and Salome, and Mary Magdalene. ℣. Woman, behold thy son: said Jesus; and to the disciple: Behold thy Mother.

Collect

O GOD, in whose passion according to the prophecy of Simeon, a sword of sorrow did pierce the most sweet soul of the glorious Virgin Mother Mary: mercifully grant; that we, who devoutly call to mind her sorrows, may obtain the blessed effects of thy passion. Who livest.

¶ On 15 September, Commemoration of St. Nicomedes, as followeth,

ASSIST, O Lord, thy people: that as they do profit by the glorious merits of blessed Nicomedes thy Martyr, so his advocacy may at all times succour them to the obtaining of thy mercy. Through.

Proper of Saints

Seven Sorrows — 15 September

Epistle. Judith 13:17

LESSED be thou, O our God, which hast this day brought to nought the enemies of thy people. O daughter, blessed art thou of the most high God above all the women upon the earth; and blessed be the Lord God, which hath created the heavens and the earth, which hath directed thee to the cutting off of the head of the chief of our enemies. For this thy confidence shall not depart from the heart of men, which remember the power of God for ever. And God turn these things to thee for a perpetual praise, to visit thee in good things because thou hast not spared thy life for the affliction of our nation, but hast revenged our ruin, walking a straight way before our God.

Gradual. Mournful and weeping art thou, O Virgin Mary, standing by the Cross of the Lord Jesus, thy Son, the Redeemer. ℣. Virgin, Mother of God, he whom the whole world containeth not, endureth this torment of the cross, the author of life made man.

Alleluia. Alleluia, alleluia, ℣. There stood mournful by the Cross of our Lord Jesus Christ, holy Mary, Queen of heaven and Lady of the world.

Sequence

At the Cross her station keeping.
Stood the mournful Mother weeping.
Where he hung, her dying Son,

Through her soul, of joy bereaved
Torn with anguish, deeply grieved,
Lo! the piercing sword hath run.

O, how sad and sore distressed,
Then was she, that Mother blessed
Of the sole-begotten One!

Torn with grief and desolation,
Mother meek, the bitter Passion
Saw she of her glorious Son.

Who, on Christ's dear Mother gazing.
Bowed with sorrow so amazing,
Born of woman, would not weep?

Who, on Christ's dear Mother think-
ing.
With her Son in sorrow sinking.
Would not share her sadness deep?

For his people's sins chastised.
She her Jesus saw despised.
Saw him by the scourges rent.

Saw her own sweet Offspring taken,
And in death by all forsaken.
While his spirit forth he sent.

Mother, fount of love o'erflowing.
Ah, that I, thy sorrow knowing.
In thy grief may mourn with thee.

That my heart, fresh ardour gaining,
Love of Christ my God attaining,
Unto him may pleasing be.

Holy Mother, be there written
Every wound of Jesus smitten
In my heart, and there remain.

15 September — **Proper of Saints** — *Seven Sorrows*

As thy Son through tribulation
Deigned to purchase my salvation.
Let me share with thee the pain.

Let me weep with thee beside him
For the sins which crucified him.
While my life remains in me.

Take beneath the Cross my station.
Share with thee thy desolation,
Humbly this I ask of thee.

Virgin, virgins all excelling,
Spurn me not, my prayer repelling;
Make me weep and mourn with thee.

So Christ's death within me bearing,
Let me, in his Passion sharing.
Keep his wounds in memory.

Let thy Son's wounds penetrate me:
Let the Cross inebriate me
And his own most precious blood.

Lest in flames I burn and perish.
On the judgment day O cherish
And defend me, Virgin good.

Christ, whene'er the world shall leave me,
Through thy Mother then receive me
To the palm of victory.

When the bonds of flesh are riven.
Glory to my soul be given
In thy Paradise with thee.
Amen. Alleluia.

Gospel. John 19:25

AT THAT TIME: There stood by the cross of Jesus his mother, and his mother's sister, Mary the wife of Cleophas, and Mary Magdalene. When Jesus therefore saw his mother, and the disciple standing by, whom he loved, he saith unto his mother, Woman, behold thy son! Then saith he to the disciple, Behold thy mother! And from that hour that disciple took her unto his own home.

Offertory. Remember, O Virgin, Mother of God, when thou standest in the sight of the Lord, that thou speak good things for us, and that he may turn away his indignation from us.

Secret

WE offer unto thee prayers and sacrifices, O Lord Jesu Christ, humbly beseeching thee: that we, who in our prayers recall the Piercing of the most sweet spirit of blessed Mary, thy Mother; may by the manifold and most loving intercession of her and of the Saints her companions beneath the Cross, through the merits of thy death, be made worthy of a portion with the blessed. Who livest.

Autumnal Emberday   Proper of Saints   Ember Wednesday

¶ On 15 September, Commemoration of St. Nicomedes, as followeth,

ERCIFULLY receive, O Lord, the gifts which we offer: and let the prayer of the blessed Martyr Nicomedes commend them unto thy Majesty. Through.

Communion. Happy the heart of the blessed Virgin Mary, which without death gained the palm of martyrdom beneath the Cross of the Lord.

Postcommunion

 LORD Jesu Christ, let the sacrifices which we have received in devout remembrance of the Piercing of thy Virgin Mother: obtain for us of thy mercy the effect of every good and saving gift. Who livest.

¶ On 15 September, Commemoration of St. Nicomedes, as followeth,

LEANSE us, O Lord, by the sacraments which we have received: that through the intercession of blessed Nicomedes, thy Martyr, they may set us free from all our offences. Through.

EMBER WEDNESDAY IN AUTUMN

Second Class Feria
Wednesday after the Exaltation of the Holy Cross (14 September)
On this day and the following Friday and Saturday, no Feast is kept unless it be a First or Second Class Double.

Introit

ING we merrily unto God our strength: make a cheerful noise unto the God of Jacob: take the merry psalm with the lute: sound the trumpet in the beginning of the month, for this was made a statute for Israel, and a law of the God of Jacob. *Ps.* This he ordained in Joseph for a testimony, when he came out of the land of Egypt: and had heard a strange language.

¶ After the Kyrie,

℣. Let us pray.   ℣. Orémus.
℣. Let us bow the knee.   ℣. Flectámus génua.
℣. Arise.   ℣. Leváte.

Collect

E beseech thee, O Lord, that our frailty may be upheld by the healing of thy loving kindness: that what by its own nature is ready to decay, may by thy mercy be renewed. Through.

Ember Wednesday — Proper of Saints — *Autumnal Emberday*

Epistle. Amos 9:13

THUS saith the Lord God: Behold, the days come: that the plowman shall overtake the reaper, and the treader of grapes him that soweth seed; and the mountains shall drop sweet wine, and all the hills shall melt. And I will bring again the captivity of my people of Israel, and they shall build the waste cities, and inhabit them; and they shall plant vineyards, and drink the wine thereof; they shall also make gardens, and eat the fruit of them. And I will plant them upon their land, and they shall no more be pulled up out of their land which I have given them, saith the LORD thy God.

Gradual. Who is like unto the Lord our God, that hath his dwelling so high, and yet humbleth himself to behold the things that are in heaven and earth? ℣. He taketh up the simple out of the dust, and lifteth the poor out of the mire.

℣. The Lord be with you.	℣. Dóminus vobíscum.
℟. And with thy spirit.	℟. Et cum spíritu tuo.
℣. Let us pray.	℣. Orémus.

Collect

GRANT, we beseech thee, O Lord, unto thy family who pray unto thee: that, as they do abstain from bodily food, so they may also spiritually fast from sin. Through.

¶ 2nd Collect is of the Saints (p. 542) & 3rd is ad libitum.

Epistle. Nehemiah 8:1

IN THOSE DAYS: All the people gathered themselves together as one man into the street that was before the water gate; and they spake unto Ezra the scribe to bring the book of the law of Moses, which the LORD had commanded to Israel. And Ezra the priest brought the law before the congregation both of men and women, and all that could hear with understanding, upon the first day of the seventh month. And he read therein before the street that was before the water gate from the morning until midday, before the men and the women, and those that could understand; and the ears of all the people were attentive unto the book of the law. And Ezra the scribe stood upon a pulpit of wood, which they had made for the purpose. And Ezra opened the book in the sight of all the people; (for he was above all the people;) and when he opened it, all the people stood up: And Ezra blessed the LORD, the great God. And all the people answered, Amen, Amen, with lifting up their hands: and they bowed

Autumnal Emberday **Proper of Saints** Ember Wednesday

their heads, and worshipped the LORD with their faces to the ground. And the Levites, caused the people to understand the law: and the people stood in their place. So they read in the book in the law of God distinctly, and gave the sense, and caused them to understand the reading. And Nehemiah, and Ezra the priest the scribe, and the Levites that taught the people, said unto all the people, This day is holy unto the LORD your God; mourn not, nor weep. For all the people wept, when they heard the words of the law. Then he said unto them, Go your way, eat the fat, and drink the sweet, and send portions unto them for whom nothing is prepared: for this day is holy unto our Lord: neither be ye sorry; for the joy of the LORD is your strength.

Gradual. Blessed are the people, whose God is the Lord: and blessed are the folk, that he hath chosen to him to be his inheritance. ℣. By the word of the Lord were the heavens made: and all the hosts of them by the breath of his mouth.

Gospel. Mark 9:17

AT THAT TIME: One of the multitude answered and said unto Jesus: Master, I have brought unto thee my son, which hath a dumb spirit; And wheresoever he taketh him, he teareth him: and he foameth, and gnasheth with his teeth, and pineth away: and I spake to thy disciples that they should cast him out; and they could not. He answereth him, and saith, O faithless generation, how long shall I be with you? how long shall I suffer you? bring him unto me. And they brought him unto him: and when he saw him, straightway the spirit tare him; and he fell on the ground, and wallowed foaming. And he asked his father, How long is it ago since this came unto him? And he said, Of a child. And ofttimes it hath cast him into the fire, and into the waters, to destroy him: but if thou canst do any thing, have compassion on us, and help us. Jesus said unto him, If thou canst believe, all things are possible to him that believeth. And straightway the father of the child cried out, and said with tears, Lord, I believe; help thou mine unbelief. When Jesus saw that the people came running together, he rebuked the foul spirit, saying unto him, Thou dumb and deaf spirit, I charge thee, come out of him, and enter no more into him. And the spirit cried, and rent him sore, and came out of him: and he was as one dead; insomuch that many said, He is dead. But Jesus took him by the hand, and lifted him up; and he arose. And when he was come into the house, his disciples asked him privately, Why could not we cast him out? And he said unto them, This kind can come forth by nothing, but by prayer and fasting.

Ember Friday — **Proper of Saints** — *Autumnal Emberday*

Offertory. My delight shall be in thy commandments, which I have loved exceedingly: my hands also will I lift up unto thy commandments, which I have loved.

Secret

E beseech thee, O Lord, that this oblation may cleanse us from our sins: and sanctify thy servants both in body and mind for the celebration of this sacrifice. Through.

¶ 2nd Secret is of the Saints (p. 542) & 3rd is ad libitum.

Communion. Eat the fat, and drink the sweet, and send portions unto them for whom nothing is prepared: for this day is holy unto our Lord, neither be ye sorry: for the joy of the Lord is your strength.

Postcommunion

E humbly beseech thee, O Lord: that like as of thy bounty we, receiving thy heavenly gifts, do with continual devotion offer the same, so by thy goodness we may worthily receive them in our souls. Through.

¶ 2nd Postcommunion is of the Saints (p. 542) & 3rd is ad libitum.

EMBER FRIDAY IN AUTUMN

Second Class Feria
Friday after Ember Wednesday

Introit

ET the heart of them rejoice that seek the Lord: seek the Lord and his strength: seek his face evermore. *Ps.* O give thanks unto the Lord, and call upon his name: tell the people what things he hath done.

Collect

RANT, we beseech thee, Almighty God: that we, who year by year devoutly keep this holy observance, may be acceptable unto thee both in body and in soul. Through.

¶ 2nd Collect is of the Saints (p. 542) & 3rd is ad libitum.

Autumnal Emberday   Proper of Saints   Ember Friday

Epistle. Hosea 14:1

THUS saith the Lord God: O Israel, return unto the LORD thy God; for thou hast fallen by thine iniquity. Take with you words, and turn to the LORD: say unto him, Take away all iniquity, and receive us graciously: so will we render the calves of our lips. Asshur shall not save us; we will not ride upon horses: neither will we say any more to the work of our hands, Ye are our gods: for in thee the fatherless findeth mercy. I will heal their backsliding, I will love them freely: for mine anger is turned away from him. I will be as the dew unto Israel: he shall grow as the lily, and cast forth his roots as Lebanon. His branches shall spread, and his beauty shall be as the olive tree, and his smell as Lebanon. They that dwell under his shadow shall return; they shall revive as the corn, and grow as the vine: the scent thereof shall be as the wine of Lebanon. Ephraim shall say, What have I to do any more with idols? I have heard him, and observed him: I am like a green fir tree. From me is thy fruit found. Who is wise, and he shall understand these things? prudent, and he shall know them? for the ways of the LORD are right, and the just shall walk in them: but the transgressors shall fall therein.

Gradual. Turn thee again, O Lord, at the last, and be gracious unto thy servants. ℣. Lord, thou hast been our refuge, from one generation to another.

Gospel. Luke 7:36

AT THAT TIME: One of the Pharisees desired Jesus that he would eat with him. And he went into the Pharisee's house, and sat down to meat. And, behold, a woman in the city, which was a sinner, when she knew that Jesus sat at meat in the Pharisee's house, brought an alabaster box of ointment, And stood at his feet behind him weeping, and began to wash his feet with tears, and did wipe them with the hairs of her head, and kissed his feet, and anointed them with the ointment. Now when the Pharisee which had bidden him saw it, he spake within himself, saying, This man, if he were a prophet, would have known who and what manner of woman this is that toucheth him: for she is a sinner. And Jesus answering said unto him, Simon, I have somewhat to say unto thee. And he saith, Master, say on. There was a certain creditor which had two debtors: the one owed five hundred pence, and the other fifty. And when they had nothing to pay, he frankly forgave them both. Tell me therefore, which of them will love him most? Simon answered and said, I suppose that he, to whom he forgave most. And he said unto him, Thou hast rightly judged. And he turned to the woman, and said unto Simon, Seest thou this woman? I entered into thine house, thou gavest me no water for

Ember Saturday — **Proper of Saints** — *Autumnal Emberday*

my feet: but she hath washed my feet with tears, and wiped them with the hairs of her head. Thou gavest me no kiss: but this woman since the time I came in hath not ceased to kiss my feet. My head with oil thou didst not anoint: but this woman hath anointed my feet with ointment. Wherefore I say unto thee, Her sins, which are many, are forgiven; for she loved much: but to whom little is forgiven, the same loveth little. And he said unto her, Thy sins are forgiven. And they that sat at meat with him began to say within themselves, Who is this that forgiveth sins also? And he said to the woman, Thy faith hath saved thee; go in peace.

Offertory. Praise the Lord, O my soul, and forget not all his benefits: who maketh thee young and lusty as an eagle.

Secret

E beseech thee, O Lord, that the offerings of our fast may be acceptable in thy sight: that we, being cleansed thereby and made worthy of thy grace, may be brought unto thine everlasting promises. Through.

¶ 2nd Secret is of the Saints (p. 542) & 3rd is ad libitum.

Communion. O turn from me shame and rebuke, for I have kept thy commandments, O Lord: for thy testimonies are my delight.

Postcommunion

E beseech thee, Almighty God: that shewing forth our thankfulness for the gifts which we have received, we may obtain yet more abundant benefits. Through.

¶ 2nd Postcommunion is of the Saints (p. 542) & 3rd is ad libitum.

Ember Saturday in Autumn

Second Class Feria
Saturday after Ember Friday

Introit

COME, let us worship and fall down, and kneel before the Lord our maker: for he is the Lord our God. *Ps.* O come, let us sing unto the Lord: let us heartily rejoice in the strength of our salvation.

Autumnal Emberday   **Proper of Saints**   Ember Saturday

¶ After the Kyrie,

℣. Let us pray.   ℣. Orémus.
℣. Let us bow the knee.   ℣. Flectámus génua.
℣. Arise.   ℣. Leváte.

Collect

ALMIGHTY and everlasting God, who by salutary continence bestowest healing in body and soul: we humbly entreat thy Majesty; that, thou wouldest mercifully look upon the devout prayers and fasting of thy people, and grant us help both in this life and that which is to come. Through.

Epistle. Leviticus 23:26

IN THOSE DAYS: The LORD spake unto Moses, saying, Also on the tenth day of this seventh month there shall be a day of atonement: it shall be an holy convocation unto you; and ye shall afflict your souls, and offer an offering made by fire unto the LORD. And ye shall do no work in that same day: for it is a day of atonement, to make an atonement for you before the LORD your God. For whatsoever soul it be that shall not be afflicted in that same day, he shall be cut off from among his people. And whatsoever soul it be that doeth any work in that same day, the same soul will I destroy from among his people. Ye shall do no manner of work: it shall be a statute for ever throughout your generations in all your dwellings. It shall be unto you a sabbath of rest, and ye shall afflict your souls: in the ninth day of the month at even, from even unto even, shall ye celebrate your sabbath.

Gradual. Be merciful unto our sins, O Lord: wherefore do the heathen say: Where is now their God? ℣. Help us, O God of our salvation: and for the glory of thy name, O Lord, deliver us.

℣. Let us pray.   ℣. Orémus.
℣. Let us bow the knee.   ℣. Flectámus génua.
℣. Arise.   ℣. Leváte.

Collect

GRANT to us, we beseech thee, Almighty God: that we may through fasting be satisfied with thy grace; and through abstinence strengthened to overcome all our enemies. Through.

Ember Saturday   **Proper of Saints**   *Autumnal Emberday*

Epistle. Leviticus 23:39

IN THOSE DAYS: The Lord spake unto Moses, saying: In the fifteenth day of the seventh month, when ye have gathered in the fruit of the land, ye shall keep a feast unto the LORD seven days: on the first day shall be a sabbath, and on the eighth day shall be a sabbath. And ye shall take you on the first day the boughs of goodly trees, branches of palm trees, and the boughs of thick trees, and willows of the brook; and ye shall rejoice before the LORD your God seven days. And ye shall keep it a feast unto the LORD seven days in the year. It shall be a statute for ever in your generations: ye shall celebrate it in the seventh month. Ye shall dwell in booths seven days; all that are Israelites born shall dwell in booths: That your generations may know that I made the children of Israel to dwell in booths, when I brought them out of the land of Egypt: I am the LORD your God.

Gradual. Behold, O God our defender: and look upon thy servants. ℣. O Lord God of hosts, hear the prayers of thy servants.

℣. Let us pray.	℣. Orémus.
℣. Let us bow the knee.	℣. Flectámus génua.
℣. Arise.	℣. Leváte.

Collect

EEP, we beseech thee, O Lord, this thy family: that as by thine inspiration we do seek thy healing unto everlasting salvation, so by thy bounty we may obtain the same. Through.

Epistle. Micah 7:14

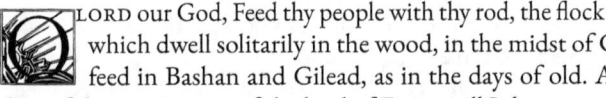LORD our God, Feed thy people with thy rod, the flock of thine heritage, which dwell solitarily in the wood, in the midst of Carmel: let them feed in Bashan and Gilead, as in the days of old. According to the days of thy coming out of the land of Egypt will I shew unto him marvellous things. The nations shall see and be confounded at all their might: they shall lay their hand upon their mouth, their ears shall be deaf. They shall lick the dust like a serpent, they shall move out of their holes like worms of the earth: they shall be afraid of the LORD our God, and shall fear because of thee. Who is a God like unto thee, that pardoneth iniquity, and passeth by the transgression of the remnant of his heritage? he retaineth not his anger for ever, because he delighteth in mercy. He will turn again, he will have compassion upon us; he will subdue our iniquities; and thou wilt cast all their sins into the depths of the

Autumnal Emberday **Proper of Saints** Ember Saturday

sea. Thou wilt perform the truth to Jacob, and the mercy to Abraham, which thou hast sworn unto our fathers from the days of old: O Lord our God.

Gradual. Turn thee again, O Lord, at the last, and be gracious unto thy servants. ℣. Lord, thou hast been our refuge, from one generation to another.

℣. Let us pray.	℣. Orémus.
℣. Let us bow the knee.	℣. Flectámus génua.
℣. Arise.	℣. Leváte.

Collect

RANT, we beseech thee, Almighty God: that we may so abstain from carnal feasting: that we may likewise fast from the vices which beset us. Through.

Epistle. Zechariah 8:14

IN THOSE DAYS: The word of the LORD came unto me, saying: Thus saith the LORD of hosts: As I thought to punish you, when your fathers provoked me to wrath, saith the LORD of hosts, and I repented not: So again have I thought in these days to do well unto Jerusalem and to the house of Judah: fear ye not. These are the things that ye shall do; Speak ye every man the truth to his neighbour; execute the judgment of truth and peace in your gates: And let none of you imagine evil in your hearts against his neighbour; and love no false oath: for all these are things that I hate, saith the LORD. And the word of the LORD of hosts came unto me, saying, Thus saith the LORD of hosts; The fast of the fourth month, and the fast of the fifth, and the fast of the seventh, and the fast of the tenth, shall be to the house of Judah joy and gladness, and cheerful feasts; therefore love the truth and peace: saith the LORD of hosts.

Gradual. Let my prayer be set forth in thy sight, O Lord, as the incense. ℣. Let the lifting up of my hands be an evening sacrifice.

℣. Let us pray.	℣. Orémus.
℣. Let us bow the knee.	℣. Flectámus génua.
℣. Arise.	℣. Leváte.

Collect

LORD, who sufferest us to offer unto thee this solemn fast: we beseech thee that thou wouldest likewise bestow upon us the succour of thy pardon. Through.

Ember Saturday   **Proper of Saints**   *Autumnal Emberday*

Epistle. Song of the Three Children 26

IN THOSE DAYS: The Angel of the Lord came down into the oven together with Azarias and his fellows, and smote the flame of the fire out of the oven; And made the midst of the furnace as it had been a moist whistling wind, so that the fire touched them not at all, neither hurt nor troubled them. Then the three, as out of one mouth, praised, glorified, and blessed, God in the furnace, saying:

℣ Thanks be to God is not said here.

Hymn

BLESSED art thou, O Lord God of our fathers. And worthy to be praised and glorious for ever.

And blessed is the name of thy glory, which is holy. And worthy to be praised and glorious for ever.

Blessed art thou in the holy temple of thy glory. And worthy to be praised and glorious for ever.

Blessed art thou on the holy throne of thy kingdom. And worthy to be praised and glorious for ever.

Blessed art thou in the sceptre of thy godhead. And worthy to be praised and glorious for ever.

Blessed art thou that beholdest the depths, and sittest upon the Cherubim. And worthy to be praised and glorious for ever.

Blessed art thou that walkest on the wings of the winds, and on the waves of the sea. And worthy to be praised and glorious for ever.

Let all thine Angels and Saints bless thee. And let them praise thee and glorify thee for ever.

Let the heavens, the earth, the sea, and all that in them is, bless thee. And let them praise thee and glorify thee for ever.

Glory be to the Father, and to the Son, and to the Holy Ghost. And worthy to be praised and glorious for ever.

As it was in the beginning, is now, and ever shall be: world without end. Amen. And worthy to be praised and glorious for ever.

Blessed art thou, O Lord God of our fathers. And worthy to be praised and glorious for ever.

℣. The Lord be with you.	℣. Dóminus vobíscum.
℟. And with thy spirit.	℟. Et cum spíritu tuo.
℣. Let us pray.	℣. Orémus.

Autumnal Emberday   Proper of Saints   *Ember Saturday*

Collect

GOD, who to the three children didst assuage the flames of fire: mercifully grant; that the flames of sin may not kindle upon us thy servants. Through.

¶ 2nd Collect is of the Saints (p. 542) & 3rd is ad libitum.

Epistle. Hebrews 9:2

BRETHREN: There was a tabernacle made; the first, wherein was the candlestick, and the table, and the shewbread; which is called the sanctuary. And after the second veil, the tabernacle which is called the Holiest of all; Which had the golden censer, and the ark of the covenant overlaid round about with gold, wherein was the golden pot that had manna, and Aaron's rod that budded, and the tables of the covenant; And over it the cherubims of glory shadowing the mercyseat; of which we cannot now speak particularly. Now when these things were thus ordained, the priests went always into the first tabernacle, accomplishing the service of God. But into the second went the high priest alone once every year, not without blood, which he offered for himself, and for the errors of the people: The Holy Ghost this signifying, that the way into the holiest of all was not yet made manifest, while as the first tabernacle was yet standing: Which was a figure for the time then present, in which were offered both gifts and sacrifices, that could not make him that did the service perfect, as pertaining to the conscience; Which stood only in meats and drinks, and divers washings, and carnal ordinances, imposed on them until the time of reformation. But Christ being come an high priest of good things to come, by a greater and more perfect tabernacle, not made with hands, that is to say, not of this building; Neither by the blood of goats and calves, but by his own blood he entered in once into the holy place, having obtained eternal redemption for us.

Tract. O praise the Lord, all ye heathen: praise him, all ye nations. ℣. For his merciful kindness is ever more and more towards us: and the truth of the Lord endureth for ever.

Gospel. Luke 13:6

AT THAT TIME: Jesus spake this parable unto the multitudes: A certain man had a fig tree planted in his vineyard; and he came and sought fruit thereon, and found none. Then said he unto the dresser of his vineyard, Behold, these three years I come seeking fruit on this fig tree, and find none: cut it down; why cumbereth it the ground? And he answering said unto

Ember Saturday **Proper of Saints** *Autumnal Emberday*

him, Lord, let it alone this year also, till I shall dig about it, and dung it: And if it bear fruit, well: and if not, then after that thou shalt cut it down. And he was teaching in one of the synagogues on the sabbath. And, behold, there was a woman which had a spirit of infirmity eighteen years, and was bowed together, and could in no wise lift up herself. And when Jesus saw her, he called her to him, and said unto her, Woman, thou art loosed from thine infirmity. And he laid his hands on her: and immediately she was made straight, and glorified God. And the ruler of the synagogue answered with indignation, because that Jesus had healed on the sabbath day, and said unto the people, There are six days in which men ought to work: in them therefore come and be healed, and not on the sabbath day. The Lord then answered him, and said, Thou hypocrite, doth not each one of you on the sabbath loose his ox or his ass from the stall, and lead him away to watering? And ought not this woman, being a daughter of Abraham, whom Satan hath bound, lo, these eighteen years, be loosed from this bond on the sabbath day? And when he had said these things, all his adversaries were ashamed: and all the people rejoiced for all the glorious things that were done by him.

Offertory. O Lord God of my salvation, I have cried day and night before thee: let my prayer enter into thy presence, O Lord.

Secret

RANT, we beseech thee, Almighty God: that the gift which we offer in the sight of thy Majesty may both obtain for us the grace of devotion, and effectually bring us to everlasting happiness. Through.

❡ 2nd Secret is of the Saints (p. 542) & 3rd is ad libitum.

Communion. In the seventh month ye shall celebrate a feast, when I made the children of Israel to dwell in booths, when I brought them out of the land of Egypt, I the Lord your God.

Postcommunion

E beseech thee, O Lord, that thy sacraments may accomplish in us that which they contain: that those things which we now offer in outward fashion, we may receive in verity and truth. Through.

❡ 2nd Postcommunion is of the Saints (p. 542) & 3rd is ad libitum.

St. Matthew

Second Class Double
21 September

Introit

HE mouth of the just is exercised in wisdom, and his tongue will be talking of judgment: the law of his God is in his heart. *Ps.* Fret not thyself because of the ungodly: neither be thou envious against the evil doers.

Collect

AY we be assisted, O Lord, by the prayers of blessed Matthew, the Apostle and Evangelist: that those things, which of ourselves we cannot obtain, may be vouchsafed unto us by his intercession. Through.

Epistle. 2 Corinthians 4:1

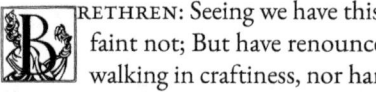RETHREN: Seeing we have this ministry, as we have received mercy, we faint not; But have renounced the hidden things of dishonesty, not walking in craftiness, nor handling the word of God deceitfully; but by manifestation of the truth commending ourselves to every man's conscience in the sight of God. But if our gospel be hid, it is hid to them that are lost: In whom the god of this world hath blinded the minds of them which believe not, lest the light of the glorious gospel of Christ, who is the image of God, should shine unto them. For we preach not ourselves, but Christ Jesus the Lord; and ourselves your servants for Jesus' sake. For God, who commanded the light to shine out of darkness, hath shined in our hearts, to give the light of the knowledge of the glory of God in the face of Jesus Christ.

Gradual. Blessed is the man that feareth the Lord: he hath great delight in his commandments. ℣. His seed shall be mighty upon earth: the generation of the faithful shall be blessed.

Alleluia. Alleluia, alleluia. ℣. The glorious company of the Apostles praise thee, O Lord. Alleluia.

21 September **Proper of Saints** St. Matthew

Gospel. Matthew 9:9

AT THAT TIME: As Jesus passed forth from thence, he saw a man, named Matthew, sitting at the receipt of custom: and he saith unto him, Follow me. And he arose, and followed him. And it came to pass, as Jesus sat at meat in the house, behold, many publicans and sinners came and sat down with him and his disciples. And when the Pharisees saw it, they said unto his disciples, Why eateth your Master with publicans and sinners? But when Jesus heard that, he said unto them, They that be whole need not a physician, but they that are sick. But go ye and learn what that meaneth, I will have mercy, and not sacrifice: for I am not come to call the righteous, but sinners to repentance.

Offertory. Thou hast set, O Lord, a crown of pure gold upon his head: he asked life of thee, and thou gavest it him, alleluia.

Secret

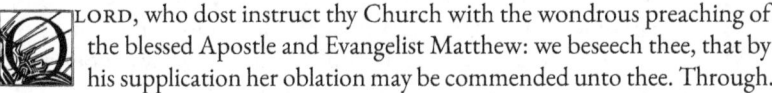

O LORD, who dost instruct thy Church with the wondrous preaching of the blessed Apostle and Evangelist Matthew: we beseech thee, that by his supplication her oblation may be commended unto thee. Through.

Communion. His honour is great in thy salvation: glory and great worship shalt thou lay upon him, O Lord.

Postcommunion

O LORD, who hast bestowed on us thy sacraments, we beseech thee: that through the mediation of blessed Matthew, thine Apostle and Evangelist, the mysteries which we have celebrated may be profitable for our healing. Through.

Michaelmas   **Proper of Saints**   29 September

St. Michael

First Class Double
29 September

Opening Sentence. The smoke of the incense ascended up before God out of the Angel's hand.

Introit

PRAISE the Lord, all ye Angels of his: ye that excel in strength ye that fulfil his commandment, and hearken unto the voice of his words. *Ps.* Praise the Lord, O my soul; and all that is within me praise his holy name

Collect

EVERLASTING God, who hast ordained and constituted the services of Angels and men in a wonderful order; Mercifully grant that, as thy holy Angels always do thee service in heaven, so, by thy appointment, they may succour and defend us on earth. Through.

Epistle. Revelation 12:7

THERE was war in heaven: Michael and his angels fought against the dragon; and the dragon fought and his angels, And prevailed not; neither was their place found any more in heaven. And the great dragon was cast out, that old serpent, called the Devil, and Satan, which deceiveth the whole world: he was cast out into the earth, and his angels were cast out with him. And I heard a loud voice saying in heaven, Now is come salvation, and strength, and the kingdom of our God, and the power of his Christ: for the accuser of our brethren is cast down, which accused them before our God day and night. And they overcame him by the blood of the Lamb, and by the word of their testimony; and they loved not their lives unto the death. Therefore rejoice, ye heavens, and ye that dwell in them. Woe to the inhabiters of the earth and of the sea! for the devil is come down unto you, having great wrath, because he knoweth that he hath but a short time.

Gradual. O praise the Lord, all ye Angels of his; ye that excel in strength, ye that fulfil his commandment. ℣. Praise the Lord, O my soul; and all that is within me praise his holy name.

Alleluia. Alleluia, alleluia. ℣. Holy Michael, Archangel, defend us in the battle: that we perish not in the dreadful judgment. Alleluia.

Proper of Saints

29 September — Michaelmas

Gospel. Matthew 18:1

T THAT TIME: The disciples came unto Jesus, saying, Who is the greatest in the kingdom of heaven? And Jesus called a little child unto him, and set him in the midst of them, And said, Verily I say unto you, Except ye be converted, and become as little children, ye shall not enter into the kingdom of heaven. Whosoever therefore shall humble himself as this little child, the same is greatest in the kingdom of heaven. And whoso shall receive one such little child in my name receiveth me. But whoso shall offend one of these little ones which believe in me, it were better for him that a millstone were hanged about his neck, and that he were drowned in the depth of the sea. Woe unto the world because of offences! for it must needs be that offences come; but woe to that man by whom the offence cometh! Wherefore if thy hand or thy foot offend thee, cut them off, and cast them from thee: it is better for thee to enter into life halt or maimed, rather than having two hands or two feet to be cast into everlasting fire. And if thine eye offend thee, pluck it out, and cast it from thee: it is better for thee to enter into life with one eye, rather than having two eyes to be cast into hell fire. Take heed that ye despise not one of these little ones; for I say unto you, That in heaven their angels do always behold the face of my Father which is in heaven.

Offertory. An Angel stood by the altar of the temple, having a golden censer in his hand, and there was given unto him much incense; and the smoke of the incense ascended up before God, alleluia.

Secret

E offer thee, O Lord, sacrifices of praise, humbly beseeching thee: that by the prayers of the Angels interceding for us, thou wouldest both graciously accept the same, and grant that they may avail to our salvation. Through.

Communion. O all ye Angels of the Lord, bless ye the Lord: sing ye praises, and magnify him above all for ever.

Postcommunion

LORD, forasmuch as we put our trust in the intercession of thy blessed Archangel Michael; we humbly beseech thee; that those things which we touch with our lips we may likewise receive into our hearts. Through.

Proper of Saints

HOLY GUARDIAN ANGELS

Greater Double
2 October

Opening Sentence. O praise the Lord, ye Angels of his. Ye that excel in strength, and hearken unto the voice of his words.

Introit

PRAISE the Lord, all ye Angels of his: ye that excel in strength, ye that fulfil his commandment, and hearken unto the voice of his words. *Ps.* Praise the Lord, O my soul: and that is within me praise his holy name.

Collect

GOD, who of thy ineffable providence dost vouchsafe to send thy holy Angels to be our guardians: grant unto us thy humble servants; that we may ever both be defended by their protection, and rejoice in their everlasting fellowship. Through.

Epistle. Exodus 23:20

HUS saith the Lord God: Behold, I send an Angel before thee, to keep thee in the way, and to bring thee into the place which I have prepared. Beware of him, and obey his voice, provoke him not; for he will not pardon your transgressions: for my name is in him. But if thou shalt indeed obey his voice, and do all that I speak; then I will be an enemy unto thine enemies, and an adversary unto thine adversaries. For mine Angel shall go before thee.

Gradual. God shall give his Angels charge over thee, to keep thee in all thy ways. ℣. They shall bear thee in their hands, that thou hurt not thy foot against a stone.

Alleluia. Alleluia, alleluia. ℣. O praise the Lord, all ye his hosts: ye servants of his that do his pleasure. Alleluia.

¶ In Votive Masses after Septuagesima, the Tract—and in Eastertide the Greater Alleluia—are as in Votives of the Holy Angels (p. 575).

Gospel. Matthew 18:1

T THAT TIME: The disciples came unto Jesus, saying, Who is the greatest in the kingdom of heaven? And Jesus called a little child unto him, and set him in the midst of them, and said, Verily I say unto you, Except ye be converted, and become as little children, ye shall not enter into the kingdom of heaven. Whosoever therefore shall humble himself as this little child, the same is greatest in the kingdom of heaven. And whoso shall receive one such little child in my name receiveth me. But whoso shall offend one of these little ones which believe in me, it were better for him that a millstone were hanged about his neck, and that he were drowned in the depth of the sea. Woe unto the world because of offences! for it must needs be that offences come; but woe to that man by whom the offence cometh! Wherefore if thy hand or thy foot offend thee, cut them off, and cast them from thee: it is better for thee to enter into life halt or maimed, rather than having two hands or two feet to be cast into everlasting fire. And if thine eye offend thee, pluck it out, and cast it from thee: it is better for thee to enter into life with one eye, rather than having two eyes to be cast into hell fire. Take heed that ye despise not one of these little ones; for I say unto you, That in heaven their angels do always behold the face of my Father which is in heaven.

Offertory. O praise the Lord, all ye Angels of his: ye servants of his, that fulfil his commandment, and hearken unto the voice of his words.

Secret

ECEIVE, O Lord, the gifts which we present in veneration of thy holy Angels: and mercifully grant; that by their continual protection we may be delivered from present dangers and attain unto everlasting life. Through.

Communion. O all ye Angels of the Lord, bless ye the Lord: sing ye praises, and magnify him above all for ever.

Postcommunion

LORD, who on this festival of thy holy Angels, hast suffered us to receive in gladness thy heavenly mysteries: we beseech thee; that by their protection we may ever be delivered from the snares of our enemies, and defended against all adversities. Through.

Holy Rosary   # Proper of Saints   7 October

Holy Rosary of the Blessed Virgin Mary

Greater Double
7 October

❧ In Low Mass, Commemoration of St. Mark of Rome and Sts. Sergius, Bacchus, Marcellus, & Apuleius is made, with the Prayers as below.
   Note, The Creed is said.

Introit

REJOICE we all in the Lord, keeping feast day in honour of the blessed Virgin Mary: in whose solemnity the Angels rejoice and glorify the Son of God. *Ps.* My heart is inditing of a good matter: I speak of the things which I have made unto the King.

Collect

O GOD, whose only-begotten Son by his life, death, and resurrection hath purchased for us the rewards of everlasting salvation: grant, we beseech thee; that we, who meditate upon these mysteries in the most sacred Rosary of the blessed Virgin Mary, may both imitate those things which they set forth, and attain unto those things which they promise. Through.

❧ Commemoration of St. Mark of Rome, as followeth,

GRACIOUSLY hear our prayers, O Lord: and at the intercession of blessed Mark, thy Confessor and Bishop, mercifully grant us pardon and peace. Through.

❧ Commemoration of Sts. Sergius, Bacchus, Marcellus, & Apuleius, as followeth,

MAY the blessed merits of thy holy Martyrs Sergius, Bacchus, Marcellus, and Apuleius uphold us, O Lord: and ever make us fervent in thy love. Through.

Epistle. Proverbs 8:22

THE Lord possessed me in the beginning of his way, before his works of old. I was set up from everlasting, from the beginning, or ever the earth was. When there were no depths, I was brought forth. Now therefore hearken unto me, O ye children: for blessed are they that keep my ways. Hear instruction, and be wise, and refuse it not. Blessed is the man that heareth me, watching daily at my gates, waiting at the posts of my doors. For whoso findeth me findeth life, and shall obtain favour of the Lord.

Gradual. Because of the word of truth, of meekness, and righteousness, and thy right hand shall teach thee terrible things. ℣. Hearken, O daughter, and consider, incline thine ear: so shall the King have pleasure in thy beauty.

Alleluia. Alleluia, alleluia. ℣. The solemnity of the glorious Virgin Mary of the seed of Abraham, sprung from the tribe of Juda, of David's noble stock. Alleluia.

Gospel. Luke 1:26

AT THAT TIME: The angel Gabriel was sent from God unto a city of Galilee, named Nazareth, to a virgin espoused to a man whose name was Joseph, of the house of David; and the virgin's name was Mary. And the angel came in unto her, and said, Hail, thou that art highly favoured, the Lord is with thee: blessed art thou among women. And when she saw him, she was troubled at his saying, and cast in her mind what manner of salutation this should be. And the angel said unto her, Fear not, Mary: for thou hast found favour with God. And, behold, thou shalt conceive in thy womb, and bring forth a son, and shalt call his name JESUS. He shall be great, and shall be called the Son of the Highest: and the Lord God shall give unto him the throne of his father David: and he shall reign over the house of Jacob for ever; and of his kingdom there shall be no end. Then said Mary unto the angel, How shall this be, seeing I know not a man? And the angel answered and said unto her, The Holy Ghost shall come upon thee, and the power of the Highest shall overshadow thee: therefore also that holy thing which shall be born of thee shall be called the Son of God. And, behold, thy cousin Elisabeth, she hath also conceived a son in her old age: and this is the sixth month with her, who was called barren. For with God nothing shall be impossible. And Mary said, Behold the handmaid of the Lord; be it unto me according to thy word.

Offertory. In me is all grace of the way and of truth: in me is all hope of life and of virtue: I have budded forth as a rose growing by the brooks of water.

Secret

GRANT, we beseech thee, O Lord, that we may be enabled worthily to offer these our gifts: and through the mysteries of the most sacred Rosary so to recall the life, the passion and the glory of thy only-begotten Son; that we may be made worthy of his promises. Who liveth and reigneth with thee.

❦ Commemoration of St. Mark of Rome, as followeth,

Holy Rosary   # Proper of Saints   7 October

Grant, O Lord, that like as thy dedicated people do acknowledge that in tribulation they have been succoured by the merits of thy Saints: so this oblation, which they offer unto thee in honour of the same, may be acceptable in thy sight. Through.

¶ Commemoration of Sts. Sergius, Bacchus, Marcellus, & Apuleius, as followeth,

We beseech thee, O Lord, that, through the meritorious supplication of thy Saints: this sacrifice, which we offer, may obtain for us the favour of thy Majesty. Through.

Communion. Put forth flowers as a lily, spread abroad a sweet smell, and bring forth leaves in grace, sing a song of praise, and bless the Lord in all his works.

Postcommunion

We beseech thee, O Lord, that we who celebrate the Rosary of thy most holy Mother, may in such wise be succoured by her prayers: that we may be partakers of the power of the mysteries which we revere; and obtain the effect of the sacraments which we have received. Who livest.

¶ Commemoration of St. Mark of Rome, as followeth,

Grant, we beseech thee, O Lord, that thy faithful people may ever rejoice in the veneration of thy Saints: and be defended by their perpetual supplication. Through.

¶ Commemoration of Sts. Sergius, Bacchus, Marcellus, & Apuleius, as followeth,

Grant, O Lord, that, being strengthened by the sacraments which we have received: we may, at the intercession of thy holy Martyrs, Sergius, Bacchus, Marcellus, and Apuleius, fight against all iniquity, and be defended by thy heavenly armour. Through.

Motherhood of the Blessed Virgin Mary

Second Class Double
11 October

Introit

EHOLD, a Virgin shall conceive, and bear a Son, and shall call his name Emmanuel. *Ps.* O sing unto the Lord a new song, for he hath done marvellous things.

Collect

GOD, who wast pleased that thy Word should take flesh of the womb of the Blessed Virgin Mary at the message of an Angel: grant to thy humble servants; that we, who believe her to be truly the Mother of God, may be aided by her intercession in thy sight. Through the same.

Epistle. Ecclesiasticus 24:17

s the vine I put forth grace; And my flowers are the fruit of glory and riches. Come unto me, ye that are desirous of me, And be ye filled with my produce. For my memorial is sweeter than honey, And mine inheritance than the honeycomb. They that eat me shall yet be hungry; And they that drink me shall yet be thirsty. He that obeyeth me shall not be ashamed; And they that work in me shall not do amiss.

Gradual. There shall come forth a rod out of the stem of Jesse: and a branch shall rise up out of his roots. ℣. And the Spirit of the Lord shall rest upon him.

Alleluia. Alleluia, alleluia. ℣. Virgin, Mother of God, he whom the whole world containeth not, being made man lay hid in thy womb. Alleluia.

Gospel. Luke 2:43

AT THAT TIME: As they returned, the child Jesus tarried behind in Jerusalem; and Joseph and his mother knew not of it. But they, supposing him to have been in the company, went a day's journey; and they sought him among their kinsfolk and acquaintance. And when they found him not, they turned back again to Jerusalem, seeking him. And it came to pass, that after three days they found him in the temple, sitting in the midst of the doctors, both hearing them, and asking them questions. And all that heard him were astonished at his understanding and answers. And when they saw him, they were amazed: and his mother said unto him, Son, why hast thou thus dealt with us? behold, thy father and I have sought thee sorrowing. And he said unto them, How is it that ye sought me? wist ye not that I must be about my Father's business? And they understood not the saying which he spake unto them. And he went down with them, and came to Nazareth, and was subject unto them.

Offertory. When Mary his Mother was espoused to Joseph, she was found with child of the Holy Ghost.

Secret

THROUGH thy mercy, O Lord, and the intercession of blessed Mary ever Virgin, Mother of thine only-begotten Son, may this oblation avail for our prosperity and peace, both now and for ever. Through the same.

Communion. Blessed is the womb of the Virgin Mary, that bore the Son of the everlasting Father.

Postcommunion

MAY this communion, O Lord, cleanse us from guilt: and at the intercession of blessed Mary, the Virgin Mother of God, make us partakers of thy heavenly healing. Through the same.

Our Lady of Walsingham

Double
15 October

Opening Sentence. How dreadful is this place! this is none other but the house of God, and this is the gate of heaven. (Gn 28:17)

Introit

HOW dreadful is this place! this is none other but the house of God, and this is the gate of heaven. *Ps.* O how amiable are thy dwellings, thou Lord of hosts! Blessed are they that dwell in thy house, they will be alway praising thee.

Collect

GOD, who in the blessed Virgin Mary didst make a fit dwelling-place for thy Son: grant, we beseech thee, that we who honour her shrine at Walsingham may also become temples of thy Holy Ghost. Through the same.

15 October   **Proper of Saints**   *Walsingham*

Epistle. Ecclesiasticus 24:8

THE Creator of all things gave me a commandment; And he that created me made my tabernacle to rest, And said, Let thy tabernacle be in Jacob, And thine inheritance in Israel. He created me from the beginning before the world; And to the end I shall not fail. In the holy tabernacle I ministered before him; And so was I established in Sion. In the beloved city likewise he gave me rest; And in Jerusalem was my authority. And I took root in a people that was glorified, Even in the portion of the Lord's own inheritance. I was exalted like a cedar in Libanus, And as a cypress tree on the mountains of Hermon. I was exalted like a palm tree on the sea shore, And as rose plants in Jericho, And as a fair olive tree in the plain; And I was exalted as a plane tree. And my flowers are the fruit of glory and riches. Come unto me, ye that are desirous of me, And be ye filled with my produce. For my memorial is sweeter than honey, And mine inheritance than the honeycomb.

Gradual. My soul hath a desire and longing to enter into the courts of the Lord. ℣. Yea, the sparrow hath found her an house, and the swallow a nest, where she may lay her young: even thy altars, O Lord of hosts, my King and my God.

Alleluia. Alleluia, alleluia. ℣. I had rather be a door-keeper in the house of my God: than to dwell in the tents of ungodliness. Alleluia.

Gospel. Luke 2:25

AT THAT TIME: There was a man in Jerusalem, whose name was Simeon; and the same man was just and devout, waiting for the consolation of Israel: and the Holy Ghost was upon him. And it was revealed unto him by the Holy Ghost, that he should not see death, before he had seen the Lord's Christ. And he came by the Spirit into the temple: and when the parents brought in the child Jesus, to do for him after the custom of the law, then took he him up in his arms, and blessed God, and said, Lord, now lettest thou thy servant depart in peace, according to thy word: for mine eyes have seen thy salvation, which thou hast prepared before the face of all people; a light to lighten the Gentiles, and the glory of thy people Israel. And Joseph and his mother marvelled at those things which were spoken of him. And Simeon blessed them, and said unto Mary his mother, Behold, this child is set for the fall and rising again of many in Israel; and for a sign which shall be spoken against; (yea, a sword shall pierce through thy own soul also,) that the thoughts of many hearts may be revealed. And there was one Anna, a prophetess, the daughter of Phanuel, of the tribe of Aser: she was of a great age, and had lived with an husband seven years from her virginity; and she was a widow of about fourscore and four years, which departed not from the temple, but served God with fastings and prayers night and day. And she coming in that instant gave thanks likewise unto the Lord, and spake of him to all them that looked for redemption in Jerusalem. And when they had performed all things according to the law of the Lord, they returned into Galilee, to their own city Nazareth. And the child grew, and waxed strong in spirit, filled with wisdom: and the grace of God was upon him.

Offertory. And Jesus went down with Mary and Joseph, and came to Nazareth, and was subject unto them. But his Mother kept all these sayings in her heart. And Jesus increased in wisdom and stature, and in favour with God and man.

Secret

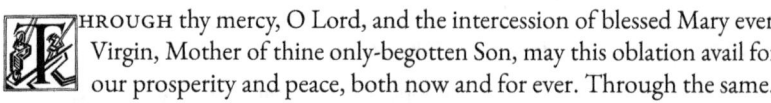THROUGH thy mercy, O Lord, and the intercession of blessed Mary ever-Virgin, Mother of thine only-begotten Son, may this oblation avail for our prosperity and peace, both now and for ever. Through the same.

Communion. Blessed is the womb of the Virgin Mary, that bare the Son of the everlasting Father.

Postcommunion

O LORD, let this holy Communion cleanse us from every guilty stain: that at the intercession of the blessed Virgin Mary, Mother of God, we may be made partakers thereby of thy healing unto life eternal. Through the same.

St. Luke

Second Class Double
18 October

Introit

RIGHT honourable are thy friends unto me, O God: right well is their princedom established. *Ps.* O Lord, thou hast searched me out, and known me: thou knowest my down-sitting and mine up-rising.

Collect

WE beseech thee, O Lord: that thy holy Evangelist Luke may intercede for us: who for the honour of thy name continually bare in his own body the mortification of the Cross. Through.

Proper of Saints

18 October — *St. Luke*

Epistle. 2 Timothy 4:5

DEARLY BELOVED: Watch thou in all things, endure afflictions, do the work of an evangelist, make full proof of thy ministry. For I am now ready to be offered, and the time of my departure is at hand. I have fought a good fight, I have finished my course, I have kept the faith: Henceforth there is laid up for me a crown of righteousness, which the Lord, the righteous judge, shall give me at that day: and not to me only, but unto all them also that love his appearing. Do thy diligence to come shortly unto me: For Demas hath forsaken me, having loved this present world, and is departed unto Thessalonica; Crescens to Galatia, Titus unto Dalmatia. Only Luke is with me. Take Mark, and bring him with thee: for he is profitable to me for the ministry. And Tychicus have I sent to Ephesus. The cloke that I left at Troas with Carpus, when thou comest, bring with thee, and the books, but especially the parchments. Alexander the coppersmith did me much evil: the Lord reward him according to his works: Of whom be thou ware also; for he hath greatly withstood our words.

Gradual. Their sound is gone out into all lands: and their words into the ends of the world. ℣. The heavens declare the glory of God: and the firmament sheweth his handy-work.

Alleluia. Alleluia, alleluia. ℣. I have chosen you out of the world, that ye should go and bring forth fruit: and that your fruit should remain. Alleluia.

Gospel. Luke 10:1

AT THAT TIME: The Lord appointed other seventy also, and sent them two and two before his face into every city and place, whither he himself would come. Therefore said he unto them, The harvest truly is great, but the labourers are few: pray ye therefore the Lord of the harvest, that he would send forth labourers into his harvest. Go your ways: behold, I send you forth as lambs among wolves. Carry neither purse, nor scrip, nor shoes: and salute no man by the way. And into whatsoever house ye enter, first say, Peace be to this house. And if the son of peace be there, your peace shall rest upon it: if not, it shall turn to you again. And in the same house remain, eating and drinking such things as they give: for the labourer is worthy of his hire.

Offertory. Right honourable are thy friends unto me, O God: right well is their princedom established.

Secret

RANT us, O Lord, we beseech thee, by thy heavenly gifts to serve thee in freedom of spirit: that, through the intercession of thy blessed Evangelist Luke, the oblations which we present may work in us for our healing and glory. Through.

Communion. Ye which have followed me shall sit upon thrones, judging the twelve tribes of Israel.

Postcommunion

RANT, we beseech thee, Almighty God: that those things which we have receive from thy holy altar may, through the prayers of thy blessed Evangelist Luke, sanctify our souls, and avail for our protection. Through.

St. Raphael

Greater Double
24 October

Opening Sentence. And there appeared an angel unto him from heaven strengthening him.

Introit

PRAISE the Lord, ye Angels of his, ye that excel in strength: ye that fulfil his commandment, and hearken unto the voice of his words. *Ps.* Praise the Lord, O my soul: and all that is within me praise his holy name.

Collect

O GOD, who didst give blessed Raphael the Archangel unto thy servant Tobias for a companion on his way: grant to us thy servants; that we may ever be guarded by his protection and strengthened by his help. Through.

Epistle. Tobit 12:7

IN THOSE DAYS: The Angel Raphael said to Tobias: It is good to keep close the secret of a king, but to reveal gloriously the works of God. Do good, and evil shall not find you. Good is prayer with fasting and alms and righteousness. A little with righteousness is better than much with unrighteousness. It is better to give alms than to lay up gold: alms doth deliver from death, and it shall purge away all sin. They that do alms and righteousness shall be filled with life; but they that sin are enemies to their own life. Surely I will keep close nothing from you. I have said, It is good to keep close the secret of a king, but to reveal gloriously the works of God. And now, when thou didst pray, and Sarah thy daughter in law, I did bring the memorial of your prayer before the Holy One: and when thou didst bury the dead, I was with thee likewise. And when thou didst not delay to rise up, and leave thy dinner, that thou mightest go and cover the dead, thy good deed was not hid from me: but I was with thee. And now God did send me to heal thee and Sarah thy daughter in law. I am Raphael, one of the seven holy angels, which present the prayers of the saints, and go in before the glory of the Holy One.

Gradual. The Angel of the Lord, Raphael, took the devil and bound him. ℣. Great is our Lord, and great is his power.

Alleluia. Alleluia, alleluia. ℣. In the sight of the Angels will I sing praise unto thee: I will worship toward thy holy temple and praise thy name, O Lord. Alleluia.

Gospel. John 5:1

AT THAT TIME: There was a feast of the Jews: and Jesus went up to Jerusalem. Now there is at Jerusalem by the sheep market a pool, which is called in the Hebrew tongue Bethesda, having five porches. In these lay a great multitude of impotent folk, of blind, halt, withered, waiting for the moving of the water. For an angel went down at a certain season into the pool, and troubled the water: whosoever then first after the troubling of the water stepped in was made whole of whatsoever disease he had.

Offertory. An Angel stood by the altar of the temple, having a golden censer in his hand, and there was given unto him much incense: and the smoke of the incense ascended up before God.

Secret

WE offer thee, O Lord, sacrifices of praise, humbly beseeching thee: that, by the prayers of the Angels interceding for us, thou wouldest both graciously accept the same, and grant that they may avail to our salvation. Through.

Communion. O all ye Angels of the Lord, bless ye the Lord: sing ye praises, and magnify him above all for ever.

Sts. Simon & Jude **Proper of Saints** 28 October

Postcommunion

OUCHSAFE, O Lord God, to direct thy holy Archangel Raphael to our succour: that, as we believe him ever to stand before thy Majesty, so he may present our unworthy supplications for thy blessing. Through.

STS. SIMON AND JUDE

Second Class Double
28 October

Introit

IGHT honourable are thy friends unto me, O God: right well is their princedom established. *Ps.* O Lord, thou hast searched me out, and known me: thou knowest my down-sitting and mine up-rising.

Collect

LMIGHTY God, who hast built thy Church upon the foundation of the Apostles and Prophets, Jesus Christ himself being the head cornerstone; Grant us so to be joined together in unity of spirit by their doctrine, that we may be made an holy temple acceptable unto thee. Through.

Epistle. Jude 1

UDE, the servant of Jesus Christ, and brother of James, to them that are sanctified by God the Father, and preserved in Jesus Christ, and called: Mercy unto you, and peace, and love, be multiplied. Beloved, when I gave all diligence to write unto you of the common salvation, it was needful for me to write unto you, and exhort you that ye should earnestly contend for the faith which was once delivered unto the saints. For there are certain men crept in unawares, who were before of old ordained to this condemnation, ungodly men, turning the grace of our God into lasciviousness, and denying the only Lord God, and our Lord Jesus Christ. I will therefore put you in remembrance, though ye once knew this, how that the Lord, having saved the people out of the land of Egypt, afterward destroyed them that believed not. And the angels which kept not their first estate, but left their own habitation, he hath reserved in everlasting chains under darkness unto the judgment of the great day. Even as Sodom and Gomorrha, and the cities about them in like manner, giving themselves over to fornication, and going after strange flesh, are set forth for an example, suffering the vengeance of eternal fire. Likewise also these filthy dreamers defile the flesh, despise dominion, and speak evil of dignities.

Gradual. Thou shalt make them princes in all lands: they shall remember thy name, O Lord. ℣. Instead of thy fathers thou shalt have children: therefore shall the people give thanks unto thee.

Alleluia. Alleluia, alleluia. ℣. Right honourable are thy friends, O God: right well is their princedom established. Alleluia.

Gospel. John 15:17

T THAT TIME: Jesus said unto his disciples: 17 These things I command you, that ye love one another. If the world hate you, ye know that it hated me before it hated you. If ye were of the world, the world would love his own: but because ye are not of the world, but I have chosen you out of the world, therefore the world hateth you. Remember the word that I said unto you, The servant is not greater than his lord. If they have persecuted me, they will also persecute you; if they have kept my saying, they will keep yours also. But all these things will they do unto you for my name's sake, because they know not him that sent me. If I had not come and spoken unto them, they had not had sin: but now they have no cloke for their sin. He that hateth me hateth my Father also. If I had not done among them the works which none other man did, they had not had sin: but now have they both seen and hated both me and my Father. But this cometh to pass, that the word might be fulfilled that is written in their law, They hated me without a cause. But when the Comforter is come, whom I will send unto you from the Father, even the Spirit of truth, which proceedeth from the Father, he shall testify of me: And ye also shall bear witness, because ye have been with me from the beginning.

Offertory. Their sound is gone out into all lands: and their words into the ends of the world.

Secret

E beseech thee, O Lord: that as we do venerate the everlasting glory of thy holy Apostles Simon and Jude; so, being cleansed by these sacred mysteries, we may more worthily celebrate the same. Through.

Communion. Ye which have followed me shall sit upon thrones, judging the twelve tribes of Israel.

Christ the King # Proper of Saints

Postcommunion

O LORD, through whom we have received these sacraments, we humbly entreat thee: that by the intercession of thy blessed Apostles Simon and Jude, the mysteries which we celebrate for their venerable passion may be profitable for our healing. Through.

OUR LORD JESUS CHRIST THE KING

First Class Double
Last Sunday in October

Opening Sentence. All power is given unto me in heaven and in earth. (Mt 28:18)

Introit

WORTHY is the Lamb that was slain to receive power, and riches, and wisdom, and strength, and honour. To him be glory and dominion for ever and ever. *Ps.* Give the King thy judgments, O God: and thy righteousness unto the King's Son.

Collect

ALMIGHTY and everlasting God, who in thy beloved Son, the King of all, hast been pleased to make all things new: mercifully grant; that all the families of the Gentiles, dispersed by the wounds of sin, may be made subject to his most gracious governance. Who liveth.

¶ Commemoration is made of the Sunday occurring.

Epistle. Colossians 1:12

BRETHREN: We give thanks unto the Father, which hath made us meet to be partakers of the inheritance of the saints in light: Who hath delivered us from the power of darkness, and hath translated us into the kingdom of his dear Son: In whom we have redemption through his blood, even the forgiveness of sins: Who is the image of the invisible God, the firstborn of every creature: For by him were all things created, that are in heaven, and that are in earth, visible and invisible, whether they be thrones, or dominions, or principalities, or powers: all things were created by him, and for him: And he is before all things, and by him all things consist. And he is the head of the body, the church: who is the beginning, the firstborn from the dead; that in all things he might have the preeminence. For it pleased the Father that in him should all fulness dwell; And, having made peace through the blood of his cross, by him to reconcile all things unto himself; by him, I say, whether they be things in earth, or things in heaven, in Christ Jesus our Lord.

Gradual. His dominion shall be from the one sea to the other, and from the flood unto the world's end. ℣. All kings shall fall down before him: all nations shall do him service.

Alleluia. Alleluia, alleluia. ℣. His dominion is an everlasting dominion, which shall not pass away: and his kingdom that which shall not be destroyed. Alleluia.

Gospel. John 18:33

T THAT TIME: Pilate said unto Jesus: Art thou the King of the Jews? Jesus answered him, Sayest thou this thing of thyself, or did others tell it thee of me? Pilate answered, Am I a Jew? Thine own nation and the chief priests have delivered thee unto me: what hast thou done? Jesus answered, My kingdom is not of this world: if my kingdom were of this world, then would my servants fight, that I should not be delivered to the Jews: but now is my kingdom not from hence. Pilate therefore said unto him, Art thou a king then? Jesus answered, Thou sayest that I am a king. To this end was I born, and for this cause came I into the world, that I should bear witness unto the truth. Every one that is of the truth heareth my voice.

Offertory. Desire of me, and I shall give thee the heathen for thine inheritance, and the utmost parts of the earth for thy possession.

Secret

E offer unto thee, O Lord, the victim of man's reconciliation: grant, we beseech thee; that he, whom we offer in these present sacrifices, may himself grant unto all nations the gifts of unity and peace, Jesus Christ thy Son our Lord. Who liveth.

¶ Commemoration is made of the Sunday occurring.

Communion. The Lord remaineth a King for ever: the Lord shall give his people the blessing of peace.

All Hallows   # Proper of Saints   1 November

Postcommunion

O LORD, who hast bestowed on us the food of immortality, we beseech thee: that we, who glory to fight beneath the banner of Christ the King, may with him be enabled to reign for ever on the heavenly throne. Who liveth.

¶ Commemoration is made of the Sunday occurring.

¶ The Last Gospel is of the Sunday occurring.

All Hallows

Second Class Double
1 November

Opening Sentence. The righteous live for evermore, but their reward is with the Lord. (Wis. 5:15)

Introit

REJOICE we all in the Lord, keeping feast day in honour of all the saints: in whose solemnity the Angels rejoice, and glorify the Son of God. *Ps.* Rejoice in the Lord, O ye righteous: for it becometh well the just to be thankful.

Collect

ALMIGHTY and everlasting God, who in one solemnity hast vouchsafed unto us to venerate the merits of all thy Saints: we beseech thee; that, at the intercession of so great a multitude, thou wouldest bestow upon us, who entreat thee, the abundance of thy mercy. Through.

Epistle. Revelation 7:2

IN THOSE DAYS: Behold, I, John, saw another angel ascending from the east, having the seal of the living God: and he cried with a loud voice to the four angels, to whom it was given to hurt the earth and the sea, Saying, Hurt not the earth, neither the sea, nor the trees, till we have sealed the servants of our God in their foreheads. And I heard the number of them which were sealed: and there were sealed an hundred and forty and four thousand of all the tribes of the children of Israel. After this I beheld, and, lo, a great multitude, which no man could number, of all nations, and kindreds, and people, and tongues, stood before the throne, and before the Lamb, clothed with white robes, and palms in their hands; And cried with a loud voice, saying, Salvation to our God which sitteth upon the throne, and unto the Lamb. And all the angels stood round about the throne, and about the elders and the four beasts, and fell before the throne on their faces, and worshipped God, Saying, Amen: Blessing, and glory, and wisdom, and thanksgiving, and honour, and power, and might, be unto our God for ever and ever. Amen. And one of the elders answered, saying unto me, What are these which are arrayed in white robes? and whence came they? And I said unto him, Sir, thou knowest. And he said to me, These are they which came out of great tribulation, and have washed their robes, and made them white in the blood of the Lamb. Therefore are they before the throne of God, and serve him day and night in his temple: and he that sitteth on the throne shall dwell among them. They shall hunger no more, neither thirst any more; neither shall the sun light on them, nor any heat. For the Lamb which is in the midst of the throne shall feed them, and shall lead them unto living fountains of waters: and God shall wipe away all tears from their eyes.

Gradual. O fear the Lord, all ye Saints of his: for they that fear him lack nothing. ℣. But they that seek the Lord, shall want no manner of thing that is good.

Alleluia. Alleluia, alleluia. ℣. Come unto me all ye that travail and are heavy laden: and I will refresh you. Alleluia.

Gospel. Matthew 5:1

AT THAT TIME: Jesus, seeing the multitudes, went up into a mountain: and when he was set, his disciples came unto him: And he opened his mouth, and taught them, saying, Blessed are the poor in spirit: for theirs is the kingdom of heaven. Blessed are they that mourn: for they shall be comforted. Blessed are the meek: for they shall inherit the earth. Blessed are they which do hunger and thirst after righteousness: for they shall be filled. Blessed are the merciful: for they shall obtain mercy. Blessed are the pure in heart: for they shall see God. Blessed are the peacemakers: for they shall be called the children of God. Blessed are they which are persecuted for righteousness' sake: for theirs is the kingdom of heaven. Blessed are ye, when men shall revile you, and persecute you, and shall say all manner of evil against you falsely, for my sake. Rejoice, and be exceeding glad: for great is your reward in heaven: for so persecuted they the prophets which were before you.

Offertory. The souls of the righteous are in the hand of God, and there shall no torment of malice touch them: in the sight of the unwise they seemed to die: but they are in peace, alleluia.

All Souls   Proper of Saints   2 November

Secret

E offer unto thee, O Lord, the gifts of our devotion: that they may both be pleasing unto thee for the honour of all the Just, and through thy mercy may be rendered profitable for our salvation. Through.

Communion. Blessed are the pure in heart, for they shall see God; blessed are the peacemakers, for they shall be called the children of God; blessed are they which are persecuted for righteousness' sake, for theirs is the kingdom of heaven.

Postcommunion

RANT, we beseech thee, O Lord, unto thy faithful people ever to rejoice in the veneration of all thy Saints: and to be defended by their perpetual supplication. Through.

ALL SOULS

Double
2 November

(The First Mass)

Introit

EST eternal grant unto them, O Lord: and let light perpetual shine upon them. *Ps.* Thou, O God, art praised in Sion, and unto thee shall the vow be performed in Jerusalem: thou that hearest the prayer, unto thee shall all flesh come.

Collect

GOD, the Creator and Redeemer of all the faithful: grant unto the souls of thy servants and handmaids the remission of all their sins: that through devout supplications they may obtain the pardon which they have alway desired. Who livest.

Epistle. 1 Corinthians 15:51

BRETHREN: Behold, I shew you a mystery; We shall not all sleep, but we shall all be changed, In a moment, in the twinkling of an eye, at the last trump: for the trumpet shall sound, and the dead shall be raised incorruptible, and we shall be changed. For this corruptible must put on incorruption, and this mortal must put on immortality. So when this corruptible

Proper of Saints

2 November — All Souls

shall have put on incorruption, and this mortal shall have put on immortality, then shall be brought to pass the saying that is written, Death is swallowed up in victory. O death, where is thy sting? O grave, where is thy victory? The sting of death is sin; and the strength of sin is the law. But thanks be to God, which giveth us the victory through our Lord Jesus Christ.

Gradual. Rest eternal grant unto them, O Lord: and let light perpetual shine upon them. ℣. The righteous shall be had in everlasting remembrance: he will not be afraid of any evil tidings.

Tract. Absolve, O Lord, the souls of all the faithful departed from every bond of sin. ℣. And by the help of thy grace may they be worthy to escape the avenging judgment. ℣. And enjoy the bliss of everlasting light.

Sequence

Day of wrath and doom impending,
David's word with Sibyl's blending:
Heaven and earth in ashes ending.

Oh, what fear man's bosom rendeth
When from heaven the judge descendeth,
On whose sentence all dependeth!

Wondrous sound the trumpet flingeth,
Through earth's sepulchres it ringeth,
All before the throne it bringeth.

Death is struck, and nature quaking,
All creation is awaking,
To its judge an answer making.

Lo! the book, exactly worded,
Wherein all hath been recorded,
Thence shall judgement be awarded.

When the judge his seat attaineth,
And each hidden deed arraigneth,
Nothing unavenged remaineth.

What shall I, frail man, be pleading?
Who for me be interceding,
When the just are mercy needing?

King of majesty tremendous,
Who dost free salvation send us,
Fount of pity, then befriend us!

Think, kind Jesu, my salvation
Caused thy wondrous Incarnation:
Leave me not to reprobation.

Faint and weary thou hast sought me:
On the Cross of suffering bought me:
Shall such grace be vainly brought me?

Righteous judge, for sin's pollution
Grant thy gift of absolution
Ere the day of retribution.

Guilty, now I pour my moaning:
All my shame with anguish owning:

All Souls # Proper of Saints 2 November

Spare, O God, thy suppliant groaning.

Through the sinful Mary shriven,
Through the dying thief forgiven,
Thou to me a hope hast given.

Worthless are my prayers and sighing:
Yet, good Lord, in grace complying,
Rescue me from fires undying.

With thy sheep a place provide me,
From the goats afar divide me,
To thy right hand do thou guide me.

When the wicked are confounded,
Doomed to flames of woe unbounded:
Call me, with thy Saints surrounded.

Low I kneel, with heart submission,
See, like ashes, my contrition:
Help me in my last condition.

Ah! that day of tears and mourning,
From the dust of earth returning,
Man for judgment must prepare him.

Spare, O God, in mercy spare him:
Lord, all-pitying, Jesu blest,
Grant them thine eternal rest. Amen.

Gospel. John 5:25

T THAT TIME: Jesus said to the multitude of the Jews: Verily, verily, I say unto you, The hour is coming, and now is, when the dead shall hear the voice of the Son of God: and they that hear shall live. For as the Father hath life in himself; so hath he given to the Son to have life in himself; And hath given him authority to execute judgment also, because he is the Son of man. Marvel not at this: for the hour is coming, in the which all that are in the graves shall hear his voice, And shall come forth; they that have done good, unto the resurrection of life; and they that have done evil, unto the resurrection of damnation.

Offertory. O Lord Jesu Christ, King of glory, deliver the souls of all the faithful departed from the pains of hell and from the depths of the pit: deliver them from the lion's mouth, that hell devour them not, that they fall not into darkness: but let the standard-bearer, Saint Michael, bring them into the holy light: Which of old thou didst promise unto Abraham and his seed. ℣. We offer unto thee, O Lord, sacrifices of prayer and praise: do thou receive them for the souls of those whose memory we this day recall: make them, O Lord, to pass from death unto life. Which of old thou didst promise unto Abraham and his seed.

Proper of Saints

2 November — All Souls

Secret

WE beseech thee, O Lord, look favourably upon the sacrifices which we offer unto thee for the souls of thy servants and handmaids: that, as thou hast bestowed on them the merit of the Christian faith, thou wouldest grant them the reward of the same. Through.

Communion. Let light eternal shine upon them, O Lord: With thy Saints for evermore: for thou art gracious. ℣. Rest eternal grant unto them, O Lord: and let light perpetual shine upon them. With thy Saints for evermore: for thou art gracious.

Postcommunion

WE beseech thee, O Lord, that the prayer of thy suppliant people may be profitable for the souls of thy servants and handmaids: that thou wouldest deliver them from all their sins, and make them to be partakers of thy redemption. Who livest.

ALL SOULS

(The Second Mass)
Introit

REST eternal grant unto them, O Lord: and let light perpetual shine upon them. *Ps.* Thou, O God, art praised in Sion, and unto thee shall the vow be performed in Jerusalem: thou that hearest the prayer, unto thee shall all flesh come.

Collect

O GOD, the Lord of mercies: grant unto the souls of thy servants and handmaids a place of refreshment, the blessedness of rest, and the brightness of thy light. Through.

Epistle. 2 Maccabees 12:43

IN THOSE DAYS: That most valiant man Judas, when he had made a collection man by man to the sum of two thousand drachmas of silver, he sent unto Jerusalem to offer a sacrifice for sin, doing therein right well and honourably, in that he took thought for a resurrection. For if he were not expecting that they that had fallen would rise again, it were superfluous and idle to pray for the dead. (And if he did it looking unto an honourable

All Souls — Proper of Saints — 2 November

memorial of gratitude laid up for them that die in godliness, holy and godly was the thought.) Wherefore he made the propitiation for them that had died, that they might be released from their sin.

Gradual. Rest eternal grant unto them, O Lord: and let light perpetual shine upon them. ℣. The righteous shall be had in everlasting remembrance: he will not be afraid of any evil tidings.

Tract. Absolve, O Lord, the souls of all the faithful departed from every bond of sin. ℣. And by the help of thy grace may they be worthy to escape the avenging judgment. ℣. And enjoy the bliss of everlasting light.

❡ The Sequence **Dies irae** is here said or sung (p. 535).

Gospel. John 6:37

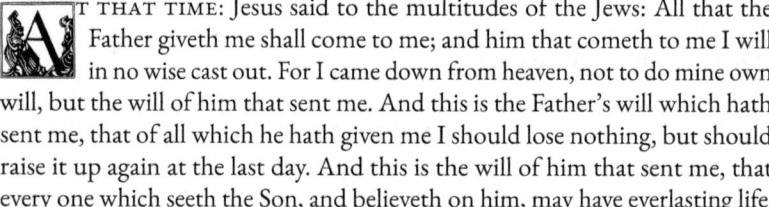T THAT TIME: Jesus said to the multitudes of the Jews: All that the Father giveth me shall come to me; and him that cometh to me I will in no wise cast out. For I came down from heaven, not to do mine own will, but the will of him that sent me. And this is the Father's will which hath sent me, that of all which he hath given me I should lose nothing, but should raise it up again at the last day. And this is the will of him that sent me, that every one which seeth the Son, and believeth on him, may have everlasting life: and I will raise him up at the last day.

Offertory. O Lord Jesu Christ, King of glory, deliver the souls of all the faithful departed from the pains of hell and from the depths of the pit: deliver them from the lion's mouth, that hell devour them not, that they fall not into darkness: but let the standard-bearer, Saint Michael, bring them into the holy light: Which of old thou didst promise unto Abraham and his seed. ℣. We offer unto thee, O Lord, sacrifices of prayer and praise: do thou receive them for the souls of those whose memory we this day recall: make them, O Lord, to pass from death unto life. Which of old thou didst promise unto Abraham and his seed.

Secret

BE favourable, O Lord, to our supplications for the souls of thy servants and handmaids, for whom we offer unto thee this sacrifice of praise: that thou wouldest vouchsafe to join them to the fellowship of thy Saints. Through.

Communion. Let light eternal shine upon them, O Lord: With thy Saints for evermore: for thou art gracious. ℣. Rest eternal grant unto them, O Lord: and let light perpetual shine upon them. With thy Saints for evermore: for thou art gracious.

Postcommunion

RANT, we beseech thee, O Lord: that the souls of thy servants and handmaids, being purged by these sacrifices, may obtain both pardon and everlasting rest. Through.

All Souls

(The Third Mass)
Introit

EST eternal grant unto them, O Lord: and let light perpetual shine upon them. *Ps.* Thou, O God, art praised in Sion, and unto thee shall the vow be performed in Jerusalem: thou that hearest the prayer, unto thee shall all flesh come.

Collect

O GOD, the giver of pardon and lover of man's salvation: we beseech thee of thy mercy to grant; that the souls of thy servants and handmaids, who have passed out of this world, may, at the intercession of the blessed Mary ever Virgin and of all thy Saints, attain unto the fellowship of eternal blessedness. Through.

Epistle. Revelation 14:13

IN THOSE DAYS: I heard a voice from heaven saying unto me, Write, Blessed are the dead which die in the Lord from henceforth: Yea, saith the Spirit, that they may rest from their labours; and their works do follow them.

Gradual. Rest eternal grant unto them, O Lord: and let light perpetual shine upon them. ℣. The righteous shall be had in everlasting remembrance: he will not be afraid of any evil tidings.

Tract. Absolve, O Lord, the souls of all the faithful departed from every bond of sin. ℣. And by the help of thy grace may they be worthy to escape the avenging judgment. ℣. And enjoy the bliss of everlasting light.

All Souls   **Proper of Saints**   2 November

℟ The Sequence **Dies irae** is here said or sung (p. 535).

Gospel. John 6:51

AT THAT TIME: Jesus said to the multitude of the Jews: I am the living bread which came down from heaven: if any man eat of this bread, he shall live for ever: and the bread that I will give is my flesh, which I will give for the life of the world. The Jews therefore strove among themselves, saying, How can this man give us his flesh to eat? Then Jesus said unto them, Verily, verily, I say unto you, Except ye eat the flesh of the Son of man, and drink his blood, ye have no life in you. Whoso eateth my flesh, and drinketh my blood, hath eternal life; and I will raise him up at the last day.

Offertory. O Lord Jesu Christ, King of glory, deliver the souls of all the faithful departed from the pains of hell and from the depths of the pit: deliver them from the lion's mouth, that hell devour them not, that they fall not into darkness: but let the standard-bearer, Saint Michael, bring them into the holy light: Which of old thou didst promise unto Abraham and his seed. ℣. We offer unto thee, O Lord, sacrifices of prayer and praise: do thou receive them for the souls of those whose memory we this day recall: make them, O Lord, to pass from death unto life. Which of old thou didst promise unto Abraham and his seed.

Secret

O GOD, whose mercies are without number, graciously receive our humble prayers: and through these sacraments of our salvation grant unto the souls of all the faithful departed, to whom thou hast given the confession of thy name, the remission of all their sins. Through.

Communion. Let light eternal shine upon them, O Lord: With thy Saints for evermore: for thou art gracious. ℣. Rest eternal grant unto them, O Lord: and let light perpetual shine upon them. With thy Saints for evermore: for thou art gracious.

Postcommunion

GRANT, we beseech thee, Almighty and Merciful God: that the souls of thy servants and handmaids, for whom we have offered unto thy Majesty this sacrifice of praise; may by the power of this sacrament be cleansed from all their sins, and by thy mercy obtain the blessedness of everlasting light. Through.

Table of Prayers

❡ These are provided for the additional Prayers during Mass.

Of St. Mary in Advent

Collect

GOD, who wast pleased that thy Word should take flesh of the womb of the blessed Virgin Mary at the message of an Angel: grant to thy humble servants; that we, who believe her to be truly the Mother of God, may be aided by her intercession in thy sight. Through the same.

Secret

E beseech thee, O Lord, stablish in our hearts the mysteries of thy true religion: that, as we believe thy Son, conceived of a Virgin, to be very God and very man; so by the power of his life-giving resurrection we may be found worthy to attain unto everlasting felicity. Through the same.

Postcommunion

E beseech thee, O Lord, pour thy grace into our hearts: that, as we have known the incarnation of thy Son Christ by the message of an Angel; so by his cross and passion we may be brought unto the glory of his resurrection. (Through the same.)

Of St. Mary after Christmas

Collect

GOD, who by the virgin child-bearing of blessed Mary hast bestowed upon mankind the rewards of eternal salvation: grant, we beseech thee; that we may perceive her intercession for us, through whom we have been counted worthy to receive the author of life, Jesus Christ thy Son, our Lord. (Who liveth.)

Secret

HROUGH thy mercy, O Lord, and the intercession of blessed Mary ever Virgin, may this oblation avail for our prosperity and peace both now and for ever. (Through.)

Postcommunion

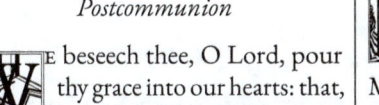AY this communion, O Lord, cleanse us from guilt: and at the intercession of blessed Mary the Virgin Mother of God, make us partakers of thy heavenly healing. (Through the same.)

Table of Prayers

Of St. Mary in Eastertide

Collect

RANT, we beseech thee, O Lord God, that we thy servants may enjoy perpetual health of mind and of body: and, at the glorious intercession of blessed Mary ever Virgin, be delivered from present sadness, and rejoice in everlasting gladness. (Through.)

Secret

HROUGH thy mercy, O Lord, and the intercession of blessed Mary ever Virgin, may this oblation avail for our prosperity and peace, both now and ever. (Through.)

Postcommunion

RANT, we beseech thee, O Lord: that we who have received these aids to our salvation may at all times and in all places be protected by the advocacy of blessed Mary ever Virgin; in whose honour we have made these offerings to thy majesty. (Through.)

Of Saints

Collect

EFEND us, O Lord, we beseech thee, from all dangers of mind and of body: and at the intercession of the blessed and glorious Mother of God, Mary ever Virgin, with blessed Joseph, thy blessed Apostles Peter and Paul, blessed *N.*, and all the Saints, graciously grant us health and peace; that all adversities and errors being done away, thy Church may serve thee in freedom and quietness. (Through the same.)

Secret

RACIOUSLY hear us, O God our Saviour: and by the power of this sacrament defend us from all enemies of mind and of body; granting us grace in this world, and glory in that which is to come. (Through.)

Postcommunion

E beseech thee, O Lord, that the gift now offered in this divine sacrament may cleanse and defend us: that at the intercession of blessed Mary the Virgin Mother of God, of blessed Joseph, of thy blessed Apostles Peter and Paul, of blessed *N.* and of all the Saints; it may set us free from every perverse way, and deliver us from all adversities. (Through the same.)

Table of Prayers

Against the Persecutors of the Church

Collect

E beseech thee, O Lord, mercifully to hear the prayers of thy Church: that all adversities and errors being done away, she may serve thee in freedom and quietness. Through.

Secret

EFEND us, O Lord, who wait upon thy mysteries: that we, cleaving fast to things heavenly, may serve thee both in body and soul. Through.

Postcommunion

E beseech thee, O Lord our God: that we, whom thou makest to rejoice in the partaking of heavenly things, may by thee be defended against all earthly perils. Through.

For the Chief Bishop

Collect

GOD, the pastor and ruler of all the faithful, mercifully look upon thy servant N., whom thou hast been pleased to set as pastor over thy Church; grant him, we beseech thee, to be in word and conversation a wholesome example to the people committed to his charge; that he with them may attain unto everlasting life. Through.

Secret

OOK favourably, we beseech thee, O Lord, upon the gifts which we offer: and guide with thy continual protection thy servant N., whom thou hast been pleased to set as pastor over thy Church. Through.

Postcommunion

E beseech thee, O Lord, that the divine sacrament which we have here received may be our protection: and together with the flock entrusted to his charge ever save and defend thy servant N.; whom thou hast been pleased to set as pastor over thy Church. Through.

Table of Prayers

OF THE HOLY GHOST

Collect

OD, who didst teach the hearts of thy faithful people, by the sending to them the light of thy Holy Spirit: grant us by the same Spirit to have a right judgment in all things; and evermore to rejoice in his holy comfort. (Through . . . in the unity of the same Holy Spirit.)

Secret

ANCTIFY, we beseech thee, O Lord, the gifts which we offer: and cleanse our hearts by the enlightening of the Holy Spirit. (Through . . . in the unity of the same Holy Spirit.)

Postcommunion

OUR thy Holy Spirit upon us, O Lord, and cleanse our hearts: that they may be made fruitful by the inward sprinkling of his dew. (Through . . . in the unity of the same Holy Spirit.)

FOR THE LIVING AND DEPARTED

Collect

LMIGHTY and everlasting God, who hast dominion both of the living and of the dead, and hast mercy upon all who thou foreknowest will be thine in faith and works: we humbly beseech thee; that all those for whom we are minded to pour forth our prayers, whether in this present world they still be held in the flesh, or being delivered from the body have passed into that which is to come, may at the intercession of all thy Saints obtain of thy bountiful goodness the remission of all their sins. Through.

Secret

GOD, to whom alone is known the number of the elect, whom thou hast appointed unto heavenly felicity: grant, we beseech thee: that at the intercession of all thy Saints, the names of all those who have been commended to our prayers, and of all thy faithful people, may ever remain written in the book of those that are predestined to everlasting blessedness. Through.

Postcommunion

LMIGHTY and merciful God, cleanse us, we pray thee, by the sacraments which we have received: and, at the intercession of all thy Saints, grant; that this thy sacrament may not bring upon us guilt to our punishment but pardon to our salvation: that it may cleanse away sins, that it may confirm the feeble, that it may defend us against every danger in this world: that it may obtain for thy faithful people both living and dead the remission of all their sins. Through.

Table of Prayers

❧ The following propers may also be used when ad libitum prayers are permitted.

To Ask the Prayers of the Saints

Collect

RANT, we beseech thee, almighty God: that the intercession of holy Mary, Mother of God, and of all the holy Apostles, Martyrs, Confessors and Virgins, and of all thy elect, may everywhere cause us to rejoice; that while we call to mind their merits, we may perceive their advocacy. Through the same.

Secret

CCEPT, O Lord, the gifts we offer: and, at the intercession of blessed Mary, ever Virgin, with all thy Saints, defend us from all perils. Through.

Postcommunion

RANT, we beseech thee, O Lord: that we who have received these heavenly sacraments, in veneration of the memory of blessed Mary, ever Virgin, and of all thy Saints; may attain in everlasting joys the fulfilment of our service in this life. Through.

For all Estates of Men in the Church

Collect

LMIGHTY and everlasting God, by whose Spirit the whole body of the Church is governed and sanctified: receive our supplications and prayers, which we offer before thee for all estates of men thy holy Church; that every member of the same, in his vocation and ministry, may truly and godly serve thee. Through . . . in the unity of the same Holy Spirit.

Secret

RANT unto thy servants, O Lord, the pardon of their sins, comfort in their life, and thy continual governance: so that they, serving thee aright, may continually obtain thy mercy. Through.

Postcommunion

ELIVER, O Lord, we beseech thee, thy servants who call upon thee from all sin and from every foe: that they, walking in godly conversation, may be hurt by no adversity. Through.

Table of Prayers

For the Emperor

Collect

GOD, the protector of all kingdoms, and specially of the Christian empire: grant unto thy servant, our emperor, *N.*, to labour with wisdom for the triumph of virtue, that he who by thy institution is a prince, may ever by thy gift be powerful. Through.

¶ Note, If he be not crowned, say Emperor-elect.

Secret

eceive, O Lord, the prayers and offerings of thy Church who calleth upon thee for the safety of thy servant: and for the protection of the faithful peoples perform with thy mighty arm thy wondrous works of old, that they may overcome the enemies of peace, and serve thee in freedom and safety. Through.

Postcommunion

GOD, who didst prepare the Roman empire for the preaching of the Gospel of the eternal King: defend thy servant, our emperor, *N.*, with thy heavenly armour, that the peace of the churches may be troubled by no war nor tumult. Through.

For the King

Collect

e beseech thee, almighty God: that thy servant *N.*, our King, who by thy mercy hath received the government of this realm, may also obtain an increase of every virtue; that, being meetly adorned therewith, he may flee from sin and iniquity, and by thy grace may attain unto thee who art the way, the truth, and the life. Through.

Secret

anctify, we beseech thee, O Lord, the gifts which we offer: that they may be made unto us the Body and Blood of thine only-begotten Son; and of thy great goodness grant that they may at all times be profitable unto our King, both for the obtaining of health of body and soul, and for the fulfilling of the charge committed unto him. Through.

Postcommunion

ay this saving oblation, O Lord, keep thy servant, *N.*, our King, from all adversity: that he may preserve peace and tranquillity for thy Church; and after the course of this life may attain unto his eternal inheritance. Through.

Table of Prayers

For Prelates & Congregations Committed to their Charge

Collect

LMIGHTY and everlasting God, who alone workest great marvels: send down upon our Bishops, and all Congregations committed to their charge, the healthful spirit of thy grace; and that they may truly please thee, pour upon them the continual dew of thy blessing. Through.

Secret

OOK down, O Lord, in mercy on the sacrifices of thy servants, which we devoutly celebrate for them unto the honour of thy name: that they may perceive the same to be profitable for the healing of their souls. Through.

Postcommunion

SSIST, O Lord, with thy continual protection those whom thou dost refresh with this heavenly gift: and grant that, as thou never failest to comfort them, so thou wouldest make them worthy of everlasting redemption. Through.

For the Congregation and Family

Collect

E beseech thee, O Lord, at the intercession of blessed Mary, ever Virgin, to defend this thy family from all adversities: that they, devoutly serving thee with all their hearts, may by thy mercy be protected from the assaults of their enemies. Through.

Secret

LMIGHTY God, we beseech thee to accept this offering of our devotion: that by the power of this sacrament we thy servants may be protected against all adversities. Through.

Postcommunion

RANT, we beseech thee, O merciful God: that we who have here received the gifts of our redemption; may through the celebration of the same obtain the help of thy defence against all adversities. Through.

Table of Prayers

For the Preservation of Concord in the Congregation

Collect

GOD, who art the author of peace and lover of charity: grant unto thy servants that true unity which is according to thy will; that we may be delivered from all the temptations which beset us. Through.

Secret

E beseech thee, O Lord, mercifully to accept these sacrifices: and grant that we who pray to be absolved from our own offences may not be burdened with the sins of other men. Through.

Postcommunion

OUR forth upon us, O Lord, the Spirit of thy charity: that as thou hast fulfilled us with one heavenly bread, so of thy goodness thou wouldest make us to be of one heart and mind. Through . . . in the unity of the same.

Against Persecutors & Malefactors

Collect

E beseech thee, O Lord, to bring down the pride of our enemies: and by the right hand of thy power destroy their obstinacy. Through.

Secret

RANT, O Lord, that by the power of this mystery, we may be cleansed from our secret faults, and delivered from the snares of our enemies. Through.

Postcommunion

EHOLD, O God our defender, and protect us against the dangers of our enemies: that we may be delivered from all distress, and serve thee in freedom of spirit. Through.

For any Necessity

Collect

GOD, our refuge and strength, who art the author of all godliness: be ready, we beseech thee, to hear the devout prayers of thy Church; and grant that those things which we ask faithfully we may obtain effectually. Through.

Secret

RANT, O merciful God: that this saving oblation may continually deliver us from our sins, and shield us from all adversities. Through.

Table of Prayers

Postcommunion

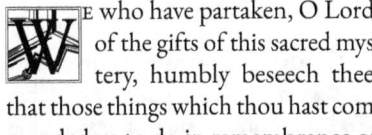E who have partaken, O Lord, of the gifts of this sacred mystery, humbly beseech thee: that those things which thou hast commanded us to do in remembrance of thee may be profitable for the assistance of our infirmity. Who livest.

In any Calamity

Collect

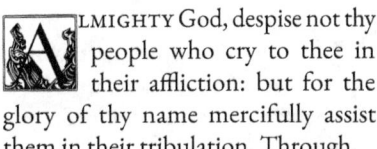LMIGHTY God, despise not thy people who cry to thee in their affliction: but for the glory of thy name mercifully assist them in their tribulation. Through.

Secret

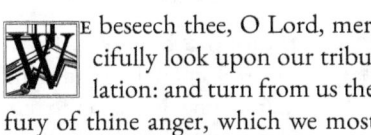ERCIFULLY accept, O Lord, these sacrifices which thou hast ordained to be the propitiation of our sins, and the means whereby of thy loving mercy we are restored to salvation. Through.

Postcommunion

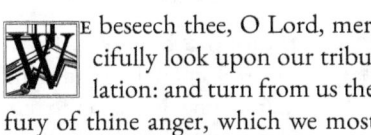E beseech thee, O Lord, mercifully look upon our tribulation: and turn from us the fury of thine anger, which we most righteously deserve. Through.

In time of Famine

Collect

RANT to us, we beseech thee, O Lord, the fulfilment of our devout supplications: and graciously turn away this famine; that the hearts of men may know that in thine anger thou sendest forth such scourges, and in thy mercy makest them to cease. Through.

Secret

GOD, who dost sustain the twofold nature of man by the food of the gifts we offer, and by this sacrament dost renew the same: grant, we beseech thee; that these thy gifts may never be lacking for our assistance both in body and soul. Through.

Postcommunion

LORD, support us, we beseech thee, with temporal food: even as thou dost vouchsafe to dwell in us in everlasting mysteries. Through.

Table of Prayers

In time of Earthquake

Collect

LMIGHTY and everlasting God, who lookest upon the earth, and makest it to tremble: spare them that fear thee, be merciful to them that call upon thee; that whereas we are sore afraid for thy wrath that shaketh the foundations of the earth, we may likewise feel thy mercy when thou healest the sores thereof. Through.

Secret

GOD, who hast laid the foundations of the earth that they should never be moved, receive the prayers and oblations of thy people: put far from us the present perils of earthquake, and turn the terrors of thy divine anger into a wholesome medicine for the safety of mankind; that they who are of the earth, and shall return to earth, may rejoice to be made citizens of heaven by holy conversation. Through.

Postcommunion

PROTECT us, O Lord, we beseech thee, who receive thy holy things: and by thy heavenly gift stablish the earth which we see trembling for our sins; that the hearts of men may know that in thine anger thou sendest forth thy scourges, and in thy mercy makest them to cease. Through.

For Rain

Collect

GOD, in whom we live, and move, and have our being: grant us such a seasonable rain; that we, receiving those things that be requisite for our necessities in this life, may the more confidently seek the things that are eternal. Through.

Secret

E beseech thee, O Lord, mercifully to receive the gifts which we offer: and send unto us a seasonable rain that may suffice for our necessities. Through.

Postcommunion

RANT us, O Lord, we beseech thee, a refreshing rain: and graciously water the parched face of the earth by showers from heaven. Through.

For Fine Weather

Collect

RACIOUSLY hear us, O Lord, who call upon thee: and grant fair weather in answer to our prayers; that we, who are justly afflicted for our sins, may by thy preventing mercy feel thy pity. Through.

Table of Prayers

Secret

ORD, we pray thee, that thy grace may alway prevent and follow us: and graciously accept these oblations which for our sins we bring for consecration unto thy name; that, through the intercession of thy Saints, they may be profitable for the safety of us all. Through.

Postcommunion

LMIGHTY God, we humbly beseech thy mercy: that thou wouldest assuage this plague of immoderate rains, and vouchsafe to shew forth on us the gladness of thy countenance. Through.

Against Storms

Collect

E beseech thee, O Lord, that all spiritual wickedness may be driven far from thy house: and that the malignity of the tempests of the air be likewise dispelled. Through.

Secret

E offer unto thee, O Lord, our praises and gifts, rendering thanks for the blessings bestowed upon us, and ever humbly praying for the continuance of the same. Through.

Postcommunion

LMIGHTY and everlasting God, who dost heal us by thy chastisement, and preserve us by thy pardon: grant unto thy suppliant people; that in tranquillity of weather we may rejoice in the comfort we have ever desired, and may alway make use of thy bountiful goodness. Through.

Against Cattle Disease

Collect

GOD, who even by the dumb beasts hast brought comfort to man's labour: we humbly beseech thee; that forasmuch as without them the sustenance of man cannot but fail, so thou wouldest preserve them for our enjoyment. Through.

Secret

OOK mercifully, O Lord, upon the sacrifices which we offer: and of thy mercy grant us thy help in our time. Through.

Postcommunion

RANT, O Lord, that thy faithful people, being filled with thy blessing, may be preserved both in body and soul: that they may render unto thee worthy service, and evermore receive the benefits of thy mercy. Through.

Table of Prayers

For the Priest Himself

Collect

LMIGHTY and merciful God, graciously give heed to my humble prayers: and make me thy servant, to whom for no merits of my own but by the boundless compassion of thy bounty thou hast vouchsafed to serve thee in these heavenly mysteries, a worthy minister at the sacred altars; that the words which I utter with my lips may by thy sanctifying power be brought to good effect. Through.

Secret

LEANSE me, O Lord, by the power of this sacrament, from all the stains of my sins: and grant; that with the help of thy grace I may be made worthy thereby to fulfil the ministry committed to my charge. Through.

Postcommunion

LMIGHTY and everlasting God, who hast vouchsafed to me, a sinner, to stand before thy sacred altars, and to praise the power of thy holy name: mercifully grant to me by the mystery of this sacrament the pardon of my sins; that I may offer unto thy majesty true and worthy service. Through.

To ask for Tears

Collect

LMIGHTY and most merciful God, who didst bring forth living water from the rock for thy thirsting people: draw out from our stony hearts the tears of repentance; that we, worthily lamenting our sins, may of thy mercy obtain forgiveness of the same. Through.

Secret

LORD God, we beseech thee, look down in mercy on this oblation, which we offer to thy majesty for our sins: and draw forth from our eyes such streams of tears, as shall quench the burning flames which we most righteously deserve. Through.

Postcommunion

LORD God, mercifully pour the grace of thy Holy Spirit into our heart: that we may be enabled thereby with tears of sorrow to wash away the defilements of our sins; that like as we do desire thy merciful pardon, so of thy bountiful goodness we may effectually receive the same. Through... in the unity of the same.

Table of Prayers

For the Remission of Sins

Collect

GOD, who dost not cast out sinners, and of thy loving mercy sparest them that are penitent, howsoever they sin against thee: mercifully incline to the prayers of thy humble servants, and enlighten our hearts; that we may be enabled to fulfil all that thou dost command. Through.

Secret

ET this present sacrifice, O Lord, which we offer to thee for our offences, be an acceptable offering unto thee: and avail for salvation both to the living and the dead. Through.

Postcommunion

LMIGHTY God, graciously hear the prayers of this thy family: and grant; that, like as we have received these holy things from thee, so of thy bounty they may be preserved pure and undefiled within us. Through.

For Public Penitents

Collect

LMIGHTY and everlasting God, of thy great goodness forgive the sins of thy servants who confess the same to thee: that they whose consciences by sin are accused may not be delivered unto punishment, but may obtain of thy loving mercy pardon and forgiveness. Through.

Secret

RANT, we beseech thee, almighty and merciful God: that this saving oblation may continually deliver thy servants from their offences, and defend them against all adversities. Through.

Postcommunion

LMIGHTY and merciful God, who wouldest not the death of sinners, but rather that they should repent, and confess to thee, and amend their lives: look down upon these thy servants; and by these holy sacraments which we have received turn from them thy wrathful indignation, and grant them forgiveness of all their sins. Through.

For the Tempted and Troubled

Collect

GOD, who dost justify the wicked, and wouldest not the death of a sinner, we humbly beseech thy majesty: that thy servants who put their trust and confidence in thy mercy may be defended by the loving-kindness of thy heavenly succour and preserved by thy continual help; that in all temptations they may steadfastly cleave unto thy service. Through.

Table of Prayers

Secret

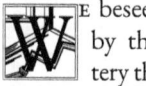E beseech thee, O Lord, that by the power of this mystery thou wouldest cleanse us from our faults, and absolve thy servants from all their offences. Through.

Postcommunion

RANT, we beseech thee, O Lord, that the sacraments which we have received may purify our hearts: and that thy servants may be delivered from all transgression; that whereas their consciences are bound by reason of their guilt, they may receive with gladness the plenteous healing of thy heavenly power. Through.

To repel Evil Thoughts

Collect

LMIGHTY and most merciful God, graciously regard our prayers: that, our hearts being delivered from the temptations of evil thoughts; we may be found worthy to be made a dwelling-place acceptable to thy Holy Spirit. Through . . . in the unity of the same Holy Spirit.

Secret

E here present unto thee, O Lord, these offerings for our salvation: that the thoughts of our hearts being purged from all uncleanness and preserved from harm, we may be enlightened by the grace of thy Holy Spirit. Through . . . in the unity of the same Holy Spirit.

Postcommunion

GOD, who lightenest every man that cometh into this world: lighten, we beseech thee, our hearts with the brightness of thy grace; that we may ever be enabled to think such things as be good and pleasing to thy majesty, and that we may love thee with an unfeigned heart. Through.

To obtain the Grace of Continence

Collect

INDLE, O Lord, with the fire of the Holy Spirit our reins and our hearts: that we, serving thee in pureness both of body and soul, may be found pleasing in thy sight. Through . . . in the unity of the same.

Secret

MITE asunder, O Lord, the chains of our sins: that we who seek to offer unto thee the sacrifice of praise in perfect freedom and in innocency of heart, may be restored by thee unto our first estate; that like as thou hast saved us by thy grace, so by thy pardon thou wouldest restore us again unto salvation. Through.

Postcommunion

SSIST us, O God, our helper and defender: that our heart and flesh being renewed by

Table of Prayers

the strength of continence and the newness of chastity, we who have offered unto thy majesty this sacrifice may be cleansed thereby from all temptations. Through.

To obtain the Grace of Humility

Collect

O GOD, who resistest the proud, and givest grace unto the humble: grant to us the virtue of true humility, after the pattern wherewith thine only-begotten Son manifested himself unto thy faithful people; that we may in no wise exalt ourselves to provoke thine anger, but may in lowliness of heart obtain thy grace. Through.

Secret

WE beseech thee, O Lord, that this oblation may obtain for us the grace of true humility: and likewise take from our hearts the lust of the flesh, and the lust of the eyes, and the pride of life; that living soberly, righteously, and godly, we may attain unto the rewards of everlasting life. Through.

Postcommunion

MAY this sacrament, O Lord, which we have received, cleanse us from every stain of sin: that we, shewing forth humility, may be brought unto thy heavenly kingdom. Through.

To obtain the Grace of Patience

Collect

O GOD, who by the long-suffering of thine only-begotten Son didst tread down the pride of our ancient enemy: grant us, we beseech thee, so rightly to call to mind the sufferings which of his goodness he bare for our sakes; that after his example we may patiently endure all our troubles and adversities. Through the same.

Secret

WE beseech thee, O Lord, graciously to receive our gifts and oblations: which we devoutly offer to thy majesty, beseeching thee that thou wouldest vouchsafe to bestow upon us the gift of patience. Through.

Postcommunion

WE beseech thee, O Lord, that we who have received these sacred mysteries may be restored thereby unto the grace from which we have fallen: that by thy continual protection both here and ever we may be enabled to endure patiently in all adversities. Through.

Table of Prayers

To obtain the Grace of Charity

Collect

GOD, who makest all things work together for good to them that love thee: pour into our hearts the steadfast affection of thy charity; that as thou dost put into our minds good desires, so we may not be turned from the same by any temptations. Through.

Secret

GOD, who by the sacraments and commandments dost renew us after thy likeness: stablish our goings in thy paths; that like as thou hast vouchsafed unto us the hope of obtaining thy gift of charity, so by these sacrifices which we offer thou wouldest make us effectually to be partakers of the same. Through.

Postcommunion

E beseech thee, O Lord, that the grace of the Holy Spirit may enlighten our hearts: that they may be abundantly renewed in the sweetness of perfect charity. Through . . . in the unity of the same Holy Spirit.

For Devoted Friends

Collect

GOD, who by the grace of thy Holy Spirit hast endued the hearts of thy faithful people with the gifts of charity: grant to thy servants and handmaids, for whom we implore thy mercy, safety of mind and body; that they may love thee with all their strength, and with pure affection perform such things as are acceptable unto thee. Through . . . in the unity of the same.

Secret

E beseech thee, O Lord, to have compassion upon thy servants and handmaids, for whom we offer unto thy majesty this sacrifice of praise: that through these holy things they may obtain the grace of thy heavenly benediction, and attain unto the glory of everlasting felicity. Through.

Postcommunion

LORD, who dost make us to taste of these divine mysteries, we humbly beseech thee: that like as we have offered these sacraments of salvation for the advancement in charity of thy servants; so they may be profitable unto them for their prosperity and peace. Through.

Table of Prayers

For Enemies

Collect

GOD, who art the lover of peace, and preserver of charity: grant unto all our enemies true peace and charity: and vouchsafe unto them remission of all their sins, and by thy mighty power deliver us from their snares. Through.

Secret

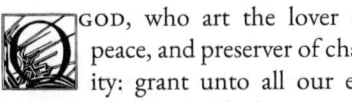E beseech thee, O Lord, graciously to accept the gifts which we offer: that by thy mercy we may be delivered from our enemies, and that they may receive of thee the pardon of their offences. Through.

Postcommunion

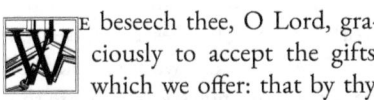AY this communion, O Lord, deliver us from our offences: and defend us against the snares of our enemies. Through.

For a Prisoner or Captive

Collect

GOD, who didst deliver blessed Peter the Apostle from his chains, and suffer him to depart unhurt: loose the chains of thy servant who now lieth in captivity; and by the merits of the same thine Apostle suffer him to depart unhurt. Through.

Secret

ET thy plenteous benediction, O Lord, descend upon these sacrifices: that they may loose the chains of this thy servant in captivity, and make us speedily to rejoice in his deliverance. Through.

Postcommunion

LORD, we beseech thee, graciously hear our prayers: and by these sacraments which we have received deliver thy servant from the chains of his captivity. Through.

For Those at Sea

Collect

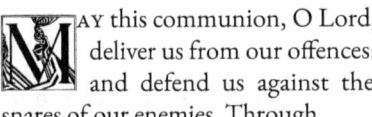GOD, who didst guide our fathers through the Red Sea, and didst bring them through the deep waters, singing praises to thy name: We humbly beseech thee; that thou wouldest defend thy servants now travelling by sea from all adversity, so that they, voyaging in tranquillity, may be brought by thee unto the haven where they would be. Through.

Secret

E beseech thee, O Lord, to receive the prayers of thy servants, with our sacrifices and oblations: that they for whom we celebrate these mysteries may be defended by thee against all adversities. Through.

Table of Prayers

Postcommunion

LORD, who hast sanctified us with this divine mystery, we humbly entreat and beseech thy majesty: that as thou dost suffer us to call to remembrance thy servants by means of these thy heavenly gifts; so through the wood of the holy Cross thou wouldest absolve them from their sins and deliver them from all perils and dangers. Through.

For the Safety of the Living

Collect

TRETCH forth, O Lord, upon thy faithful people the right hand of thy heavenly succour: that they, seeking thee with their whole heart, may be found worthy to obtain those things which they ask according to thy will. Through.

Secret

E beseech thee, O Lord, to have compassion on our prayers, and graciously to accept these oblations of thy faithful people, which we present before thee for their safety: and that none may ask amiss or fail in his petition; grant that those things which we ask faithfully, we may obtain effectually. Through.

Postcommunion

RANT, we beseech thee, O Lord, unto thy faithful people steadfastness in faith and singleness of heart: that they, being stablished in divine charity, may not by any temptations be parted from the fulness of the same. Through.

For the Living & Departed

Collect

LMIGHTY and everlasting God, who hast dominion both of the living and of the dead, and hast mercy upon all whom thou foreknowest will be thine in faith and works: we humbly beseech thee; that all those for whom we are minded to pour forth our prayers, whether in this present world they still be held in the flesh, or being delivered from the body have passed into that which is to come, may at the intercession of all thy Saints obtain of thy bountiful goodness the remission of all their sins. Through.

Secret

GOD, to whom alone is known the number of the elect, whom thou hast appointed unto heavenly felicity: grant, we beseech thee; that at the intercession of all thy Saints, the names of all those who have been commended to our prayers, and of all thy faithful people, may ever remain written in the book of those that are predestined to everlasting blessedness. Through.

Table of Prayers

Postcommunion

LMIGHTY and merciful God, cleanse us we pray thee, by the sacraments which we have received: and, at the intercession of all thy Saints, grant; that this thy sacrament may not bring upon us guilt to our punishment but pardon to our salvation: that it may cleanse away sins, that it may confirm the feeble, that it may defend us against every danger in this world: that it may obtain for thy faithful people both living and dead the remission of all their sins. Through.

¶ *The following propers are used for the faithful departed.*

For a Chief Bishop Departed

Collect

GOD, who of thy unspeakable providence didst vouchsafe to number thy servant *N.* in the company of thy high Priests: grant, we beseech thee; that like as he did fulfil on earth the office of thine Only-begotten Son, so he may be numbered in the everlasting fellowship of the same thy Saints. Through the same.

Secret

ECEIVE, O Lord, we beseech thee, these our sacrifices for the soul of thy servant *N.*, thy high Priest: that forasmuch as in this life thou didst give him the dignity of a Bishop, so thou wouldest bid him to be joined to the company of the Saints in thy heavenly kingdom. Through.

Postcommunion

AY thy merciful lovingkindness, which we implore, benefit, we beseech thee, O Lord, the soul of thy servant the *Metropolitan N.*: that, by thy mercy he may attain the eternal fellowship of him in whom he hoped and believed. Through.

For a Departed Bishop

Collect

GOD, who didst cause thy servant *N.* to enjoy the dignity of a Bishop in the apostolic Priesthood: grant, we beseech thee; that he may evermore be joined unto the fellowship of the same. Through.

Secret

CCEPT, O Lord, we beseech thee, the sacrifice which we offer to thee for the soul of thy servant and Bishop *N.*: that forasmuch as in this life thou didst bestow on him the dignity of a Bishop, so thou wouldest bid him to be joined unto the fellowship of thy Saints in the heavenly kingdom. Through.

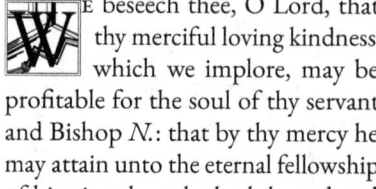

Table of Prayers

Postcommunion

E beseech thee, O Lord, that thy merciful loving kindness, which we implore, may be profitable for the soul of thy servant and Bishop *N*.: that by thy mercy he may attain unto the eternal fellowship of him in whom he hath hoped and believed. Through.

or,

Collect

RANT unto us, O Lord, that the *soul* of thy *servant* and *Bishop N.* (and *N.*), which thou hast taken out of the toil and conflict of this world, may be *partaker* of the fellowship of thy Saints. Through.

Secret

GRANT unto us, we beseech thee, O Lord: that like as by the offering of this oblation thou didst grant unto the whole world remission of sins so the *soul* of thy *servant* and *Bishop N.* (and *N.*) may be profited by the same. Through.

Postcommunion

E beseech thee, almighty God, that the *soul* of thy *servant* and *Bishop N.* (and *N.*), being purified by these sacrifices, may be found worthy to obtain thy pardon and everlasting refreshment. Through.

For a Departed Priest

Collect

GOD, who didst cause thy *servant N.* (and *N.*) to enjoy the dignity of a Priest in the apostolic Priesthood: grant, we beseech thee, that *he* may evermore be joined unto the fellowship of the same. Through.

Secret

CCEPT, O Lord, we beseech thee, the sacrifice which we offer to thee for the *soul* of thy *servant* and *Priest N.* (and *N.*): that forasmuch as in this life thou didst bestow on him the dignity of a Priest, so thou wouldest bid him to be joined unto the fellowship of thy Saints in the heavenly kingdom.

Postcommunion

E beseech thee, O Lord, that thy merciful loving kindness, which we implore, may be profitable for the *soul* of thy *servant* and *Priest N.* (and *N.*): that by thy mercy *he* may attain unto the eternal fellowship of him in whom in whom *he* hath hoped and believed. Through.

or,

Collect

RANT, we beseech thee, O Lord, that the *soul* of thy *servant N.* (and *N.*): whom while *he* lived in this world thou didst

Table of Prayers

adorn with the holy gifts of Priesthood; may ever rejoice in the glory of thy heavenly abode. Through.

Secret

ECEIVE, O Lord, we beseech thee, these sacrifices, which we offer for the *soul* of *N.* (and *N.*) thy *servant* and *Priest*: that as thou hast given *him* the dignity of the Priesthood, thou wouldest also give him the reward of the same. Through.

Postcommunion

RANT, we beseech thee, almighty God: to the *soul* of *N.* (and *N.*) thy *servant* and *Priest*, the fellowship of eternal blessedness in the congregation of the just. Through.

For a Man Departed

Collect

NCLINE thine ear, O Lord, unto the prayers wherewith we humbly entreat thy mercy: that thou wouldest set the *soul* of thy *servant N.* (and *N.*), which thou hast bidden depart this life, in a place of peace and light; and make *him* to be joined unto the fellowship of thy Saints. Through.

Secret

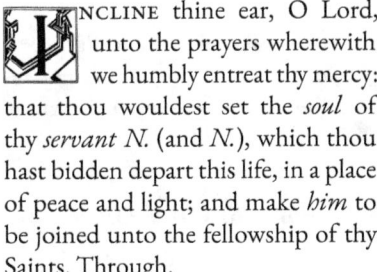RANT to us, we beseech thee, O Lord: that like as by the offering of this oblation thou didst bestow upon the whole world remission of sins: so the *soul* of thy *servant N.* (and *N.*) may be profited by the same. Through.

Postcommunion

BSOLVE, O Lord, we beseech thee, the *soul* of thy *servant N.* (and *N.*), from every bond of sin: that in the glory of the resurrection *he* may be raised up amid thy Saints and elect unto newness of life. Through.

For a Woman Departed

Collect

E beseech thee, O Lord, of thy loving-kindness to have mercy on the *soul* of thy *handmaid N.* (and *N.*): that being purged from the defilements of our mortal nature, *she* may be restored to the portion of everlasting salvation. Through.

Secret

E beseech thee, O Lord, that by these sacrifices, whereby alone we have deliverance from our sins, the *soul* of thy *handmaid N.* (and *N.*) may be absolved from all *her* offences: that through this our bounden duty of propitiation she may obtain thine everlasting mercy. Through.

Table of Prayers

Postcommunion

E beseech thee, O Lord, that forasmuch as the *soul* of thine *handmaid N.* (and *N.*) hath received this pledge of thy never-failing mercy: *she* may be made partaker of thine everlasting brightness. Through.

For a Father and Mother

Collect

 GOD, who hast bidden us to honour our father and our mother: of thy loving-kindness have mercy on the souls of *my father and mother* and forgive them their sins; and grant that *I* may behold them in the joy of the eternal brightness. Through.

Secret

ECEIVE, O Lord, the sacrifice which I offer unto thee for the souls of *my father and mother*: and grant them in the land of the living everlasting blessedness; and join *me* with them in the felicity of thy Saints. Through.

Postcommunion

E beseech thee, O Lord, that this partaking of thy heavenly sacrament may obtain for the souls of *my father and mother* rest and light perpetual: and that with them *I* may receive the crown of thy everlasting grace. Through.

For a Father Only

Collect

 GOD, who hast bidden us to honour our father and our mother: of thy loving-kindness have mercy on the soul of *my* father and forgive him his sins; and grant that *I* may behold him in the joy of the eternal brightness. Through.

Secret

ECEIVE, O Lord, the sacrifice which I offer unto thee for the soul of *my* father: and grant him in the land of the living everlasting blessedness; and join *me* with him in the felicity of thy Saints. Through.

Postcommunion

E beseech thee, O Lord, that this partaking of thy heavenly sacrament may obtain for the soul of *my* father rest and light perpetual; and that with him *I* may receive the crown of thy everlasting grace. Through.

For a Mother Only

Collect

 GOD, who hast bidden us to honour our father and our mother: of thy loving-kindness have mercy on the soul of *my* mother and forgive her her sins; and

Table of Prayers

grant that *I* may behold her in the joy of the eternal brightness. Through.

Secret

ECEIVE, O Lord, the sacrifice which *I* offer unto thee for the soul of *my* mother: and grant her in the land of the living everlasting blessedness; and join *me* with her in the felicity of thy Saints. Through.

Postcommunion

E beseech thee, O Lord, that this partaking of thy heavenly sacrament may obtain for the soul of *my* mother rest and light perpetual: and that with her *I* may receive the crown of thy everlasting grace. Through.

For Departed Brethren, Kinsfolk, & Benefactors

Collect

GOD, the giver of pardon and lover man's salvation: we beseech thee of thy mercy to grant; that the brethren, kinsfolk, and benefactors of our congregation who have passed out of this world, may at the intercession of blessed Mary, ever Virgin, and of all thy Saints attain unto the fellowship of eternal blessedness. Through.

Secret

GOD, whose mercies are without number, graciously receive our humble prayers: and through these sacraments of our salvation grant unto the souls of our brethren, kinsfolk, and benefactors, to whom thou hast given the confession of thy name, the remission of all their sins. Through.

Postcommunion

RANT, we beseech thee, almighty and merciful God: that the souls of our brethren, kinsfolk, and benefactors, for whom we have offered unto thy majesty this sacrifice of praise; may by the power of this sacrament be cleansed from all their sins, and by thy mercy obtain the blessedness of everlasting light. Through.

For Those who Rest in a Cemetery

Collect

GOD, through whose mercy the souls of the faithful are at rest: mercifully grant to thy servants and handmaids, and to all that here and in all places do rest in Christ, the remission of their sins; that being delivered from all their iniquities, they may rejoice with thee for evermore. Through the same.

Table of Prayers

Secret

RACIOUSLY receive, O Lord, this sacrifice which we offer for the souls of thy servants and handmaids, and of all Christian people who here and in all places are asleep in Christ: that by this wondrous sacrifice they may be delivered from the dreadful bonds of death, and be found worthy to enter into everlasting life. Through the same.

Postcommunion

GOD, the light of the souls of the faithful, assist our supplications: and grant unto thy servants and handmaids, whose bodies both here and in all places do rest in Christ, a place of refreshing, the blessedness of thy rest, and the glory of everlasting light. Through the same.

For Many Persons Departed

Collect

GOD, whose property is ever to have mercy and to forgive: have compassion upon the souls of thy servants and handmaids, and forgive them all their sins; that being delivered from the bonds of this our mortal nature, they may be found worthy to enter into life. Through.

Secret

RANT to us, we beseech thee, O Lord, that like as by the offering of this oblation thou didst bestow upon the whole world remission of sins: so the souls of thy servants and handmaids may be profited by the same. Through.

Postcommunion

GOD, to whom alone it belongeth to bestow healing after death: grant, we beseech thee; that the souls of thy servants and handmaids, being cleansed from the defilements of this earthly life, may be numbered in the portion of thy redeemed. Who livest and reignest.

Other Prayers for Many Persons Departed

Collect

RANT, O Lord, we pray thee, to the souls of thy servants and handmaids thy perpetual mercy: that as they have hoped and believed in thee, so it may be profitable unto them for evermore. Through.

Secret

E beseech thee, O Lord, mercifully to look upon these our gifts: that these things which we humbly offer to the glory of thy name, may be profitable unto them that are departed for the forgiveness of their sins. Through.

Postcommunion

E humbly offer unto thee, O Lord, our prayers for the souls of thy servants and handmaids: beseeching thee; that whatsoever they may have contracted in their earthly conversation being pardoned by thy goodness, they may be made partakers of the gladness of thy redeemed. Through.

Votive Masses

Our Lady on Saturday

Advent

Introit

DROP down dew, ye heavens, from above, and let the skies pour down righteousness: let the earth open, and bring forth a Saviour. *Ps.* Lord, thou art become gracious unto thy land: thou hast turned away the captivity of Jacob.

¶ The Collects of St. Mary in Advent (p. 541), of the Advent Feria, and of the Holy Ghost (p. 544) are here said.

Epistle. Isaiah 7:10

IN THOSE DAYS: The LORD spake again unto Ahaz, saying, Ask thee a sign of the LORD thy God; ask it either in the depth, or in the height above. But Ahaz said, I will not ask, neither will I tempt the LORD. And he said, Hear ye now, O house of David; Is it a small thing for you to weary men, but will ye weary my God also? Therefore the Lord himself shall give you a sign; Behold, a virgin shall conceive, and bear a son, and shall call his name Immanuel. Butter and honey shall he eat, that he may know to refuse the evil, and choose the good.

Gradual. Lift up your heads, O ye gates: and be ye lift up, ye everlasting doors: and the King of glory shall come in. ℣. Who shall ascend into the hill of the Lord? or who shall rise up in his holy place? Even he that hath clean hands, and a pure heart.

Alleluia. Alleluia, alleluia. ℣. Hail, Mary, full of grace; the Lord is with thee: blessed art thou among women. Alleluia.

Gospel. Luke 1:26

AT THAT TIME: The Angel Gabriel was sent from God unto a city of Galilee, named Nazareth, To a virgin espoused to a man whose name was Joseph, of the house of David; and the virgin's name was Mary. And the angel came in unto her, and said, Hail, thou that art highly favoured, the Lord is with thee: blessed art thou among women. And when she saw him, she was troubled at his saying, and cast in her mind what manner of salutation this should be. And the angel said unto her, Fear not, Mary: for thou hast found favour with God. And, behold, thou shalt conceive in thy womb, and bring forth a son, and shalt call his name JESUS. He shall be great, and shall be called the Son of the Highest: and the Lord God shall give unto him the throne of his father David: And he shall reign over the house of Jacob for ever; and of his kingdom there shall be no end. Then said Mary unto the angel, How shall this be, seeing I know not a man? And the angel answered and said unto her, The Holy Ghost shall come upon thee, and the power of the Highest shall overshadow thee: therefore also that holy thing which shall be born of thee shall be called the Son of God. And, behold, thy cousin Elisabeth, she hath also conceived a son in her old age: and this is the sixth month with her, who was called barren. For with God nothing shall be impossible. And Mary said, Behold the handmaid of the Lord; be it unto me according to thy word.

Offertory. Hail, Mary, full of grace; the Lord is with thee: blessed art thou among women, and blessed is the fruit of thy womb.

¶ The Secrets of St. Mary in Advent (p. 541), of the Advent Feria, and of the Holy Ghost (p. 544) are here said.

Communion. Behold, a Virgin shall conceive, and bear a son: and shall call his name Immanuel.

¶ The Postcommunions of St. Mary in Advent (p. 541), of the Advent Feria, and of the Holy Ghost (p. 544) are here said.

Epiphanytide

¶ From the Octave of the Epiphany (or in Votive Masses, from 26 December) until 1 February, inclusive.

Introit

ALL the rich among the people shall make their supplication before thee: the Virgins that be her fellows shall be brought unto the King: they that bear her company shall be brought unto thee with joy and gladness. *Ps.* My heart is inditing of a good matter: I speak of the things which I have made unto the King.

Collect

O GOD, who by the virgin child-bearing of blessed Mary hast bestowed upon mankind the rewards of eternal salvation: grant, we beseech thee; that we may perceive her intercession for us, through whom we have been counted worthy to receive the author of life, Jesus Christ thy Son our Lord. Who liveth.

Our Lady on Saturday   **Votive Masses**   Epiphanytide

Epistle. Titus 3:4

EARLY BELOVED: The kindness and love of God our Saviour toward man appeared, Not by works of righteousness which we have done, but according to his mercy he saved us, by the washing of regeneration, and renewing of the Holy Ghost; Which he shed on us abundantly through Jesus Christ our Saviour; That being justified by his grace, we should be made heirs according to the hope of eternal life: in Christ Jesus our Lord.

Gradual. Thou art fairer than the children of men: full of grace are thy lips. ℣. My heart is inditing of a good matter: I speak of the things which I have made unto the King: my tongue is the pen of a ready writer.

Alleluia. Alleluia, alleluia. ℣. After childbirth, O Virgin, thou didst remain inviolate: Mother of God, intercede for us. Alleluia.

Gospel. Luke 2:15

T THAT TIME: The shepherds said one to another, Let us now go even unto Bethlehem, and see this thing which is come to pass, which the Lord hath made known unto us. And they came with haste, and found Mary, and Joseph, and the babe lying in a manger. And when they had seen it, they made known abroad the saying which was told them concerning this child. And all they that heard it wondered at those things which were told them by the shepherds. But Mary kept all these things, and pondered them in her heart. And the shepherds returned, glorifying and praising God for all the things that they had heard and seen, as it was told unto them.

Offertory. Happy indeed art thou, O sacred Virgin Mary, and most worthy of all praise: for out of thee hath arisen the sun of righteousness, Christ our God.

Secret

THROUGH thy mercy, O Lord, and the intercession of blessed Mary, ever Virgin, may this oblation avail for our prosperity and peace, both now and for ever. Through.

Communion. Blessed is the womb of the Virgin Mary, that bore the Son of the everlasting Father.

Postcommunion

AY this communion, O Lord, cleanse us from guilt: and at the intercession of blessed Mary, the Virgin Mother of God, make us partakers of thy heavenly healing. Through the same.

Septuagesimatide

¶ From the Saturday after the Purification of the Blessed Virgin Mary to the Saturday after Sexagesima Sunday, or in Votive Masses till the Saturday after Passion Sunday, inclusive, according to the Rubrics.

Introit

HAIL, O Mother most holy, who in childbirth didst bring forth the Monarch: him who o'er heaven and earth reigneth for ever and ever. *Ps.* My heart is inditing of a good matter: I speak of the things which I have made unto the King.

Collect

GRANT, we beseech thee, O Lord God, that we thy servants may enjoy perpetual health of mind and of body: and, by the glorious intercession of blessed Mary ever Virgin, be delivered from present sadness, and rejoice in everlasting gladness. Through.

¶ The Collects of the Holy Ghost (p. 544) and Against the Persecutors of the Church (p. 543), or for the Chief Bishop (p. 543), are then said.

Epistle. Ecclesiasticus 24:9

HE created me from the beginning before the world; And to the end I shall not fail. In the holy tabernacle I ministered before him; And so was I established in Sion. In the beloved city likewise he gave me rest; And in Jerusalem was my authority. And I took root in a people that was glorified, Even in the portion of the Lord's own inheritance.

Gradual. Blessed and venerable art thou O Virgin Mary: who without spot wast found Mother of the Saviour. ℣. Virgin Mother of God, he whom the whole world containeth not, being made man lay hid in thy womb.

Alleluia. Alleluia, alleluia. ℣. Now hath blossomed Jesse's rod: a Virgin bears both man and God: God restoreth peace to men, high and low are one again. Alleluia.

¶ After Septuagesima Sunday, use the following Tract instead of the Alleluia.

Tract. Rejoice, O Virgin Mary, alone thou hast destroyed all heresies. ℣. Who didst believe the words of the Archangel Gabriel. ℣. Whilst a Virgin, thou didst bring forth him who is God and man: and after childbirth, O Virgin, inviolate didst remain. ℣. Mother of God, intercede for us.

Gospel. Luke 11:27

T THAT TIME: As Jesus spake to the multitudes, a certain woman of the company lifted up her voice, and said unto him, Blessed is the womb that bare thee, and the paps which thou hast sucked. But he said, Yea rather, blessed are they that hear the word of God, and keep it.

Offertory. Happy indeed art thou, O sacred Virgin Mary, and most worthy of all praise: for out of thee hath arisen the sun of righteousness, Christ our God.

Secret

HROUGH thy mercy, O Lord, and the intercession of blessed Mary ever Virgin, may this oblation avail for our prosperity and peace, both now and ever. Through.

¶ The Secrets of the Holy Ghost (p. 544) and Against the Persecutors of the Church (p. 543), or for the Chief Bishop (p. 543), are then said.

Communion. Blessed is the womb of the Virgin Mary, that bore the Son of the everlasting Father.

Postcommunion

RANT, we beseech thee, O Lord: that we, who have received these aids to our salvation, may at all times and in all places be protected by the advocacy of blessed Mary ever Virgin; in whose honour we have made these offerings to thy majesty. Through.

¶ The Postcommunions of the Holy Ghost (p. 544) and Against the Persecutors of the Church (p. 543), or for the Chief Bishop (p. 543), are then said.

Eastertide   **Votive Masses**   *Our Lady on Saturday*

Eastertide

¶ From Saturday after Low Sunday until Saturday after the Fourth Sunday after Easter; or in Votive Masses from Wednesday after Easter till Saturday in the Octave of Pentecost, inclusive, according to the Rubrics.

Introit

HAIL, O Mother most holy, who in childbirth didst bring forth the Monarch: him who o'er heaven and earth reigneth for ever and ever, alleluia, alleluia. *Ps.* My heart is inditing of a good matter: I speak of the things which I have made unto the King.

¶ On Saturday, Gloria in excelsis is said.

Collect

GRANT, we beseech thee, O Lord God, that we thy servants may enjoy perpetual health of mind and of body: and at the glorious intercession of blessed Mary ever Virgin, be delivered from present sadness, and rejoice in everlasting gladness. Through.

¶ The Collects of the Holy Ghost (p. 544) and Against the Persecutors of the Church (p. 543), or for the Chief Bishop (p. 543), are then said.

Epistle. Ecclesiasticus 24:9

HE created me from the beginning before the world; And to the end I shall not fail. In the holy tabernacle I ministered before him; And so was I established in Sion. In the beloved city likewise he gave me rest; And in Jerusalem was my authority. And I took root in a people that was glorified, Even in the portion of the Lord's own inheritance.

Alleluia. Alleluia, alleluia. ℣. Now hath blossomed Jesse's rod: a Virgin bears both man and God: God restoreth peace to men, high and low are one again. Alleluia. ℣. Hail, Mary, full of grace; the Lord is with thee: blessed art thou among women. Alleluia.

Gospel. John 19:25

AT THAT TIME: There stood by the cross of Jesus his mother, and his mother's sister, Mary the wife of Cleophas, and Mary Magdalene. When Jesus therefore saw his mother, and the disciple standing by, whom he loved, he saith unto his mother, Woman, behold thy son! Then saith

Our Lady on Saturday   **Votive Masses**   Eastertide

he to the disciple, Behold thy mother! And from that hour that disciple took her unto his own home.

Offertory. Blessed art thou, O Virgin Mary, who didst bear the Creator of all things: thou broughtest forth him who made thee, and for ever remainest a Virgin, alleluia.

Secret

THROUGH thy mercy, O Lord, and the intercession of blessed Mary ever Virgin, may this oblation avail for our prosperity and peace, both now and ever. Through.

¶ The Secrets of the Holy Ghost (p. 544) and Against the Persecutors of the Church (p. 543), or for the Chief Bishop (p. 543), are then said.

Communion. Blessed is the womb of the Virgin Mary, that bore the Son of the everlasting Father, alleluia.

Postcommunion

GRANT, we beseech thee, O Lord: that we who have received these aids to our salvation, may at all times and in all places be protected by the advocacy of blessed Mary ever Virgin; in whose honour we have made these offerings to thy majesty. Through.

¶ The Postcommunions of the Holy Ghost (p. 544) and Against the Persecutors of the Church (p. 543), or for the Chief Bishop (p. 543), are then said.

Votive Masses — Our Lady on Saturday

TRINITYTIDE

¶ From the Saturday after the Divine Compassion Octave, or in Votives from the Monday after Trinity Sunday, until the Saturday before the First Sunday in Advent, inclusive.

Introit

HAIL, O Mother most holy, who in childbirth didst bring forth the Monarch: him who o'er heaven and earth reigneth for ever and ever. *Ps.* My heart is inditing of a good matter: I speak of the things which I have made unto the King.

¶ On Saturday, **Gloria in excelsis** is said.

Collect

GRANT, we beseech thee, O Lord God, that we thy servants may enjoy perpetual health of mind and of body: and, by the glorious intercession of blessed Mary ever Virgin, be delivered from present sadness, and rejoice in everlasting gladness. Through.

¶ The Collects of the Holy Ghost (p. 544) and Against the Persecutors of the Church (p. 543), or for the Chief Bishop (p. 543), are then said.

Epistle. Ecclesiasticus 24:9

HE created me from the beginning before the world; And to the end I shall not fail. In the holy tabernacle I ministered before him; And so was I established in Sion. In the beloved city likewise he gave me rest; And in Jerusalem was my authority. And I took root in a people that was glorified, Even in the portion of the Lord's own inheritance.

Gradual. Blessed and venerable art thou, O Virgin Mary: who without spot wast found Mother of the Saviour. ℣. Virgin Mother of God, he whom the whole world containeth not, being made man lay hid in thy womb.

Alleluia. Alleluia, alleluia. ℣. After childbirth, O Virgin, thou didst remain inviolate : Mother of God, intercede for us. Alleluia.

Our Lady on Saturday   **Votive Masses**   Trinitytide

Gospel. Luke 11:27

T THAT TIME: As Jesus spake to the multitudes, a certain woman of the company lifted up her voice, and said unto him, Blessed is the womb that bare thee, and the paps which thou hast sucked. But he said, Yea rather, blessed are they that hear the word of God, and keep it.

Offertory. Hail, Mary, full of grace; the Lord is with thee: blessed art thou among women, and blessed is the fruit of thy womb.

Secret

HROUGH thy mercy, Lord, and the intercession of blessed Mary ever Virgin, may this oblation avail for our prosperity and peace, both now and ever. Through.

¶ The Secrets of the Holy Ghost (p. 544) and Against the Persecutors of the Church (p. 543), or for the Chief Bishop (p. 543), are then said.

Communion. Blessed is the womb of the Virgin Mary, that bore the Son of the everlasting Father.

Postcommunion

RANT, we beseech thee, O Lord: that we who have received these aids to our salvation may at all times and in all places be protected by the advocacy of blessed Mary ever Virgin; in whose honour we have made these offerings to thy majesty. Through.

¶ The Postcommunions of the Holy Ghost (p. 544) and Against the Persecutors of the Church (p. 543), or for the Chief Bishop (p. 543), are then said.

Votive Masses *Angels*

Mass of the Angels

¶ It is custom, when rubrics permit, to celebrate a Votive Mass for the Angels on Tuesday and for the death of a departed baptised Child.

Introit

O PRAISE the Lord, ye Angels of his: ye that excel in strength, ye that fulfil his commandment, and hearken unto the voice of his words (Alleluia, alleluia.) *Ps.* Praise the Lord, O my soul: and all that is within me praise his holy name.

¶ Gloria in excelsis is always said.

Collect

O EVERLASTING God, who hast ordained and constituted the services of Angels and men in a wonderful order: mercifully grant; that as thy holy Angels alway do thee service in heaven, so by thy appointment they may succour and defend us on earth. Through.

Epistle. Revelation 5:11

IN THOSE DAYS: I heard the voice of many Angels round about the throne and the beasts and the elders: and the number of them was ten thousand times ten thousand, and thousands of thousands; Saying with a loud voice, Worthy is the Lamb that was slain to receive power, and riches, and wisdom, and strength, and honour, and glory, and blessing. And every creature which is in heaven, and on the earth, and under the earth, and such as are in the sea, and all that are in them, heard I saying, Blessing, and honour, and glory, and power, be unto him that sitteth upon the throne, and unto the Lamb for ever and ever. And the four beasts said, Amen. And the four and twenty elders fell down and worshipped him that liveth for ever and ever.

Gradual. O praise the Lord of heaven: praise in him in the height. ℣. Praise him, all ye Angels of his: praise him, all his host.

Alleluia. Alleluia, alleluia. ℣. In the presence of the Angels will I sing praise unto thee: I will worship toward thy holy temple, and praise thy name. Alleluia.

Angels

Votive Masses

¶ After Septuagesima, the following Tract is said instead of the Gradual & Alleluia Verse.

Tract. O praise the Lord, ye Angels of his: ye that excel in strength, ye that fulfil his commandment. ℣. O praise the Lord, all ye his hosts: ye servants of his that do his pleasure. ℣. O speak good of the Lord, all ye works of his: in all places of his dominion, praise thou the Lord, O my soul.

¶ In Eastertide, the following Greater Alleluia is said instead of the Gradual & the Lesser Alleluia Verse.

Alleluia. Alleluia, alleluia. ℣. In the presence of the Angels will I sing praise unto thee: I will worship toward thy holy temple, and praise thy name. Alleluia. ℣. The Angel of the Lord descended from heaven, and came and rolled back the stone, and sat upon it. Alleluia.

Epistle. John 1:47

T THAT TIME: Jesus saw Nathanael coming to him, and saith of him, Behold an Israelite indeed, in whom is no guile! Nathanael saith unto him, Whence knowest thou me? Jesus answered and said unto him, Before that Philip called thee, when thou wast under the fig tree, I saw thee. Nathanael answered and saith unto him, Rabbi, thou art the Son of God; thou art the King of Israel. Jesus answered and said unto him, Because I said unto thee, I saw thee under the fig tree, believest thou? thou shalt see greater things than these. And he saith unto him, Verily, verily, I say unto you, Hereafter ye shall see heaven open, and the angels of God ascending and descending upon the Son of man.

Offertory. An Angel stood at the altar of the temple, having a golden censer in his hand: and there was given unto him much incense: and the smoke of the incense ascended up before God. (Alleluia.)

Secret

E offer thee, O Lord, sacrifices of praise, humbly beseeching thee: that, by the prayers of the Angels interceding for us, thou wouldest both graciously accept the same, and grant that they may avail to our salvation. Through.

Communion. Angels, Archangels, Thrones and Dominations, Principalities and Powers, Virtues of heaven, Cherubim and Seraphim, bless ye the Lord for ever. (Alleluia.)

Votive Masses — *Angels*

POSTCOMMUNION

O LORD, who hast filled us with thy heavenly benediction, we humbly beseech thee: that through the assistance of thy holy Angels and Archangels we may feel the benefit of the mystery which in our weakness we celebrate. Through.

Matrimony

Votive Masses

Holy Matrimony

℟ On a Sunday or 1ˢᵗ or 2ⁿᵈ Double, or Vigil of Whitsunday, or within the Octaves of Epiphany, Easter, Whitsunday, or Corpus Christi; Mass of the Day is said, with Creed and **Gloria in excelsis**, if the Mass require them, with Commemoration of the following Mass at a wedding, and the other things that belong.

On other days (excepting All Souls' Day, on which both the Votive Mass and the solemn Nuptial benediction are forbidden) the following Mass is said, even if a Greater Double or less occur.

Introit

THE God of Israel make you one: and may he be with you, even as he had mercy of two that were the only-begotten of their fathers: and now, O Lord, grant them to bless thee yet more abundantly. (Alleluia, alleluia.) *Ps.* Blessed are all they that fear the Lord: and walk in his ways.

Collect

ETERNAL God, we humbly beseech thee, favourably to behold these thy servants now joined in wedlock according to thy holy ordinance; and grant that they, seeking first thy kingdom and thy righteousness, may obtain the manifold blessings of thy grace. Through.

Epistle. Ephesians 5:20

BRETHREN: Give thanks always for all things unto God and the Father in the name of our Lord Jesus Christ; submit-ting yourselves one to another in the fear of God. Wives, submit yourselves unto your own husbands, as unto the Lord. For the husband is the head of the wife, even as Christ is the head of the church: and he is the saviour of the body. Therefore as the church is subject unto Christ, so let the wives be to their own husbands in every thing. Husbands, love your wives, even as Christ also loved the church, and gave himself for it; that he might sanctify and cleanse it with the washing of water by the word, that he might present it to himself a glorious church, not having spot, or wrinkle, or any such thing; but that it should be holy and without blemish. So ought men to love their wives as their own bodies. He that loveth his wife loveth himself. For no man ever yet hated his own flesh; but nourisheth and cherisheth it, even as the Lord the church: for we are members of his body, of his flesh, and of his bones. For this cause shall a man leave his father and mother, and shall be joined unto his wife, and they two shall be one flesh. This is a great mystery: but I speak concerning Christ and the church. Nevertheless let every one of you in particular so love his wife even as himself; and the wife see that she reverence her husband.

Gradual. Thy wife shall be as the fruitful vine upon the walls of thine house. ℣. Thy children like the olive-branches round about thy table.

Alleluia. Alleluia, alleluia. ℣. The Lord send you help from the sanctuary: and strengthen you out of Sion. Alleluia.

❧ After Septuagesima, the following Tract is said instead of the Gradual & Alleluia Verse.

Tract. Lo, thus shall the man be blessed, that feareth the Lord. ℣. The Lord from out of Sion shall so bless thee: that thou shalt see Jerusalem in prosperity all thy life long. ℣. Yea, that thou shalt see thy children's children: and peace upon Israel.

❧ In Eastertide, the following Greater Alleluia is said instead of the Gradual & the Lesser Alleluia Verse.

Alleluia. Alleluia, alleluia. ℣. The Lord send you help from the sanctuary: and strengthen you out of Sion. Alleuia. ℣. The Lord that made heaven and earth: give you blessing out of Sion. Alleluia.

Gospel. Matthew 19:4

AT THAT TIME: The Pharisees came unto Jesus, tempting him, and saying unto him: Is it lawful for a man to put away his wife for every cause? And he answered and said unto them, Have ye not read, that he which made them at the beginning made them male and female, and said, For this cause shall a man leave father and mother, and shall cleave to his wife: and they twain shall be one flesh? Wherefore they are no more twain, but one flesh. What therefore God hath joined together, let not man put asunder.

Offertory. My hope hath been in thee, O Lord: I have said: Thou art my God: my time is in thy hand. (Alleluia.)

Secret

O LORD, we beseech thee to accept this gift which we present unto thee for the sacred ordinance of matrimony: that this work begun by the bounty of thy goodness may be disposed according to thy will. Through.

Matrimony # Votive Masses

❡ Once the Lord's Prayer is ended, the Priest immediately moves to the Epistle corner and turning towards the Bridegroom and Bride kneeling before the Altar, says the following prayers over them.

❡ NOTE, The following prayers are not said in second or third marriages.

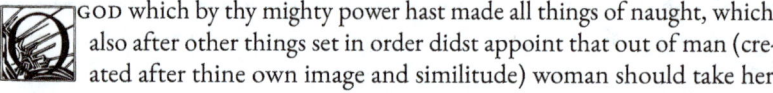MERCIFUL Lord, and heavenly Father, by whose gracious gift mankind is increased: We beseech thee assist with thy blessing these two persons, that they may both be fruitful in procreation of children; and also live together so long in godly love and honesty, that they may see their children's children, unto the third and fourth generation, unto thy praise and honour: through Jesus Christ our Lord. *Amen.*

O GOD which by thy mighty power hast made all things of naught, which also after other things set in order didst appoint that out of man (created after thine own image and similitude) woman should take her beginning: and, knitting them together, didst teach, that it should never be lawful to put asunder those, whom thou by matrimony hadst made one: O God, which hast consecrated the state of matrimony to such an excellent mystery, that in it is signified and represented the spiritual marriage and unity betwixt Christ and his Church: Look mercifully upon these thy servants, that both this man may love his wife, according to thy Word, (as Christ did love his spouse the Church, who gave himself for it, loving and cherishing it even as his own flesh;) And also that this woman may be loving and amiable to her husband as Rachel, wise as Rebecca, faithful and obedient as Sara; And in all quietness, sobriety, and peace, be a follower of holy and godly matrons. O Lord, bless them both, and grant them to inherit thy everlasting kingdom, through Jesu Christ our Lord. *Amen.*

❡ The Priest then moving to the middle of the Altar, he continues with the Deliver us.
  NOTE, during the Distribution of Communion, the Bridegroom and Bride should be communed first.

Communion. Lo, thus shall the man be blessed that feareth the Lord: yea, thou shalt see thy children's children: and peace upon Israel. (Alleluia.)

POSTCOMMUNION

E beseech thee, almighty God: let thy gracious favour accompany the institution of thy providence; that those whom thou hast joined together in lawful union thou wouldest preserve in lasting peace. Through.

Votive Masses *Matrimony*

¶ Having said the Dismissal, the Priest, before blessing the People, turns to the Bridegroom and Bride and says:

ALMIGHTY God, which at the beginning did create our first parents Adam and Eve, and did sanctify and join them together in marriage: Pour upon you the riches of his grace, sanctify and ✠ bless you, that ye may please him both in body and soul; and live together in holy love unto your lives' end. *Amen.*

¶ The Priest shall solemnly charge them that they shall be faithful to each other; that they shall remain chaste at the time of prayer, and especially during fasts and solemnities; that they shall love each other, and remain in the fear of God. Then he sprinkles them with holy water, and having said **Let this my bounden duty,** gives the blessing, and reads the Last Gospel as usual.

Votive Masses

Masses for the Dead

❧ Instead of Gloria Patri is said the Rest eternal.

On the Commemoration of all the Faithful Departed

❧ On this day, Masses are said of All Souls' Day (p. 534).

❧ For a departed Bishop or Priest, as well on the Day of burial as on the Anniversary, the first of the All Souls' Day Masses is said, with the special prayers in Various Prayers (p. 559).

On the Day of Death or Burial of a Departed Person

❧ The Mass is said of All Souls' Day's First Mass (p. 534), except for the following.

Collect

O GOD, whose property is ever to have mercy and to forgive, we humbly entreat thee for the soul of thy *servant N.*, which thou hast this day commanded to depart from this world: deliver it not into the hands of the enemy, neither forget it at the last, but command that it be received by thy holy Angels, and brought unto the fatherland of paradise; that forasmuch as *he* hoped and believed in thee, *he* may not undergo the pains of hell, but may obtain everlasting felicity. Through.

❧ On the 3rd, 7th, and 30th Day, the following Collect is instead said,

WE beseech thee, O Lord, that thou wouldest vouchsafe to grant unto the soul of thy *servant N.*, whose burial *three* days since, we now commemorate, the fellowship of thy Saints and elect: and that thou wouldest pour upon it the continual dew of thy mercy. Through.

Epistle. 1 Thessalonians 4:13

BRETHREN: I would not have you to be ignorant concerning them which are asleep, that ye sorrow not, even as others which have no hope. For if we believe that Jesus died and rose again: even so them also which sleep in Jesus will God bring with him. For this we say unto you by the word of the Lord, that we which are alive and remain unto the coming of the Lord shall not prevent them which are asleep. For the Lord himself shall descend from heaven with a shout, with the voice of the Archangel, and with the trump of God: and the dead in Christ shall rise first. Then we which are alive and remain

Votive Masses *Requiem Masses*

shall be caught up together with them in the clouds, to meet the Lord in the air, and so shall we ever be with the Lord. Wherefore comfort one another with these words.

Gospel. John 11:21

AT THAT TIME: Martha said unto Jesus: Lord, if thou hadst been here, my brother had not died: but I know, that even now, whatsoever thou wilt ask of God, God will give it thee. Jesus saith unto her: Thy brother shall rise again. Martha saith unto him: know that he shall rise again in the resurrection at the last day. Jesus said unto her: I am the resurrection, and the life: he that believeth in me, though he were dead, yet shall he live: and whosoever liveth and believeth in me shall never die. Believest thou this? She saith unto him: Yea, Lord, I believe that thou art the Christ, the Son of God, which should come into the world.

Secret

WE beseech thee, O Lord, to have mercy upon the soul of thy *servant N.*, for which we offer unto thee the sacrifice of praise, humbly entreating thy majesty: that by these offices of loving atonement, it may be worthy to attain unto everlasting rest. Through.

¶ On the 3rd, 7th, and 30th Day, the following Secret is instead said,

WE beseech thee, O Lord, graciously to regard the gifts which we offer unto thee for the soul of thy *servant N.*: that, being cleansed by heavenly remedies, it may rest in thy mercy. Through.

Postcommunion

GRANT, we beseech thee, almighty God: that the soul of thy *servant N.*, which hath this day passed from this world, being cleansed by these sacrifices and delivered from sins, may obtain thy pardon and everlasting rest. Through.

¶ On the 3rd, 7th, and 30th Day, the following Secret is instead said,

RECEIVE, O Lord, our prayers for the soul of thy *servant N.*: that whatsoever stains of earthly defilement cleave to it may by thy merciful pardon be done away. Through.

Requiem Masses # Votive Masses

ON THE ANNIVERSARY OF THE DEPARTED

❧ All is said of All Souls' Day's Second Mass (p. 537), except the following.

Collect

GOD, the Lord of mercies: grant unto the *soul* of thy *servant N.*, the anniversary of whose burial we now commemorate, a place of refreshment, the blessedness of rest, and the brightness of thy light. Through.

Secret

E favourable, O Lord, to our supplications for the *soul* of thy *servant N.*, whose anniversary is kept this day: for which we offer unto thee this sacrifice of praise; that thou wouldest vouchsafe to join *it* to the fellowship of thy Saints. Through.

Postcommunion

RANT, we beseech thee, O Lord: that the *soul* of thy *servant N.*, the anniversary of whose burial we commemorate; being purged by these sacrifices, may obtain both pardon and everlasting rest. Through.

IN DAILY MASSES OF THE DEAD

❧ All is said of All Souls' Day's Third Mass (p. 539), except the following.

Collect

❧ If the Mass is said for the all the faithful departed, then all three Collects are said.

❧ If the Mass is said for specified persons, the 1st Collect is for him (p. 559), or say the second Collect following if the name is unknown), the 2nd Collect is ad libitum, & the 3rd Collect is the third Collect following.

GOD, who didst cause thy servants to enjoy the dignity of Priest or Bishop in the apostolic Priesthood: grant, we beseech thee; that they may evermore be joined unto the fellowship of the same. Through.

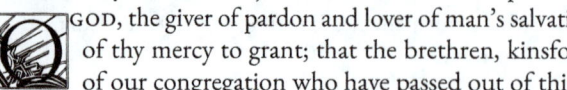GOD, the giver of pardon and lover of man's salvation: we beseech thee of thy mercy to grant; that the brethren, kinsfolk, and benefactors of our congregation who have passed out of this world, may, at the intercession of blessed Mary ever Virgin and of all thy Saints, attain unto the fellowship of eternal blessedness. (Through.)

Votive Masses *Requiem Masses*

GOD, the Creator and Redeemer of all the faithful: grant unto the souls of thy servants and handmaids the remission of all their sins; that through devout supplications they may obtain the pardon which they have alway desired. Who livest and reignest.

Secret

CCEPT, O Lord, we beseech thee, the sacrifices which we offer to thee for the souls of thy servants, Bishops or Priests: that forasmuch as in this life thou didst bestow on them the dignity of Bishop or Priest, so thou wouldest bid them be joined unto the fellowship of thy Saints in the heavenly kingdom. Through.

GOD, whose mercies are without number, graciously receive our humble prayers: and through these sacraments of our salvation grant unto the souls of our brethren, kinsfolk, and benefactors, to whom thou hast given the confession of thy name, the remission of all their sins. (Through.)

E beseech thee, O Lord, look favourably upon the sacrifices which we offer unto thee for the souls of thy servants and handmaids: that as thou hast bestowed on them the merit of the Christian faith, thou wouldest grant them the reward of the same. Through.

Postcommunion

E beseech thee, O Lord, that thy merciful loving kindness, which we implore, may be profitable for the souls of thy servants, Bishops or Priests: that by thy mercy they may attain unto the eternal fellowship of him in whom they have hoped and believed. Through.

RANT, we beseech thee, almighty and merciful God: that the souls of our brethren, kinsfolk, and benefactors, for whom we have offered unto thy majesty this sacrifice of praise; may by the power of this sacrament be cleansed from all their sins, and by thy mercy obtain the blessedness of everlasting light. (Through.)

E beseech thee, O Lord, that the prayer of thy suppliant people may be profitable for the souls of thy servants and handmaids: that thou wouldest deliver them from all their sins, and make them to be partakers of thy redemption. Who livest.

Pastoral Rites

Baptism of Infants   ## Pastoral Rites

Sacrament of Baptism for Infants

¶The clean Baptismal Font is filled with clear water. The container for salt and the phials of Holy Chrism and Oil of Catchumens are placed nearby. The Priest, with acolytes and other clergy, the Cross and candles going before, and with thurible and incense, comes to the Font, and there, or before the Altar of the Baptistery, begins with the questioning at the Doors of the Church.

℣. N., what dost thou ask of the Church of God?
℟. Faith.
℣. What doth Faith bring to thee?
℟. Life everlasting.
℣. If then thou desirest to enter into life, keep the commandments. Thou shalt love the Lord thy God with all thy heart, and with all thy soul, and with all thy mind; and thy neighbour as thyself.

℣. N., Quid petis ab Ecclesia Dei?
℟. Fidem.
℣. Fides quid tibi præstat?
℟. Vitam æternam.
℣. Si igitur vis ad vitam íngredi, serva mandáta. Díliges Dóminum Deum tuum ex toto corde tuo, ex tota ánima tua, et ex tota mente tua, et próximum tuum sicut teípsum.

¶ The Priest now breathes three times softly upon the face of the Infant, and says:

Depart from *him*, O unclean spirit, and give place to the Holy Spirit, the Comforter.

Exi ab *eo*, immúnde spíritus, et da locum Spirítui Sancto Paráclito.

¶ He then makes the sign of the cross upon the forehead and breast of the Child, while he saith:

Accept the sign of the Cross both on thy forehead ✠ and on thy breast ✠; receive the faith of the heavenly precepts; and be such in thy conduct, that thou mayest be the temple of God.

Accipe signum Crucis tam in fron ✠ te, quam in cor ✠ de, sume fidem cæléstium præceptórum: et talis esto móribus, ut templum Dei jam esse possis.

Let us pray.

MERCIFULLY hear our prayers, we beseech thee, O Lord; and, with thy ever-abiding power, preserve this thy chosen *servant N.*, who hath been marked with the sign of the Lord's Cross; that, observing the beginnings of the greatness of thy glory, he may, by keeping thy commandments, deserve to arrive at the

Orémus.

PRECES nostras, quæsumus Dómine, cleménter exáudi: et *hunc Eléctum tuum, N.*, Crucis Domínicæ impressióne *signátum* perpétua virtúte custódi: ut magnitúdinis glóriæ tuæ rudiménta servans, per custódiam mandatórum tuórum ad regeneratiónis glóriam pervenére mereátur. Per Christum Dominum no-glory of regeneration. Through Christ our Lord.

℞. Amen.

¶ The Priest then places his hand on the head of the child, and says:

Let us pray.

ALMIGHTY, everlasting God, Father of our Lord Jesus Christ, deign to look upon this thy *servant N.*, whom thou hast vouchsafed to call to the rudiments of faith; drive out from *him* all blindness of heart; break all the chains of Satan wherewith *he* hath been bound: open to *him*, O Lord, the gate of thy mercy, that, being imbued with the seal of thy wisdom, *he* may be free from the filth of all evil desires, and, by the sweet odour of thy precepts, may joyfully serve thee in thy Church, and advance from day to day. Through the same Christ our Lord.

℞. Amen.

strum.

℞. Amen.

Orémus.

MNÍPOTENS, sempitérne Deus, Pater Dómini nostri Jesu Christi, respícere dignáre super *hunc fámulum tuum N.*, quem ad rudiménta fídei vocáre dignátus es: omnem cæcitátem cordis ab *eo* expélle: disrúmpe omnes láqueos sátanæ, quibus fúerat *colligátus*: áperi ei, Dómine, jánuam pietátis tuæ, ut signo sapiéntiæ tuæ *imbútus*, ómnium cupiditátum fœtóribus cáreat, et ad suávem odórem præceptórum tuórum *lætus* tibi in Ecclésia tua desérviat, et profíciat de die in diem. Per eúmdem Christum Dóminum nostrum.

℞. Amen.

BLESSING OF SALT

¶ If the salt has not already been blest, it is here blest by the Priest.

EXORCISE thee, creature of salt, in the name of God the Father ✠ Almighty, and in the charity of our Lord Jesus ✠ Christ, and in the power of the Holy ✠ Ghost.

I exorcise thee by the living ✠ God, by the true ✠ God, by the holy ✠ God; by God ✠ who hath created thee for the preservation of mankind, and hath appointed thee to be consecrated by his servants for the people coming unto the faith, that, in the name of the holy

XORCÍZO te, creatúra salis, in nómine Dei ✠ Patris omnipoténtis, et in caritáte Dómini nostri Jesu ✠ Christi, et in virtúte Spíritus ✠ Sancti.

Exorízo te per Deum ✠ vivum, per Deum ✠ verum, per Deum ✠ sanctum, per Deum ✠, qui te ad tutélam humáni géneris procreávit, et pópulo veniénti ad credulitátem per servos suos consecrári præcépit: ut in nómine sanctæ Trinitátis efficiáris salutáre Sacramén-

Baptism of Infants # Pastoral Rites

Trinity, thou mayest be made a salutary sacrament to drive away the enemy.

Wherefore, we beseech thee, O Lord our God, that, sanctifying this creature of salt, thou wouldst sanctify it, and blessing thou wouldst bless it, that it may become unto all who receive it a perfect medicine, abiding in their hearts, in the name of the same our Lord Jesus Christ, who will come to judge the living and the dead, and the world by fire.

℞. Amen.

tum ad effugándum inimícum.

Proínde rogámus te, Dómine, Deus noster, ut hanc creatúram salis sanctificándo sanctí ✠ fices, et benedicéndo bene ✠ dícas ut fiat ómnibus accipiéntibus perfécta medicína, pérmanens in viscéribus eórum, in nómine ejúsdem Dómini nostri Jesu Christi, qui ventúrus est judicáre vivos et mórtuos, et sæculum per ignem.

℞. Amen.

Imposition of Salt

❡ The Priest now puts a small quantity of the blessed salt into the mouth of the Child, saying:

N., receive the salt of wisdom; may it be to thee a propitiation unto life everlasting.

℞. Amen.

℣. Peace be with thee.

℞. And with thy spirit.

Let us pray.

GOD of our fathers, O God, the author of all truth, we humbly beseech thee, graciously vouchsafe to look upon this thy *servant N.*, now tasting this first nutriment of salt, and do not suffer *him* to hunger any longer through want of being filled with heavenly food, so that *he* may always be fervent in spirit, rejoicing in hope, always serving thy name.

Bring *him*, O Lord, we beseech thee, to the laver of the new regeneration, that, with thy faithful, *he* may deserve

N., Accipe sal sapiéntiæ: propitiátio sit tibi in vitam ætérnam.

℞. Amen.

℣. Pax tibi.

℞. Et cum spíritu tuo.

Orémus.

EUS patrum nostrórum, Deus univérsæ cónditor veritátis, te súpplices exorámus, ut *hunc fámulum tuum N.* respícere dignéris propítius, et hoc primum pábulum salis gustántem, non diútius esuríre permíttas, quo minus cibo expleátur cælésti, quátenus sit semper spíritu fervens, spe gaudens, tuo semper nómini sérviens.

Per duc *eum*, Dómine, quæsumus, ad novæ regeneratiónis lavácrum, ut cum fidélibus tuis promissiónum tuá-

Pastoral Rites *Baptism of Infants*

to attain unto the everlasting rewards of thy promises. Through Christ our Lord.

℟. Amen.

rum ætérna præmia cónsequi reátur. Per Christum Dóminum nostrum.

℟. Amen.

Exorcism of the Infant

I EXORCISE thee, unclean spirit, in the name of the Father ✠, and of the Son ✠, and of the Holy ✠ Ghost, that thou go out and depart from this *servant* of God, *N.* For he who walked on foot upon the sea, and stretched out his right hand to Peter when sinking, commands thee, accursed one.

Therefore, accursed devil, acknowledge thy sentence, and give honour to the living and true God; give honour to Jesus Christ his Son, and to the Holy Ghost; and depart from this *servant* of God, *N.*, because God, even our Lord Jesus Christ, hath deigned to call *him* to his holy grace and blessing, and to the font of baptism.

E XORCÍZO te, immúnde spiritus, in nómine Pa ✠ tris, et Fí ✠ lii, et Spíritus ✠ Sancti, ut éxeas, et recédas ab *hoc fámulo* Dei *N.*: Ipse enim tibi ímperat, maledícte damnáte, qui pédibus super mare ambulávit, et Petro mergénti déxteram porréxit.

Ergo, maledícte diábole, recognósce senténtiam tuam, et da honórem Deo vivo et vero, da honórem Jesu Christo Fílio ejus, et Spirítui Sancto, et recéde ab *hoc fámulo* Dei *N.*, quia *istum* sibi Deus, et Dóminus noster Jesus Christus ad suam sanctam grátiam, et benedictiónem, fontémque Baptísmatis vocáre dignátus est.

¶ With his right thumb, the Priest now makes the sign of the cross on the Child's forehead, saying:

And this sign of the holy Cross ✠ which we make upon *his* forehead, do thou, accursed devil, never dare to violate. Through the same Christ our Lord.

℟. Amen.

Et hoc signum sanctæ Cru ✠ cis, quod nos fronti ejus damus, tu, maledícte diábole, numquam áudeas violáre. Per eúmdem Christum Dóminum nostrum.

℟. Amen.

¶ Then the Priest places his hand on the head of the Child and says:

Let us pray.

I ENTREAT thy eternal and most just mercy, O holy Lord, Father Almighty, eternal God, Author of light and truth, in

Orémus.

Æ TÉRNAM, ac justíssimam pietátem tuam déprecor, Dómine sancte, Pater omnípotens, ætérne Deus, auctor lúminis et veritá-

behalf of this thy *servant N.*, that thou wouldst vouchsafe to enlighten *him* with the light of thy wisdom; cleanse *him*, and sanctify *him*; give unto *him* true knowledge, that, being made worthy of the grace of thy baptism, *he* may retain firm hope, right counsel, and holy doctrine. Through Christ our Lord.

℟. Amen.

tis, super *hunc fámulum tuum N.* ut dignéris *eum* illumináre lúmine intelligéntiæ tuæ: munda *eum*, et sanctífica: da ei sciéntiam veram, ut *dignus* grátia Baptísmi tui *efféctus*, téneat firmam spem, consílium rectum, doctrínam sanctam. Per Christum Dóminum nostrum.

℟. Amen.

❡ The Priest now places one end of his stole upon the Child that is to be baptised, and leads it into the church, saying:

N., Come into the Temple of God, that thou mayest have part with Christ unto Life Everlasting.

℟. Amen.

N., Ingrédere in templum Dei, ut hábeas partem cum Christo in vitam ætérnam.

℟. Amen.

❡ When they have entered the church, the Priest, as he proceeds to the font, says in a loud tone, the Creed and the Our Father. The Godparents also say them with the Priest.

Nicene Creed

I BELIEVE in one God, the Father Almighty, Maker of heaven and earth, And of all things visible and invisible:

And in one Lord Jesus Christ, the only-begotten Son of God; Begotten of his Father before all worlds, God of God, Light of Light, Very God of very God; Begotten, not made; Being of one substance with the Father; By whom all things were made: Who for us men and for our salvation came down from heaven, And was incarnate by the Holy Ghost of the Virgin Mary, And was made man: And was crucified also for us under Pontius Pilate; He suffered and was buried: And the third day he rose again according

CREDO in unum Deum, Patrem omnipoténtem, factórem cæli et terræ, visibílium ómnium et invisibílium.

Et in unum Dóminum Jesum Christum, Fílium Dei unigénitum. Et ex Patre natum ante ómnia sǽcula. Deum de Deo, lumen de lúmine, Deum verum de Deo vero. Génitum, non factum, consubstantiálem Patri: per quem ómnia facta sunt. Qui propter nos hómines et propter nostram salútem descéndit de cælis. Et incarnátus est de Spíritu Sancto ex María Vírgine: Et homo factus est. Crucifíxus étiam pro nobis: sub Póntio Piláto passus, et sepúltus est. Et resurréxit tértia die, secúndum Scriptúras. Et ascéndit in cæ-

to the Scriptures: And ascended into heaven, And sitteth on the right hand of the Father: And he shall come again, with glory, to judge both the quick and the dead; Whose kingdom shall have no end.

And I believe in the Holy Ghost, The Lord, and Giver of Life, Who proceedeth from the Father; Who with the Father and the Son together is worshiped and glorified; Who spake by the Prophets: And I believe one, holy, catholic, and apostolic Church: I acknowledge one Baptism for the remission of sins: And I look for the Resurrection of the dead: ✠ And the Life of the world to come. Amen.

lum: sedet ad déxteram Patris. Et íterum ventúrus est cum glória judicáre vivos et mórtuos: cujus regni non erit finis.

Et in Spíritum Sanctum, Dóminum et vivificántem: qui ex Patre procédit. Qui cum Patre et Fílio simul adorátur et conglorificátur: qui locútus est per Prophétas. Et unam sanctam cathólicam et apostólicam Ecclésiam. Confíteor unum baptísma in remissiónem peccatórum. Et exspécto resurrectiónem mortuórum. ✠ Et vitam ventúri sǽculi. Amen.

Lord's Prayer

OUR Father, who art in heaven, Hallowed be thy Name. Thy kingdom come. Thy will be done on earth, As it is in heaven. Give us this day our daily bread. And forgive us our trespasses, As we forgive those who trespass against us. And lead us not into temptation; But deliver us from evil. Amen.

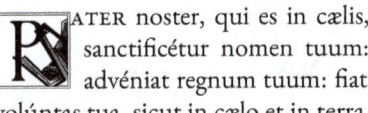ATER noster, qui es in cælis, sanctificétur nomen tuum: advéniat regnum tuum: fiat volúntas tua, sicut in cælo et in terra. Panem nostrum quotidiánum da nobis hódie: et dimítte nobis débita nostra, sicut et nos dimíttimus debitóribus nostris: et ne nos indúcas in tentatiónem: sed líbera nos a malo. Amen.

¶ Before entering the Baptistery the Priest again exorcises the Child, saying:

EXORCISE thee, every unclean spirit, in the name of God the Father ✠ Almighty, and in the name of Jesus Christ his Son, ✠ our Lord and judge, and in the power of the Holy ✠ Ghost, that thou depart from this creature of God *N.*, which our Lord hath vouchsafed to call unto his holy temple, that it may be made the temple of the living God, and that

XORCÍZO te, omnis spíritus immúnde, in nómine Dei ✠ Patris omnipoténtis, et in nómine Jesu ✠ Christi Fílii ejus, Dómini et Júdicis nostri, et in virtúte Spíritus ✠ Sancti, ut discédas ab hoc plásmate Dei *N.*, quod Dóminus noster ad templum sanctum suum vocáre dignátus est, ut fiat templum Dei vivi, et Spíritus Sanctus hábitet in eo. Per eú-

Baptism of Infants   # Pastoral Rites

the Holy Ghost may dwell therein. Through the same Christ our Lord, who will come to judge the living and the dead, and the world by fire.

℞. Amen.

mdem Christum Dóminum nostrum, qui ventúrus est judicáre vivos, et mórtuos et sǽculum per ignem.

℞. Amen.

¶ Then the Priest puts spit from his mouth into his thumb, then makes the sign of the Cross on the right, and afterwards on the left, ear of the Child that is to be baptised, and says once only:

Ephpheta, ✠ that is ✠, Be thou opened.

Ephpheta, ✠ quod est ✠, Adaperíre.

¶ And then, signing the nostrils, he adds:

For an odour ✠ of sweetness.

In odórem ✠ suavitátis.

¶ Lastly, in a louder tone of voice, he says:

But do thou depart, O devil; for the judgment of God will come.

Tu autem effugáre, diábole; appropinquábit enim judícium Dei.

¶ He then, by name, questions the Child (the Godparents responding):

℣. *N.*, Dost thou renounce Satan?
℞. I do renounce him.
℣. And all his works?
℞. I do renounce them.
℣. And all his pomps?
℞. I do renounce them.

℣. *N.*, Abrenúntias Sátanæ?
℞. Abrenúntio.
℣. Et ómnibus opéribus ejus?
℞. Abrenúntio.
℣. Et ómnibus pompis ejus?
℞. Abrenúntio.

¶ The Priest then dips his right thumb into the Oil of Catechumens, and with it makes the sign of the Cross on the breast and between the shoulders of the Child, saying:

I anoint thee ✠ with the oil of salvation, in Christ ✠ Jesus our Lord, that thou mayest have life everlasting.

℞. Amen.

Ego te línio ✠ óleo salútis in Christo ✠ Jesu Dómino nostro, ut habeas vitam ætérnam.

℞. Amen.

¶ The Priest now removes the oil from his thumb, and from the breast and back of the child with some cotton wool, and changes the purple stole, which he had hitherto worn, for a white one; and then, by name, questions the Child as follows (the Godparents responding):

℣. *N.*, Dost thou believe in God the Father Almighty, Creator of heaven and earth?
℞. I do believe.
℣. Dost thou believe in Jesus Christ, his only Son our Lord, who was born into this world, and who suffered for

℣. *N.*, Credis in Deum Patrem omnipoténtem, Creatórem cæli et terræ?
℞. Credo.
℣. Credis in Jesum Christum Fílium ejus únicum, Dóminum nostrum, natum et passum?

us?

℟. I do believe.

℣. Dost thou also believe in the Holy Ghost, the Holy Catholic Church, the Communion of Saints, the Forgiveness of Sins, the Resurrection of the Body, and Life Everlasting?

℟. I do believe.

℣. *N.*, Wilt thou be baptised?

℟. I will.

℟. Credo.

℣. Credis et in Spíritum Sanctum, sanctam Ecclésiam Cathólicam, Sanctórum communiónem, remissiónem peccatórum, carnis resurrectiónem et vitam ætérnam?

℟. Credo.

℣. *N.*, Vis baptizári?

℟. Volo.

❡ Then the Priest places the Child in a Font sufficient for immersion.

N., I baptise thee in the name of the Father, (he immerses) and of the Son, (he immerses) and of the Holy Ghost (he immerses).

N. Ego te baptízo in nómine Patris, (mergit) et Fílii, (mergit) et Spíritus Sancti (mergit).

❡ After cleansing his hands, the Priest immediately moves onto Confirmation (p. 629).

Baptism of Adults

Pastoral Rites

Sacrament of Baptism for Adults

℣ The clean Baptismal font is filled with clear water. The container for salt and the phials of Holy Chrism and Oil of Catechumens are placed nearby. The Baptismal Candle and Chrisom (white cloth) are prepared. The Priest (vested in surplice and purple stole and cope), with acolytes and assisting clerics, kneels at the steps of the Altar and silently offers devout prayers to God that he may worthily administer this great Sacrament. Rising, he makes the sign of the Cross and says or sings:

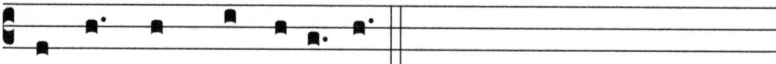

℣. O God, make speed to save us.

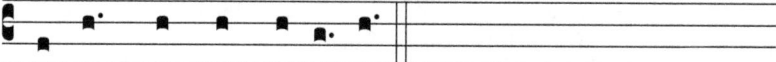

℟. O Lord, make haste to help us.

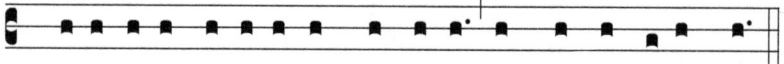

℣. Glo-ry be to the Father, and to the Son, and to the Ho-ly Ghost.

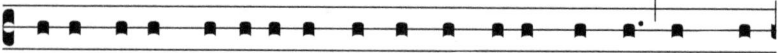

℟. As it was in the be-ginning, is now, and ev-er shall be, world with-

out end. Amen.

Pastoral Rites — *Baptism of Adults*

Psalm 8. *Domine, Dominus noster*

Ant. I will pour clean water over you, and ye shall be washed of all your iniquities, saith the Lord.

O LORD our Governor, how excellent is thy Name in all the world : thou that hast set thy glory above the heavens!

2 Out of the mouth of very babes and sucklings hast thou ordained strength, because of thine enemies : that thou mightest still the enemy and the avenger.

3 For I will consider thy heavens, even the works of thy fingers : the moon and the stars, which thou hast ordained.

4 What is man, that thou art mindful of him : and the son of man, that thou visitest him?

5 Thou madest him lower than the angels : to crown him with glory and worship.

6 Thou makest him to have dominion of the works of thy hands : and thou hast put all things in subjection under his feet;

7 All sheep and oxen : yea, and the beasts of the field;

8 The fowls of the air, and the fishes of the sea : and whatsoever walketh through the paths of the seas.

9 O Lord our Governor : how excellent is thy Name in all the world!

℣. Glory be to the Father, and to the Son, and to the Holy Ghost.

℟. As it was in the beginning, is now, and ever shall be, world without end. Amen.

Psalm 29. *Afferte Domino*

BRING unto the Lord, O ye mighty, bring young rams unto the Lord : ascribe unto the Lord worship and strength.

2 Give the Lord the honour due unto his Name : worship the Lord with holy worship.

3 It is the Lord that commandeth the waters : it is the glorious God that maketh the thunder.

4 It is the Lord that ruleth the sea; the voice of the Lord is mighty in operation : the voice of the Lord is a glorious voice.

5 The voice of the Lord breaketh the cedar-trees : yea, the Lord breaketh the cedars of Libanus.

6 He maketh them also to skip like a calf : Libanus also, and Sirion, like a young unicorn.

7 The voice of the Lord divideth the flames of fire; the voice of the Lord shaketh the wilderness : yea, the Lord shaketh the wilderness of Cades.

8 The voice of the Lord maketh the hinds to bring forth young, and discovereth the thick bushes : in his temple doth every man speak of his honour.

9 The Lord sitteth above the water-flood : and the Lord remaineth a King for ever.

10 The Lord shall give strength unto his people : the Lord shall give his people the blessing of peace.

℣. Glory be to the Father, and to the Son, and to the Holy Ghost.

℟. As it was in the beginning, is now, and ever shall be, world without end. Amen.

Psalm 42. *Quemadmodum*

Like as the hart desireth the water-brooks : so longeth my soul after thee, O God.

2 My soul is athirst for God, yea, even for the living God : when shall I come to appear before the presence of God?

3 My tears have been my meat day and night : while they daily say unto me, Where is now thy God?

4 Now when I think thereupon, I pour out my heart by myself : for I went with the multitude, and brought them forth into the house of God;

5 In the voice of praise and thanksgiving : among such as keep holy-day.

6 Why art thou so full of heaviness, O my soul : and why art thou so disquieted within me?

7 Put thy trust in God : for I will yet give him thanks for the help of his countenance.

8 My God, my soul is vexed within me : therefore will I remember thee concerning the land of Jordan, and the little hill of Hermon.

9 One deep calleth another, because of the noise of the water-pipes : all thy waves and storms are gone over me.

10 The Lord hath granted his loving-kindness in the day-time : and in the night-season did I sing of him, and made my prayer unto the God of my life.

11 I will say unto the God of my strength, Why hast thou forgotten me : why go I thus heavily, while the enemy oppresseth me?

12 My bones are smitten asunder as with a sword : while mine enemies that trouble me cast me in the teeth;

13 Namely, while they say daily unto me : Where is now thy God?

14 Why art thou so vexed, O my soul : and why art thou so disquieted within me?

Pastoral Rites *Baptism of Adults*

15 O put thy trust in God : for I will yet thank him, which is the help of my countenance, and my God.

℣. Glory be to the Father, and to the Son, and to the Holy Ghost.

℟. As it was in the beginning, is now, and ever shall be, world without end. Amen.

Ant. I will pour clean water over you, and ye shall be washed of all your iniquities, saith the Lord.

℣. Lord, have mercy upon us.
℟. Christ, have mercy upon us.
℣. Lord, have mercy upon us.

℣. Kýrie, eléison.
℟. Christe, eléison.
℣. Kýrie, eléison.

UR Father, who art in heaven, Hallowed be thy Name. Thy kingdom come. Thy will be done on earth, As it is in heaven. Give us this day our daily bread. And forgive us our trespasses, As we forgive those who trespass against us.

℣. And lead us not into temptation;
℟. But deliver us from evil.
℣. O Lord, hear my prayer.
℟. And let my cry come unto thee.
℣. The Lord be with you.
℟. And with thy spirit.

Let us pray.

LMIGHTY and everlasting God, who hast given unto us thy servants grace, by the confession of a true faith, to acknowledge the glory of the eternal Trinity, and in the power of the Divine Majesty to worship the Unity; We beseech thee that thou wouldest keep us stedfast in this faith, and evermore defend us from all adversities.

LMIGHTY God, we beseech thee to hear our prayers: may the working of thy power accomplish what is to be done through our lowly ministry.

ATER noster, qui es in cælis, sanctificétur nomen tuum: advéniat regnum tuum: fiat volúntas tua, sicut in cælo et in terra. Panem nostrum quotidiánum da nobis hódie: et dimítte nobis débita nostra, sicut et nos dimíttimus debitóribus nostris:

℣. Et ne nos indúcas in tentatiónem:
℟. Sed líbera nos a malo.
℣. Dómine, exáudi oratiónem meam.
℟. Et clamor meus ad te véniat.
℣. Dóminus vobíscum.
℟. Et cum spíritu tuo.

Orémus.

MNÍPOTENS sempitérne Deus, qui dedísti fámulis tuis in confessióne veræ Fídei, ætérnæ Trinitátis glóriam agnóscere, et in poténtia majestátis adoráre unitatem, quæsumus, ut ejusdem Fidei firmitáte ab ómnibus semper muniámur advérsis.

DÉSTO supplicatiónibus nostris, Omnípotens Deus; et quod humilitátis nostræ geréndum est ministério, tuæ virtútis impleátur efféctu.

Baptism of Adults   # Pastoral Rites

GRANT, O Lord, we beseech thee, to thy *servant*, that, being instructed in thy holy mysteries, *he* may be born again in the water of baptism and counted among the members of thy holy Church. Through Christ our Lord.
℟. Amen.

DA, quæsumus, Dómine,* *Elécto nostro*, ut sanctis * *edóctus* mystériis, et renovétur Fonte Baptísmatis, et inter Ecclésiæ tuæ membra numerétur. Per Christum Dóminum nostrum.
℟. Amen.

¶ The Priest then interrogates the Catechumen.

℣. N., what dost thou ask of the Church of God?
℟. Faith.
℣. What doth Faith bring to thee?
℟. Life everlasting.
℣. If then thou desirest to enter into life, keep the commandments: Thou shalt love the Lord thy God with all thy heart, and with all thy soul, and with all thy mind and thy neighbour as thyself. On these two commandments hang all the Law and the Prophets. And the Faith is, that we worship one God in Trinity, and Trinity in Unity; neither confusing the Persons: nor dividing the substance. For there is one Person of the Father, another of the Son: and another of the Holy Ghost. But the Godhead of these three is all one.

℣. N., Quid petis ab Ecclesia Dei?
℟. Fidem.
℣. Fides quid tibi præstat?
℟. Vitam ætérnam.
℣. Si vis habére vitam ætérnam, serva mandáta. Díliges Dóminum Deum tuum ex toto corde tuo, et ex tota ánima tua, et ex tota mente tua, et próximum tuum sicut te ipsum. In his duóbus mandátis tota Lex pendet, et Prophétæ. Fides autem est, ut unum Deum in Trinitáte, et Trinitátem in unitáte veneréris, neque confundéndo persónas, neque substántiam separándo. Alia est enim persóna Patris, ália Fílii, ália Spíritus Sancti: sed horum trium una est substántia, et nónnisi una Divínitas.

¶ The Priest then questions the Catechumen,

℣. N., Dost thou renounce Satan?
℟. I do renounce him.
℣. And all his works?
℟. I do renounce them.
℣. And all his allurements?
℟. I do renounce them.
℣. N., Dost thou believe in God the Father Almighty, Maker of heaven and earth?

℣. Abrenúntias Sátanæ?
℟. Abrenúntio.
℣. Et ómnibus opéribus ejus?
℟. Abrenúntio.
℣. Et ómnibus pompis ejus?
℟. Abrenúntio.
℣. Credis in Deum Patrem omnipoténtem, Creatórem cæli et terræ?

Pastoral Rites *Baptism of Adults*

℟. I do believe.

℣. Dost thou believe in Jesus Christ, his only Son, our Lord, who was born into this world, and who suffered?

℟. I do believe.

℣. Dost thou also believe in the Holy Ghost, the Holy Catholic Church, the Communion of Saints, the Forgiveness of Sins, the Resurrection of the Body, and the Life Everlasting?

℟. I do believe.

℟. Credo.

℣. Credis in Jesum Christum Fílium ejus únicum, Dóminum nostrum, natum et passum?

℟. Credo.

℣. Credis et in Spíritum Sanctum, sanctam Ecclésiam Cathólicam, Sanctórum communiónem, remissiónem peccatórum, carnis resurrectiónem et vitam ætérnam?

℟. Credo.

¶ *The Priest now breathes three times softly upon the face of the Catechumen, and says:*

Go out of *him* thou unclean spirit, and give place unto the Holy Spirit the Paraclete.

Exi ab *eo*, spíritus immúnde, et da locum Spirítui Sancto Paráclito.

¶ *The Priest then breathes in the form of the Cross upon his face, saying,*

N., through this rite of breathing upon thee, receive the good spirit and the bless ✠ ing of God. Peace be with thee.

℟. And with thy spirit.

N. Accipe Spíritum bonum per istam insufflatiónem, et Dei bene ✠ dictiónem. Pax tibi.

℟. Et cum spíritu tuo.

¶ *He then makes the sign of the cross upon the forehead and breast of the Catechumen, while he says:*

Receive the sign of the Cross both upon thy forehead ✠ and also on the heart ✠; take unto thee the faith of the heavenly precepts: and be thou such in thy conversation, that thou mayest now be the temple of God. Having entered into the Church of God, be happy in knowing that thou hast escaped the snares of death.

Accipe signum Crucis tam in fron ✠ te, quam in cor ✠ de, sume fidem cæléstium præceptórum. Talis esto móribus, ut templum Dei jam esse possis: *ingressúsque* ecclésiam Dei, evasísse te láqueos mortis, *lætus* agnósce.

¶ *If the Catechumen is from paganism or idolatry,*

Abhor false gods. Reject idols.

Horrésce idóla, réspue simulácra.

¶ *from Judaism,*

Abhor the Jewish perfidy. Reject the Hebrew superstition.

Horrésce Judáicam perfídiam, réspue Hebráicam superstitiónem.

Baptism of Adults

Pastoral Rites

¶ from Islam,

Abhor the perfidy of the Mahotemans. Reject the depraved sect of infidelity.

Horrésce Mahuméticam perfídiam, réspue pravam sectam infidelitátis.

¶ from Heretics, whose Baptism is not accepted,

Abhor heretical depravity. Reject the foul sects of the impious.

Horrésce hæréticam pravitátem, réspue nefárias sectas impiórum.

¶ For all, it continues,

Worship only God, the Father almighty, and Jesus Christ, his only Son, our Lord, who shall come to judge the quick and the dead, and the world by fire.

℟. Amen.

Cole Deum Patrem omnipoténtem, et Jesum Christum, Fílium ejus únicum, Dóminum nostrum, qui ventúrus est judicáre vivos et mórtuos, et sæculum per ignem.

℟. Amen.

Let us pray.

Orémus.

O LORD, holy Father, almighty and eternal God, I pray thee, show thy *servant, N.*, the way of the true faith and the knowledge of thyself. For *he* wandereth in uncertainty and doubt through the darkness of this world. Then, when the eyes of *his* heart have been opened, *he* will profess thee to be the one God, the Father, the Son, and the Holy Spirit. May *he* enjoy the fruit of this profession of faith both here and in the world to come. Through Christ our Lord.

℟. Amen.

TE déprecor, Dómine sancte, Pater omnípotens, ætérne Deus: ut huic *fámulo tuo N., qui* in hujus sæculi nocte vagátur *incértus* ac *dúbius*, viam veritátis et agnitiónis tuæ júbeas demonstrári; quátenus, reserátis óculis cordis sui, te unum Deum Patrem in Fílio, et Fílium in Patre cum Spíritu Sancto recognóscat, atque hujus confessiónis fructum, et hic, et in futúro sæculo percípere mereátur. Per Christum Dóminum nostrum.

℟. Amen.

¶ The Priest, with his thumb, then signs the seven parts of the Body with the Cross, starting with the forehead,

I sign thee on the forehead, ✠ that thou mayest take up the Lord's Cross.
(On the ears:) I sign thee on the ears, ✠ that thou mayest listen attentively to God's commands.
(On the eyes:) I sign thee on the eyes, ✠ that thou mayest see God's glory.

Signo tibi fron ✠ tem, ut suscípias Crucem Dómini.
(In auribus:) Signo tibi au ✠ res, ut áudias divína præcépta.
(In oculis:) Signo tibi ócu ✠ los, ut vídeas claritátem Dei.

Pastoral Rites *Baptism of Adults*

(On the nostrils:) I sign thee on the nostrils, ✠ that thou mayest perceive the sweet fragrance of Christ.
(On the mouth:) I sign thee on the mouth, ✠ that thou mayest speak the words of life.
(On the breast:) I sign thee on the breast, ✠ that thou mayest believe in God.
(On the shoulders:) I sign thee on the shoulders, ✠ that thou mayest take upon thyself the yoke of his service.

(In naribus:) Signo tibi na ✠ res, ut odórem suavitátis Christi sántias.
(In ore:) Signo tibi os ✠, ut loquáris verba vitæ.
(In pectore:) Signo tibi pe ✠ ctus, ut credas in Deum.
(In scapulis:) Signo tibi scá ✠ pulas, ut suscípias jugum servitútis ejus.

℟ *The Priest then signs the Catechumen's whole body (without physical touch),*

I sign thy whole being, in the name of the Father, ✠ and of the Son, ✠ and of the Holy ✠ Spirit, that thou mayest have etenal life and live for ever.
℞. Amen.

Signo te totum in nómine Pa ✠ tris, et Fí ✠ lii, et Spíritus ✠ Sancti, ut hábeas vitam ætérnam, et vivas in sæcula sæculórum.
℞. Amen.

Let us pray.

E beseech thee, O Lord, graciously hear our prayers, and keep with thy perpetual power this thine Elect, *N.*, who hath been signed with the sign of the Cross of the Lord: that *he,* preserving the rudiments of the greatness of thy glory, may by keeping of thy commandments be worthy to attain unto the glory of regeneration. Through Christ our Lord.
℞. Amen.

Orémus.

RECES nostras, quæsumus Dómine, cleménter exáudi: et hunc Eléctum tuum, *N.*, Crucis Dominicæ impressióne *signátum* perpétua virtúte custódi: ut magnitúdinis glóriæ tuæ rudiménta servans, per custódiam mandatórum tuórum ad regeneratiónis glóriam perveníre mereátur. Per Christum Dominum nostrum.
℞. Amen.

Let us pray.

GOD, Creator of the human race and also its Redeemer, be merciful to the people thou hast adopted. Enrol these reborn children in the New Covenant. Then, as children of promise, they will joyfully receive by grace what they could not attain by nature. Through Christ our

Orémus.

EUS, qui humáni géneris ita es cónditor, ut sis étiam reformátor, propitiáre pópulis adoptívis, et novo testaménto sóbolem novæ prolis adscríbe: ut fílii promissiónis, quod non potuérunt ássequi per naúram, gáudeant suscepísse per grátiam. Per Christum Dóminum no-

Baptism of Adults   # Pastoral Rites

Lord. ℟. Amen.	strum. ℟. Amen.

❧ The Priest imposes his hands upon the hand of the Elect and then extends them over him, saying,

Let us pray.	*Orémus.*
LMIGHTY and everlasting God, Father of Our Lord Jesus Christ, vouchsafe to look upon this thy *servant N.*, whom thou hast been pleased to call to the rudiments of the faith: drive far from *him* all blindness of heart: break all the snares of Satan, wherewith *he* hath been bound: open to *him*, O Lord, the gate of thy mercy, that, being filled with the sign of thy wisdom, *he* may be free from all evil desires, and in the sweet savour of thy commandments may joyfully serve thee in thy Church, and prosper from day to day. Through the same Christ our Lord. ℟. Amen.	MNÍPOTENS, sempitérne Deus, Pater Dómini nostri Jesu Christi, respícere dignáre super *hunc fámulum tuum N., quem* ad rudiménta fídei vocáre dignátus es: omnem cæcitátem cordis ab *eo* expélle: disrúmpe omnes láqueos sátanæ, quibus fúerat *colligátus*: áperi ei, Dómine, jánuam pietátis tuæ, ut signo sapiéntiæ tuæ *imbútus*, ómnium cupiditátum fœtóribus cáreat, et ad suávem odórem præceptórum tuórum *lætus* tibi in Ecclésia tua desérviat, et profíciat de die in diem, ut *idóneus* efficiátur accédere ad grátiam Baptísmi tui, percépta medicína. Per eúmdem Christum Dóminum nostrum. ℟. Amen.

❧ If the salt has not already been blest, it is here blest by the Priest.

Blessing of Salt

XORCISE thee, O creature of salt, in the Name of God the Father ✠ almighty, and in the charity of our Lord Jesus ✠ Christ, and in the power of the Holy ✠ Ghost. XORCISE thee through God ✠ the living, through God ✠ the true, through God ✠ the holy, through God ✠ who created thee for the protection of mankind, and commanded thee to be consecrated	XORCÍZO te, creatúra salis, in nómine Dei ✠ Patris omnipoténtis, et in caritáte Dómini nostri Jesu ✠ Christi, et in virtúte Spíritus ✠ Sancti. XORÍZO te per Deum ✠ vivum, per Deum ✠ verum, per Deum ✠ sanctum, per Deum ✠, qui te ad tutélam humáni géneris procreávit, et pópulo veniénti ad credulitátem per servos suos consecrári

through his servants for the people that should come to believe; that in the Name fo the holy Trinity thou be made a saving sacrament to put to flight the enemy.

HEREFORE, we pray thee, O Lord our God, that sanctifying thou wouldest ✠ sanctify, and blessing thou wouldest ✠ bless this creature of salt, that it be made to all who receive it perfect healing, abiding in their members, in the Name of the same our Lord Jesus Christ, who shall come to judge the living and the dead, and the world by fire.

℟. Amen.

præcépit: ut in nómine sanctæ Trinitátis efficiáris salutáre Sacraméntum ad effugándum inimícum.

ROÍNDE rogámus te, Dómine, Deus noster, ut hanc creatúram salis sanctificándo sanctí ✠ fices, et benedicéndo bene ✠ dícas ut fiat ómnibus accipiéntibus perfécta medicína, pérmanens in viscéribus eórum, in nómine ejúsdem Dómini nostri Jesu Christi, qui ventúrus est judicáre vivos et mórtuos, et sæculum per ignem.

℟. Amen.

Imposition of Salt

¶ If the Catechumen comes from paganism or idolatry, the following Collect is said by the Priest,

Let us pray.

LORD, holy Father, almighty and eternal God, yesterday, who art, who wast, and who remainest even unto the end, whose beginning is unknown, nor can the end be found out; we humbly beseech thee for this thy *servant, N.*, whom thou hast delivered from the error of the Gentiles, and their abominable conversation; vouchsafe to hear *him* who bows down unto thee *his* neck unto the font of purification, that being regenerate by water and the Holy Spirit, having put off the old man, *he* may put on the new, which is created according to thee, may receive the uncorrupt and spotless garment, and may

Orémus.

ÓMINE, sancte, Pater omnípotens, ætérne Deus, qui es, qui eras, et qui pérmanes usque in finem, cujus orígo nescítur, nec finis comprehéndi potest: te súpplices invocámus super *hunc fámulum tuum N., quem* liberásti de erróre gentílium, et conversatióne turpíssima: dignáre exaudíre *eum, qui* tibi cervíces suas humíliat ad lavácri fontem, ut, *renátus* ex aqua et Spíritu Sancto, *exspoliátus* véterem hóminem, índuat novum, qui secúndum te creátus est; accípiat vestem incorrúptam, et immaculátam, tibíque Deo nostro servíre mereátur. Per Christum Dóminum nostrum.

℟. Amen.

merit to serve thee, our God. Through Christ our Lord. Through Christ our Lord.

℟. Amen.

❡ The Priest now puts a small quantity of the blessed salt into the mouth of the Catechumen, saying:

N., receive the salt of wisdom: may it be to thee a propitiation unto life everlasting.

℟. Amen.
℣. Peace be with thee.
℟. And with thy spirit.

Let us pray.

GOD of our fathers, O God the author of all truth, we humbly beseech thee, that thou wouldest vouchsafe mercifully to look upon this thy *servant N.*, and that thou wouldest suffer *him* no longer to hunger, now tasting this first relish of salt, to the end that, being fulfilled with heavenly food, *he* may ever be fervent in spirit, rejoicing in hope, ever serving thy Name.

EAD *him*, O Lord, we beseech thee, to the washing of the new birth, that *he* may with thy faithful be worthy to attain unto the eternal rewards of thy promises. Through Christ our Lord.

℟. Amen.

N., Accipe sal sapiéntiæ: propitiátio sit tibi in vitam ætérnam.

℟. Amen.
℣. Pax tibi.
℟. Et cum spíritu tuo.

Orémus.

EUS patrum nostrórum, Deus universæ cónditor veritátis, te súpplices exorámus, ut *hunc fámulum tuum N.* respícere dignéris propítius, et hoc primum pábulum salis gustántem, non diútius esuríre permíttas, quo minus cibo expleátur cælésti, quátenus sit semper spíritu fervens, spe gaudens, tuo semper nómini sérviens.

ᴘᴇʀ duc *eum*, Dómine, quæsumus, ad novæ regeneratiónis lavácrum, ut cum fidélibus tuis promissiónum tuárum ætérna præmia cónsequi mereátur. Per Christum Dóminum nostrum.

℟. Amen.

Pastoral Rites *Baptism of Adults*

Exorcisms for Men

¶ If there be women among the Elect, they stand to the side for while the males receive the following exorcisms.

℣. Pray, O elect, and bow the knee, and say: Our Father.

℟. Our Father, who art in heaven, Hallowed be thy Name. Thy kingdom come. Thy will be done on earth, As it is in heaven. Give us this day our daily bread. And forgive us our trespasses, As we forgive those who trespass against us. And lead us not into temptation; But deliver us from evil.

℣. Arise, complete thy prayer, and say: Amen.

℟. Amen.

℣. (To the Godfather:) Make the sign of the Cross on him.

¶ The Priest says,

℣. (To the Elect:) Come forward.

¶ The Godfather approaches and signs the Elect on the forehead, saying:

In the Name of the Father, and of the Son, and of the Holy Spirit.

¶ The Priest then also makes the sign of the Cross on the forehead of the Elect (only once), saying,

In the name of the Father, and of the Son, and of the Holy Spirit.

¶ The Priest imposes his hand upon the Elect, then stretches them out over him, saying,

Let us pray.

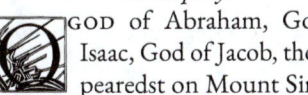GOD of Abraham, God of Isaac, God of Jacob, thou appearedst on Mount Sinai to thy servant, Moses; thou leddest the children of Israel out of Egypt, gra-

℣. Ora, Elécte, flecte génua, et dic: Pater noster.

℟. Pater noster, qui es in cælis, sanctificétur nomen tuum: advéniat regnum tuum: fiat volúntas tua, sicut in cælo et in terra. Panem nostrum quotidiánum da nobis hódie: et dimítte nobis débita nostra, sicut et nos dimíttimus debitóribus nostris: et ne nos indúcas in tentatiónem: sed líbera nos a malo.

℣. Leva, comple oratiónem tuam, et dic: Amen.

℟. Amen.

℣. (Patrino:) Signa eum.

℣. (Electo:) Accéde.

In nómine Patris, et Fílii, et Spíritus Sancti.

In nómine Patris, et Fílii, et Spíritus Sancti.

Orémus.

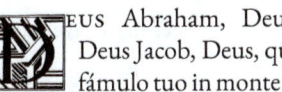EUS Abraham, Deus Isaac, Deus Jacob, Deus, qui Móysi fámulo tuo in monte Sínai apparuísti, et fílios Israël de terra Ægypti eduxísti, députans eis Angelum pietá-

Baptism of Adults   # Pastoral Rites

ciously appointing an Angel to guard them day and night. We ask thee, Lord, to send thy holy Angel from heaven to guard in the same way thy servant, *N.*, and to lead him to the grace of thy baptism. Through Christ our Lord.

℟. Amen.

HEREFORE, accursed devil, acknowledge thy condemnation, and pay homage to the living and true God; pay homage to Jesus Christ, his Son, and to the Holy Spirit, and depart from this servant of God, *N.*, for Jesus Christ, our God and Lord, hath called him to his holy grace and to the Font of baptism. Accursed devil, never dare to desecrate this sign of the holy ✠ Cross which we are tracing upon his forehead. Through the same Christ our Lord, who is come to judge the living and the dead, and the world by fire.

℟. Amen.

℣. Pray, O elect, and bow the knee, and say: Our Father.

℟. Our Father, who art in heaven, Hallowed be thy Name. Thy kingdom come. Thy will be done on earth, As it is in heaven. Give us this day our daily bread. And forgive us our trespasses, As we forgive those who trespass against us. And lead us not into temptation; But deliver us from evil.

℣. Arise, complete thy prayer, and say: Amen.

℟. Amen.

℣. (To the Godfather:) **Make the sign of the Cross on him.**

tis tuæ, qui custodíret eos die ac nocte: te quæsumus, Dómine; ut míttere dignéris sanctum Angelum tuum de cælis, qui simíliter custódiat et hunc fámulum tuum *N.* et perdúcat eum ad grátiam Baptísmi tui. Per Christum Dóminum nostrum.

℟. Amen.

RGO, maledícte diábole, recognósce senténtiam tuam, et da honórem Deo vivo et vero, da honórem Jesu Christo Fílio ejus, et Spirítui Sancto, et recéde ab hoc fámulo Dei *N.*, quia istum sibi Deus et Dóminus noster Jesus Christus ad suam sanctam grátiam, fontémque Baptísmatis vocáre dignátus est: et hoc signum sanctæ cru ✠ cis (signat singulos), quod nos fronti ejus damus, tu, maledícte diábole, numquam áudeas violáre. Per eúmdem Christum Dóminum nostrum, qui ventúrus est judicáre vivos et mórtuos, et sæculum per ignem.

℟. Amen.

℣. Ora, Elécte, flecte génua, et dic: Pater noster.

℟. Pater noster, qui es in cælis, sanctificétur nomen tuum: advéniat regnum tuum: fiat volúntas tua, sicut in cælo et in terra. Panem nostrum quotidiánum da nobis hódie: et dimítte nobis débita nostra, sicut et nos dimíttimus debitóribus nostris: et ne nos indúcas in tentatiónem: sed líbera nos a malo.

℣. Leva, comple oratiónem tuam, et dic: Amen.

℟. Amen.

℣. (Patrino:) **Signa eum.**

Pastoral Rites *Baptism of Adults*

¶ The Priest says,

℣. (To the Elect:) **Come forward.** | ℣. (Electo:) **Accéde.**

¶ The Godfather approaches and signs the Elect on the forehead, saying:

In the Name of the Father, and of the Son, and of the Holy Spirit. | In nómine Patris, et Fílii, et Spíritus Sancti.

¶ The Priest then also makes the sign of the Cross on the forehead of the Elect (only once), saying,

In the name of the Father, and of the Son, and of the Holy Spirit. | In nómine Patris, et Fílii, et Spíritus Sancti.

¶ The Priest imposes his hand upon the Elect, then stretches them out over him, saying,

Let us pray. | *Orémus.*

O GOD, thou art the unfailing support of those who call upon thee, the liberator of those who pray to thee, the peace of those who appeal to thee, the life of those who believe in thee, the resurrection of those who die in thee. I call upon thee in behalf of thy servant, *N.*, that asketh for the gift of baptism and hopeth to obtain, through this spiritual rebirth, everlasting grace. Accept him, O Lord. Thou hast graciously said, 'Ask, and ye shall receive' seek, and ye shall find; knock, and it shall be opened unto you.' Then grant thy favour to him that knocketh, so that, having received an everlasting blessing in his baptism, he may possess the kingdom of grace that thou hast promised. Who, with the Father and the Holy Spirit, livest and reignest ever one God, world without end.

℟. Amen.

DEUS, immortále præsídium ómnium postulántium, liberátio súpplicum, pax rogántium, vita credéntium, resurréctio mortuórum: te ínvoco super hunc fámulum tuum *N.*, qui, Baptísmi tui donum petens, ætérnam cónsequi grátiam spirituáli regeneratióne desíderat: áccipe eum, Dómine, et quia dignátus es dícere: Pétite, et accipiétis; quǽrite, et inveniétis; pulsáte, et aperiétur vobis: peténti præmium pórrige, et jánuam pande pulsánti, ut, ætérnam cæléstis lavácri benedictiónem consecútus, promíssa tui múneris regna percípiat: Qui cum Patre, et Spíritu Sancto vivis et regnas Deus, in sǽcula sæculórum.

℟. Amen.

HEAR, accursed Satan, I adjure thee by the Name of the eternal God and of our Saviour Jesus Christ his Son. Depart | AUDI, maledícte sátana, adjurátus per nomen ætérni Dei, et Salvatóris nostri Jesu Christi Fílii ejus, cum tua victus invídia, tre-

Baptism of Adults

Pastoral Rites

with thy envy: conquered, trembling and groaning. May have thou no part in the servant of God, *N.*, that already hath thoughts of heaven and is about to renounce thee and thy world and achieve a blessed immortality. Therefore, give honour to the Holy Spirit who, descending from the high throne of heaven, cometh to upset thy wiles and to make perfect the heart cleansed at the divine fountain, a temple and dwelling place dedicated to God. And thus entirely freed from the harmful effects of past sins, may this servant of God give thanks always to the eternal God and bless his Holy Name for ever and ever.

℞. Amen.

℣. Pray, O elect, and bow the knee, and say: Our Father.

℞. Our Father, who art in heaven, Hallowed be thy Name. Thy kingdom come. Thy will be done on earth, As it is in heaven. Give us this day our daily bread. And forgive us our trespasses, As we forgive those who trespass against us. And lead us not into temptation; But deliver us from evil.

℣. Arise, complete thy prayer, and say: Amen.

℞. Amen.

℣. (To the Godfather:) Make the sign of the Cross on him.

¶ The Priest says,

℣. (To the Elect:) Come forward.

¶ The Godfather approaches and signs the Elect on the forehead, saying:

In the Name of the Father, and of the Son, and of the Holy Spirit.

mens, geménsque discéde: nihil tibi sit commúne cum servo Dei *N.*, jam cæléstia cogitánte, renuntiatúro tibi et sæculo tuo, et beátæ immortalitáti victúro. Da ígitur honórem adveniénti Spirítui Sancto, qui, ex summa cæli arce descéndens, proturbátis fráudibus tuis, divíno fonte purgátum pectus, sanctificátum Deo templum et habitáculum perfíciat ut, ab ómnibus pénitus nóxiis prætéritórum críminum liberátus, servus Dei grátias perénni Deo réferat semper, et benedícat nomen sanctum ejus in sǽcula sæculórum.

℞. Amen.

℣. Ora, Elécte, flecte génua, et dic: Pater noster.

℞. Pater noster, qui es in cælis, sanctificétur nomen tuum: advéniat regnum tuum: fiat volúntas tua, sicut in cælo et in terra. Panem nostrum quotidiánum da nobis hódie: et dimítte nobis débita nostra, sicut et nos dimíttimus debitóribus nostris: et ne nos indúcas in tentatiónem: sed líbera nos a malo.

℣. Leva, comple oratiónem tuam, et dic: Amen.

℞. Amen.

℣. (Patrino:) Signa eum.

℣. (Electo:) Accéde.

In nómine Patris, et Fílii, et Spíritus Sancti.

Pastoral Rites — *Baptism of Adults*

¶ The Priest then also makes the sign of the Cross on the forehead of the Elect (only once), saying,

In the name of the Father, and of the Son, and of the Holy Spirit.	In nómine Patris, et Fílii, et Spíritus Sancti.

¶ The Priest imposes his hand upon the Elect, then stretches them out over him, saying,

I EXORCISE thee, unclean spirit, in the Name of the Father ✠, and of the Son ✠, and of the Holy ✠ Ghost. Come forth, depart from this servant of God, *N.*, for he commandeth thee, accursed and damned spirit, he who walked upon the sea and extended his right hand to Peter as he was sinking.

T HEREFORE, accursed devil, acknowledge thy condemnation and pay homage to the living and true God; pay homage to Jesus Christ, his Son, and to the Holy Spirit, and depart from this servant of God, *N.*, for Jesus Christ, our Lord and God, hath called him to his holy grace and to the Font of baptism. Accursed devil, never dare to desecrate this sign of the holy ✠ Cross which we are tracing upon his forehead. Through the same Christ our Lord, who is come to judge the living and the dead, and the world by fire. ℟. Amen.

E XORCÍZO te, immúnde spíritus, in nómine Pa ✠ tris, et Fí ✠ lii, et Spíritus ✠ Sancti, ut éxeas, et recédas ab hoc fámulo Dei *N.* Ipse enim tibi ímperat, maledícte damnáte, qui pédibus super mare ambulávit, et Petro mergénti déxteram porréxit.

E RGO, maledícte diábole, recognósce senténtiam tuam, et da honórem Deo vivo et vero, da honórem Jesu Christo Fílio ejus, et Spirítui Sancto, et recéde ab hoc fámulo Dei *N.*, quia istum sibi Deus et Dóminus noster Jesus Christus ad suam sanctam grátiam, fontémque Baptísmatis vocáre dignátus est: et hoc signum sanctæ cru ✠ cis (signat singulos), quod nos fronti ejus damus, tu, maledícte diábole, numquam áudeas violáre. Per eúmdem Christum Dóminum nostrum, qui ventúrus est judicáre vivos et mórtuos, et sæculum per ignem. ℟. Amen.

Baptism of Adults # Pastoral Rites

Exorcisms for Women

¶ If there be women among the Elect, the men stand to the side for while the females receive the following exorcisms.

℣. Pray, O elect, and bow the knee, and say: Our Father.

℟. Our Father, who art in heaven, Hallowed be thy Name. Thy kingdom come. Thy will be done on earth, As it is in heaven. Give us this day our daily bread. And forgive us our trespasses, As we forgive those who trespass against us. And lead us not into temptation; But deliver us from evil.

℣. Arise, complete thy prayer, and say: Amen.

℟. Amen.

℣. (To the Godfather or Godmother:) Make the sign of the Cross on her.

℣. Ora, Elécta, flecte génua, et dic: Pater noster.

℟. Pater noster, qui es in cælis, sanctificétur nomen tuum: advéniat regnum tuum: fiat volúntas tua, sicut in cælo et in terra. Panem nostrum quotidiánum da nobis hódie: et dimítte nobis débita nostra, sicut et nos dimíttimus debitóribus nostris: et ne nos indúcas in tentatiónem: sed líbera nos a malo.

℣. Leva, comple oratiónem tuam, et dic: Amen.

℟. Amen.

℣. (Patrino:) Signa eam.

¶ The Priest says

℣. (To the Elect:) **Come forward.**

℣. (Electo:) **Accéde.**

¶ The Godfather or Godmother approaches and signs the Elect on the forehead, saying:

In the Name of the Father, and of the Son, and of the Holy Spirit.

In nómine Patris, et Fílii, et Spíritus Sancti.

¶ The Priest then also makes the sign of the Cross on the forehead of the Elect (only once), saying,

In the Name of the Father, and of the Son, and of the Holy Spirit.

In nómine Patris, et Fílii, et Spíritus Sancti.

¶ The Priest imposes his hand upon the Elect, then stretches it out over her, saying,

Let us pray.

Orémus.

GOD of heaven, God of earth, God of angels, God of archangels, God of patriarchs, God of prophets, God of apostles, God of martyrs, God of

EUS cæli, Deus terræ, Deus Angelórum, Deus Archangelórum, Deus Patriarchárum, Deus Prophetárum, Deus Apostolórum, Deus Mártyrum, Deus Confessó-

confessors, God of virgins, God of all that live well, God, to whom every tongue confesseth, and every knee boweth, of those that are in heaven, on earth, and under the earth; I call upon thee, O Lord, for this thy handmaid, *N.*, that thou mayest vouchsafe to guard her, and to bring her to the grace of thy baptism. Through Christ our Lord.

℟. Amen.

HEREFORE, accursed devil, acknowledge thy condemnation, and pay homage to the living and true God; pay homage to Jesus Christ, his Son, and to the Holy Spirit, and depart from this handmaid of God, *N.*, for Jesus Christ, our God and Lord, hath called her to his holy grace and to the Font of baptism. Accursed devil, never dare to desecrate this sign of the holy ✠ Cross which we are tracing upon her forehead. Through the same Christ our Lord, who is come to judge the living and the dead, and the world by fire.

℟. Amen.

℣. Pray, O elect, and bow the knee, and say: Our Father.

℟. Our Father, who art in heaven, Hallowed be thy Name. Thy kingdom come. Thy will be done on earth, As it is in heaven. Give us this day our daily bread. And forgive us our trespasses, As we forgive those who trespass against us. And lead us not into temptation; But deliver us from evil.

℣. Arise, complete thy prayer, and say: Amen.

rum, Deus Vírginum, Deus ómnium bene vivéntium, Deus, cui omnis lingua confitétur, et omne genu fléctitur, cæléstium, terréstrium, et infernórum: te ínvoco, Dómine, super hanc fámulam tuam *N.*, ut eam custodíre, et perdúcere dignéris ad grátiam Baptísmi tui. Per Christum Dóminum nostrum.

℟. Amen.

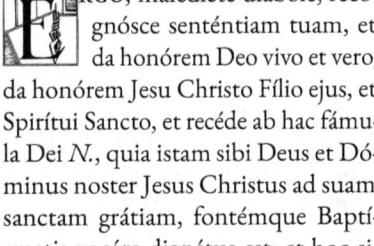RGO, maledícte diábole, recognósce senténtiam tuam, et da honórem Deo vivo et vero, da honórem Jesu Christo Fílio ejus, et Spirítui Sancto, et recéde ab hac fámula Dei *N.*, quia istam sibi Deus et Dóminus noster Jesus Christus ad suam sanctam grátiam, fontémque Baptísmatis vocáre dignátus est: et hoc signum sanctæ cru ✠ cis (signat singulos), quod nos fronti ejus damus, tu, maledícte diábole, numquam áudeas violáre. Per eúmdem Christum Dóminum nostrum, qui ventúrus est judicáre vivos et mórtuos, et sǽculum per ignem.

℟. Amen.

℣. Ora, Elécta, flecte génua, et dic: Pater noster.

℟. Pater noster, qui es in cælis, sanctificétur nomen tuum: advéniat regnum tuum: fiat volúntas tua, sicut in cælo et in terra. Panem nostrum quotidiánum da nobis hódie: et dimítte nobis débita nostra, sicut et nos dimíttimus debitóribus nostris: et ne nos indúcas in tentatiónem: sed líbera nos a malo.

℣. Leva, comple oratiónem tuam, et dic: Amen.

Baptism of Adults

Pastoral Rites

℟. Amen.

℣. (To the Godfather or Godmother:) Make the sign of the Cross on her.

¶ The Priest says

℣. (To the Elect:) Come forward.

¶ The Godfather or Godmother approaches and signs the Elect on the forehead, saying:

In the Name of the Father, and of the Son, and of the Holy Spirit.

¶ The Priest then also makes the sign of the Cross on the forehead of the Elect (only once), saying,

In the Name of the Father, and of the Son, and of the Holy Spirit.

¶ The Priest imposes his hand upon the Elect, then stretches it out over her, saying,

Let us pray.

GOD of Abraham, God of Isaac, God of Jacob, thou appearedst on Mount Sinai to thy servant, Moses; thou leddest the children of Israel out of Egypt, graciously appointing an Angel to guard them day and night. We ask thee, Lord, to send thy holy Angel from heaven to guard in the same way thy handmaid, *N.*, and to lead her to the grace of thy baptism. Through Christ our Lord.

℟. Amen.

℟. Amen.

℣. (Patrino:) Signa eam.

℣. (Electo:) Accéde.

In nómine Patris, et Fílii, et Spíritus Sancti.

In nómine Patris, et Fílii, et Spíritus Sancti.

Orémus.

EUS Abraham, Deus Isaac, Deus Jacob, Deus, qui Móysi fámulo tuo in monte Sínai apparuísti, et fílios Israël de terra Ægypti eduxísti, députans eis Angelum pietátis tuæ, qui custodíret eos die ac nocte: te quæsumus, Dómine; ut míttere dignéris sanctum Angelum tuum de cælis, qui simíliter custódiat et hanc fámulam tuam *N.* et perdúcat eam ad grátiam Baptísmi tui. Per Christum Dóminum nostrum.

℟. Amen.

Exorcism

HEREFORE, accursed devil, acknowledge thy condemnation, and pay homage to the living and true God; pay homage to Jesus Christ, his Son, and to the Holy Spirit, and depart from this handmaid of God, *N.*, for Jesus Christ, our God and Lord, hath called her to his

RGO, maledícte diábole, recognósce senténtiam tuam, et da honórem Deo vivo et vero, da honórem Jesu Christo Fílio ejus, et Spirítui Sancto, et recéde ab hac fámula Dei *N.*, quia istam sibi Deus et Dóminus noster Jesus Christus ad suam sanctam grátiam, fontémque Baptí-

Pastoral Rites — *Baptism of Adults*

holy grace and to the Font of baptism. Accursed devil, never dare to desecrate this sign of the holy ✠ Cross which we are tracing upon her forehead. Through the same Christ our Lord, who is come to judge the living and the dead, and the world by fire.

℟. Amen.

℣. Pray, O elect, and bow the knee, and say: Our Father.

℟. Our Father, who art in heaven, Hallowed be thy Name. Thy kingdom come. Thy will be done on earth, As it is in heaven. Give us this day our daily bread. And forgive us our trespasses, As we forgive those who trespass against us. And lead us not into temptation; But deliver us from evil.

℣. Arise, complete thy prayer, and say: Amen.

℟. Amen.

℣. (To the Godfather or Godmother:) Make the sign of the Cross on her.

¶ The Priest says

℣. (To the Elect:) **Come forward.**

¶ The Godfather or Godmother approaches and signs the Elect on the forehead, saying:

In the Name of the Father, and of the Son, and of the Holy Spirit.

¶ The Priest then also makes the sign of the Cross on the forehead of the Elect (only once), saying,

In the Name of the Father, and of the Son, and of the Holy Spirit.

¶ The Priest imposes his hand upon the Elect, then stretches it out over her, saying,

Let us pray.

EXORCISE thee, unclean spirit, by the Fa ✠ ther, and the ✠ Son, and the Holy ✠ Ghost,

---

smatis vocáre dignátus est: et hoc signum sanctæ cru ✠ cis (signat singulos), quod nos fronti ejus damus, tu, maledícte diábole, numquam áudeas violáre. Per eúmdem Christum Dóminum nostrum, qui ventúrus est judicáre vivos et mórtuos, et sæculum per ignem.

℟. Amen.

℣. Ora, Elécta, flecte génua, et dic: Pater noster.

℟. Pater noster, qui es in cælis, sanctificétur nomen tuum: advéniat regnum tuum: fiat volúntas tua, sicut in cælo et in terra. Panem nostrum quotidiánum da nobis hódie: et dimítte nobis débita nostra, sicut et nos dimíttimus debitóribus nostris: et ne nos indúcas in tentatiónem: sed líbera nos a malo.

℣. Leva, comple oratiónem tuam, et dic: Amen.

℟. Amen.

℣. (Patrino:) **Signa eam.**

℣. (Electo:) **Accéde.**

In nómine Patris, et Fílii, et Spíritus Sancti.

In nómine Patris, et Fílii, et Spíritus Sancti.

Orémus.

EXORCÍZO te, immúnde spíritus, per Pa ✠ trem, et Fí ✠ lium, et Spíritum ✠ Sanctum, ut éxeas,

that thou go out and depart from this handmaid of God, *N.*; for he commandeth thee, accursed one, who opened the eyes of him that was born blind, and raised Lazarus, after four days, from the grave.

HEREFORE, accursed devil, acknowledge thy condemnation, and pay homage to the living and true God; pay homage to Jesus Christ, his Son, and to the Holy Spirit, and depart from this handmaid of God, *N.*, for Jesus Christ, our God and Lord, hath called her to his holy grace and to the Font of baptism. Accursed devil, never dare to desecrate this sign of the holy ✠ Cross (He signs each one individually.) which we are tracing upon her forehead. Through the same Christ our Lord, who is come to judge the living and the dead, and the world by fire.

℟. Amen.

et recédas ab hac fámula Dei *N.* Ipse enim tibi ímperat, maledícte damnáte, qui cæco nato óculos apéruit, et quatriduánum Lázarum de monuménto suscitávit.

RGO, maledícte diábole, recognósce senténtiam tuam, et da honórem Deo vivo et vero, da honórem Jesu Christo Fílio ejus, et Spirítui Sancto, et recéde ab hac fámula Dei *N.*, quia istam sibi Deus et Dóminus noster Jesus Christus ad suam sanctam grátiam, fontémque Baptísmatis vocáre dignátus est: et hoc signum sanctæ cru ✠ cis (Signat singulos), quod nos fronti ejus damus, tu, maledícte diábole, numquam áudeas violáre. Per eúmdem Christum Dóminum nostrum, qui ventúrus est judicáre vivos et mórtuos, et sæculum per ignem.

℟. Amen.

Blessing of the Catechumens

❧ *If there be many Catechumens of both sexes, the men return, the men being on the Priest's right and the women on his left, as at the beginning.*

❧ *The Priest then imposes his hand upon the Catechumen (if there be many, he imposes on each individually and then raises it over all of them) and says,*

Let us pray.

ENTREAT thy eternal and most just mercy, O Lord holy, Father Almighty, everlasting God, author of light and truth, upon *this servant* of God, *N.*, that thou wouldest vouchsafe to enlighten *him* with the light of thine understand-

Orémus.

TÉRNAM, ac justíssimam pietátem tuam déprecor, Dómine sancte, Pater omnípotens, ætérne Deus, auctor lúminis et veritátis, super *hunc fámulum tuum N.* ut dignéris *eum* illumináre lúmine intelligéntiæ tuæ: munda *eum*, et sanctífi-

Pastoral Rites — *Baptism of Adults*

ing: cleanse *him* and sanctify *him*: give *him* true knowledge, that being made worthy of the grace of thy Baptism, *he* may hold firm hope, right counsel, and holy doctrine. Through Christ our Lord.

℟. Amen.

ca: da ei sciéntiam veram, ut *dignus* efficiátur accédere ad grátiam Baptísmi tui, téneat firmam spem, consílium rectum, doctrínam sanctam, ut *aptus* sit ad percipiéndam grátiam tuam. Per Christum Dóminum nostrum.

℟. Amen.

Entrance into the Church

¶ The Priest holds out his left hand on the Elect's right arm, or the end of his stole on the left side to the Elect, introducing him into the Church (if there be many Catechumens, it is done individually with each), while saying,

N., Enter into the holy Church of God, that thou mayest receive heavenly blessing from the Lord Jesus Christ, and may have thy portion with him and with his saints.

℟. Amen.

N., Ingrédere in sanctam ecclésiam Dei, ut accípias benedictiónem cæléstem a Dómino Jesu Christo, et hábeas partem cum illo et Sanctis ejus.

℟. Amen.

¶ When the Elect enters, he either prostrates at the entrance or prostrates himself on the Pavement (in the centre right before the Altar Rail and Chancel) and adores (if there be many, they all do so together).

¶ Then he rises (if there be many, they all do so together), and the Priest lays his hand on his head (each individually, if there be many), and the Elect recites with him the Nicene Creed and the Lord's Prayer (if there be many, they all do so together).

I BELIEVE in one God, the Father Almighty, Maker of heaven and earth, And of all things visible and invisible:

And in one Lord Jesus Christ, the only-begotten Son of God; Begotten of his Father before all worlds, God of God, Light of Light, Very God of very God; Begotten, not made; Being of one substance with the Father; By whom all things were made: Who for us men and for our salvation came down from heaven, And was incarnate by the Holy Ghost of the Virgin

REDO in unum Deum, Patrem omnipoténtem, factórem cæli et terræ, visibílium ómnium et invisibílium.

Et in unum Dóminum Jesum Christum, Fílium Dei unigénitum. Et ex Patre natum ante ómnia sǽcula. Deum de Deo, lumen de lúmine, Deum verum de Deo vero. Génitum, non factum, consubstantiálem Patri: per quem ómnia facta sunt. Qui propter nos hómines et propter nostram salútem descéndit de cælis. Et incarnátus est de Spíritu Sancto ex María Vírgine:

Baptism of Adults   # Pastoral Rites

Mary, And was made man: And was crucified also for us under Pontius Pilate; He suffered and was buried: And the third day he rose again according to the Scriptures: And ascended into heaven, And sitteth on the right hand of the Father: And he shall come again, with glory, to judge both the quick and the dead; Whose kingdom shall have no end.

And I believe in the Holy Ghost, The Lord, and Giver of Life, Who proceedeth from the Father; Who with the Father and the Son together is worshiped and glorified; Who spake by the Prophets: And I believe one, holy, catholic, and apostolic Church: I acknowledge one Baptism for the remission of sins: And I look for the Resurrection of the dead: ✠ And the Life of the world to come. Amen.

UR Father, who art in heaven, Hallowed be thy Name. Thy kingdom come. Thy will be done on earth, As it is in heaven. Give us this day our daily bread. And forgive us our trespasses, As we forgive those who trespass against us. And lead us not into temptation; But deliver us from evil. Amen.

Et homo factus est. Crucifíxus étiam pro nobis: sub Póntio Piláto passus, et sepúltus est. Et resurréxit tértia die, secúndum Scriptúras. Et ascéndit in cælum: sedet ad déxteram Patris. Et íterum ventúrus est cum glória judicáre vivos et mórtuos: cujus regni non erit finis.

Et in Spíritum Sanctum, Dóminum et vivificántem: qui ex Patre procédit. Qui cum Patre et Fílio simul adorátur et conglorificátur: qui locútus est per Prophétas. Et unam sanctam cathólicam et apostólicam Ecclésiam. Confíteor unum baptísma in remissiónem peccatórum. Et exspécto resurrectiónem mortuórum. ✠ Et vitam ventúri sǽculi. Amen.

ATER noster, qui es in cælis, sanctificétur nomen tuum: advéniat regnum tuum: fiat volúntas tua, sicut in cælo et in terra. Panem nostrum quotidiánum da nobis hódie: et dimítte nobis débita nostra, sicut et nos dimíttimus debitóribus nostris: et ne nos indúcas in tentatiónem: sed líbera nos a malo. Amen.

¶ *The Priest then turning his back to the doors of the Baptistry, imposes his hand upon the head of the Elect (each Elect), and afterwards, extending his hands, he says,*

HE threats of punishments and tortures are not hidden from thee, Satan, the day of judgement, the day of pain, the day which is to come like a fiery furnace, in which unending destruction is prepared for thee and all thine angels. Therefore, ac-

EC te latet, sátana, imminére tibi pœnas, imminére tibi torménta, imminére tibi diem judícii, diem supplícii sempitérni; diem, qui ventúrus est velut clíbanus ardens, in quo tibi, atque univérsis ángelis tuis præparátus sempitérnus erit intéritus.

Pastoral Rites — *Baptism of Adults*

cursed and damnable one, pay homage to the living and true God; pay homage to Jesus Christ, his Son, give homage to the Holy Spirit, the Consoler, in whose Name and power I command thee, unclean spirit, whoever thou mayest be, go forth and depart from *this servant* of God, *N.*, whom this day Jesus Christ, our God and Lord, hath called to his holy grace and blessing, and to the Font of baptism. May *he* become the temple of God through the water of rebirth unto remission of all *his* sins. In the Name of the same Jesus Christ our Lord, who shall come to judge the living and the dead, and the world by fire.

℟. Amen.

Proínde, damnáte, atque damnánde, da honórem Deo vivo et vero, da honórem Jesu Christo Fílio ejus, da honórem Spirítui Sancto Paráclito, in cujus nómine atque virtúte præcípio tibi, quicúmque es, spíritus immúnde, ut éxeas, et recédas ab *hoc fámulo Dei N.*, *quem* hódie idem Deus et Dóminus noster Jesus Christus ad suam sanctam grátiam et benedictiónem, fontémque Baptísmatis dono vocáre dignátus est: ut fiat ejus templum per aquam regeneratiónis in remissiónem ómnium peccatórum. In nómine ejúsdem Dómini nostri Jesu Christi, qui ventúrus est judicáre vivos et mórtuos et sæculum per ignem.

℟. Amen.

❧ *Then the Priest puts spit from his mouth into his thumb, then makes the sign of the Cross on the right, and afterwards on the left, ear of the Catechumen, and says once only:*

Ephthatha, ✠ that is, ✠ Be thou opened.

Ephpheta, ✠ quod est, ✠ Adaperíre.

❧ *And then, signing the nostrils, he adds:*

For a savour ✠ of sweetness.

In odórem suavitátis.

❧ *Lastly, in a louder tone of voice, he says,*

But thou, devil, flee away; for the judgement of God draweth nigh.

Tu autem effugáre, diábole; appropinquábit enim judícium Dei.

❧ *He then questions the Catechumen, asking,*

℣. What is thy name?
℟. N.
℣. *N.*, Dost thou renounce Satan?
℟. I do renounce him.
℣. And all his works?
℟. I do renounce them.
℣. And all his allurements?
℟. I do renounce them.

℣. Quis vocáris?
℟. N.
℣. *N.*, Abrenúntias Sátanæ?
℟. Abrenúntio.
℣. Et ómnibus opéribus ejus?
℟. Abrenúntio.
℣. Et ómnibus pompis ejus?
℟. Abrenúntio.

Baptism of Adults # Pastoral Rites

❡ The Priest then dips his right thumb into the Oil of Catechumens, and with it makes the sign of the Cross on the breast, and between the shoulders of the Catechumen, saying:

I anoint thee ✠ with the Oil of salvation, in Christ Jesus our Lord, that thou mayest have eternal life. ℟. Amen. ℣. Peace be to thee. ℟. And with thy spirit.	Ego te línio ✠ óleo salútis in Christo Jesu Dómino nostro, ut habeas vitam ætérnam. ℟. Amen. ℣. Pax tibi. ℟. Et cum spíritu tuo.

❡ Then he wipes his thumb and the places anointed with cotton or something similar and says,

o forth, unclean spirit, and pay homage to the living and true God. Depart, unclean spirit, and give place to Jesus Christ, his Son. Depart, unclean spirit, and give place to the Holy Spirit, the Consoler.

xi, immúnde spíritus, et da honórem Deo vivo et vero. Fuge, immúnde spíritus, et da locum Jesu Christo Fílio ejus. Recéde, immúnde spíritus, et da locum Spirítui Sancto Parácleto.

❡ Standing outside the Chancel, the Priest takes off his violet cope and stole and puts on the same of white colour.

❡ The Priest leads the Catechumen to the Baptistry, where if the water has not been blessed, it is blessed according to the appropriate rite (p. 94).

❡ When at the Font, the Priest asks,

℣. What is thy name? ℟. N. ℣. *N.*, Dost thou believe in God the Father Almighty, Creator of heaven and earth? ℟. I do believe. ℣. Dost thou believe in Jesus Christ, his only Son our Lord, who was born into this world, and who suffered for us? ℟. I do believe. ℣. Dost thou also believe in the Holy Ghost, the Holy Catholic Church, the Communion of Saints, the Forgiveness of Sins, the Resurrection of the Body, and Life	℣. Quis vocáris? ℟. N. ℣. *N.*, Credis in Deum Patrem omnipoténtem, Creatórem cæli et terræ? ℟. Credo. ℣. Credis in Jesum Christum Fílium ejus únicum, Dóminum nostrum, natum et passum? ℟. Credo. ℣. Credis et in Spíritum Sanctum, sanctam Ecclésiam Cathólicam, Sanctórum communiónem, remissiónem peccatórum, carnis resurrectiónem et vitam ætérnam?

Pastoral Rites *Baptism of Adults*

Everlasting?
℟. I do believe.
℣. *N.*, What seekest thou?
℟. Baptism.
℣. Wilt thou be baptised?
℟. I will.

℟. Credo.
℣. *N.*, Quid petis?
℟. Baptísmum.
℣. Vis baptizári?
℟. Volo.

¶ The Priest takes the Elect by his arms, near the shoulders, and, the upper part of his body being uncovered, the rest decently covered, the Priest, thrice immersing him, and raising him as often, thus invoking the Most Holy Trinity once only.

¶ Meanwhile, the Godfather or Godmother, or both, either holds or touches him.

N., I baptise thee in the name of the Father, (he immerses) and of the Son, (he immerses) and of the Holy Ghost (he immerses).

N. Ego te baptízo in nómine Patris, (mergit) et Fílii, (mergit) et Spíritus Sancti (mergit).

¶ After cleansing his hands, the Priest immediately moves onto Confirmation (p. 629).

Pastoral Rites

Sacrament of Penance

¶ The Penitent begins with the following.

Bless me, Father, for I have sinned.

℣. The Lord be in thy heart and upon thy lips, that so thou mayest worthily confess all thy sins; In the Name of the Father, ✠ and of the Son, and of the Holy Ghost. Amen.

¶ The Penitent then confesses his sins using the following or similar formula:

I confess to God Almighty, to Blessed Mary Ever-Virgin, to blessed Michael the Archangel, to blessed John Baptist, to the holy Apostles Peter and Paul, to all the Saints, and to thee, Father, that I have sinned exceedingly in thought, word, and deed, by my fault, by my own fault, by my own most grievous fault,

Especially I accuse myself that since my last Confession, which was (Say how long) ago, I have committed the following sins. (Confess your sins and conclude with:)

For these and for all my other sins which I cannot now remember, I am heartily sorry, firmly purpose amendment, and humbly ask pardon of God; and of thee, my spiritual father, penance, counsel, and Absolution.

Wherefore I beg blessed Mary Ever-Virgin, blessed Michael the Archangel, blessed John Baptist, the holy Apostles Peter and Paul, all the Saints, and thee, father, to pray for me to the Lord our God.

¶ Here the Priest gives penance, counsel, and then absolution saying,

LMIGHTY God have mercy upon thee, forgive thee thy sins, and bring thee to everlasting life. *Amen.*

HE Almighty and merciful Lord grant thee pardon, ✠ absolution, and remission of thy sins. *Amen.*

UR Lord Jesus Christ, who hath left power to his Church to absolve all sinners who truly repent and believe in him, of his great mercy forgive thee thine offences: And by his authority committed to me, I absolve thee from all thy sins, In the Name of the Father, ✠ and of the Son, and of the Holy Ghost. *Amen.*

HE merits of the Passion of our Lord Jesus Christ, the prayers of his holy Mother the Blessed Virgin Mary, and of all the Saints, whatsoever good thou hast done, or evil thou hast endured, be unto thee for the remission of sins, the increase of grace, and the reward of eternal life: And the blessing of God Almighty, the Father, ✠ the Son, and the Holy Ghost, be upon thee and remain with thee for ever. *Amen.*

Go in peace, the Lord hath put away all thy sins. And pray for me, a sinner.

Pastoral Rites —*Reception of Converts*

Reception of Converts

¶ The Rite of Reception is to be used for catechumens who are to be received by Confirmation immediately before the Rite of Confirmation.

¶ If there be many such catechumens, then each such catechumen must recite the Profession of Faith and individually receive absolution.

¶ The Priest, kneeling before the middle of the altar, says alternately with the attendants:

Veni, Creator Spiritus

Come, Holy Ghost, Creator blest,
Vouchsafe within our souls to rest;
Come with thy grace and heav'nly aid
And fill the hearts which thou hast made.

To thee, the Comforter, we cry,
To thee, the Gift of God Most High,
The Fount of life, the Fire of love,
The soul's Anointing from above.

The sev'n-fold gifts of grace are thine,
O Finger of the Hand Divine;
True Promise of the Father thou,
Who dost the tongue with speech endow.

Thy light to every thought impart
And shed thy love in every heart;
Thine own unfailing might supply
To strengthen our infirmity.

Drive far away our ghostly foe,
And thine abiding peace bestow;
If thou be our preventing Guide,
No evil can our steps betide.

Make thou to us the Father known;
Teach us the eternal Son to own
Be this our never-changing creed,
That from the Father dost proceed.

To thee who, dead, again dost live,
All glory, Lord, thy people give;
Whom with the Father we adore
And Holy Ghost for evermore. Amen.

℣. O send forth thy Spirit and they shall be made.
℟. And thou shalt renew the face of the earth.

Reception of Converts # Pastoral Rites

Let us pray.

GOD, who as at this time didst teach the hearts of thy faithful people, by sending to them the light of thy Holy Spirit; Grant us by the same Spirit to have a right judgment in all things, and evermore to rejoice in his holy comfort. Through Christ our Lord. *Amen.*

¶ The Priest then sits, and the new convert kneels before him: who, touching the Holy Gospel with his right hand, utters the profession of faith as stated below; or, if he does not know how to read, the Priest recites the same profession to him slowly, so that he can understand it when he turns and pronounce it with the priest in distinct words.

PROFESSION OF FAITH

N.N., having before my eyes the Holy Gospels, which I touch with my hand, and knowing that no one can be saved without that faith which the Holy, Catholic, and Apostolic Orthodox Church holds, believes, and teaches; against which I grieve that I have greatly erred, inasmuch as, I have held and believed doctrines opposed to her teaching.

NOW by the help of God's grace, profess that I believe the Holy, Catholic Apostolic Orthodox Church to be the only and true Church established on earth by Jesus Christ, to which I submit myself with my whole heart. I firmly believe all the articles that she proposes to my belief; I reject and condemn all that she rejects and condemns, and I am ready to observe all that she commands me. And especially I profess that I believe:

One only God in three divine Persons, distinct from and equal to each other – that is to say, the Father, the Son, and the Holy Ghost;

The Catholic doctrine of the Incarnation, Passion, Death, and Resurrection of our Lord Jesus Christ; and the personal union of the two Natures, the divine and the human: the Divine Maternity of the most holy Mary together with her most spotless virginity; and also her Assumption into heaven;

The true, real, and substantial presence of the Body of our Lord Jesus Christ, together with his Soul and Divinity, in the most holy sacrament of the Eucharist;

The seven Sacraments instituted by Jesus Christ, for the salvation of mankind: that is to say, Baptism, Confirmation, Holy Eucharist, Penance, Holy Unction, Holy Orders, Matrimony;

I also believe in the Resurrection of the Dead and Everlasting Life;

That Our Lord Jesus Christ is the Head of the Catholic Church; that no man can be the head of Christ's Body, that is to say, of the whole Church.

That the holy Apostles received from Our Lord equal spiritual power, and every bishop is equally successor of the Apostles.

The veneration of the Saints, and of their images;

Pastoral Rites *Reception of Converts*

The authority of the apostolic and ecclesiastical Traditions, and of the Holy Scriptures, which we must interpret and understand only in the sense which our holy Mother the Catholic Church has held, and does hold, to whom alone it belongs to judge of their meaning and interpretation.

And everything else that has been defined and declared by the sacred Canons, by the Seven Holy Ecumenical Councils, and the other traditions of the Holy Orthodox Catholic Apostolic Church.

With a sincere heart, therefore, and with unfeigned faith, I detest and abjure every error, heresy, and sect opposed to the said Catholic, Apostolic, and Orthodox Church. So help me God, and these his holy Gospels, which I touch with my hand.

¶ *The new convert then kneels—the Priest remaining sitting—and says either Psalm 51 as follows (or Psalm 130), ending in the* **Gloria Patri,**

Psalm 51

Have mercy upon me, O God, after thy great goodness : according to the multitude of thy mercies do away mine offences.

2 Wash me throughly from my wickedness : and cleanse me from my sin.

3 For I acknowledge my faults : and my sin is ever before me.

4 Against thee only have I sinned, and done this evil in thy sight : that thou mightest be justified in thy saying, and clear when thou art judged.

5 Behold, I was shapen in wickedness : and in sin hath my mother conceived me.

6 But lo, thou requirest truth in the inward parts : and shalt make me to understand wisdom secretly.

7 Thou shalt purge me with hyssop, and I shall be clean : thou shalt wash me, and I shall be whiter than snow.

8 Thou shalt make me hear of joy and gladness : that the bones which thou hast broken may rejoice.

9 Turn thy face from my sins : and put out all my misdeeds.

10 Make me a clean heart, O God : and renew a right spirit within me.

11 Cast me not away from thy presence : and take not thy holy Spirit from me.

12 O give me the comfort of thy help again : and stablish me with thy free Spirit.

13 Then shall I teach thy ways unto the wicked : and sinners shall be converted unto thee.

14 Deliver me from blood-guiltiness, O God, thou that art the God of my health : and my tongue shall sing of thy righteousness.

Reception of Converts # Pastoral Rites

15 Thou shalt open my lips, O Lord : and my mouth shall shew thy praise.

16 For thou desirest no sacrifice, else would I give it thee : but thou delightest not in burnt-offerings.

17 The sacrifice of God is a troubled spirit : a broken and contrite heart, O God, shalt thou not despise.

18 O be favourable and gracious unto Sion : build thou the walls of Jerusalem.

19 Then shalt thou be pleased with the sacrifice of righteousness, with the burnt-offerings and oblations : then shall they offer young bullocks upon thine altar.

℣. Glory be to the Father, and to the Son, and to the Holy Ghost.
℟. As it was in the beginning, is now, and ever shall be, world without end. Amen.

Preces

℣. Lord, have mercy upon us.
℟. Christ, have mercy upon us.
℣. Lord, have mercy upon us.

¶ *Our Father is said secretly until,*

℣. And lead us not into temptation;
℟. But deliver us from evil.
℣. Save thy *servant*, O Lord.
℟. My God, that putteth *his* trust in thee.
℣. O Lord, hear my prayer.
℟. And let my cry come unto thee.
℣. The Lord be with you.
℟. And with thy spirit.

Let us pray.

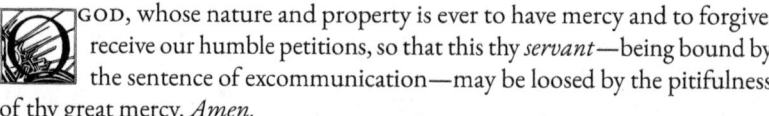GOD, whose nature and property is ever to have mercy and to forgive: receive our humble petitions, so that this thy *servant*—being bound by the sentence of excommunication—may be loosed by the pitifulness of thy great mercy. *Amen.*

¶ *A conditional baptism here follows, if it is to be conferred.*

Pastoral Rites *Reception of Converts*

Absolution

¶ The Priest immediately sits down, turns to the convert, and—covering his head with the stole—absolves him of heresy in the following manner.

WITH Apostolic Authority, I, by such authority, absolve thee from the bond of excommunication, which thou hadst incurred,[a] and I restore thee to the Sacred Sacraments of the Church, Communion, and the Unity of the Faithful, in the Name of the Father, and of the Son, ✠ and of the Holy Ghost. Amen.

[a] *In grave or light doubt as to whether the penitent incurred excommunication by the profession of heresy, the priest here inserts the word 'perchance'.*

¶ The Priest then enjoins some salutary penance upon the convert.

Te Deum laudamus

WE praise thee, O God; we acknowledge thee to be the Lord.
All the earth doth worship thee, the Father everlasting.
To thee all Angels cry aloud; the Heavens, and all the Powers therein;
To thee Cherubim and Seraphim continually do cry,
Holy, Holy, Holy, Lord God of Sabaoth;
Heaven and earth are full of the Majesty of thy glory.
The glorious company of the Apostles praise thee.
The goodly fellowship of the Prophets praise thee.
The noble army of Martyrs praise thee.
The holy Church throughout all the world doth acknowledge thee;
The Father of an infinite Majesty;
Thine honourable, true and only Son;
Also the Holy Ghost the Comforter.

THOU art the King of Glory, O Christ.
Thou art the everlasting Son of the Father.
When thou tookest upon thee to deliver man, thou didst not abhor the Virgin's womb.
When thou hadst overcome the sharpness of death, thou didst open the Kingdom of Heaven to all believers.
Thou sittest at the right hand of God, in the glory of the Father.
We believe that thou shalt come to be our Judge. (The following is said kneeling.)
We therefore pray thee, help thy servants, whom thou hast redeemed with thy precious blood.
Make them to be numbered with thy Saints, in glory everlasting.

O LORD, save thy people, and bless thine heritage.
Govern them and lift them up for ever.
Day by day we magnify thee;

And we worship thy Name ever, world without end.
Vouchsafe, O Lord, to keep us this day without sin.
O Lord, have mercy upon us, have mercy upon us.
O Lord, let thy mercy lighten upon us, as our trust is in thee.
O Lord, in thee have I trusted; let me never be confounded.

CONCLUSION

¶ The Priest then stands and says,

℣. Blessed art thou, O Lord, in the firmament of heaven.
℟. And above all to be praised and glorified for ever.
℣. The Lord be with you.
℟. And with thy spirit.

Let us pray.

ALMIGHTY and everlasting God, who hast given unto us thy servants grace by the confession of a true faith to acknowledge the glory of the eternal Trinity, and in the power of the Divine Majesty to worship the Unity: We beseech thee; that thou wouldest keep us stedfast in this faith, and evermore defend us from all adversities. Who livest and reignest, one God, world without end. *Amen.*

℣. The Lord be with you.
℟. And with thy spirit.
℣. Let us bless the Lord.
℟. Thanks be to God.

THE Blessing of Almighty God, the Father, ✠ the Son, and the Holy Ghost, descend upon you and remain with you always. *Amen.*

Pastoral Rites *Confirmation*

Sacrament of Confirmation

℟ Immediately after Baptism, or if the persons are not to be baptised – immediately after the Rite of Reception.

℟ This rite assumes multiple confirmands. When there is just one, the gender and number should be changed.

℟ The Bishop or Priest proceeds to the faldstool, before the altar, or in some other convenient place, and sits thereon, with his face to the people (if he be a bishop, holding his pastoral staff in his left hand). Having washed his hands, he rises up, and stands with his face towards the persons to be confirmed, who kneel before him with their hands joined before their breasts. He then says:

May the Holy Ghost come upon *you*, and may the power of the Most High preserve *you* from sins. ℟. Amen.	Spíritus Sanctus supervéniat in *vos*, et virtus Altíssimi costódiat *vos* a peccátis. ℟. Amen.

℟ Then, signing himself with his right hand with the sign of the cross ✠ from his forehead to his breast, he says:

℣. Our help ✠ is in the name of the Lord. ℟. Who hath made heaven and earth. ℣. O Lord, hear my prayer. ℟. And let my cry come unto thee. ℣. The Lord be with you. ℟. And with thy spirit.	℣. Adjutórium ✠ nostrum in nómine Dómini. ℟. Qui fecit cœlum et terram. ℣. Dómine, exáudi oratiónem meam. ℟. Et clamor meus ad te véniat. ℣. Dóminus vobíscum. ℟. Et cum spíritu tuo.

Invocation

℟ Then, with his hands extended towards those to be confirmed, he says:

Let us pray.	Orémus.
LMIGHTY everlasting God, who hast vouchsafed to regenerate *these thy servants* by water and the Holy Ghost, and hast given unto *them* the remission of all *their* sins, send forth upon *them* thy sevenfold Spirit, the Holy Paraclete from heaven. ℟. Amen.	MNÍPOTENS sempitérne Deus, qui regeneráre dignátus es *hos fámulos* tuos ex aqua, et Spíritu sancto; quique dedísti *eis* remissiónem ómnium *peccatórum*: emitte in *eos* septifórmem Spíritum tuum Sanctum Paráclitum de cœlis. ℟. Amen.

Confirmation

Pastoral Rites

℣. The Spirit of wisdom and understanding.
℟. Amen.
℣. The Spirit of counsel and ghostly strength.
℟. Amen.
℣. The Spirit of knowledge and true godliness.
℟. Amen.

EPLENISH *them* with the Spirit of thy fear, and sign *them* with the sign of the Cross ✠ of Christ, in thy mercy unto life eternal. Through the same Jesus Christ, thy Son, our Lord, who liveth and reigneth with thee in the unity of the same Holy Spirit, God, world without end.
℟. Amen.

℣. Spiritum sapientiæ, et intellectus.
℟. Amen.
℣. Spiritum consilii, et fortitudinis.
℟. Amen.
℣. Spiritum scientiæ et pietatis.
℟. Amen.

DIMPLE *eos* Spiritu timoris tui, et consigna *eos* signo cru ✠ cis Christi, in yitam propitiatus æternam. Per eumdem Dominum nostrum Jesum Christum Filium tuum, qui tecum vivit, et regnat in unitate ejusdem Spiritus Sancti Deus, per omnia sæcula sæculorum.
℟. Amen.

Chrismation

¶ The Bishop inquires separately the name of each person to be confirmed, who is presented to him by the Godfather or Godmother, kneeling; and having dipped the end of his right thumb in Chrism, chrismating upon each person's forehead, he says:

N., I sign thee with the sign of the ✠ Cross. And I confirm thee with the Chrism of salvation. The Seal of the Gift of the Holy Ghost. In the name of the Fa ✠ ther, and of the ✠ Son, and of the Holy ✠ Ghost.
℟. Amen.

N., Signo te signo cru ✠ cis: Et confirmo te Chrismate salútis. Signáculum Doni Spíritus Sancti. In nómine Pat ✠ ris, et Fí ✠ lii, et Spíritus ✠ Sancti.

℟. Amen.

¶ The Bishop or Priest, strikes the person gently on the cheek saying,

℣. Peace be with thee.
℣. Pax tecum.

Pastoral Rites *Confirmation*

¶ When all have been confirmed, the Bishop or Priest wipes his hands with bread crumb, and washes them over a basin. Whilst he is washing his hands, the following antiphon is said or sung:

Ant. Confirm, O Lord, what thou hast wrought in us, from thy holy temple which is in Jerusalem.

℣. Glory be to the Father, and to the Son, and to the Holy Ghost.

℟. As it was in the beginning, is now, and ever shall be, world without end. Amen.

Ant. Confirm, O Lord, what thou hast wrought in us, from thy holy temple which is in Jerusalem.

℣. O Lord, show thy mercy upon us.

℟. And grant us thy salvation.

℣. O Lord, hear my prayer.

℟. And let my cry come unto thee.

℣. The Lord be with you.

℟. And with thy spirit.

Ant. Confirma hoc Deus, quod operátus es in nobis a templo sancto tuo, quod est in Jerúsalem,

℣. Glória Patri, et Fílio, * et Spirítui Sancto:

℟. Sicut erat in princípio, et nunc, et semper, * et in sǽcula sæculórum. Amen.

Ant. Confirma hoc Deus, quod operátus es in nobis a templo sancto tuo, quod est in Jerúsalem.

℣. Osténde nobis, Dómine, misericórdiam tuam.

℟. Et salutáre tuum da nobis.

℣. Dómine, exáudi oratiónem meam.

℟. Et clamor meus ad te véniat.

℣. Dóminus vobíscum.

℟. Et cum spíritu tuo.

¶ Then with his hands still joined before his breast, while all the persons confirmed devoutly kneel, he says:

Let us pray.

GOD, who didst give to thine Apostles the Holy Spirit, and didst will that by them and their successors, he should be delivered to the rest of the faithful; look mercifully on the service of our humility; and grant that the *hearts of those* whose *foreheads* we have anointed with the sacred Chrism, and signed with the sign of the holy Cross, may, by the same Holy Spirit descending therein, be made the temple of his glory. Who, with the Father and the same Holy Spirit, liveth and reignest, God, world

Orémus.

EUS, qui Apóstolis tuis sanctum dedísti Spíritum, et per eos, eorúmque successores cæteris fidélibus tradéndum esse voluísti: réspice propítius ad humilitátis nostræ famulátum; et præsta, ut eórum corda, quorum frontes sacro Chrismáte delinívimus, et signo sanctæ crucis signávimus, idem Spíritus Sanctus in eis supervéniens, templum gloriæ suæ dignanter inhabitando perfíciat. Qui cum Patre, et eodem Spíritu Sancto vivis, et regnas Deus, in sæcula sæculorum.

without end.

℟. Amen.

℣. Behold, thus shall every man be blessed that feareth the Lord.

℟. Amen.

℣. Ecce sic benedicétur omnis homo, qui timet Dóminum.

Bestowal of Candle & White Garment

¶ The Priest or Bishop then places on the head of the Elect a Chrismal, or white linen cloth, and gives him a white garment, saying,

Receive this white garment, and see thou carry it without stain before the judgement-seat of our Lord Jesus Christ, that thou mayest have eternal life.

Accipe vestem cándidam, quam pérferas immaculátam ante tribúnal Dómini nostri Jesu Christi, ut hábeas vitam ætérnam.

¶ And the elect lays aside his former garments, and puts on new ones of white; or at least that white outer garment which he has received from the Priest. Afterwards the Priest gives to him a waxen taper, or lighted candle, in his right hand, saying,

Receive this burning light, and keep thy Baptism, so as to be without blame: keep the commandments of God; that, when the Lord shall come to the nuptials, thou mayest meet him in the company of all the Saints in the heavenly court, and have eternal life, and live for ever and ever.

℟. Amen.

Accipe lámpadem ardéntem, et irreprehensíbilis custódi Baptísmum tuum: serva Dei mandáta, ut, cum Dóminus vénerit ad núptias, possis occúrrere ei una cum ómnibus Sanctis in aula cælésti et vivas in sæcula sæculórum.

℟. Amen.

¶ And, turning to the persons confirmed, he makes over them the sign of the cross, saying,

May the Lord ✠ bless *you* out of Sion, that *you* may see the good things of Jerusalem all the days of *your* life, and have life everlasting.

℟. Amen.

Bene ✠ dicat *vos* Dominus ex Sion, at *videatis* bona Jerusalem omnibus diebus vitæ *vestræ*, et *habeatis* vitam ætérnam.

℟. Amen.

¶ The Holy Sacrifice of the Mass immediately follows.

Pastoral Rites *Matrimony*

Sacrament of Matrimony

¶ First the banns must be posted for three Sundays or Holy Days. If the persons that would be married dwell in divers parishes, the banns must be posted in both parishes, and the Curate of the one parish shall not solemnise matrimony betwixt them, without a certificate of the banns being thrice asked from the Curate of the other parish.

At the day appointed for Solemnisation of Matrimony, the persons to be married shall come into the body of the church, with their friends and neighbours. And there the priest shall thus say,

EARLY beloved friends, we are gathered together here in the sight of God, and in the face of his congregation, to join together this man and this woman in holy matrimony, which is an honourable estate instituted of God in paradise, in the time of man's innocency, signifying unto us the mystical union that is betwixt Christ and his Church: which holy estate, Christ adorned and beautified with his presence, and first miracle that he wrought in Cana of Galilee, and is commended by Saint Paul to be honourable among all men; and therefore is not to be enterprised, nor taken in hand unadvisedly, lightly, or wantonly, to satisfy men's carnal lusts and appetites, like brute beasts that have no understanding: but reverently, discretely, advisedly, soberly, and in the fear of God. Duly considering the causes for the which matrimony was ordained.

Exhortation

First it was ordained for the procreation of children, to be brought up in the fear and nurture of the Lord, and praise of God.

Secondly it was ordained for a remedy against sin, and to avoid fornication, that such persons as be married, might live chastely in matrimony, and keep themselves undefiled members of Christ's body.

Thirdly for the mutual society, help, and comfort, that the one ought to have of the other, both in prosperity and adversity. Into the which holy estate these two persons present: come now to be joined. Therefore if any man can shew any just cause why they may not lawfully be joined so together: Let him now speak, or else hereafter for ever hold his peace.

¶ And also speaking to the persons that shall be married, he shall say,

REQUIRE and charge you (as you will answer at the dreadful day of judgement, when the secrets of all hearts shall be disclosed) that if either of you do know any impediment, why ye may not be lawfully joined together in matrimony, that ye confess it. For be ye well assured, that so many as be coupled together otherwise than God's Word doth allow: are not joined of God, neither is their matrimony lawful.

Matrimony

Pastoral Rites

¶ At which day of Marriage, if any man do allege and declare any impediment, why they may not be coupled together in Matrimony, by God's law, or the laws of this Realm; and will be bound, and sufficient sureties with him, to the parties; or else put in a caution (to the full value of such charges as the persons to be married do thereby sustain) to prove his allegation: then the solemnisation must be deferred, until such time as the truth be tried.

Vows

¶ If no impediment be alleged, then shall the Curate say unto the Man,

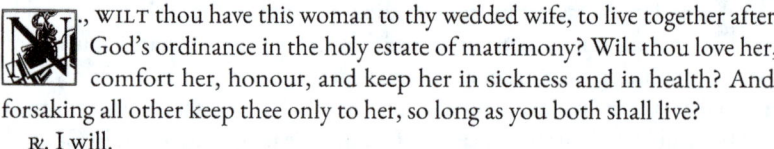

N., WILT thou have this woman to thy wedded wife, to live together after God's ordinance in the holy estate of matrimony? Wilt thou love her, comfort her, honour, and keep her in sickness and in health? And forsaking all other keep thee only to her, so long as you both shall live?

℟. I will.

¶ Then shall the Curate say unto the Woman,

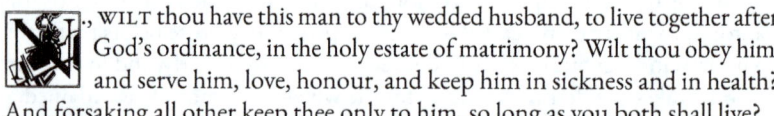

N., WILT thou have this man to thy wedded husband, to live together after God's ordinance, in the holy estate of matrimony? Wilt thou obey him, and serve him, love, honour, and keep him in sickness and in health? And forsaking all other keep thee only to him, so long as you both shall live?

℟. I will.

¶ Then shall the Minister say,

Who giveth this woman to be married to this man?

¶ And the Minister receiving the Woman at her father's or friend's hands: shall cause the Man to take the Woman by the right hand, and so to give their troth to each other: The Man first saying,

I N. take thee *N.* to my wedded wife, to have and to hold from this day forward, for better, for worse, for richer, for poorer, in sickness, and in health, to love and to cherish, til death us depart: according to God's holy ordinance: And thereto I plight thee my troth.

¶ Then shall they loose their hands, and the Woman taking again the Man by the right hand shall say,

I N. take thee *N.* to my wedded husband, to have and to hold from this day forward, for better, for worse, for richer, for poorer, in sickness, and in health, to love, cherish, and to obey, till death us depart: according to God's holy ordinance: And thereto I give thee my troth.

¶ Then shall they again loose their hands, and the Man shall give unto the Woman a ring, and optionally other tokens of spousage, as gold or silver, laying the same upon the

Pastoral Rites *Matrimony*

book: And the Priest taking the ring shall deliver it unto the Man: to put it upon the fourth finger of the Woman's left hand. And the Man taught by the Priest, shall say,

With this ring I thee wed: (This gold and silver I thee give:) with my body I thee worship: and with all my worldly goods I thee endow. In the name of the Father, and of the Son, and of the Holy Ghost. Amen.

SOLEMNISATION OF MATRIMONY

¶ Then the Man leaving the ring upon the fourth finger of the Woman's left hand, the Minister shall say,

Let us pray.

ETERNAL God, Creator and preserver of all mankind, giver of all spiritual grace, the author of everlasting life: Send thy blessing upon these thy servants, this man, and this woman, whom we bless in thy name, that as Isaac and Rebecca (after bracelets and Jewels of gold given of the one to the other for tokens of their matrimony) lived faithfully together; So these persons may surely perform and keep the vow and covenant betwixt them made, whereof this ring given, and received, is a token and pledge. And may ever remain in perfect love and peace together; And live according to thy laws; through Jesus Christ our Lord. *Amen.*

¶ Then shall the Priest join their right hands together, and say,

THOSE WHOM GOD HATH JOINED TOGETHER:
LET NO MAN PUT ASUNDER.

¶ Then shall the Priest speak unto the people.

FORASMUCH as *N.* and *N.* have consented together in holy wedlock, and have witnessed the same here before God and this company; And thereto have given and pledged their troth either to other, and have declared the same by giving and receiving gold and silver, and by joining of hands: I pronounce that they be man and wife together. In the name of the Father, of the Son, and of the Holy Ghost. Amen.

¶ And the Minister shall add this Blessing.

GOD the Father bless you ✠ God the Son keep you: God the Holy Ghost lighten your understanding: The Lord mercifully with his favour look upon you, and so fill you with all spiritual benediction, and grace, that you may have remission of your sins in this life, and in the world to come life everlasting. *Amen.*

Matrimony # Pastoral Rites

Thanksgiving

¶ Then shall they go into the choir, and the Ministers or Clerks shall say or sing, this psalm following.

Psalm 128. Beati omnes

BLESSED are all they that fear the Lord : and walk in his ways.
2 For thou shalt eat the labours of thine hands : O well is thee, and happy shalt thou be.
3 Thy wife shall be as the fruitful vine : upon the walls of thine house.
4 Thy children like the olive-branches : round about thy table.
5 Lo, thus shall the man be blessed : that feareth the Lord.
6 The Lord from out of Sion shall so bless thee : that thou shalt see Jerusalem in prosperity all thy life long.
7 Yea, that thou shalt see thy children's children : and peace upon Israel.
℣. Glory be to the Father and to the Son and to the Holy Ghost.
℟. As it was in the beginning, is now, and ever shall be, world without end. Amen.

or,

Psalm 67. Deus misereatur

GOD be merciful unto us, and bless us : and shew us the light of his countenance, and be merciful unto us;
2 That thy way may be known upon earth : thy saving health among all nations.
3 Let the people praise thee, O God : yea, let all the people praise thee.
4 O let the nations rejoice and be glad : for thou shalt judge the folk righteously, and govern the nations upon earth.
5 Let the people praise thee, O God : let all the people praise thee.
6 Then shall the earth bring forth her increase : and God, even our own God, shall give us his blessing.
7 God shall bless us : and all the ends of the world shall fear him.
℣. Glory be to the Father and to the Son and to the Holy Ghost.
℟. As it was in the beginning, is now, and ever shall be, world without end. Amen.

Pastoral Rites *Matrimony*

¶ The Psalm ended, and the Man and Woman kneeling before the Altar: the Priest standing toward the Altar, and turning his face toward them, shall say,

℣. Lord have mercy upon us.
℟. Christ have mercy upon us.
℣. Lord have mercy upon us.
℣. Our Father, who art in heaven, Hallowed be thy Name. Thy kingdom come. Thy will be done, On earth as it is in heaven. Give us this day our daily bread. And forgive us our trespasses, As we forgive those who trespass against us. And lead us not into temptation,
℟. But deliver us from evil. Amen.
℣. O Lord save thy servant, and thy handmaiden.
℟. Which put their trust in thee.
℣. O Lord send them help from thy holy place.
℟. And evermore defend them.
℣. Be unto them a tower of strength.
℟. From the face of their enemy.
℣. O Lord, hear my prayer.
℟. And let my cry come unto thee.

Let us pray.

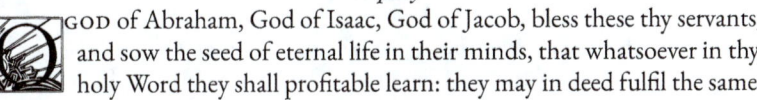GOD of Abraham, God of Isaac, God of Jacob, bless these thy servants, and sow the seed of eternal life in their minds, that whatsoever in thy holy Word they shall profitable learn: they may in deed fulfil the same. Look, O Lord, mercifully upon them from heaven, and bless them: And as thou didst send thy Angel Raphael to Tobit, and Sara, the daughter of Raguel, to their great comfort; so vouchsafe to send thy blessing upon these thy servants, that they obeying thy will, and alway being in safety under thy protection: may abide in thy love unto their lives' end: through Jesu Christ our Lord. *Amen.*

¶ It is to be noted that the prayers O eternal God and God the Father bless you is not to be said in second or third marriages. For neither the Man nor the Woman, entering into a second union, ought to be blessed again by the Priest; forasmuch as they were blessed on a former occasion, their blessing is not to be repeated. For blessed flesh draweth unto itself flesh that is not blessed.

Blessed Ambrose testifieth to this, saying: 'The first marriage is instituted by the Lord; the second is permitted. The first is celebrated with every blessing; the second is without any blessing.'

¶ While there are various blessings given in the solemnisation of matrimony, the prayers specified here, as well as 'O merciful Lord' and 'O God, which by thy' (as specified in the Votive Mass), are to be omitted. For it is unfitting for a blessing to speak of the unity of Christ and the Church, which is figured in the first marriage, but not in the second. As the Apostle saith to the Corinthians: 'They two shall be one flesh.' But he who cleaveth to more than one dissolveth the unity or the covenant of unity. Therefore, that blessing which speaketh of such unity is not to be said in second marriages. And this is true whether the Man be digamous or the Woman a widow: for blessed flesh draweth unto itself flesh that is not blessed.

¶ Although the second marriage, in itself considered, is a true and perfect sacrament, yet when considered in relation to the first, it hath some defect as a sacrament. For it doth not have the fullness of signification, inasmuch as it no longer represents 'one flesh,' as doth the marriage betwixt Christ and the Church. For this reason the blessing is withheld from second marriages.

This is to be understood particularly when both parties are entering into second marriage—that is, second on the part of both the Man and the Woman. For if a virgin be joined to a Man who had before another wife, the nuptial blessing may nonetheless be given, for something of the signification is retained in regard to the first nuptials. Even as a bishop, though he have but one bride (the Church), hath yet many souls espoused within her; but the soul itself may not be the spouse of any other than Christ. To do so were to commit spiritual fornication with the devil, and such union were no true marriage. Wherefore, when a woman marrieth again, the nuptial blessing is not given, by reason of the defect in the sacramental sign.

Sermon

¶ Then shall Holy Communion begin (p. 578). Then be said after the Creed a sermon, wherein ordinarily (so oft as there is any marriage) the office of Man and Wife shall be declared according to Holy Scripture. Or if there be no sermon, the Minister shall read this that followeth.

ALL ye which be married, or which intend to take the holy estate of matrimony upon you: hear what Holy Scripture doth say, as touching the duty of husbands toward their wives, and wives toward their husbands.

Saint Paul (in his epistle to the Ephesians the fifth chapter) doth give this commandment to all married men.

Ye husbands love your wives, even as Christ loved the Church, and hath given himself for it, to sanctify it, purging it in the fountain of water, through the word, that he might make it unto himself, a glorious congregation, not having spot or wrinkle, or any such thing; but that it should be holy and blameless. So men are bound to love their own wives as their own bodies: he that loveth his own wife, loveth himself. For never did any man hate his own flesh, but nourisheth and cherisheth it, even as the Lord doth the congregation, for we are members of his body, of his flesh, and of his bones. For this cause shall a man leave father and mother, and shall be joined unto his wife, and they two shall be one flesh. This mystery is great, but I speak of Christ and of the congregation. Nevertheless let every one of you so love his own wife, even as himself.

Pastoral Rites *Matrimony*

Likewise the same Saint Paul (writing to the Colossians) speaketh thus to all men that be married: Ye men, love your wives and be not bitter unto them.

Hear also what Saint Peter the apostle of Christ, (which was himself a married man,) sayeth unto all men that are married.

Ye husbands, dwell with your wives according to knowledge: Giving honour unto the wife, as unto the weaker vessel, and as heirs together of the grace of life, so that your prayers be not hindered.

Hitherto ye have heard the duty of the husband toward the wife.

Now likewise, ye wives, hear and learn your duty toward your husbands, even as it is plainly set forth in holy scripture.

Saint Paul (in the forenamed epistle to the Ephesians) teacheth you thus:

Ye women submit yourselves unto your own husbands as unto the Lord: for the husband is the wife's head, even as Christ is the head of the Church: And he also is the Saviour of the whole body. Therefore as the Church, or congregation, is subject unto Christ: So likewise let the wives also be in subjection unto their own husbands in all things.

And again he sayeth: Let the wife reverence her husband. And (in his epistle to the Colossians) Saint Paul giveth you this short lesson. Ye wives, submit yourselves unto your own husbands, as it is convenient in the Lord.

Saint Peter also doth instruct you very godly, thus saying, Let wives be subject to their own husbands, so that if any obey not the Word, they may be won without the Word, by the conversation of the wives; While they behold your chaste conversation, coupled with fear, whose apparel let it not be outward, with plaited hair, and trimming about with gold, either in putting on of gorgeous apparel: But let the hid man which is in the heart, be without all corruption, so that the spirit be mild and quiet, which is a precious thing in the sight of God. For after this manner (in the old time) did the holy women, which trusted in God, apparel themselves, being subject to their own husbands: as Sara obeyed Abraham calling him lord, whose daughters ye are made, doing well, and being not dismayed with any fear.

¶ The newly married persons (the same day of their marriage) shall receive Holy Communion.

Pastoral Rites

Purification of Women after Childbirth

¶ The Woman, at the usual time after her delivery, shall come into the Church decently apparelled, and there shall kneel down in some convenient place nigh the door of the Church, and the Priest standing by her shall say these words.

NOTE, The Priest shall come vested in surplice and white stole, with a Minister bearing the aspersorium. It is a laudable custom for the Woman to hold a lighted candle.

FORASMUCH as it hath pleased Almighty God, of his goodness, to give you safe deliverance, and your Child Baptism, and hath preserved you in the great danger of Child-birth: ye shall therefore give hearty thanks unto God, and pray,

Psalm 121. *Levavi oculus*

¶ Then shall be said by both of them the following Psalm, the Woman still kneeling.

I WILL lift up mine eyes unto the hills : from whence cometh my help.

2 My help cometh even from the Lord : who hath made heaven and earth.

3 He will not suffer thy foot to be moved : and he that keepeth thee will not sleep.

4 Behold, he that keepeth Israel : shall neither slumber nor sleep.

5 The Lord himself is thy keeper : the Lord is thy defence upon thy right hand;

6 So that the sun shall not burn thee by day : neither the moon by night.

7 The Lord shall preserve thee from all evil : yea, it is even he that shall keep thy soul.

8 The Lord shall preserve thy going out, and thy coming in : from this time forth for evermore.

℣. Glory be to the Father, and to the Son, and to the Holy Ghost.

℟. As it was in the beginning, is now, and ever shall be, world without end. Amen.

℣. Lord, have mercy upon us.
℟. Christ, have mercy upon us.
℣. Lord, have mercy upon us.

Pastoral Rites *Purification of Women*

¶ Then shall the Minister say the Lord's Prayer, with what followeth.

OUR Father, who art in heaven, Hallowed be thy Name. Thy kingdom come. Thy will be done on earth, As it is in heaven. Give us this day our daily bread. And forgive us our trespasses, As we forgive those who trespass against us. And lead us not into temptation; But deliver us from evil. Amen.

℣. O Lord, save this woman thy servant;
℟. Who putteth her trust in thee.
℣. Be thou to her a strong tower;
℟. From the face of her enemy.
℣. O Lord hear our prayer.
℟. And let our cry come unto thee.
℣. The Lord be with you.
℟. And with thy spirit.

Let us pray.

ALMIGHTY God, we give thee humble thanks for that thou hast been graciously pleased to preserve, through the great pain and peril of childbirth, this woman, thy servant, who desireth now to offer her praises and thanksgivings unto thee. Grant, we beseech thee, most merciful Father, that she, through thy help, may faithfully live according to thy will in this life, and also may be partaker of everlasting glory in the life to come. Through.

¶ The Priest sprinkles her with Holy Water and then leadeth the Woman into the Church, with what followeth.

Come into the Temple of God, that thou mayest have life everlasting and live for ever. Amen.

Pastoral Rites

Sacrament of Holy Unction

Exhortation before Holy Unction

¶ The Priest may, before administering Holy Unction, exhort the sick person with these words,

OUR Lord and Saviour Jesus Christ has been pleased to institute, besides the Holy Communion, another heavenly medicine for the benefit of the sick, which is the Sacrament of Holy Unction; according to what we read in the Epistle of St. James, where it is said: Is any man sick among you, let him bring in the priests of the Church, and let them pray over him, anointing him with oil in the name of the Lord: and the prayer of faith shall save the sick man; and the Lord shall raise him up, and if he be in sins, they shall be forgiven him (v. 14). — You see here the authority for administering to the sick this holy Unction, from the express word of God. And also the great graces and benefits which God promises to bestow on every one who receives this Sacrament with proper dispositions, namely, that he will save the sick man, will raise him up from his sick bed, if he sees his recovery expedient for the welfare of his soul; and, what is infinitely more desirable than corporal health, will impart to him the forgiveness of his sins. Acknowledge, then, the infinite goodness of your Redeemer, and with the most lively sentiments of gratitude and love, embrace the great grace which is here prepared for you in this heavenly institution: and join your attention and devotion, with the prayers we shall now make to our Lord, for the healing of your soul and body, and to obtain for you the full remission of all your sins.

And as the eyes, the ears, and the other organs of sense, are the instruments by which men are led to offend Almighty God, they will on that account be anointed with the holy Oil: whilst we apply this holy Oil to your eyes, your ears, and your other senses, do you, with a contrite and humble heart, implore the mercy of God for the forgiveness of all the sins which through these avenues have made their way into your soul. Pray also for his supporting grace in this your illness, and that you may continue to the end ever faithful to him.

Pastoral Rites — *Holy Unction*

Devotion during Holy Unction

¶ While the Priest is administering this Sacrament to the sick person, one of the assistants may, before each Unction, read one of the following short prayers, corresponding to the organ of sense that is next to be anointed, that it may be repeated by the sick person.

My eyes have seen vanities, but now let them be shut to the world, and open to thee alone, my Jesus; and pardon me all the sins I have committed by my seeing.

My ears have been open to detraction, profaneness, and unprofitable discourses: let me now give ear to thy word, to thy commands, and thy call; and pardon me, O Jesus, all the sins I have committed by my hearing.

I have taken delight in the perfumes of this world, which are nothing but corruptions: now let my heart and prayers ascend like incense in thy sight, and pardon me, O Lord, all the sins I have committed by my sense of smell.

My tongue has many ways offended, both in speaking and tasting; now let its whole business be to cry for mercy: pardon me, dear Jesus, all the sins I have committed by words, or by any excess in eating and drinking.

My hands have offended in contributing to many follies injurious to myself and my neighbour: now let them be lifted up to Heaven in testimony of a penitent heart; and pardon me, O Lord, all the sins I have committed by the ill use of my hands.

My feet have gone astray in the paths of vanity and sin: now let me walk in the way of thy commandments; and forgive me, O Lord, all the sins I have committed by my disordered steps.

Unction of the Sick

¶ In case of necessity, it suffices to anoint one sense only, or more fittingly the forehead, with this shorter form:

Through this holy ✠ Unction the Lord pardon thee whatsoever thou hast done amiss. Amen.

¶ But the obligation remains, when the danger ceases, of supplying each of the anointings and all the prayers. If there be doubt whether the sick person yet lives, the Priest shall anoint conditionally saying:

If thou livest, through this holy ✠ Unction, etc.

¶ The Priest, who is to administer the Sacrament of Holy Unction, shall take care that there be made ready, as far as possible, in the sick person's house, a table covered with a white cloth, and a vessel, wherein is cotton-wool or the like, divided into six small pellets, for wiping the places anointed; bread crumbs for cleansing the fingers; water for washing the Priest's hands, and a wax candle, to give him light as he anoints.

Holy Unction # Pastoral Rites

¶ Then with the Clergy or at least with one Clerk, who carries a Cross, the holy Water with sprinkler, and the Ritual, the Parish Priest himself takes the vessel of sacred Oil, enclosed in a bag of violet silk, and carries it with care; for greater safety he may hang it around his neck. No bell is rung.

¶ When he comes to the place where the sick person lies, the Priest entering the room, says:

℣. Peace be to this house.
℟. And to all that dwell in it.

℣. Pax huic dómui.
℟. Et ómnibus habitántibus in ea.

¶ Having placed the Oil upon the table and (if not already vested) having put on surplice and violet stole, the Priest gives the sick person a Cross to kiss. Then he shall sprinkle him, the bystanders, and the room, in the form of a Cross, saying:

Thou shalt purge me, O Lord, with hyssop, and I shall be clean: thou shalt wash me, and I shall be whiter than snow.

¶ If the sick person wishes to confess, he shall hear him and absolve him. Then he shall comfort him, and, if time permit, briefly admonish him concerning the power and efficacy of this Sacrament.

℣. Our help ✠ is in the name of the Lord.
℟. Who hath made heaven and earth.
℣. The Lord be with you.
℟. And with thy spirit.

℣. Adjutórium ✠ nostrum in nómine Dómini.
℟. Qui fecit cœlum et terram.
℣. Dóminus vobíscum.
℟. Et cum spíritu tuo.

Let us pray.

LET there enter into this house, O Lord, Jesu Christ, with the coming of us unworthy, everlasting happiness, divine prosperity, serene gladness, fruitful charity, and everlasting health: let no evil spirits approach this place: may Angels of peace be present, and all evil discord far removed from this house: magnify upon us thy holy Name, O Lord, and ✠ bless our conversation; sanctify our unworthy coming, who art holy and gracious, and abidest with the Father and the Holy Ghost, world without end. *Amen.*

LET us pray and beseech our Lord Jesus Christ, that in blessing he may ✠ bless this dwelling-place, and all that inhabit it, and give to them a good Angel guardian, and make them so to serve him, that they may consider the wondrous things of his law: may he turn from them all adverse powers: deliver them from all fear, and from every disquiet, and vouchsafe to preserve them in safety in this dwelling-place: Who with the Father and the Holy Ghost liveth and reigneth, world without end. *Amen.*

Pastoral Rites *Holy Unction*

Let us pray.

GRACIOUSLY hear us, O Lord holy, Father almighty, everlasting God: and vouchsafe to send from heaven thy holy Angel to guard and cherish, protect, visit, and defend all who dwell in this place. Through Christ our Lord. *Amen.*

¶ These prayers, if time does not allow, may be omitted in whole or in part. Then the General Confession is made in the accustomed manner (p. 622), and the Priest says in the singular number:

℟. God Almighty have mercy upon thee, forgive thee thy sins, and bring thee to everlasting life.

℟. Amen.

℣. The Almighty and merciful Lord grant thee pardon, ✠ absolution, and remission of thy sins.

℟. Amen.

℟. Misereátur tui omnípotens Deus, et, dimíssis peccátis tuis, perdúcat te ad vitam ætérnam.

℟. Amen.

℣. Indulgéntiam, ✠ absolutiónem et remissiónem peccatórum tuórum tríbuat tibi omnípotens et miséricors Dóminus.

℟. Amen.

¶ The Priest, extending his right hand over the head of the sick person, says:

In the Name of the ✠ Father, and of the ✠ Son, and of the ✠ Holy Ghost, may there be extinguished in thee all power of the devil, through the imposition of our hands, and through the invocation of the glorious and holy Virgin Mary Mother of God, and of her illustrious Spouse Joseph, and of all the holy Angels, Archangels, Patriarchs, Prophets, Apostles, Martyrs, Confessors and Virgins, and of all the Saints. *Amen.*

Anointings

¶ Then, dipping his thumb in the holy Oil, he anoints the sick person in the form of a Cross on the parts mentioned below, adapting the words of the form to the appropriate place in this manner,

¶ The Clerk, if he be in Holy Orders, or the Priest himself, after each anointing shall wipe the place anointed with a fresh pellet of cotton-wool, and place it in a clean vessel, and afterwards carry it to the Church, burn it, and cast the ashes into the sacrarium.

¶ During the anointings, the bystanders should say suitable prayers for the sick person, e.g., one or more of the Penitential Psalms (6, 32, 38, 51, 102, 130, 143) or the Litany of the Saints (p. 98).

At the eyes

Through this holy ✠ Unction, and his most tender mercy, the Lord pardon thee whatsoever thou hast done amiss by seeing. Amen.

At the ears

Through this holy ✠ Unction, and his most tender mercy, the Lord pardon thee whatsoever thou hast done amiss by hearing. Amen.

At the nostrils

Through this holy ✠ Unction, and his most tender mercy, the Lord pardon thee whatsoever thou hast done amiss by smelling. Amen.

At the mouth, the lips being closed

Through this holy ✠ Unction, and his most tender mercy, the Lord pardon thee whatsoever thou hast done amiss by tasting and speaking. Amen.

At the hands

¶ NOTE, The hands of Priests are not anointed on the inside, but on the outside.

Through this holy ✠ Unction, and his most tender mercy, the Lord pardon thee whatsoever thou hast done amiss by touching. Amen.

Pastoral Rites *Holy Unction*

At the feet

℣ Note, This unction of the feet may be omitted for any reasonable cause.

Through this holy ✠ Unction, and his most tender mercy, the Lord pardon thee whatsoever thou hast done amiss by walking. Amen.

℣ All these things being done, the Priest rubs his thumb with bread crumbs, washes his hands, and wipes them with the towel. The water and bread shall in due course be cast into the sacrarium or the fire. Then he says:

℣. Lord, have mercy upon us.	℣. Kýrie, eléison.
℟. Christ, have mercy upon us.	℟. Christe, eléison.
℣. Lord, have mercy upon us.	℣. Kýrie, eléison.

Conclusion

℣ The Lord's Prayer is said secretly until,

℣. And lead us not into temptation;	℣. Et ne nos indúcas in tentatiónem.
℟. But deliver us from evil.	℟. Sed líbera nos a malo.
℣. O Lord, save thy *servant*.	℣. Salvum fac *servum tuum*.
℟. Who putteth *his* trust in thee.	℟. Deus meus, sperántem in te.
℣. Send *him* help from thy holy place.	℣. Mitte ei, Dómine, auxílium de sancto.
℟. And evermore mightily defend *him*.	℟. Et de Sion tuére *eum*.
℣. Be unto *him*, O Lord, a tower of strength.	℣. Esto ei, Dómine, turris fortitúdinis.
℟. From the face of the enemy.	℟. A fácie inimíci.
℣. Let the enemy have no advantage over *him*.	℣. Nihil profíciat inimícus in *eo*.
℟. Nor the wicked approach to hurt *him*.	℟. Et fílius iniquitátis non appónat nocére ei.
℣. O Lord, hear my prayer.	℣. Dómine, exáudi oratiónem meam.
℟. And let my cry come unto thee.	℟. Et clamor meus ad te véniat.
℣. The Lord be with you.	℣. Dóminus vobíscum.
℟. And with thy spirit.	℟. Et cum spíritu tuo.

Let us pray.

O LORD God, who through thine Apostle James hast said: Is any sick among you? Let him call for the elders of the Church and let them pray over him, anointing him with oil in the Name of the Lord: and the prayer of faith shall save the sick, and the Lord shall raise him up: and if he have committed sins, they shall be forgiven him; cure, we beseech thee, O our Redeemer, by the grace of the Holy Ghost, the weakness of this sick person; heal *his* wounds and put away *his* sins; cast out from *him* all pain of mind and body and mercifully give back to *him* full health, both inwardly and outwardly, that, being restored by the help of thy mercy, *he* may return to *his* duties as of old: Who with the Father and the same Holy Ghost livest and reignest God, world without end. *Amen.*

Let us pray.

LOOK, O Lord, we beseech thee, upon this thy *servant N.*, languishing in weakness of body, and comfort again the soul which thou hast created: that, being amended by thy chastisement, *he* may feel *himself* to be saved by thy healing. Through Christ our Lord. *Amen.*

Let us pray.

O LORD holy, Father almighty, everlasting God, who in pouring the grace of thy blessing upon sick bodies dost preserve by thy manifold goodness thy handy-work: graciously assist us who call upon thy Name; deliver thy *servant* from *his* sickness, and give *him* health; raise *him* up by thy right hand; strengthen *him* by thy might; protect *him* by thy power, and with all the prosperity which *he* desires restore *him* to thy holy Church. Through Christ our Lord. *Amen.*

¶ At the end, the Priest may give brief and salutary exhortations to enable the sick person to die in the Lord, and to strengthen him to put to flight the temptations of evil spirits.

¶ Finally, he should leave with him holy water and a Cross, that he may frequently look up on it, and according to his devotion kiss it and embrace it.

¶ He should also warn the relatives and servants of the sick man to send at once for the Parish Priest, if the disease grows worse, that he may help the dying man, and commend his soul to God; but if death is at hand, the Priest, before he departs, shall duly commend the soul to God.

¶ When this Sacrament is administered to several sick persons at the same time, the Priest shall present the Cross to each to be devoutly kissed, and shall say all the prayers which precede and follow the anointing once for all in the plural number; but he shall perform the anointings with their respective forms separately on each sick person.

Pastoral Rites   *Holy Unction*

After Holy Unction

RETURN thanks now to your loving Saviour with your whole heart, for having favoured you with all these helps in your sickness. Reflect how many are carried off by sudden death, or otherwise die without the holy Sacraments, or any of the extraordinary graces which God has afforted you! Beg of him that this holy Unction may produce in you all the happy fruits for which it was instituted by the goodness of your Saviour, by healing your soul of all its weaknesses and spiritual maladies: by fortifying you against all the temptations of the enemy: by supporting and comforting you under all your pains and anguish: by preparing and disposing you for whatever may be the holy will of God in your regard: and, if he sees it expedient for you, by restoring you to your bodily health and strength. In the meantime, keep yourself, as much as you can in the company of your Saviour Jesus Christ: but let it be with the dispositions of a true penitent, often bewailing your sins at his feet, and calling upon him for mercy. Hide yourself in his Wounds and bathe yourself in his precious Blood. A truly penitent spirit will be your best security both in life and death. But then, let this be joined with a great confidence in the mercy of God, and in the merits of Jesus Christ who died for you. Keep your eyes fixed upon him: contemplate the infinite and eternal happiness he has prepared for you in his heavenly kingdom: relinquish from this moment all worldly concerns, and all desires of remaining any longer in this place of banishment : and frequently say with St. Paul: I desire to be dissolved and to be with Christ : resign yourself entirely into his hands: let the consideration of the holy will of God, the glory he has prepared for you, and the sufferings your Saviour endured for your sake, animate you to bear with patience all your sufferings. Offer up all your pains and troubles to him: accept them as a penance justly inflicted on you for your sins: and pray that they may be sanctified and accepted through him. Beg also the intercession of the Blessed Virgin, and of all the glorious Angels and Saints of God, that you may be helped by their prayers both in life and death.

Holy Unction # Pastoral Rites

Questions Proper to be Asked of the Sick, to Excite them to Make Acts of the Necessary Virtues

Do you firmly believe all the Articles of Faith which the Holy, Catholic, Apostolic, Orthodox Church believes and teaches?

℞. I do believe them.

Do you firmly hope that God will be merciful to you: and that through the merits of Jesus Christ you will obtain from him the forgiveness of your sins, and life everlasting?

℞. I do.

Do you love God with your whole heart? and do you desire to love him as the blessed do in heaven?

℞. I do.

Are you, for the love of God, sorry from your heart, for every offence you have committed against him, and against your neighbour?

℞. I am.

Do you, for God's sake, forgive from your heart every one who has ever offended you, or been your enemy?

℞. I do.

Do you now, from your heart, ask pardon of every one whom you have offended by word or deed?

℞. I do.

Do you receive your present and future sufferings as penance justly inflicted on you by Almighty God; and will you endeavour to bear them with the patience becoming a Christian?

℞. I do so receive them: and will endeavour to bear them with patience and resignation to the holy will of God.

If it shall please God to restore you again to your bodily health and strength, will you, during the remainder of your life, carefully endeavour to avoid sin, and keep all his divine commandments?

℞. This is my determined resolution.

Pastoral Rites — *Communion of the Sick*

Communion of the Sick

¶ Upon entering the room, the Priest makes preparation and says,

℣. Peace be to this house.	℣. Pax huic dómui.
℟. And to all that dwell in it.	℟. Et ómnibus habitántibus in ea.

¶ The Priest then takes Holy Water and sprinkles the sick person and the room while saying,

Thou shalt purge me, * O Lord, with hyssop, and I shall be clean: thou shalt wash me, and I shall be whiter than snow. *Ps.* Have mercy upon me, O God, after thy great goodness. ℣. Glory be to the Father, and to the Son, and to the Holy Ghost; ℟. As it was in the beginning, is now and ever shall be, world without end. Amen.

Thou shalt purge me, * O Lord, with hyssop, and I shall be clean: thou shalt wash me, and I shall be whiter than snow.

℣. O Lord, show thy mercy upon us.	℣. Osténde nobis, Dómine, misericórdiam tuam.
℟. And grant us thy salvation.	℟. Et salutáre tuum da nobis.
℣. O Lord, hear my prayer.	℣. Dómine, exáudi oratiónem meam.
℟. And let my cry come unto thee.	℟. Et clamor meus ad te véniat.
℣. The Lord be with you.	℣. Dóminus vobíscum.
℟. And with thy spirit.	℟. Et cum spíritu tuo.

Let us pray.

RACIOUSLY hear us, O Lord holy, Father almighty, everlasting God: and vouchsafe to send thy holy Angel from heaven; to guard and cherish, to protect and visit, and to defend all who dwell in this place. Through Christ our Lord. *Amen.*

¶ The following General Confession is then said, unless a private confession be made.

CONFESS to God Almighty, to Blessed Mary ever Virgin, to blessed Michael the Archangel, to blessed John Baptist, to the holy Apostles Peter and Paul, to all the Saints, and to thee, Father, that I have sinned exceedingly in thought, word, and deed; (Strike breast thrice.) by my fault, my own fault, my own most grievous fault. Therefore I beg blessed

ONFÍTEOR Deo omnipoténti, beátæ Maríæ semper Vírgini, beáto Michaéli Archángelo, beáto Joánni Baptístæ, sanctis Apóstolis Petro et Paulo, ómnibus Sanctis, et tibi, pater: quia peccávi nimis cogitatióne, verbo et ópere: (Strike breast thrice.) mea culpa, mea culpa, mea máxima culpa. Ideo precor beátam Maríam semper Vírginem, beátum Michaélem

Communion of the Sick   # Pastoral Rites

Mary ever Virgin, blessed Michael the Archangel, blessed John Baptist, the holy Apostles Peter and Paul, all the Saints, and thee, Father, to pray for me to the Lord our God.	Archángelum, beátum Joánnem Baptístam, sanctos Apóstolos Petrum et Paulum, omnes Sanctos, et te, pater, oráre pro me ad Dóminum, Deum nostrum.
℣. God Almighty have mercy upon *you*, forgive *you your* sins, and bring *you* to everlasting life.	℣. Misereátur *vestri* omnípotens Deus, et, dimíssis peccátis *vestris*, perdúcat *vos* ad vitam ætérnam.
℟. Amen.	℟. Amen.
℣. The almighty and merciful Lord grant unto *you* pardon, absolution, ✠ and remission of *your* sins.	℣. Indulgéntiam, ✠ absolutiónem et remissiónem peccatórum *vestrórum* tríbuat *vobis* omnípotens et miséricors Dóminus.
℟. Amen.	℟. Amen.

¶ The Priest then takes the Sacrament from the Pyx and raises it saying,

℣. Behold ✠ the Lamb of God; behold him who taketh away the sins of the world.	℣. Ecce Agnus Dei, ecce, qui tollit peccáta mundi.
℟. Lord, I am not worthy that thou shouldest come under my roof, but speak the word only, and my soul shall be healed.	℟. Dómine, non sum dignus, ut intres sub tectum meum, sed tantum dic verbo, et sanábitur ánima mea.
℟. Lord, I am not worthy that thou shouldest come under my roof, but speak the word only, and my soul shall be healed.	℟. Dómine, non sum dignus, ut intres sub tectum meum, sed tantum dic verbo, et sanábitur ánima mea.
℟. Lord, I am not worthy that thou shouldest come under my roof, but speak the word only, and my soul shall be healed.	℟. Dómine, non sum dignus, ut intres sub tectum meum, sed tantum dic verbo, et sanábitur ánima mea.

¶ The Priest administers the Sacrament to the sick person saying,
    Note, the Priest may use a form of delivering the Sacrament to the People from the Mass.

THE BODY AND BLOOD OF OUR LORD JESUS CHRIST PRESERVE THY SOUL UNTO EVERLASTING LIFE.

Pastoral Rites *Communion of the Sick*

℣ The Priest cleanses his fingers and then says.

℣. The Lord be with you.
℟. And with thy spirit.

℣. Dóminus vobíscum.
℟. Et cum spíritu tuo.

Let us pray.

LORD holy, Father almighty, everlasting God, we faithfully beseech thee that the most Sacred Body of our Lord Jesus Christ thy Son, which our *brother* hath received, may avail for the healing both of body and soul: who liveth and reigneth with thee, in the unity of the Holy Ghost, ever one God, world without end. *Amen.*

HE blessing of God almighty, the Father, ✠ the Son, and the Holy Ghost, descend upon *you* and remain with *you* always. *Amen.*

Burial of the Dead   # Pastoral Rites

The Order for the Burial of the Dead

Reception of the Body

¶ The Priest, meeting the Body at the entrance of the church yard, and prior to going before it either into the church or towards the grave, shall say or sing,

Note, The Priest should be vested in surplice and black stole, and also, on more solemn occasions, in black cope.

I am the resurrection and the life, saith the Lord: he that believeth in me, though he were dead, yet shall he live: and whosoever liveth and believeth in me, shall never die.

I know that my redeemer liveth, and that he shall stand at the latter day upon the earth: and though this body be destroyed, yet shall I see God: whom I shall see for myself, and mine eyes shall behold, and not as a stranger.

We brought nothing into this world, and it is certain we can carry nothing out. The LORD gave, and the LORD hath taken away; blessed be the name of the LORD.

Procession

¶ A Clerk carrying the Cross goes before (and, on more solemn occasions, with two acolytes with candles), accompanied by another bearing Holy Water. As the Ministers and Clerks proceed into the Church, the following Responsory is begun.

Subvenite

Come to *his* aid, ye Saints of God, come to meet *him*, ye Angels of the Lord. Receiving *his* soul, offering it in the sight of the Most High.

℣. May Christ receive thee, who hath called thee: and may the Angels lead thee unto Abraham's bosom.

℟. Receiving *his* soul, offering it in the sight of the Most High.

℣. Rest eternal grant unto *him*, O Lord: and let light perpetual shine upon *him*.

℟. Offering it in the sight of the Most High.

¶ The Coffin is set down in the midst of the Church, so that the feet of the departed, unless he be a Priest, are toward the High Altar; but if he be a Priest, his head is toward the Altar. Then Candles should be lighted about the Body.

Pastoral Rites *Burial of the Dead*

Service in the Church

¶ *After they are come into the Church, and the Responsory hath been said, then shall be said one or more or the following Selections, taken from the Psalms. Instead of the Gloria Patri shall be said the following at the end of each Psalm.*

℣. Rest eternal * grant unto them, O Lord.
℟. And let light perpetual * shine upon them.

Psalm 39. Dixi, Custodiam

LORD, let me know mine end, and the number of my days : that I may be certified how long I have to live.

6 Behold, thou hast made my days as it were a span long : and mine age is even as nothing in respect of thee; and verily every man living is altogether vanity.

7 For man walketh in a vain shadow, and disquieteth himself in vain : he heapeth up riches, and cannot tell who shall gather them.

8 And now, Lord, what is my hope : truly my hope is even in thee.

9 Deliver me from all mine offences : and make me not a rebuke unto the foolish.

10 I became dumb, and opened not my mouth : for it was thy doing.

11 Take thy plague away from me : I am even consumed by the means of thy heavy hand.

12 When thou with rebukes dost chasten man for sin, thou makest his beauty to consume away, like as it were a moth fretting a garment : every man therefore is but vanity.

13 Hear my prayer, O Lord, and with thine ears consider my calling : hold not thy peace at my tears.

14 For I am a stranger with thee : and a sojourner, as all my fathers were.

15 O spare me a little, that I may recover my strength : before I go hence, and be no more seen.

Psalm 90. Domine, refugium

LORD, thou hast been our refuge : from one generation to another.

2 Before the mountains were brought forth, or ever the earth and the world were made : thou art God from everlasting, and world without end.

3 Thou turnest man to destruction : again thou sayest, Come again, ye children of men.

4 For a thousand years in thy sight are but as yesterday : seeing that is past as a watch in the night.

5 As soon as thou scatterest them they are even as a sleep : and fade away suddenly like the grass.

6 In the morning it is green, and groweth up : but in the evening it is cut down, dried up, and withered.

7 For we consume away in thy displeasure : and are afraid at thy wrathful indignation.

8 Thou hast set our misdeeds before thee : and our secret sins in the light of thy countenance.

9 For when thou art angry all our days are gone : we bring our years to an end, as it were a tale that is told.

10 The days of our age are threescore years and ten; and though men be so strong that they come to fourscore years : yet is their strength then but labour and sorrow; so soon passeth it away, and we are gone.

11 But who regardeth the power of thy wrath : for even thereafter as a man feareth, so is thy displeasure.

12 So teach us to number our days : that we may apply our hearts unto wisdom.

Psalm 27. *Dominus illuminatio*

THE Lord is my light and my salvation ; whom then shall I fear : the Lord is the strength of my life; of whom then shall I be afraid?

2 When the wicked, even mine enemies and my foes, came upon me to eat up my flesh : they stumbled and fell.

3 Though an host of men were laid against me, yet shall not my heart be afraid : and though there rose up war against me, yet will I put my trust in him.

4 One thing have I desired of the Lord, which I will require : even that I may dwell in the house of the Lord all the days of my life, to behold the fair beauty of the Lord, and to visit his temple.

5 For in the time of trouble he shall hide me in his tabernacle : yea, in the secret place of his dwelling shall he hide me, and set me up upon a rock of stone.

6 And now shall he lift up mine head : above mine enemies round about me.

7 Therefore will I offer in his dwelling an oblation with great gladness : I will sing, and speak praises unto the Lord.

8 Hearken unto my voice, O Lord, when I cry unto thee : have mercy upon me, and hear me.

9 My heart hath talked of thee, Seek ye my face : Thy face, Lord, will I seek.

10 O hide not thou thy face from me : nor cast thy servant away in displeasure.

11 Thou hast been my succour : leave me not, neither forsake me, O God of my salvation.

12 When my father and my mother forsake me : the Lord taketh me up.

13 Teach me thy way, O Lord : and lead me in the right way, because of mine enemies.

14 Deliver me not over into the will of mine adversaries : for there are false witnesses risen up against me, and such as speak wrong.

15 I should utterly have fainted : but that I believe verily to see the goodness of the Lord in the land of the living.

16 O tarry thou the Lord's leisure : be strong, and he shall comfort thine heart; and put thou thy trust in the Lord.

Psalm 46. Deus noster refugium

OD is our hope and strength : a very present help in trouble.

2 Therefore will we not fear, though the earth be moved : and though the hills be carried into the midst of the sea;

3 Though the waters thereof rage and swell : and though the mountains shake at the tempest of the same.

4 The rivers of the flood thereof shall make glad the city of God : the holy place of the tabernacle of the most Highest.

5 God is in the midst of her, therefore shall she not be removed : God shall help her, and that right early.

6 The heathen make much ado, and the kingdoms are moved : but God hath shewed his voice, and the earth shall melt away.

7 The Lord of hosts is with us : the God of Jacob is our refuge.

8 O come hither, and behold the works of the Lord : what destruction he hath brought upon the earth.

9 He maketh wars to cease in all the world : he breaketh the bow, and knappeth the spear in sunder, and burneth the chariots in the fire.

10 Be still then, and know that I am God : I will be exalted among the heathen, and I will be exalted in the earth.

11 The Lord of hosts is with us : the God of Jacob is our refuge.

Burial of the Dead   # Pastoral Rites

Psalm 121. Levavi oculus

I WILL lift up mine eyes unto the hills : from whence cometh my help.

2 My help cometh even from the Lord : who hath made heaven and earth.

3 He will not suffer thy foot to be moved : and he that keepeth thee will not sleep.

4 Behold, he that keepeth Israel : shall neither slumber nor sleep.

5 The Lord himself is thy keeper : the Lord is thy defence upon thy right hand;

6 So that the sun shall not burn thee by day : neither the moon by night.

7 The Lord shall preserve thee from all evil : yea, it is even he that shall keep thy soul.

8 The Lord shall preserve thy going out, and thy coming in : from this time forth for evermore.

Psalm 130. De profundis

OUT of the deep have I called unto thee, O Lord : Lord, hear my voice.

2 O let thine ears consider well : the voice of my complaint.

3 If thou, Lord, wilt be extreme to mark what is done amiss : O Lord, who may abide it?

4 For there is mercy with thee : therefore shalt thou be feared.

5 I look for the Lord; my soul doth wait for him : in his word is my trust.

6 My soul fleeth unto the Lord : before the morning watch, I say, before the morning watch.

7 O Israel, trust in the Lord, for with the Lord there is mercy : and with him is plenteous redemption.

8 And he shall redeem Israel : from all his sins.

Lesson. 1 Corinthians 15:20

¶ Then shall follow the Lesson.

¶ NOTE, Either Romans 8:14-39 or John 14:1-6 may be said instead.

NOW is Christ risen from the dead, and become the first-fruits of them that slept. For since by man came death, by man came also the resurrection of the dead. For as in Adam all die, even so in Christ shall all be made alive. But every man in his own order: Christ the first-fruits; afterward they that are Christ's, at his coming. Then cometh the end, when he shall have delivered up the kingdom to God, even the Father; when he shall have put down all rule,

Pastoral Rites *Burial of the Dead*

and all authority, and power. For he must reign, till he hath put all enemies under his feet. The last enemy that shall be destroyed is death. For he hath put all things under his feet. But when he saith, all things are put under him, it is manifest that he is excepted, which did put all things under him. And when all things shall be subdued unto him, then shall the Son also himself be subject unto Him that put all things under him that God may be all in all.

Else what shall they do which are baptized for the dead, if the dead rise not at all? Why are they then baptized for the dead? and why stand we in jeopardy every hour? I protest by your rejoicing, which I have in Christ Jesus our Lord, I die daily. If after the manner of men I have fought with beasts at Ephesus, what advantageth it me, if the dead rise not? let us eat and drink, for tomorrow we die. Be not deceived: evil communications corrupt good manners. Awake to righteousness, and sin not; for some have not the knowledge of God. I speak this to your shame. But some man will say, How are the dead raised up? and with what body do they come? Thou fool! that which thou sowest is not quickened, except it die. And that which thou sowest, thou sowest not that body that shall be, but bare grain, it may chance of wheat, or of some other grain. But God giveth it a body as it hath pleased him, and to every seed his own body. All flesh is not the same flesh; but there is one kind of flesh of men, another flesh of beasts, another of fishes, and another of birds. There are also celestial bodies, and bodies terrestrial; but the glory of the celestial is one, and the glory of the terrestrial is another. There is one glory of the sun, and another glory of the moon, and another glory of the stars; for one star differeth from another star in glory. So also is the resurrection of the dead. It is sown in corruption; it is raised in incorruption: it is sown in dishonour; it is raised in glory: it is sown in weakness; it is raised in power: it is sown a natural body; it is raised a spiritual body. There is a natural body, and there is a spiritual body. And so it is written, The first man Adam was made a living soul; the last Adam was made a quickening spirit. Howbeit, that was not first which is spiritual, but that which is natural; and afterward that which is spiritual. The first man is of the earth, earthy: the second man is the Lord from heaven. As is the earthy, such are they also that are earthy: and as is the heavenly, such are they also that are heavenly. And as we have borne the image of the earthy, we shall also bear the image of the heavenly.

Now this I say, brethren, that flesh and blood cannot inherit the kingdom of God; neither doth corruption inherit incorruption Behold, I show you a mystery: we shall not all sleep, but we shall all be changed, in a moment, in the twinkling of an eye, at the last trump: for the trumpet shall sound, and the dead shall be raised incorruptible, and we shall be changed. For this corruptible must put on incorruption, and this mortal must put on immortality. So when

Burial of the Dead # Pastoral Rites

this corruptible shall have put on incorruption, and this mortal shall have put on immortality; then shall be brought to pass the saying that is written, Death is swallowed up in victory. O death, where is thy sting? O grave, where is thy victory? The sting of death is sin; and the strength of sin is the Law. But thanks be to God, which giveth us the victory through our Lord Jesus Christ. Therefore, my beloved brethren, be ye steadfast, unmoveable, always abounding in the work of the Lord, forasmuch as ye know that your labour is not in vain in the Lord.

❡ Here may be sung a Hymn or Anthem; and at the discretion of the Minister, the Apostles' Creed, the Lord's Prayer, and such other fitting Prayers as are elsewhere provided in this Book, ending with the prayers which followeth and the Blessing; the Minister, before the Prayers, first pronouncing,

℣. The Lord be with you.
℟. And with thy spirit.

Let us pray.

ABSOLVE, we beseech thee, O Lord, the soul of thy *servant N.* from every bond of sin: that in the glory of the resurrection *he* may be raised up amid thy Saints and elect unto newness of life. Through Christ, our Lord. *Amen.*

REMEMBER thy servant, O Lord, according to the favour which thou bearest unto thy people, and grant that, increasing in knowledge and love of thee, *he* may go from strength to strength, in the life of perfect service, in thy heavenly kingdom; through Jesus Christ our Lord, who liveth and reigneth with thee and the Holy Ghost, ever, one God, world without end. *Amen.*

UNTO God's gracious mercy and protection we commit you. The Lord bl ✠ ess you and keep you. The Lord make his face to shine upon you, and be gracious unto you. The Lord lift up his countenance upon you, and give you peace, both now and evermore. *Amen.*

❡ If a Requiem Mass be said, it may be offered here (p. 582).

Pastoral Rites *Burial of the Dead*

Absolution of the Dead

¶ If this office follow a Requiem Mass, the Priest takes off his chasuble and maniple, and puts on a black cope. He then proceeds to stand at the foot of the bier, where he says the following prayer.

ENTER not into judgment with thy servant, O Lord, for in thy sight shall no man living be justified, except thou grant unto him remission of all his sins. Therefore, we beseech thee, let not the sentence of thy judgment fall upon him, whom the faithful prayer of Christian people commendeth unto thee: but by the succour of thy grace let him who while he lived was sealed with the sign of the Holy Trinity be found worthy to escape the avenging judgment: Who livest and reignest world without end. *Amen.*

¶ Then, the Cantor beginning, the Clerks standing around sing the following Responsory:

Deliver me, O Lord, * from death eternal in that fearful day: * When the heavens and the earth shall be shaken: * When thou shalt come to judge the world by fire. ℣. I am in fear and trembling till the sifting be upon us, and the wrath to come, * When the heavens and the earth shall be shaken. ℣. O that day that day of anger, of calamity and misery, a great day and exceeding bitter. * When thou shalt come to judge the world by fire. ℣. Rest eternal grant unto them, O Lord: and let light perpetual shine upon them.

℟. Deliver me, O Lord, * from death eternal in that fearful day: * When the heavens and the earth shall be shaken: * When thou shalt come to judge the world by fire.

¶ Towards the end of the Responsory, the Celebrant puts incense into the thurible, blessing it as usual, the Deacon ministering the boat.

¶ The Responsory ended, the Priest says,

℣. Lord, have mercy upon us.
℟. Christ, have mercy upon us.
℣. Lord, have mercy upon us.

¶ While the Lord's Prayer is said silently, the Priest goeth about the bier, sprinkling it with Holy Water, thrice on each side; and then in like manner he censes it, thrice on each side. He then says aloud,

℣. And lead us not into temptation.
℟. But deliver us from evil.

℣. From the gate of hell.
℟. Deliver *his* soul, O Lord.
℣. May *he* rest in peace.

℟. Amen.
℣. O Lord, hear my prayer.
℟. And let my cry come unto thee.
℣. The Lord be with you.
℟. And with thy spirit.
℣. Let us pray.

❡ If the Body be present, the following Collect shall be said.

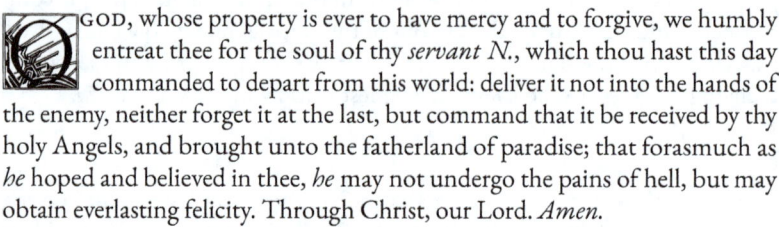GOD, whose property is ever to have mercy and to forgive, we humbly entreat thee for the soul of thy *servant N.*, which thou hast this day commanded to depart from this world: deliver it not into the hands of the enemy, neither forget it at the last, but command that it be received by thy holy Angels, and brought unto the fatherland of paradise; that forasmuch as *he* hoped and believed in thee, *he* may not undergo the pains of hell, but may obtain everlasting felicity. Through Christ, our Lord. *Amen.*

❡ If the Body be not present, the following shall be said.

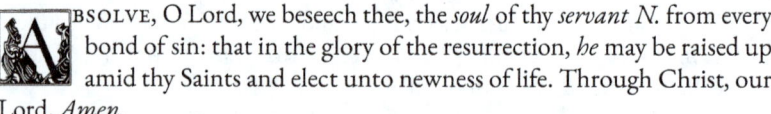BSOLVE, O Lord, we beseech thee, the *soul* of thy *servant N.* from every bond of sin: that in the glory of the resurrection, *he* may be raised up amid thy Saints and elect unto newness of life. Through Christ, our Lord. *Amen.*

❡ Then, the Priest making a cross with his right hand over the bier, says,

℣. Rest eternal grant unto *him,* O Lord.
℟. And let light perpetual shine upon *him.*
℣. May *he* rest in peace.
℟. Amen.

❡ The Celebrant, again making a cross over the bier, says without inflexion:

℣. May *his* soul and the souls of all the faithful departed through the mercy of God rest in peace.
℟. Amen.

Pastoral Rites *Burial of the Dead*

Service at the Grave

¶ While the Body is being borne from the Church to the Grave, the following shall be sung,

INTO Paradise * may the Angels lead thee: at thy coming may the Martyrs receive thee, and bring thee into the holy city Jerusalem. May the Choirs of Angels receive thee, and with Lazarus, once poor, mayest thou have eternal rest.

Blessing of the Grave

¶ If the ground be unconsecrated, when the Priest and People arrive, the following blessing is said.

Let us pray.

O LORD Jesu Christ, who wast laid in the new tomb of Joseph, and didst thereby sanctify the grave to be a bed of hope to thy people: Vouchsafe, we beseech thee, to bless, ha ✠ llow, and consecrate this grave, that it may be a resting-place, peaceful and secure, for the body of thy servant which we are about to commit to thy gracious keeping; who art the resurrection and the life, and who livest and reignest with the Father and the Holy Ghost, one God, world without end. *Amen.*

¶ The Priest then sprinkles the grave with Holy Water, and then censes the Body and the Grave.

At the Grave

¶ When they come to the Grave, while the Body is made ready to be laid into the earth, shall be sung or said,

MAN, that is born of a woman, hath but a short time to live, and is full of misery. He cometh up, and is cut down, like a flower; he fleeth as it were a shadow, and never continueth in one stay.

In the midst of life we are in death; of whom may we seek for succour, but of thee, O Lord, who for our sins art justly displeased?

Yet, O Lord God most holy, O Lord most mighty, O holy and most merciful Saviour, deliver us not into the bitter pains of eternal death.

Thou knowest, Lord, the secrets of our hearts; shut not thy merciful ears to our prayer; but spare us, Lord most holy, O God most mighty, O holy and merciful Saviour, thou most worthy Judge eternal, suffer us not, at our last hour, for any pains of death, to fall from thee.

or,

Pastoral Rites

Burial of the Dead

ALL that the Father giveth me shall come to me: and him that cometh to me I will in no wise cast out.

He that raised up Jesus from the dead: will also quicken your mortal bodies by the spirit which dwelleth in you.

Wherefore my heart is glad, and my glory rejoiceth: my flesh also shall rest in hope.

Thou shalt show me the path of life; in thy presence is the fulness of joy: and at thy right hand there is pleasure for evermore.

¶ Then, while the earth shall be cast upon the Body by some standing by, the Priest shall say,

UNTO Almighty God we commend the soul of our *brother* departed, and we commit *his* body to the ground; earth to earth, ashes to ashes, dust to dust; in sure and certain hope of the Resurrection unto eternal life, through our Lord Jesus Christ, at whose coming in glorious majesty to judge the world, the earth and the sea shall give up their dead; and the corruptible bodies of those who sleep in him shall be changed, and made like unto his own glorious body; according to the mighty working whereby he is able to subdue all things unto himself.

¶ Then shall be said or sung,

Ant. I heard a voice from heaven, saying unto me, Write, From henceforth blessed are the dead who die in the Lord: even so saith the Spirit; for they rest from their labours.

BLESSED ✠ be the Lord God of Israel; * for he hath visited and redeemed his people;

And hath raised up a mighty salvation for us, * in the house of his servant David;

As he spake by the mouth of his holy Prophets, * which have been since the world began;

That we should be saved from our enemies, * and from the hand of all that hate us.

To perform the mercy promised to our forefathers, * and to remember his holy covenant;

To perform the oath which he sware to our forefather Abraham, * that he would give us;

That we being delivered out of the hand of our enemies * might serve him without fear;

In holiness and righteousness before him, * all the days of our life.

And thou, child, shalt be called the prophet of the Highest: * for thou shalt go before the face of the Lord to prepare his ways;

Pastoral Rites *Burial of the Dead*

To give knowledge of salvation unto his people * for the remission of their sins,

Through the tender mercy of our God; * whereby the day-spring from on high hath visited us;

To give light to them that sit in darkness, and in the shadow of death, * and to guide our feet into the way of peace.

℣. Rest eternal * grant unto them, O Lord.

℟. And let light perpetual * shine upon them.

Ant. I heard a voice from heaven, saying unto me, Write, From henceforth blessed are the dead who die in the Lord: even so saith the Spirit; for they rest from their labours.

℣. The Lord be with you.

℟. And with thy spirit.

℣. Let us pray.

℣. Lord, have mercy upon us.

℟. Christ, have mercy upon us.

℣. Lord, have mercy upon us.

OUR Father, who art in heaven, Hallowed be thy Name. Thy kingdom come. Thy will be done on earth, As it is in heaven. Give us this day our daily bread. And forgive us our trespasses, As we forgive those who trespass against us. And lead us not into temptation; But deliver us from evil. Amen.

¶ Meanwhile, the Priest sprinkles the body with Holy Water.

¶ Then the Priest shall say that which followeth.

GRANT, we beseech thee, O Lord, this mercy to thy *servant* departed; that, forasmuch as *he* desired to do thy will, *he* may not suffer the punishment of *his* misdeed: that, as true faith joined *him* to the company of the faithful here below, so in heaven thy mercy may number *him* among the angelic choirs. Through Christ, our Lord. *Amen.*

¶ The Priest may say one or more of the following Prayers, at his discretion.

O GOD, whose mercies cannot be numbered; Accept our prayers on behalf of the soul of thy *servant* departed, and grant *him* an entrance into the land of light and joy, in the fellowship of thy saints; through Jesus Christ our Lord. *Amen.*

ALMIGHTY God, with whom do live the spirits of those who depart hence in the Lord, and with whom the souls of the faithful, after they are delivered from the burden of the flesh, are in joy and felicity; We give

Burial of the Dead   **Pastoral Rites**

thee hearty thanks for the good examples of all those thy servants, who, having finished their course in faith, do now rest from their labours. And we beseech thee, that we, with all those who are departed in the true faith of thy holy Name, may have our perfect consummation and bliss, both in body and soul, in thy eternal and everlasting glory; through Jesus Christ our Lord. *Amen.*

MERCIFUL God, the Father of our Lord Jesus Christ, who is the Resurrection and the Life; in whom whosoever believeth, shall live, though he die; and whosoever liveth, and believeth in him, shall not die eternally; who also hath taught us, by his holy Apostle Saint Paul, not to be sorry, as men without hope, for those who sleep in him; We humbly beseech thee, O Father, to raise us from the death of sin unto the life of righteousness; that, when we shall depart this life, we may rest in him; and that, at the general Resurrection in the last day, we may be found acceptable in thy sight; and receive that blessing, which thy well-beloved Son shall then pronounce to all who love and fear thee, saying, Come, ye blessed children of my Father, receive the kingdom prepared for you from the beginning of the world. Grant this, we beseech thee, O merciful Father, through Jesus Christ, our Mediator and Redeemer. *Amen.*

THE God of peace, who brought again from the dead our Lord Jesus Christ, the great Shepherd of the sheep, through the blood of the everlasting covenant; Make you perfect in every good work to do his will, working in you that which is well pleasing in his sight; through Jesus Christ, to whom be glory for ever and ever. *Amen.*

ALMIGHTY God, the God of the spirits of all flesh, who by a voice from heaven didst proclaim, Blessed are the dead who die in the Lord; Multiply, we beseech thee, to those who rest in Jesus, the manifold blessings of thy love, that the good work which thou didst begin in them may be perfected unto the day of Jesus Christ. And of thy mercy, O heavenly Father, vouchsafe that we, who now serve thee here on earth, may at last, together with them, be found meet to be partakers of the inheritance of the saints in light; for the sake of the same thy Son Jesus Christ our Lord. *Amen.*

MOST merciful Father, who hast been pleased to take unto thyself the soul of this thy servant; Grant to us who are still in our pilgrimage, and who walk as yet by faith, that having served thee with constancy on earth, we may be joined hereafter with thy blessed saints in glory everlasting; through Jesus Christ our Lord. *Amen.*

LORD Jesus Christ, who by thy death didst take away the sting of death; Grant unto us thy servants so to follow in faith where thou hast led the way, that we may at length fall asleep peacefully in thee, and awake up after thy likeness; through thy mercy, who livest with the Father and the Holy Ghost, one God, world without end. *Amen.*

Almighty and everliving God, we yield unto thee most high praise and hearty thanks, for the wonderful grace and virtue declared in all thy saints, who have been the choice vessels of thy grace, and the lights of the world in their several generations; most humbly beseeching thee to give us grace so to follow the example of their stedfastness in thy faith, and obedience to thy holy commandments, that at the day of the general Resurrection, we, with all those who are of the mystical body of thy Son, may be set on his right hand, and hear that his most joyful voice: Come, ye blessed of my Father, inherit the kingdom prepared for you from the foundation of the world. Grant this, O Father, for the sake of the same, thy Son Jesus Christ, our only Mediator and Advocate. *Amen.*

¶ The Priest then continues,

℣. Rest eternal grant unto *him*, O Lord.
℟. And let light perpetual shine upon *him*.
℣. May *he* rest in peace.
℟. Amen.

May *his* soul, ✠ and the souls of all the faithful departed, through the mercy of God, rest in peace. *Amen.*

¶ The Priest then sprinkles the grave with Holy Water.

At the Burial of the Dead at Sea

¶ The same office may be used; but instead of the Sentence of Committal, the Minister shall say,

Unto Almighty God we commend the soul of our brother departed, and we commit his body to the deep; in sure and certain hope of the Resurrection unto eternal life, through our Lord Jesus Christ; at whose coming in glorious majesty to judge the world, the sea shall give up her dead; and the corruptible bodies of those who sleep in him shall be changed, and made like unto his glorious body; according to the mighty working whereby he is able to subdue all things unto himself.

Burial of a Child

Pastoral Rites

At the Burial of a Child

¶ When a baptised Child dies before the age of reason, it receives this special funeral rite. Note, the Ministers, Holy Water, and incense should be present similar to the standard Burial rite.

¶ Unlike funerals for adults, bells should be rung joyfully. The Altar should be decorated festively, and the liturgical colour is white.

¶ The Priest, vested in surplice and white stole, meeting the Body, and going before it, either into the Church or towards the Grave, shall say:

AM the resurrection and the life, saith the Lord: he that believeth in me, though he were dead, yet shall he live: and whosoever liveth and believeth in me, shall never die.

ESUS called them unto him and said, Suffer the little children to come unto me, and forbid them not: for of such is the kingdom of God.

E shall feed his flock like a shepherd: he shall gather the lambs with his arms, and carry them in his bosom.

¶ When they are come into the Church, shall be said the following Psalms.

Psalm 23. *Dominus regit me.*

HE Lord is my shepherd : therefore can I lack nothing.

2 He shall feed me in a green pasture : and lead me forth beside the waters of comfort.

3 He shall convert my soul : and bring me forth in the paths of righteousness, for his Name's sake.

4 Yea, though I walk through the valley of the shadow of death, I will fear no evil : for thou art with me; thy rod and thy staff comfort me.

5 Thou shalt prepare a table before me against them that trouble me : thou hast anointed my head with oil, and my cup shall be full.

6 But thy loving-kindness and mercy shall follow me all the days of my life : and I will dwell in the house of the Lord for ever.

℣. Glory be to the Father, and to the Son, and to the Holy Ghost.

℟. As it was in the beginning, is now, and ever shall be, world without end. Amen.

Pastoral Rites   *Burial of a Child*

Psalm 121. *Levavi oculus*

I will lift up mine eyes unto the hills : from whence cometh my help.

2 My help cometh even from the Lord : who hath made heaven and earth.

3 He will not suffer thy foot to be moved : and he that keepeth thee will not sleep.

4 Behold, he that keepeth Israel : shall neither slumber nor sleep.

5 The Lord himself is thy keeper : the Lord is thy defence upon thy right hand;

6 So that the sun shall not burn thee by day : neither the moon by night.

7 The Lord shall preserve thee from all evil : yea, it is even he that shall keep thy soul.

8 The Lord shall preserve thy going out, and thy coming in : from this time forth for evermore.

℣. Glory be to the Father, and to the Son, and to the Holy Ghost.

℟. As it was in the beginning, is now, and ever shall be, world without end. Amen.

Lesson. Matthew 18:1

At the same time came the disciples unto Jesus, saying, Who is the greatest in the kingdom of heaven? And Jesus called a little child unto him, and set him in the midst of them, and said, Verily I say unto you, Except ye be converted, and become as little children, ye shall not enter into the kingdom of heaven. Whosoever therefore shall humble himself as this little child, the same is greatest in the kingdom of heaven. And whoso shall receive one such little child in my name receiveth me. Take heed that ye despise not one of these little ones; for I say unto you, That in heaven their angels do always behold the face of my Father which is in heaven.

¶ If a Mass is to be said, it may be offered here, either a Votive Mass for the Holy Angels (p. 575)—if rubrics permit—or the Mass of the Day.

Otherwise, Here may be sung a Hymn or an Anthem; then shall the Minister say,

℣. The Lord be with you.
℟. And with thy spirit.
℣. Let us pray.
℣. Lord, have mercy upon us.
℟. Christ, have mercy upon us.
℣. Lord, have mercy upon us.

Burial of a Child   # Pastoral Rites

UR Father, who art in heaven, Hallowed be thy Name. Thy kingdom come. Thy will be done on earth, As it is in heaven. Give us this day our daily bread. And forgive us our trespasses, As we forgive those who trespass against us. And lead us not into temptation; But deliver us from evil. Amen.

¶ While the Lord's Prayer is said, the Priest thrice sprinkles the Coffin with Holy Water. NOTE, He does not go round it, nor is it censed.

℣. Blessed are the pure in heart;
℟. For they shall see God.
℣. Blessed be the name of the Lord;
℟. Henceforth, world without end.
℣. O Lord, hear our prayer;
℟. And let our cry come unto thee.

¶ Here shall be said the following Prayers.

MERCIFUL Father, whose face the angels of thy little ones do always behold in heaven; Grant us stedfastly to believe that this thy child hath been taken into the safe keeping of thine eternal love. Through.

LMIGHTY and merciful Father, who dost grant to children an abundant entrance into thy kingdom; Grant us grace so to conform our lives to their innocency and perfect faith, that at length, united with them, we may stand in thy presence in fulness of joy. Through.

HE grace of our Lord Jesus ✠ Christ, and the love of God, and the fellowship of the Holy Ghost, be with us all evermore. *Amen.*

¶ While the Body is being borne from the church to the Grave, the following is said or sung,

PSALM 148. *LAUDATE DOMINUM*

PRAISE the Lord of heaven : praise him in the height.
2 Praise him, all ye angels of his : praise him, all his host.
3 Praise him, sun and moon : praise him, all ye stars and light.
4 Praise him, all ye heavens : and ye waters that are above the heavens.
5 Let them praise the Name of the Lord : for he spake the word, and they were made; he commanded, and they were created.
6 He hath made them fast for ever and ever : he hath given them a law which shall not be broken.
7 Praise the Lord upon earth : ye dragons, and all deeps;
8 Fire and hail, snow and vapours : wind and storm, fulfilling his word;

9 Mountains and all hills : fruitful trees and all cedars;
10 Beasts and all cattle : worms and feathered fowls;
11 Kings of the earth and all people : princes and all judges of the world;
12 Young men and maidens, old men and children, praise the Name of the Lord : for his Name only is excellent, and his praise above heaven and earth.
13 He shall exalt the horn of his people; all his saints shall praise him : even the children of Israel, even the people that serveth him.

℣. Glory be to the Father, and to the Son, and to the Holy Ghost.

℞. As it was in the beginning, is now, and ever shall be, world without end. Amen.

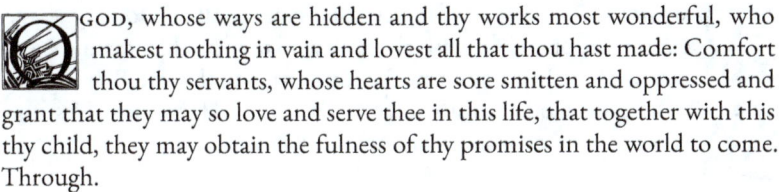GOD, whose ways are hidden and thy works most wonderful, who makest nothing in vain and lovest all that thou hast made: Comfort thou thy servants, whose hearts are sore smitten and oppressed and grant that they may so love and serve thee in this life, that together with this thy child, they may obtain the fulness of thy promises in the world to come. Through.

At the Grave

¶ *When they are come to the Grave shall be said or sung,*

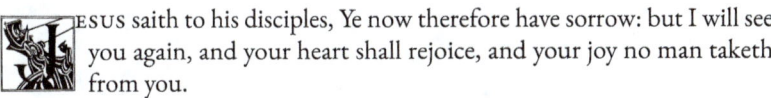ESUS saith to his disciples, Ye now therefore have sorrow: but I will see you again, and your heart shall rejoice, and your joy no man taketh from you.

¶ *Meanwhile the Priest sprinkles both the coffin and the Grave with Holy Water and censes them.*

While the earth is being cast upon the Body, the Minister shall say,

IN sure and certain hope of the Resurrection to eternal life through our Lord Jesus Christ, we commit the body of this child to the ground. The LORD bless *him* and keep *him*, the LORD make his face to shine upon *him* and be gracious unto *him*, the LORD lift up his countenance upon *him*, and give *him* peace, both now and evermore.

¶ *Then shall be said or sung,*

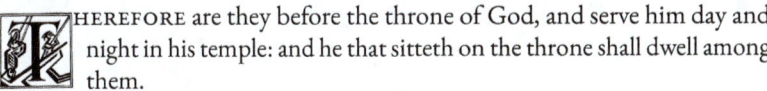HEREFORE are they before the throne of God, and serve him day and night in his temple: and he that sitteth on the throne shall dwell among them.

They shall hunger no more, neither thirst any more; neither shall the sun light on them, nor any heat.

Pastoral Rites
Burial of a Child

For the Lamb which is in the midst of the throne shall feed them, and shall lead them unto living fountains of waters: and God shall wipe away all tears from their eyes.

℣. The Lord be with you.

℟. And with thy spirit.

Let us pray.

O GOD, whose most dear Son did take little children into his arms and bless them; Give us grace, we beseech thee, to entrust the soul of this child to thy neverfailing care and love, and bring us all to thy heavenly kingdom. Through the same.

ALMIGHTY God, Father of mercies and giver of all comfort; Deal graciously, we pray thee, with all those who mourn, that, casting every care on thee, they may know the consolation of thy love. Through.

MAY Almighty God, the Father, the ✠ Son, and the Holy Ghost, bless you and keep you, now and for evermore. *Amen.*

¶ Before leaving, the Priest sprinkles the Grave one more time with Holy Water.

Forms of Prayer to be used in Families

Forms of Prayer to be used in Families

Morning Prayer

¶ *The Master or Mistress having called together as many of the Family as can conveniently be present, let one of them, or any other who may be appointed, say as followeth, all kneeling, and repeating with him the Lord's Prayer & Angelic Salutation.*

OUR Father, who art in heaven, Hallowed be thy Name. Thy kingdom come. Thy will be done, On earth as it is in heaven. Give us this day our daily bread. And forgive us our trespasses, As we forgive those who trespass against us. And lead us not into temptation, But deliver us from evil. For thine is the kingdom, and the power, and the glory, for ever and ever. Amen.

HAIL Mary, full of grace; The Lord is with thee; Blessed art thou amongst women, And blessed is the fruit of thy womb, Jesus. Holy Mary, Mother of God, Pray for us sinners, now and at the hour of our death. Amen.

¶ *Here may follow the Collect for the day.*

Acknowledgment of God's Mercy and Preservation, especially through the Night past.

ALMIGHTY and everlasting God, in whom we live and move and have our being; We, thy needy creatures, render thee our humble praises, for thy preservation of us from the beginning of our lives to this day, and especially for having delivered us from the dangers of the past night. For these thy mercies, we bless and magnify thy glorious Name; humbly beseeching thee to accept this our morning sacrifice of praise and thanksgiving; for his sake who lay down in the grave, and rose again for us, thy Son our Saviour Jesus Christ. *Amen.*

Dedication of Soul and Body to God's Service, with a Resolution to be growing daily in Goodness.

AND since it is of thy mercy, O gracious Father, that another day is added to our lives; We here dedicate both our souls and our bodies to thee and thy service, in a sober, righteous, and godly life: in which resolution, do thou, O merciful God, confirm and strengthen us; that, as we grow in age, we may grow in grace, and in the knowledge of our Lord and Saviour Jesus Christ. *Amen.*

Forms of Prayer to be used in Families

PRAYER FOR GRACE TO ENABLE US TO PERFORM THAT RESOLUTION.

BUT, O God, who knowest the weakness and corruption of our nature, and the manifold temptations which we daily meet with; We humbly beseech thee to have compassion on our infirmities, and to give us the constant assistance of thy Holy Spirit; that we may be effectually restrained from sin, and incited to our duty. Imprint upon our hearts such a dread of thy judgments, and such a grateful sense of thy goodness to us, as may make us both afraid and ashamed to offend thee. And, above all, keep in our minds a lively remembrance of that great day, in which we must give a strict account of our thoughts, words, and actions to him whom thou hast appointed the Judge of quick and dead, thy Son Jesus Christ our Lord. *Amen.*

FOR GRACE TO GUIDE AND KEEP US THE FOLLOWING DAY, AND FOR GOD'S BLESSING ON THE BUSINESS OF THE SAME.

IN particular, we implore thy grace and protection for the ensuing day. Keep us temperate in all things, and diligent in our several callings. Grant us patience under our afflictions. Give us grace to be just and upright in all our dealings; quiet and peaceable; full of compassion; and ready to do good to all men, according to our abilities and opportunities. Direct us in all our ways. Defend us from all dangers and adversities; and be graciously pleased to take us, and all who are dear to us, under thy fatherly care and protection. These things, and whatever else thou shalt see to be necessary and convenient to us, we humbly beg, through the merits and mediation of thy Son Jesus Christ, our Lord and Saviour. *Amen.*

THE grace of our Lord Jesus Christ, ✠ and the love of God, and the fellowship of the Holy Ghost, be with us all evermore. *Amen.*

Forms of Prayer to be used in Families

Evening Prayer

¶ The Family being together, a little before bedtime, let the Master or Mistress, or any other who may be appointed, say as followeth, all kneeling, and repeating with him the Lord's Prayer & Angelic Salutation.

Our Father, who art in heaven, Hallowed be thy Name. Thy kingdom come. Thy will be done, On earth as it is in heaven. Give us this day our daily bread. And forgive us our trespasses, As we forgive those who trespass against us. And lead us not into temptation, But deliver us from evil. For thine is the kingdom, and the power, and the glory, for ever and ever. Amen.

Hail Mary, full of grace; The Lord is with thee; Blessed art thou amongst women, And blessed is the fruit of thy womb, Jesus. Holy Mary, Mother of God, Pray for us sinners, now and at the hour of our death. Amen.

¶ Here may follow the Collect for the day.

CONFESSION OF SINS, WITH A PRAYER FOR CONTRITION AND PARDON.

Most merciful God, who art of purer eyes than to behold iniquity, and hast promised forgiveness to all those who confess and forsake their sins; We come before thee in an humble sense of our own unworthiness, acknowledging our manifold transgressions of thy righteous laws.[a] But, O gracious Father, who desirest not the death of a sinner, look upon us, we beseech thee, in mercy, and forgive us all our transgressions. Make us deeply sensible of the great evil of them; and work in us an hearty contrition; that we may obtain forgiveness at thy hands, who art ever ready to receive humble and penitent sinners; for the sake of thy Son Jesus Christ, our only Saviour and Redeemer. Amen.

[a] *Here let him who reads make a short pause, that every one may secretly confess the sins and failings of that day.*

PRAYER FOR GRACE TO REFORM AND GROW BETTER.

And lest, through our own frailty, or the temptations which encompass us, we be drawn again into sin, vouchsafe us, we beseech thee, the direction and assistance of thy Holy Spirit. Reform whatever is amiss in the temper and disposition of our souls; that no unclean thoughts, unlawful designs, or inordinate desires, may rest there. Purge our hearts from envy, hatred, and malice; that we may never suffer the sun to go down upon our wrath; but may always go to our rest in peace, charity, and good-will, with a conscience void of offence towards thee, and towards men; that so we may be preserved

Forms of Prayer to be used in Families

pure and blameless, unto the coming of our Lord and Saviour Jesus Christ. *Amen.*

The Intercession.

And accept, O Lord, our intercessions for all mankind. Let the light of thy Gospel shine upon all nations; and may as many as have received it, live as becomes it. Be gracious unto thy Church; and grant that every member of the same, in his vocation and ministry, may serve thee faithfully. Bless all in authority over us; and so rule their hearts and strengthen their hands, that they may punish wickedness and vice, and maintain thy true religion and virtue. Send down thy blessings, temporal and spiritual, upon all our relations, friends, and neighbours. Reward all who have done us good, and pardon all those who have done or wish us evil, and give them repentance and better minds. Be merciful to all who are in any trouble; and do thou, the God of pity, administer to them according to their several necessities; for his sake who went about doing good, thy Son our Saviour Jesus Christ. *Amen.*

The Thanksgiving.

To our prayers, O Lord, we join our unfeigned thanks for all thy mercies; for our being, our reason, and all other endowments and faculties of soul and body; for our health, friends, food, and raiment, and all the other comforts and conveniences of life. Above all, we adore thy mercy in sending thy only Son into the world, to redeem us from sin and eternal death, and in giving us the knowledge and sense of our duty towards thee. We bless thee for thy patience with us, notwithstanding our many and great provocations; for all the directions, assistances, and comforts of thy Holy Spirit; for thy continual care and watchful providence over us through the whole course of our lives; and particularly for the mercies and benefits of the past day; beseeching thee to continue these thy blessings to us, and to give us grace to show our thankfulness in a sincere obedience to his laws, through whose merits and inter-cession we received them all, thy Son our Saviour Jesus Christ. *Amen.*

Prayer for God's Protection through the Night following.

In particular, we beseech thee to continue thy gracious protection to us this night. Defend us from all dangers and mischiefs, and from the fear of them; that we may enjoy such refreshing sleep as may fit us for the duties of the coming day. And grant us grace always to live in such a state that we may never be afraid to die; so that, living and dying, we may be thine,

Forms of Prayer to be used in Families

through the merits and satisfaction of thy Son Christ Jesus, in whose Name we offer up these our imperfect prayers. *Amen.*

THE grace of our Lord Jesus Christ, ✠ and the love of God, and the fellowship of the Holy Ghost, be with us all evermore. *Amen.*

❧ On Sundays, and on other days when it may be convenient, it will be proper to begin with a Chapter, or part of a Chapter, from the New Testament.

A Shorter Form of Morning Prayer

❧ After the reading of a brief portion of Holy Scripture, let the Head of the Household, or some other member of the family, say as followeth, all kneeling, and repeating with him the Lord's Prayer & Angelic Salutation.

OUR Father, who art in heaven, Hallowed be thy Name. Thy kingdom come. Thy will be done, On earth as it is in heaven. Give us this day our daily bread. And forgive us our trespasses, As we forgive those who trespass against us. And lead us not into temptation, But deliver us from evil. For thine is the kingdom, and the power, and the glory, for ever and ever. Amen.

HAIL Mary, full of grace; The Lord is with thee; Blessed art thou amongst women, And blessed is the fruit of thy womb, Jesus. Holy Mary, Mother of God, Pray for us sinners, now and at the hour of our death. Amen.

O LORD, our heavenly Father, Almighty and everlasting God, who hast safely brought us to the beginning of this day; Defend us in the same with thy mighty power; and grant that this day we fall into no sin, neither run into any kind of danger; but that all our doings, being ordered by thy governance, may be righteous in thy sight; through Jesus Christ our Lord. *Amen.*

❧ Here may be added any special Prayers.

THE grace of our Lord Jesus Christ, ✠ and the love of God, and the fellowship of the Holy Ghost, be with us all evermore. *Amen.*

Forms of Prayer to be used in Families

A Shorter Form of Evening Prayer

❡ After the reading of a brief portion of Holy Scripture, let the Head of the Household, or some other member of the family, say as followeth, all kneeling and repeating with him the Lord's Prayer & Angelic Salutation.

OUR Father, who art in heaven, Hallowed be thy Name. Thy kingdom come. Thy will be done, On earth as it is in heaven. Give us this day our daily bread. And forgive us our trespasses, As we forgive those who trespass against us. And lead us not into temptation, But deliver us from evil. For thine is the kingdom, and the power, and the glory, for ever and ever. Amen.

HAIL Mary, full of grace; The Lord is with thee; Blessed art thou amongst women, And blessed is the fruit of thy womb, Jesus. Holy Mary, Mother of God, Pray for us sinners, now and at the hour of our death. Amen.

LIGHTEN our darkness, we beseech thee, O Lord; and by thy great mercy defend us from all perils and dangers of this night; for the love of thy only Son, our Saviour, Jesus Christ. *Amen.*

❡ Here may be added any special Prayers.

THE Lord bless us and keep us. The Lord make his face to shine upon us, and be gracious unto us. The Lord ✠ lift up his countenance upon us, and give us peace, this night and evermore. *Amen.*

Forms of Prayer to be used in Families

Additional Prayers

For the Spirit of Prayer.

ALMIGHTY God, who pourest out on all who desire it, the spirit of grace and of supplication; Deliver us, when we draw nigh to thee, from coldness of heart and wanderings of mind, that with stedfast thoughts and kindled affections, we may worship thee in spirit and in truth; through Jesus Christ our Lord. *Amen.*

In the Morning.

O GOD, the King eternal, who dividest the day from the darkness, and turnest the shadow of death into the morning; Drive far off from us all wrong desires, incline our hearts to keep thy law, and guide our feet into the way of peace; that having done thy will with cheerfulness while it was day, we may, when the night cometh, rejoice to give thee thanks; through Jesus Christ our Lord. *Amen.*

ALMIGHTY God, who alone gavest us the breath of life, and alone canst keep alive in us the holy desires thou dost impart; We beseech thee, for thy compassion's sake, to sanctify all our thoughts and endeavours; that we may neither begin an action without a pure intention nor continue it without thy blessing. And grant that, having the eyes of the mind opened to behold things invisible and unseen, we may in heart be inspired by thy wisdom, and in work be upheld by thy strength, and in the end be accepted of thee as thy faithful servants; through Jesus Christ our Saviour. *Amen.*

At Night.

O LORD, support us all the day long, until the shadows lengthen and the evening comes, and the busy world is hushed, and the fever of life is over, and our work is done. Then in thy mercy grant us a safe lodging, and a holy rest, and peace at the last. *Amen.*

O GOD, who art the life of mortal men, the light of the faithful, the strength of those who labour, and the repose of the dead; We thank thee for the timely blessings of the day, and humbly supplicate thy merciful protection all this night. Bring us, we beseech thee, in safety to the morning hours; through him who died for us and rose again, thy Son, our Saviour Jesus Christ. *Amen.*

Forms of Prayer to be used in Families

Sunday Morning.

O GOD, who makest us glad with the weekly remembrance of the glorious resurrection of thy Son our Lord; Vouchsafe us this day such blessing through our worship of thee, that the days to come may be spent in thy service; through the same Jesus Christ our Lord. *Amen.*

For Quiet Confidence.

O GOD of peace, who hast taught us that in returning and rest we shall be saved, in quietness and in confidence shall be our strength; By the might of thy Spirit lift us, we pray thee, to thy presence, where we may be still and know that thou art God; through Jesus Christ our Lord. *Amen.*

For Guidance.

O GOD, by whom the meek are guided in judgment, and light riseth up in darkness for the godly; Grant us, in all our doubts and uncertainties, the grace to ask what thou wouldest have us to do, that the Spirit of Wisdom may save us from all false choices, and that in thy light we may see light, and in thy straight path may not stumble; through Jesus Christ our Lord. *Amen.*

For Trustfulness.

O MOST loving Father, who willest us to give thanks for all things, to dread nothing but the loss of thee, and to cast all our care on thee, who carest for us; Preserve us from faithless fears and worldly anxieties, and grant that no clouds of this mortal life may hide from us the light of that love which is immortal, and which thou hast manifested unto us in thy Son, Jesus Christ our Lord. *Amen.*

O HEAVENLY Father, thou understandest all thy children; through thy gift of faith we bring our perplexities to the light of thy wisdom, and receive the blessed encouragement of thy sympathy, and a clearer knowledge of thy will. Glory be to thee for all thy gracious gifts. *Amen.*

For Joy in God's Creation.

O HEAVENLY Father, who hast filled the world with beauty; Open, we beseech thee, our eyes to behold thy gracious hand in all thy works; that rejoicing in thy whole creation, we may learn to serve thee with

Forms of Prayer to be used in Families

gladness; for the sake of him by whom all things were made, thy Son, Jesus Christ our Lord. *Amen.*

For the Children.

ALMIGHTY God, heavenly Father, who hast blessed us with the joy and care of children; Give us light and strength so to train them, that they may love whatsoever things are true and pure and lovely and of good report, following the example of their Saviour Jesus Christ. *Amen.*

For the Absent.

O GOD, whose fatherly care reacheth to the uttermost parts of the earth; We humbly beseech thee graciously to behold and bless those whom we love, now absent from us. Defend them from all dangers of soul and body; and grant that both they and we, drawing nearer to thee, may be bound together by thy love in the communion of thy Holy Spirit, and in the fellowship of thy saints; through Jesus Christ our Lord. *Amen.*

For Those We Love.

ALMIGHTY God, we entrust all who are dear to us to thy never-failing care and love, for this life and the life to come; knowing that thou art doing for them better things than we can desire or pray for; through Jesus Christ our Lord. *Amen.*

For the Recovery of a Sick Person.

O MERCIFUL God, giver of life and health; Bless, we pray thee, thy *servant*, *N.*, and those who administer to *him* of thy healing gifts; that *he* may be restored to health of body and of mind; through Jesus Christ our Lord. *Amen.*

For One about to undergo an Operation.

ALMIGHTY God our heavenly Father, we beseech thee graciously to comfort thy servant in his suffering, and to bless the means made use of for his cure. Fill his heart with confidence, that though he be sometime afraid, he yet may put his trust in thee; through Jesus Christ our Lord. *Amen.*

Forms of Prayer to be used in Families

For a Birthday.

WATCH over thy child, O Lord, as his days increase; bless and guide him wherever he may be, keeping him unspotted from the world. Strengthen him when he stands; comfort him when discouraged or sorrowful; raise him up if he fall; and in his heart may thy peace which passeth understanding abide all the days of his life; through Jesus Christ our Lord. *Amen.*

For an Anniversary of One Departed.

ALMIGHTY God, we remember this day before thee thy faithful servant *N.*, and we pray thee that, having opened to him the gates of larger life, thou wilt receive him more and more into thy joyful service; that he may win, with thee and thy servants everywhere, the eternal victory; through Jesus Christ our Lord. *Amen.*

For Those in Mental Darkness.

O HEAVENLY Father, we beseech thee to have mercy upon all thy children who are living in mental darkness. Restore them to strength of mind and cheerfulness of spirit, and give them health and peace; through Jesus Christ our Lord. *Amen.*

For a Blessing on the Families of the Land.

ALMIGHTY God, our heavenly Father, who settest the solitary in families; We commend to thy continual care the homes in which thy people dwell. Put far from them, we beseech thee, every root of bitterness, the desire of vain-glory, and the pride of life. Fill them with faith, virtue, knowledge, temperance, patience, godliness. Knit together in constant affection those who, in holy wedlock, have been made one flesh; turn the heart of the fathers to the children, and the heart of the children to the fathers; and so enkindle fervent charity among us all, that we be evermore kindly affectioned with brotherly love; through Jesus Christ our Lord. *Amen.*

For all Poor, Homeless, and Neglected Folk.

O GOD, Almighty and merciful, who healest those that are broken in heart, and turnest the sadness of the sorrowful to joy; Let thy fatherly goodness be upon all that thou hast made. Remember in pity such as are this day destitute, homeless, or forgotten of their fellow-men. Bless the

Forms of Prayer to be used in Families

congregation of thy poor. Uplift those who are cast down. Mightily befriend innocent sufferers, and sanctify to them the endurance of their wrongs. Cheer with hope all discouraged and unhappy people, and by thy heavenly grace preserve from falling those whose penury tempteth them to sin; though they be troubled on every side, suffer them not to be distressed; though they be perplexed, save them from despair. Grant this, O Lord, for the love of him, who for our sakes became poor, thy Son, our Saviour Jesus Christ. *Amen.*

For Faithfulness in the Use of this World's Goods.

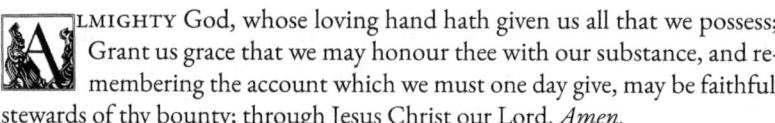LMIGHTY God, whose loving hand hath given us all that we possess; Grant us grace that we may honour thee with our substance, and remembering the account which we must one day give, may be faithful stewards of thy bounty; through Jesus Christ our Lord. *Amen.*

A General Intercession.

O GOD, at whose word man goeth forth to his work and to his labour until the evening; Be merciful to all whose duties are difficult or burdensome, and comfort them concerning their toil. Shield from bodily accident and harm the workmen at their work. Protect the efforts of sober and honest industry, and suffer not the hire of the labourers to be kept back by fraud. Incline the heart of employers and of those whom they employ to mutual forbearance, fairness, and good-will. Give the spirit of governance and of a sound mind to all in places of authority. Bless all those who labour in works of mercy or in schools of good learning. Care for all aged persons, and all little children, the sick and the afflicted, and those who travel by land or by sea. Remember all who by reason of weakness are overtasked, or because of poverty are forgotten. Let the sorrowful sighing of the prisoners come before thee; and according to the greatness of thy power, preserve thou those that are appointed to die. Give ear unto our prayer, O merciful and gracious Father, for the love of thy dear Son, our Saviour Jesus Christ. *Amen.*

Grace before Meat.

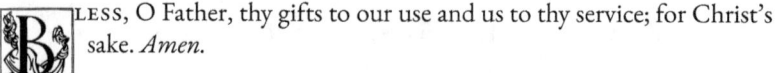LESS, O Father, thy gifts to our use and us to thy service; for Christ's sake. *Amen.*

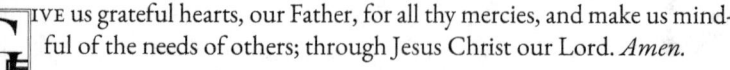IVE us grateful hearts, our Father, for all thy mercies, and make us mindful of the needs of others; through Jesus Christ our Lord. *Amen.*

Psalter of David

Psalter

Day 1. Morning Prayer

Psalm 1. *Beatus vir, qui non abiit, &c.*

LESSED is the man that hath not walked in the counsel of the ungodly, nor stood in the way of sinners : and hath not sat in the seat of the scornful.

2 But his delight is in the law of the Lord : and in his law will he exercise himself day and night.

3 And he shall be like a tree planted by the water-side : that will bring forth his fruit in due season.

4 His leaf also shall not wither : and look, whatsoever he doeth, it shall prosper.

5 As for the ungodly, it is not so with them : but they are like the chaff, which the wind scattereth away from the face of the earth.

6 Therefore the ungodly shall not be able to stand in the judgement : neither the sinners in the congregation of the righteous.

7 But the Lord knoweth the way of the righteous : and the way of the ungodly shall perish.

Psalm 2. *Quare fremuerunt gentes?*

HY do the heathen so furiously rage together : and why do the people imagine a vain thing?

2 The kings of the earth stand up, and the rulers take counsel together : against the Lord, and against his Anointed.

3 Let us break their bonds asunder : and cast away their cords from us.

4 He that dwelleth in heaven shall laugh them to scorn : the Lord shall have them in derision.

5 Then shall he speak unto them in his wrath : and vex them in his sore displeasure.

6 Yet have I set my King : upon my holy hill of Sion.

7 I will preach the law, whereof the Lord hath said unto me : Thou art my Son, this day have I begotten thee.

8 Desire of me, and I shall give thee the heathen for thine inheritance : and the utmost parts of the earth for thy possession.

9 Thou shalt bruise them with a rod of iron : and break them in pieces like a potter's vessel.

10 Be wise now therefore, O ye kings : be learned, ye that are judges of the earth.

11 Serve the Lord in fear : and rejoice unto him with reverence.

12 Kiss the Son, lest he be angry, and so ye perish from the right way : if his wrath be kindled, (yea, but a little,) blessed are all they that put their trust in him.

Psalm 3. *Domine, quid multiplicati,*

Lord, how are they increased that trouble me : many are they that rise against me.

2 Many one there be that say of my soul : There is no help for him in his God.

3 But thou, O Lord, art my defender : thou art my worship, and the lifter up of my head.

4 I did call upon the Lord with my voice : and he heard me out of his holy hill.

5 I laid me down and slept, and rose up again : for the Lord sustained me.

6 I will not be afraid for ten thousands of the people : that have set themselves against me round about.

7 Up, Lord, and help me, O my God : for thou smitest all mine enemies upon the cheekbone; thou hast broken the teeth of the ungodly.

8 Salvation belongeth unto the Lord : and thy blessing is upon thy people.

Psalm 4. *Cum invocarem*

Hear me when I call, O God of my righteousness : thou hast set me at liberty when I was in trouble; have mercy upon me, and hearken unto my prayer.

2 O ye sons of men, how long will ye blaspheme mine honour : and have such pleasure in vanity, and seek after leasing?

3 Know this also, that the Lord hath chosen to himself the man that is godly : when I call upon the Lord, he will hear me.

4 Stand in awe, and sin not : commune with your own heart, and in your chamber, and be still.

5 Offer the sacrifice of righteousness : and put your trust in the Lord.

6 There be many that say : Who will shew us any good?

7 Lord, lift thou up : the light of thy countenance upon us.

8 Thou hast put gladness in my heart : since the time that their corn and wine and oil increased.

9 I will lay me down in peace, and take my rest : for it is thou, Lord, only, that makest me dwell in safety.

Psalm 5. *Verba mea auribus.*

PONDER my words, O Lord : consider my meditation
2 O hearken thou unto the voice of my calling, my King, and my God : for unto thee will I make my prayer.

3 My voice shalt thou hear betimes, O Lord : early in the morning will I direct my prayer unto thee, and will look up.

4 For thou art the God that hast no pleasure in wickedness : neither shall any evil dwell with thee.

5 Such as be foolish shall not stand in thy sight : for thou hatest all them that work vanity.

6 Thou shalt destroy them that speak leasing : the Lord will abhor both the blood-thirsty and deceitful man.

7 But as for me, I will come into thine house, even upon the multitude of thy mercy : and in thy fear will I worship toward thy holy temple.

8 Lead me, O Lord, in thy righteousness, because of mine enemies : make thy way plain before my face.

9 For there is no faithfulness in his mouth : their inward parts are very wickedness.

10 Their throat is an open sepulchre : they flatter with their tongue.

11 Destroy thou them, O God; let them perish through their own imaginations : cast them out in the multitude of their ungodliness; for they have rebelled against thee.

12 And let all them that put their trust in thee rejoice : they shall ever be giving of thanks, because thou defendest them; they that love thy Name shall be joyful in thee;

13 For thou, Lord, wilt give thy blessing unto the righteous : and with thy favourable kindness wilt thou defend him as with a shield.

Day 1. Evening Prayer

Psalm 6. *Domine, ne in furore*

LORD, rebuke me not in thine indignation : neither chasten me in thy displeasure.

2 Have mercy upon me, O Lord, for I am weak : O Lord, heal me, for my bones are vexed.

3 My soul also is sore troubled : but, Lord, how long wilt thou punish me?

4 Turn thee, O Lord, and deliver my soul : O save me for thy mercy's sake.

5 For in death no man remembereth thee : and who will give thee thanks in the pit?

6 I am weary of my groaning; every night wash I my bed : and water my couch with my tears.

7 My beauty is gone for very trouble : and worn away because of all mine enemies.

8 Away from me, all ye that work vanity : for the Lord hath heard the voice of my weeping.

9 The Lord hath heard my petition : the Lord will receive my prayer.

10 All mine enemies shall be confounded, and sore vexed : they shall be turned back, and put to shame suddenly.

Psalm 7. *Domine, Deus meus*

LORD my God, in thee have I put my trust : save me from all them that persecute me, and deliver me;

2 Lest he devour my soul, like a lion, and tear it in pieces : while there is none to help.

3 O Lord my God, if I have done any such thing : or if there be any wickedness in my hands;

4 If I have rewarded evil unto him that dealt friendly with me : yea, I have delivered him that without any cause is mine enemy,

5 Then let mine enemy persecute my soul, and take me : yea, let him tread my life down upon the earth, and lay mine honour in the dust.

6 Stand up, O Lord, in thy wrath, and lift up thyself, because of the indignation of mine enemies : arise up for me in the judgement that thou hast commanded.

7 And so shall the congregation of the people come about thee : for their sakes therefore lift up thyself again.

8 The Lord shall judge the people; give sentence with me, O Lord : according to my righteousness, and according to the innocency that is in me.

9 O let the wickedness of the ungodly come to an end : but guide thou the just.

10 For the righteous God : trieth the very hearts and reins.

11 My help cometh of God : who preserveth them that are true of heart.

12 God is a righteous Judge, strong and patient : and God is provoked every day.

13 If a man will not turn, he will whet his sword : he hath bent his bow, and made it ready.

14 He hath prepared for him the instruments of death : he ordaineth his arrows against the persecutors.

15 Behold, he travaileth with mischief : he hath conceived sorrow, and brought forth ungodliness.

16 He hath graven and digged up a pit : and is fallen on himself into the destruction that he made for other.

17 For his travail shall come upon his own head : and his wickedness shall fall on his own pate.

18 I will give thanks unto the Lord, according to his righteousness : and I will praise the Name of the Lord most High.

Psalm 8. *Domine, Dominus noster*

O LORD our Governor, how excellent is thy Name in all the world : thou that hast set thy glory above the heavens!

2 Out of the mouth of very babes and sucklings hast thou ordained strength, because of thine enemies : that thou mightest still the enemy and the avenger.

3 For I will consider thy heavens, even the works of thy fingers : the moon and the stars, which thou hast ordained.

4 What is man, that thou art mindful of him : and the son of man, that thou visitest him?

5 Thou madest him lower than the angels : to crown him with glory and worship.

6 Thou makest him to have dominion of the works of thy hands : and thou hast put all things in subjection under his feet;

7 All sheep and oxen : yea, and the beasts of the field;

8 The fowls of the air, and the fishes of the sea : and whatsoever walketh through the paths of the seas.

9 O Lord our Governor : how excellent is thy Name in all the world!

Day 2. Morning Prayer

Psalm 9. *Confitebor tibi*

I WILL give thanks unto thee, O Lord, with my whole heart : I will speak of all thy marvellous works.

2 I will be glad and rejoice in thee : yea, my songs will I make of thy Name, O thou most Highest.

3 While mine enemies are driven back : they shall fall and perish at thy presence.

4 For thou hast maintained my right and my cause : thou art set in the throne that judgest right.

5 Thou hast rebuked the heathen, and destroyed the ungodly : thou hast put out their name for ever and ever.

6 O thou enemy, destructions are come to a perpetual end : even as the cities which thou hast destroyed, their memorial is perished with them.

7 But the Lord shall endure for ever : he hath also prepared his seat for judgement.

8 For he shall judge the world in righteousness : and minister true judgement unto the people.

9 The Lord also will be a defence for the oppressed : even a refuge in due time of trouble.

10 And they that know thy Name will put their trust in thee : for thou, Lord, hast never failed them that seek thee.

11 O praise the Lord which dwelleth in Sion : shew the people of his doings.

12 For when he maketh inquisition for blood, he remembereth them : and forgetteth not the complaint of the poor.

13 Have mercy upon me, O Lord; consider the trouble which I suffer of them that hate me : thou that liftest me up from the gates of death.

14 That I may shew all thy praises within the ports of the daughter of Sion : I will rejoice in thy salvation.

15 The heathen are sunk down in the pit that they made : in the same net which they hid privily, is their foot taken.

16 The Lord is known to execute judgement : the ungodly is trapped in the work of his own hands.

17 The wicked shall be turned into hell : and all the people that forget God.

18 For the poor shall not alway be forgotten : the patient abiding of the meek shall not perish for ever.

19 Up, Lord, and let not man have the upper hand : let the heathen be judged in thy sight.

20 Put them in fear, O Lord : that the heathen may know themselves to be but men.

Psalm 10. Ut quid, Domine?

WHY standest thou so far off, O Lord : and hidest thy face in the needful time of trouble?

2 The ungodly for his own lust doth persecute the poor : let them be taken in the crafty wiliness that they have imagined.

3 For the ungodly hath made boast of his own heart's desire : and speaketh good of the covetous, whom God abhorreth.

4 The ungodly is so proud, that he careth not for God : neither is God in all his thoughts.

5 His ways are alway grievous : thy judgements are far above out of his sight, and therefore defieth he all his enemies.

6 For he hath said in his heart, Tush, I shall never be cast down : there shall no harm happen unto me.

7 His mouth is full of cursing, deceit, and fraud : under his tongue is ungodliness and vanity.

8 He sitteth lurking in the thievish corners of the streets : and privily in his lurking dens doth he murder the innocent; his eyes are set against the poor.

9 For he lieth waiting secretly, even as a lion lurketh he in his den : that he may ravish the poor.

10 He doth ravish the poor : when he getteth him into his net.

11 He falleth down, and humbleth himself : that the congregation of the poor may fall into the hands of his captains.

12 He hath said in his heart, Tush, God hath forgotten : he hideth away his face, and he will never see it.

13 Arise, O Lord God, and lift up thine hand : forget not the poor.

14 Wherefore should the wicked blaspheme God : while he doth say in his heart, Tush, thou God carest not for it.

15 Surely thou hast seen it : for thou beholdest ungodliness and wrong.

16 That thou mayest take the matter into thy hand : the poor committeth himself unto thee; for thou art the helper of the friendless.

17 Break thou the power of the ungodly and malicious : take away his ungodliness, and thou shalt find none.

18 The Lord is King for ever and ever : and the heathen are perished out of the land.

19 Lord, thou hast heard the desire of the poor : thou preparest their heart, and thine ear hearkeneth thereto;

20 To help the fatherless and poor unto their right : that the man of the earth be no more exalted against them.

Psalm 11. *In Domino confido*

IN the Lord put I my trust : how say ye then to my soul, that she should flee as a bird unto the hill?

2 For lo, the ungodly bend their bow, and make ready their arrows within the quiver : that they may privily shoot at them which are true of heart.

3 For the foundations will be cast down : and what hath the righteous done?

4 The Lord is in his holy temple : the Lord's seat is in heaven.

5 His eyes consider the poor : and his eye-lids try the children of men.

6 The Lord alloweth the righteous : but the ungodly, and him that delighteth in wickedness, doth his soul abhor.

7 Upon the ungodly he shall rain snares, fire and brimstone, storm and tempest : this shall be their portion to drink.

8 For the righteous Lord loveth righteousness : his countenance will behold the thing that is just.

Day 2. Evening Prayer

Psalm 12. *Salvum me fac*

HELP me, Lord, for there is not one godly man left : for the faithful are minished from among the children of men,

2 They talk of vanity every one with his neighbour : they do but flatter with their lips, and dissemble in their double heart.

3 The Lord shall root out all deceitful lips : and the tongue that speaketh proud things;

4 Which have said, With our tongue will we prevail : we are they that ought to speak, who is lord over us?

5 Now for the comfortless trouble's sake of the needy : and because of the deep sighing of the poor,

6 I will up, saith the Lord : and will help every one from him that swelleth against him, and will set him at rest.

7 The words of the Lord are pure words : even as the silver, which from the earth is tried, and purified seven times in the fire.

8 Thou shalt keep them, O Lord : thou shalt preserve him from this generation for ever.

9 The ungodly walk on every side : when they are exalted, the children of men are put to rebuke.

Psalm 13. *Usque quo, Domine?*

How long wilt thou forget me, O Lord, for ever : how long wilt thou hide thy face from me?

2 How long shall I seek counsel in my soul, and be so vexed in my heart : how long shall mine enemies triumph over me?

3 Consider, and hear me, O Lord my God : lighten mine eyes, that I sleep not in death.

4 Lest mine enemy say, I have prevailed against him : for if I be cast down, they that trouble me will rejoice at it.

5 But my trust is in thy mercy : and my heart is joyful in thy salvation.

6 I will sing of the Lord, because he hath dealt so lovingly with me : yea, I will praise the Name of the Lord most Highest.

Psalm 14. *Dixit insipiens*

The fool hath said in his heart : There is no God.

2 They are corrupt, and become abominable in their doings : there is none that doeth good, no not one.

3 The Lord looked down from heaven upon the children of men : to see if there were any that would understand, and seek after God.

4 But they are all gone out of the way, they are altogether become abominable : there is none that doeth good, no not one.

5 Their throat is an open sepulchre, with their tongues have they deceived : the poison of asps is under their lips.

6 Their mouth is full of cursing and bitterness : their feet are swift to shed blood.

7 Destruction and unhappiness is in their ways, and the way of peace have they not known : there is no fear of God before their eyes.

8 Have they no knowledge, that they are all such workers of mischief : eating up my people as it were bread, and call not upon the Lord?

9 There were they brought in great fear, even where no fear was : for God is in the generation of the righteous.

10 As for you, ye have made a mock at the counsel of the poor : because he putteth his trust in the Lord.

11 Who shall give salvation unto Israel out of Sion? When the Lord turneth the captivity of his people : then shall Jacob rejoice, and Israel shall be glad.

Day 3. Morning Prayer

Psalm 15. *Domine, quis habitabit?*

Lord, who shall dwell in thy tabernacle : or who shall rest upon thy holy hill?

2 Even he that leadeth an uncorrupt life : and doeth the thing which is right, and speaketh the truth from his heart.

3 He that hath used no deceit in his tongue, nor done evil to his neighbour : and hath not slandered his neighbour.

4 He that setteth not by himself, but is lowly in his own eyes : and maketh much of them that fear the Lord.

5 He that sweareth unto his neighbour, and disappointeth him not : though it were to his own hindrance.

6 He that hath not given his money upon usury : nor taken reward against the innocent.

7 Whoso doeth these things : shall never fall.

Psalm 16. *Conserva me, Domine*

Preserve me, O God : for in thee have I put my trust.

2 O my soul, thou hast said unto the Lord : Thou art my God, my goods are nothing unto thee.

3 All my delight is upon the saints, that are in the earth : and upon such as excel in virtue.

4 But they that run after another god : shall have great trouble.

5 Their drink-offerings of blood will I not offer : neither make mention of their names within my lips.

6 The Lord himself is the portion of mine inheritance, and of my cup : thou shalt maintain my lot.

7 The lot is fallen unto me in a fair ground : yea, I have a goodly heritage.

8 I will thank the Lord for giving me warning : my reins also chasten me in the night-season.

9 I have set God always before me : for he is on my right hand, therefore I shall not fall.

10 Wherefore my heart was glad, and my glory rejoiced : my flesh also shall rest in hope.

11 For why? thou shalt not leave my soul in hell : neither shalt thou suffer thy Holy One to see corruption.

12 Thou shalt shew me the path of life; in thy presence is the fulness of joy : and at thy right hand there is pleasure for evermore.

Psalm 17. *Exaudi, Domine*

Hear the right, O Lord, consider my complaint : and hearken unto my prayer, that goeth not out of feigned lips.

2 Let my sentence come forth from thy presence : and let thine eyes look upon the thing that is equal.

3 Thou hast proved and visited mine heart in the night-season; thou hast tried me, and shalt find no wickedness in me : for I am utterly purposed that my mouth shall not offend.

4 Because of men's works, that are done against the words of thy lips : I have kept me from the ways of the destroyer.

5 O hold thou up my goings in thy paths : that my footsteps slip not.

6 I have called upon thee, O God, for thou shalt hear me : incline thine ear to me, and hearken unto my words.

7 Shew thy marvellous loving-kindness, thou that art the Saviour of them which put their trust in thee : from such as resist thy right hand.

8 Keep me as the apple of an eye : hide me under the shadow of thy wings.

9 From the ungodly that trouble me : mine enemies compass me round about to take away my soul.

10 They are inclosed in their own fat : and their mouth speaketh proud things.

11 They lie waiting in our way on every side : turning their eyes down to the ground.

12 Like as a lion that is greedy of his prey : and as it were a lion's whelp, lurking in secret places.

13 Up, Lord, disappoint him, and cast him down : deliver my soul from the ungodly, which is a sword of thine;

14 From the men of thy hand, O Lord, from the men, I say, and from the evil world : which have their portion in this life, whose bellies thou fillest with thy hid treasure.

15 They have children at their desire : and leave the rest of their substance for their babes.

16 But as for me, I will behold thy presence in righteousness : and when I awake up after thy likeness, I shall be satisfied with it.

Day 3. Evening Prayer

Psalm 18. *Diligam te, Domine*

I WILL love thee, O Lord, my strength; the Lord is my stony rock, and my defence : my saviour, my God, and my might, in whom I will trust, my buckler, the horn also of my salvation, and my refuge.

2 I will call upon the Lord, which is worthy to be praised : so shall I be safe from mine enemies.

3 The sorrows of death compassed me : and the overflowings of ungodliness made me afraid.

4 The pains of hell came about me : the snares of death overtook me.

5 In my trouble I will call upon the Lord : and complain unto my God.

6 So shall he hear my voice out of his holy temple : and my complaint shall come before him, it shall enter even into his ears.

7 The earth trembled and quaked : the very foundations also of the hills shook, and were removed, because he was wroth.

8 There went a smoke out in his presence : and a consuming fire out of his mouth, so that coals were kindled at it.

9 He bowed the heavens also, and came down : and it was dark under his feet.

10 He rode upon the cherubins, and did fly : he came flying upon the wings of the wind.

11 He made darkness his secret place : his pavilion round about him, with dark water and thick clouds to cover him.

12 At the brightness of his presence his clouds removed : hail-stones, and coals of fire.

13 The Lord also thundered out of heaven, and the Highest gave his thunder : hail-stones, and coals of fire.

14 He sent out his arrows, and scattered them : he cast forth lightnings, and destroyed them.

15 The springs of water were seen, and the foundations of the round world were discovered, at thy chiding, O Lord : at the blasting of the breath of thy displeasure.

16 He shall send down from on high to fetch me : and shall take me out of many waters.

17 He shall deliver me from my strongest enemy, and from them which hate me : for they are too mighty for me.

18 They prevented me in the day of my trouble : but the Lord was my upholder.

19 He brought me forth also into a place of liberty : he brought me forth, even because he had a favour unto me.
20 The Lord shall reward me after my righteous dealing : according to the cleanness of my hands shall he recompense me.
21 Because I have kept the ways of the Lord : and have not forsaken my God, as the wicked doth.
22 For I have an eye unto all his laws : and will not cast out his commandments from me.
23 I was also uncorrupt before him : and eschewed mine own wickedness.
24 Therefore shall the Lord reward me after my righteous dealing : and according unto the cleanness of my hands in his eye-sight.
25 With the holy thou shalt be holy : and with a perfect man thou shalt be perfect.
26 With the clean thou shalt be clean : and with the froward thou shalt learn frowardness.
27 For thou shalt save the people that are in adversity : and shalt bring down the high looks of the proud.
28 Thou also shalt light my candle : the Lord my God shall make my darkness to be light.
29 For in thee I shall discomfit an host of men : and with the help of my God I shall leap over the wall.
30 The way of God is an undefiled way : the word of the Lord also is tried in the fire; he is the defender of all them that put their trust in him.
31 For who is God, but the Lord : or who hath any strength, except our God?
32 It is God, that girdeth me with strength of war : and maketh my way perfect.
33 He maketh my feet like harts' feet : and setteth me up on high.
34 He teacheth mine hands to fight : and mine arms shall break even a bow of steel.
35 Thou hast given me the defence of thy salvation : thy right hand also shall hold me up, and thy loving correction shall make me great.
36 Thou shalt make room enough under me for to go : that my footsteps shall not slide.
37 I will follow upon mine enemies, and overtake them : neither will I turn again till I have destroyed them.
38 I will smite them, that they shall not be able to stand : but fall under my feet.
39 Thou hast girded me with strength unto the battle : thou shalt throw down mine enemies under me.

40 Thou hast made mine enemies also to turn their backs upon me : and I shall destroy them that hate me.
41 They shall cry, but there shall be none to help them : yea, even unto the Lord shall they cry, but he shall not hear them.
42 I will beat them as small as the dust before the wind : I will cast them out as the clay in the streets.
43 Thou shalt deliver me from the strivings of the people : and thou shalt make me the head of the heathen.
44 A people whom I have not known : shall serve me.
45 As soon as they hear of me, they shall obey me : but the strange children shall dissemble with me.
46 The strange children shall fail : and be afraid out of their prisons.
47 The Lord liveth, and blessed be my strong helper : and praised be the Lord of my salvation;
48 Even the God that seeth that I be avenged : and subdueth the people unto me.
49 It is he that delivereth me from my cruel enemies, and setteth me up above mine adversaries : thou shalt rid me from the wicked man.
50 For this cause will I give thanks unto thee, O Lord, among the Gentiles : and sing praises unto thy Name.
51 Great prosperity giveth he unto his King : and sheweth loving-kindness unto David his Anointed, and unto his seed for evermore.

Day 4. Morning Prayer

Psalm 19. *Caeli enarrant*

THE heavens declare the glory of God : and the firmament sheweth his handywork.
2 One day telleth another : and one night certifieth another.
3 There is neither speech nor language : but their voices are heard among them.
4 Their sound is gone out into all lands : and their words into the ends of the world.
5 In them hath he set a tabernacle for the sun : which cometh forth as a bridegroom out of his chamber, and rejoiceth as a giant to run his course.
6 It goeth forth from the uttermost part of the heaven, and runneth about unto the end of it again : and there is nothing hid from the heat thereof.

7 The law of the Lord is an undefiled law, converting the soul : the testimony of the Lord is sure, and giveth wisdom unto the simple.

8 The statutes of the Lord are right, and rejoice the heart : the commandment of the Lord is pure, and giveth light unto the eyes.

9 The fear of the Lord is clean, and endureth for ever : the judgements of the Lord are true, and righteous altogether.

10 More to be desired are they than gold, yea, than much fine gold : sweeter also than honey, and the honey-comb.

11 Moreover, by them is thy servant taught : and in keeping of them there is great reward.

12 Who can tell how oft he offendeth : O cleanse thou me from my secret faults.

13 Keep thy servant also from presumptuous sins, lest they get the dominion over me : so shall I be undefiled, and innocent from the great offence.

14 Let the words of my mouth, and the meditation of my heart : be alway acceptable in thy sight,

15 O Lord : my strength, and my redeemer.

Psalm 20. *Exaudiat te Dominus*

THE Lord hear thee in the day of trouble : the Name of the God of Jacob defend thee;

2 Send thee help from the sanctuary : and strengthen thee out of Sion;

3 Remember all thy offerings : and accept thy burnt-sacrifice;

4 Grant thee thy heart's desire : and fulfil all thy mind.

5 We will rejoice in thy salvation, and triumph in the Name of the Lord our God : the Lord perform all thy petitions.

6 Now know I that the Lord helpeth his Anointed, and will hear him from his holy heaven : even with the wholesome strength of his right hand.

7 Some put their trust in chariots, and some in horses : but we will remember the Name of the Lord our God.

8 They are brought down, and fallen : but we are risen, and stand upright.

9 Save, Lord, and hear us, O King of heaven : when we call upon thee.

Psalm 21. *Domine, in virtute tua*

THE King shall rejoice in thy strength, O Lord : exceeding glad shall he be of thy salvation.

2 Thou hast given him his heart's desire : and hast not denied him the request of his lips.

3 For thou shalt prevent him with the blessings of goodness : and shalt set a crown of pure gold upon his head.

4 He asked life of thee, and thou gavest him a long life : even for ever and ever.

5 His honour is great in thy salvation : glory and great worship shalt thou lay upon him.

6 For thou shalt give him everlasting felicity : and make him glad with the joy of thy countenance.

7 And why? because the King putteth his trust in the Lord : and in the mercy of the most Highest he shall not miscarry.

8 All thine enemies shall feel thine hand : thy right hand shall find out them that hate thee.

9 Thou shalt make them like a fiery oven in time of thy wrath : the Lord shall destroy them in his displeasure, and the fire shall consume them.

10 Their fruit shalt thou root out of the earth : and their seed from among the children of men.

11 For they intended mischief against thee : and imagined such a device as they are not able to perform.

12 Therefore shalt thou put them to flight : and the strings of thy bow shalt thou make ready against the face of them.

13 Be thou exalted, Lord, in thine own strength : so we will sing, and praise thy power.

Day 4. Evening Prayer

Psalm 22. *Deus, Deus meus*

My God, my God, look upon me; why hast thou forsaken me : and art so far from my health, and from the words of my complaint?

2 O my God, I cry in the day-time, but thou hearest not : and in the night-season also I take no rest.

3 And thou continuest holy : O thou worship of Israel.

4 Our fathers hoped in thee : they trusted in thee, and thou didst deliver them.

5 They called upon thee, and were holpen : they put their trust in thee, and were not confounded.

6 But as for me, I am a worm, and no man : a very scorn of men, and the outcast of the people.

7 All they that see me laugh me to scorn : they shoot out their lips, and shake their heads, saying,

8 He trusted in God, that he would deliver him : let him deliver him, if he will have him.

9 But thou art he that took me out of my mother's womb : thou wast my hope, when I hanged yet upon my mother's breasts.

10 I have been left unto thee ever since I was born : thou art my God, even from my mother's womb.

11 O go not from me, for trouble is hard at hand : and there is none to help me.

12 Many oxen are come about me : fat bulls of Basan close me in on every side.

13 They gape upon me with their mouths : as it were a ramping and a roaring lion.

14 I am poured out like water, and all my bones are out of joint : my heart also in the midst of my body is even like melting wax.

15 My strength is dried up like a potsherd, and my tongue cleaveth to my gums : and thou shalt bring me into the dust of death.

16 For many dogs are come about me : and the council of the wicked layeth siege against me.

17 They pierced my hands and my feet; I may tell all my bones : they stand staring and looking upon me.

18 They part my garments among them : and casts lots upon my vesture.

19 But be not thou far from me, O Lord : thou art my succour, haste thee to help me.

20 Deliver my soul from the sword : my darling from the power of the dog.

21 Save me from the lion's mouth : thou hast heard me also from among the horns of the unicorns.

22 I will declare thy Name unto my brethren : in the midst of the congregation will I praise thee.

23 O praise the Lord, ye that fear him : magnify him, all ye of the seed of Jacob, and fear him, all ye seed of Israel.

24 For he hath not despised, nor abhorred, the low estate of the poor : he hath not hid his face from him, but when he called unto him he heard him.

25 My praise is of thee in the great congregation : my vows will I perform in the sight of them that fear him.

26 The poor shall eat and be satisfied : they that seek after the Lord shall praise him; your heart shall live for ever.

27 All the ends of the world shall remember themselves, and be turned unto the Lord : and all the kindreds of the nations shall worship before him.

28 For the kingdom is the Lord's : and he is the Governor among the people.

29 All such as be fat upon earth : have eaten and worshipped.

30 All they that go down into the dust shall kneel before him : and no man hath quickened his own soul.

31 My seed shall serve him : they shall be counted unto the Lord for a generation.

32 They shall come, and the heavens shall declare his righteousness : unto a people that shall be born, whom the Lord hath made.

Psalm 23. *Dominus regit me.*

THE Lord is my shepherd : therefore can I lack nothing.

2 He shall feed me in a green pasture : and lead me forth beside the waters of comfort.

3 He shall convert my soul : and bring me forth in the paths of righteousness, for his Name's sake.

4 Yea, though I walk through the valley of the shadow of death, I will fear no evil : for thou art with me; thy rod and thy staff comfort me.

5 Thou shalt prepare a table before me against them that trouble me : thou hast anointed my head with oil, and my cup shall be full.

6 But thy loving-kindness and mercy shall follow me all the days of my life : and I will dwell in the house of the Lord for ever.

Day 5. Morning Prayer

Psalm 24. *Domini est terra*

THE earth is the Lord's, and all that therein is : the compass of the world, and they that dwell therein.

2 For he hath founded it upon the seas : and prepared it upon the floods.

3 Who shall ascend into the hill of the Lord : or who shall rise up in his holy place?

4 Even he that hath clean hands, and a pure heart : and that hath not lift up his mind unto vanity, nor sworn to deceive his neighbour.

5 He shall receive the blessing from the Lord : and righteousness from the God of his salvation.

6 This is the generation of them that seek him : even of them that seek thy face, O Jacob.

7 Lift up your heads, O ye gates, and be ye lift up, ye everlasting doors : and the King of glory shall come in.

8 Who is the King of glory : it is the Lord strong and mighty, even the Lord mighty in battle.

9 Lift up your heads, O ye gates, and be ye lift up, ye everlasting doors : and the King of glory shall come in.

10 Who is the King of glory : even the Lord of hosts, he is the King of glory.

Psalm 25. *Ad te, Domine, levavi*

NTO thee, O Lord, will I lift up my soul; my God, I have put my trust in thee : O let me not be confounded, neither let mine enemies triumph over me.

2 For all they that hope in thee shall not be ashamed : but such as transgress without a cause shall be put to confusion.

3 Shew me thy ways, O Lord : and teach me thy paths.

4 Lead me forth in thy truth, and learn me : for thou art the God of my salvation; in thee hath been my hope all the day long.

5 Call to remembrance, O Lord, thy tender mercies : and thy loving-kindnesses, which have been ever of old.

6 O remember not the sins and offences of my youth : but according to thy mercy think thou upon me, O Lord, for thy goodness.

7 Gracious and righteous is the Lord : therefore will he teach sinners in the way.

8 Them that are meek shall he guide in judgement : and such as are gentle, them shall he learn his way.

9 All the paths of the Lord are mercy and truth : unto such as keep his covenant and his testimonies.

10 For thy Name's sake, O Lord : be merciful unto my sin, for it is great.

11 What man is he that feareth the Lord : him shall he teach in the way that he shall choose.

12 His soul shall dwell at ease : and his seed shall inherit the land.

13 The secret of the Lord is among them that fear him : and he will shew them his covenant.

14 Mine eyes are ever looking unto the Lord : for he shall pluck my feet out of the net.

15 Turn thee unto me, and have mercy upon me : for I am desolate and in misery.

16 The sorrows of my heart are enlarged : O bring thou me out of my troubles.

17 Look upon my adversity and misery : and forgive me all my sin.

18 Consider mine enemies, how many they are : and they bear a tyrannous hate against me.

19 O keep my soul, and deliver me : let me not be confounded, for I have put my trust in thee.

20 Let perfectness and righteous dealing wait upon me : for my hope hath been in thee.

21 Deliver Israel, O God : out of all his troubles.

Psalm 26. *Judica me, Domine*

Be thou my judge, O Lord, for I have walked innocently : my trust hath been also in the Lord, therefore shall I not fall.

2 Examine me, O Lord, and prove me : try out my reins and my heart.

3 For thy loving-kindness is ever before mine eyes : and I will walk in thy truth.

4 I have not dwelt with vain persons : neither will I have fellowship with the deceitful.

5 I have hated the congregation of the wicked : and will not sit among the ungodly.

6 I will wash my hands in innocency, O Lord : and so will I go to thine altar.

7 That I may shew the voice of thanksgiving : and tell of all thy wondrous works.

8 Lord, I have loved the habitation of thy house : and the place where thine honour dwelleth.

9 O shut not up my soul with the sinners : nor my life with the blood-thirsty.

10 In whose hands is wickedness : and their right hand is full of gifts.

11 But as for me, I will walk innocently : O deliver me, and be merciful unto me.

12 My foot standeth right : I will praise the Lord in the congregations.

Day 5. Evening Prayer

Psalm 27. *Dominus illuminatio*

The Lord is my light and my salvation; whom then shall I fear : the Lord is the strength of my life; of whom then shall I be afraid?

2 When the wicked, even mine enemies and my foes, came upon me to eat up my flesh : they stumbled and fell.

3 Though an host of men were laid against me, yet shall not my heart be afraid : and though there rose up war against me, yet will I put my trust in him.

4 One thing have I desired of the Lord, which I will require : even that I may dwell in the house of the Lord all the days of my life, to behold the fair beauty of the Lord, and to visit his temple.

5 For in the time of trouble he shall hide me in his tabernacle : yea, in the secret place of his dwelling shall he hide me, and set me up upon a rock of stone.

6 And now shall he lift up mine head : above mine enemies round about me.

7 Therefore will I offer in his dwelling an oblation with great gladness : I will sing, and speak praises unto the Lord.

8 Hearken unto my voice, O Lord, when I cry unto thee : have mercy upon me, and hear me.

9 My heart hath talked of thee, Seek ye my face : Thy face, Lord, will I seek.

10 O hide not thou thy face from me : nor cast thy servant away in displeasure.

11 Thou hast been my succour : leave me not, neither forsake me, O God of my salvation.

12 When my father and my mother forsake me : the Lord taketh me up.

13 Teach me thy way, O Lord : and lead me in the right way, because of mine enemies.

14 Deliver me not over into the will of mine adversaries : for there are false witnesses risen up against me, and such as speak wrong.

15 I should utterly have fainted : but that I believe verily to see the goodness of the Lord in the land of the living.

16 O tarry thou the Lord's leisure : be strong, and he shall comfort thine heart; and put thou thy trust in the Lord.

PSALM 28. *AD TE, DOMINE*

UNTO thee will I cry, O Lord my strength : think no scorn of me; lest, if thou make as though thou hearest not, I become like them that go down into the pit.

2 Hear the voice of my humble petitions, when I cry unto thee : when I hold up my hands towards the mercy-seat of thy holy temple.

3 O pluck me not away, neither destroy me, with the ungodly and wicked doers : which speak friendly to their neighbours, but imagine mischief in their hearts.

4 Reward them according to their deeds : and according to the wickedness of their own inventions.

5 Recompense them after the work of their hands : pay them that they have deserved.

6 For they regard not in their mind the works of the Lord, nor the operation of his hands : therefore shall he break them down, and not build them up.

7 Praised be the Lord : for he hath heard the voice of my humble petitions.

8 The Lord is my strength and my shield; my heart hath trusted in him, and I am helped : therefore my heart danceth for joy, and in my song will I praise him.

9 The Lord is my strength : and he is the wholesome defence of his Anointed.

10 O save thy people, and give thy blessing unto thine inheritance : feed them, and set them up for ever.

Psalm 29. *Afferte Domino*

BRING unto the Lord, O ye mighty, bring young rams unto the Lord : ascribe unto the Lord worship and strength.

2 Give the Lord the honour due unto his Name : worship the Lord with holy worship.

3 It is the Lord that commandeth the waters : it is the glorious God that maketh the thunder.

4 It is the Lord that ruleth the sea; the voice of the Lord is mighty in operation : the voice of the Lord is a glorious voice.

5 The voice of the Lord breaketh the cedar-trees : yea, the Lord breaketh the cedars of Libanus.

6 He maketh them also to skip like a calf : Libanus also, and Sirion, like a young unicorn.

7 The voice of the Lord divideth the flames of fire; the voice of the Lord shaketh the wilderness : yea, the Lord shaketh the wilderness of Cades.

8 The voice of the Lord maketh the hinds to bring forth young, and discovereth the thick bushes : in his temple doth every man speak of his honour.

9 The Lord sitteth above the water-flood : and the Lord remaineth a King for ever.

10 The Lord shall give strength unto his people : the Lord shall give his people the blessing of peace.

Day 6. Morning Prayer

Psalm 30. *Exaltabo te, Domine*

I WILL magnify thee, O Lord, for thou hast set me up : and not made my foes to triumph over me.

2 O Lord my God, I cried unto thee : and thou hast healed me.

3 Thou, Lord, hast brought my soul out of hell : thou hast kept my life from them that go down to the pit.

4 Sing praises unto the Lord, O ye saints of his : and give thanks unto him for a remembrance of his holiness.

5 For his wrath endureth but the twinkling of an eye, and in his pleasure is life : heaviness may endure for a night, but joy cometh in the morning.

6 And in my prosperity I said, I shall never be removed : thou, Lord, of thy goodness hast made my hill so strong.

7 Thou didst turn thy face from me : and I was troubled.

8 Then cried I unto thee, O Lord : and gat me to my Lord right humbly.

9 What profit is there in my blood : when I go down to the pit?

10 Shall the dust give thanks unto thee : or shall it declare thy truth?

11 Hear, O Lord, and have mercy upon me : Lord, be thou my helper.

12 Thou hast turned my heaviness into joy : thou hast put off my sackcloth, and girded me with gladness.

13 Therefore shall every good man sing of thy praise without ceasing : O my God, I will give thanks unto thee for ever.

Psalm 31. *In te, Domine, speravi*

In thee, O Lord, have I put my trust : let me never be put to confusion, deliver me in thy righteousness.

2 Bow down thine ear to me : make haste to deliver me.

3 And be thou my strong rock, and house of defence : that thou mayest save me.

4 For thou art my strong rock, and my castle : be thou also my guide, and lead me for thy Name's sake.

5 Draw me out of the net that they have laid privily for me : for thou art my strength.

6 Into thy hands I commend my spirit : for thou hast redeemed me, O Lord, thou God of truth.

7 I have hated them that hold of superstitious vanities : and my trust hath been in the Lord.

8 I will be glad and rejoice in thy mercy : for thou hast considered my trouble, and hast known my soul in adversities.

9 Thou hast not shut me up into the hand of the enemy : but hast set my feet in a large room.

10 Have mercy upon me, O Lord, for I am in trouble : and mine eye is consumed for very heaviness; yea, my soul and my body.

11 For my life is waxen old with heaviness : and my years with mourning.

12 My strength faileth me, because of mine iniquity : and my bones are consumed.

13 I became a reproof among all mine enemies, but especially among my neighbours : and they of mine acquaintance were afraid of me; and they that did see me without conveyed themselves from me.

14 I am clean forgotten, as a dead man out of mind : I am become like a broken vessel.

15 For I have heard the blasphemy of the multitude : and fear is on every side, while they conspire together against me, and take their counsel to take away my life.

16 But my hope hath been in thee, O Lord : I have said, Thou art my God.

17 My time is in thy hand; deliver me from the hand of mine enemies : and from them that persecute me.

18 Shew thy servant the light of thy countenance : and save me for thy mercy's sake.

19 Let me not be confounded, O Lord, for I have called upon thee : let the ungodly be put to confusion, and be put to silence in the grave.

20 Let the lying lips be put to silence : which cruelly, disdainfully, and despitefully, speak against the righteous.

21 O how plentiful is thy goodness, which thou hast laid up for them that fear thee : and that thou hast prepared for them that put their trust in thee, even before the sons of men!

22 Thou shalt hide them privily by thine own presence from the provoking of all men : thou shalt keep them secretly in thy tabernacle from the strife of tongues.

23 Thanks be to the Lord : for he hath shewed me marvellous great kindness in a strong city.

24 And when I made haste, I said : I am cast out of the sight of thine eyes.

25 Nevertheless, thou heardest the voice of my prayer : when I cried unto thee.

26 O love the Lord, all ye his saints : for the Lord preserveth them that are faithful, and plenteously rewardeth the proud doer.

27 Be strong, and he shall establish your heart : all ye that put your trust in the Lord.

Day 6. Evening Prayer

PSALM 32. *BEATI, QUORUM*

BLESSED is he whose unrighteousness is forgiven : and whose sin is covered.

2 Blessed is the man unto whom the Lord imputeth no sin : and in whose spirit there is no guile.

3 For while I held my tongue : my bones consumed away through my daily complaining.

4 For thy hand is heavy upon me day and night : and my moisture is like the drought in summer.

5 I will acknowledge my sin unto thee : and mine unrighteousness have I not hid.

6 I said, I will confess my sins unto the Lord : and so thou forgavest the wickedness of my sin.

7 For this shall every one that is godly make his prayer unto thee, in a time when thou mayest be found : but in the great water-floods they shall not come nigh him.

8 Thou art a place to hide me in, thou shalt preserve me from trouble : thou shalt compass me about with songs of deliverance.

9 I will inform thee, and teach thee in the way wherein thou shalt go : and I will guide thee with mine eye.

10 Be ye not like to horse and mule, which have no understanding : whose mouths must be held with bit and bridle, lest they fall upon thee.

11 Great plagues remain for the ungodly : but whoso putteth his trust in the Lord, mercy embraceth him on every side.

12 Be glad, O ye righteous, and rejoice in the Lord : and be joyful, all ye that are true of heart.

Psalm 33. *Exultate, justi*

REJOICE in the Lord, O ye righteous : for it becometh well the just to be thankful.

2 Praise the Lord with harp : sing praises unto him with the lute, and instrument of ten strings.

3 Sing unto the Lord a new song : sing praises lustily unto him with a good courage.

4 For the word of the Lord is true : and all his works are faithful.

5 He loveth righteousness and judgement : the earth is full of the goodness of the Lord.

6 By the word of the Lord were the heavens made : and all the hosts of them by the breath of his mouth.

7 He gathereth the waters of the sea together, as it were upon an heap : and layeth up the deep, as in a treasure-house.

8 Let all the earth fear the Lord : stand in awe of him, all ye that dwell in the world.

9 For he spake, and it was done : he commanded, and it stood fast.

10 The Lord bringeth the counsel of the heathen to nought : and maketh the devices of the people to be of none effect, and casteth out the counsels of princes.

11 The counsel of the Lord shall endure for ever : and the thoughts of his heart from generation to generation.

12 Blessed are the people, whose God is the Lord JEHOVAH : and blessed are the folk, that he hath chosen to him to be his inheritance.

13 The Lord looked down from heaven, and beheld all the children of men : from the habitation of his dwelling he considereth all them that dwell on the earth.

14 He fashioneth all the hearts of them : and understandeth all their works.

15 There is no king that can be saved by the multitude of an host : neither is any mighty man delivered by much strength.

16 A horse is counted but a vain thing to save a man : neither shall he deliver any man by his great strength.

17 Behold, the eye of the Lord is upon them that fear him : and upon them that put their trust in his mercy;

18 To deliver their soul from death : and to feed them in the time of dearth.

19 Our soul hath patiently tarried for the Lord : for he is our help and our shield.

20 For our heart shall rejoice in him : because we have hoped in his holy Name.

21 Let thy merciful kindness, O Lord, be upon us : like as we do put our trust in thee.

PSALM 34. *BENEDICAM DOMINO*

I WILL alway give thanks unto the Lord : his praise shall ever be in my mouth.

2 My soul shall make her boast in the Lord : the humble shall hear thereof, and be glad.

3 O praise the Lord with me : and let us magnify his Name together.

4 I sought the Lord, and he heard me : yea, he delivered me out of all my fear.

5 They had an eye unto him, and were lightened : and their faces were not ashamed.

6 Lo, the poor crieth, and the Lord heareth him : yea, and saveth him out of all his troubles.

7 The angel of the Lord tarrieth round about them that fear him : and delivereth them.

8 O taste, and see, how gracious the Lord is : blessed is the man that trusteth in him.

9 O fear the Lord, ye that are his saints : for they that fear him lack nothing.

10 The lions do lack, and suffer hunger : but they who seek the Lord shall want no manner of thing that is good.

11 Come, ye children, and hearken unto me : I will teach you the fear of the Lord.

12 What man is he that lusteth to live : and would fain see good days?

13 Keep thy tongue from evil : and thy lips, that they speak no guile.

14 Eschew evil, and do good : seek peace, and ensue it.

15 The eyes of the Lord are over the righteous : and his ears are open unto their prayers.

16 The countenance of the Lord is against them that do evil : to root out the remembrance of them from the earth.

17 The righteous cry, and the Lord heareth them : and delivereth them out of all their troubles.

18 The Lord is nigh unto them that are of a contrite heart : and will save such as be of an humble spirit.

19 Great are the troubles of the righteous : but the Lord delivereth him out of all.

20 He keepeth all his bones : so that not one of them is broken.

21 But misfortune shall slay the ungodly : and they that hate the righteous shall be desolate.

22 The Lord delivereth the souls of his servants : and all they that put their trust in him shall not be destitute.

Day 7. Morning Prayer

Psalm 35. *Judica, Domine*

Plead thou my cause, O Lord, with them that strive with me : and fight thou against them that fight against me.

2 Lay hand upon the shield and buckler : and stand up to help me.

3 Bring forth the spear, and stop the way against them that persecute me : say unto my soul, I am thy salvation.

4 Let them be confounded and put to shame, that seek after my soul : let them be turned back and brought to confusion, that imagine mischief for me.

5 Let them be as the dust before the wind : and the angel of the Lord scattering them.

6 Let their way be dark and slippery : and let the angel of the Lord persecute them.

7 For they have privily laid their net to destroy me without a cause : yea, even without a cause have they made a pit for my soul.

8 Let a sudden destruction come upon him unawares, and his net, that he hath laid privily, catch himself : that he may fall into his own mischief.

9 And, my soul, be joyful in the Lord : it shall rejoice in his salvation.

10 All my bones shall say, Lord, who is like unto thee, who deliverest the poor from him that is too strong for him : yea, the poor, and him that is in misery, from him that spoileth him?

11 False witnesses did rise up : they laid to my charge things that I knew not.

12 They rewarded me evil for good : to the great discomfort of my soul.

13 Nevertheless, when they were sick, I put on sackcloth, and humbled my soul with fasting : and my prayer shall turn into mine own bosom.

14 I behaved myself as though it had been my friend or my brother : I went heavily, as one that mourneth for his mother.

15 But in mine adversity they rejoiced, and gathered themselves together : yea, the very abjects came together against me unawares, making mouths at me, and ceased not.

16 With the flatterers were busy mockers : who gnashed upon me with their teeth.

17 Lord, how long wilt thou look upon this : O deliver my soul from the calamities which they bring on me, and my darling from the lions.

18 So will I give thee thanks in the great congregation : I will praise thee among much people.

19 O let not them that are mine enemies triumph over me ungodly : neither let them wink with their eyes that hate me without a cause.

20 And why? their communing is not for peace : but they imagine deceitful words against them that are quiet in the land.

21 They gaped upon me with their mouths, and said : Fie on thee, fie on thee, we saw it with our eyes.

22 This thou hast seen, O Lord : hold not thy tongue then, go not far from me, O Lord.

23 Awake, and stand up to judge my quarrel : avenge thou my cause, my God, and my Lord.

24 Judge me, O Lord my God, according to thy righteousness : and let them not triumph over me.

25 Let them not say in their hearts, There, there, so would we have it : neither let them say, We have devoured him.

26 Let them be put to confusion and shame together, that rejoice at my trouble : let them be clothed with rebuke and dishonour, that boast themselves against me.

27 Let them be glad and rejoice, that favour my righteous dealing : yea, let them say alway, Blessed be the Lord, who hath pleasure in the prosperity of his servant.

28 And as for my tongue, it shall be talking of thy righteousness : and of thy praise all the day long.

Psalm 36. *Dixit injustus*

My heart sheweth me the wickedness of the ungodly : that there is no fear of God before his eyes.

2 For he flattereth himself in his own sight : until his abominable sin be found out.

3 The words of his mouth are unrighteous, and full of deceit : he hath left off to behave himself wisely, and to do good.

4 He imagineth mischief upon his bed, and hath set himself in no good way : neither doth he abhor any thing that is evil.

5 Thy mercy, O Lord, reacheth unto the heavens : and thy faithfulness unto the clouds.

6 Thy righteousness standeth like the strong mountains : thy judgements are like the great deep.

7 Thou, Lord, shalt save both man and beast; How excellent is thy mercy, O God : and the children of men shall put their trust under the shadow of thy wings.

8 They shall be satisfied with the plenteousness of thy house : and thou shalt give them drink of thy pleasures, as out of the river.

9 For with thee is the well of life : and in thy light shall we see light.

10 O continue forth thy loving-kindness unto them that know thee : and thy righteousness unto them that are true of heart.

11 O let not the foot of pride come against me : and let not the hand of the ungodly cast me down.

12 There are they fallen, all that work wickedness : they are cast down, and shall not be able to stand.

Day 7. Evening Prayer

Psalm 37. *Noli aemulari*

Fret not thyself because of the ungodly : neither be thou envious against the evil-doers.

2 For they shall soon be cut down like the grass : and be withered even as the green herb.

3 Put thou thy trust in the Lord, and be doing good : dwell in the land, and verily thou shalt be fed.

4 Delight thou in the Lord : and he shall give thee thy heart's desire.

5 Commit thy way unto the Lord, and put thy trust in him : and he shall bring it to pass.

6 He shall make thy righteousness as clear as the light : and thy just dealing as the noon-day.

7 Hold thee still in the Lord, and abide patiently upon him : but grieve not thyself at him whose way doth prosper, against the man that doeth after evil counsels.

8 Leave off from wrath, and let go displeasure : fret not thyself, else shalt thou be moved to do evil.

9 Wicked doers shall be rooted out : and they that patiently abide the Lord, those shall inherit the land.

10 Yet a little while, and the ungodly shall be clean gone : thou shalt look after his place, and he shall be away.

11 But the meek-spirited shall possess the earth : and shall be refreshed in the multitude of peace.

12 The ungodly seeketh counsel against the just : and gnasheth upon him with his teeth.

13 The Lord shall laugh him to scorn : for he hath seen that his day is coming.

14 The ungodly have drawn out the sword, and have bent their bow : to cast down the poor and needy, and to slay such as are of a right conversation.

15 Their sword shall go through their own heart : and their bow shall be broken.

16 A small thing that the righteous hath : is better than great riches of the ungodly.

17 For the arms of the ungodly shall be broken : and the Lord upholdeth the righteous.

18 The Lord knoweth the days of the godly : and their inheritance shall endure for ever.

19 They shall not be confounded in the perilous time : and in the days of dearth they shall have enough.

20 As for the ungodly, they shall perish; and the enemies of the Lord shall consume as the fat of lambs : yea, even as the smoke shall they consume away.

21 The ungodly borroweth, and payeth not again : but the righteous is merciful and liberal.

22 Such as are blessed of God shall possess the land : and they that are cursed of him shall be rooted out.

23 The Lord ordereth a good man's going : and maketh his way acceptable to himself.

24 Though he fall, he shall not be cast away : for the Lord upholdeth him with his hand.

25 I have been young, and now am old : and yet saw I never the righteous forsaken, nor his seed begging their bread.

26 The righteous is ever merciful, and lendeth : and his seed is blessed.

27 Flee from evil, and do the thing that is good : and dwell for evermore.

28 For the Lord loveth the thing that is right : he forsaketh not his that be godly, but they are preserved for ever.

29 The unrighteous shall be punished : as for the seed of the ungodly, it shall be rooted out.

30 The righteous shall inherit the land : and dwell therein for ever.

31 The mouth of the righteous is exercised in wisdom : and his tongue will be talking of judgement.

32 The law of his God is in his heart : and his goings shall not slide.

33 The ungodly seeth the righteous : and seeketh occasion to slay him.

34 The Lord will not leave him in his hand : nor condemn him when he is judged.

35 Hope thou in the Lord, and keep his way, and he shall promote thee, that thou shalt possess the land : when the ungodly shall perish, thou shalt see it.

36 I myself have seen the ungodly in great power : and flourishing like a green bay-tree.

37 I went by, and lo, he was gone : I sought him, but his place could no where be found.

38 Keep innocency, and take heed unto the thing that is right : for that shall bring a man peace at the last.

39 As for the transgressors, they shall perish together : and the end of the ungodly is, they shall be rooted out at the last.

40 But the salvation of the righteous cometh of the Lord : who is also their strength in the time of trouble.

41 And the Lord shall stand by them, and save them : he shall deliver them from the ungodly, and shall save them, because they put their trust in him.

Day 8. Morning Prayer

Psalm 38. *Domine, ne in furore*

Put me not to rebuke, O Lord, in thine anger : neither chasten me in thy heavy displeasure.

2 For thine arrows stick fast in me : and thy hand presseth me sore.

3 There is no health in my flesh, because of thy displeasure : neither is there any rest in my bones, by reason of my sin.

4 For my wickednesses are gone over my head : and are like a sore burden, too heavy for me to bear.

5 My wounds stink, and are corrupt : through my foolishness.

6 I am brought into so great trouble and misery : that I go mourning all the day long.

7 For my loins are filled with a sore disease : and there is no whole part in my body.

8 I am feeble, and sore smitten : I have roared for the very disquietness of my heart.

9 Lord, thou knowest all my desire : and my groaning is not hid from thee.

10 My heart panteth, my strength hath failed me : and the sight of mine eyes is gone from me.

11 My lovers and my neighbours did stand looking upon my trouble : and my kinsmen stood afar off.

12 They also that sought after my life laid snares for me : and they that went about to do me evil talked of wickedness, and imagined deceit all the day long.

13 As for me, I was like a deaf man, and heard not : and as one that is dumb, who doth not open his mouth.

14 I became even as a man that heareth not : and in whose mouth are no reproofs.

15 For in thee, O Lord, have I put my trust : thou shalt answer for me, O Lord my God.

16 I have required that they, even mine enemies, should not triumph over me : for when my foot slipped, they rejoiced greatly against me.

17 And I, truly, am set in the plague : and my heaviness is ever in my sight.

18 For I will confess my wickedness : and be sorry for my sin.

Day 8. Morning Prayer   **Psalter**   Psalm 39

19 But mine enemies live, and are mighty : and they that hate me wrongfully are many in number.

20 They also that reward evil for good are against me : because I follow the thing that good is.

21 Forsake me not, O Lord my God : be not thou far from me.

22 Haste thee to help me : O Lord God of my salvation.

Psalm 39. *Dixi, Custodiam*

I SAID, I will take heed to my ways : that I offend not in my tongue.

2 I will keep my mouth as it were with a bridle : while the ungodly is in my sight.

3 I held my tongue, and spake nothing : I kept silence, yea, even from good words; but it was pain and grief to me.

4 My heart was hot within me, and while I was thus musing the fire kindled : and at the last I spake with my tongue;

5 Lord, let me know mine end, and the number of my days : that I may be certified how long I have to live.

6 Behold, thou hast made my days as it were a span long : and mine age is even as nothing in respect of thee; and verily every man living is altogether vanity.

7 For man walketh in a vain shadow, and disquieteth himself in vain : he heapeth up riches, and cannot tell who shall gather them.

8 And now, Lord, what is my hope : truly my hope is even in thee.

9 Deliver me from all mine offences : and make me not a rebuke unto the foolish.

10 I became dumb, and opened not my mouth : for it was thy doing.

11 Take thy plague away from me : I am even consumed by the means of thy heavy hand.

12 When thou with rebukes dost chasten man for sin, thou makest his beauty to consume away, like as it were a moth fretting a garment : every man therefore is but vanity.

13 Hear my prayer, O Lord, and with thine ears consider my calling : hold not thy peace at my tears.

14 For I am a stranger with thee : and a sojourner, as all my fathers were.

15 O spare me a little, that I may recover my strength : before I go hence, and be no more seen.

Psalm 40. *Expectans expectavi*

I waited patiently for the Lord : and he inclined unto me, and heard my calling.

2 He brought me also out of the horrible pit, out of the mire and clay : and set my feet upon the rock, and ordered my goings.

3 And he hath put a new song in my mouth : even a thanksgiving unto our God.

4 Many shall see it, and fear : and shall put their trust in the Lord.

5 Blessed is the man that hath set his hope in the Lord : and turned not unto the proud, and to such as go about with lies.

6 O Lord my God, great are the wondrous works which thou hast done, like as be also thy thoughts which are to us-ward : and yet there is no man that ordereth them unto thee:

7 If I should declare them, and speak of them : they should be more than I am able to express.

8 Sacrifice and meat-offering thou wouldest not : but mine ears hast thou opened.

9 Burnt-offerings, and sacrifice for sin, hast thou not required : then said I, Lo, I come,

10 In the volume of the book it is written of me, that I should fulfil thy will, O my God : I am content to do it; yea, thy law is within my heart.

11 I have declared thy righteousness in the great congregation : lo, I will not refrain my lips, O Lord, and that thou knowest.

12 I have not hid thy righteousness within my heart : my talk hath been of thy truth and of thy salvation.

13 I have not kept back thy loving mercy and truth : from the great congregation.

14 Withdraw not thou thy mercy from me, O Lord : let thy loving-kindness and thy truth alway preserve me.

15 For innumerable troubles are come about me; my sins have taken such hold upon me that I am not able to look up : yea, they are more in number than the hairs of my head, and my heart hath failed me.

16 O Lord, let it be thy pleasure to deliver me : make haste, O Lord, to help me.

17 Let them be ashamed and confounded together, that seek after my soul to destroy it : let them be driven backward and put to rebuke, that wish me evil.

18 Let them be desolate, and rewarded with shame : that say unto me, Fie upon thee, fie upon thee.

19 Let all those that seek thee be joyful and glad in thee : and let such as love thy salvation say alway, The Lord be praised.
20 As for me, I am poor and needy : but the Lord careth for me.
21 Thou art my helper and redeemer : make no long tarrying, O my God.

Day 8. Evening Prayer

Psalm 41. *Beatus qui intelligit*

Blessed is he that considereth the poor and needy : the Lord shall deliver him in the time of trouble.
2 The Lord preserve him, and keep him alive, that he may be blessed upon earth : and deliver not thou him into the will of his enemies.
3 The Lord comfort him, when he lieth sick upon his bed : make thou all his bed in his sickness.
4 I said, Lord, be merciful unto me : heal my soul, for I have sinned against thee.
5 Mine enemies speak evil of me : When shall he die, and his name perish?
6 And if he come to see me, he speaketh vanity : and his heart conceiveth falsehood within himself, and when he cometh forth he telleth it.
7 All mine enemies whisper together against me : even against me do they imagine this evil.
8 Let the sentence of guiltiness proceed against him : and now that he lieth, let him rise up no more.
9 Yea, even mine own familiar friend, whom I trusted : who did also eat of my bread, hath laid great wait for me.
10 But be thou merciful unto me, O Lord : raise thou me up again, and I shall reward them.
11 By this I know thou favourest me : that mine enemy doth not triumph against me.
12 And when I am in my health, thou upholdest me : and shalt set me before thy face for ever.
13 Blessed be the Lord God of Israel : world without end. Amen.

Psalm 42. *Quemadmodum*

Like as the hart desireth the water-brooks : so longeth my soul after thee, O God.
2 My soul is athirst for God, yea, even for the living God : when shall I come to appear before the presence of God?

3 My tears have been my meat day and night : while they daily say unto me, Where is now thy God?

4 Now when I think thereupon, I pour out my heart by myself : for I went with the multitude, and brought them forth into the house of God;

5 In the voice of praise and thanksgiving : among such as keep holy-day.

6 Why art thou so full of heaviness, O my soul : and why art thou so disquieted within me?

7 Put thy trust in God : for I will yet give him thanks for the help of his countenance.

8 My God, my soul is vexed within me : therefore will I remember thee concerning the land of Jordan, and the little hill of Hermon.

9 One deep calleth another, because of the noise of the water-pipes : all thy waves and storms are gone over me.

10 The Lord hath granted his loving-kindness in the day-time : and in the night-season did I sing of him, and made my prayer unto the God of my life.

11 I will say unto the God of my strength, Why hast thou forgotten me : why go I thus heavily, while the enemy oppresseth me?

12 My bones are smitten asunder as with a sword : while mine enemies that trouble me cast me in the teeth;

13 Namely, while they say daily unto me : Where is now thy God?

14 Why art thou so vexed, O my soul : and why art thou so disquieted within me?

15 O put thy trust in God : for I will yet thank him, which is the help of my countenance, and my God.

Psalm 43. *Judica me, Deus*

Give sentence with me, O God, and defend my cause against the ungodly people : O deliver me from the deceitful and wicked man.

2 For thou art the God of my strength, why hast thou put me from thee : and why go I so heavily, while the enemy oppresseth me?

3 O send out thy light and thy truth, that they may lead me : and bring me unto thy holy hill, and to thy dwelling.

4 And that I may go unto the altar of God, even unto the God of my joy and gladness : and upon the harp will I give thanks unto thee, O God, my God.

5 Why art thou so heavy, O my soul : and why art thou so disquieted within me?

6 O put thy trust in God : for I will yet give him thanks, which is the help of my countenance, and my God.

Day 9. Morning Prayer

PSALM 44. *DEUS, AURIBUS*

WE have heard with our ears, O God, our fathers have told us : what thou hast done in their time of old;

2 How thou hast driven out the heathen with thy hand, and planted them in : how thou hast destroyed the nations and cast them out.

3 For they gat not the land in possession through their own sword : neither was it their own arm that helped them;

4 But thy right hand, and thine arm, and the light of thy countenance : because thou hadst a favour unto them.

5 Thou art my King, O God : send help unto Jacob.

6 Through thee will we overthrow our enemies : and in thy Name will we tread them under, that rise up against us.

7 For I will not trust in my bow : it is not my sword that shall help me;

8 But it is thou that savest us from our enemies : and puttest them to confusion that hate us.

9 We make our boast of God all day long : and will praise thy Name for ever.

10 But now thou art far off, and puttest us to confusion : and goest not forth with our armies.

11 Thou makest us to turn our backs upon our enemies : so that they which hate us spoil our goods.

12 Thou lettest us be eaten up like sheep : and hast scattered us among the heathen.

13 Thou sellest thy people for nought : and takest no money for them.

14 Thou makest us to be rebuked of our neighbours : to be laughed to scorn, and had in derision of them that are round about us.

15 Thou makest us to be a by-word among the heathen : and that the people shake their heads at us.

16 My confusion is daily before me : and the shame of my face hath covered me;

17 For the voice of the slanderer and blasphemer : for the enemy and avenger.

18 And though all this be come upon us, yet do we not forget thee : nor behave ourselves frowardly in thy covenant.

19 Our heart is not turned back : neither our steps gone out of thy way;

20 No, not when thou hast smitten us into the place of dragons : and covered us with the shadow of death.

21 If we have forgotten the Name of our God, and holden up our hands to any strange god : shall not God search it out? for he knoweth the very secrets of

the heart.

22 For thy sake also are we killed all the day long : and are counted as sheep appointed to be slain.

23 Up, Lord, why sleepest thou : awake, and be not absent from us for ever.

24 Wherefore hidest thou thy face : and forgettest our misery and trouble?

25 For our soul is brought low, even unto the dust : our belly cleaveth unto the ground.

26 Arise, and help us : and deliver us for thy mercy's sake.

PSALM 45. *ERUCTAVIT COR MEUM*

My heart is inditing of a good matter : I speak of the things which I have made unto the King.

2 My tongue is the pen : of a ready writer.

3 Thou art fairer than the children of men : full of grace are thy lips, because God hath blessed thee for ever.

4 Gird thee with thy sword upon thy thigh, O thou most Mighty : according to thy worship and renown.

5 Good luck have thou with thine honour : ride on, because of the word of truth, of meekness, and righteousness; and thy right hand shall teach thee terrible things.

6 Thy arrows are very sharp, and the people shall be subdued unto thee : even in the midst among the King's enemies.

7 Thy seat, O God, endureth for ever : the sceptre of thy kingdom is a right sceptre.

8 Thou hast loved righteousness, and hated iniquity : wherefore God, even thy God, hath anointed thee with the oil of gladness above thy fellows.

9 All thy garments smell of myrrh, aloes, and cassia : out of the ivory palaces, whereby they have made thee glad.

10 Kings' daughters were among thy honourable women : upon thy right hand did stand the queen in a vesture of gold, wrought about with divers colours.

11 Hearken, O daughter, and consider, incline thine ear : forget also thine own people, and thy father's house.

12 So shall the King have pleasure in thy beauty : for he is thy Lord God, and worship thou him.

13 And the daughter of Tyre shall be there with a gift : like as the rich also among the people shall make their supplication before thee.

14 The King's daughter is all glorious within : her clothing is of wrought gold.

15 She shall be brought unto the King in raiment of needle-work : the virgins that be her fellows shall bear her company, and shall be brought unto thee.

16 With joy and gladness shall they be brought : and shall enter into the King's palace.

17 Instead of thy fathers thou shalt have children : whom thou mayest make princes in all lands.

18 I will remember thy Name from one generation to another : therefore shall the people give thanks unto thee, world without end.

Psalm 46. *Deus noster refugium*

OD is our hope and strength : a very present help in trouble.

2 Therefore will we not fear, though the earth be moved : and though the hills be carried into the midst of the sea;

3 Though the waters thereof rage and swell : and though the mountains shake at the tempest of the same.

4 The rivers of the flood thereof shall make glad the city of God : the holy place of the tabernacle of the most Highest.

5 God is in the midst of her, therefore shall she not be removed : God shall help her, and that right early.

6 The heathen make much ado, and the kingdoms are moved : but God hath shewed his voice, and the earth shall melt away.

7 The Lord of hosts is with us : the God of Jacob is our refuge.

8 O come hither, and behold the works of the Lord : what destruction he hath brought upon the earth.

9 He maketh wars to cease in all the world : he breaketh the bow, and knappeth the spear in sunder, and burneth the chariots in the fire.

10 Be still then, and know that I am God : I will be exalted among the heathen, and I will be exalted in the earth.

11 The Lord of hosts is with us : the God of Jacob is our refuge.

Day 9. Evening Prayer

Psalm 47. *Omnes gentes, plaudite*

CLAP your hands together, all ye people : O sing unto God with the voice of melody.

2 For the Lord is high, and to be feared : he is the great King upon all the earth.

3 He shall subdue the people under us : and the nations under our feet.

4 He shall choose out an heritage for us : even the worship of Jacob, whom he loved.

5 God is gone up with a merry noise : and the Lord with the sound of the trump.

6 O sing praises, sing praises unto our God : O sing praises, sing praises unto our King.

7 For God is the King of all the earth : sing ye praises with understanding.

8 God reigneth over the heathen : God sitteth upon his holy seat.

9 The princes of the people are joined unto the people of the God of Abraham : for God, which is very high exalted, doth defend the earth, as it were with a shield.

PSALM 48. *MAGNUS DOMINUS*

GREAT is the Lord, and highly to be praised : in the city of our God, even upon his holy hill.

2 The hill of Sion is a fair place, and the joy of the whole earth : upon the north-side lieth the city of the great King; God is well known in her palaces as a sure refuge.

3 For lo, the kings of the earth : are gathered, and gone by together.

4 They marvelled to see such things : they were astonished, and suddenly cast down.

5 Fear came there upon them, and sorrow : as upon a woman in her travail.

6 Thou shalt break the ships of the sea : through the east-wind.

7 Like as we have heard, so have we seen in the city of the Lord of hosts, in the city of our God : God upholdeth the same for ever.

8 We wait for thy loving-kindness, O God : in the midst of thy temple.

9 O God, according to thy Name, so is thy praise unto the world's end : thy right hand is full of righteousness.

10 Let the mount Sion rejoice, and the daughters of Judah be glad : because of thy judgements.

11 Walk about Sion, and go round about her : and tell the towers thereof.

12 Mark well her bulwarks, set up her houses : that ye may tell them that come after.

13 For this God is our God for ever and ever : he shall be our guide unto death.

Psalm 49. *Audite haec, omnes*

HEAR ye this, all ye people : ponder it with your ears, all ye that dwell in the world;

2 High and low, rich and poor : one with another.

3 My mouth shall speak of wisdom : and my heart shall muse of understanding.

4 I will incline mine ear to the parable : and shew my dark speech upon the harp.

5 Wherefore should I fear in the days of wickedness : and when the wickedness of my heels compasseth me round about?

6 There be some that put their trust in their goods : and boast themselves in the multitude of their riches.

7 But no man may deliver his brother : nor make agreement unto God for him;

8 For it cost more to redeem their souls : so that he must let that alone for ever;

9 Yea, though he live long : and see not the grave.

10 For he seeth that wise men also die, and perish together : as well as the ignorant and foolish, and leave their riches for other.

11 And yet they think that their houses shall continue for ever : and that their dwelling-places shall endure from one generation to another; and call the lands after their own names.

12 Nevertheless, man will not abide in honour : seeing he may be compared unto the beasts that perish; this is the way of them.

13 This is their foolishness : and their posterity praise their saying.

14 They lie in the hell like sheep, death gnaweth upon them, and the righteous shall have domination over them in the morning : their beauty shall consume in the sepulchre out of their dwelling.

15 But God hath delivered my soul from the place of hell : for he shall receive me.

16 Be not thou afraid, though one be made rich : or if the glory of his house be increased;

17 For he shall carry nothing away with him when he dieth : neither shall his pomp follow him.

18 For while he lived, he counted himself an happy man : and so long as thou doest well unto thyself, men will speak good of thee.

19 He shall follow the generation of his fathers : and shall never see light.

20 Man being in honour hath no understanding : but is compared unto the beasts that perish.

Day 10. Morning Prayer

PSALM 50. *DEUS DEORUM*

THE Lord, even the most mighty God, hath spoken : and called the world, from the rising up of the sun unto the going down thereof.

2 Out of Sion hath God appeared : in perfect beauty.

3 Our God shall come, and shall not keep silence : there shall go before him a consuming fire, and a mighty tempest shall be stirred up round about him.

4 He shall call the heaven from above : and the earth, that he may judge his people.

5 Gather my saints together unto me : those that have made a covenant with me with sacrifice.

6 And the heavens shall declare his righteousness : for God is Judge himself.

7 Hear, O my people, and I will speak : I myself will testify against thee, O Israel; for I am God, even thy God.

8 I will not reprove thee because of thy sacrifices, or for thy burnt-offerings : because they were not alway before me.

9 I will take no bullock out of thine house : nor he-goat out of thy folds.

10 For all the beasts of the forest are mine : and so are the cattle upon a thousand hills.

11 I know all the fowls upon the mountains : and the wild beasts of the field are in my sight.

12 If I be hungry, I will not tell thee : for the whole world is mine, and all that is therein.

13 Thinkest thou that I will eat bulls' flesh : and drink the blood of goats?

14 Offer unto God thanksgiving : and pay thy vows unto the most Highest.

15 And call upon me in the time of trouble : so will I hear thee, and thou shalt praise me.

16 But unto the ungodly said God : Why dost thou preach my laws, and takest my covenant in thy mouth;

17 Whereas thou hatest to be reformed : and hast cast my words behind thee?

18 When thou sawest a thief, thou consentedst unto him : and hast been partaker with the adulterers.

19 Thou hast let thy mouth speak wickedness : and with thy tongue thou hast set forth deceit.

20 Thou satest, and spakest against thy brother : yea, and hast slandered thine own mother's son.

21 These things hast thou done, and I held my tongue, and thou thoughtest wickedly, that I am even such a one as thyself : but I will reprove thee, and set

before thee the things that thou hast done.

22 O consider this, ye that forget God : lest I pluck you away, and there be none to deliver you.

23 Whoso offereth me thanks and praise, he honoureth me : and to him that ordereth his conversation right will I shew the salvation of God.

Psalm 51. *Miserere mei, Deus*

Have mercy upon me, O God, after thy great goodness : according to the multitude of thy mercies do away mine offences.

2 Wash me throughly from my wickedness : and cleanse me from my sin.

3 For I acknowledge my faults : and my sin is ever before me.

4 Against thee only have I sinned, and done this evil in thy sight : that thou mightest be justified in thy saying, and clear when thou art judged.

5 Behold, I was shapen in wickedness : and in sin hath my mother conceived me.

6 But lo, thou requirest truth in the inward parts : and shalt make me to understand wisdom secretly.

7 Thou shalt purge me with hyssop, and I shall be clean : thou shalt wash me, and I shall be whiter than snow.

8 Thou shalt make me hear of joy and gladness : that the bones which thou hast broken may rejoice.

9 Turn thy face from my sins : and put out all my misdeeds.

10 Make me a clean heart, O God : and renew a right spirit within me.

11 Cast me not away from thy presence : and take not thy holy Spirit from me.

12 O give me the comfort of thy help again : and stablish me with thy free Spirit.

13 Then shall I teach thy ways unto the wicked : and sinners shall be converted unto thee.

14 Deliver me from blood-guiltiness, O God, thou that art the God of my health : and my tongue shall sing of thy righteousness.

15 Thou shalt open my lips, O Lord : and my mouth shall shew thy praise.

16 For thou desirest no sacrifice, else would I give it thee : but thou delightest not in burnt-offerings.

17 The sacrifice of God is a troubled spirit : a broken and contrite heart, O God, shalt thou not despise.

18 O be favourable and gracious unto Sion : build thou the walls of Jerusalem.

19 Then shalt thou be pleased with the sacrifice of righteousness, with the burnt-offerings and oblations : then shall they offer young bullocks upon thine altar.

Psalm 52. *Quid gloriaris?*

WHY boastest thou thyself, thou tyrant : that thou canst do mischief;

2 Whereas the goodness of God : endureth yet daily?

3 Thy tongue imagineth wickedness : and with lies thou cuttest like a sharp rasor.

4 Thou hast loved unrighteousness more than goodness : and to talk of lies more than righteousness.

5 Thou hast loved to speak all words that may do hurt : O thou false tongue.

6 Therefore shall God destroy thee for ever : he shall take thee, and pluck thee out of thy dwelling, and root thee out of the land of the living.

7 The righteous also shall see this, and fear : and shall laugh him to scorn;

8 Lo, this is the man that took not God for his strength : but trusted unto the multitude of his riches, and strengthened himself in his wickedness.

9 As for me, I am like a green olive-tree in the house of God : my trust is in the tender mercy of God for ever and ever.

10 I will always give thanks unto thee for that thou hast done : and I will hope in thy Name, for thy saints like it well.

Day 10. Evening Prayer

Psalm 53. *Dixit insipiens*

THE foolish body hath said in his heart : There is no God.

2 Corrupt are they, and become abominable in their wickedness : there is none that doeth good.

3 God looked down from heaven upon the children of men : to see if there were any that would understand, and seek after God.

4 But they are all gone out of the way, they are altogether become abominable : there is also none that doeth good, no not one.

5 Are not they without understanding, that work wickedness : eating up my people as if they would eat bread? they have not called upon God.

6 They were afraid where no fear was : for God hath broken the bones of him that besieged thee; thou hast put them to confusion, because God hath despised them.

7 O that the salvation were given unto Israel out of Sion : O that the Lord would deliver his people out of captivity!

8 Then should Jacob rejoice : and Israel should be right glad.

Psalm 54. *Deus, in nomine*

Save me, O God, for thy Name's sake : and avenge me in thy strength.

2 Hear my prayer, O God : and hearken unto the words of my mouth.

3 For strangers are risen up against me : and tyrants, which have not God before their eyes, seek after my soul.

4 Behold, God is my helper : the Lord is with them that uphold my soul.

5 He shall reward evil unto mine enemies : destroy thou them in thy truth.

6 An offering of a free heart will I give thee, and praise thy Name, O Lord : because it is so comfortable.

7 For he hath delivered me out of all my trouble : and mine eye hath seen his desire upon mine enemies.

Psalm 55. *Exaudi, Deus*

Hear my prayer, O God : and hide not thyself from my petition.

2 Take heed unto me, and hear me : how I mourn in my prayer, and am vexed.

3 The enemy crieth so, and the ungodly cometh on so fast : for they are minded to do me some mischief; so maliciously are they set against me.

4 My heart is disquieted within me : and the fear of death is fallen upon me.

5 Fearfulness and trembling are come upon me : and an horrible dread hath overwhelmed me.

6 And I said, O that I had wings like a dove : for then would I flee away, and be at rest.

7 Lo, then would I get me away far off : and remain in the wilderness.

8 I would make haste to escape : because of the stormy wind and tempest.

9 Destroy their tongues, O Lord, and divide them : for I have spied unrighteousness and strife in the city.

10 Day and night they go about within the walls thereof : mischief also and sorrow are in the midst of it.

11 Wickedness is therein : deceit and guile go not out of their streets.

12 For it is not an open enemy, that hath done me this dishonour : for then I could have borne it.

13 Neither was it mine adversary, that did magnify himself against me : for then peradventure I would have hid myself from him.

14 But it was even thou, my companion : my guide, and mine own familiar friend.

15 We took sweet counsel together : and walked in the house of God as friends.

16 Let death come hastily upon them, and let them go down quick into hell : for wickedness is in their dwellings, and among them.

17 As for me, I will call upon God : and the Lord shall save me.

18 In the evening, and morning, and at noonday will I pray, and that instantly : and he shall hear my voice.

19 It is he that hath delivered my soul in peace from the battle that was against me : for there were many with me.

20 Yea, even God, that endureth for ever, shall hear me, and bring them down : for they will not turn, nor fear God.

21 He laid his hands upon such as be at peace with him : and he brake his covenant.

22 The words of his mouth were softer than butter, having war in his heart : his words were smoother than oil, and yet be they very swords.

23 O cast thy burden upon the Lord, and he shall nourish thee : and shall not suffer the righteous to fall for ever.

24 And as for them : thou, O God, shalt bring them into the pit of destruction.

25 The blood-thirsty and deceitful men shall not live out half their days : nevertheless, my trust shall be in thee, O Lord.

Day 11. Morning Prayer

Psalm 56. *Miserere mei, Deus*

BE merciful unto me, O God, for man goeth about to devour me : he is daily fighting, and troubling me.

2 Mine enemies are daily in hand to swallow me up : for they be many that fight against me, O thou most Highest.

3 Nevertheless, though I am sometime afraid : yet put I my trust in thee.

4 I will praise God, because of his word : I have put my trust in God, and will not fear what flesh can do unto me.

5 They daily mistake my words : all that they imagine is to do me evil.

6 They hold all together, and keep themselves close : and mark my steps, when they lay wait for my soul.

7 Shall they escape for their wickedness : thou, O God, in thy displeasure shalt cast them down.

8 Thou tellest my flittings; put my tears into thy bottle : are not these things noted in thy book?

9 Whensoever I call upon thee, then shall mine enemies be put to flight : this I know; for God is on my side.

10 In God's word I will rejoice : in the Lord's word will I comfort me.

11 Yea, in God have I put my trust : I will not be afraid what man can do unto me.

12 Unto thee, O God, will I pay my vows : unto thee will I give thanks.

13 For thou hast delivered my soul from death, and my feet from falling : that I may walk before God in the light of the living.

Psalm 57. *Miserere mei, Deus*

BE merciful unto me, O God, be merciful unto me, for my soul trusteth in thee : and under the shadow of thy wings shall be my refuge, until this tyranny be over-past.

2 I will call unto the most high God : even unto the God that shall perform the cause which I have in hand.

3 He shall send from heaven : and save me from the reproof of him that would eat me up.

4 God shall send forth his mercy and truth : my soul is among lions.

5 And I lie even among the children of men, that are set on fire : whose teeth are spears and arrows, and their tongue a sharp sword.

6 Set up thyself, O God, above the heavens : and thy glory above all the earth.

7 They have laid a net for my feet, and pressed down my soul : they have digged a pit before me, and are fallen into the midst of it themselves.

8 My heart is fixed, O God, my heart is fixed : I will sing, and give praise.

9 Awake up, my glory; awake, lute and harp : I myself will awake right early.

10 I will give thanks unto thee, O Lord, among the people : and I will sing unto thee among the nations.

11 For the greatness of thy mercy reacheth unto the heavens : and thy truth unto the clouds.

12 Set up thyself, O God, above the heavens : and thy glory above all the earth.

Psalm 58. *Si vere utique*

ARE your minds set upon righteousness, O ye congregation : and do ye judge the thing that is right, O ye sons of men?

2 Yea, ye imagine mischief in your heart upon the earth : and your hands deal with wickedness.

3 The ungodly are froward, even from their mother's womb : as soon as they are born, they go astray, and speak lies.

4 They are as venomous as the poison of a serpent : even like the deaf adder that stoppeth her ears;

5 Which refuseth to hear the voice of the charmer : charm he never so wisely.

6 Break their teeth, O God, in their mouths; smite the jaw-bones of the lions, O Lord : let them fall away like water that runneth apace; and when they shoot their arrows let them be rooted out.

7 Let them consume away like a snail, and be like the untimely fruit of a woman : and let them not see the sun.

8 Or ever your pots be made hot with thorns : so let indignation vex him, even as a thing that is raw.

9 The righteous shall rejoice when he seeth the vengeance : he shall wash his footsteps in the blood of the ungodly.

10 So that a man shall say, Verily there is a reward for the righteous : doubtless there is a God that judgeth the earth.

Day 11. Evening Prayer

Psalm 59. *Eripe me de inimicis*

DELIVER me from mine enemies, O God : defend me from them that rise up against me.

2 O deliver me from the wicked doers : and save me from the blood-thirsty men.

3 For lo, they lie waiting for my soul : the mighty men are gathered against me, without any offence or fault of me, O Lord.

4 They run and prepare themselves without my fault : arise thou therefore to help me, and behold.

5 Stand up, O Lord God of hosts, thou God of Israel, to visit all the heathen : and be not merciful unto them that offend of malicious wickedness.

6 They go to and fro in the evening : they grin like a dog, and run about through the city.

7 Behold, they speak with their mouth, and swords are in their lips : for who doth hear?

8 But thou, O Lord, shalt have them in derision : and thou shalt laugh all the heathen to scorn.

9 My strength will I ascribe unto thee : for thou art the God of my refuge.

10 God sheweth me his goodness plenteously : and God shall let me see my desire upon mine enemies.

11 Slay them not, lest my people forget it : but scatter them abroad among the people, and put them down, O Lord, our defence.

12 For the sin of their mouth, and for the words of their lips, they shall be taken in their pride : and why? their preaching is of cursing and lies.

13 Consume them in thy wrath, consume them, that they may perish : and know that it is God that ruleth in Jacob, and unto the ends of the world.

14 And in the evening they will return : grin like a dog, and will go about the city.

15 They will run here and there for meat : and grudge if they be not satisfied.

16 As for me, I will sing of thy power, and will praise thy mercy betimes in the morning : for thou hast been my defence and refuge in the day of my trouble.

17 Unto thee, O my strength, will I sing : for thou, O God, art my refuge, and my merciful God.

PSALM 60. *DEUS, REPULISTI NOS*

GOD, thou hast cast us out, and scattered us abroad : thou hast also been displeased; O turn thee unto us again.

2 Thou hast moved the land, and divided it : heal the sores thereof, for it shaketh.

3 Thou hast shewed thy people heavy things : thou hast given us a drink of deadly wine.

4 Thou hast given a token for such as fear thee : that they may triumph because of the truth.

5 Therefore were thy beloved delivered : help me with thy right hand, and hear me.

6 God hath spoken in his holiness, I will rejoice, and divide Sichem : and mete out the valley of Succoth.

7 Gilead is mine, and Manasses is mine : Ephraim also is the strength of my head; Judah is my law-giver;

8 Moab is my wash-pot; over Edom will I cast out my shoe : Philistia, be thou glad of me.

9 Who will lead me into the strong city : who will bring me into Edom?

10 Hast not thou cast us out, O God : wilt not thou, O God, go out with our hosts?

11 O be thou our help in trouble : for vain is the help of man.

12 Through God will we do great acts : for it is he that shall tread down our enemies.

Psalm 61. *Exaudi, Deus*

Hear my crying, O God : give ear unto my prayer.

2 From the ends of the earth will I call upon thee : when my heart is in heaviness.

3 O set me up upon the rock that is higher than I : for thou hast been my hope, and a strong tower for me against the enemy.

4 I will dwell in thy tabernacle for ever : and my trust shall be under the covering of thy wings.

5 For thou, O Lord, hast heard my desires : and hast given an heritage unto those that fear thy Name.

6 Thou shalt grant the King a long life : that his years may endure throughout all generations.

7 He shall dwell before God for ever : O prepare thy loving mercy and faithfulness, that they may preserve him.

8 So will I always sing praise unto thy Name : that I may daily perform my vows.

Day 12. Morning Prayer

Psalm 62. *Nonne Deo?*

My soul truly waiteth still upon God : for of him cometh my salvation.

2 He verily is my strength and my salvation : he is my defence, so that I shall not greatly fall.

3 How long will ye imagine mischief against every man : ye shall be slain all the sort of you; yea, as a tottering wall shall ye be, and like a broken hedge.

4 Their device is only how to put him out whom God will exalt : their delight is in lies; they give good words with their mouth, but curse with their heart.

5 Nevertheless, my soul, wait thou still upon God : for my hope is in him.

6 He truly is my strength and my salvation : he is my defence, so that I shall not fall.

7 In God is my health, and my glory : the rock of my might, and in God is my trust.

8 O put your trust in him alway, ye people : pour out your hearts before him, for God is our hope.

9 As for the children of men, they are but vanity : the children of men are deceitful upon the weights, they are altogether lighter than vanity itself.

10 O trust not in wrong and robbery, give not yourselves unto vanity : if riches increase, set not your heart upon them.

11 God spake once, and twice I have also heard the same : that power belongeth unto God;

12 And that thou, Lord, art merciful : for thou rewardest every man according to his work.

Psalm 63. *Deus, Deus meus*

O GOD, thou art my God : early will I seek thee.

2 My soul thirsteth for thee, my flesh also longeth after thee : in a barren and dry land where no water is.

3 Thus have I looked for thee in holiness : that I might behold thy power and glory.

4 For thy loving-kindness is better than the life itself : my lips shall praise thee.

5 As long as I live will I magnify thee on this manner : and lift up my hands in thy Name.

6 My soul shall be satisfied, even as it were with marrow and fatness : when my mouth praiseth thee with joyful lips.

7 Have I not remembered thee in my bed : and thought upon thee when I was waking?

8 Because thou hast been my helper : therefore under the shadow of thy wings will I rejoice.

9 My soul hangeth upon thee : thy right hand hath upholden me.

10 These also that seek the hurt of my soul : they shall go under the earth.

11 Let them fall upon the edge of the sword : that they may be a portion for foxes.

12 But the King shall rejoice in God; all they also that swear by him shall be commended : for the mouth of them that speak lies shall be stopped.

Psalm 64. *Exaudi, Deus*

HEAR my voice, O God, in my prayer : preserve my life from fear of the enemy.

2 Hide me from the gathering together of the froward : and from the insurrection of wicked doers;

3 Who have whet their tongue like a sword : and shoot out their arrows, even bitter words;

4 That they may privily shoot at him that is perfect : suddenly do they hit him, and fear not.

5 They encourage themselves in mischief : and commune among themselves how they may lay snares, and say that no man shall see them.

6 They imagine wickedness, and practise it : that they keep secret among themselves, every man in the deep of his heart.

7 But God shall suddenly shoot at them with a swift arrow : that they shall be wounded.

8 Yea, their own tongues shall make them fall : insomuch that whoso seeth them shall laugh them to scorn.

9 And all men that see it shall say, This hath God done : for they shall perceive that it is his work.

10 The righteous shall rejoice in the Lord, and put his trust in him : and all they that are true of heart shall be glad.

Day 12. Evening Prayer

PSALM 65. *TE DECET HYMNUS*

THOU, O God, art praised in Sion : and unto thee shall the vow be performed in Jerusalem.

2 Thou that hearest the prayer : unto thee shall all flesh come.

3 My misdeeds prevail against me : O be thou merciful unto our sins.

4 Blessed is the man whom thou choosest, and receivest unto thee : he shall dwell in thy court, and shall be satisfied with the pleasures of thy house, even of thy holy temple.

5 Thou shalt shew us wonderful things in thy righteousness, O God of our salvation : thou that art the hope of all the ends of the earth, and of them that remain in the broad sea.

6 Who in his strength setteth fast the mountains : and is girded about with power.

7 Who stilleth the raging of the sea : and the noise of his waves, and the madness of the people.

8 They also that dwell in the uttermost parts of the earth shall be afraid at thy tokens : thou that makest the outgoings of the morning and evening to praise thee.

9 Thou visitest the earth, and blessest it : thou makest it very plenteous.

10 The river of God is full of water : thou preparest their corn, for so thou providest for the earth.

11 Thou waterest her furrows, thou sendest rain into the little valleys thereof : thou makest it soft with the drops of rain, and blessest the increase of it.

12 Thou crownest the year with thy goodness : and thy clouds drop fatness.

13 They shall drop upon the dwellings of the wilderness : and the little hills shall rejoice on every side.

14 The folds shall be full of sheep : the valleys also shall stand so thick with corn, that they shall laugh and sing.

Psalm 66. *Jubilate Deo*

BE joyful in God, all ye lands : sing praises unto the honour of his Name, make his praise to be glorious.

2 Say unto God, O how wonderful art thou in thy works : through the greatness of thy power shall thine enemies be found liars unto thee.

3 For all the world shall worship thee : sing of thee, and praise thy Name.

4 O come hither, and behold the works of God : how wonderful he is in his doing toward the children of men.

5 He turned the sea into dry land : so that they went through the water on foot; there did we rejoice thereof.

6 He ruleth with his power for ever; his eyes behold the people : and such as will not believe shall not be able to exalt themselves.

7 O praise our God, ye people : and make the voice of his praise to be heard;

8 Who holdeth our soul in life : and suffereth not our feet to slip.

9 For thou, O God, hast proved us : thou also hast tried us, like as silver is tried.

10 Thou broughtest us into the snare : and laidest trouble upon our loins.

11 Thou sufferedst men to ride over our heads : we went through fire and water, and thou broughtest us out into a wealthy place.

12 I will go into thine house with burnt-offerings : and will pay thee my vows, which I promised with my lips, and spake with my mouth, when I was in trouble.

13 I will offer unto thee fat burnt-sacrifices, with the incense of rams : I will offer bullocks and goats.

14 O come hither, and hearken, all ye that fear God : and I will tell you what he hath done for my soul.

15 I called unto him with my mouth : and gave him praises with my tongue.

16 If I incline unto wickedness with mine heart : the Lord will not hear me.

17 But God hath heard me : and considered the voice of my prayer.

18 Praised be God, who hath not cast out my prayer : nor turned his mercy from me.

Psalm 67. *Deus misereatur*

God be merciful unto us, and bless us : and shew us the light of his countenance, and be merciful unto us;

2 That thy way may be known upon earth : thy saving health among all nations.

3 Let the people praise thee, O God : yea, let all the people praise thee.

4 O let the nations rejoice and be glad : for thou shalt judge the folk righteously, and govern the nations upon earth.

5 Let the people praise thee, O God : let all the people praise thee.

6 Then shall the earth bring forth her increase : and God, even our own God, shall give us his blessing.

7 God shall bless us : and all the ends of the world shall fear him.

Day 13. Morning Prayer

Psalm 68. *Exurgat Deus*

Let God arise, and let his enemies be scattered : let them also that hate him flee before him.

2 Like as the smoke vanisheth, so shalt thou drive them away : and like as wax melteth at the fire, so let the ungodly perish at the presence of God.

3 But let the righteous be glad and rejoice before God : let them also be merry and joyful.

4 O sing unto God, and sing praises unto his Name : magnify him that rideth upon the heavens, as it were upon an horse; praise him in his Name Jah, and rejoice before him.

5 He is a father of the fatherless, and defendeth the cause of the widows : even God in his holy habitation.

6 He is the God that maketh men to be of one mind in an house, and bringeth the prisoners out of captivity : but letteth the runagates continue in scarceness.

7 O God, when thou wentest forth before the people : when thou wentest through the wilderness;

8 The earth shook, and the heavens dropped at the presence of God : even as Sinai also was moved at the presence of God, who is the God of Israel.

9 Thou, O God, sentest a gracious rain upon thine inheritance : and refreshedst it when it was weary.

10 Thy congregation shall dwell therein : for thou, O God, hast of thy goodness prepared for the poor.

11 The Lord gave the word : great was the company of the preachers.

12 Kings with their armies did flee, and were discomfited : and they of the household divided the spoil.

13 Though ye have lien among the pots, yet shall ye be as the wings of a dove : that is covered with silver wings, and her feathers like gold.

14 When the Almighty scattered kings for their sake : then were they as white as snow in Salmon.

15 As the hill of Basan, so is God's hill : even an high hill, as the hill of Basan.

16 Why hop ye so, ye high hills? this is God's hill, in the which it pleaseth him to dwell : yea, the Lord will abide in it for ever.

17 The chariots of God are twenty thousand, even thousands of angels : and the Lord is among them, as in the holy place of Sinai.

18 Thou art gone up on high, thou hast led captivity captive, and received gifts for men : yea, even for thine enemies, that the Lord God might dwell among them.

19 Praised be the Lord daily : even the God who helpeth us, and poureth his benefits upon us.

20 He is our God, even the God of whom cometh salvation : God is the Lord, by whom we escape death.

21 God shall wound the head of his enemies : and the hairy scalp of such a one as goeth on still in his wickedness.

22 The Lord hath said, I will bring my people again, as I did from Basan : mine own will I bring again, as I did sometime from the deep of the sea.

23 That thy foot may be dipped in the blood of thine enemies : and that the tongue of thy dogs may be red through the same.

24 It is well seen, O God, how thou goest : how thou, my God and King, goest in the sanctuary.

25 The singers go before, the minstrels follow after : in the midst are the damsels playing with the timbrels.

26 Give thanks, O Israel, unto God the Lord in the congregations : from the ground of the heart.

27 There is little Benjamin their ruler, and the princes of Judah their counsel : the princes of Zabulon, and the princes of Nephthali.

28 Thy God hath sent forth strength for thee : stablish the thing, O God, that thou hast wrought in us,

29 For thy temple's sake at Jerusalem : so shall kings bring presents unto thee.

30 When the company of the spear-men, and multitude of the mighty are scattered abroad among the beasts of the people, so that they humbly bring pieces of silver : and when he hath scattered the people that delight in war;

31 Then shall the princes come out of Egypt : the Morians' land shall soon stretch our her hands unto God.

32 Sing unto God, O ye kingdoms of the earth : O sing praises unto the Lord;

33 Who sitteth in the heavens over all from the beginning : lo, he doth send out his voice, yea, and that a mighty voice.

34 Ascribe ye the power to God over Israel : his worship and strength is in the clouds.

35 O God, wonderful art thou in thy holy places : even the God of Israel, he will give strength and power unto his people; blessed be God.

Day 13. Evening Prayer

PSALM 69. *SALVUM ME FAC*

Save me, O God : for the waters are come in, even unto my soul.

2 I stick fast in the deep mire, where no ground is : I am come into deep waters, so that the floods run over me.

3 I am weary of crying; my throat is dry : my sight faileth me for waiting so long upon my God.

4 They that hate me without a cause are more than the hairs of my head : they that are mine enemies, and would destroy me guiltless, are mighty.

5 I paid them the things that I never took : God, thou knowest my simpleness, and my faults are not hid from thee.

6 Let not them that trust in thee, O Lord God of hosts, be ashamed for my cause : let not those that seek thee be confounded through me, O Lord God of Israel.

7 And why? for thy sake have I suffered reproof : shame hath covered my face.

8 I am become a stranger unto my brethren : even an alien unto my mother's children.

9 For the zeal of thine house hath even eaten me : and the rebukes of them that rebuked thee are fallen upon me.

10 I wept, and chastened myself with fasting : and that was turned to my reproof.

11 I put on sackcloth also : and they jested upon me.

12 They that sit in the gate speak against me : and the drunkards make songs upon me.

13 But, Lord, I make my prayer unto thee : in an acceptable time.

14 Hear me, O God, in the multitude of thy mercy : even in the truth of thy salvation.

15 Take me out of the mire, that I sink not : O let me be delivered from them that hate me, and out of the deep waters.

16 Let not the water-flood drown me, neither let the deep swallow me up : and let not the pit shut her mouth upon me.

17 Hear me, O Lord, for thy loving-kindness is comfortable : turn thee unto me according to the multitude of thy mercies.

18 And hide not thy face from thy servant, for I am in trouble : O haste thee, and hear me.

19 Draw nigh unto my soul, and save it : O deliver me, because of mine enemies.

20 Thou hast known my reproof, my shame, and my dishonour : mine adversaries are all in thy sight.

21 Thy rebuke hath broken my heart; I am full of heaviness : I looked for some to have pity on me, but there was no man, neither found I any to comfort me.

22 They gave me gall to eat : and when I was thirsty they gave me vinegar to drink.

23 Let their table be made a snare to take themselves withal : and let the things that should have been for their wealth be unto them an occasion of falling.

24 Let their eyes be blinded, that they see not : and ever bow thou down their backs.

25 Pour out thine indignation upon them : and let thy wrathful displeasure take hold of them.

26 Let their habitation be void : and no man to dwell in their tents.

27 For they persecute him whom thou hast smitten : and they talk how they may vex them whom thou hast wounded.

28 Let them fall from one wickedness to another : and not come into thy righteousness.

29 Let them be wiped out of the book of the living : and not be written among the righteous.

30 As for me, when I am poor and in heaviness : thy help, O God, shall lift me up.

31 I will praise the Name of God with a song : and magnify it with thanksgiving.

32 This also shall please the Lord : better than a bullock that hath horns and hoofs.

33 The humble shall consider this, and be glad : seek ye after God, and your soul shall live.

34 For the Lord heareth the poor : and despiseth not his prisoners.

35 Let heaven and earth praise him : the sea, and all that moveth therein.

36 For God will save Sion, and build the cities of Judah : that men may dwell there, and have it in possession.

37 The posterity also of his servants shall inherit it : and they that love his Name shall dwell therein.

Psalm 70. *Deus, in adjutorium*

Haste thee, O God, to deliver me : make haste to help me, O Lord.

2 Let them be ashamed and confounded that seek after my soul : let them be turned backward and put to confusion that wish me evil.

3 Let them for their reward be soon brought to shame : that cry over me, There, there.

4 But let all those that seek thee be joyful and glad in thee : and let all such as delight in thy salvation say alway, The Lord be praised.

5 As for me, I am poor and in misery : haste thee unto me, O God.

6 Thou art my helper and my redeemer : O Lord, make no long tarrying.

Day 14. Morning Prayer

Psalm 71. *In te, Domine, speravi*

In thee, O Lord, have I put my trust, let me never be put to confusion : but rid me and deliver me in thy righteousness, incline thine ear unto me, and save me.

2 Be thou my strong hold, whereunto I may alway resort : thou hast promised to help me, for thou art my house of defence and my castle.

3 Deliver me, O my God, out of the hand of the ungodly : out of the hand of the unrighteous and cruel man.

4 For thou, O Lord God, art the thing that I long for : thou art my hope, even from my youth.

5 Through thee have I been holden up ever since I was born : thou art he that took me out of my mother's womb; my praise shall be always of thee.

6 I am become as it were a monster unto many : but my sure trust is in thee.

7 O let my mouth be filled with thy praise : that I may sing of thy glory and honour all the day long.

8 Cast me not away in the time of age : forsake me not when my strength faileth me.

9 For mine enemies speak against me, and they that lay wait for my soul take their counsel together, saying : God hath forsaken him; persecute him, and take him, for there is none to deliver him.

10 Go not far from me, O God : my God, haste thee to help me.

11 Let them be confounded and perish that are against my soul : let them be covered with shame and dishonour that seek to do me evil.

12 As for me, I will patiently abide alway : and will praise thee more and more.

13 My mouth shall daily speak of thy righteousness and salvation : for I know no end thereof.

14 I will go forth in the strength of the Lord God : and will make mention of thy righteousness only.

15 Thou, O God, hast taught me from my youth up until now : therefore will I tell of thy wondrous works.

16 Forsake me not, O God, in mine old age, when I am gray-headed : until I have shewed thy strength unto this generation, and thy power to all them that are yet for to come.

17 Thy righteousness, O God, is very high : and great things are they that thou hast done; O God, who is like unto thee?

18 O what great troubles and adversities hast thou shewed me, and yet didst thou turn and refresh me : yea, and broughtest me from the deep of the earth again.

19 Thou hast brought me to great honour : and comforted me on every side.

20 Therefore will I praise thee and thy faithfulness, O God, playing upon an instrument of musick : unto thee will I sing upon the harp, O thou Holy One of Israel.

21 My lips will be fain when I sing unto thee : and so will my soul whom thou hast delivered.

22 My tongue also shall talk of thy righteousness all the day long : for they are confounded and brought unto shame that seek to do me evil.

PSALM 72. *DEUS, JUDICIUM*

GIVE the King thy judgements, O God : and thy righteousness unto the King's son.

2 Then shall he judge thy people according unto right : and defend the poor.

3 The mountains also shall bring peace : and the little hills righteousness unto the people.

4 He shall keep the simple folk by their right : defend the children of the poor, and punish the wrong-doer.

5 They shall fear thee, as long as the sun and moon endureth : from one generation to another.

6 He shall come down like the rain into a fleece of wool : even as the drops that water the earth.

7 In his time shall the righteous flourish : yea, and abundance of peace, so long as the moon endureth.

8 His dominion shall be also from the one sea to the other : and from the flood unto the world's end.

9 They that dwell in the wilderness shall kneel before him : his enemies shall lick the dust.

10 The kings of Tharsis and of the isles shall give presents : the kings of Arabia and Saba shall bring gifts.

11 All kings shall fall down before him : all nations shall do him service.

12 For he shall deliver the poor when he crieth : the needy also, and him that hath no helper.

13 He shall be favourable to the simple and needy : and shall preserve the souls of the poor.

14 He shall deliver their souls from falsehood and wrong : and dear shall their blood be in his sight.

15 He shall live, and unto him shall be given of the gold of Arabia : prayer shall be made ever unto him, and daily shall he be praised.

16 There shall be an heap of corn in the earth, high upon the hills : his fruit shall shake like Libanus, and shall be green in the city like grass upon the earth.

17 His Name shall endure for ever; his Name shall remain under the sun among the posterities : which shall be blessed through him; and all the heathen shall praise him.

18 Blessed be the Lord God, even the God of Israel : which only doeth wondrous things;

19 And blessed be the Name of his majesty for ever : and all the earth shall be filled with his majesty. Amen, Amen.

Day 14. Evening Prayer

PSALM 73. *QUAM BONUS ISRAEL!*

TRULY God is loving unto Israel : even unto such as are of a clean heart.

2 Nevertheless, my feet were almost gone : my treadings had well-nigh slipt.

3 And why? I was grieved at the wicked : I do also see the ungodly in such prosperity.

4 For they are in no peril of death : but are lusty and strong.

5 They come in no misfortune like other folk : neither are they plagued like other men.

6 And this is the cause that they are so holden with pride : and overwhelmed with cruelty.

7 Their eyes swell with fatness : and they do even what they lust.

8 They corrupt other, and speak of wicked blasphemy : their talking is against the most High.

9 For they stretch forth their mouth unto the heaven : and their tongue goeth through the world.

10 Therefore fall the people unto them : and thereout suck they no small advantage.

11 Tush, say they, how should God perceive it : is there knowledge in the most High?

12 Lo, these are the ungodly, these prosper in the world, and these have riches in possession : and I said, Then have I cleansed my heart in vain, and washed mine hands in innocency.

13 All the day long have I been punished : and chastened every morning.

14 Yea, and I had almost said even as they : but lo, then I should have condemned the generation of thy children.

15 Then thought I to understand this : but it was too hard for me,

16 Until I went into the sanctuary of God : then understood I the end of these men;

17 Namely, how thou dost set them in slippery places : and castest them down, and destroyest them.

18 O how suddenly do they consume : perish, and come to a fearful end!

19 Yea, even like as a dream when one awaketh : so shalt thou make their image to vanish out of the city.

20 Thus my heart was grieved : and it went even through my reins.

21 So foolish was I, and ignorant : even as it were a beast before thee.

22 Nevertheless, I am alway by thee : for thou hast holden me by my right hand.

23 Thou shalt guide me with thy counsel : and after that receive me with glory.

24 Whom have I in heaven but thee : and there is none upon earth that I desire in comparison of thee.

25 My flesh and my heart faileth : but God is the strength of my heart, and my portion for ever.

26 For lo, they that forsake thee shall perish : thou hast destroyed all them that commit fornication against thee.

27 But it is good for me to hold me fast by God, to put my trust in the Lord God : and to speak of all thy works in the gates of the daughter of Sion.

Psalm 74. *Ut quid, Deus?*

O GOD, wherefore art thou absent from us so long : why is thy wrath so hot against the sheep of thy pasture?

2 O think upon thy congregation : whom thou hast purchased and redeemed of old.

3 Think upon the tribe of thine inheritance : and mount Sion, wherein thou hast dwelt.

4 Lift up thy feet, that thou mayest utterly destroy every enemy : which hath done evil in thy sanctuary.

5 Thine adversaries roar in the midst of thy congregations : and set up their banners for tokens.

6 He that hewed timber afore out of the thick trees : was known to bring it to an excellent work.

7 But now they break down all the carved work thereof : with axes and hammers.

8 They have set fire upon thy holy places : and have defiled the dwelling-place of thy Name, even unto the ground.

9 Yea, they said in their hearts, Let us make havock of them altogether : thus have they burnt up all the houses of God in the land.

10 We see not our tokens, there is not one prophet more : no, not one is there among us, that understandeth any more.

11 O God, how long shall the adversary do this dishonour : how long shall the enemy blaspheme thy Name, for ever?

12 Why withdrawest thou thy hand : why pluckest thou not thy right hand out of thy bosom to consume the enemy?

13 For God is my King of old : the help that is done upon earth he doeth it himself.

14 Thou didst divide the sea through thy power : thou brakest the heads of the dragons in the waters.

15 Thou smotest the heads of Leviathan in pieces : and gavest him to be meat for the people in the wilderness.

16 Thou broughtest out fountains and waters out of the hard rocks : thou driedst up mighty waters.

17 The day is thine, and the night is thine : thou hast prepared the light and the sun.

18 Thou hast set all the borders of the earth : thou hast made summer and winter.

19 Remember this, O Lord, how the enemy hath rebuked : and how the foolish people hath blasphemed thy Name.

Day 15. Morning Prayer # Psalter Psalm 76

20 O deliver not the soul of thy turtle-dove unto the multitude of the enemies : and forget not the congregation of the poor for ever.

21 Look upon the covenant : for all the earth is full of darkness and cruel habitations.

22 O let not the simple go away ashamed : but let the poor and needy give praise unto thy Name.

23 Arise, O God, maintain thine own cause : remember how the foolish man blasphemeth thee daily.

24 Forget not the voice of thine enemies : the presumption of them that hate thee increaseth ever more and more.

Day 15. Morning Prayer

Psalm 75. *Confitebimur tibi*

Unto thee, O God, do we give thanks : yea, unto thee do we give thanks.

2 Thy Name also is so nigh : and that do thy wondrous works declare.

3 When I receive the congregation : I shall judge according unto right.

4 The earth is weak, and all the inhabiters thereof : I bear up the pillars of it.

5 I said unto the fools, Deal not so madly : and to the ungodly, Set not up your horn.

6 Set not up your horn on high : and speak not with a stiff neck.

7 For promotion cometh neither from the east, nor from the west : nor yet from the south.

8 And why? God is the Judge : he putteth down one, and setteth up another.

9 For in the hand of the Lord there is a cup, and the wine is red : it is full mixed, and he poureth out of the same.

10 As for the dregs thereof : all the ungodly of the earth shall drink them, and suck them out.

11 But I will talk of the God of Jacob : and praise him for ever.

12 All the horns of the ungodly also will I break : and the horns of the righteous shall be exalted.

Psalm 76. *Notus in Judaea*

In Jewry is God known : his Name is great in Israel.

2 At Salem is his tabernacle : and his dwelling in Sion.

3 There brake he the arrows of the bow : the shield, the sword, and the battle.

4 Thou art of more honour and might : than the hills of the robbers.

5 The proud are robbed, they have slept their sleep : and all the men whose hands were mighty have found nothing.

6 At thy rebuke, O God of Jacob : both the chariot and horse are fallen.

7 Thou, even thou art to be feared : and who may stand in thy sight when thou art angry?

8 Thou didst cause thy judgement to be heard from heaven : the earth trembled, and was still;

9 When God arose to judgement : and to help all the meek upon earth.

10 The fierceness of man shall turn to thy praise : and the fierceness of them shalt thou refrain.

11 Promise unto the Lord your God, and keep it, all ye that are round about him : bring presents unto him that ought to be feared.

12 He shall refrain the spirit of princes : and is wonderful among the kings of the earth.

Psalm 77. *Voce mea ad Dominum*

I will cry unto God with my voice : even unto God will I cry with my voice, and he shall hearken unto me.

2 In the time of my trouble I sought the Lord : my sore ran and ceased not in the night-season; my soul refused comfort.

3 When I am in heaviness, I will think upon God : when my heart is vexed, I will complain.

4 Thou holdest mine eyes waking : I am so feeble, that I cannot speak.

5 I have considered the days of old : and the years that are past.

6 I call to remembrance my song : and in the night I commune with mine own heart, and search out my spirits.

7 Will the Lord absent himself for ever : and will he be no more intreated?

8 Is his mercy clean gone for ever : and is his promise come utterly to an end for evermore?

9 Hath God forgotten to be gracious : and will he shut up his loving-kindness in displeasure?

10 And I said, It is mine own infirmity : but I will remember the years of the right hand of the most Highest.

11 I will remember the works of the Lord : and call to mind thy wonders of old time.

12 I will think also of all thy works : and my talking shall be of thy doings.

13 Thy way, O God, is holy : who is so great a God as our God?

14 Thou art the God that doeth wonders : and hast declared thy power among the people.

15 Thou hast mightily delivered thy people : even the sons of Jacob and Joseph.

16 The waters saw thee, O God, the waters saw thee, and were afraid : the depths also were troubled.

17 The clouds poured out water, the air thundered : and thine arrows went abroad.

18 The voice of thy thunder was heard round about : the lightnings shone upon the ground; the earth was moved, and shook withal.

19 Thy way is in the sea, and thy paths in the great waters : and thy footsteps are not known.

20 Thou leddest thy people like sheep : by the hand of Moses and Aaron.

Day 15. Evening Prayer

PSALM 78. *ATTENDITE, POPULE*

Hear my law, O my people : incline your ears unto the words of my mouth.

2 I will open my mouth in a parable : I will declare hard sentences of old;

3 Which we have heard and known : and such as our fathers have told us;

4 That we should not hide them from the children of the generations to come : but to shew the honour of the Lord, his mighty and wonderful works that he hath done.

5 He made a covenant with Jacob, and gave Israel a law : which he commanded our forefathers to teach their children;

6 That their posterity might know it : and the children which were yet unborn;

7 To the intent that when they came up : they might shew their children the same;

8 That they might put their trust in God : and not to forget the works of God, but to keep his commandments;

9 And not to be as their forefathers, a faithless and stubborn generation : a generation that set not their heart aright, and whose spirit cleaveth not stedfastly unto God;

10 Like as the children of Ephraim : who being harnessed, and carrying bows, turned themselves back in the day of battle.

11 They kept not the covenant of God : and would not walk in his law;

12 But forgat what he had done : and the wonderful works that he had shewed for them.

13 Marvellous things did he in the sight of our forefathers, in the land of Egypt : even in the field of Zoan.

14 He divided the sea, and let them go through : he made the waters to stand on an heap.

15 In the day-time also he led them with a cloud : and all the night through with a light of fire.

16 He clave the hard rocks in the wilderness : and gave them drink thereof, as it had been out of the great depth.

17 He brought waters out of the stony rock : so that it gushed out like the rivers.

18 Yet for all this they sinned more against him : and provoked the most Highest in the wilderness.

19 They tempted God in their hearts : and required meat for their lust.

20 They spake against God also, saying : Shall God prepare a table in the wilderness?

21 He smote the stony rock indeed, that the waters gushed out, and the streams flowed withal : but can he give bread also, or provide flesh for his people?

22 When the Lord heard this, he was wroth : so the fire was kindled in Jacob, and there came up heavy displeasure against Israel;

23 Because they believed not in God : and put not their trust in his help.

24 So he commanded the clouds above : and opened the doors of heaven.

25 He rained down manna also upon them for to eat : and gave them food from heaven.

26 So man did eat angels' food : for he sent them meat enough.

27 He caused the east-wind to blow under heaven : and through his power he brought in the south-west-wind.

28 He rained flesh upon them as thick as dust : and feathered fowls like as the sand of the sea.

29 He let it fall among their tents : even round about their habitation.

30 So they did eat and were well filled, for he gave them their own desire : they were not disappointed of their lust.

31 But while the meat was yet in their mouths, the heavy wrath of God came upon them, and slew the wealthiest of them : yea, and smote down the chosen men that were in Israel.

32 But for all this they sinned yet more : and believed not his wondrous works.

33 Therefore their days did he consume in vanity : and their years in trouble.

34 When he slew them, they sought him : and turned them early, and inquired after God.

35 And they remembered that God was their strength : and that the high God was their redeemer.

36 Nevertheless, they did but flatter him with their mouth : and dissembled with him in their tongue.

37 For their heart was not whole with him : neither continued they stedfast in his covenant.

38 But he was so merciful, that he forgave their misdeeds : and destroyed them not.

39 Yea, many a time turned he his wrath away : and would not suffer his whole displeasure to arise.

40 For he considered that they were but flesh : and that they were even a wind that passeth away, and cometh not again.

41 Many a time did they provoke him in the wilderness : and grieved him in the desert.

42 They turned back, and tempted God : and moved the Holy One in Israel.

43 They thought not of his hand : and of the day when he delivered them from the hand of the enemy;

44 How he had wrought his miracles in Egypt : and his wonders in the field of Zoan.

45 He turned their waters into blood : so that they might not drink of the rivers.

46 He sent lice among them, and devoured them up : and frogs to destroy them.

47 He gave their fruit unto the caterpillar : and their labour unto the grasshopper.

48 He destroyed their vines with hail-stones : and their mulberry-trees with the frost.

49 He smote their cattle also with hail-stones : and their flocks with hot thunderbolts.

50 He cast upon them the furiousness of his wrath, anger, displeasure, and trouble : and sent evil angels among them.

51 He made a way to his indignation, and spared not their soul from death : but gave their life over to the pestilence;

52 And smote all the first-born in Egypt : the most principal and mightiest in the dwellings of Ham.

53 But as for his own people, he led them forth like sheep : and carried them in the wilderness like a flock.

54 He brought them out safely, that they should not fear : and overwhelmed their enemies with the sea.

55 And brought them within the borders of his sanctuary : even to his mountain which he purchased with his right hand.

56 He cast out the heathen also before them : caused their land to be divided among them for an heritage, and made the tribes of Israel to dwell in their tents.

57 So they tempted and displeased the most high God : and kept not his testimonies;

58 But turned their backs, and fell away like their forefathers : starting aside like a broken bow.

59 For they grieved him with their hill-altars : and provoked him to displeasure with their images.

60 When God heard this, he was wroth : and took sore displeasure at Israel.

61 So that he forsook the tabernacle in Silo : even the tent that he had pitched among men.

62 He delivered their power into captivity : and their beauty into the enemy's hand.

63 He gave his people over also unto the sword : and was wroth with his inheritance.

64 The fire consumed their young men : and their maidens were not given to marriage.

65 Their priests were slain with the sword : and there were no widows to make lamentation.

66 So the Lord awaked as one out of sleep : and like a giant refreshed with wine.

67 He smote his enemies in the hinder parts : and put them to a perpetual shame.

68 He refused the tabernacle of Joseph : and chose not the tribe of Ephraim;

69 But chose the tribe of Judah : even the hill of Sion which he loved.

70 And there he built his temple on high : and laid the foundation of it like the ground which he hath made continually.

71 He chose David also his servant : and took him away from the sheep-folds.

72 As he was following the ewes great with young ones he took him : that he might feed Jacob his people, and Israel his inheritance.

73 So he fed them with a faithful and true heart : and ruled them prudently with all his power.

Day 16. Morning Prayer

Psalm 79. *Deus, venerunt*

O GOD, the heathen are come into thine inheritance : thy holy temple have they defiled, and made Jerusalem an heap of stones.

2 The dead bodies of thy servants have they given to be meat unto the fowls of the air : and the flesh of thy saints unto the beasts of the land.

3 Their blood have they shed like water on every side of Jerusalem : and there was no man to bury them.

4 We are become an open shame to our enemies : a very scorn and derision unto them that are round about us.

5 Lord, how long wilt thou be angry : shall thy jealousy burn like fire for ever?

6 Pour out thine indignation upon the heathen that have not known thee : and upon the kingdoms that have not called upon thy Name.

7 For they have devoured Jacob : and laid waste his dwelling-place.

8 O remember not our old sins, but have mercy upon us, and that soon : for we are come to great misery.

9 Help us, O God of our salvation, for the glory of thy Name : O deliver us, and be merciful unto our sins, for thy Name's sake.

10 Wherefore do the heathen say : Where is now their God?

11 O let the vengeance of thy servants' blood that is shed : be openly shewed upon the heathen in our sight.

12 O let the sorrowful sighing of the prisoners come before thee : according to the greatness of thy power, preserve thou those that are appointed to die.

13 And for the blasphemy wherewith our neighbours have blasphemed thee : reward thou them, O Lord, seven-fold into their bosom.

14 So we, that are thy people, and sheep of thy pasture, shall give thee thanks for ever : and will alway be shewing forth thy praise from generation to generation.

Psalm 80. *Qui regis Israel*

HEAR, O thou Shepherd of Israel, thou that leadest Joseph like a sheep : shew thyself also, thou that sittest upon the cherubims.

2 Before Ephraim, Benjamin, and Manasses : stir up thy strength, and come, and help us.

3 Turn us again, O God : shew the light of thy countenance, and we shall be whole.

4 O Lord God of hosts : how long wilt thou be angry with thy people that prayeth?

5 Thou feedest them with the bread of tears : and givest them plenteousness of tears to drink.

6 Thou hast made us a very strife unto our neighbours : and our enemies laugh us to scorn.

7 Turn us again, thou God of hosts : shew the light of thy countenance, and we shall be whole.

8 Thou hast brought a vine out of Egypt : thou hast cast out the heathen, and planted it.

9 Thou madest room for it : and when it had taken root it filled the land.

10 The hills were covered with the shadow of it : and the boughs thereof were like the goodly cedar-trees.

11 She stretched out her branches unto the sea : and her boughs unto the river.

12 Why hast thou then broken down her hedge : that all they that go by pluck off her grapes?

13 The wild boar out of the wood doth root it up : and the wild beasts of the field devour it.

14 Turn thee again, thou God of hosts, look down from heaven : behold, and visit this vine;

15 And the place of the vineyard that thy right hand hath planted : and the branch that thou madest so strong for thyself.

16 It is burnt with fire, and cut down : and they shall perish at the rebuke of thy countenance.

17 Let thy hand be upon the man of thy right hand : and upon the son of man, whom thou madest so strong for thine own self.

18 And so will not we go back from thee : O let us live, and we shall call upon thy Name.

19 Turn us again, O Lord God of hosts : shew the light of thy countenance, and we shall be whole.

Psalm 81. *Exultate Deo*

Sing we merrily unto God our strength : make a cheerful noise unto the God of Jacob.

2 Take the psalm, bring hither the tabret : the merry harp with the lute.

3 Blow up the trumpet in the new-moon : even in the time appointed, and upon our solemn feast-day.

4 For this was made a statute for Israel : and a law of the God of Jacob.

5 This he ordained in Joseph for a testimony : when he came out of the land of Egypt, and had heard a strange language.

6 I eased his shoulder from the burden : and his hands were delivered from making the pots.

7 Thou calledst upon me in troubles, and I delivered thee : and heard thee what time as the storm fell upon thee.

8 I proved thee also : at the waters of strife.

9 Hear, O my people, and I will assure thee, O Israel : if thou wilt hearken unto me,

10 There shall no strange god be in thee : neither shalt thou worship any other god.

11 I am the Lord thy God, who brought thee out of the land of Egypt : open thy mouth wide, and I shall fill it.

12 But my people would not hear my voice : and Israel would not obey me.

13 So I gave them up unto their own hearts' lusts : and let them follow their own imaginations.

14 O that my people would have hearkened unto me : for if Israel had walked in my ways,

15 I should soon have put down their enemies : and turned my hand against their adversaries.

16 The haters of the Lord should have been found liars : but their time should have endured for ever.

17 He should have fed them also with the finest wheat-flour : and with honey out of the stony rock should I have satisfied thee.

Day 16. Evening Prayer

Psalm 82. *Deus stetit*

GOD standeth in the congregation of princes : he is a Judge among gods.

2 How long will ye give wrong judgement : and accept the persons of the ungodly?

3 Defend the poor and fatherless : see that such as are in need and necessity have right.

4 Deliver the outcast and poor : save them from the hand of the ungodly.

5 They will not be learned nor understand, but walk on still in darkness : all the foundations of the earth are out of course.

6 I have said, Ye are gods : and ye are all the children of the most Highest.

7 But ye shall die like men : and fall like one of the princes.

8 Arise, O God, and judge thou the earth : for thou shalt take all heathen to thine inheritance.

Psalm 83. *Deus, quis similis?*

Hold not thy tongue, O God, keep not still silence : refrain not thyself, O God.

2 For lo, thine enemies make a murmuring : and they that hate thee have lift up their head.

3 They have imagined craftily against thy people : and taken counsel against thy secret ones.

4 They have said, Come, and let us root them out, that they be no more a people : and that the name of Israel may be no more in remembrance.

5 For they have cast their heads together with one consent : and are confederate against thee;

6 The tabernacles of the Edomites, and the Ismaelites : the Moabites and Hagarenes;

7 Gebal, and Ammon, and Amalek : the Philistines, with them that dwell at Tyre.

8 Assur also is joined with them : and have holpen the children of Lot.

9 But do thou to them as unto the Madianites : unto Sisera, and unto Jabin at the brook of Kison;

10 Who perished at Endor : and became as the dung of the earth.

11 Make them and their princes like Oreb and Zeb : yea, make all their princes like as Zeba and Salmana;

12 Who say, Let us take to ourselves : the houses of God in possession.

13 O my God, make them like unto a wheel : and as the stubble before the wind;

14 Like as the fire that burneth up the wood : and as the flame that consumeth the mountains.

15 Persecute them even so with thy tempest : and make them afraid with thy storm.

16 Make their faces ashamed, O Lord : that they may seek thy Name.

17 Let them be confounded and vexed ever more and more : let them be put to shame, and perish.

18 And they shall know that thou, whose Name is JEHOVAH : art only the most Highest over all the earth.

Psalm 84. *Quam dilecta!*

How amiable are thy dwellings : thou Lord of hosts!

2 My soul hath a desire and longing to enter into the courts of the Lord : my heart and my flesh rejoice in the living God.

Day 16. Evening Prayer

3 Yea, the sparrow hath found her an house, and the swallow a nest where she may lay her young : even thy altars, O Lord of hosts, my King and my God.

4 Blessed are they that dwell in thy house : they will be alway praising thee.

5 Blessed is the man whose strength is in thee : in whose heart are thy ways.

6 Who going through the vale of misery use it for a well : and the pools are filled with water.

7 They will go from strength to strength : and unto the God of gods appeareth every one of them in Sion.

8 O Lord God of hosts, hear my prayer : hearken, O God of Jacob.

9 Behold, O God our defender : and look upon the face of thine Anointed.

10 For one day in thy courts : is better than a thousand.

11 I had rather be a door-keeper in the house of my God : than to dwell in the tents of ungodliness.

12 For the Lord God is a light and defence : the Lord will give grace and worship, and no good thing shall he withhold from them that live a godly life.

13 O Lord God of hosts : blessed is the man that putteth his trust in thee.

PSALM 85. *BENEDIXISTI, DOMINE*

LORD, thou art become gracious unto thy land : thou hast turned away the captivity of Jacob.

2 Thou hast forgiven the offence of thy people : and covered all their sins.

3 Thou hast taken away all thy displeasure : and turned thyself from thy wrathful indignation.

4 Turn us then, O God our Saviour : and let thine anger cease from us.

5 Wilt thou be displeased at us for ever : and wilt thou stretch out thy wrath from one generation to another?

6 Wilt thou not turn again, and quicken us : that thy people may rejoice in thee?

7 Shew us thy mercy, O Lord : and grant us thy salvation.

8 I will hearken what the Lord God will say concerning me : for he shall speak peace unto his people, and to his saints, that they turn not again.

9 For his salvation is nigh them that fear him : that glory may dwell in our land.

10 Mercy and truth are met together : righteousness and peace have kissed each other.

11 Truth shall flourish out of the earth : and righteousness hath looked down from heaven.

12 Yea, the Lord shall shew loving-kindness : and our land shall give her increase.

13 Righteousness shall go before him : and he shall direct his going in the way.

Day 17. Morning Prayer

Psalm 86. *Inclina, Domine*

Bow down thine ear, O Lord, and hear me : for I am poor, and in misery.

2 Preserve thou my soul, for I am holy : my God, save thy servant that putteth his trust in thee.

3 Be merciful unto me, O Lord : for I will call daily upon thee.

4 Comfort the soul of thy servant : for unto thee, O Lord, do I lift up my soul.

5 For thou, Lord, art good and gracious : and of great mercy unto all them that call upon thee.

6 Give ear, Lord, unto my prayer : and ponder the voice of my humble desires.

7 In the time of my trouble I will call upon thee : for thou hearest me.

8 Among the gods there is none like unto thee, O Lord : there is not one that can do as thou doest.

9 All nations whom thou hadst made shall come and worship thee, O Lord : and shall glorify thy Name.

10 For thou art great, and doest wondrous things : thou art God alone.

11 Teach me thy way, O Lord, and I will walk in thy truth : O knit my heart unto thee, that I may fear thy Name.

12 I will thank thee, O Lord my God, with all my heart : and will praise thy Name for evermore.

13 For great is thy mercy toward me : and thou hast delivered my soul from the nethermost hell.

14 O God, the proud are risen against me : and the congregations of naughty men have sought after my soul, and have not set thee before their eyes.

15 But thou, O Lord God, art full of compassion and mercy : long-suffering, plenteous in goodness and truth.

16 O turn thee then unto me, and have mercy upon me : give thy strength unto thy servant, and help the son of thine handmaid.

17 Shew some token upon me for good, that they who hate me may see it and be ashamed : because thou, Lord, hast holpen me and comforted me.

Psalm 87. *Fundamenta ejus*

Her foundations are upon the holy hills : the Lord loveth the gates of Sion more than all the dwellings of Jacob.

2 Very excellent things are spoken of thee : thou city of God.

3 I will think upon Rahab and Babylon : with them that know me.

4 Behold ye the Philistines also : and they of Tyre, with the Morians; lo, there was he born.

5 And of Sion it shall be reported that he was born in her : and the most High shall stablish her.

6 The Lord shall rehearse it when he writeth up the people : that he was born there.

7 The singers also and trumpeters shall he rehearse : All my fresh springs shall be in thee.

Psalm 88. *Domine Deus*

O Lord God of my salvation, I have cried day and night before thee : O let my prayer enter into thy presence, incline thine ear unto my calling.

2 For my soul is full of trouble : and my life draweth nigh unto hell.

3 I am counted as one of them that go down into the pit : and I have been even as a man that hath no strength.

4 Free among the dead, like unto them that are wounded, and lie in the grave : who are out of remembrance, and are cut away from thy hand.

5 Thou hast laid me in the lowest pit : in a place of darkness, and in the deep.

6 Thine indignation lieth hard upon me : and thou hast vexed me with all thy storms.

7 Thou hast put away mine acquaintance far from me : and made me to be abhorred of them.

8 I am so fast in prison : that I cannot get forth.

9 My sight faileth for very trouble : Lord, I have called daily upon thee, I have stretched forth my hands unto thee.

10 Dost thou shew wonders among the dead : or shall the dead rise up again, and praise thee?

11 Shall thy loving-kindness be shewed in the grave : or thy faithfulness in destruction?

12 Shall thy wondrous works be known in the dark : and thy righteousness in the land where all things are forgotten?

13 Unto thee have I cried, O Lord : and early shall my prayer come before thee.

14 Lord, why abhorrest thou my soul : and hidest thou thy face from me?
15 I am in misery, and like unto him that is at the point to die : even from my youth up thy terrors have I suffered with a troubled mind.
16 Thy wrathful displeasure goeth over me : and the fear of thee hath undone me.
17 They came round about me daily like water : and compassed me together on every side.
18 My lovers and friends hast thou put away from me : and hid mine acquaintance out of my sight.

Day 17. Evening Prayer

Psalm 89. *Misericordias Domini*

My song shall be alway of the loving-kindness of the Lord : with my mouth will I ever be shewing thy truth from one generation to another.
2 For I have said, Mercy shall be set up for ever : thy truth shalt thou stablish in the heavens.
3 I have made a covenant with my chosen : I have sworn unto David my servant;
4 Thy seed will I stablish for ever : and set up thy throne from one generation to another.
5 O Lord, the very heavens shall praise thy wondrous works : and thy truth in the congregation of the saints.
6 For who is he among the clouds : that shall be compared unto the Lord?
7 And what is he among the gods : that shall be like unto the Lord?
8 God is very greatly to be feared in the council of the saints : and to be had in reverence of all them that are round about him.
9 O Lord God of hosts, who is like unto thee : thy truth, most mighty Lord, is on every side.
10 Thou rulest the raging of the sea : thou stillest the waves thereof when they arise.
11 Thou hast subdued Egypt, and destroyed it : thou hast scattered thine enemies abroad with thy mighty arm.
12 The heavens are thine, the earth also is thine : thou hast laid the foundation of the round world, and all that therein is.
13 Thou hast made the north and the south : Tabor and Hermon shall rejoice in thy Name.
14 Thou hast a mighty arm : strong is thy hand, and high is thy right hand.

Day 17. Evening Prayer — Psalter — Psalm 89

15 Righteousness and equity are the habitation of thy seat : mercy and truth shall go before thy face.

16 Blessed is the people, O Lord, that can rejoice in thee : they shall walk in the light of thy countenance.

17 Their delight shall be daily in thy Name : and in thy righteousness shall they make their boast.

18 For thou art the glory of their strength : and in thy loving-kindness thou shalt lift up our horns.

19 For the Lord is our defence : the Holy One of Israel is our King.

20 Thou spakest sometime in visions unto thy saints, and saidst : I have laid help upon one that is mighty; I have exalted one chosen out of the people.

21 I have found David my servant : with my holy oil have I anointed him.

22 My hand shall hold him fast : and my arm shall strengthen him.

23 The enemy shall not be able to do him violence : the son of wickedness shall not hurt him.

24 I will smite down his foes before his face : and plague them that hate him.

25 My truth also and my mercy shall be with him : and in my Name shall his horn be exalted.

26 I will set his dominion also in the sea : and his right hand in the floods.

27 He shall call me, Thou art my Father : my God, and my strong salvation.

28 And I will make him my first-born : higher than the kings of the earth.

29 My mercy will I keep for him for evermore : and my covenant shall stand fast with him.

30 His seed also will I make to endure for ever : and his throne as the days of heaven.

31 But if his children forsake my law : and walk not in my judgements;

32 If they break my statutes, and keep not my commandments : I will visit their offences with the rod, and their sin with scourges.

33 Nevertheless, my loving-kindness will I not utterly take from him : nor suffer my truth to fail.

34 My covenant I will not break, nor alter the thing that is gone out of my lips : I have sworn once by my holiness, that I will not fail David.

35 His seed shall endure for ever : and his seat is like as the sun before me.

36 He shall stand fast for evermore as the moon : and as the faithful witness in heaven.

37 But thou hast abhorred and forsaken thine Anointed : and art displeased at him.

38 Thou hast broken the covenant of thy servant : and cast his crown to the ground.

39 Thou hast overthrown all his hedges : and broken down his strong holds.

40 All they that go by spoil him : and he is become a reproach to his neighbours.

41 Thou hast set up the right hand of his enemies : and made all his adversaries to rejoice.

42 Thou hast taken away the edge of his sword : and givest him not victory in the battle.

43 Thou hast put out his glory : and cast his throne down to the ground.

44 The days of his youth hast thou shortened : and covered him with dishonour.

45 Lord, how long wilt thou hide thyself, for ever : and shall thy wrath burn like fire?

46 O remember how short my time is : wherefore hast thou made all men for nought?

47 What man is he that liveth, and shall not see death : and shall he deliver his soul from the hand of hell?

48 Lord, where are thy old loving-kindnesses : which thou swarest unto David in thy truth?

49 Remember, Lord, the rebuke that thy servants have : and how I do bear in my bosom the rebukes of many people.

50 Wherewith thine enemies have blasphemed thee, and slandered the footsteps of thine Anointed : Praised be the Lord for evermore. Amen, and Amen.

Day 18. Morning Prayer

Psalm 90. *Domine, refugium*

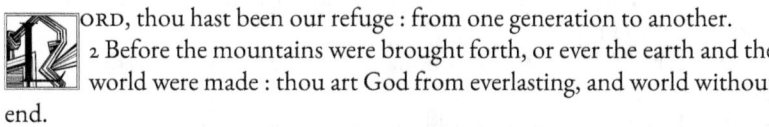

Lord, thou hast been our refuge : from one generation to another.

2 Before the mountains were brought forth, or ever the earth and the world were made : thou art God from everlasting, and world without end.

3 Thou turnest man to destruction : again thou sayest, Come again, ye children of men.

4 For a thousand years in thy sight are but as yesterday : seeing that is past as a watch in the night.

5 As soon as thou scatterest them they are even as a sleep : and fade away suddenly like the grass.

6 In the morning it is green, and groweth up : but in the evening it is cut down, dried up, and withered.

7 For we consume away in thy displeasure : and are afraid at thy wrathful indignation.

8 Thou hast set our misdeeds before thee : and our secret sins in the light of thy countenance.

9 For when thou art angry all our days are gone : we bring our years to an end, as it were a tale that is told.

10 The days of our age are threescore years and ten; and though men be so strong that they come to fourscore years : yet is their strength then but labour and sorrow; so soon passeth it away, and we are gone.

11 But who regardeth the power of thy wrath : for even thereafter as a man feareth, so is thy displeasure.

12 So teach us to number our days : that we may apply our hearts unto wisdom.

13 Turn thee again, O Lord, at the last : and be gracious unto thy servants.

14 O satisfy us with thy mercy, and that soon : so shall we rejoice and be glad all the days of our life.

15 Comfort us again now after the time that thou hast plagued us : and for the years wherein we have suffered adversity.

16 Shew thy servants thy work : and their children thy glory.

17 And the glorious majesty of the Lord our God be upon us : prosper thou the work of our hands upon us, O prosper thou our handywork.

PSALM 91. *QUI HABITAT*

WHOSO dwelleth under the defence of the most High : shall abide under the shadow of the Almighty.

2 I will say unto the Lord, Thou art my hope, and my strong hold : my God, in him will I trust.

3 For he shall deliver thee from the snare of the hunter : and from the noisome pestilence.

4 He shall defend thee under his wings, and thou shalt be safe under his feathers : his faithfulness and truth shall be thy shield and buckler.

5 Thou shalt not be afraid for any terror by night : nor for the arrow that flieth by day;

6 For the pestilence that walketh in darkness : nor for the sickness that destroyeth in the noon-day.

7 A thousand shall fall beside thee, and ten thousand at thy right hand : but it shall not come nigh thee.

8 Yea, with thine eyes shalt thou behold : and see the reward of the ungodly.

9 For thou, Lord, art my hope : thou hast set thine house of defence very high.

10 There shall no evil happen unto thee : neither shall any plague come nigh thy dwelling.

11 For he shall give his angels charge over thee : to keep thee in all thy ways.

12 They shall bear thee in their hands : that thou hurt not thy foot against a stone.

13 Thou shalt go upon the lion and adder : the young lion and the dragon shalt thou tread under thy feet.

14 Because he hath set his love upon me, therefore will I deliver him : I will set him up, because he hath known my Name.

15 He shall call upon me, and I will hear him : yea, I am with him in trouble; I will deliver him, and bring him to honour.

16 With long life will I satisfy him : and shew him my salvation.

Psalm 92. *Bonum est confiteri*

It is a good thing to give thanks unto the Lord : and to sing praises unto thy Name, O most Highest;

2 To tell of thy loving-kindness early in the morning : and of thy truth in the night-season;

3 Upon an instrument of ten strings, and upon the lute : upon a loud instrument, and upon the harp.

4 For thou, Lord, hast made me glad through thy works : and I will rejoice in giving praise for the operations of thy hands.

5 O Lord, how glorious are thy works : thy thoughts are very deep.

6 An unwise man doth not well consider this : and a fool doth not understand it.

7 When the ungodly are green as the grass, and when all the workers of wickedness do flourish : then shall they be destroyed for ever; but thou, Lord, art the most Highest for evermore.

8 For lo, thine enemies, O Lord, lo, thine enemies shall perish : and all the workers of wickedness shall be destroyed.

9 But mine horn shall be exalted like the horn of an unicorn : for I am anointed with fresh oil.

10 Mine eye also shall see his lust of mine enemies : and mine ear shall hear his desire of the wicked that arise up against me.

11 The righteous shall flourish like a palm-tree : and shall spread abroad like a cedar in Libanus.

12 Such as are planted in the house of the Lord : shall flourish in the courts of the house of our God.

13 They also shall bring forth more fruit in their age : and shall be fat and well-liking.

14 That they may shew how true the Lord my strength is : and that there is no unrighteousness in him.

Day 18. Evening Prayer

PSALM 93. *DOMINUS REGNAVIT*

THE Lord is King, and hath put on glorious apparel : the Lord hath put on his apparel, and girded himself with strength.

2 He hath made the round world so sure : that it cannot be moved.

3 Ever since the world began hath thy seat been prepared : thou art from everlasting.

4 The floods are risen, O Lord, the floods have lift up their voice : the floods lift up their waves.

5 The waves of the sea are mighty, and rage horribly : but yet the Lord, who dwelleth on high, is mightier.

6 Thy testimonies, O Lord, are very sure : holiness becometh thine house for ever.

PSALM 94. *DEUS ULTIONUM*

LORD God, to whom vengeance belongeth : thou God, to whom vengeance belongeth, shew thyself.

2 Arise, thou Judge of the world : and reward the proud after their deserving.

3 Lord, how long shall the ungodly : how long shall the ungodly triumph?

4 How long shall all wicked doers speak so disdainfully : and make such proud boasting?

5 They smite down thy people, O Lord : and trouble thine heritage.

6 They murder the widow and the stranger : and put the fatherless to death.

7 And yet they say, Tush, the Lord shall not see : neither shall the God of Jacob regard it.

8 Take heed, ye unwise among the people : O ye fools, when will ye understand?

9 He that planted the ear, shall he not hear : or he that made the eye, shall he not see?

10 Or he that nurtureth the heathen : it is he that teacheth man knowledge, shall not he punish?

11 The Lord knoweth the thoughts of man : that they are but vain.

12 Blessed is the man whom thou chastenest, O Lord : and teachest him in thy law;

13 That thou mayest give him patience in time of adversity : until the pit be digged up for the ungodly.

14 For the Lord will not fail his people : neither will he forsake his inheritance;

15 Until righteousness turn again unto judgement : all such as are true in heart shall follow it.

16 Who will rise up with me against the wicked : or who will take my part against the evil-doers?

17 If the Lord had not helped me : it had not failed but my soul had been put to silence.

18 But when I said, My foot hath slipt : thy mercy, O Lord, held me up.

19 In the multitude of the sorrows that I had in my heart : thy comforts have refreshed my soul.

20 Wilt thou have any thing to do with the stool of wickedness : which imagineth mischief as a law?

21 They gather them together against the soul of the righteous : and condemn the innocent blood.

22 But the Lord is my refuge : and my God is the strength of my confidence.

23 He shall recompense them their wickedness, and destroy them in their own malice : yea, the Lord our God shall destroy them.

Day 19. Morning Prayer

PSALM 95. *VENITE, EXULTEMUS*

COME, let us sing unto the Lord : let us heartily rejoice in the strength of our salvation.

2 Let us come before his presence with thanksgiving : and shew ourselves glad in him with psalms.

3 For the Lord is a great God : and a great King above all gods.

4 In his hand are all the corners of the earth : and the strength of the hills is his also.

5 The sea is his, and he made it : and his hands prepared the dry land.

6 O come, let us worship and fall down : and kneel before the Lord our Maker.

7 For he is the Lord our God : and we are the people of his pasture, and the sheep of his hand.

8 To-day if ye will hear his voice, harden not your hearts : as in the provocation, and as in the day of temptation in the wilderness.

9 When your fathers tempted me : proved me, and saw my works.

10 Forty years long was I grieved with this generation, and said : It is a people that do err in their hearts, for they have not known my ways;

11 Unto whom I sware in my wrath : that they should not enter into my rest.

Psalm 96. *Cantate Domino*

Sing unto the Lord a new song : sing unto the Lord, all the whole earth.

2 Sing unto the Lord, and praise his Name : be telling of his salvation from day to day.

3 Declare his honour unto the heathen : and his wonders unto all people.

4 For the Lord is great, and cannot worthily be praised : he is more to be feared than all gods.

5 As for all the gods of the heathen, they are but idols : but it is the Lord that made the heavens.

6 Glory and worship are before him : power and honour are in his sanctuary.

7 Ascribe unto the Lord, O ye kindreds of the people : ascribe unto the Lord worship and power.

8 Ascribe unto the Lord the honour due unto his Name : bring presents, and come into his courts.

9 O worship the Lord in the beauty of holiness : let the whole earth stand in awe of him.

10 Tell it out among the heathen that the Lord is King : and that it is he who hath made the round world so fast that it cannot be moved; and how that he shall judge the people righteously.

11 Let the heavens rejoice, and let the earth be glad : let the sea make a noise, and all that therein is.

12 Let the field be joyful, and all that is in it : then shall all the trees of the wood rejoice before the Lord.

13 For he cometh, for he cometh to judge the earth : and with righteousness to judge the world, and the people with his truth.

Psalm 97. *Dominus regnavit*

THE Lord is King, the earth may be glad thereof : yea, the multitude of the isles may be glad thereof.

2 Clouds and darkness are round about him : righteousness and judgement are the habitation of his seat.

3 There shall go a fire before him : and burn up his enemies on every side.

4 His lightnings gave shine unto the world : the earth saw it, and was afraid.

5 The hills melted like wax at the presence of the Lord : at the presence of the Lord of the whole earth.

6 The heavens have declared his righteousness : and all the people have seen his glory.

7 Confounded be all they that worship carved images, and that delight in vain gods : worship him, all ye gods.

8 Sion heard of it, and rejoiced : and the daughters of Judah were glad, because of thy judgements, O Lord.

9 For thou, Lord, art higher than all that are in the earth : thou art exalted far above all gods.

10 O ye that love the Lord, see that ye hate the thing which is evil : the Lord preserveth the souls of his saints; he shall deliver them from the hand of the ungodly.

11 There is sprung up a light for the righteous : and joyful gladness for such as are true-hearted.

12 Rejoice in the Lord, ye righteous : and give thanks for a remembrance of his holiness.

Day 19. Evening Prayer

Psalm 98. *Cantate Domino*

SING unto the Lord a new song : for he hath done marvellous things.

2 With his own right hand, and with his holy arm : hath he gotten himself the victory.

3 The Lord declared his salvation : his righteousness hath he openly shewed in the sight of the heathen.

4 He hath remembered his mercy and truth toward the house of Israel : and all the ends of the world have seen the salvation of our God.

5 Shew yourselves joyful unto the Lord, all ye lands : sing, rejoice, and give thanks.

6 Praise the Lord upon the harp : sing to the harp with a psalm of thanksgiving.

7 With trumpets also and shawms : O shew yourselves joyful before the Lord the King.

8 Let the sea make a noise, and all that therein is : the round world, and they that dwell therein.

9 Let the floods clap their hands, and let the hills be joyful together before the Lord : for he is come to judge the earth.

10 With righteousness shall he judge the world : and the people with equity.

PSALM 99. *DOMINUS REGNAVIT*

THE Lord is King, be the people never so unpatient : he sitteth between the cherubims, be the earth never so unquiet.

2 The Lord is great in Sion : and high above all people.

3 They shall give thanks unto thy Name : which is great, wonderful, and holy.

4 The King's power loveth judgement; thou hast prepared equity : thou hast executed judgement and righteousness in Jacob.

5 O magnify the Lord our God : and fall down before his footstool, for he is holy.

6 Moses and Aaron among his priests, and Samuel among such as call upon his Name : these called upon the Lord, and he heard them.

7 He spake unto them out of the cloudy pillar : for they kept his testimonies, and the law that he gave them.

8 Thou heardest them, O Lord our God : thou forgavest them, O God, and punishedst their own inventions.

9 O magnify the Lord our God, and worship him upon his holy hill : for the Lord our God is holy.

PSALM 100. *JUBILATE DEO*

BE joyful in the Lord, all ye lands : serve the Lord with gladness, and come before his presence with a song.

2 Be ye sure that the Lord he is God : it is he that hath made us, and not we ourselves; we are his people, and the sheep of his pasture.

3 O go your way into his gates with thanksgiving, and into his courts with praise : be thankful unto him, and speak good of his Name.

4 For the Lord is gracious, his mercy is everlasting : and his truth endureth from generation to generation.

Psalm 101. *Misericordiam et judicium*

My song shall be of mercy and judgement : unto thee, O Lord, will I sing.

2 O let me have understanding : in the way of godliness.

3 When wilt thou come unto me : I will walk in my house with a perfect heart.

4 I will take no wicked thing in hand; I hate the sins of unfaithfulness : there shall no such cleave unto me.

5 A froward heart shall depart from me : I will not know a wicked person.

6 Whoso privily slandereth his neighbour : him will I destroy.

7 Whoso hath also a proud look and high stomach : I will not suffer him.

8 Mine eyes look upon such as are faithful in the land : that they may dwell with me.

9 Whoso leadeth a godly life : he shall be my servant.

10 There shall no deceitful person dwell in my house : he that telleth lies shall not tarry in my sight.

11 I shall soon destroy all the ungodly that are in the land : that I may root out all wicked doers from the city of the Lord.

Day 20. Morning Prayer

Psalm 102. *Domine, exaudi*

Hear my prayer, O Lord : and let my crying come unto thee.

2 Hide not thy face from me in the time of my trouble : incline thine ear unto me when I call; O hear me, and that right soon.

3 For my days are consumed away like smoke : and my bones are burnt up as it were a firebrand.

4 My heart is smitten down, and withered liked grass : so that I forget to eat my bread.

5 For the voice of my groaning : my bones will scarce cleave to my flesh.

6 I am become like a pelican in the wilderness : and like an owl that is in the desert.

7 I have watched, and am even as it were a sparrow : that sitteth alone upon the house-top.

8 Mine enemies revile me all the day long : and they that are mad upon me are sworn together against me.

9 For I have eaten ashes as it were bread : and mingled my drink with weeping;

10 And that because of thine indignation and wrath : for thou hast taken me up, and cast me down.

Day 20. Morning Prayer   **Psalter**   Psalm 103

11 My days are gone like a shadow : and I am withered like grass.

12 But thou, O Lord, shalt endure for ever : and thy remembrance throughout all generations.

13 Thou shalt arise, and have mercy upon Sion : for it is time that thou have mercy upon her, yea, the time is come.

14 And why? thy servants think upon her stones : and it pitieth them to see her in the dust.

15 The heathen shall fear thy Name, O Lord : and all the kings of the earth thy majesty;

16 When the Lord shall build up Sion : and when his glory shall appear;

17 When he turneth him unto the prayer of the poor destitute : and despiseth not their desire.

18 This shall be written for those that come after : and the people which shall be born shall praise the Lord.

19 For he hath looked down from his sanctuary : out of the heaven did the Lord behold the earth;

20 That he might hear the mournings of such as are in captivity : and deliver the children appointed unto death;

21 That they may declare the Name of the Lord in Sion : and his worship at Jerusalem;

22 When the people are gathered together : and the kingdoms also, to serve the Lord.

23 He brought down my strength in my journey : and shortened my days.

24 But I said, O my God, take me not away in the midst of mine age : as for thy years, they endure throughout all generations.

25 Thou, Lord, in the beginning hast laid the foundation of the earth : and the heavens are the work of thy hands.

26 They shall perish, but thou shalt endure : they all shall wax old as doth a garment;

27 And as a vesture shalt thou change them, and they shall be changed : but thou art the same, and thy years shall not fail.

28 The children of thy servants shall continue : and their seed shall stand fast in thy sight.

Psalm 103. *Benedic, anima mea*

PRAISE the Lord, O my soul : and all that is within me praise his holy Name.

2 Praise the Lord, O my soul : and forget not all his benefits;

3 Who forgiveth all thy sin : and healeth all thine infirmities;

4 Who saveth thy life from destruction : and crowneth thee with mercy and loving-kindness;

5 Who satisfieth thy mouth with good things : making thee young and lusty as an eagle.

6 The Lord executeth righteousness and judgement : for all them that are oppressed with wrong.

7 He shewed his ways unto Moses : his works unto the children of Israel.

8 The Lord is full of compassion and mercy : long-suffering, and of great goodness.

9 He will not alway be chiding : neither keepeth he his anger for ever.

10 He hath not dealt with us after our sins : nor rewarded us according to our wickednesses.

11 For look how high the heaven is in comparison of the earth : so great is his mercy also toward them that fear him.

12 Look how wide also the east is from the west : so far hath he set our sins from us.

13 Yea, like as a father pitieth his own children : even so is the Lord merciful unto them that fear him.

14 For he knoweth whereof we are made : he remembereth that we are but dust.

15 The days of man are but as grass : for he flourisheth as a flower of the field.

16 For as soon as the wind goeth over it, it is gone : and the place thereof shall know it no more.

17 But the merciful goodness of the Lord endureth for ever and ever upon them that fear him : and his righteousness upon children's children;

18 Even upon such as keep his covenant : and think upon his commandments to do them.

19 The Lord hath prepared his seat in heaven : and his kingdom ruleth over all.

20 O praise the Lord, ye angels of his, ye that excel in strength : ye that fulfil his commandment, and hearken unto the voice of his words.

21 O praise the Lord, all ye his hosts : ye servants of his that do his pleasure.

22 O speak good of the Lord, all ye works of his, in all places of his dominion : praise thou the Lord, O my soul.

Day 20. Evening Prayer

Psalm 104. *Benedic, anima mea*

PRAISE the Lord, O my soul : O Lord my God, thou art become exceeding glorious; thou art clothed with majesty and honour.

2 Thou deckest thyself with light as it were with a garment : and spreadest out the heavens like a curtain.

3 Who layeth the beams of his chambers in the waters : and maketh the clouds his chariot, and walketh upon the wings of the wind.

4 He maketh his angels spirits : and his ministers a flaming fire.

5 He laid the foundations of the earth : that it never should move at any time.

6 Thou coveredst it with the deep like as with a garment : the waters stand in the hills.

7 At thy rebuke they flee : at the voice of thy thunder they are afraid.

8 They go up as high as the hills, and down to the valleys beneath : even unto the place which thou hast appointed for them.

9 Thou hast set them their bounds which they shall not pass : neither turn again to cover the earth.

10 He sendeth the springs into the rivers : which run among the hills.

11 All beasts of the field drink thereof : and the wild asses quench their thirst.

12 Beside them shall the fowls of the air have their habitation : and sing among the branches.

13 He watereth the hills from above : the earth is filled with the fruit of thy works.

14 He bringeth forth grass for the cattle : and green herb for the service of men;

15 That he may bring food out of the earth, and wine that maketh glad the heart of man : and oil to make him a cheerful countenance, and bread to strengthen man's heart.

16 The trees of the Lord also are full of sap : even the cedars of Libanus which he hath planted;

17 Wherein the birds make their nests : and the fir-trees are a dwelling for the stork.

18 The high hills are a refuge for the wild goats : and so are the stony rocks for the conies.

19 He appointed the moon for certain seasons : and the sun knoweth his going down.

20 Thou makest darkness that it may be night : wherein all the beasts of the forest do move.

21 The lions roaring after their prey : do seek their meat from God.

22 The sun ariseth, and they get them away together : and lay them down in their dens.

23 Man goeth forth to his work, and to his labour : until the evening.

24 O Lord, how manifold are thy works : in wisdom hast thou made them all; the earth is full of thy riches.

25 So is the great and wide sea also : wherein are things creeping innumerable, both small and great beasts.

26 There go the ships, and there is that Leviathan : whom thou hast made to take his pastime therein.

27 These wait all upon thee : that thou mayest give them meat in due season.

28 When thou givest it them they gather it : and when thou openest thy hand they are filled with good.

29 When thou hidest thy face they are troubled : when thou takest away their breath they die, and are turned again to their dust.

30 When thou lettest thy breath go forth they shall be made : and thou shalt renew the face of the earth.

31 The glorious majesty of the Lord shall endure for ever : the Lord shall rejoice in his works.

32 The earth shall tremble at the look of him : if he do but touch the hills, they shall smoke.

33 I will sing unto the Lord as long as I live : I will praise my God while I have my being.

34 And so shall my words please him : my joy shall be in the Lord.

35 As for sinners, they shall be consumed out of the earth, and the ungodly shall come to an end : praise thou the Lord, O my soul, praise the Lord.

Day 21. Morning Prayer

PSALM 105. *CONFITEMINI DOMINO*

GIVE thanks unto the Lord, and call upon his Name : tell the people what things he hath done.

2 O let your songs be of him, and praise him : and let your talking be of all his wondrous works.

3 Rejoice in his holy Name : let the heart of them rejoice that seek the Lord.

4 Seek the Lord and his strength : seek his face evermore.

5 Remember the marvellous works that he hath done : his wonders, and the judgements of his mouth.

Day 21. Morning Prayer # Psalter *Psalm 105*

6 O ye seed of Abraham his servant : ye children of Jacob his chosen.

7 He is the Lord our God : his judgements are in all the world.

8 He hath been alway mindful of his covenant and promise : that he made to a thousand generations;

9 Even the covenant that he made with Abraham : and the oath that he sware unto Isaac;

10 And appointed the same unto Jacob for a law : and to Israel for an everlasting testament;

11 Saying, Unto thee will I give the land of Canaan : the lot of your inheritance;

12 When there were yet but a few of them : and they strangers in the land;

13 What time as they went from one nation to another : from one kingdom to another people;

14 He suffered no man to do them wrong : but reproved even kings for their sakes;

15 Touch not mine Anointed : and do my prophets no harm.

16 Moreover, he called for a dearth upon the land : and destroyed all the provision of bread.

17 But he had sent a man before them : even Joseph, who was sold to be a bond-servant;

18 Whose feet they hurt in the stocks : the iron entered into his soul;

19 Until the time came that his cause was known : the word of the Lord tried him.

20 The king sent, and delivered him : the prince of the people let him go free.

21 He made him lord also of his house : and ruler of all his substance;

22 That he might inform his princes after his will : and teach his senators wisdom.

23 Israel also came into Egypt : and Jacob was a stranger in the land of Ham.

24 And he increased his people exceedingly : and made them stronger than their enemies;

25 Whose heart turned, so that they hated his people : and dealt untruly with his servants.

26 Then sent he Moses his servant : and Aaron whom he had chosen.

27 And these shewed his tokens among them : and wonders in the land of Ham.

28 He sent darkness, and it was dark : and they were not obedient unto his word.

29 He turned their waters into blood : and slew their fish.

30 Their land brought forth frogs : yea, even in their kings' chambers.

31 He spake the word, and there came all manner of flies : and lice in all their quarters.

32 He gave them hail-stones for rain : and flames of fire in their land.

33 He smote their vines also and fig-trees : and destroyed the trees that were in their coasts.

34 He spake the word, and the grasshoppers came, and caterpillars innumerable : and did eat up all the grass in their land, and devoured the fruit of their ground.

35 He smote all the first-born in their land : even the chief of all their strength.

36 He brought them forth also with silver and gold : there was not one feeble person among their tribes.

37 Egypt was glad at their departing : for they were afraid of them.

38 He spread out a cloud to be a covering : and fire to give light in the night-season.

39 At their desire he brought quails : and he filled them with the bread of heaven.

40 He opened the rock of stone, and the waters flowed out : so that rivers ran in the dry places.

41 For why? he remembered his holy promise : and Abraham his servant.

42 And he brought forth his people with joy : and his chosen with gladness;

43 And gave them the lands of the heathen : and they took the labours of the people in possession;

44 That they might keep his statutes : and observe his laws.

Day 21. Evening Prayer

Psalm 106. *Confitemini Domino*

GIVE thanks unto the Lord, for he is gracious : and his mercy endureth for ever.

2 Who can express the noble acts of the Lord : or shew forth all his praise?

3 Blessed are they that alway keep judgement : and do righteousness.

4 Remember me, O Lord, according to the favour that thou bearest unto thy people : O visit me with thy salvation;

5 That I may see the felicity of thy chosen : and rejoice in the gladness of thy people, and give thanks with thine inheritance.

6 We have sinned with our fathers : we have done amiss, and dealt wickedly.

7 Our fathers regarded not thy wonders in Egypt, neither kept they thy great goodness in remembrance : but were disobedient at the sea, even at the Red sea.

Day 21. Evening Prayer   **Psalter**   Psalm 106

8 Nevertheless, he helped them for his Name's sake : that he might make his power to be known.

9 He rebuked the Red sea also, and it was dried up : so he led them through the deep, as through a wilderness.

10 And he saved them from the adversaries' hand : and delivered them from the hand of the enemy.

11 As for those that troubled them, the waters overwhelmed them : there was not one of them left.

12 Then believed they his words : and sang praise unto him.

13 But within a while they forgat his works : and would not abide his counsel.

14 But lust came upon them in the wilderness : and they tempted God in the desert.

15 And he gave them their desire : and sent leanness withal into their soul.

16 They angered Moses also in the tents : and Aaron the saint of the Lord.

17 So the earth opened, and swallowed up Dathan : and covered the congregation of Abiram.

18 And the fire was kindled in their company : the flame burnt up the ungodly.

19 They made a calf in Horeb : and worshipped the molten image.

20 Thus they turned their glory : into the similitude of a calf that eateth hay.

21 And they forgat God their Saviour : who had done so great things in Egypt;

22 Wondrous works in the land of Ham : and fearful things by the Red sea.

23 So he said, he would have destroyed them, had not Moses his chosen stood before him in the gap : to turn away his wrathful indignation, lest he should destroy them.

24 Yea, they thought scorn of that pleasant land : and gave no credence unto his word;

25 But murmured in their tents : and hearkened not unto the voice of the Lord.

26 Then lift he up his hand against them : to overthrow them in the wilderness;

27 To cast out their seed among the nations : and to scatter them in the lands.

28 They joined themselves unto Baal-peor : and ate the offerings of the dead.

29 Thus they provoked him to anger with their own inventions : and the plague was great among them.

30 Then stood up Phinees and prayed : and so the plague ceased.

31 And that was counted unto him for righteousness : among all posterities for evermore.

32 They angered him also at the waters of strife : so that he punished Moses for their sakes;

33 Because they provoked his spirit : so that he spake unadvisedly with his lips.

34 Neither destroyed they the heathen : as the Lord commanded them;

35 But were mingled among the heathen : and learned their works.

36 Insomuch that they worshipped their idols, which turned to their own decay : yea, they offered their sons and their daughters unto devils;

37 And shed innocent blood, even the blood of their sons and of their daughters : whom they had offered unto the idols of Canaan; and the land was defiled with blood.

38 Thus were they stained with their own works : and went a whoring with their own inventions.

39 Therefore was the wrath of the Lord kindled against his people : insomuch that he abhorred his own inheritance.

40 And he gave them over into the hands of the heathen : and they that hated them were lords over them.

41 Their enemies oppressed them : and had them in subjection.

42 Many a time did he deliver them : but they rebelled against him with their own inventions, and were brought down in their wickedness.

43 Nevertheless, when he saw their adversity : he heard their complaint.

44 He thought upon his covenant, and pitied them according unto the multitude of his mercies : yea, he made all those that led them away captive to pity them.

45 Deliver us, O Lord our God, and gather us from among the heathen : that we may give thanks unto thy holy Name, and make our boast of thy praise.

46 Blessed be the Lord God of Israel from everlasting and world without end : and let all the people say, Amen.

Day 22. Morning Prayer

Psalm 107. *Confitemini Domino*

GIVE thanks unto the Lord, for he is gracious : and his mercy endureth for ever.

2 Let them give thanks whom the Lord hath redeemed : and delivered from the hand of the enemy;

3 And gathered them out of the lands, from the east and from the west : from the north and from the south.

4 They went astray in the wilderness out of the way : and found no city to dwell in;

Day 22. Morning Prayer   **Psalter**   Psalm 107

5 Hungry and thirsty : their soul fainted in them.
6 So they cried unto the Lord in their trouble : and he delivered them from their distress.
7 He led them forth by the right way : that they might go to the city where they dwelt.
8 O that men would therefore praise the Lord for his goodness : and declare the wonders that he doeth for the children of men!
9 For he satisfieth the empty soul : and filleth the hungry soul with goodness.
10 Such as sit in darkness, and in the shadow of death : being fast bound in misery and iron;
11 Because they rebelled against the words of the Lord : and lightly regarded the counsel of the most Highest;
12 He also brought down their heart through heaviness : they fell down, and there was none to help them.
13 So when they cried unto the Lord in their trouble : he delivered them out of their distress.
14 For he brought them out of darkness, and out of the shadow of death : and brake their bonds in sunder.
15 O that men would therefore praise the Lord for his goodness : and declare the wonders that he doeth for the children of men!
16 For he hath broken the gates of brass : and smitten the bars of iron in sunder.
17 Foolish men are plagued for their offence : and because of their wickedness.
18 Their soul abhorred all manner of meat : and they were even hard at death's door.
19 So when they cried unto the Lord in their trouble : he delivered them out of their distress.
20 He sent his word, and healed them : and they were saved from their destruction.
21 O that men would therefore praise the Lord for his goodness : and declare the wonders that he doeth for the children of men!
22 That they would offer unto him the sacrifice of thanksgiving : and tell out his works with gladness!
23 They that go down to the sea in ships : and occupy their business in great waters;
24 These men see the works of the Lord : and his wonders in the deep.
25 For at his word the stormy wind ariseth : which lifteth up the waves thereof.
26 They are carried up to the heaven, and down again to the deep : their soul melteth away because of the trouble.

27 They reel to and fro, and stagger like a drunken man : and are at their wits' end.
28 So when they cry unto the Lord in their trouble : he delivereth them out of their distress.
29 For he maketh the storm to cease : so that the waves thereof are still.
30 Then are they glad, because they are at rest : and so he bringeth them unto the haven where they would be.
31 O that men would therefore praise the Lord for his goodness : and declare the wonders that he doeth for the children of men!
32 That they would exalt him also in the congregation of the people : and praise him in the seat of the elders!
33 Who turneth the floods into a wilderness : and drieth up the water-springs.
34 A fruitful land maketh he barren : for the wickedness of them that dwell therein.
35 Again, he maketh the wilderness a standing water : and water-springs of a dry ground.
36 And there he setteth the hungry : that they may build them a city to dwell in;
37 That they may sow their land, and plant vineyards : to yield them fruits of increase.
38 He blesseth them so that they multiply exceedingly : and suffereth not their cattle to decrease.
39 And again, when they are minished and brought low : through oppression, through any plague or trouble;
40 Though he suffer them to be evil intreated through tyrants : and let them wander out of the way in the wilderness;
41 Yet helpeth he the poor out of misery : and maketh him households like a flock of sheep.
42 The righteous will consider this, and rejoice : and the mouth of all wickedness shall be stopped.
43 Whoso is wise will ponder these things : and they shall understand the loving-kindness of the Lord.

Day 22. Evening Prayer

PSALM 108. *PARATUM COR MEUM*

GOD, my heart is ready, my heart is ready : I will sing and give praise with the best member that I have.

2 Awake, thou lute, and harp : I myself will awake right early.

3 I will give thanks unto thee, O Lord, among the people : I will sing praises unto thee among the nations.

4 For thy mercy is greater than the heavens : and thy truth reacheth unto the clouds.

5 Set up thyself, O God, above the heavens : and thy glory above all the earth.

6 That thy beloved may be delivered : let thy right hand save them, and hear thou me.

7 God hath spoken in his holiness : I will rejoice therefore, and divide Sichem, and mete out the valley of Succoth.

8 Gilead is mine, and Manasses is mine : Ephraim also is the strength of my head.

9 Judah is my law-giver, Moab is my wash-pot : over Edom will I cast out my shoe, upon Philistia will I triumph.

10 Who will lead me into the strong city : and who will bring me into Edom?

11 Hast not thou forsaken us, O God : and wilt not thou, O God, go forth with our hosts?

12 O help us against the enemy : for vain is the help of man.

13 Through God we shall do great acts : and it is he that shall tread down our enemies.

PSALM 109. *DEUS, LAUDEM*

HOLD not thy tongue, O God of my praise : for the mouth of the ungodly, yea, the mouth of the deceitful is opened upon me.

2 And they have spoken against me with false tongues : they compassed me about also with words of hatred, and fought against me without a cause.

3 For the love that I had unto them, lo, they take now my contrary part : but I give myself unto prayer.

4 Thus have they rewarded me evil for good : and hatred for my good will.

5 Set thou an ungodly man to be ruler over him : and let Satan stand at his right hand.

6 When sentence is given upon him, let him be condemned : and let his prayer be turned into sin.

7 Let his days be few : and let another take his office.

8 Let his children be fatherless : and his wife a widow.

9 Let his children be vagabonds, and beg their bread : let them seek it also out of desolate places.

10 Let the extortioner consume all that he hath : and let the stranger spoil his labour.

11 Let there be no man to pity him : nor to have compassion upon his fatherless children.

12 Let his posterity be destroyed : and in the next generation let his name be clean put out.

13 Let the wickedness of his fathers be had in remembrance in the sight of the Lord : and let not the sin of his mother be done away.

14 Let them alway be before the Lord : that he may root out the memorial of them from off the earth.

15 And that, because his mind was not to do good : but persecuted the poor helpless man, that he might slay him that was vexed at the heart.

16 His delight was in cursing, and it shall happen unto him : he loved not blessing, therefore shall it be far from him.

17 He clothed himself with cursing, like as with a raiment : and it shall come into his bowels like water, and like oil into his bones.

18 Let it be unto him as the cloke that he hath upon him : and as the girdle that he is alway girded withal.

19 Let it thus happen from the Lord unto mine enemies : and to those that speak evil against my soul.

20 But deal thou with me, O Lord God, according unto thy Name : for sweet is thy mercy.

21 O deliver me, for I am helpless and poor : and my heart is wounded within me.

22 I go hence like the shadow that departeth : and am driven away as the grasshopper.

23 My knees are weak through fasting : my flesh is dried up for want of fatness.

24 I became also a reproach unto them : they that looked upon me shaked their heads.

25 Help me, O Lord my God : O save me according to thy mercy.

26 And they shall know, how that this is thy hand : and that thou, Lord, hast done it.

27 Though they curse, yet bless thou : and let them be confounded that rise up against me; but let thy servant rejoice.

28 Let mine adversaries be clothed with shame : and let them cover themselves with their own confusion, as with a cloke.

29 As for me, I will give great thanks unto the Lord with my mouth : and praise him among the multitude.

30 For he shall stand at the right hand of the poor : to save his soul from the unrighteous judges.

Day 23. Morning Prayer

Psalm 110. *Dixit Dominus*

THE Lord said unto my Lord : Sit thou on my right hand, until I make thine enemies thy footstool.

2 The Lord shall send the rod of thy power out of Sion : be thou ruler, even in the midst among thine enemies.

3 In the day of thy power shall the people offer thee free-will offerings with an holy worship : the dew of thy birth is of the womb of the morning.

4 The Lord sware, and will not repent : Thou art a priest for ever after the order of Melchisedech.

5 The Lord upon thy right hand : shall wound even kings in the day of his wrath.

6 He shall judge among the heathen; he shall fill the places with the dead bodies : and smite in sunder the heads over divers countries.

7 He shall drink of the brook in the way : therefore shall he lift up his head.

Psalm 111. *Confitebor tibi*

I WILL give thanks unto the Lord with my whole heart : secretly among the faithful, and in the congregation.

2 The works of the Lord are great : sought out of all them that have pleasure therein.

3 His work is worthy to be praised and had in honour : and his righteousness endureth for ever.

4 The merciful and gracious Lord hath so done his marvellous works : that they ought to be had in remembrance.

5 He hath given meat unto them that fear him : he shall ever be mindful of his covenant.

6 He hath shewed his people the power of his works : that he may give them the heritage of the heathen.

7 The works of his hands are verity and judgement : all his commandments are true.

8 They stand fast for ever and ever : and are done in truth and equity.

9 He sent redemption unto his people : he hath commanded his covenant for ever; holy and reverend is his Name.

10 The fear of the Lord is the beginning of wisdom : a good understanding have all they that do thereafter; the praise of it endureth for ever.

Psalm 112. *Beatus vir*

Blessed is the man that feareth the Lord : he hath great delight in his commandments.

2 His seed shall be mighty upon earth : the generation of the faithful shall be blessed.

3 Riches and plenteousness shall be in his house : and his righteousness endureth for ever.

4 Unto the godly there ariseth up light in the darkness : he is merciful, loving, and righteous.

5 A good man is merciful, and lendeth : and will guide his words with discretion.

6 For he shall never be moved : and the righteous shall be had in everlasting remembrance.

7 He will not be afraid of any evil tidings : for his heart standeth fast, and believeth in the Lord.

8 His heart is established, and will not shrink : until he see his desire upon his enemies.

9 He hath dispersed abroad, and given to the poor : and his righteousness remaineth for ever; his horn shall be exalted with honour.

10 The ungodly shall see it, and it shall grieve him : he shall gnash with his teeth, and consume away; the desire of the ungodly shall perish.

Psalm 113. *Laudate, pueri*

Praise the Lord, ye servants : O praise the Name of the Lord.

2 Blessed be the Name of the Lord : from this time forth for evermore.

3 The Lord's Name is praised : from the rising up of the sun unto the going down of the same.

4 The Lord is high above all heathen : and his glory above the heavens.

5 Who is like unto the Lord our God, that hath his dwelling so high : and yet humbleth himself to behold the things that are in heaven and earth?

6 He taketh up the simple out of the dust : and lifteth the poor out of the mire;

7 That he may set him with the princes : even with the princes of his people.

8 He maketh the barren woman to keep house : and to be a joyful mother of children.

Day 23. Evening Prayer

Psalm 114. *In exitu Israel*

WHEN Israel came out of Egypt : and the house of Jacob from among the strange people,

2 Judah was his sanctuary : and Israel his dominion.

3 The sea saw that, and fled : Jordan was driven back.

4 The mountains skipped like rams : and the little hills like young sheep.

5 What aileth thee, O thou sea, that thou fleddest : and thou Jordan, that thou wast driven back?

6 Ye mountains, that ye skipped like rams : and ye little hills, like young sheep?

7 Tremble, thou earth, at the presence of the Lord : at the presence of the God of Jacob;

8 Who turned the hard rock into a standing water : and the flint-stone into a springing well.

Psalm 115. *Non nobis, Domine*

NOT unto us, O Lord, not unto us, but unto thy Name give the praise : for thy loving mercy and for thy truth's sake.

2 Wherefore shall the heathen say : Where is now their God?

3 As for our God, he is in heaven : he hath done whatsoever pleased him.

4 Their idols are silver and gold : even the work of men's hands.

5 They have mouths, and speak not : eyes have they, and see not.

6 They have ears, and hear not : noses have they, and smell not.

7 They have hands, and handle not; feet have they, and walk not : neither speak they through their throat.

8 They that make them are like unto them : and so are all such as put their trust in them.

9 But thou, house of Israel, trust thou in the Lord : he is their succour and defence.

10 Ye house of Aaron, put your trust in the Lord : he is their helper and defender.

11 Ye that fear the Lord, put your trust in the Lord : he is their helper and defender.

12 The Lord hath been mindful of us, and he shall bless us : even he shall bless the house of Israel, he shall bless the house of Aaron.

13 He shall bless them that fear the Lord : both small and great.

14 The Lord shall increase you more and more : you and your children.

15 Ye are the blessed of the Lord : who made heaven and earth.

16 All the whole heavens are the Lord's : the earth hath he given to the children of men.

17 The dead praise not thee, O Lord : neither all they that go down into silence.

18 But we will praise the Lord : from this time forth for evermore. Praise the Lord.

Day 24. Morning Prayer

Psalm 116. *Dilexi, quoniam*

I AM well pleased : that the Lord hath heard the voice of my prayer;

2 That he hath inclined his ear unto me : therefore will I call upon him as long as I live.

3 The snares of death compassed me round about : and the pains of hell gat hold upon me.

4 I shall find trouble and heaviness, and I will call upon the Name of the Lord : O Lord, I beseech thee, deliver my soul.

5 Gracious is the Lord, and righteous : yea, our God is merciful.

6 The Lord preserveth the simple : I was in misery, and he helped me.

7 Turn again then unto thy rest, O my soul : for the Lord hath rewarded thee.

8 And why? thou hast delivered my soul from death : mine eyes from tears, and my feet from falling.

9 I will walk before the Lord : in the land of the living.

10 I believed, and therefore will I speak; but I was sore troubled : I said in my haste, All men are liars.

11 What reward shall I give unto the Lord : for all the benefits that he hath done unto me?

12 I will receive the cup of salvation : and call upon the Name of the Lord.

13 I will pay my vows now in the presence of all his people : right dear in the sight of the Lord is the death of his saints.

14 Behold, O Lord, how that I am thy servant : I am thy servant, and the son of thine handmaid; thou hast broken my bonds in sunder.

15 I will offer to thee the sacrifice of thanksgiving : and will call upon the Name of the Lord.

16 I will pay my vows unto the Lord, in the sight of all his people : in the courts of the Lord's house, even in the midst of thee, O Jerusalem. Praise the Lord.

Psalm 117. *Laudate Dominum*

PRAISE the Lord, all ye heathen : praise him, all ye nations.

2 For his merciful kindness is ever more and more towards us : and the truth of the Lord endureth for ever. Praise the Lord.

Psalm 118. *Confitemini Domino*

GIVE thanks unto the Lord, for he is gracious : because his mercy endureth for ever.

2 Let Israel now confess that he is gracious : and that his mercy endureth for ever.

3 Let the house of Aaron now confess : that his mercy endureth for ever.

4 Yea, let them now that fear the Lord confess : that his mercy endureth for ever.

5 I called upon the Lord in trouble : and the Lord heard me at large.

6 The Lord is on my side : I will not fear what man doeth unto me.

7 The Lord taketh my part with them that help me : therefore shall I see my desire upon mine enemies.

8 It is better to trust in the Lord : than to put any confidence in man.

9 It is better to trust in the Lord : than to put any confidence in princes.

10 All nations compassed me round about : but in the Name of the Lord will I destroy them.

11 They kept me in on every side, they kept me in, I say, on every side : but in the Name of the Lord will I destroy them.

12 They came about me like bees, and are extinct even as the fire among the thorns : for in the Name of the Lord I will destroy them.

13 Thou hast thrust sore at me, that I might fall : but the Lord was my help.

14 The Lord is my strength, and my song : and is become my salvation.

15 The voice of joy and health is in the dwellings of the righteous : the right hand of the Lord bringeth mighty things to pass.

16 The right hand of the Lord hath the pre-eminence : the right hand of the Lord bringeth mighty things to pass.

17 I shall not die, but live : and declare the works of the Lord.

18 The Lord hath chastened and corrected me : but he hath not given me over unto death.

19 Open me the gates of righteousness : that I may go into them, and give thanks unto the Lord.

20 This is the gate of the Lord : the righteous shall enter into it.

21 I will thank thee, for thou hast heard me : and art become my salvation.

22 The same stone which the builders refused : is become the head-stone in the corner.

23 This is the Lord's doing : and it is marvellous in our eyes.

24 This is the day which the Lord hath made : we will rejoice and be glad in it.

25 Help me now, O Lord : O Lord, send us now prosperity.

26 Blessed be he that cometh in the Name of the Lord : we have wished you good luck, ye that are of the house of the Lord.

27 God is the Lord who hath shewed us light : bind the sacrifice with cords, yea, even unto the horns of the altar.

28 Thou art my God, and I will thank thee : thou art my God, and I will praise thee.

29 O give thanks unto the Lord, for he is gracious : and his mercy endureth for ever.

Day 24. Evening Prayer

Psalm 119. *Beati immaculati*

BLESSED are those that are undefiled in the way : and walk in the law of the Lord.

2 Blessed are they that keep his testimonies : and seek him with their whole heart.

3 For they who do no wickedness : walk in his ways.

4 Thou hast charged : that we shall diligently keep thy commandments.

5 O that my ways were made so direct : that I might keep thy statutes!

6 So shall I not be confounded : while I have respect unto all thy commandments.

7 I will thank thee with an unfeigned heart : when I shall have learned the judgements of thy righteousness.

8 I will keep thy ceremonies : O forsake me not utterly.

Day 24. Evening Prayer   # Psalter   Psalm 119:25

IN QUO CORRIGET?

WHEREWITHAL shall a young man cleanse his way : even by ruling himself after thy word.

10 With my whole heart have I sought thee : O let me not go wrong out of thy commandments.

11 Thy words have I hid within my heart : that I should not sin against thee.

12 Blessed art thou, O Lord : O teach me thy statutes.

13 With my lips have I been telling : of all the judgements of thy mouth.

14 I have had as great delight in the way of thy testimonies : as in all manner of riches.

15 I will talk of thy commandments : and have respect unto thy ways.

16 My delight shall be in thy statutes : and I will not forget thy word.

RETRIBUE SERVO TUO

O DO well unto thy servant : that I may live, and keep thy word.

18 Open thou mine eyes : that I may see the wondrous things of thy law.

19 I am a stranger upon earth : O hide not thy commandments from me.

20 My soul breaketh out for the very fervent desire : that it hath alway unto thy judgements.

21 Thou hast rebuked the proud : and cursed are they that do err from thy commandments.

22 O turn from me shame and rebuke : for I have kept thy testimonies.

23 Princes also did sit and speak against me : but thy servant is occupied in thy statutes.

24 For thy testimonies are my delight : and my counsellors.

ADHÆSIT PAVIMENTO

MY soul cleaveth to the dust : O quicken thou me, according to thy word.

26 I have acknowledged my ways, and thou heardest me : O teach me thy statutes.

27 Make me to understand the way of thy commandments : and so shall I talk of thy wondrous works.

28 My soul melteth away for very heaviness : comfort thou me according unto thy word.

29 Take from me the way of lying : and cause thou me to make much of thy law.

30 I have chosen the way of truth : and thy judgements have I laid before me.

31 I have stuck unto thy testimonies : O Lord, confound me not.

32 I will run the way of thy commandments : when thou hast set my heart at liberty.

Day 25. Morning Prayer

LEGEM PONE

TEACH me, O Lord, the way of thy statutes : and I shall keep it unto the end.

34 Give me understanding, and I shall keep thy law : yea, I shall keep it with my whole heart.

35 Make me to go in the path of thy commandments : for therein is my desire.

36 Incline my heart unto thy testimonies : and not to covetousness.

37 O turn away mine eyes, lest they behold vanity : and quicken thou me in thy way.

38 O stablish thy word in thy servant : that I may fear thee.

39 Take away the rebuke that I am afraid of : for thy judgements are good.

40 Behold, my delight is in thy commandments : O quicken me in thy righteousness.

ET VENIAT SUPER ME

LET thy loving mercy come also unto me, O Lord : even thy salvation, according unto thy word.

42 So shall I make answer unto my blasphemers : for my trust is in thy word.

43 O take not the word of thy truth utterly out of my mouth : for my hope is in thy judgements.

44 So shall I alway keep thy law : yea, for ever and ever.

45 And I will walk at liberty : for I seek thy commandments.

46 I will speak of thy testimonies also, even before kings : and will not be ashamed.

47 And my delight shall be in thy commandments : which I have loved.

48 My hands also will I lift up unto thy commandments, which I have loved : and my study shall be in thy statutes.

Psalter

Memor esto servi tui

O THINK upon thy servant, as concerning thy word : wherein thou hast caused me to put my trust.

50 The same is my comfort in my trouble : for thy word hath quickened me.

51 The proud have had me exceedingly in derision : yet have I not shrinked from thy law.

52 For I remembered thine everlasting judgements, O Lord : and received comfort.

53 I am horribly afraid : for the ungodly that forsake thy law.

54 Thy statutes have been my songs : in the house of my pilgrimage.

55 I have thought upon thy Name, O Lord, in the night-season : and have kept thy law.

56 This I had : because I kept thy commandments.

Portio mea, Domine

THOU art my portion, O Lord : I have promised to keep thy law.

58 I made my humble petition in thy presence with my whole heart : O be merciful unto me, according to thy word.

59 I called mine own ways to remembrance : and turned my feet unto thy testimonies.

60 I made haste, and prolonged not the time : to keep thy commandments.

61 The congregations of the ungodly have robbed me : but I have not forgotten thy law.

62 At midnight I will rise to give thanks unto thee : because of thy righteous judgements.

63 I am a companion of all them that fear thee : and keep thy commandments.

64 The earth, O Lord, is full of thy mercy : O teach me thy statutes.

Bonitatem fecisti

O LORD, thou hast dealt graciously with thy servant : according unto thy word.

66 O learn me true understanding and knowledge : for I have believed thy commandments.

67 Before I was troubled, I went wrong : but now have I kept thy word.

68 Thou art good and gracious : O teach me thy statutes.

69 The proud have imagined a lie against me : but I will keep thy commandments with my whole heart.

70 Their heart is as fat as brawn : but my delight hath been in thy law.
71 It is good for me that I have been in trouble : that I may learn thy statutes.
72 The law of thy mouth is dearer unto me : than thousands of gold and silver.

Day 25. Evening Prayer

Manus tuae fecerunt me

THY hands have made me and fashioned me : O give me understanding, that I may learn thy commandments.
74 They that fear thee will be glad when they see me : because I have put my trust in thy word.
75 I know, O Lord, that thy judgements are right : and that thou of very faithfulness hast caused me to be troubled.
76 O let thy merciful kindness be my comfort : according to thy word unto thy servant.
77 O let thy loving mercies come unto me, that I may live : for thy law is my delight.
78 Let the proud be confounded, for they go wickedly about to destroy me : but I will be occupied in thy commandments.
79 Let such as fear thee, and have known thy testimonies : be turned unto me.
80 O let my heart be sound in thy statutes : that I be not ashamed.

Defecit anima mea

MY soul hath longed for thy salvation : and I have a good hope because of thy word.
82 Mine eyes long sore for thy word : saying, O when wilt thou comfort me?
83 For I am become like a bottle in the smoke : yet do I not forget thy statutes.
84 How many are the days of thy servant : when wilt thou be avenged of them that persecute me?
85 The proud have digged pits for me : which are not after thy law.
86 All thy commandments are true : they persecute me falsely; O be thou my help.
87 They had almost made an end of me upon earth : but I forsook not thy commandments.

88 O quicken me after thy loving-kindness : and so shall I keep the testimonies of thy mouth.

In aeternum, Domine

LORD, thy word : endureth for ever in heaven.

90 Thy truth also remaineth from one generation to another : thou hast laid the foundation of the earth, and it abideth.

91 They continue this day according to thine ordinance : for all things serve thee.

92 If my delight had not been in thy law : I should have perished in my trouble.

93 I will never forget thy commandments : for with them thou hast quickened me.

94 I am thine, O save me : for I have sought thy commandments.

95 The ungodly laid wait for me to destroy me : but I will consider thy testimonies.

96 I see that all things come to an end : but thy commandment is exceeding broad.

Quomodo dilexi!

LORD, what love have I unto thy law : all the day long is my study in it.

98 Thou through thy commandments hast made me wiser than mine enemies : for they are ever with me.

99 I have more understanding than my teachers : for thy testimonies are my study.

100 I am wiser than the aged : because I keep thy commandments.

101 I have refrained my feet from every evil way : that I may keep thy word.

102 I have not shrunk from thy judgements : for thou teachest me.

103 O how sweet are thy words unto my throat : yea, sweeter than honey unto my mouth.

104 Through thy commandments I get understanding : therefore I hate all evil ways.

Day 26. Morning Prayer

Lucerna pedibus meis

THY word is a lantern unto my feet : and a light unto my paths.
106 I have sworn, and am stedfastly purposed : to keep thy righteous judgements.
107 I am troubled above measure : quicken me, O Lord, according to thy word.
108 Let the free-will offerings of my mouth please thee, O Lord : and teach me thy judgements.
109 My soul is alway in my hand : yet do I not forget thy law.
110 The ungodly have laid a snare for me : but yet I swerved not from thy commandments.
111 Thy testimonies have I claimed as mine heritage for ever : and why? they are the very joy of my heart.
112 I have applied my heart to fulfil thy statutes alway : even unto the end.

Iniquos odio habui

HATE them that imagine evil things : but thy law do I love.
114 Thou art my defence and shield : and my trust is in thy word.
115 Away from me, ye wicked : I will keep the commandments of my God.
116 O stablish me according to thy word, that I may live : and let me not be disappointed of my hope.
117 Hold thou me up, and I shall be safe : yea, my delight shall be ever in thy statutes.
118 Thou hast trodden down all them that depart from thy statutes : for they imagine but deceit.
119 Thou puttest away all the ungodly of the earth like dross : therefore I love thy testimonies.
120 My flesh trembleth for fear of thee : and I am afraid of thy judgements.

Feci judicium

I DEAL with the thing that is lawful and right : O give me not over unto mine oppressors.
122 Make thou thy servant to delight in that which is good : that the proud do me no wrong.

123 Mine eyes are wasted away with looking for thy health : and for the word of thy righteousness.

124 O deal with thy servant according unto thy loving mercy : and teach me thy statutes.

125 I am thy servant, O grant me understanding : that I may know thy testimonies.

126 It is time for thee, Lord, to lay to thine hand : for they have destroyed thy law.

127 For I love thy commandments : above gold and precious stone.

128 Therefore hold I straight all thy commandments : and all false ways I utterly abhor.

Mirabilia

THY testimonies are wonderful : therefore doth my soul keep them.

130 When thy word goeth forth : it giveth light and understanding unto the simple.

131 I opened my mouth, and drew in my breath : for my delight was in thy commandments.

132 O look thou upon me, and be merciful unto me : as thou usest to do unto those that love thy Name.

133 Order my steps in thy word : and so shall no wickedness have dominion over me.

134 O deliver me from the wrongful dealings of men : and so shall I keep thy commandments.

135 Shew the light of thy countenance upon thy servant : and teach me thy statutes.

136 Mine eyes gush out with water : because men keep not thy law.

Justus es, Domine

RIGHTEOUS art thou, O Lord : and true is thy judgement.

138 The testimonies that thou hast commanded : are exceeding righteous and true.

139 My zeal hath even consumed me : because mine enemies have forgotten thy words.

140 Thy word is tried to the uttermost : and thy servant loveth it.

141 I am small, and of no reputation : yet do I not forget thy commandments.

142 Thy righteousness is an everlasting righteousness : and thy law is the truth.

143 Trouble and heaviness have taken hold upon me : yet is my delight in thy commandments.

144 The righteousness of thy testimonies is everlasting : O grant me understanding, and I shall live.

Day 26. Evening Prayer

Clamavi in toto corde meo

I CALL with my whole heart : hear me, O Lord, I will keep thy statutes.

146 Yea, even unto thee do I call : help me, and I shall keep thy testimonies.

147 Early in the morning do I cry unto thee : for in thy word is my trust.

148 Mine eyes prevent the night-watches : that I might be occupied in thy words.

149 Hear my voice, O Lord, according unto thy loving-kindness : quicken me, according as thou art wont.

150 They draw nigh that of malice persecute me : and are far from thy law.

151 Be thou nigh at hand, O Lord : for all thy commandments are true.

152 As concerning thy testimonies, I have known long since : that thou hast grounded them for ever.

Vide humilitatem

CONSIDER mine adversity, and deliver me : for I do not forget thy law.

154 Avenge thou my cause, and deliver me : quicken me, according to thy word.

155 Health is far from the ungodly : for they regard not thy statutes.

156 Great is thy mercy, O Lord : quicken me, as thou art wont.

157 Many there are that trouble me, and persecute me : yet do I not swerve from thy testimonies.

158 It grieveth me when I see the transgressors : because they keep not thy law.

159 Consider, O Lord, how I love thy commandments : O quicken me, according to thy loving-kindness.

160 Thy word is true from everlasting : all the judgements of thy righteousness endure for evermore.

Principes persecuti sunt

PRINCES have persecuted me without a cause : but my heart standeth in awe of thy word.

162 I am as glad of thy word : as one that findeth great spoils.

163 As for lies, I hate and abhor them : but thy law do I love.

164 Seven times a day do I praise thee : because of thy righteous judgements.

165 Great is the peace that they have who love thy law : and they are not offended at it.

166 Lord, I have looked for thy saving health : and done after thy commandments.

167 My soul hath kept thy testimonies : and loved them exceedingly.

168 I have kept thy commandments and testimonies : for all my ways are before thee.

Appropinquet deprecatio

LET my complaint come before thee, O Lord : give me understanding, according to thy word.

170 Let my supplication come before thee : deliver me, according to thy word.

171 My lips shall speak of thy praise : when thou hast taught me thy statutes.

172 Yea, my tongue shall sing of thy word : for all thy commandments are righteous.

173 Let thine hand help me : for I have chosen thy commandments.

174 I have longed for thy saving health, O Lord : and in thy law is my delight.

175 O let my soul live, and it shall praise thee : and thy judgements shall help me.

176 I have gone astray like a sheep that is lost : O seek thy servant, for I do not forget thy commandments.

Day 27. Morning Prayer

Psalm 120. *Ad Dominum*

WHEN I was in trouble I called upon the Lord : and he heard me.

2 Deliver my soul, O Lord, from lying lips : and from a deceitful tongue.

3 What reward shall be given or done unto thee, thou false tongue : even mighty and sharp arrows, with hot burning coals.

4 Woe is me, that I am constrained to dwell with Mesech : and to have my habitation among the tents of Kedar.
5 My soul hath long dwelt among them : that are enemies unto peace.
6 I labour for peace, but when I speak unto them thereof : they make them ready to battle.

Psalm 121. *Levavi oculus*

will lift up mine eyes unto the hills : from whence cometh my help.
2 My help cometh even from the Lord : who hath made heaven and earth.
3 He will not suffer thy foot to be moved : and he that keepeth thee will not sleep.
4 Behold, he that keepeth Israel : shall neither slumber nor sleep.
5 The Lord himself is thy keeper : the Lord is thy defence upon thy right hand;
6 So that the sun shall not burn thee by day : neither the moon by night.
7 The Lord shall preserve thee from all evil : yea, it is even he that shall keep thy soul.
8 The Lord shall preserve thy going out, and thy coming in : from this time forth for evermore.

Psalm 122. *Laetatus sum*

I was glad when they said unto me : We will go into the house of the Lord.
2 Our feet shall stand in thy gates : O Jerusalem.
3 Jerusalem is built as a city : that is at unity in itself.
4 For thither the tribes go up, even the tribes of the Lord : to testify unto Israel, to give thanks unto the Name of the Lord.
5 For there is the seat of judgement : even the seat of the house of David.
6 O pray for the peace of Jerusalem : they shall prosper that love thee.
7 Peace be within thy walls : and plenteousness within thy palaces.
8 For my brethren and companions' sakes : I will wish thee prosperity.
9 Yea, because of the house of the Lord our God : I will seek to do thee good.

Psalm 123. *Ad te levavi oculos meos*

Unto thee lift I up mine eyes : O thou that dwellest in the heavens.
2 Behold, even as the eyes of servants look unto the hand of their masters, and as the eyes of a maiden unto the hand of her mistress : even

so our eyes wait upon the Lord our God, until he have mercy upon us.

3 Have mercy upon us, O Lord, have mercy upon us : for we are utterly despised.

4 Our soul is filled with the scornful reproof of the wealthy : and with the despitefulness of the proud.

Psalm 124. *Nisi quia Dominus*

If the Lord himself had not been on our side, now may Israel say : if the Lord himself had not been on our side, when men rose up against us;

2 They had swallowed us up quick : when they were so wrathfully displeased at us.

3 Yea, the waters had drowned us : and the stream had gone over our soul.

4 The deep waters of the proud : had gone even over our soul.

5 But praised be the Lord : who hath not given us over for a prey unto their teeth.

6 Our soul is escaped even as a bird out of the snare of the fowler : the snare is broken, and we are delivered.

7 Our help standeth in the Name of the Lord : who hath made heaven and earth.

Psalm 125. *Qui confidunt*

They that put their trust in the Lord shall be even as the mount Sion : which may not be removed, but standeth fast for ever.

2 The hills stand about Jerusalem : even so standeth the Lord round about his people, from this time forth for evermore.

3 For the rod of the ungodly cometh not into the lot of the righteous : lest the righteous put their hand unto wickedness.

4 Do well, O Lord : unto those that are good and true of heart.

5 As for such as turn back unto their own wickedness : the Lord shall lead them forth with the evil-doers; but peace shall be upon Israel.

Day 27. Evening Prayer

Psalm 126. *In convertendo*

When the Lord turned again the captivity of Sion : then were we like unto them that dream.

2 Then was our mouth filled with laughter : and our tongue with joy.

3 Then said they among the heathen : The Lord hath done great things for them.
4 Yea, the Lord hath done great things for us already : whereof we rejoice.
5 Turn our captivity, O Lord : as the rivers in the south.
6 They that sow in tears : shall reap in joy.
7 He that now goeth on his way weeping, and beareth forth good seed : shall doubtless come again with joy, and bring his sheaves with him.

Psalm 127. *Nisi Dominus*

EXCEPT the Lord build the house : their labour is but lost that build it.
2 Except the Lord keep the city : the watchman waketh but in vain.
3 It is but lost labour that ye haste to rise up early, and so late take rest, and eat the bread of carefulness : for so he giveth his beloved sleep.
4 Lo, children and the fruit of the womb : are an heritage and gift that cometh of the Lord.
5 Like as the arrows in the hand of the giant : even so are the young children.
6 Happy is the man that hath his quiver full of them : they shall not be ashamed when they speak with their enemies in the gate.

Psalm 128. *Beati omnes*

BLESSED are all they that fear the Lord : and walk in his ways.
2 For thou shalt eat the labours of thine hands : O well is thee, and happy shalt thou be.
3 Thy wife shall be as the fruitful vine : upon the walls of thine house.
4 Thy children like the olive-branches : round about thy table.
5 Lo, thus shall the man be blessed : that feareth the Lord.
6 The Lord from out of Sion shall so bless thee : that thou shalt see Jerusalem in prosperity all thy life long.
7 Yea, that thou shalt see thy children's children : and peace upon Israel.

Psalm 129. *Saepe expugnaverunt*

MANY a time have they fought against me from my youth up : may Israel now say.
2 Yea, many a time have they vexed me from my youth up : but they have not prevailed against me.
3 The plowers plowed upon my back : and made long furrows.
4 But the righteous Lord : hath hewn the snares of the ungodly in pieces.

5 Let them be confounded and turned backward : as many as have evil will at Sion.

6 Let them be even as the grass growing upon the house-tops : which withereth afore it be plucked up;

7 Whereof the mower filleth not his hand : neither he that bindeth up the sheaves his bosom.

8 So that they who go by say not so much as, The Lord prosper you : we wish you good luck in the Name of the Lord.

Psalm 130. *De profundis*

OUT of the deep have I called unto thee, O Lord : Lord, hear my voice.

2 O let thine ears consider well : the voice of my complaint.

3 If thou, Lord, wilt be extreme to mark what is done amiss : O Lord, who may abide it?

4 For there is mercy with thee : therefore shalt thou be feared.

5 I look for the Lord; my soul doth wait for him : in his word is my trust.

6 My soul fleeth unto the Lord : before the morning watch, I say, before the morning watch.

7 O Israel, trust in the Lord, for with the Lord there is mercy : and with him is plenteous redemption.

8 And he shall redeem Israel : from all his sins.

Psalm 131. *Domine, non est*

LORD, I am not high-minded : I have no proud looks.

2 I do not exercise myself in great matters : which are too high for me.

3 But I refrain my soul, and keep it low, like as a child that is weaned from his mother : yea, my soul is even as a weaned child.

4 O Israel, trust in the Lord : from this time forth for evermore.

Day 28. Morning Prayer

Psalm 132. *Memento, Domine*

LORD, remember David : and all his trouble;

2 How he sware unto the Lord : and vowed a vow unto the Almighty God of Jacob;

3 I will not come within the tabernacle of mine house : nor climb up into my bed;

4 I will not suffer mine eyes to sleep, nor mine eye-lids to slumber : neither the temples of my head to take any rest;

5 Until I find out a place for the temple of the Lord : an habitation for the mighty God of Jacob.

6 Lo, we heard of the same at Ephrata : and found it in the wood.

7 We will go into his tabernacle : and fall low on our knees before his footstool.

8 Arise, O Lord, into thy resting-place : thou, and the ark of thy strength.

9 Let thy priests be clothed with righteousness : and let thy saints sing with joyfulness.

10 For thy servant David's sake : turn not away the presence of thine Anointed.

11 The Lord hath made a faithful oath unto David : and he shall not shrink from it;

12 Of the fruit of thy body : shall I set upon thy seat.

13 If thy children will keep my covenant, and my testimonies that I shall learn them : their children also shall sit upon thy seat for evermore.

14 For the Lord hath chosen Sion to be an habitation for himself : he hath longed for her.

15 This shall be my rest for ever : here will I dwell, for I have a delight therein.

16 I will bless her victuals with increase : and will satisfy her poor with bread.

17 I will deck her priests with health : and her saints shall rejoice and sing.

18 There shall I make the horn of David to flourish : I have ordained a lantern for mine Anointed.

19 As for his enemies, I shall clothe them with shame : but upon himself shall his crown flourish.

Psalm 133. *Ecce, quam bonum!*

Behold, how good and joyful a thing it is : brethren, to dwell together in unity!

2 It is like the precious ointment upon the head, that ran down unto the beard : even unto Aaron's beard, and went down to the skirts of his clothing.

3 Like as the dew of Hermon : which fell upon the hill of Sion.

4 For there the Lord promised his blessing : and life for evermore.

Psalm 134. *Ecce nunc*

Behold now, praise the Lord : all ye servants of the Lord;

2 Ye that by night stand in the house of the Lord : even in the courts of the house of our God.

3 Lift up your hands in the sanctuary : and praise the Lord.

4 The Lord that made heaven and earth : give thee blessing out of Sion.

Day 28. Morning Prayer   **Psalter**   Psalm 135

Psalm 135. *Laudate Nomen*

O PRAISE the Lord, laud ye the Name of the Lord : praise it, O ye servants of the Lord;

2 Ye that stand in the house of the Lord : in the courts of the house of our God.

3 O praise the Lord, for the Lord is gracious : O sing praises unto his Name, for it is lovely.

4 For why? the Lord hath chosen Jacob unto himself : and Israel for his own possession.

5 For I know that the Lord is great : and that our Lord is above all gods.

6 Whatsoever the Lord pleased, that did he in heaven and in earth : and in the sea, and in all deep places.

7 He bringeth forth the clouds from the ends of the world : and sendeth forth lightnings with the rain, bringing the winds out of his treasures.

8 He smote the first-born of Egypt : both of man and beast.

9 He hath sent tokens and wonders into the midst of thee, O thou land of Egypt : upon Pharaoh, and all his servants.

10 He smote divers nations : and slew mighty kings;

11 Sehon king of the Amorites, and Og the king of Basan : and all the kingdoms of Canaan;

12 And gave their land to be an heritage : even an heritage unto Israel his people.

13 Thy Name, O Lord, endureth for ever : so doth thy memorial, O Lord, from one generation to another.

14 For the Lord will avenge his people : and be gracious unto his servants.

15 As for the images of the heathen, they are but silver and gold : the work of men's hands.

16 They have mouths, and speak not : eyes have they, but they see not.

17 They have ears, and yet they hear not : neither is there any breath in their mouths.

18 They that make them are like unto them : and so are all they that put their trust in them.

19 Praise the Lord, ye house of Israel : praise the Lord, ye house of Aaron.

20 Praise the Lord, ye house of Levi : ye that fear the Lord, praise the Lord.

21 Praised be the Lord out of Sion : who dwelleth at Jerusalem.

Day 28. Evening Prayer

Psalm 136. *Confitemini*

O GIVE thanks unto the LORD, for he is gracious : and his mercy endureth for ever.

2 O give thanks unto the God of all gods : for his mercy endureth for ever.

3 O thank the Lord of all lords : for his mercy endureth for ever.

4 Who only doeth great wonders : for his mercy endureth for ever.

5 Who by his excellent wisdom made the heavens : for his mercy endureth for ever.

6 Who laid out the earth above the waters : for his mercy endureth for ever.

7 Who hath made great lights : for his mercy endureth for ever;

8 The sun to rule the day : for his mercy endureth for ever;

9 The moon and the stars to govern the night : for his mercy endureth for ever.

10 Who smote Egypt with their first-born : for his mercy endureth for ever;

11 And brought out Israel from among them : for his mercy endureth for ever;

12 With a mighty hand, and stretched out arm : for his mercy endureth for ever.

13 Who divided the Red sea in two parts : for his mercy endureth for ever;

14 And made Israel to go through the midst of it : for his mercy endureth for ever.

15 But as for Pharaoh and his host, he overthrew them in the Red sea : for his mercy endureth for ever.

16 Who led his people through the wilderness : for his mercy endureth for ever.

17 Who smote great kings : for his mercy endureth for ever;

18 Yea, and slew mighty kings : for his mercy endureth for ever;

19 Sehon king of the Amorites : for his mercy endureth for ever;

20 And Og the king of Basan : for his mercy endureth for ever;

21 And gave away their land for an heritage : for his mercy endureth for ever;

22 Even for an heritage unto Israel his servant : for his mercy endureth for ever.

23 Who remembered us when we were in trouble : for his mercy endureth for ever;

24 And hath delivered us from our enemies : for his mercy endureth for ever.

25 Who giveth food to all flesh : for his mercy endureth for ever.

26 O give thanks unto the God of heaven : for his mercy endureth for ever.
27 O give thanks unto the Lord of lords : for his mercy endureth for ever.

Psalm 137. *Super flumina*

By the waters of Babylon we sat down and wept : when we remembered thee, O Sion.

2 As for our harps, we hanged them up : upon the trees that are therein.

3 For they that led us away captive required of us then a song, and melody in our heaviness : Sing us one of the songs of Sion.

4 How shall we sing the Lord's song : in a strange land?

5 If I forget thee, O Jerusalem : let my right hand forget her cunning.

6 If I do not remember thee, let my tongue cleave to the roof of my mouth : yea, if I prefer not Jerusalem in my mirth.

7 Remember the children of Edom, O Lord, in the day of Jerusalem : how they said, Down with it, down with it, even to the ground.

8 O daughter of Babylon, wasted with misery : yea, happy shall he be that rewardeth thee, as thou hast served us.

9 Blessed shall he be that taketh thy children : and throweth them against the stones.

Psalm 138. *Confitebor tibi*

I will give thanks unto thee, O Lord, with my whole heart : even before the gods will I sing praise unto thee.

2 I will worship toward thy holy temple, and praise thy Name, because of thy loving-kindness and truth : for thou hast magnified thy Name and thy word above all things.

3 When I called upon thee, thou heardest me : and enduedst my soul with much strength.

4 All the kings of the earth shall praise thee, O Lord : for they have heard the words of thy mouth.

5 Yea, they shall sing in the ways of the Lord : that great is the glory of the Lord.

6 For though the Lord be high, yet hath he respect unto the lowly : as for the proud, he beholdeth them afar off.

7 Though I walk in the midst of trouble, yet shalt thou refresh me : thou shalt stretch forth thy hand upon the furiousness of mine enemies, and thy right hand shall save me.

8 The Lord shall make good his loving-kindness toward me : yea, thy mercy, O Lord, endureth for ever; despise not then the works of thine own hands.

Day 29. Morning Prayer

Psalm 139. *Domine, probasti*

LORD, thou hast searched me out and known me : thou knowest my down-sitting and mine up-rising, thou understandest my thoughts long before.

2 Thou art about my path, and about my bed : and spiest out all my ways.

3 For lo, there is not a word in my tongue : but thou, O Lord, knowest it altogether.

4 Thou hast fashioned me behind and before : and laid thine hand upon me.

5 Such knowledge is too wonderful and excellent for me : I cannot attain unto it.

6 Whither shall I go then from thy Spirit : or whither shall I go then from thy presence?

7 If I climb up into heaven, thou art there : if I go down to hell, thou art there also.

8 If I take the wings of the morning : and remain in the uttermost parts of the sea;

9 Even there also shall thy hand lead me : and thy right hand shall hold me.

10 If I say, Peradventure the darkness shall cover me : then shall my night be turned to day.

11 Yea, the darkness is no darkness with thee, but the night is as clear as the day : the darkness and light to thee are both alike.

12 For my reins are thine : thou hast covered me in my mother's womb.

13 I will give thanks unto thee, for I am fearfully and wonderfully made : marvellous are thy works, and that my soul knoweth right well.

14 My bones are not hid from thee : though I be made secretly, and fashioned beneath in the earth.

15 Thine eyes did see my substance, yet being unperfect : and in thy book were all my members written;

16 Which day by day were fashioned : when as yet there was none of them.

17 How dear are thy counsels unto me, O God : O how great is the sum of them!

18 If I tell them, they are more in number than the sand : when I wake up I am present with thee.

19 Wilt thou not slay the wicked, O God : depart from me, ye blood-thirsty men.

20 For they speak unrighteously against thee : and thine enemies take thy Name in vain.

21 Do not I hate them, O Lord, that hate thee : and am not I grieved with those that rise up against thee?

22 Yea, I hate them right sore : even as though they were mine enemies.

23 Try me, O God, and seek the ground of my heart : prove me, and examine my thoughts.

24 Look well if there be any way of wickedness in me : and lead me in the way everlasting.

Psalm 140. *Eripe me, Domine*

Deliver me, O Lord, from the evil man : and preserve me from the wicked man.

2 Who imagine mischief in their hearts : and stir up strife all the day long.

3 They have sharpened their tongues like a serpent : adders' poison is under their lips.

4 Keep me, O Lord, from the hands of the ungodly : preserve me from the wicked men, who are purposed to overthrow my goings.

5 The proud have laid a snare for me, and spread a net abroad with cords : yea, and set traps in my way.

6 I said unto the Lord, Thou art my God : hear the voice of my prayers, O Lord.

7 O Lord God, thou strength of my health : thou hast covered my head in the day of the battle.

8 Let not the ungodly have his desire, O Lord : let not his mischievous imagination prosper, lest they be too proud.

9 Let the mischief of their own lips fall upon the head of them : that compass me about.

10 Let hot burning coals fall upon them : let them be cast into the fire and into the pit, that they never rise up again.

11 A man full of words shall not prosper upon the earth : evil shall hunt the wicked person to overthrow him.

12 Sure I am that the Lord will avenge the poor : and maintain the cause of the helpless.

13 The righteous also shall give thanks unto thy Name : and the just shall continue in thy sight.

Psalm 141. *Domine, clamavi*

LORD, I call upon thee, haste thee unto me : and consider my voice when I cry unto thee.

2 Let my prayer be set forth in thy sight as the incense : and let the lifting up of my hands be an evening sacrifice.

3 Set a watch, O Lord, before my mouth : and keep the door of my lips.

4 O let not mine heart be inclined to any evil thing : let me not be occupied in ungodly works with the men that work wickedness, lest I eat of such things as please them.

5 Let the righteous rather smite me friendly : and reprove me.

6 But let not their precious balms break my head : yea, I will pray yet against their wickedness.

7 Let their judges be overthrown in stony places : that they may hear my words, for they are sweet.

8 Our bones lie scattered before the pit : like as when one breaketh and heweth wood upon the earth.

9 But mine eyes look unto thee, O Lord God : in thee is my trust, O cast not out my soul.

10 Keep me from the snare that they have laid for me : and from the traps of the wicked doers.

11 Let the ungodly fall into their own nets together : and let me ever escape them.

Day 29. Evening Prayer

Psalm 142. *Voce mea ad Dominum*

I CRIED unto the Lord with my voice : yea, even unto the Lord did I make my supplication.

2 I poured out my complaints before him : and shewed him of my trouble.

3 When my spirit was in heaviness thou knewest my path : in the way wherein I walked have they privily laid a snare for me.

4 I looked also upon my right hand : and saw there was no man that would know me.

5 I had no place to flee unto : and no man cared for my soul.

6 I cried unto thee, O Lord, and said : Thou art my hope, and my portion in the land of the living.

7 Consider my complaint : for I am brought very low.

Day 29. Evening Prayer   **Psalter**   Psalm 143

8 O deliver me from my persecutors : for they are too strong for me.

9 Bring my soul out of prison, that I may give thanks unto thy Name : which thing if thou wilt grant me, then shall the righteous resort unto my company.

Psalm 143. *Domine, exaudi*

Hear my prayer, O Lord, and consider my desire : hearken unto me for thy truth and righteousness' sake.

2 And enter not into judgement with thy servant : for in thy sight shall no man living be justified.

3 For the enemy hath persecuted my soul; he hath smitten my life down to the ground : he hath laid me in the darkness, as the men that have been long dead.

4 Therefore is my spirit vexed within me : and my heart within me is desolate.

5 Yet do I remember the time past; I muse upon all thy works : yea, I exercise myself in the works of thy hands.

6 I stretch forth my hands unto thee : my soul gaspeth unto thee as a thirsty land.

7 Hear me, O Lord, and that soon, for my spirit waxeth faint : hide not thy face from me, lest I be like unto them that go down into the pit.

8 O let me hear thy loving-kindness betimes in the morning, for in thee is my trust : shew thou me the way that I should walk in, for I lift up my soul unto thee.

9 Deliver me, O Lord, from mine enemies : for I flee unto thee to hide me.

10 Teach me to do the thing that pleaseth thee, for thou art my God : let thy loving Spirit lead me forth into the land of righteousness.

11 Quicken me, O Lord, for thy Name's sake : and for thy righteousness' sake bring my soul out of trouble.

12 And of thy goodness slay mine enemies : and destroy all them that vex my soul; for I am thy servant.

Day 30. Morning Prayer

¶ The Psalms for the 30th Day are repeated on the 31st Day, if there be one.

Psalm 144. *Benedictus Dominus*

BLESSED be the Lord my strength : who teacheth my hands to war, and my fingers to fight;

2 My hope and my fortress, my castle and deliverer, my defender in whom I trust : who subdueth my people that is under me.

3 Lord, what is man, that thou hast such respect unto him : or the son of man, that thou so regardest him?

4 Man is like a thing of nought : his time passeth away like a shadow.

5 Bow thy heavens, O Lord, and come down : touch the mountains, and they shall smoke.

6 Cast forth thy lightning, and tear them : shoot out thine arrows, and consume them.

7 Send down thine hand from above : deliver me, and take me out of the great waters, from the hand of strange children;

8 Whose mouth talketh of vanity : and their right hand is a right hand of wickedness.

9 I will sing a new song unto thee, O God : and sing praises unto thee upon a ten-stringed lute.

10 Thou hast given victory unto kings : and hast delivered David thy servant from the peril of the sword.

11 Save me, and deliver me from the hand of strange children : whose mouth talketh of vanity, and their right hand is a right hand of iniquity.

12 That our sons may grow up as the young plants : and that our daughters may be as the polished corners of the temple.

13 That our garners may be full and plenteous with all manner of store : that our sheep may bring forth thousands and ten thousands in our streets.

14 That our oxen may be strong to labour, that there be no decay : no leading into captivity, and no complaining in our streets.

15 Happy are the people that are in such a case : yea, blessed are the people who have the Lord for their God.

Psalm 145. *Exaltabo te, Deus*

I will magnify thee, O God, my King : and I will praise thy Name for ever and ever.

2 Every day will I give thanks unto thee : and praise thy Name for ever and ever.

3 Great is the Lord, and marvellous worthy to be praised : there is no end of his greatness.

4 One generation shall praise thy works unto another : and declare thy power.

5 As for me, I will be talking of thy worship : thy glory, thy praise, and wondrous works;

6 So that men shall speak of the might of thy marvellous acts : and I will also tell of thy greatness.

7 The memorial of thine abundant kindness shall be shewed : and men shall sing of thy righteousness.

8 The Lord is gracious and merciful : long-suffering and of great goodness.

9 The Lord is loving unto every man : and his mercy is over all his works.

10 All thy works praise thee, O Lord : and thy saints give thanks unto thee.

11 They shew the glory of thy kingdom : and talk of thy power;

12 That thy power, thy glory, and mightiness of thy kingdom : might be known unto men.

13 Thy kingdom is an everlasting kingdom : and thy dominion endureth throughout all ages.

14 The Lord upholdeth all such as fall : and lifteth up all those that are down.

15 The eyes of all wait upon thee, O Lord : and thou givest them their meat in due season.

16 Thou openest thine hand : and fillest all things living with plenteousness.

17 The Lord is righteous in all his ways : and holy in all his works.

18 The Lord is nigh unto all them that call upon him : yea, all such as call upon him faithfully.

19 He will fulfil the desire of them that fear him : he also will hear their cry, and will help them.

20 The Lord preserveth all them that love him : but scattereth abroad all the ungodly.

21 My mouth shall speak the praise of the Lord : and let all flesh give thanks unto his holy Name for ever and ever.

Psalm 146. *Lauda, anima mea*

Praise the Lord, O my soul; while I live will I praise the Lord : yea, as long as I have any being, I will sing praises unto my God.

2 O put not your trust in princes, nor in any child of man : for there is no help in them.

3 For when the breath of man goeth forth he shall turn again to his earth : and then all his thoughts perish.

4 Blessed is he that hath the God of Jacob for his help : and whose hope is in the Lord his God;

5 Who made heaven and earth, the sea, and all that therein is : who keepeth his promise for ever;

6 Who helpeth them to right that suffer wrong : who feedeth the hungry.

7 The Lord looseth men out of prison : the Lord giveth sight to the blind.

8 The Lord helpeth them that are fallen : the Lord careth for the righteous.

9 The Lord careth for the strangers, he defendeth the fatherless and widow : as for the way of the ungodly, he turneth it upside down.

10 The Lord thy God, O Sion, shall be King for evermore : and throughout all generations.

Day 30. Evening Prayer

Psalm 147. *Laudate Dominum*

O praise the Lord, for it is a good thing to sing praises unto our God : yea, a joyful and pleasant thing it is to be thankful.

2 The Lord doth build up Jerusalem : and gather together the out-casts of Israel.

3 He healeth those that are broken in heart : and giveth medicine to heal their sickness.

4 He telleth the number of the stars : and calleth them all by their names.

5 Great is our Lord, and great is his power : yea, and his wisdom is infinite.

6 The Lord setteth up the meek : and bringeth the ungodly down to the ground.

7 O sing unto the Lord with thanksgiving : sing praises upon the harp unto our God;

8 Who covereth the heaven with clouds, and prepareth rain for the earth : and maketh the grass to grow upon the mountains, and herb for the use of men;

9 Who giveth fodder unto the cattle : and feedeth the young ravens that call upon him.

10 He hath no pleasure in the strength of an horse : neither delighteth he in any man's legs.

11 But the Lord's delight is in them that fear him : and put their trust in his mercy.

12 Praise the Lord, O Jerusalem : praise thy God, O Sion.

13 For he hath made fast the bars of thy gates : and hath blessed thy children within thee.

14 He maketh peace in thy borders : and filleth thee with the flour of wheat.

15 He sendeth forth his commandment upon earth : and his word runneth very swiftly.

16 He giveth snow like wool : and scattereth the hoar-frost like ashes.

17 He casteth forth his ice like morsels : who is able to abide his frost?

18 He sendeth out his word, and melteth them : he bloweth with his wind, and the waters flow.

19 He sheweth his word unto Jacob : his statutes and ordinances unto Israel.

20 He hath not dealt so with any nation : neither have the heathen knowledge of his laws.

PSALM 148. *LAUDATE DOMINUM*

O PRAISE the Lord of heaven : praise him in the height.

2 Praise him, all ye angels of his : praise him, all his host.

3 Praise him, sun and moon : praise him, all ye stars and light.

4 Praise him, all ye heavens : and ye waters that are above the heavens.

5 Let them praise the Name of the Lord : for he spake the word, and they were made; he commanded, and they were created.

6 He hath made them fast for ever and ever : he hath given them a law which shall not be broken.

7 Praise the Lord upon earth : ye dragons, and all deeps;

8 Fire and hail, snow and vapours : wind and storm, fulfilling his word;

9 Mountains and all hills : fruitful trees and all cedars;

10 Beasts and all cattle : worms and feathered fowls;

11 Kings of the earth and all people : princes and all judges of the world;

12 Young men and maidens, old men and children, praise the Name of the Lord : for his Name only is excellent, and his praise above heaven and earth.

13 He shall exalt the horn of his people; all his saints shall praise him : even the children of Israel, even the people that serveth him.

Psalm 149. *Cantate Domino*

SING unto the Lord a new song : let the congregation of saints praise him.

2 Let Israel rejoice in him that made him : and let the children of Sion be joyful in their King.

3 Let them praise his Name in the dance : let them sing praises unto him with tabret and harp.

4 For the Lord hath pleasure in his people : and helpeth the meek-hearted.

5 Let the saints be joyful with glory : let them rejoice in their beds.

6 Let the praises of God be in their mouth : and a two-edged sword in their hands;

7 To be avenged of the heathen : and to rebuke the people;

8 To bind their kings in chains : and their nobles with links of iron.

9 That they may be avenged of them, as it is written : Such honour have all his saints.

Psalm 150. *Laudate Dominum*

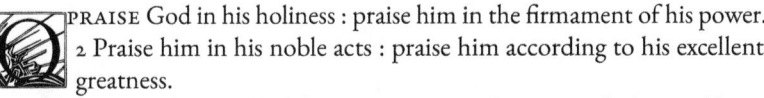

PRAISE God in his holiness : praise him in the firmament of his power.

2 Praise him in his noble acts : praise him according to his excellent greatness.

3 Praise him in the sound of the trumpet : praise him upon the lute and harp.

4 Praise him in the cymbals and dances : praise him upon the strings and pipe.

5 Praise him upon the well-tuned cymbals : praise him upon the loud cymbals.

6 Let every thing that hath breath : praise the Lord.

Most Holy Trinity, Save Us.
St. Mary Ever-Virgin, Pray for Us.
St. John the Divine, Pray for Us.
St. Alban the Martyr, Pray for Us.
St. Augustine of Canterbury, Pray for Us.
St. Gregory the Great, Pray for Us.
St. Tikhon of Moscow, Pray for Us.
St. John of San Francisco, Pray for Us.
All Ye Holy Angels & Saints, Pray for Us.

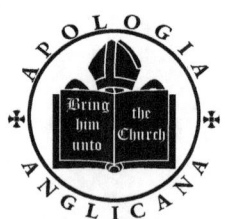

© 2025 Some Rights Reserved (CC-BY-SA-4.0)
Apologia Anglicana, LLC
Boston, MA
www.ApologiaAnglicana.org

www.ingramcontent.com/pod-product-compliance
Lightning Source LLC
Chambersburg PA
CBHW070313010526
44107CB00004B/327